For Dana and Sky

THE OFFICIAL GUIDE TO THE

AMERICAN MARKETPLACE

FIRST EDITION

The _real_ facts about how
well-educated, healthy,
family-oriented, rich,
productive, demanding,
and opinionated we are.

Margaret Ambry and Cheryl Russell

New Strategist Publications & Consulting
Ithaca, New York

New Strategist Publications & Consulting
P.O. Box 242, Ithaca, NY 14851
607 / 273-0913

Copyright 1992, NEW STRATEGIST PUBLICATIONS

First published USA 1992

Ambry, Margaret, 1947—
Russell, Cheryl, 1953—
The Official Guide to the American Marketplace.

ISBN 0-9628092-1-7

Printed in the United States of America.

Contents

Tables and Maps

CHAPTER 1. *Population Trends*

CHAPTER 2. *Household Trends*

CHAPTER 3. *Income Trends*

CHAPTER 4. *Spending and Wealth Trends*

CHAPTER 5. *Labor Force Trends*

CHAPTER 6. *Education Trends*

CHAPTER 7. *Health Trends*

CHAPTER 8. *Attitude Trends*

Introduction

Americans know more about themselves than probably any people in history. Yet the more we know, the more elusive the truth. If you're a business person trying to market consumer products or services, it's hard to sort through all the numbers and find direction. There are so many statistics collected and published about Americans that, depending on who is doing the picking and choosing, the statistics could support any point of view. Is our educational system failing or are Americans increasingly well educated? Is our leisure time shrinking or expanding? Are we a multicultural society, or are we still predominantly white? Is our health improving or worsening? Has the traditional family disappeared, or is it staging a comeback?

All of the above are true, depending on which numbers you examine. More and more, the facts you hear about these and other issues are hand-picked to bolster the political agendas of proliferating special interest groups. These groups issue press releases to a media more concerned with ratings than with reason. The next thing you know, political opinions are lead stories on the evening news—hailed as certified trends.

What you need are facts, not opinions, about your customers. This book presents you with those facts, a straightforward and honest picture of Americans in all their complexity. You will find your customers in this book. You also will find many Americans who are not your customers. But armed with the big picture, you can spot your customers, see how they fit in the overall scheme of things, and devise products, services, and marketing campaigns that will work for you.

The Trends

There are a lot of numbers in this book. At first glance, the numbers may seem overwhelming. But most of them sort themselves into a few recognizable trends. These trends will drive consumer markets during the 1990s. As we see it, the most important trends are these:

☞ *Multicultural* By the end of the 1990s, the United States will have made the transition from a predominantly non-Hispanic white to a multicultural society. This trend is most powerful among American youth.

☞ *Stable* After decades of dramatic lifestyle change, look for household stability in the 1990s as the burgeoning middle-aged population settles into family life.

☞ *Affluent* Once the impact of the recession is behind us, look for continued gains in household affluence, making the 1990s the most affluent decade in American history.

☞ *Careful* Despite growing affluence, spending patterns have changed permanently. With so many Americans raising children, spending is no longer impulsive, but planned.

☞ **Productive** As the baby boom inflates the number of experienced, middle-aged workers, look for substantial productivity gains in the labor force.

☞ **Demanding** Though the population as a whole is becoming increasingly well educated, minorities are losing ground at the college level. During the 1990s, minorities will demand the opportunity to get ahead.

☞ **Transforming** As the oldest baby boomers enter their late 40s and early 50s during the 1990s, chronic health problems will increase. This will ensure the transformation of health care financing by the end of the decade.

☞ **Longing for leisure** With a record proportion of Americans working, people will feel busier than ever during the 1990s. Consequently, leisure time will become more valued than it already is.

How to Use This Book

This book is meant to be easy to use. It is organized into chapters based on the major demographic factors that drive consumer markets: population characteristics, household characteristics, income, spending, labor force, education, health, and attitudes. When appropriate, we present the latest 1990 census results. Note that some of the tables include adjustments of 1990 census totals for the known undercount of minorities. After all, many of the 5 million Americans not counted by the census are your customers.

Each chapter begins with a short introduction, highlighting major trends of the 1980s and the trends you can expect in the 1990s. If you want to know what will happen in the next few years, scan the introductions. If you're looking for a particular piece of information, start with the table of contents or look it up in the detailed index at the end of the book. If a term confuses you, find out what it means in the glossary.

Most of our sources for this book are publicly available information from the Census Bureau, the Bureau of Labor Statistics, the Federal Reserve Board, and so on. The federal government continues to be the best source of information about the characteristics of Americans. Occasionally, we rely on private sources of information—particularly in the chapter on attitudes. The federal government rarely asks Americans for their opinions. Opinion polling is most often done by private companies such as The Roper Organization and The Gallup Poll. In combination, the facts about the characteristics and attitudes of Americans collected here present a complete picture of American life in the last decade of the 20th century. We hope you find the picture profitable.

Margaret Ambry
Cheryl Russell

1

Population Trends

Slowing population growth, the middle-aging of the population, and increasing racial and ethnic diversity are the defining trends of the 1990s. In the decade ahead, the U.S. population will grow more slowly than in any decade since the Great Depression of the 1930s—a projected increase of just 7.7 percent. Immigrants now account for more than one-fourth of our annual population gain, contributing to the increasing diversity of our population. Most immigrants settle in the nation's largest metropolitan areas—driving metropolitan growth.

Major Population Trends

☞ Businesses will need to explore local markets and market niches for revenue growth as overall population growth slows. Expect large metropolitan areas to continue to dominate population gains as immigrants settle in those areas.

☞ Middle-aged consumers will drive the nation's economy as the number of 45-to-54-year-olds increases by 47 percent during the 1990s.

☞ Racial and ethnic diversity will be the rule among American children as the number of Hispanic preschoolers rises by 20 percent, versus a 4 percent increase in all preschoolers.

Population by Regions and Divisions, 1970 to 2000

The U.S. population will grow more slowly in the 1990s than in any decade since the 1930s. Growth will slow even in the rapidly growing West.

(resident population by region and division, 1970, 1980, 1990, and projected population in 2000; growth rates for the 1970s, 1980s, and projected growth rate for the 1990s; numbers in thousands)

	1970	1980	1990	2000	percent change 1970-80	percent change 1980-90	percent change 1990-2000
United States	**203,213**	**226,546**	**248,710**	**267,747**	**11.5%**	**9.8%**	**7.7%**
Northeast	**49,041**	**49,135**	**50,809**	**51,810**	**0.2**	**3.4**	**2.0**
New England	11,842	12,348	13,207	13,775	4.3	7.0	4.3
Middle Atlantic	37,199	36,787	37,602	38,035	-1.1	2.2	1.2
Midwest	**56,572**	**58,866**	**59,669**	**59,596**	**4.1**	**1.4**	**-0.1**
East North Central	40,253	41,682	42,009	41,746	3.6	0.8	-0.6
West North Central	16,320	17,183	17,660	17,850	5.3	2.8	1.1
South	**62,795**	**75,372**	**85,446**	**96,919**	**20.0**	**13.4**	**13.4**
South Atlantic	30,671	36,959	43,567	50,002	20.5	17.9	14.8
East South Central	12,804	14,666	15,176	16,285	14.5	3.5	7.3
West South Central	19,320	23,747	26,703	30,632	22.9	12.4	14.7
West	**34,804**	**43,172**	**52,786**	**59,422**	**24.0**	**22.3**	**12.6**
Mountain	8,281	11,373	13,659	16,022	37.3	20.1	17.3
Pacific	26,523	31,800	39,127	43,400	19.9	23.0	10.9

Source: Bureau of the Census.

Population by Race and Hispanic Origin

The Asian population nearly doubled in every region during the 1980s, while the Hispanic population grew by half in the West and South. The white population fell in both the Northeast and Midwest.

(regional populations by race and Hispanic origin, number and percent distribution, 1990, percent change, 1980-90; numbers in thousands)

	total	white	black	Asian	other race	Hispanic*
Number						
United States	**248,710**	**199,686**	**29,986**	**7,274**	**11,764**	**22,354**
Northeast	50,809	42,069	5,613	1,335	1,792	3,754
Midwest	59,669	52,018	5,716	768	1,167	1,727
South	85,446	65,582	15,829	1,122	2,913	6,767
West	52,786	40,017	2,828	4,048	5,893	10,106
Percent distribution						
United States	**100.0%**	**80.3%**	**12.1%**	**2.9%**	**4.7%**	**9.0%**
Northeast	100.0	82.8	11.0	2.6	3.5	7.4
Midwest	100.0	87.2	9.6	1.3	2.0	2.9
South	100.0	76.8	18.5	1.3	3.4	7.9
West	100.0	75.8	5.4	7.7	11.2	19.1
Percent change, 1980-90						
United States	**9.8%**	**6.0%**	**13.2%**	**107.8%**	**43.8%**	**53.0%**
Northeast	3.4	-0.6	15.8	138.6	27.9	44.2
Midwest	1.4	-0.3	7.1	96.9	23.6	35.2
South	13.4	11.2	12.7	138.9	53.7	51.3
West	22.3	14.7	25.0	94.5	49.6	61.6

*Hispanics may be of any race.
Source: Bureau of the Census

U.S. Population by Age, 1990 to 2000

The number of people aged 25 to 34 will fall by 10 percent during the 1990s, while the number aged 45 to 54 will grow by 47 percent.

(resident U.S. population by age in 1990 and projected resident population by age in 1995 and 2000; numbers in thousands)

	total			change			percent change		
	1990	*1995*	*2000*	*1990-1995*	*1995-2000*	*1990-2000*	*1990-1995*	*1995-2000*	*1990-2000*
Total	**253,979**	**266,986**	**278,473**	**13,007**	**11,488**	**24,495**	**5.1%**	**4.3%**	**9.6%**
Under age 6	22,526	23,508	23,462	982	-46	936	4.4	-0.2	4.2
Under age 1	3,816	3,906	3,924	90	18	109	2.4	0.5	2.8
Aged 1	3,707	3,825	3,817	119	-9	110	3.2	-0.2	3.0
Aged 2	3,698	3,876	3,848	179	-28	150	4.8	-0.7	4.1
Aged 3	3,754	3,994	3,950	240	-44	196	6.4	-1.1	5.2
Aged 4	3,791	4,089	4,034	297	-54	243	7.8	-1.3	6.4
Aged 5	3,761	3,818	3,889	57	71	128	1.5	1.9	3.4
Aged 6 to 12	25,487	26,730	27,831	1,243	1,101	2,344	4.9	4.1	9.2
Aged 6	3,633	3,838	3,940	205	102	307	5.6	2.6	8.4
Aged 7	3,770	3,900	4,064	130	164	294	3.4	4.2	7.8
Aged 8	3,636	3,769	3,984	132	215	348	3.6	5.7	9.6
Aged 9	3,701	3,877	4,154	177	277	454	4.8	7.1	12.3
Aged 10	3,734	3,879	3,921	145	42	187	3.9	1.1	5.0
Aged 11	3,566	3,704	3,894	139	190	329	3.9	5.1	9.2
Aged 12	3,447	3,762	3,874	315	111	427	9.1	3.0	12.4
Aged 13 to 17	17,139	18,381	19,230	1,242	849	2,091	7.2	4.6	12.2
Aged 13	3,442	3,769	3,889	327	120	447	9.5	3.2	13.0
Aged 14	3,310	3,744	3,906	434	162	596	13.1	4.3	18.0
Aged 15	3,491	3,749	3,884	259	135	393	7.4	3.6	11.3
Aged 16	3,410	3,617	3,747	208	129	337	6.1	3.6	9.9
Aged 17	3,486	3,500	3,803	14	303	318	0.4	8.7	9.1
Aged 18 to 24	27,200	25,385	25,617	-1,815	232	-1,583	-6.7	0.9	-5.8
Aged 18	3,638	3,432	3,741	-206	309	103	-5.7	9.0	2.8
Aged 19	4,128	3,431	3,859	-697	429	-268	-16.9	12.5	-6.5
Aged 20 to 24	19,435	18,523	18,017	-911	-506	-1,418	-4.7	-2.7	-7.3
Aged 25 to 29	21,770	20,170	19,100	-1,600	-1,070	-2,670	-7.4	-5.3	-12.3
Aged 30 to 34	22,328	22,370	20,640	42	-1,729	-1,688	0.2	-7.7	-7.6
Aged 35 to 39	20,383	22,536	22,516	2,153	-20	2,133	10.6	-0.1	10.5
Aged 40 to 44	17,979	20,362	22,477	2,382	2,115	4,497	13.3	10.4	25.0
Aged 45 to 49	14,156	17,854	20,196	3,698	2,343	6,041	26.1	13.1	42.7
Aged 50 to 54	11,583	13,917	17,542	2,333	3,626	5,959	20.1	26.1	51.4
Aged 55 to 59	10,746	11,222	13,488	476	2,267	2,743	4.4	20.2	25.5

(continued on next page)

(continued from previous page)
(resident U.S. population by age in 1990 and projected resident population by age in 1995 and 2000; numbers in thousands)

	total			change			percent change		
	1990	*1995*	*2000*	*1990-1995*	*1995-2000*	*1990-2000*	*1990-1995*	*1995-2000*	*1990-2000*
Aged 60 to 64	10,829	10,183	10,656	-645	472	-173	-6.0%	4.6%	-1.6%
Aged 65 to 69	10,312	9,935	9,374	-377	-561	-938	-3.7	-5.6	-9.1
Aged 70 to 74	8,151	9,014	8,730	863	-284	579	10.6	-3.1	7.1
Aged 75 to 79	6,241	6,645	7,409	404	764	1,168	6.5	11.5	18.7
Aged 80 to 84	4,010	4,602	4,970	592	368	960	14.8	8.0	24.0
Aged 85 or older	3,140	4,173	5,233	1,033	1,059	2,093	32.9	25.4	66.7

Source: TGE Demographics, Inc., Ithaca, New York
Note: The 1990 population here has been adjusted by the Census Bureau's estimated undercount. The undercount is distributed by age, race, and Hispanic origin.
Numbers may not add to total due to rounding.

White Population by Age, 1990 to 2000

The number of white Americans under age 6 will grow by only 5 percent during the 1990s, while the number aged 85 or older will climb by 65 percent.

(white resident population by age in 1990 and projected white resident population by age in 1995 and 2000; numbers in thousands)

	white population			change			percent change		
	1990	1995	2000	1990-1995	1995-2000	1990-2000	1990-1995	1995-2000	1990-2000
Total	**202,967**	**211,154**	**218,288**	**8,187**	**7,134**	**15,322**	**4.0%**	**3.4%**	**7.5%**
Under age 6	16,682	17,593	17,591	911	-2	909	5.5	0.0	5.4
Under age 1	2,825	2,927	2,941	101	14	116	3.6	0.5	4.1
Aged 1	2,753	2,877	2,870	124	-7	118	4.5	-0.2	4.3
Aged 2	2,736	2,907	2,885	171	-22	149	6.3	-0.8	5.4
Aged 3	2,778	2,998	2,965	220	-33	187	7.9	-1.1	6.7
Aged 4	2,782	3,066	3,026	284	-40	244	10.2	-1.3	8.8
Aged 5	2,809	2,818	2,904	10	86	96	0.4	3.0	3.4
Aged 6 to 12	19,052	19,832	20,738	780	906	1,686	4.1	4.6	8.9
Aged 6	2,723	2,841	2,953	118	112	230	4.3	4.0	8.5
Aged 7	2,823	2,885	3,049	63	163	226	2.2	5.7	8.0
Aged 8	2,720	2,787	2,990	67	203	270	2.5	7.3	9.9
Aged 9	2,765	2,841	3,112	76	271	347	2.7	9.5	12.5
Aged 10	2,784	2,896	2,894	112	-2	110	4.0	-0.1	3.9
Aged 11	2,657	2,769	2,877	112	107	219	4.2	3.9	8.3
Aged 12	2,580	2,813	2,864	233	52	285	9.0	1.8	11.0
Aged 13 to 17	12,774	13,691	14,249	917	558	1,475	7.2	4.1	11.5
Aged 13	2,571	2,814	2,872	243	57	301	9.5	2.0	11.7
Aged 14	2,473	2,799	2,865	327	66	392	13.2	2.4	15.9
Aged 15	2,606	2,785	2,889	178	104	282	6.8	3.7	10.8
Aged 16	2,536	2,685	2,790	149	104	253	5.9	3.9	10.0
Aged 17	2,587	2,608	2,834	21	226	247	0.8	8.7	9.5
Aged 18 to 24	20,595	18,942	19,075	-1,652	133	-1,520	-8.0	0.7	-7.4
Aged 18	2,718	2,558	2,790	-160	231	72	-5.9	9.0	2.6
Aged 19	3,114	2,563	2,888	-551	325	-226	-17.7	12.7	-7.3
Aged 20 to 24	14,763	13,821	13,398	-942	-423	-1,365	-6.4	-3.1	-9.2
Aged 25 to 29	16,912	15,322	14,261	-1,590	-1,061	-2,650	-9.4	-6.9	-15.7
Aged 30 to 34	17,637	17,297	15,625	-340	-1,672	-2,011	-1.9	-9.7	-11.4
Aged 35 to 39	16,346	17,729	17,359	1,384	-370	1,013	8.5	-2.1	6.2
Aged 40 to 44	14,745	16,290	17,658	1,546	1,367	2,913	10.5	8.4	19.8
Aged 45 to 49	11,776	14,622	16,150	2,846	1,528	4,374	24.2	10.4	37.1
Aged 50 to 54	9,661	11,563	14,362	1,902	2,800	4,701	19.7	24.2	48.7
Aged 55 to 59	9,116	9,349	11,204	234	1,855	2,088	2.6	19.8	22.9

(continued on next page)

(continued from previous page)
(white resident population by age in 1990 and projected white resident population by age in 1995 and 2000; numbers in thousands)

	white population			change			percent change		
	1990	1995	2000	1990-1995	1995-2000	1990-2000	1990-1995	1995-2000	1990-2000
Aged 60 to 64	9,362	8,631	8,876	-731	245	-486	-7.8%	2.8%	-5.2%
Aged 65 to 69	9,046	8,586	7,945	-460	-641	-1,101	-5.1	-7.5	-12.2
Aged 70 to 74	7,244	7,915	7,555	671	-360	311	9.3	-4.5	4.3
Aged 75 to 79	5,575	5,917	6,520	341	604	945	6.1	10.2	17.0
Aged 80 to 84	3,611	4,120	4,433	508	314	822	14.1	7.6	22.8
Aged 85 or older	2,834	3,756	4,685	922	929	1,851	32.6	24.7	65.3

Source: TGE Demographics, Inc., Ithaca, New York
Note: The 1990 population here has been adjusted by the Census Bureau's estimated undercount. The undercount is distributed by age, race, and Hispanic origin.
Numbers may not add to total due to rounding.

Black Population by Age, 1990 to 2000

The number of blacks under the age of 6 will actually decline during the 1990s, but the number aged 45 to 54 will increase by 57 percent.

(black resident population by age in 1990 and projected black resident population by age in 1995 and 2000; numbers in thousands)

	black population			change			percent change		
	1990	1995	2000	1990-1995	1995-2000	1990-2000	1990-1995	1995-2000	1990-2000
Total	**31,662**	**33,787**	**35,771**	**2,126**	**1,984**	**4,110**	**6.7%**	**5.9%**	**13.0%**
Under age 6	3,520	3,527	3,501	8	-27	-19	0.2	-0.8	-0.5
Under age 1	600	589	592	-11	3	-9	-1.9	0.5	-1.4
Aged 1	575	566	566	-9	0	-9	-1.6	0.1	-1.6
Aged 2	580	577	575	-3	-3	-6	-0.5	-0.5	-1.0
Aged 3	586	591	585	4	-6	-1	0.8	-1.0	-0.2
Aged 4	600	611	602	11	-9	2	1.8	-1.4	0.4
Aged 5	578	594	581	16	-13	3	2.8	-2.2	0.6
Aged 6 to 12	3,932	4,103	4,189	170	86	257	4.3	2.1	6.5
Aged 6	548	593	582	45	-11	34	8.2	-1.8	6.2
Aged 7	571	605	600	34	-5	29	6.0	-0.8	5.2
Aged 8	555	586	588	31	2	33	5.6	0.4	6.0
Aged 9	568	605	615	37	10	47	6.5	1.6	8.2
Aged 10	590	593	607	2	14	17	0.4	2.4	2.8
Aged 11	564	558	602	-6	44	38	-1.1	7.9	6.7
Aged 12	535	563	594	28	31	59	5.1	5.6	11.0
Aged 13 to 17	2,684	2,853	2,940	170	86	256	6.3	3.0	9.5
Aged 13	540	571	600	30	30	60	5.6	5.2	11.1
Aged 14	516	568	604	51	36	88	9.9	6.4	17.0
Aged 15	539	593	594	53	2	55	9.9	0.3	10.2
Aged 16	534	575	567	41	-8	33	7.6	-1.4	6.1
Aged 17	554	548	575	-6	27	21	-1.1	4.9	3.8
Aged 18 to 24	3,903	3,900	3,935	-3	35	32	-0.1	0.9	0.8
Aged 18	563	535	563	-28	28	0	-5.0	5.3	0.1
Aged 19	617	523	573	-94	49	-44	-15.2	9.5	-7.2
Aged 20 to 24	2,723	2,842	2,799	119	-43	76	4.4	-1.5	2.8
Aged 25 to 29	2,859	2,771	2,877	-88	106	18	-3.1	3.8	0.6
Aged 30 to 34	2,832	2,903	2,804	72	-99	-28	2.5	-3.4	-1.0
Aged 35 to 39	2,467	2,837	2,903	370	66	436	15.0	2.3	17.7
Aged 40 to 44	1,981	2,447	2,811	466	364	830	23.5	14.9	41.9
Aged 45 to 49	1,484	1,947	2,405	463	457	921	31.2	23.5	62.0
Aged 50 to 54	1,245	1,440	1,892	195	452	647	15.7	31.4	52.0
Aged 55 to 59	1,090	1,182	1,372	92	190	282	8.4	16.1	25.8

(continued on next page)

(continued from previous page)

(black resident population by age in 1990 and projected black resident population by age in 1995 and 2000; numbers in thousands)

	black population			change			percent change		
	1990	*1995*	*2000*	*1990-1995*	*1995-2000*	*1990-2000*	*1990-1995*	*1995-2000*	*1990-2000*
Aged 60 to 64	1,015	1,002	1,093	-13	91	78	-1.3%	9.1%	7.7%
Aged 65 to 69	911	897	893	-14	-4	-18	-1.6	-0.5	-2.0
Aged 70 to 74	676	760	756	84	-4	79	12.4	-0.6	11.8
Aged 75 to 79	508	525	598	17	73	90	3.3	14.0	17.7
Aged 80 to 84	310	361	380	51	19	70	16.6	5.3	22.7
Aged 85 or older	243	330	423	87	93	180	35.6	28.3	74.0

Source: TGE Demographics, Inc., Ithaca, New York
Note: The 1990 population here has been adjusted by the Census Bureau's estimated undercount. The undercount is distributed by age, race, and Hispanic origin.
Numbers may not add to total due to rounding.

Asian and Other Population by Age, 1990 to 2000

The Asian and other population will grow by 26 percent during the 1990s, but the biggest growth will be among those aged 35 and older.

(Asian and other resident population by age in 1990 and projected Asian and other resident population by age in 1995 and 2000; numbers in thousands)

	Asian and other population			change			percent change		
	1990	1995	2000	1990-1995	1995-2000	1990-2000	1990-1995	1995-2000	1990-2000
Total	**19,350**	**22,045**	**24,414**	**2,694**	**2,369**	**5,063**	**13.9%**	**10.7%**	**26.2%**
Under age 6	2,324	2,389	2,366	65	-23	41	2.8	-1.0	1.8
Under age 1	397	393	394	-5	1	-3	-1.2	0.4	-0.8
Aged 1	387	386	385	-1	-1	-2	-0.3	-0.4	-0.6
Aged 2	385	390	386	5	-4	2	1.4	-0.9	0.5
Aged 3	391	402	397	12	-5	7	3.0	-1.2	1.7
Aged 4	391	411	405	20	-6	14	5.2	-1.4	3.7
Aged 5	374	407	398	33	-9	24	8.9	-2.1	6.5
Aged 6 to 12	2,503	2,792	2,924	289	132	421	11.5	4.7	16.8
Aged 6	362	410	405	48	-5	43	13.2	-1.3	11.7
Aged 7	376	416	418	41	1	42	10.9	0.3	11.3
Aged 8	362	402	410	40	8	48	11.1	1.9	13.2
Aged 9	368	410	427	42	17	59	11.4	4.0	15.9
Aged 10	359	394	424	34	30	64	9.6	7.6	17.9
Aged 11	343	377	421	34	45	78	9.8	11.9	22.8
Aged 12	333	382	420	50	37	87	14.9	9.7	26.0
Aged 13 to 17	1,667	1,839	2,023	173	184	357	10.4	10.0	21.4
Aged 13	332	383	421	51	38	89	15.3	9.9	26.7
Aged 14	319	381	420	61	39	100	19.3	10.2	31.5
Aged 15	342	371	402	29	31	59	8.3	8.2	17.3
Aged 16	333	358	388	24	30	55	7.3	8.4	16.4
Aged 17	340	347	394	7	47	54	2.2	13.4	15.9
Aged 18 to 24	2,715	2,543	2,609	-173	67	-106	-6.4	2.6	-3.9
Aged 18	357	341	388	-16	47	31	-4.6	13.8	8.6
Aged 19	409	341	401	-68	60	-8	-16.5	17.6	-1.9
Aged 20 to 24	1,949	1,860	1,820	-89	-40	-129	-4.5	-2.2	-6.6
Aged 25 to 29	1,999	2,077	1,962	78	-115	-37	3.9	-5.6	-1.9
Aged 30 to 34	1,860	2,170	2,211	310	42	352	16.7	1.9	18.9
Aged 35 to 39	1,570	1,969	2,254	399	284	684	25.4	14.4	43.5
Aged 40 to 44	1,254	1,624	2,008	371	383	754	29.6	23.6	60.2
Aged 45 to 49	896	1,284	1,642	389	358	746	43.4	27.8	83.3
Aged 50 to 54	678	914	1,288	236	374	611	34.9	41.0	90.1
Aged 55 to 59	539	690	912	151	222	373	28.0	32.2	69.2

(continued on next page)

(continued from previous page)

(Asian and other resident population by age in 1990 and projected Asian and other resident population by age in 1995 and 2000; numbers in thousands)

	Asian and other population			change			percent change		
	1990	1995	2000	1990-1995	1995-2000	1990-2000	1990-1995	1995-2000	1990-2000
Aged 60 to 64	451	550	686	99	136	235	22.0%	24.7%	52.2%
Aged 65 to 69	355	451	536	97	85	181	27.2	18.8	51.1
Aged 70 to 74	232	339	420	108	80	188	46.5	23.7	81.2
Aged 75 to 79	158	204	291	47	87	133	29.5	42.6	84.7
Aged 80 to 84	89	121	157	33	35	68	36.6	29.2	76.6
Aged 85 or older	63	87	125	24	37	62	38.7	42.7	97.9

Source: TGE Demographics, Inc., Ithaca, New York
Note: The 1990 population here has been adjusted by the Census Bureau's estimated undercount. The undercount is distributed by age, race, and Hispanic origin.
Numbers may not add to total due to rounding.

Hispanic Population by Age, 1990 to 2000

The number of Hispanics under age 6 will grow by fully 20 percent during the 1990s. By 2000, one in six preschoolers in the U.S. will be Hispanic.

(Hispanic resident population by age in 1990 and projected Hispanic resident population by age in 1995 and 2000; numbers in thousands)

	Hispanic population			change			percent change		
	1990	1995	2000	1990-1995	1995-2000	1990-2000	1990-1995	1995-2000	1990-2000
Total	**23,722**	**27,823**	**32,085**	**4,101**	**4,262**	**8,362**	**17.3%**	**15.3%**	**35.3%**
Under age 6	3,039	3,339	3,635	300	296	596	9.9	8.9	19.6
Under age 1	533	573	626	40	53	93	7.5	9.2	17.4
Aged 1	520	564	615	44	51	95	8.5	9.0	18.3
Aged 2	507	555	605	49	50	99	9.6	9.0	19.5
Aged 3	494	547	598	54	50	104	10.9	9.2	21.1
Aged 4	481	540	592	59	51	110	12.3	9.5	22.9
Aged 5	505	559	599	54	41	95	10.7	7.3	18.8
Aged 6 to 12	3,125	3,701	4,085	575	384	959	18.4	10.4	30.7
Aged 6	490	549	593	58	45	103	11.8	8.1	20.9
Aged 7	474	537	586	63	49	112	13.3	9.1	23.6
Aged 8	434	524	579	90	55	145	20.7	10.4	33.3
Aged 9	424	510	570	86	60	146	20.2	11.7	34.4
Aged 10	445	544	598	99	54	153	22.3	9.9	34.4
Aged 11	434	527	586	93	59	152	21.4	11.2	35.0
Aged 12	423	509	573	86	63	149	20.4	12.4	35.3
Aged 13 to 17	2,118	2,296	2,751	177	456	633	8.4	19.9	29.9
Aged 13	414	468	558	54	90	144	13.0	19.3	34.8
Aged 14	408	458	544	50	86	136	12.3	18.8	33.5
Aged 15	432	464	563	31	99	131	7.2	21.4	30.2
Aged 16	431	456	549	25	93	118	5.8	20.3	27.3
Aged 17	432	450	537	17	87	104	4.0	19.4	24.2
Aged 18 to 24	3,329	3,323	3,513	-6	190	184	-0.2	5.7	5.5
Aged 18	437	448	502	11	54	65	2.4	12.1	14.8
Aged 19	446	448	498	1	50	51	0.3	11.2	11.5
Aged 20 to 24	2,446	2,428	2,514	-18	86	68	-0.7	3.6	2.8
Aged 25 to 29	2,485	2,857	2,840	373	-17	356	15.0	-0.6	14.3
Aged 30 to 34	2,189	2,748	3,120	560	372	931	25.6	13.5	42.6
Aged 35 to 39	1,762	2,300	2,858	538	557	1,095	30.5	24.2	62.1
Aged 40 to 44	1,363	1,813	2,347	450	534	984	33.0	29.5	72.2
Aged 45 to 49	1,012	1,394	1,839	382	445	827	37.7	31.9	81.7
Aged 50 to 54	802	1,026	1,401	223	376	599	27.8	36.6	74.6
Aged 55 to 59	678	803	1,021	125	218	343	18.4	27.1	50.5

(continued on next page)

(continued from previous page)
(Hispanic resident population by age in 1990 and projected Hispanic resident population by age in 1995 and 2000; numbers in thousands)

	Hispanic population			change			percent change		
	1990	**1995**	**2000**	**1990-1995**	**1995-2000**	**1990-2000**	**1990-1995**	**1995-2000**	**1990-2000**
Aged 60 to 64	588	666	786	78	121	199	13.3%	18.1%	33.8
Aged 65 to 69	463	556	630	93	74	167	20.2	13.3	36.1
Aged 70 to 74	304	419	503	114	85	199	37.5	20.2	65.3
Aged 75 to 79	226	259	357	33	98	131	14.6	37.6	57.7
Aged 80 to 84	138	176	204	38	27	65	27.4	15.5	47.3
Aged 85 or older	100	143	192	42	50	92	42.3	34.8	91.8

Source: TGE Demographics, Inc., Ithaca, New York
Note: The 1990 population here has been adjusted by the Census Bureau's estimated undercount. The undercount is distributed by age, race, and Hispanic origin.
Numbers may not add to total due to rounding. Hispanics may be of any race.

Median Age, 1950 to 2020

The median age of Americans fell in the 1960s and 1970s because the baby boomers were children and teenagers. By 2020, the median age will reach 40 as baby boomers reach retirement age.

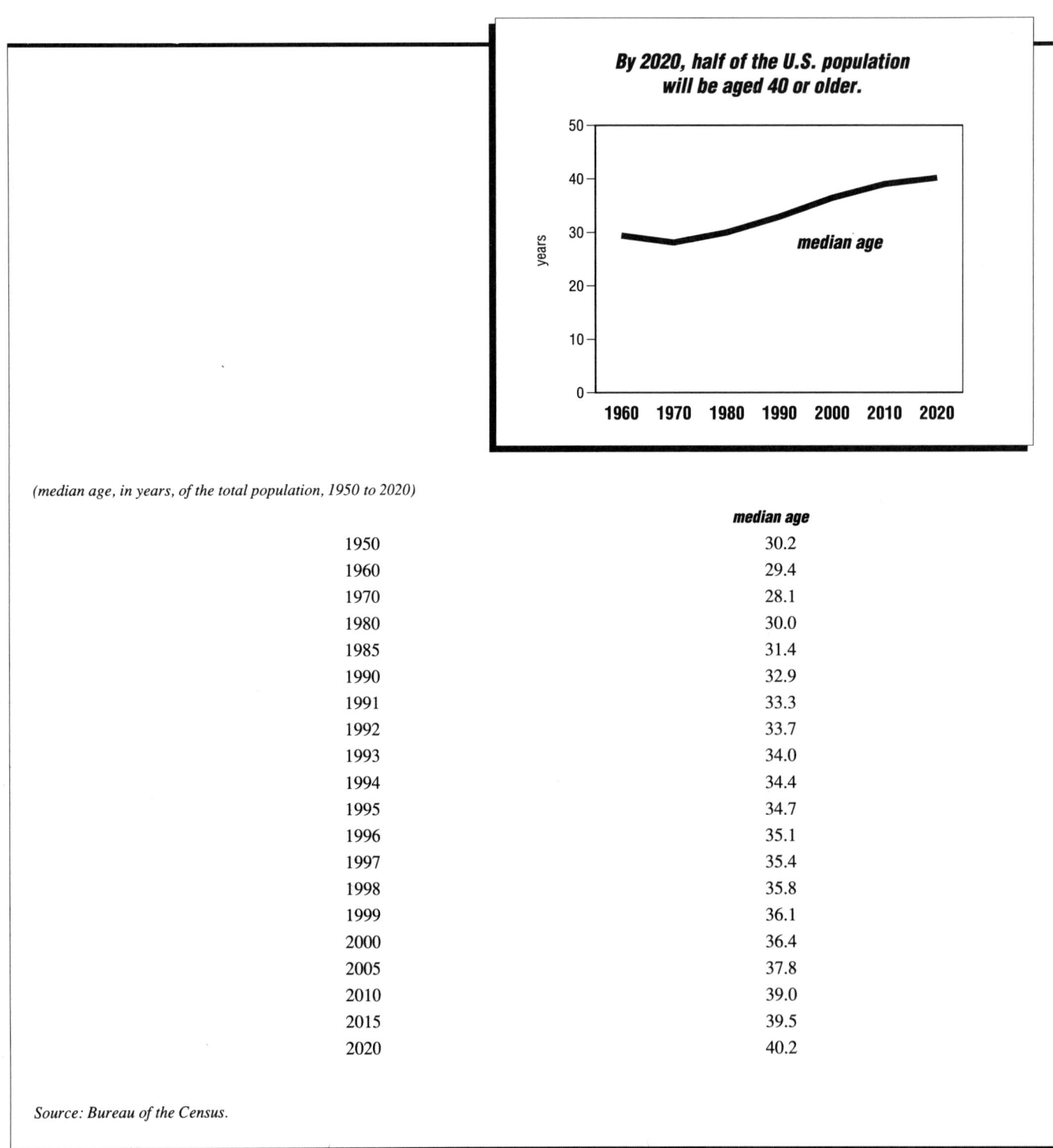

(median age, in years, of the total population, 1950 to 2020)

	median age
1950	30.2
1960	29.4
1970	28.1
1980	30.0
1985	31.4
1990	32.9
1991	33.3
1992	33.7
1993	34.0
1994	34.4
1995	34.7
1996	35.1
1997	35.4
1998	35.8
1999	36.1
2000	36.4
2005	37.8
2010	39.0
2015	39.5
2020	40.2

Source: Bureau of the Census.

Median Age of the Baby Boom and Baby Bust, 1980 to 2020

In any year, the median age of the baby boom is a good indicator of major trends in American society. The median age of the baby bust marks the trough in the generation following the baby boom.

(age, median age, and size of the baby boom and the baby bust, 1980 to 2020; baby boom born 1946-64; baby bust born 1965-76; numbers in thousands)

	baby boom			baby bust		
	age	median age	number	age	median age	number
1980	16 to 34	24	75,509	4 to 15	9	42,144
1990	26 to 44	34	77,745	14 to 25	19	43,454
1991	27 to 45	35	77,773	15 to 26	20	43,533
1992	28 to 46	36	77,780	16 to 27	21	43,620
1993	29 to 47	37	78,004	17 to 28	22	43,555
1994	30 to 48	38	77,761	18 to 29	23	43,806
1995	31 to 49	39	77,597	19 to 30	24	44,071
1996	32 to 50	40	77,570	20 to 31	25	44,083
1997	33 to 51	41	77,416	21 to 32	26	44,146
1998	34 to 52	42	77,294	22 to 33	27	44,241
1999	35 to 53	43	77,067	23 to 34	28	44,484
2000	36 to 54	44	76,947	24 to 35	29	44,670
2005	41 to 59	49	75,979	29 to 40	34	45,186
2010	46 to 64	54	74,590	34 to 45	39	44,758
2015	51 to 69	58	72,139	39 to 50	44	44,531
2020	56 to 74	63	68,055	44 to 55	49	44,060

Source: Bureau of the Census

Population Growth Due to Immigration, 1980 to 1990

For most years during the 1980s, immigration accounted for more than one-quarter of U.S. population growth. In 1990, immigrants represented 25 percent of our annual growth.

(total annual population gain, annual number of immigrants, and percent of population gain due to immigration, 1980-90; numbers in thousands)

	change in population	number of immigrants	share of population gain due to immigration
1980	2,236	531	23.7%
1981	2,234	597	26.7
1982	2,129	594	27.9
1983	2,049	560	27.3
1984	2,122	544	25.6
1985	2,188	570	26.1
1986	2,156	602	27.9
1987	2,221	602	27.1
1988	2,286	643	28.1
1989	2,632	612*	23.3
1990	2,651	656*	24.7

* Does not include aliens who had been living in the U.S. under temporary residence status since 1982—478,814 in 1989, 880,372 in 1990—who were granted permanent status.
Source: Bureau of the Census

Immigrants by Country of Birth

Nearly 20 percent of new immigrants in 1989 were from Mexico and the Philippines. In 1990, the number of legal immigrants from Mexico declined, while the number coming from the former Soviet Union increased by 130 percent.

(immigrants admitted from the top 15 countries of birth, excluding IRCA legalization of aliens in residence, 1989 and 1990)

			percent distribution	
	1990	*1989*	*1990*	*1989*
Total	**656,111**	**612,110**	**100.0%**	**100.0%**
Mexico	56,549	66,445	8.6	10.9
Philippines	54,907	49,749	8.4	8.1
Vietnam	48,662	37,572	7.4	6.1
Dominican Republic	32,064	25,622	4.9	4.2
Korea	29,548	32,218	4.5	5.3
China (Mainland)	28,746	27,489	4.4	4.5
India	28,679	28,517	4.4	4.7
Soviet Union	25,350	11,009	3.9	1.8
Jamaica	18,828	21,991	2.9	3.6
Iran	18,031	17,155	2.7	2.8
Taiwan	13,839	12,470	2.1	2.0
United Kingdom	13,730	12,892	2.1	2.1
Canada	13,717	10,618	2.1	1.7
Poland	13,334	9,610	2.0	1.6
Haiti	11,862	9,700	1.8	1.6
Other	248,265	239,053	37.8	39.1

Source: Immigration and Naturalization Service

American Mobility, 1950-1990

The share of Americans who move each year has dropped since the 1950s. Most moves in 1989-90 were to a different house in the same county.

(number of persons aged 1 or older moving per year and annual mobility rates by type of move, selected years 1950-90; numbers in thousands)

Number	total	total movers	total	different house, same county	total	same state	different state	different region	not living in U.S. in beginning of year
					residing in U.S. at beginning of year				
						different county			
1989-90	242,208	43,381	41,821	25,726	16,094	8,061	8,033	3,761	1,560
1985-86	232,998	43,237	42,037	26,401	15,636	8,665	6,971	3,778	1,200
1980-81	221,641	38,200	36,887	23,097	13,789	7,614	6,175	3,363	1,313
1970-71	201,506	37,705	36,161	23,018	13,143	6,197	6,946	3,936	1,544
1960-61	177,354	36,533	35,535	24,289	11,246	5,493	5,753	3,097	998
1950-51	148,400	31,464	31,158	20,694	10,464	5,276	5,188	na	306
Percent									
1989-90	100.0%	17.9%	17.3%	10.6%	6.6%	3.3%	3.3%	1.6%	0.6%
1985-86	100.0	18.6	18.0	11.3	6.7	3.7	3.0	1.6	0.5
1980-81	100.0	17.2	16.6	10.4	6.2	3.4	2.8	1.5	0.6
1970-71	100.0	18.7	17.9	11.4	6.5	3.1	3.4	2.0	0.8
1960-61	100.0	20.6	20.0	13.7	6.3	3.1	3.2	1.7	0.6
1950-51	100.0	21.2	21.0	13.9	7.1	3.6	3.5	na	0.2

Source: Bureau of the Census
Note: (na) means data not available.

Characteristics of Movers

Americans in their 20s and early 30s are most likely to move. Men and people who are unemployed have higher mobility rates than women and employed workers.

(number of persons aged 1 or older moving between 1989 and 1990 and annual mobility rate by type of move, age, sex, and employment status; numbers in thousands)

Number	total	total movers	total	local move (same county)	long-distance (different county) total	same state	different state	movers from abroad
All persons	**242,208**	**43,381**	**41,821**	**25,726**	**16,094**	**8,061**	**8,033**	**1,560**
Age								
Aged 1 to 4	14,948	3,553	3,474	2,275	1,199	555	644	79
Aged 5 to 9	18,300	3,480	3,373	2,238	1,135	545	590	107
Aged 10 to 14	17,168	2,559	2,452	1,559	892	398	494	107
Aged 15 to 19	17,266	3,068	2,874	1,789	1,085	557	528	194
Aged 20 to 24	17,988	6,810	6,532	4,046	2,486	1,340	1,146	278
Aged 25 to 29	21,200	7,080	6,861	4,172	2,689	1,386	1,303	219
Aged 30 to 34	22,040	5,116	4,953	3,023	1,929	931	999	163
Aged 35 to 39	19,891	3,572	3,433	2,077	1,355	621	734	139
Aged 40 to 44	17,304	2,421	2,342	1,406	936	466	470	79
Aged 45 to 49	13,860	1,456	1,408	813	595	339	256	48
Aged 50 to 54	11,444	1,041	1,008	625	383	182	201	33
Aged 55 to 59	10,549	870	841	477	364	171	194	29
Aged 60 to 64	10,683	742	700	355	345	189	155	42
Aged 65 to 69	10,126	583	567	314	253	141	112	16
Aged 70 to 74	7,853	334	328	187	141	79	62	6
Aged 75 to 79	5,791	336	327	178	149	80	69	9
Aged 80 to 84	3,563	218	212	114	97	44	54	6
Aged 85 or older	2,233	143	137	76	61	39	23	6
Median age	33.2	26.5	26.6	26.1	27.3	27.3	27.4	25.3
Sex								
Male	117,791	21,681	20,838	12,698	8,140	4,089	4,052	843
Female	124,416	21,700	20,983	13,029	7,954	3,973	3,982	717
Employment status								
Employed	116,669	22,569	21,950	13,471	8,479	4,454	4,026	619
Unemployed	6,830	2,019	1,931	1,131	800	386	414	88
Percent								
All persons	**100.0%**	**17.9%**	**17.3%**	**10.6%**	**6.6%**	**3.3%**	**3.3%**	**0.6%**
Age								
Aged 1 to 4	100.0	23.8	23.2	15.2	8.0	3.7	4.3	0.5
Aged 5 to 9	100.0	19.0	18.4	12.2	6.2	3.0	3.2	0.6

(continued on next page)

(continued from previous page)

(number of persons aged 1 or older moving between 1989 and 1990 and annual mobility rates by type of move, age, sex, and employment status; numbers in thousands)

	total	total movers	total	local move (same county)	long-distance (different county) total	same state	different state	movers from abroad
					different house in the U.S.			
Aged 10 to 14	100.0%	14.9%	14.3%	9.1%	5.2%	2.3%	2.9%	0.6%
Aged 15 to 19	100.0	17.8	16.6	10.4	6.3	3.2	3.1	1.1
Aged 20 to 24	100.0	37.9	36.3	22.5	13.8	7.4	6.4	1.5
Aged 25 to 29	100.0	33.4	32.4	19.7	12.7	6.5	6.1	1.0
Aged 30 to 34	100.0	23.2	22.5	13.7	8.8	4.2	4.5	0.7
Aged 35 to 39	100.0	18.0	17.3	10.4	6.8	3.1	3.7	0.7
Aged 40 to 44	100.0	14.0	13.5	8.1	5.4	2.7	2.7	0.5
Aged 45 to 49	100.0	10.5	10.2	5.9	4.3	2.4	1.8	0.3
Aged 50 to 54	100.0	9.1	8.8	5.5	3.3	1.6	1.8	0.3
Aged 55 to 59	100.0	8.2	8.0	4.5	3.5	1.6	1.8	0.3
Aged 60 to 64	100.0	6.9	6.6	3.3	3.2	1.8	1.5	0.4
Aged 65 to 69	100.0	5.8	5.6	3.1	2.5	1.4	1.1	0.2
Aged 70 to 74	100.0	4.3	4.2	2.4	1.8	1.0	0.8	0.1
Aged 75 to 79	100.0	5.8	5.6	3.1	2.6	1.4	1.2	0.2
Aged 80 to 84	100.0	6.1	6.0	3.2	2.7	1.2	1.5	0.2
Aged 85 or older	100.0	6.4	6.1	3.4	2.7	1.7	1.0	0.3
Sex								
Male	100.0	18.4	17.7	10.8	6.9	3.5	3.4	0.7
Female	100.0	17.4	16.9	10.5	6.4	3.2	3.2	0.6
Employment status								
Employed	100.0	19.3	18.8	11.5	7.3	3.8	3.5	0.5
Unemployed	100.0	29.6	28.3	16.6	11.7	5.7	6.1	1.3

Source: Bureau of the Census

State Populations, 1980 and 1990

California is the most populous state in the nation, and one of the fastest growing. During the 1980s, it gained over 6 million new residents.

(state population size in 1990 and 1980, change and percent change in state populations, 1980-90; states ranked by resident population in 1990; numbers in thousands)

	1990 population	1980 population	change 1980-90 number	change 1980-90 percent change
Total	**248,710**	**226,546**	**22,164**	**9.8%**
1. California	29,760	23,668	6,092	25.7
2. New York	17,990	17,558	432	2.5
3. Texas	16,987	14,229	2,758	19.4
4. Florida	12,938	9,746	3,192	32.7
5. Pennsylvania	11,882	11,864	18	0.1
6. Illinois	11,431	11,427	4	0.0
7. Ohio	10,847	10,798	49	0.5
8. Michigan	9,295	9,262	33	0.4
9. New Jersey	7,730	7,365	365	5.0
10. North Carolina	6,629	5,882	747	12.7
11. Georgia	6,478	5,463	1,015	18.6
12. Virginia	6,187	5,347	840	15.7
13. Massachusetts	6,016	5,737	279	4.9
14. Indiana	5,544	5,490	54	1.0
15. Missouri	5,117	4,917	200	4.1
16. Wisconsin	4,892	4,706	186	4.0
17. Tennessee	4,877	4,591	286	6.2
18. Washington	4,867	4,132	735	17.8
19. Maryland	4,781	4,217	564	13.4
20. Minnesota	4,375	4,076	299	7.3
21. Louisiana	4,220	4,206	14	0.3
22. Alabama	4,041	3,894	147	3.8
23. Kentucky	3,685	3,661	24	0.7
24. Arizona	3,665	2,718	947	34.8
25. South Carolina	3,487	3,122	365	11.7
26. Colorado	3,294	2,890	404	14.0
27. Connecticut	3,287	3,108	179	5.8
28. Oklahoma	3,146	3,025	121	4.0
29. Oregon	2,842	2,633	209	7.9
30. Iowa	2,777	2,914	-137	-4.7
31. Mississippi	2,573	2,521	52	2.1
32. Kansas	2,478	2,364	114	4.8
33. Arkansas	2,351	2,286	65	2.8
34. West Virginia	1,793	1,950	-157	-8.0
35. Utah	1,723	1,461	262	17.9

(continued on next page)

(continued from previous page)

(state population size in 1990 and 1980, change and percent change in state populations, 1980 to 1990; states ranked by resident population in 1990; numbers in thousands)

	1990 population	1980 population	change 1980 to 1990	
			number	percent change
36. Nebraska	1,578	1,570	8	0.5%
37. New Mexico	1,515	1,303	212	16.3
38. Maine	1,228	1,125	103	9.2
39. Nevada	1,202	800	402	50.1
40. New Hampshire	1,109	921	188	20.5
41. Hawaii	1,108	965	143	14.9
42. Idaho	1,007	944	63	6.7
43. Rhode Island	1,003	947	56	5.9
44. Montana	799	787	12	1.6
45. South Dakota	696	691	5	0.8
46. Delaware	666	594	72	12.1
47. North Dakota	639	653	-14	-2.1
48. District of Columbia	607	638	-31	-4.9
49. Vermont	563	511	52	10.0
50. Alaska	550	402	148	36.9
51. Wyoming	454	470	-16	-3.4

Source: Bureau of the Census

State Populations by Age

The baby-boom generation is inflating the number of 25-to-44-year-olds in every state. Three states have more than 1 million residents aged 75 or older—California, New York, and Florida.

(state resident populations by age, 1990; numbers in thousands)

	all ages	under 5	5 to 17	18 to 24	25 to 44	45 to 54	55 to 64	65 to 74	75+
United States	**248,710**	**18,354**	**45,250**	**26,738**	**80,755**	**25,223**	**21,148**	**18,107**	**13,135**
Alabama	4,041	283	775	443	1,232	419	364	301	222
Alaska	550	55	117	56	216	54	29	16	7
Arizona	3,665	293	688	393	1,164	350	300	290	189
Arkansas	2,351	165	456	237	686	243	213	196	154
California	29,760	2,398	5,353	3,412	10,326	2,903	2,233	1,857	1,278
Colorado	3,294	253	608	336	1,180	337	252	195	135
Connecticut	3,287	228	521	345	1,095	356	295	256	190
Delaware	666	49	115	76	218	68	60	50	31
District of Columbia	607	37	80	83	216	62	51	45	33
Florida	12,938	850	2,017	1,216	3,927	1,292	1,268	1,370	1,000
Georgia	6,478	496	1,232	739	2,191	669	499	388	266
Hawaii	1,108	83	197	121	379	109	94	79	46
Idaho	1,007	80	228	98	302	99	78	70	52
Illinois	11,431	848	2,098	1,213	3,693	1,167	975	822	615
Indiana	5,544	399	1,057	605	1,734	571	482	402	294
Iowa	2,777	193	526	284	824	274	250	227	199
Kansas	2,478	188	473	254	774	235	209	185	158
Kentucky	3,685	251	703	400	1,159	382	323	268	199
Louisiana	4,220	335	893	465	1,310	406	343	275	194
Maine	1,228	86	223	124	399	125	108	92	72
Maryland	4,781	358	804	505	1,677	522	397	314	203
Massachusetts	6,016	412	941	709	2,020	600	515	460	359
Michigan	9,295	703	1,756	1,005	2,981	948	795	656	453
Minnesota	4,375	337	830	443	1,446	428	344	295	252
Mississippi	2,573	195	551	293	750	248	214	180	141
Missouri	5,117	369	946	517	1,587	523	457	394	323
Montana	799	59	163	70	250	82	68	61	46
Nebraska	1,578	120	309	156	486	149	135	118	105
Nevada	1,202	92	205	119	414	136	108	86	42
New Hampshire	1,109	85	194	118	387	112	88	71	54
New Jersey	7,730	533	1,267	779	2,557	843	719	610	422
New Mexico	1,515	126	321	152	484	147	122	98	65
New York	17,990	1,256	3,004	1,953	5,863	1,914	1,637	1,348	1,015
North Carolina	6,629	459	1,147	781	2,151	699	587	483	321
North Dakota	639	48	128	68	194	57	53	48	44
Ohio	10,847	785	2,015	1,136	3,411	1,113	980	828	579

(continued on next page)

(continued from previous page)

(state resident populations by age, 1990; numbers in thousands)

	all ages	under 5	5 to 17	18 to 24	25 to 44	45 to 54	55 to 64	65 to 74	75+
Oklahoma	3,146	227	610	321	962	323	278	235	189
Oregon	2,842	201	523	268	926	297	236	224	167
Pennsylvania	11,882	797	1,998	1,227	3,657	1,214	1,160	1,070	759
Rhode Island	1,003	67	159	120	321	96	89	86	65
South Carolina	3,487	256	664	407	1,115	356	293	246	151
South Dakota	696	55	144	68	205	63	60	54	48
Tennessee	4,877	333	883	528	1,553	526	435	357	261
Texas	16,987	1,390	3,446	1,891	5,625	1,629	1,289	998	718
Utah	1,723	170	458	200	500	138	107	88	62
Vermont	563	41	102	63	188	57	45	37	29
Virginia	6,187	443	1,062	720	2,132	663	503	401	264
Washington	4,867	367	895	489	1,659	502	381	336	239
West Virginia	1,793	107	337	180	533	191	177	156	113
Wisconsin	4,892	361	928	512	1,547	479	414	358	293
Wyoming	454	35	101	41	148	45	35	28	19

Source: Bureau of the Census

Share of State Populations Under Age 18

The percentage of the population under age 18 is below average in the Northeast and much of the South, while it is above average in the central part of the country.

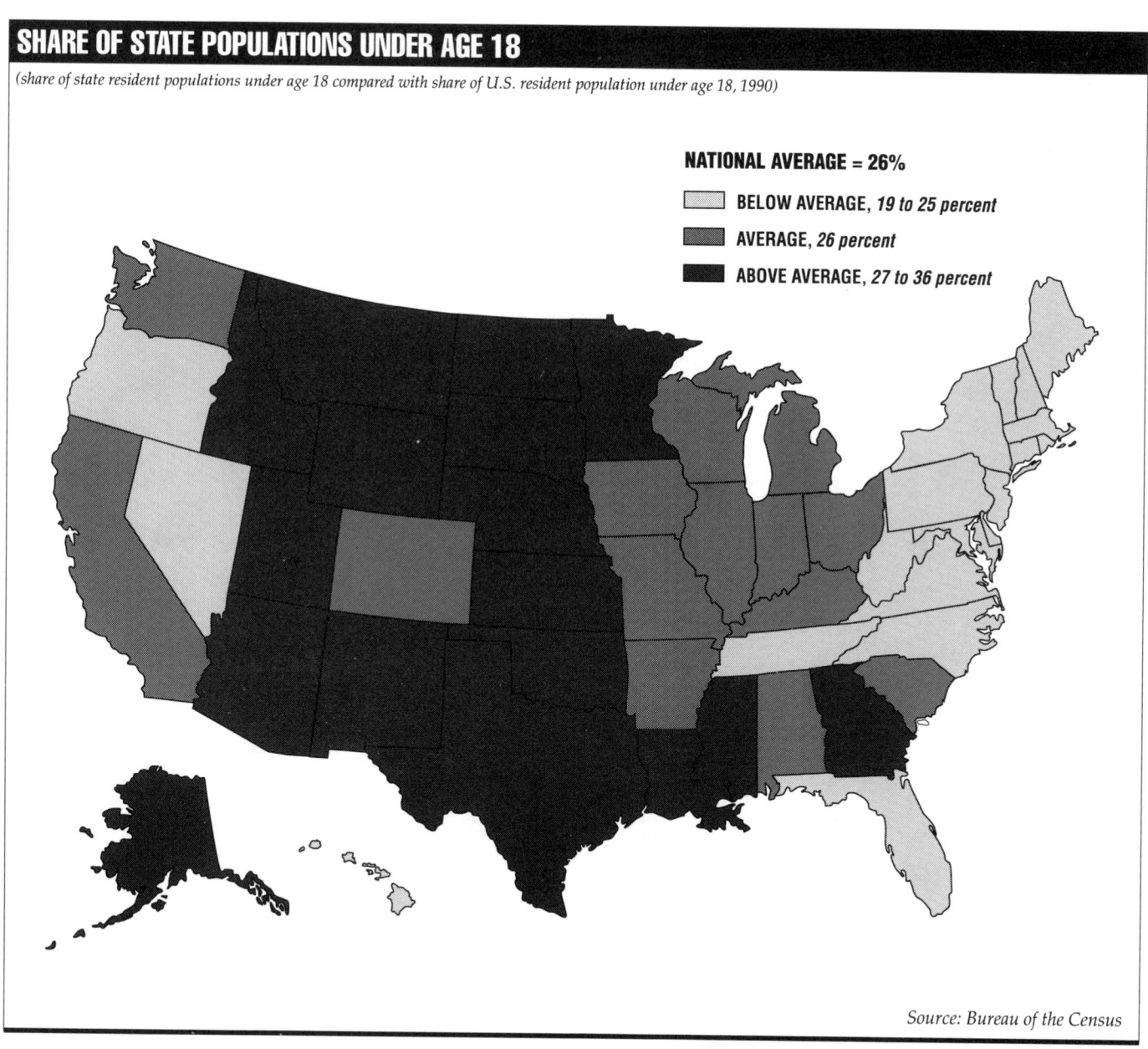

SHARE OF STATE POPULATIONS UNDER AGE 18

(share of state resident populations under age 18 compared with share of U.S. resident population under age 18, 1990)

NATIONAL AVERAGE = 26%

BELOW AVERAGE, *19 to 25 percent*

AVERAGE, *26 percent*

ABOVE AVERAGE, *27 to 36 percent*

Source: Bureau of the Census

Share of State Populations Aged 18 to 24

The share of the population aged 18 to 24 is above average in only a few states such as Utah, Virginia, and Massachusetts.

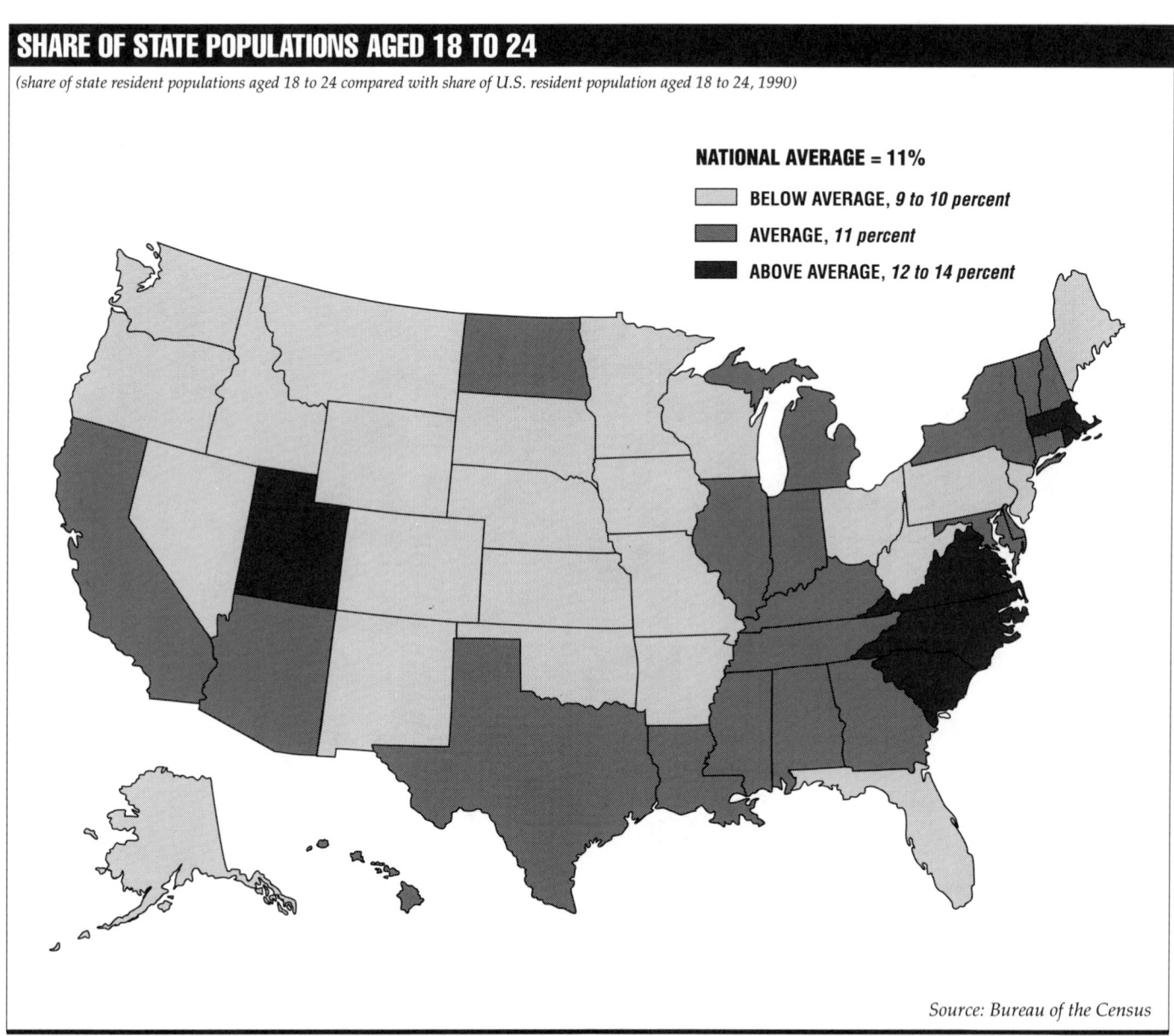

SHARE OF STATE POPULATIONS AGED 18 TO 24

(share of state resident populations aged 18 to 24 compared with share of U.S. resident population aged 18 to 24, 1990)

NATIONAL AVERAGE = 11%

BELOW AVERAGE, *9 to 10 percent*

AVERAGE, *11 percent*

ABOVE AVERAGE, *12 to 14 percent*

Source: Bureau of the Census

Share of State Populations Aged 25 to 44

The percentage of people aged 25 to 44 (baby boomers) is above average in some of the most populous states in the country—California, New York, and Texas.

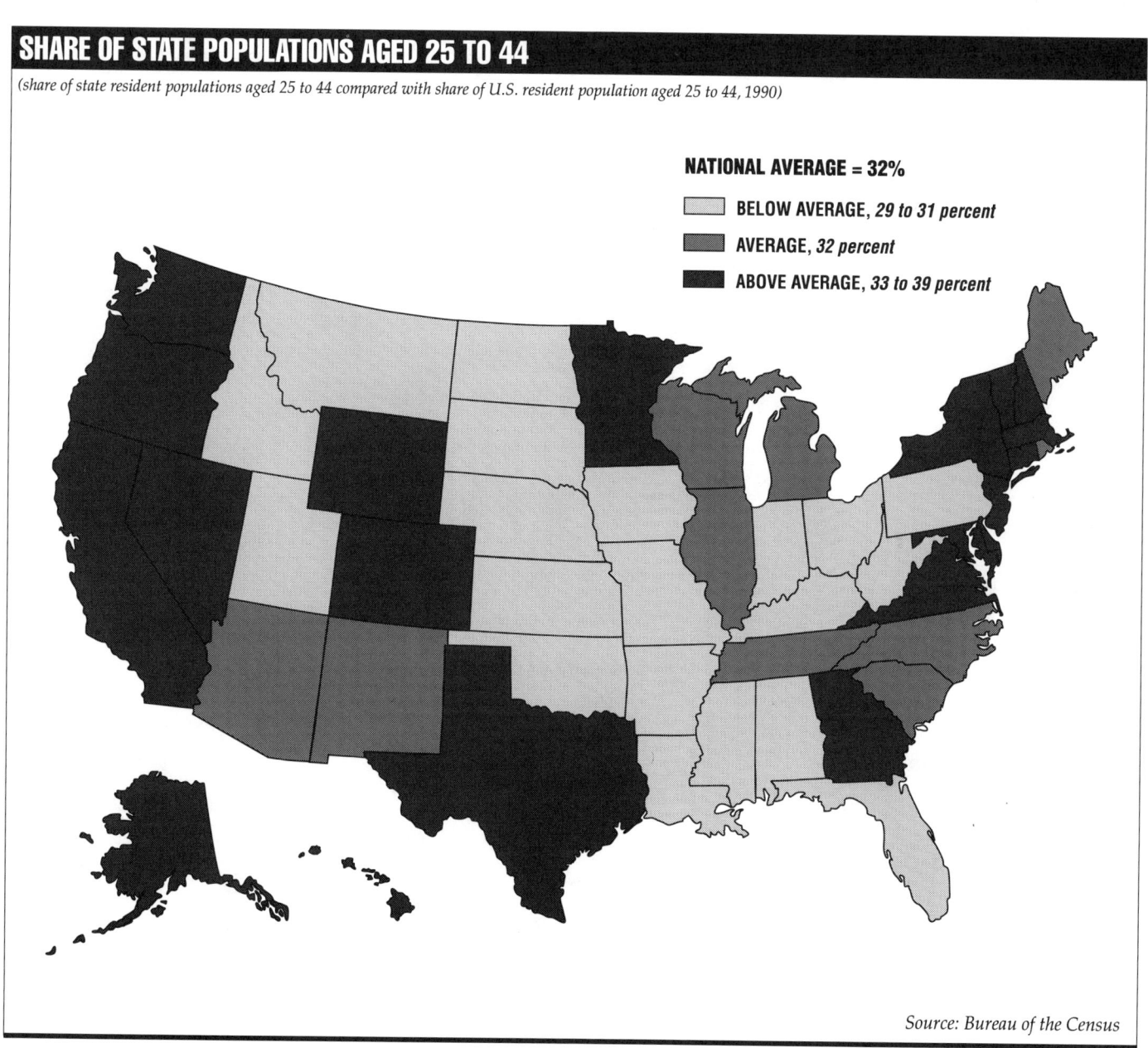

SHARE OF STATE POPULATIONS AGED 25 TO 44

(share of state resident populations aged 25 to 44 compared with share of U.S. resident population aged 25 to 44, 1990)

NATIONAL AVERAGE = 32%

BELOW AVERAGE, *29 to 31 percent*

AVERAGE, *32 percent*

ABOVE AVERAGE, *33 to 39 percent*

Source: Bureau of the Census

Share of State Populations Aged 45 to 64

The percentage of people aged 45 to 64 is below average in many states, particularly in the West.

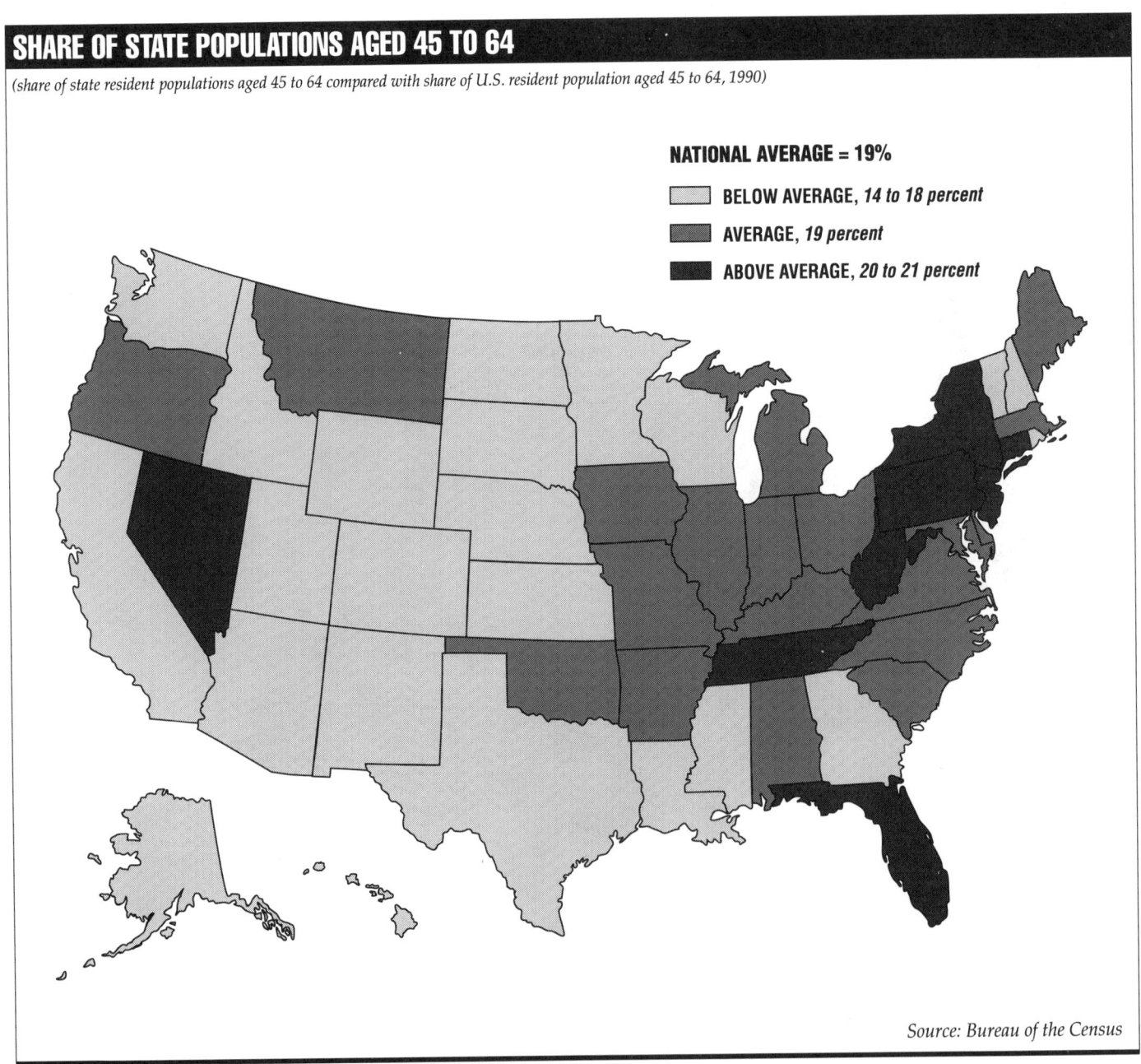

SHARE OF STATE POPULATIONS AGED 45 TO 64

(share of state resident populations aged 45 to 64 compared with share of U.S. resident population aged 45 to 64, 1990)

NATIONAL AVERAGE = 19%

- BELOW AVERAGE, *14 to 18 percent*
- AVERAGE, *19 percent*
- ABOVE AVERAGE, *20 to 21 percent*

Source: Bureau of the Census

Share of State Populations Aged 65 or Older

The percentage of people aged 65 or older is above average in retirement states like Florida, and also in the Midwest, which younger people have fled, looking for jobs elsewhere.

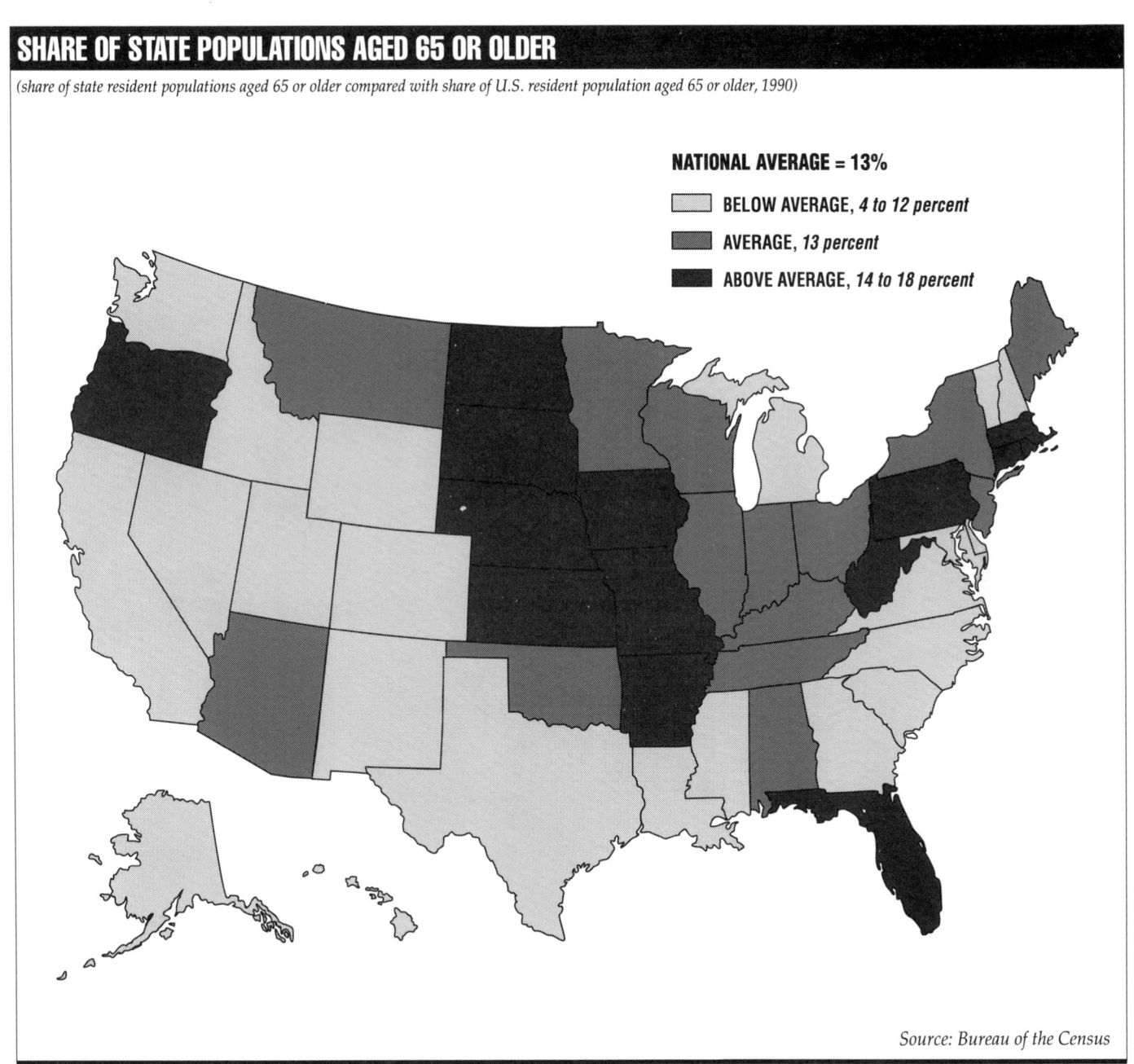

SHARE OF STATE POPULATIONS AGED 65 OR OLDER

(share of state resident populations aged 65 or older compared with share of U.S. resident population aged 65 or older, 1990)

NATIONAL AVERAGE = 13%

BELOW AVERAGE, *4 to 12 percent*

AVERAGE, *13 percent*

ABOVE AVERAGE, *14 to 18 percent*

Source: Bureau of the Census

State Populations, 1990 to 2000

By 2000, Texas will be the second most populous state in the nation, while New York will slip to third. Florida's population will not surpass New York's until after the turn of the century.

(resident population in 1990 and projected resident population in 2000; states ranked by population in 2000; percent change in population, 1990 to 2000)

	1990	*2000*	*percent change 1990–2000*
United States	**248,710**	**267,747**	**7.7%**
1. California	29,760	33,500	12.6
2. Texas	16,987	20,211	19.0
3. New York	17,990	17,986	0.0
4. Florida	12,938	15,415	19.1
5. Illinois	11,431	11,580	1.3
6. Pennsylvania	11,882	11,503	-3.2
7. Ohio	10,847	10,629	-2.0
8. Michigan	9,295	9,250	-0.5
9. New Jersey	7,730	8,546	10.6
10. Georgia	6,478	7,957	22.8
11. North Carolina	6,629	7,483	12.9
12. Virginia	6,187	6,877	11.2
13. Massachusetts	6,016	6,087	1.2
14. Indiana	5,544	5,502	-0.8
15. Missouri	5,117	5,383	5.2
16. Maryland	4,781	5,274	10.3
17. Tennessee	4,877	5,266	8.0
18. Washington	4,867	4,991	2.5
19. Wisconsin	4,892	4,784	-2.2
20. Arizona	3,665	4,618	26.0
21. Louisiana	4,220	4,516	7.0
22. Minnesota	4,375	4,490	2.6
23. Alabama	4,041	4,410	9.1
24. South Carolina	3,487	3,906	12.0
25. Colorado	3,294	3,813	15.8
26. Kentucky	3,685	3,733	1.3
27. Connecticut	3,287	3,445	4.8
28. Oklahoma	3,146	3,376	7.3
29. Oregon	2,842	2,877	1.2
30. Mississippi	2,573	2,877	11.8
31. Iowa	2,777	2,549	-8.2
32. Kansas	2,478	2,529	2.1
33. Arkansas	2,351	2,529	7.6
34. Utah	1,723	1,991	15.6
35. New Mexico	1,515	1,968	29.9

(continued on next page)

(continued from previous page)

(resident population in 1990 and projected resident population in 2000; states ranked by population in 2000; percent change in population, 1990 to 2000)

	1990	2000	percent change 1990–2000
36. West Virginia	1,793	1,722	-4.0%
37. Nebraska	1,578	1,556	-1.4
38. Hawaii	1,108	1,345	21.4
39. New Hampshire	1,109	1,333	20.2
40. Nevada	1,202	1,303	8.4
41. Maine	1,228	1,271	3.5
42. Rhode Island	1,003	1,049	4.6
43. Idaho	1,007	1,047	4.0
44. Montana	799	794	-0.6
45. Delaware	666	734	10.2
46. South Dakota	696	714	2.6
47. Alaska	550	687	24.9
48. District of Columbia	607	634	4.4
49. North Dakota	639	629	-1.6
50. Vermont	563	591	5.0
51. Wyoming	454	489	7.7

Source: Bureau of the Census.
Note: Numbers may not add to total due to rounding.

State Population Changes, 1990–2000

The most rapidly growing states during the 1990s are projected to be those in the South and West.

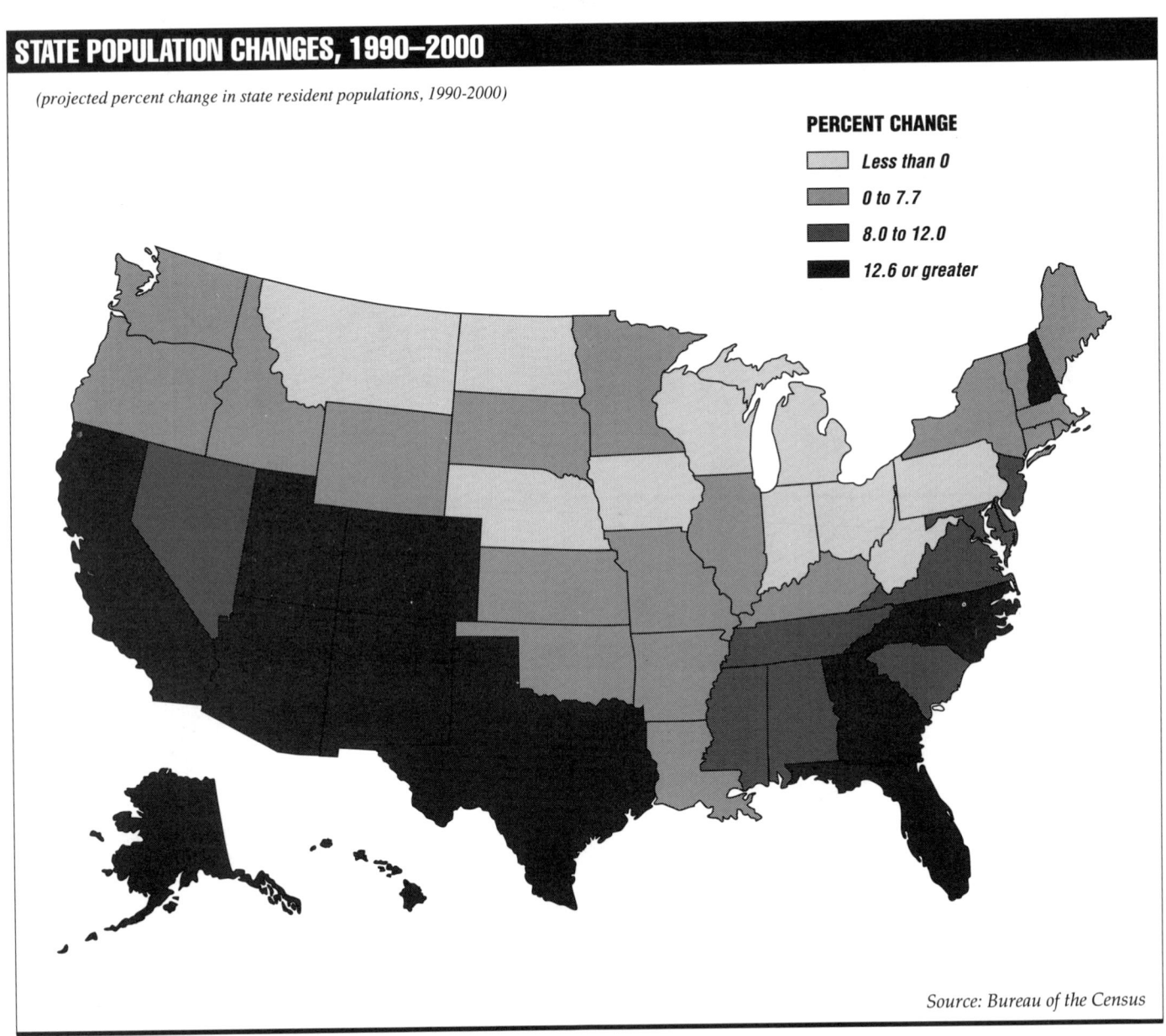

STATE POPULATION CHANGES, 1990–2000

(projected percent change in state resident populations, 1990-2000)

PERCENT CHANGE

- Less than 0
- 0 to 7.7
- 8.0 to 12.0
- 12.6 or greater

Source: Bureau of the Census

State Populations by Race and Hispanic Origin

Blacks numbered more than 1 million in 16 states in 1990, while Hispanics reached the 1 million mark in only 4 states. California is the only state with more than 1 million Asians.

(white and minority populations of states in 1990; states ranked by resident population in 1990; numbers in thousands)

	total	white	black	Am. Indian Eskimo, Aleut	Asian Pac. Islander	other races	Hispanic
United States	248,710	199,686	29,986	1,959	7,274	9,805	22,354
1. California	29,760	20,524	2,209	242	2,846	3,939	7,688
2. New York	17,990	13,385	2,859	63	694	990	2,214
3. Texas	16,987	12,775	2,022	66	319	1,805	4,340
4. Florida	12,938	10,749	1,760	36	154	238	1,574
5. Pennsylvania	11,882	10,520	1,090	15	137	119	232
6. Illinois	11,431	8,953	1,694	22	285	476	904
7. Ohio	10,847	9,522	1,155	20	91	59	140
8. Michigan	9,295	7,756	1,292	56	105	87	202
9. New Jersey	7,730	6,130	1,037	15	273	275	740
10. North Carolina	6,629	5,008	1,456	80	52	32	77
11. Georgia	6,478	4,600	1,747	13	76	42	109
12. Virginia	6,187	4,792	1,163	15	159	58	160
13. Massachusetts	6,016	5,405	300	12	143	155	288
14. Indiana	5,544	5,021	432	13	38	41	99
15. Missouri	5,117	4,486	548	20	41	22	62
16. Wisconsin	4,892	4,513	245	39	54	42	93
17. Tennessee	4,877	4,048	778	10	32	9	33
18. Washington	4,867	4,309	150	81	211	116	215
19. Maryland	4,781	3,394	1,190	13	140	45	125
20. Minnesota	4,375	4,130	95	50	78	22	54
21. Louisiana	4,220	2,839	1,299	19	41	22	93
22. Alabama	4,041	2,976	1,021	17	22	6	25
23. Kentucky	3,685	3,392	263	6	18	7	22
24. Arizona	3,665	2,963	111	204	55	333	688
25. South Carolina	3,487	2,407	1,040	8	22	9	31
26. Colorado	3,294	2,905	133	28	60	168	424
27. Connecticut	3,287	2,859	274	7	51	96	213
28. Oklahoma	3,146	2,584	234	252	34	42	86
29. Oregon	2,842	2,637	46	38	69	52	113
30. Iowa	2,777	2,683	48	7	25	13	33
31. Mississippi	2,573	1,633	915	9	13	3	16
32. Kansas	2,478	2,232	143	22	32	49	94
33. Arkansas	2,351	1,945	374	13	13	7	20
34. West Virginia	1,793	1,726	56	2	7	2	8
35. Utah	1,723	1,616	12	24	33	38	85

(continued on next page)

(continued from previous page)

(white and minority populations of states in 1990; states ranked by resident population in 1990; numbers in thousands)

	total	white	black	Am. Indian Eskimo, Aleut	Asian Pac. Islander	other races	Hispanic
36. Nebraska	1,578	1,481	57	12	12	16	37
37. New Mexico	1,515	1,146	30	134	14	190	579
38. Maine	1,228	1,208	5	6	7	2	7
39. Nevada	1,202	1,013	79	20	38	53	124
40. New Hampshire	1,109	1,087	7	2	9	3	11
41. Hawaii	1,108	370	27	5	685	21	81
42. Idaho	1,007	950	3	14	9	30	53
43. Rhode Island	1,003	917	39	4	18	25	46
44. Montana	799	741	2	48	4	4	12
45. South Dakota	696	638	3	51	3	2	5
46. Delaware	666	535	112	2	9	8	16
47. North Dakota	639	604	4	26	3	2	5
48. District of Columbia	607	180	400	1	11	15	33
49. Vermont	563	555	2	2	3	1	4
50. Alaska	550	415	22	86	20	7	18
51. Wyoming	454	427	4	9	3	11	26

Source: Bureau of the Census
Note: Hispanics may be of any race.

Percent Change in Racial and Ethnic Populations by State, 1980 to 1990

The white population fell in 12 states during the 1980s. The Hispanic population more than doubled in 5 states, while the Asian population more than doubled in 30 states and the District of Columbia.

(percent change in racial and ethnic groups by state, 1980-90; states ranked by resident population in 1990)

		total	white	black	Asian Pac. Islander	Hispanic
1.	California	25.7%	13.8%	21.4%	127.0%	69.2%
2.	New York	2.5	-4.1	19.0	123.4	33.4
3.	Texas	19.4	14.1	18.2	165.5	45.4
4.	Florida	32.7	31.3	31.0	171.9	83.4
5.	Pennsylvania	0.1	-1.2	4.1	113.5	50.9
6.	Illinois	0.0	-3.0	1.1	78.7	42.3
7.	Ohio	0.5	-0.8	7.3	90.7	16.5
8.	Michigan	0.4	-1.5	7.7	84.9	24.1
9.	New Jersey	5.0	0.0	12.1	162.4	50.4
10.	North Carolina	12.7	12.4	10.4	146.3	35.4
11.	Georgia	18.6	16.5	19.2	208.6	77.8
12.	Virginia	15.7	13.3	15.3	140.2	100.7
13.	Massachusetts	4.9	0.8	35.6	187.7	103.9
14.	Indiana	1.0	0.3	4.2	83.0	13.5
15.	Missouri	4.1	3.2	6.6	78.7	19.5
16.	Wisconsin	4.0	1.6	33.9	195.0	48.0
17.	Tennessee	6.2	5.5	7.2	128.0	-3.9
18.	Washington	17.8	14.0	41.9	105.7	78.8
19.	Maryland	13.4	7.4	24.2	117.4	93.2
20.	Minnesota	7.3	4.9	78.0	193.5	67.7
21.	Louisiana	0.3	-2.5	4.9	72.8	-6.1
22.	Alabama	3.8	3.6	2.4	123.9	-26.0
23.	Kentucky	0.7	0.4	1.3	78.7	-19.8
24.	Arizona	34.8	32.2	47.4	150.6	56.2
25.	South Carolina	11.7	12.1	9.6	89.1	-8.6
26.	Colorado	14.0	13.0	30.9	100.1	24.9
27.	Connecticut	5.8	2.1	26.1	167.3	71.2
28.	Oklahoma	4.0	-0.5	14.2	94.3	50.1
29.	Oregon	7.9	5.9	24.6	99.2	71.2
30.	Iowa	4.7	-5.5	15.3	120.1	27.8
31.	Mississippi	2.1	1.1	3.1	75.6	-35.6
32.	Kansas	4.8	2.9	13.4	110.6	47.9
33.	Arkansas	2.8	2.9	0.0	85.9	11.0
34.	West Virginia	-8.0	-8.0	-13.5	43.6	-33.2
35.	Utah	17.9	16.9	25.5	121.4	40.3
36.	Nebraska	0.5	-0.7	18.6	77.4	31.9

(continued on next page)

(continued from previous page)

(percent change in racial and ethnic groups by state, 1980 to 1990; states ranked by resident population in 1990)

	total	white	black	Asian Pac. Islander	Hispanic
37. New Mexico	16.3%	17.2%	25.8%	106.9%	21.4%
38. Maine	9.2	8.9	64.3	126.8	36.4
39. Nevada	50.1	44.6	54.5	169.2	130.9
40. New Hampshire	20.5	19.5	80.4	219.0	102.8
41. Hawaii	14.9	16.0	56.6	17.5	14.2
42. Idaho	6.7	5.4	24.1	57.4	44.6
43. Rhode Island	5.9	2.3	40.9	245.6	132.2
44. Montana	1.6	0.1	33.3	70.2	22.1
45. South Dakota	0.8	12.1	52.0	79.1	30.5
46. Delaware	12.1	9.7	17.3	120.3	63.8
47. North Dakota	-2.1	-3.4	37.2	74.9	19.6
48. District of Columbia	-4.9	4.6	-11.0	120.3	85.0
49. Vermont	10.0	9.5	71.9	137.3	10.8
50. Alaska	36.9	34.1	64.6	144.9	87.3
51. Wyoming	-3.4	-4.4	7.2	42.5	5.1

Source: Bureau of the Census
Note: Hispanics may be of any race.

State Populations, Percent White and Minority

Blacks were more than one-fourth of residents in five states and the District of Columbia in 1990. Hispanics were at least one-fourth of residents in three states, while Asians were a majority of Hawaii's population.

(percent distribution of white and minority groups by state, 1990; states ranked by resident state population, 1990)

	total	white	black	Am. Indian, Eskimo, Aleut	Asian, Pac. Islander	other races	Hispanic
United States	**100.0%**	**80.3%**	**12.1%**	**0.8%**	**2.9%**	**3.9%**	**9.0%**
1. California	100.0	69.0	7.4	0.8	9.6	13.2	25.8
2. New York	100.0	74.4	15.9	0.3	3.9	5.5	12.3
3. Texas	100.0	75.2	11.9	0.4	1.9	10.6	25.5
4. Florida	100.0	83.1	13.6	0.3	1.2	1.8	12.2
5. Pennsylvania	100.0	88.5	9.2	0.1	1.2	1.0	2.0
6. Illinois	100.0	78.3	14.8	0.2	2.5	4.2	7.9
7. Ohio	100.0	87.8	10.6	0.2	0.8	0.5	1.3
8. Michigan	100.0	83.4	13.9	0.6	1.1	0.9	2.2
9. New Jersey	100.0	79.3	13.4	0.2	3.5	3.6	9.6
10. North Carolina	100.0	75.6	22.0	1.2	0.8	0.5	1.2
11. Georgia	100.0	71.0	27.0	0.2	1.2	0.7	1.7
12. Virginia	100.0	77.4	18.8	0.2	2.6	0.9	2.6
13. Massachusetts	100.0	89.8	5.0	0.2	2.4	2.6	4.8
14. Indiana	100.0	90.6	7.8	0.2	0.7	0.7	1.8
15. Missouri	100.0	87.7	10.7	0.4	0.8	0.4	1.2
16. Wisconsin	100.0	92.2	5.0	0.8	1.1	0.9	1.9
17. Tennessee	100.0	83.0	16.0	0.2	0.7	0.2	0.7
18. Washington	100.0	88.5	3.1	1.7	4.3	2.4	4.4
19. Maryland	100.0	71.0	24.9	0.3	2.9	0.9	2.6
20. Minnesota	100.0	94.4	2.2	1.1	1.8	0.5	1.2
21. Louisiana	100.0	67.3	30.8	0.4	1.0	0.5	2.2
22. Alabama	100.0	73.6	25.3	0.4	0.5	0.1	0.6
23. Kentucky	100.0	92.0	7.1	0.2	0.5	0.2	0.6
24. Arizona	100.0	80.8	3.0	5.6	1.5	9.1	18.8
25. South Carolina	100.0	69.0	29.8	0.2	0.6	0.3	0.9
26. Colorado	100.0	88.2	4.0	0.8	1.8	5.1	12.9
27. Connecticut	100.0	87.0	8.3	0.2	1.5	2.9	6.5
28. Oklahoma	100.0	82.1	7.4	8.0	1.1	1.3	2.7
29. Oregon	100.0	92.8	1.6	1.4	2.4	1.8	4.0
30. Iowa	100.0	96.6	1.7	0.3	0.9	0.5	1.2
31. Mississippi	100.0	63.5	35.6	0.3	0.5	0.1	0.6
32. Kansas	100.0	90.1	5.8	0.9	1.3	2.0	3.8
33. Arkansas	100.0	82.7	15.9	0.5	0.5	0.3	0.8
34. West Virginia	100.0	96.2	3.1	0.1	0.4	0.1	0.5
35. Utah	100.0	93.8	0.7	1.4	1.9	2.2	4.9

(continued on next page)

(continued from previous page)

(percent distribution of white and minority groups by state, 1990; states ranked by resident state population, 1990)

	total	white	black	Am. Indian Eskimo, Aleut	Asian Pac. Islander	other races	Hispanic
36. Nebraska	100.0%	93.8%	3.6%	0.8%	0.8%	1.0%	2.3%
37. New Mexico	100.0	75.6	2.0	8.9	0.9	12.6	38.2
38. Maine	100.0	98.4	0.4	0.5	0.5	0.1	0.6
39. Nevada	100.0	84.3	6.6	1.6	3.2	4.4	10.4
40. New Hampshire	100.0	98.0	0.6	0.2	0.8	0.3	1.0
41. Hawaii	100.0	33.4	2.5	0.5	61.8	1.9	7.3
42. Idaho	100.0	94.4	0.3	1.4	0.9	3.0	5.3
43. Rhode Island	100.0	91.4	3.9	0.4	1.8	2.5	4.6
44. Montana	100.0	92.7	0.3	6.0	0.5	0.5	1.5
45. South Dakota	100.0	91.6	0.5	7.3	0.4	0.2	0.8
46. Delaware	100.0	80.3	16.9	0.3	1.4	1.1	2.4
47. North Dakota	100.0	94.6	0.6	4.1	0.5	0.3	0.7
48. District of Columbia	100.0	29.6	65.8	0.2	1.8	2.5	5.4
49. Vermont	100.0	98.6	0.3	0.3	0.6	0.1	0.7
50. Alaska	100.0	75.5	4.1	15.6	3.6	1.2	3.2
51. Wyoming	100.0	94.2	0.8	2.1	0.6	2.3	5.7

Source: Bureau of the Census
Note: Hispanics may be of any race.

State Populations, Percent Black, 1990

Blacks represent a large share of the populations of a number of southern states, including the Carolinas, Georgia, Alabama, Mississippi, and Louisiana.

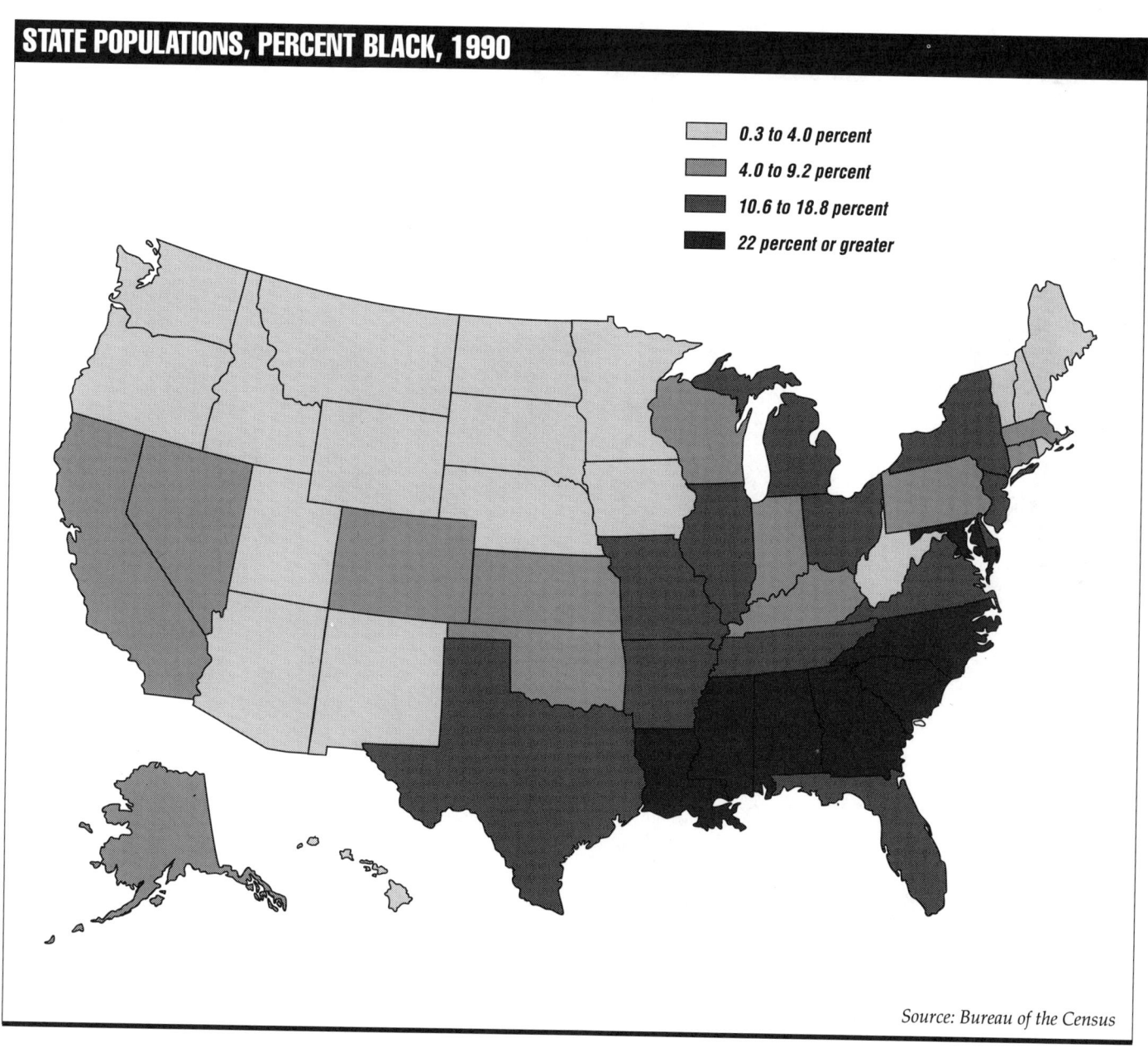

STATE POPULATIONS, PERCENT BLACK, 1990

0.3 to 4.0 percent
4.0 to 9.2 percent
10.6 to 18.8 percent
22 percent or greater

Source: Bureau of the Census

State Populations, Percent Asian and Pacific Islander, 1990

Only a handful of states have an above-average share of Asians, including New York and New Jersey on the East Coast and Hawaii, California, and Washington in the West.

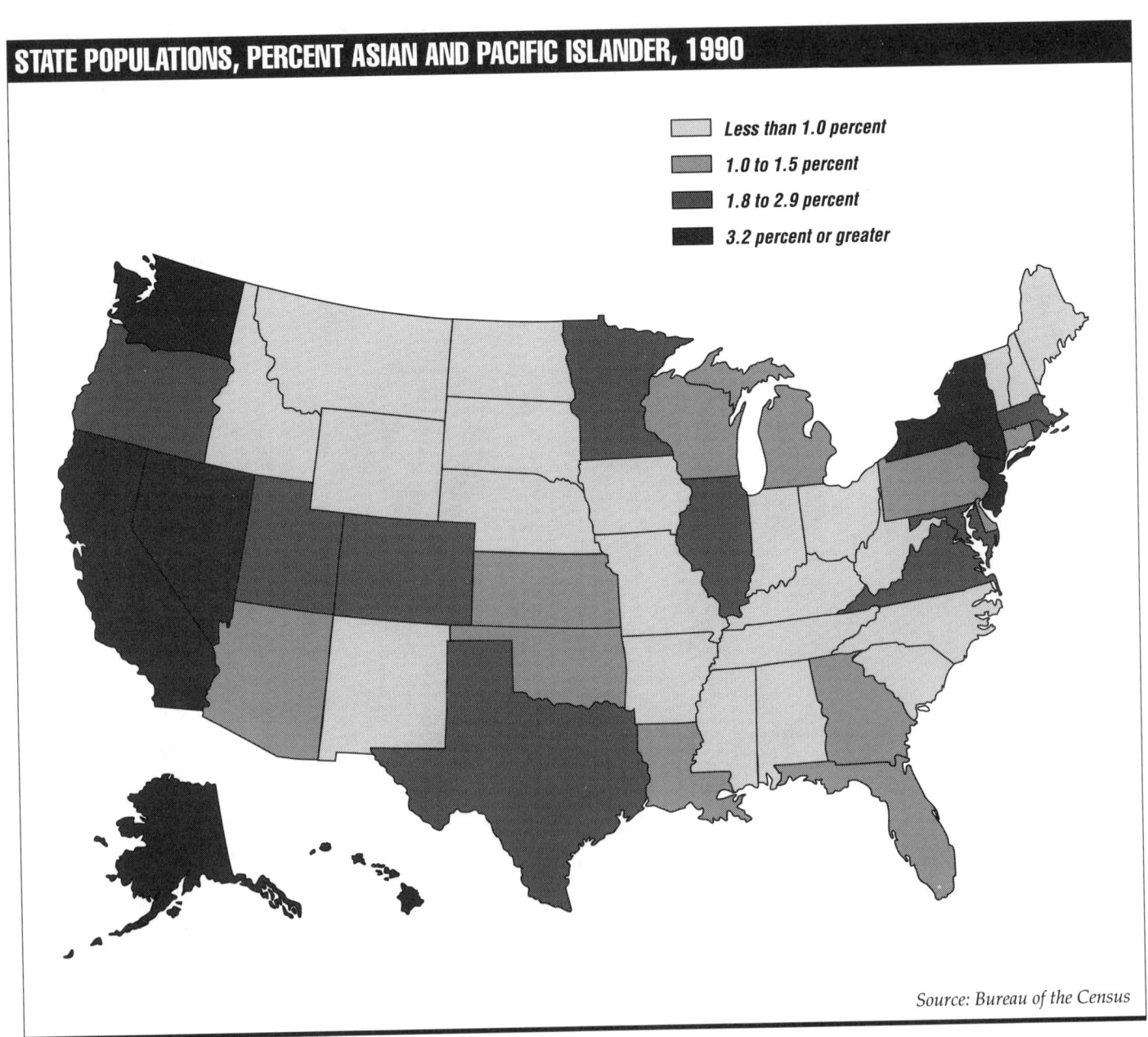

STATE POPULATIONS, PERCENT ASIAN AND PACIFIC ISLANDER, 1990

Less than 1.0 percent
1.0 to 1.5 percent
1.8 to 2.9 percent
3.2 percent or greater

Source: Bureau of the Census

State Populations, Percent Hispanic, 1990

More than 10 percent of the population of the nation's largest states—California, New York, Texas, and Florida—are Hispanic.

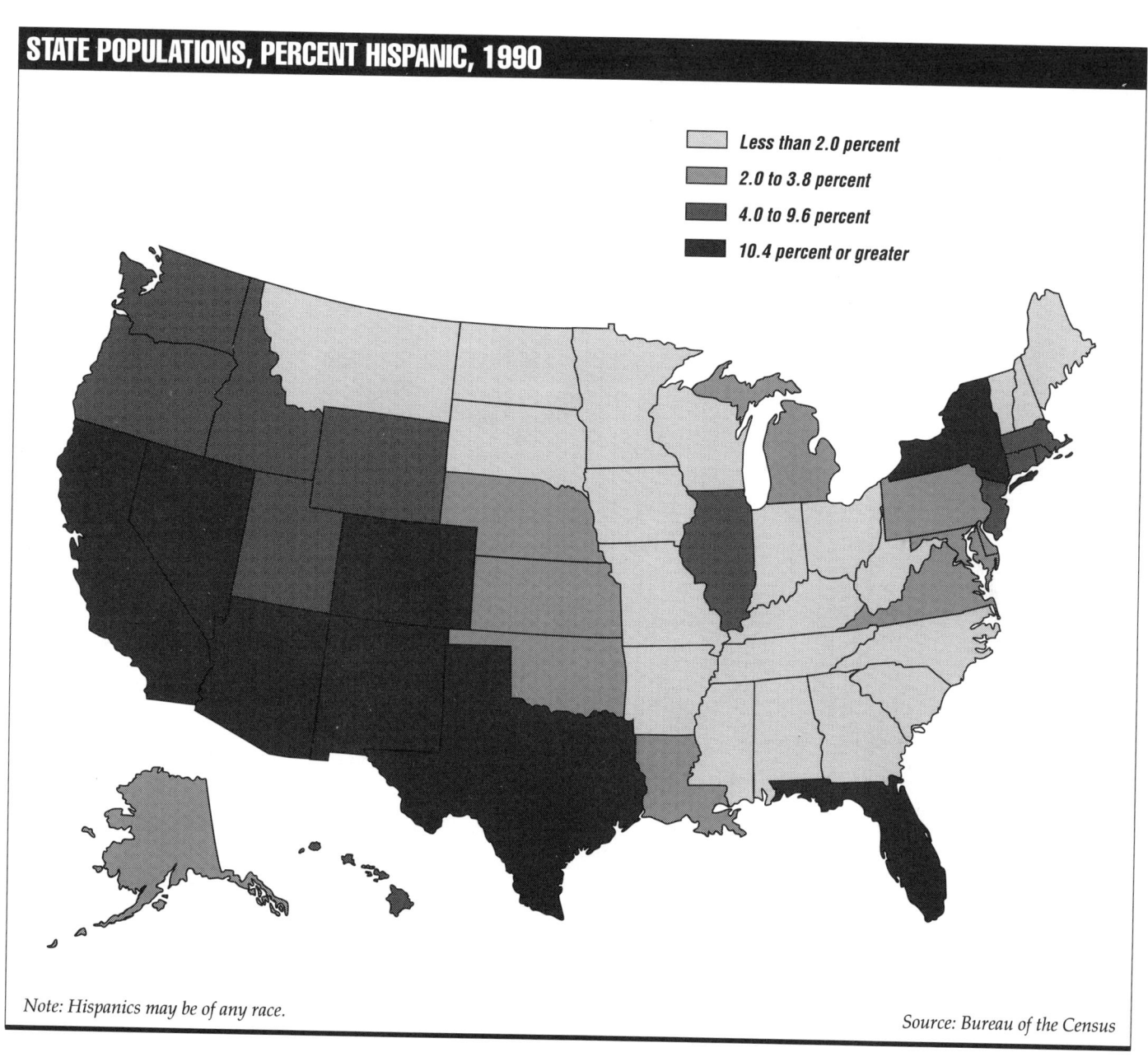

STATE POPULATIONS, PERCENT HISPANIC, 1990

Legend:
- Less than 2.0 percent
- 2.0 to 3.8 percent
- 4.0 to 9.6 percent
- 10.4 percent or greater

Note: Hispanics may be of any race.

Source: Bureau of the Census

Growth of Metropolitan Areas by Size of Area, 1960 to 1990

After slow growth in the 1970s, the nation's largest metropolitan areas grew faster than nonmetropolitan areas during the 1980s.

(percent change in metropolitan areas with populations of 1 million or more, other metropolitan areas, and nonmetropolitan areas, by census region, 1960 to 1990)

	population 1990 (in millions)	percent change		
		1980–1990	1970–1980	1960–1970
Total U.S.				
Large metro areas	124.9	12.1%	8.1%	18.5%
Other metro areas	68.2	10.8	15.5	14.6
Nonmetro areas	55.6	3.9	14.3	2.7
Northeast/Midwest				
Large metro areas	62.9	2.8	-0.9	12.0
Other metro areas	25.5	3.3	5.2	11.1
Nonmetro areas	22.6	0.1	8.0	2.6
South				
Large metro areas	28.2	22.3	23.4	30.9
Other metro areas	31.9	13.4	20.9	15.5
Nonmetro areas	24.9	4.6	16.3	1.1
West				
Large metro areas	33.8	24.2	20.0	29.1
Other metro areas	10.8	22.8	32.2	24.8
Nonmetro areas	8.1	14.1	30.6	9.0

Source: William H. Frey and Alden Speare, Jr., "Metropolitan Revival in the United States: An Assessment of 1990 Census Findings" Population and Development Review, Volume 18, No. 1, March 1992.

Thirty-nine metropolitan areas had populations of 1 million or more in 1990. New York remains the largest, but Los Angeles is catching up.

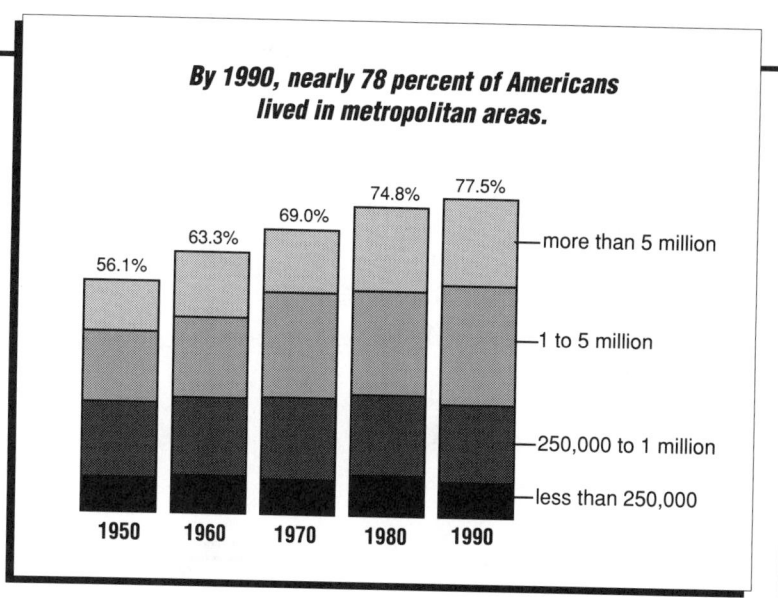

By 1990, nearly 78 percent of Americans lived in metropolitan areas.

56.1%   63.3%   69.0%   74.8%   77.5%

more than 5 million

1 to 5 million

250,000 to 1 million

less than 250,000

1950   1960   1970   1980   1990

(metropolitan areas with populations of 1 million or more, 1990)

	population 1990	percent change 1980–90
1. New York-Northern New Jersey-Long Island, NY-NJ-CT	18,087,251	3.1%
2. Los Angeles-Anaheim-Riverside, CA	14,531,529	26.4
3. Chicago-Gary-Lake County, IL-IN-WI	8,065,633	1.6
4. San Francisco-Oakland-San Jose, CA	6,253,311	16.5
5. Philadelphia-Wilmington-Trenton, PA-NJ-DE-MD	5,899,345	3.9
6. Detroit-Ann Arbor, MI	4,665,236	-1.8
7. Boston-Lawrence-Salem, MA-NH	4,171,643	5.0
8. Washington, DC-MD-VA	3,923,574	20.7
9. Dallas-Fort Worth, TX	3,885,415	32.6
10. Houston-Galveston-Brazoria, TX	3,711,043	19.7
11. Miami-Fort Lauderdale, FL	3,192,582	20.8
12. Atlanta, GA	2,833,511	32.5
13. Cleveland-Akron-Lorain, OH	2,759,823	-2.6
14. Seattle-Tacoma, WA	2,559,164	22.3
15. San Diego, CA	2,498,016	34.2
16. Minneapolis-St. Paul, MN-WI	2,464,124	15.3
17. St. Louis, MO-IL	2,444,099	2.8
18. Baltimore, MD	2,382,172	8.3
19. Pittsburgh-Beaver Valley, PA	2,242,798	-7.4
20. Phoenix, AZ	2,122,101	40.6
21. Tampa-St. Petersburg-Clearwater, FL	2,067,959	28.2

(continued on next page)

(continued from previous page)

(metropolitan areas with populations of 1 million or more, 1990)

	population 1990	percent change 1980–90
22. Denver-Boulder, CO	1,848,319	14.2%
23. Cincinnati-Hamilton, OH-KY-IN	1,744,124	5.1
24. Milwaukee-Racine, WI	1,607,183	2.4
25. Kansas City, MO-KS	1,566,280	9.3
26. Sacramento, CA	1,481,102	34.7
27. Portland-Vancouver, OR-WA	1,477,895	13.9
28. Norfolk-Virginia Beach-Newport News, VA	1,396,107	20.3
29. Columbus, OH	1,377,419	10.7
30. San Antonio, TX	1,302,099	21.5
31. Indianapolis, IN	1,249,822	7.1
32. New Orleans, LA	1,238,816	-1.4
33. Buffalo-Niagara Falls, NY	1,189,288	-4.3
34. Charlotte-Gastonia-Rock Hill, NC-SC	1,162,093	19.6
35. Providence-Pawtucket-Fall River, RI-MA	1,141,510	5.4
36. Hartford-New Britain-Middletown, CT	1,085,837	7.1
37. Orlando, FL	1,072,748	53.3
38. Salt Lake City-Ogden, UT	1,072,227	17.8
39. Rochester, NY	1,002,410	3.2

Source: Bureau of the Census

Growth of Large Metropolitan Areas, 1980 to 1990

Among the nation's 50 largest metro areas, Orlando, Florida, grew the fastest during the 1980s, up by over 50 percent. Six of the nation's largest metros lost population.

(populations of the 50 largest metropolitan areas in 1990 and 1980; ranked by rate of growth, 1980-90; numbers in thousands)

	population 1990	population 1980	percent change 1980–90
Population of 50 largest metropolitan areas	**134,965**	**120,487**	**12.0%**
1. Orlando, FL	1,073	700	53.3
2. West Palm Beach-Boca Raton-Delray Beach, FL	864	577	49.7
3. Phoenix, AZ	2,122	1,509	40.6
4. Sacramento, CA	1,481	1,100	34.7
5. San Diego, CA	2,498	1,862	34.2
6. Dallas-Fort Worth, TX	3,885	2,931	32.6
7. Atlanta, GA	2,834	2,138	32.5
8. Tampa-St. Petersburg-Clearwater, FL	2,068	1,614	28.2
9. Los Angeles-Anaheim-Riverside, CA	14,532	11,498	26.4
10. Jacksonville, FL	907	722	25.5
11. Seattle-Tacoma, WA	2,559	2,093	22.3
12. San Antonio, TX	1,302	1,072	21.5
13. Miami-Fort Lauderdale, FL	3,193	2,644	20.8
14. Washington, DC-MD-VA	3,924	3,251	20.7
15. Norfolk-Virginia Beach-Newport News, VA	1,396	1,160	20.3
16. Houston-Galveston-Brazoria, TX	3,711	3,100	19.7
17. Charlotte-Gastonia-Rock Hill, NC-SC	1,162	971	19.6
18. Salt Lake City-Ogden, UT	1,072	910	17.8
19. San Francisco-Oakland-San Jose, CA	6,253	5,368	16.5
20. Nashville, TN	985	851	15.8
21. Minneapolis-St. Paul, MN-WI	2,464	2,137	15.3
22. Denver-Boulder, CO	1,848	1,618	14.2
23. Portland-Vancouver, OR-WA	1,478	1,298	13.9
24. Richmond-Petersburg, VA	866	761	13.7
25. Oklahoma City, OK	959	861	11.4
26. Columbus, OH	1,377	1,244	10.7
27. Greensboro–Winston-Salem–High Point, NC	942	851	10.6
28. Kansas City, MO-KS	1,566	1,433	9.3
29. Baltimore, MD	2,382	2,199	8.3
30. Memphis, TN-AR-MS	982	913	7.5
31. Indianapolis, IN	1,250	1,167	7.1
32. Hartford-New Britain-Middletown, CT	1,086	1,014	7.1
33. Providence-Pawtucket-Fall River, RI-MA	1,142	1,083	5.4
34. Cincinnati-Hamilton, OH-KY-IN	1,744	1,660	5.1
35. Boston-Lawrence-Salem, MA-NH	4,172	3,972	5.0

(continued on next page)

(continued from previous page)

(populations of the 50 largest metropolitan areas in 1990 and 1980; ranked by rate of growth, 1980 to 1990; numbers in thousands)

	population 1990	population 1980	percent change 1980–90
36. Albany-Schenectady-Troy, NY	874	836	4.6%
37. Philadelphia-Wilmington-Trenton, PA-NJ-DE-MD	5,899	5,681	3.9
38. Rochester, NY	1,002	971	3.2
39. New York-Northern New Jersey-Long Island, NY-NJ-CT	18,087	17,540	3.1
40. St. Louis, MO-IL	2,444	2,377	2.8
41. Birmingham, AL	908	884	2.7
42. Milwaukee-Racine, WI	1,607	1,570	2.4
43. Chicago-Gary-Lake County, IL-IN-WI	8,066	7,937	1.6
44. Dayton-Springfield, OH	951	942	1.0
45. Louisville, KY-IN	953	956	-0.4
46. New Orleans, LA	1,239	1,257	-1.4
47. Detroit-Ann Arbor, MI	4,665	4,753	-1.8
48. Cleveland-Akron-Lorain, OH	2,760	2,834	-2.6
49. Buffalo-Niagara Falls, NY	1,189	1,243	-4.3
50. Pittsburgh-Beaver Valley, PA	2,243	2,423	-7.4

Source: Bureau of the Census

Minority Populations of the 50 Largest Metropolitan Areas

Just over half of all Americans lived in the 50 largest metro areas in 1990, but more than 70 percent of Asians and Hispanics lived in these areas.

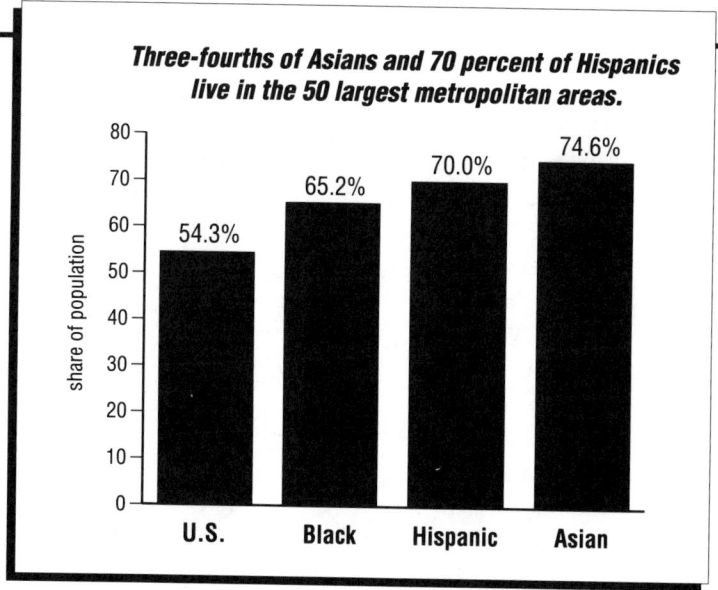

Three-fourths of Asians and 70 percent of Hispanics live in the 50 largest metropolitan areas.

(racial and ethnic populations of 50 largest metropolitan areas, 1990; metropolitan areas ranked by resident population, 1990; numbers in thousands)

	total	black	Am. Indian, Eskimo, Aleut	Asian, Pac. Islander	other races	Hispanic
United States	**248,710**	**29,986**	**1,959**	**7,274**	**9,805**	**22,354**
Population of 50 largest metropolitan areas	**134,966**	**19,552**	**597**	**5,426**	**6,945**	**15,654**
Share of U.S. population in 50 largest metropolitan areas	**54.3%**	**65.2%**	**30.5%**	**74.6%**	**70.8%**	**70.0%**
1. New York-Northern New Jersey-Long Island, NY-NJ-CT	18,087	3,289	46	873	1,179	2,778
2. Los Angeles-Anaheim-Riverside, CA	14,532	1,230	87	1,339	2,486	4,779
3. Chicago-Gary-Lake County, IL-IN-WI	8,066	1,548	16	256	474	893
4. San Francisco-Oakland-San Jose, CA	6,253	538	41	927	414	970
5. Philadelphia-Wilmington-Trenton, PA-NJ-DE-MD	5,899	1,100	11	123	126	226
6. Detroit-Ann Arbor, MI	4,665	975	18	69	34	91
7. Boston-Lawrence-Salem, MA-NH	4,172	239	8	121	95	193
8. Washington, DC-MD-VA	3,924	1,042	11	202	90	225
9. Dallas-Fort Worth, TX	3,885	555	19	98	290	519
10. Houston-Galveston-Brazoria, TX	3,711	665	11	132	395	772
11. Miami-Fort Lauderdale, FL	3,193	591	6	43	113	1,062
12. Atlanta, GA	2,834	736	6	51	20	57
13. Cleveland-Akron-Lorain, OH	2,760	442	5	28	23	53
14. Seattle-Tacoma, WA	2,559	123	32	164	28	76

(continued on next page)

(racial and ethnic populations of 50 largest metropolitan areas, 1990; metropolitan areas ranked by resident population, 1990; numbers in thousands)

	total	black	Am. Indian, Eskimo, Aleut	Asian, Pac. Islander	other races	Hispanic
15. San Diego, CA	2,498	159	20	198	248	511
16. Minneapolis-St. Paul, MN-WI	2,464	90	24	65	15	37
17. St. Louis, MO-IL	2,444	423	5	24	7	26
18. Baltimore, MD	2,382	616	6	43	8	30
19. Pittsburgh-Beaver Valley, PA	2,243	179	2	16	4	13
20. Phoenix, AZ	2,122	74	38	36	174	345
21. Tampa-St. Petersburg-Clearwater, FL	2,068	186	5	23	26	139
22. Denver-Boulder, CO	1,848	98	14	43	94	226
23. Cincinnati-Hamilton, OH-KY-IN	1,744	204	2	14	3	9
24. Milwaukee-Racine, WI	1,607	214	9	20	29	60
25. Kansas City, MO-KS	1,566	201	8	17	20	45
26. Sacramento, CA	1,481	102	17	115	77	172
27. Portland-Vancouver, OR-WA	1,478	42	14	52	20	50
28. Norfolk-Virginia Beach-Newport News, VA	1,396	398	5	35	11	32
29. Columbus, OH	1,377	165	3	21	4	11
30. San Antonio, TX	1,302	89	5	16	214	620
31. Indianapolis, IN	1,250	172	3	10	4	11
32. New Orleans, LA	1,239	430	4	21	13	53
33. Buffalo-Niagara Falls, NY	1,189	122	8	11	11	24
34. Charlotte-Gastonia-Rock Hill, NC-SC	1,162	232	4	11	3	11
35. Providence-Pawtucket-Fall River, RI-MA	1,142	37	4	20	25	47
36. Hartford-New Britain-Middletown, CT	1,086	95	2	16	40	76
37. Orlando, FL	1,073	133	3	20	27	96
38. Salt Lake City-Ogden, UT	1,072	10	8	26	28	62
39. Rochester, NY	1,002	94	3	14	16	31
40. Nashville, TN	985	152	2	10	2	8
41. Memphis, TN-AR-MS	982	399	2	8	2	8
42. Oklahoma City, OK	959	101	46	18	17	34
43. Louisville, KY-IN	953	125	2	6	2	6
44. Dayton-Springfield, OH	951	126	2	9	2	7
45. Greensboro–Winston-Salem–High Point, NC	942	182	3	6	2	7
46. Birmingham, AL	908	246	2	4	1	4
47. Jacksonville, FL	907	181	3	15	6	22
48. Albany-Schenectady-Troy, NY	874	41	2	11	6	16
49. Richmond-Petersburg, VA	866	252	3	12	3	9
50. West Palm Beach-Boca Raton-Delray Beach, FL	864	108	1	9	13	67

Source: Bureau of the Census
Note: Hispanics may be of any race.

Minority Share of the 50 Largest Metropolitan Areas

Blacks were more than one-fourth of the populations of eight large metropolitan areas in 1990. Hispanics were more than one-fourth of the population of three large metropolitan areas.

(percent distribution of racial and ethnic populations of 50 largest metropolitan areas, 1990; metropolitan areas ranked by resident population, 1990)

	total	white	black	Am. Indian, Eskimo, Aleut	Asian, Pac. Islander	other races	Hispanic
Population of 50 largest metropolitan areas	100.0%	75.9%	14.5%	0.4%	4.0%	5.1%	11.6%
1. New York-Northern New Jersey-Long Island, NY-NJ-CT	100.0	70.2	18.2	0.3	4.8	6.5	15.4
2. Los Angeles-Anaheim-Riverside, CA	100.0	64.6	8.5	0.6	9.2	17.1	32.9
3. Chicago-Gary-Lake County, IL-IN-WI	100.0	71.6	19.2	0.2	3.2	5.9	11.1
4. San Francisco-Oakland-San Jose, CA	100.0	69.3	8.6	0.7	14.8	6.6	15.5
5. Philadelphia-Wilmington-Trenton, PA-NJ-DE-MD	100.0	76.9	18.7	0.2	2.1	2.1	4.3
6. Detroit-Ann Arbor, MI	100.0	76.5	20.9	0.4	1.5	0.7	1.9
7. Boston-Lawrence-Salem, MA-NH	100.0	88.9	5.7	0.2	2.9	2.3	4.6
8. Washington, DC-MD-VA	100.0	65.7	26.6	0.3	5.2	2.3	5.7
9. Dallas-Fort Worth, TX	100.0	75.2	14.3	0.5	2.5	7.5	13.4
10. Houston-Galveston-Brazoria, TX	100.0	67.6	17.9	0.3	3.6	10.6	20.8
11. Miami-Fort Lauderdale, FL	100.0	76.4	18.5	0.2	1.4	3.6	33.3
12. Atlanta, GA	100.0	71.3	26.0	0.2	1.8	0.7	2.0
13. Cleveland-Akron-Lorain, OH	100.0	82.0	16.0	0.2	1.0	0.8	1.9
14. Seattle-Tacoma, WA	100.0	86.4	4.8	1.3	6.4	1.1	3.0
15. San Diego, CA	100.0	75.0	6.4	0.8	7.9	9.9	20.4
16. Minneapolis-St. Paul, MN-WI	100.0	92.1	3.6	1.0	2.6	0.6	1.5
17. St. Louis, MO-IL	100.0	81.2	17.3	0.2	1.0	0.3	1.1
18. Baltimore, MD	100.0	71.7	25.9	0.3	1.8	0.3	1.3
19. Pittsburgh-Beaver Valley, PA	100.0	91.0	8.0	0.1	0.7	0.2	0.6
20. Phoenix, AZ	100.0	84.8	3.5	1.8	1.7	8.2	16.3
21. Tampa-St. Petersburg-Clearwater, FL	100.0	88.4	9.0	0.3	1.1	1.3	6.7
22. Denver-Boulder, CO	100.0	86.5	5.3	0.8	2.3	5.1	12.2
23. Cincinnati-Hamilton, OH-KY-IN	100.0	87.2	11.7	0.1	0.8	0.2	0.5
24. Milwaukee-Racine, WI	100.0	83.1	13.3	0.5	1.2	1.8	3.8
25. Kansas City, MO-KS	100.0	84.3	12.8	0.5	1.1	1.3	2.9
26. Sacramento, CA	100.0	79.0	6.9	1.1	7.7	5.2	11.6
27. Portland-Vancouver, OR-WA	100.0	91.3	2.8	0.9	3.5	1.4	3.4
28. Norfolk-Virginia Beach-Newport News, VA	100.0	67.8	28.5	0.3	2.5	0.8	2.3
29. Columbus, OH	100.0	86.0	12.0	0.2	1.5	0.3	0.8
30. San Antonio, TX	100.0	75.1	6.8	0.4	1.2	16.4	47.6
31. Indianapolis, IN	100.0	84.9	13.8	0.2	0.8	0.3	0.9
32. New Orleans, LA	100.0	62.2	34.7	0.3	1.7	1.0	4.3
33. Buffalo-Niagara Falls, NY	100.0	87.2	10.3	0.6	0.9	1.0	2.0

(continued on next page)

(percent distribution of racial and ethnic populations of 50 largest metropolitan areas, 1990; metropolitan areas ranked by resident population, 1990)

	total	white	black	Am. Indian, Eskimo, Aleut	Asian, Pac. Islander	other races	Hispanic
34. Charlotte-Gastonia-Rock Hill, NC-SC	100.0%	78.5%	19.9%	0.4%	1.0%	0.3%	0.9%
35. Providence-Pawtucket-Fall River, RI-MA	100.0	92.5	3.3	0.3	1.8	2.2	4.2
36. Hartford-New Britain-Middletown, CT	100.0	85.9	8.7	0.2	1.5	3.7	7.0
37. Orlando, FL	100.0	83.0	12.4	0.3	1.9	2.5	9.0
38. Salt Lake City-Ogden, UT	100.0	93.3	1.0	0.8	2.4	2.6	5.8
39. Rochester, NY	100.0	87.3	9.4	0.3	1.4	1.6	3.1
40. Nashville, TN	100.0	83.1	15.5	0.2	1.0	0.2	0.8
41. Memphis, TN-AR-MS	100.0	58.2	40.6	0.2	0.8	0.2	0.8
42. Oklahoma City, OK	100.0	81.0	10.5	4.8	1.9	1.7	3.6
43. Louisville, KY-IN	100.0	85.9	13.1	0.2	0.6	0.2	0.6
44. Dayton-Springfield, OH	100.0	85.4	13.3	0.2	1.0	0.3	0.8
45. Greensboro–Winston-Salem–High Point, NC	100.0	79.5	19.3	0.3	0.7	0.3	0.8
46. Birmingham, AL	100.0	72.2	27.1	0.2	0.4	0.1	0.4
47. Jacksonville, FL	100.0	77.4	20.0	0.3	1.7	0.6	2.5
48. Albany-Schenectady-Troy, NY	100.0	93.1	4.7	0.2	1.2	0.6	1.8
49. Richmond-Petersburg, VA	100.0	68.9	29.2	0.3	1.4	0.3	1.1
50. West Palm Beach-Boca Raton-Delray Beach, FL	100.0	84.9	12.5	0.1	1.0	1.5	7.7

Source: Bureau of the Census
Note: Hispanics may be of any race.

The 50 Metropolitan Areas With the Most Blacks

The black population grew rapidly in many of the 50 metropolitan areas with the most blacks. In Little Rock, San Diego, and Miami, the black population grew by more than half.

(50 metropolitan areas with the largest black populations, 1990, black population in 1980, change and percent change in black population, 1980-90; numbers in thousands)

	population 1990	population 1980	change 1980–90 number	change 1980–90 percent
Total number of blacks in top 50 black metropolitan areas	**20,270**	**17,662**	**2,608**	**14.8%**
1. New York-Northern New Jersey-Long Island, NY-NJ-CT	3,289	2,825	464	16.4
2. Chicago-Gary-Lake County, IL-IN-WI	1,548	1,557	-9	-0.6
3. Los Angeles-Anaheim-Riverside, CA	1,230	1,059	171	16.1
4. Philadelphia-Wilmington-Trenton, PA-NJ-DE-ME	1,100	1,033	67	6.5
5. Washington, DC-MD-VA	1,042	871	171	19.7
6. Detroit-Ann Arbor, MI	975	921	54	5.9
7. Atlanta, GA	736	526	210	40.0
8. Houston-Galveston-Brazoria, TX	665	565	100	17.8
9. Baltimore, MD	616	561	55	9.8
10. Miami-Fort Lauderdale, FL	591	394	197	50.1
11. Dallas-Fort Worth, TX	555	419	136	32.4
12. San Francisco-Oakland-San Jose, CA	538	468	70	14.8
13. Cleveland-Akron-Lorain, OH	442	426	16	3.8
14. New Orleans, LA	430	409	21	5.2
15. St. Louis, MO-IL	423	408	15	3.7
16. Memphis, TN-AR-MS	399	364	35	9.5
17. Norfolk-Virginia Beach-Newport News, VA	398	326	72	22.1
18. Richmond-Petersburg, VA	252	221	31	13.9
19. Birmingham, AL	246	240	6	2.3
20. Boston-Lawrence-Salem, MA-NH	239	176	63	35.6
21. Charlotte-Gastonia-Rock Hill, NC-SC	232	194	38	19.4
22. Milwaukee-Racine, WI	214	165	49	30.1
23. Cincinnati-Hamilton, OH-KY-IN	204	186	18	9.6
24. Kansas City, MO-KS	201	180	21	11.3
25. Tampa-St. Petersburg-Clearwater, FL	186	148	38	24.9
26. Raleigh-Durham, NC	183	147	36	25.1
27. Greensboro–Winston-Salem–High Point, NC	182	162	20	12.4
28. Jacksonville, FL	181	156	25	16.2
29. Pittsburgh-Beaver Valley, PA	179	182	-3	-1.5
30. Indianapolis, IN	172	157	15	9.6
31. Jackson, MS	168	149	19	12.3
32. Columbus, OH	165	137	28	19.9
33. San Diego, CA	159	104	55	52.5
34. Baton Rouge, LA	157	138	19	13.8
35. Charleston, SC	153	133	20	14.8

(continued on next page)

(continued from previous page)

(50 metropolitan areas with the largest black populations, 1990, black population in 1980, change and percent change in black population, 1980-90; numbers in thousands)

	population 1990	population 1980	change 1980–90 number	change 1980–90 percent
36. Nashville, TN	152	137	15	10.9%
37. Columbia, SC	138	118	20	17.0
38. Orlando, FL	133	91	42	47.1
39. Mobile, AL	131	127	4	2.9
40. Dayton-Springfield, OH	126	118	8	6.7
41. Louisville, KY-IN	125	121	4	3.4
42. Augusta, GA-SC	123	107	16	15.7
43. Seattle-Tacoma, WA	123	88	35	40.1
44. Buffalo-Niagara Falls, NY	122	114	8	7.0
45. Shreveport, LA	117	110	7	5.8
46. Greenville-Spartanburg, SC	111	98	13	14.1
47. West Palm Beach-Boca Raton-Delray Beach, FL	108	78	30	38.8
48. Montgomery, AL	105	94	11	11.3
49. Sacramento, CA	102	62	40	65.5
50. Little Rock-North Little Rock, AR	102	91	11	12.2

Source: Bureau of the Census

The 50 Metropolitan Areas
With the Most Asians

The Asian population grew by more than 300 percent during the 1980s in 4 of the 50 metropolitan areas with the most Asians.

(50 metropolitan areas with the largest Asian populations, 1990, Asian population in 1980, change and percent change in Asian population, 1980-90; numbers in thousands)

	population 1990	population 1980	change 1980–90 number	change 1980–90 percent
Total number of Asians in top 50 Asian metropolitan areas	**6,128**	**2,895**	**3,233**	**111.7%**
1. Los Angeles-Anaheim-Riverside, CA	1,339	562	777	138.3
2. San Francisco-Oakland-San Jose, CA	927	455	472	103.9
3. New York-Northern New Jersey-Long Island, NY-NJ-CT	873	371	502	135.5
4. Honolulu, HI	526	456	70	15.3
5. Chicago-Gary-Lake County, IL-IN-MI	256	145	111	77.0
6. Washington, DC-MD-VA	202	83	119	143.9
7. San Diego, CA	198	90	108	120.7
8. Seattle-Tacoma, WA	164	78	86	109.9
9. Houston-Galveston-Brazoria, TX	132	53	79	149.0
10. Philadelphia-Wilmington-Trenton, PA-NJ-DE-MD	123	53	70	131.7
11. Boston-Lawrence-Salem, MA-NH	121	43	79	183.9
12. Sacramento, CA	115	46	69	146.4
13. Dallas-Fort Worth, TX	98	24	74	298.4
14. Detroit-Ann Arbor, MI	69	39	30	77.3
15. Minneapolis-St. Paul, MN-WI	65	20	45	230.2
16. Stockton, CA	60	20	40	200.1
17. Fresno, CA	57	15	42	287.4
18. Portland-Vancouver, OR-WA	52	24	28	113.5
19. Atlanta, GA	51	12	39	332.7
20. Miami-Fort Lauderdale, FL	43	17	26	152.6
21. Denver-Boulder, CO	43	20	23	108.2
22. Baltimore, MD	43	22	21	96.3
23. Phoenix, AZ	36	13	23	176.7
24. Norfolk-Virginia Beach-Newport News, VA	35	19	16	82.0
25. Cleveland-Akron-Lorain, OH	28	17	11	64.3
26. Salinas-Seaside-Monterey, CA	28	20	8	41.4
27. Las Vegas, NV	26	9	17	182.9
28. Salt Lake City-Ogden, UT	26	11	15	129.7
29. St. Louis, MO-IL	24	13	11	86.7
30. Tampa-St. Petersburg-Clearwater, FL	23	7	16	209.4
31. New Orleans, LA	21	14	7	54.7
32. Columbus, OH	21	7	14	185.2
33. Orlando, FL	20	5	15	287.0
34. Providence-Pawtucket-Fall River, RI-MA	20	5	15	277.0
35. Milwaukee-Racine, WI	20	8	12	141.1

(continued on next page)

(continued from previous page)

(50 metropolitan areas with the largest Asian populations, 1990, Asian population in 1980, change and percent change in Asian population, 1980-90; numbers in thousands)

	population 1990	population 1980	change 1980–90	
			number	percent
36. Modesto, CA	19	4	15	368.2%
37. Austin, TX	19	5	14	303.5
38. Oklahoma City, OK	18	8	10	129.6
39. Kansas City, MO-KS	17	9	8	93.0
40. Bakersfield, CA	17	8	9	114.2
41. Santa Barbara-Santa Maria-Lompoc, CA	16	8	8	96.9
42. Pittsburgh-Beaver Valley, PA	16	10	6	63.2
43. San Antonio, TX	16	8	8	107.4
44. Hartford-New Britain-Middletown, CT	16	5	11	188.8
45. Jacksonville, FL	15	7	8	128.6
46. Merced, CA	15	3	12	423.3
47. Cincinnati-Hamilton, OH-KY-IN	14	7	7	99.0
48. Rochester, NY	14	6	8	134.1
49. Raleigh-Durham, NC	14	4	10	239.7
50. Visalia-Tulare-Porterville, CA	13	5	8	162.9

Source: Bureau of the Census

The 50 Metropolitan Areas With the Most Hispanics

The Hispanic population in Los Angeles is nearing 5 million, up by 73 percent during the 1980s. Hispanics more than doubled in 10 of the 50 metropolitan areas with the most Hispanics.

(50 metropolitan areas with the largest Hispanic populations, 1990, Hispanic population in 1980, change and percent change in Hispanic population, 1980-90; numbers in thousands)

	population 1990	population 1980	change 1980–90 number	change 1980–90 percent
Total number of Hispanics in top 50 Hispanic metropolitan areas	**18,355**	**11,669**	**6,656**	**57.3%**
1. Los Angeles-Anaheim-Riverside, CA	4,779	2,756	2,023	73.4
2. New York-Northern New Jersey-Long Island, NY-NJ-CT	2,778	2,051	727	35.4
3. Miami-Fort Lauderdale, FL	1,062	621	441	70.9
4. San Francisco-Oakland-San Jose, CA	970	660	310	47.0
5. Chicago-Gary-Lake County, IL-IN-WI	893	632	261	41.3
6. Houston-Galveston-Brazoria, TX	772	448	324	72.2
7. San Antonio, TX	620	482	138	28.8
8. Dallas-Fort Worth, TX	519	248	271	109.4
9. San Diego, CA	511	275	236	85.6
10. El Paso, TX	412	297	115	38.6
11. Phoenix, AZ	345	199	146	73.6
12. McAllen-Edinburg-Mission, TX	327	230	97	42.0
13. Fresno, CA	237	151	86	56.9
14. Denver-Boulder, CO	226	174	52	30.2
15. Philadelphia-Wilmington-Trenton, PA-NJ-DE-MD	256	148	78	52.7
16. Washington, DC-MD-VA	225	95	130	136.7
17. Brownsville-Harlingen, TX	213	162	51	31.8
18. Boston-Lawrence-Salem, MA-NH	193	92	101	108.9
19. Corpus Christi, TX	182	158	24	15.0
20. Albuquerque, NM	178	155	23	15.3
21. Sacramento, CA	172	106	66	63.1
22. Tucson, AZ	163	111	52	46.5
23. Austin, TX	160	94	66	69.5
24. Bakersfield, CA	152	87	65	74.7
25. Tampa-St. Petersburg-Clearwater, FL	139	80	59	73.5
26. Laredo, TX	125	91	34	37.7
27. Visalia-Tulare-Porterville, CA	121	73	48	64.9
28. Salinas-Seaside-Monterey, CA	120	75	45	59.2
29. Stockton, CA	113	67	46	69.3
30. Santa Barbara-Santa Maria-Lompoc, CA	98	55	43	77.4
31. Orlando, FL	96	26	70	271.2
32. Detroit-Ann Arbor, MI	91	77	13	17.4
33. Las Vegas, NV	83	35	48	136.3
34. Modesto, CA	81	40	41	102.8
35. Las Cruces, NM	76	50	26	52.3

(continued on next page)

(continued from previous page)

(50 metropolitan areas with the largest Hispanic populations, 1990, Hispanic population in 1980, change and percent change in Hispanic population, 1980-90; numbers in thousands)

	population 1990	population 1980	change 1980–90	
			number	percent
36. Hartford-New Britain-Middletown, CT	76	44	32	73.2%
37. Seattle-Tacoma, WA	76	45	31	68.0
38. West Palm Beach-Boca Raton-Delray Beach, FL	67	29	38	133.7
39. Salt Lake City-Ogden, UT	62	45	17	38.1
40. Milwaukee-Racine, WI	60	42	18	45.2
41. Merced, CA	58	34	24	70.6
42. Atlanta, GA	57	24	33	135.8
43. Honolulu, HI	57	55	2	4.3
44. New Orleans, LA	53	50	3	6.6
45. Cleveland-Akron-Lorain, OH	53	43	10	24.6
46. Lubbock, TX	51	41	10	23.1
47. Santa Fe, NM	51	44	7	16.1
48. Portland-Vancouver, OR-WA	50	26	24	90.7
49. Springfield, MA	48	24	24	102.3
50. Providence-Pawtucket-Fall River, RI-MA	47	22	25	114.6

Source: Bureau of the Census
Note: Hispanics may be of any race.

The 40 Largest American Cities

Among the 40 largest American cities, 14 lost population between 1980 and 1990. New York City's population is twice as large as second-ranking Los Angeles.

(city populations, 1990, percent change in city populations, 1980-90, and land area of cities; population in thousands)

	population 1990	percent change in population 1980–90	land area (square miles)
1. New York, NY	7,323	3.5%	309
2. Los Angeles, CA	3,485	17.4	469
3. Chicago, IL	2,784	-7.4	227
4. Houston, TX	1,631	2.2	540
5. Philadelphia, PA	1,586	-6.1	135
6. San Diego, CA	1,111	26.8	324
7. Detroit, MI	1,028	-14.6	139
8. Dallas, TX	1,007	11.3	342
9. Phoenix, AZ	983	24.5	420
10. San Antonio, TX	936	19.1	333
11. San Jose, CA	782	24.3	171
12. Indianapolis, IN*	742	4.3	367
13. Baltimore, MD	736	-6.4	81
14. San Francisco, CA	724	6.6	47
15. Jacksonville, FL*	673	17.9	774
16. Columbus, OH	633	12.0	191
17. Milwaukee, WI	628	-1.3	96
18. Memphis, TN	610	-5.5	256
19. Washington, DC	607	-4.9	61
20. Boston, MA	574	2.0	48
21. Seattle, WA	516	4.5	84
22. El Paso, TX	515	21.2	245
23. Nashville-Davidson, TN*	511	6.9	502
24. Cleveland, OH	506	-11.9	77
25. New Orleans, LA	497	-10.9	181
26. Denver, CO	468	-5.1	153
27. Austin, TX	466	34.6	218
28. Fort Worth, TX	448	16.2	281
29. Oklahoma City, OK	445	10.1	608
30. Portland, OR	437	18.8	125
31. Kansas City, MO	435	-2.9	312
32. Long Beach, CA	429	18.8	50
33. Tucson, AZ	405	22.6	156
34. St. Louis, MO	397	-12.4	62
35. Charlotte, NC	396	25.5	174
36. Atlanta, GA	394	-7.3	132
37. Virginia Beach, VA	393	49.9	248
38. Albuquerque, NM	385	15.6	132
39. Oakland, CA	372	9.7	56
40. Pittsburgh, PA	370	-12.8	56

* Data are for city-county consolidated area. Source: Bureau of the Census

CHAPTER

2

Household Trends

The past two decades have been marked by dramatic household change in the U.S. The number of married couples without children surpassed the number of couples with children. The number of two-parent families grew much more slowly than the number of single-parent families. People who live alone were one of the fastest-growing household types. Behind these changes were a rising age at marriage, a rising divorce rate, and a rising proportion of out-of-wedlock births. In contrast to the household turmoil of the past 20 years, the 1990s promise greater stability.

Major Household Trends

☞ The 1990s will be a family oriented decade as the number of householders aged 35 to 54, most of whom are married couples, grows by 30 percent.

☞ After two decades of decline, the number of married couples with children is projected to grow during the 1990s with the middle-aging of the baby-boom generation. For the next ten years, spending by the nation's parents will drive many markets.

☞ A growing share of American households will be headed by minorities. The numbers of black and Hispanic households are projected to grow many times faster than white households.

Households by Type

Married couples are a majority of householders, but over half of married couples have no children living with them.

(number and percent distribution of households by type, 1991; numbers in thousands)

	number	percent
Total	**94,312**	**100.0%**
Family households	**66,322**	**70.3**
Married couples, total	52,147	55.3
With children under age 18	25,410	26.9
Without children under age 18	26,737	28.3
Male householder	2,907	3.1
Female householder	11,268	11.9
Nonfamily households	**27,990**	**29.7**
Male householder	12,150	12.9
Living alone	9,450	10.0
Female householder	15,840	16.8
Living alone	14,141	15.0

Source: Bureau of the Census

Households by Type, 1970 to 1990

Only one household type has declined in number since 1970—married couples with children under age 18 at home. The number of male-headed households and people living alone have grown the fastest.

(households by type, 1970 to 1990, and percent change 1970 to 1990; numbers in thousands)

	1990	1980	1970	percent change 1970-90
Total	**93,347**	**80,776**	**63,401**	**47.2%**
Family households	**66,090**	**59,550**	**51,456**	**28.4**
Married couples, total	52,317	49,112	44,728	17.0
With children under age 18	24,537	24,961	25,532	-3.9
Without children under age 18	27,780	24,151	19,196	44.7
Male householders	2,884	1,733	1,228	134.9
Female householders	10,890	8,705	5,500	98.0
Nonfamily householders	**27,257**	**21,226**	**11,945**	**128.2**
Male householders	11,606	8,807	4,063	185.7
Living alone	9,049	6,966	3,532	156.2
Female householders	15,651	12,419	7,882	98.6
Living alone	13,950	11,330	7,319	90.6

Source: Bureau of the Census

Households by Type and Race of Householder

More than 80 percent of all households in the U.S. are headed by whites, but blacks head over 30 percent of female-headed households.

(number and percent distribution of households by type and race of householder, 1991; numbers in thousands)

	total		white		black		Hispanic*	
	number	percent	number	percent	number	percent	number	percent
Total	**94,312**	**100.0%**	**80,968**	**85.9%**	**10,672**	**11.3%**	**6,220**	**6.6%**
Family households	**66,322**	**100.0**	**56,803**	**85.6**	**7,471**	**11.3**	**4,981**	**7.5**
Married couples, total	52,147	100.0	47,014	90.2	3,569	6.8	3,454	6.6
With children under age 18	25,410	100.0	22,289	87.7	2,104	8.3	2,405	9.5
Without children under age 18	26,737	100.0	24,726	92.5	1,465	5.5	1,049	3.9
Male householders	2,907	100.0	2,276	78.3	472	16.2	342	11.8
Female householders	11,268	100.0	7,512	66.7	3,430	30.4	1,186	10.5
Nonfamily householders	**27,990**	**100.0**	**24,166**	**86.3**	**3,200**	**11.4**	**1,238**	**4.4**
Male householders	12,150	100.0	10,312	84.9	1,531	12.6	669	5.5
Living alone	9,450	100.0	7,963	84.3	1,266	13.4	456	4.8
Female householders	15,840	100.0	13,853	87.5	1,670	10.5	569	3.6
Living alone	14,141	100.0	12,356	87.4	1,511	10.7	469	3.3

* Hispanics may be of any race.
Note: White and black do not sum to total because other races are not shown.
Source: Census Bureau

Projections of Households by Household Type, 1990 to 2000

After declining for decades, the number of married couples with children is projected to grow by 12 percent during the 1990s.

(number of households by type of household, 1990-2000, and percent change 1990-2000; numbers in thousands)

	1990	1995	2000	percent change 1990–2000
Total	**91,950**	**98,265**	**103,828**	**12.9%**
Family households	**65,337**	**70,073**	**74,174**	**13.5**
Married couples, total	51,725	55,535	58,878	13.8
With children under age 18	24,930	26,945	27,981	12.2
Without children under age 18	26,795	28,590	30,896	15.3
Male householder	2,855	3,047	3,227	13.0
Female householder	10,759	11,494	12,073	12.2
Nonfamily households	**26,613**	**28,192**	**29,654**	**11.4**
Male householder	11,429	12,005	12,479	9.2
Living alone	8,898	9,422	9,859	10.8
Female householder	15,184	16,187	17,174	13.1
Living alone	13,500	14,477	15,422	14.2

Note: Household counts for 1990 in this projection series are based on 1990 census figures and will differ from household estimates for 1990 based on the Current Population Survey shown elsewhere in this book.
Source: TGE Demographics, Inc., Ithaca, New York

Households by Age and Race of Householder

Younger householders are more likely to be black than older householders, in part because blacks have more children than whites.

(number and percent distribution of households by age and race of householder, 1991; numbers in thousands)

	total		white		black		Hispanic*	
	number	percent	number	percent	number	percent	number	percent
Total	**94,311**	**100.0%**	**80,969**	**85.9%**	**10,671**	**11.3%**	**6,219**	**6.6%**
Under age 25	4,882	100.0	4,046	82.9	683	14.0	594	12.2
Aged 25 to 34	20,323	100.0	17,069	84.0	2,591	12.7	1,808	8.9
Aged 35 to 44	21,304	100.0	18,013	84.6	2,578	12.1	1,524	7.2
Aged 45 to 54	14,751	100.0	12,534	85.0	1,693	11.5	957	6.5
Aged 55 to 64	12,524	100.0	10,876	86.8	1,337	10.7	682	5.4
Aged 65 to 74	12,001	100.0	10,663	88.9	1,118	9.3	434	3.6
Aged 75 or older	8,526	100.0	7,768	91.1	671	7.9	220	2.6

Hispanics may be of any race.
Note: White and black do not sum to total because other races are not shown.
Source: Census Bureau

Projections of Households by Age of Householder, 1990 to 2000

Households are projected to increase by 13 percent between 1990 and 2000, but those headed by people aged 45 to 54 should grow by 47 percent.

(number of households by age of householder, 1990-2000, and percent change 1990-2000; numbers in thousands)

	1990	1995	2000	percent change 1990–2000
Total	**91,950**	**98,265**	**103,828**	**12.9%**
Under age 25	5,141	4,953	5,066	-1.5
Aged 25 to 34	19,997	19,321	18,007	-10.0
Aged 35 to 44	20,503	22,951	24,089	17.5
Aged 45 to 54	14,555	17,971	21,351	46.7
Aged 55 to 64	12,549	12,438	14,012	11.7
Aged 65 to 74	11,577	11,910	11,385	-1.7
Aged 75 or older	7,628	8,721	9,918	30.0

Note: Household counts for 1990 in this projection series are based on 1990 census figures and will differ from household estimates for 1990 based on the Current Population Survey shown elsewhere in this book.
Source: TGE Demographics, Inc., Ithaca, New York

Projections of Family Households by Age of Householder, 1990 to 2000

Family households are projected to grow slightly faster than all households during the 1990s, with those headed by 45-to-54-year-olds leading the way.

(number of family households by age of householder, 1990-2000, and percent change 1990-2000; numbers in thousands)

	1990	1995	2000	percent change 1990–2000
Total	**65,337**	**70,073**	**74,174**	**13.5%**
Under age 25	2,864	2,759	2,822	-1.5
Aged 25 to 34	14,506	14,048	13,083	-9.8
Aged 35 to 44	16,654	18,644	19,582	17.6
Aged 45 to 54	11,745	14,503	17,228	46.7
Aged 55 to 64	9,265	9,190	10,362	11.8
Aged 65 to 74	7,134	7,307	6,978	-2.2
Aged 75 or older	3,168	3,622	4,119	30.0

Note: Household counts for 1990 in this projection series are based on 1990 census figures and will differ from household estimates for 1990 based on the Current Population Survey shown elsewhere in this book.
Source: TGE Demographics, Inc., Ithaca, New York

Projections of Married Couples by Age of Householder, 1990 to 2000

The number of married couples under age 35 is projected to decline by more than 1 million between 1990 and 2000.

(number of married-couple households by age of householder, 1990-2000, and percent change, 1990-2000; numbers in thousands)

	1990	1995	2000	percent change 1990–2000
Total	**51,725**	**55,535**	**58,878**	**13.8%**
Under age 25	1,642	1,582	1,618	-1.5
Aged 25 to 34	11,119	10,773	10,031	-9.8
Aged 35 to 44	13,051	14,611	15,345	17.6
Aged 45 to 54	9,498	11,723	13,939	46.8
Aged 55 to 64	7,856	7,788	8,774	11.7
Aged 65 to 74	6,065	6,207	5,927	-2.3
Aged 75 or older	2,494	2,851	3,243	30.0

Note: Household counts for 1990 in this projection series are based on 1990 census figures and will differ from household estimates for 1990 based on the Current Population Survey shown elsewhere in this book.
Source: TGE Demographics, Inc., Ithaca, New York

Projections of Married Couple Households With and Without Children, 1990 to 2000

After several decades of decline, the number of married couples with children is projected to grow during the 1990s, particularly among households headed by 45-to-54-year-olds.

(number of married-couple households without children under age 18 living at home by age of householder, and percent change 1990-2000; numbers in thousands)

Without children under age 18	1990	1995	2000	percent change 1990–2000
Total	26,795	28,590	30,896	15.3%
Under age 25	802	773	790	-1.5
Aged 25 to 34	2,914	2,794	2,610	-10.4
Aged 35 to 44	2,443	2,743	2,913	19.2
Aged 45 to 54	5,395	6,624	7,966	47.7
Aged 55 to 64	6,920	6,842	7,684	11.0
Aged 65 to 74	5,858	5,999	5,729	-2.2
Aged 75 or older	2,463	2,816	3,203	30.0
With children under age 18				
Total	24,930	26,945	27,981	12.2
Under age 25	840	810	828	-1.5
Aged 25 to 34	8,205	7,979	7,421	-9.6
Aged 35 to 44	10,608	11,868	12,432	17.2
Aged 45 to 54	4,104	5,100	5,972	45.5
Aged 55 to 64	936	945	1,091	16.5
Aged 65 to 74	207	208	198	-4.3
Aged 75 or older	31	35	40	30.0

Note: Household counts for 1990 in this projection series are based on 1990 census figures and will differ from household estimates for 1990 based on the Current Population Survey shown elsewhere in this book.
Source: TGE Demographics, Inc., Ithaca, New York

Projections of Male- and Female-Headed Families, 1990 to 2000

By the turn of the century, there should be more than 12 million female-headed families in the U.S., versus just over 3 million male-headed families.

(number of male- and female-headed families by age of householder, 1990-2000, and percent change, 1990-2000; numbers in thousands)

Male-headed families	1990	1995	2000	percent change 1990–2000
Total	**2,855**	**3,047**	**3,227**	**13.0%**
Under age 25	315	304	311	-1.5
Aged 25 to 34	657	634	591	-10.1
Aged 35 to 44	681	762	802	17.9
Aged 45 to 54	531	656	780	46.8
Aged 55 to 64	329	328	372	13.2
Aged 65 to 74	225	230	219	-2.7
Aged 75 or older	117	134	152	30.0
Female-headed families				
Total	**10,759**	**11,494**	**12,073**	**12.2**
Under age 25	908	874	894	-1.5
Aged 25 to 34	2,731	2,642	2,461	-9.9
Aged 35 to 44	2,922	3,271	3,435	17.6
Aged 45 to 54	1,717	2,125	2,510	46.2
Aged 55 to 64	1,081	1,075	1,215	12.4
Aged 65 to 74	844	870	832	-1.4
Aged 75 or older	557	637	724	30.0

Note: Household counts for 1990 in this projection series are based on 1990 census figures and will differ from household estimates for 1990 based on the Current Population Survey shown elsewhere in this book.
Source: TGE Demographics, Inc., Ithaca, New York

Projections of Nonfamily Households by Age of Householder, 1990 to 2000

Nonfamily households are projected to grow more slowly than family households between 1990 and 2000, after years of faster growth.

(number of nonfamily households by age of householder, 1990-2000, and percent change, 1990-2000; numbers in thousands)

	1990	1995	2000	percent change 1990–2000
Total	**26,613**	**28,192**	**29,654**	**11.4%**
Under age 25	2,277	2,194	2,243	-1.5
Aged 25 to 34	5,491	5,273	4,924	-10.3
Aged 35 to 44	3,850	4,306	4,507	17.1
Aged 45 to 54	2,810	3,468	4,124	46.8
Aged 55 to 64	3,284	3,248	3,650	11.1
Aged 65 to 74	4,443	4,604	4,407	-0.8
Aged 75 or older	4,460	5,099	5,799	30.0

Note: Household counts for 1990 in this projection series are based on 1990 census figures and will differ from household estimates for 1990 based on the Current Population Survey shown elsewhere in this book.
Source: TGE Demographics, Inc., Ithaca, New York

Projections of Male- and Female-Headed Nonfamily Households, 1990 to 2000

The number of female-headed nonfamily households is projected to grow faster than the number of male-headed nonfamily households through the 1990s.

(number of male- and female-headed non-family households by age of householder, 1990-2000, and percent change, 1990-2000; numbers in thousands)

Male-headed nonfamily households	1990	1995	2000	percent change 1990–2000
Total	**11,430**	**12,005**	**12,480**	**9.2%**
Under age 25	1,241	1,196	1,223	-1.5
Aged 25 to 34	3,388	3,259	3,041	-10.2
Aged 35 to 44	2,307	2,578	2,689	16.6
Aged 45 to 54	1,414	1,747	2,073	46.6
Aged 55 to 64	1,128	1,120	1,266	12.2
Aged 65 to 74	1,108	1,140	1,090	-1.6
Aged 75 or older	844	965	1,098	30.1
Female-headed nonfamily households				
Total	**15,183**	**16,187**	**17,175**	**13.1**
Under age 25	1,036	998	1,021	-1.4
Aged 25 to 34	2,103	2,014	1,882	-10.5
Aged 35 to 44	1,542	1,728	1,818	17.9
Aged 45 to 54	1,395	1,721	2,051	47.0
Aged 55 to 64	2,156	2,128	2,384	10.6
Aged 65 to 74	3,335	3,464	3,317	-0.5
Aged 75 or older	3,616	4,134	4,702	30.0

Note: Household counts for 1990 in this projection series are based on 1990 census figures and will differ from household estimates for 1990 based on the Current Population Survey shown elsewhere in this book.
Source: TGE Demographics, Inc., Ithaca, New York

Projections of Male and Female Householders Living Alone, 1990 to 2000

By 2000, there will be more than 15 million women living alone, up by 14 percent over the decade. In contrast, fewer than 10 million men will live alone by 2000.

(number of male and female householders living alone by age of householder 1990-2000, and percent change, 1990-2000; numbers in thousands)

Male householders living alone	1990	1995	2000	percent change 1990–2000
Total	**8,898**	**9,422**	**9,859**	**10.8%**
Under age 25	678	653	668	-1.5
Aged 25 to 34	2,340	2,257	2,104	-10.1
Aged 35 to 44	1,830	2,045	2,133	16.6
Aged 45 to 54	1,169	1,444	1,715	46.6
Aged 55 to 64	1,038	1,031	1,166	12.3
Aged 65 to 74	1,028	1,059	1,013	-1.4
Aged 75 or older	816	933	1,061	30.0
Female householders living alone				
Total	**13,500**	**14,477**	**15,422**	**14.2**
Under age 25	537	517	529	-1.5
Aged 25 to 34	1,542	1,480	1,382	-10.4
Aged 35 to 44	1,300	1,456	1,532	17.9
Aged 45 to 54	1,259	1,552	1,851	47.0
Aged 55 to 64	2,047	2,020	2,262	10.5
Aged 65 to 74	3,261	3,388	3,244	-0.5
Aged 75 or older	3,554	4,064	4,622	30.0

Note: Household counts for 1990 in this projection series are based on 1990 census figures and will differ from household estimates for 1990 based on the Current Population Survey shown elsewhere in this book.
Source: TGE Demographics, Inc., Ithaca, New York

Projections of White Households by Age of Householder, 1990 to 2000

The number of white households is projected to grow by just 4 percent between 1990 and 2000, much slower than total household growth.

(number of white households by age of householder, 1990-2000, and percent change, 1990-2000; numbers in thousands)

	1990	1995	2000	percent change 1990–2000
Total	**76,028**	**76,117**	**79,411**	**4.4%**
Under age 25	3,945	3,501	3,524	-10.7
Aged 25 to 34	15,790	14,097	13,240	-16.1
Aged 35 to 44	16,511	17,040	17,606	6.6
Aged 45 to 54	12,035	14,234	16,442	36.6
Aged 55 to 64	10,684	10,112	11,168	4.5
Aged 65 to 74	10,229	10,095	9,398	-8.1
Aged 75 or older	6,834	7,037	8,032	17.5

Note: Household counts for 1990 in this projection series are based on 1990 census figures and will differ from household estimates for 1990 based on the Current Population Survey shown elsewhere in this book.
Source: TGE Demographics, Inc., Ithaca, New York

Projections of White Households by Type of Household, 1990 to 2000

The fastest-growing household type among white households during the 1990s will be married couples without children.

(number of white households by type of household, 1990-2000, and percent change, 1990-2000; numbers in thousands)

	1990	1995	2000	percent change 1990–2000
Total	**76,028**	**76,117**	**79,411**	**4.4%**
Family households	**53,836**	**54,168**	**56,604**	**5.1**
Married couples, total	44,727	45,030	47,074	5.2
With children under age 18	20,801	20,907	21,459	3.2
Without children under age 18	23,926	24,123	25,616	7.1
Male householder	2,185	2,185	2,287	4.7
Female householder	6,921	6,951	7,240	4.6
Nonfamily households	**22,192**	**21,949**	**22,807**	**2.8**
Male householder	9,377	9,189	9,447	0.7
Living alone	7,285	7,205	7,453	2.3
Female householder	12,815	12,759	13,359	4.2
Living alone	11,446	11,470	12,055	5.3

Note: Household counts for 1990 in this projection series are based on 1990 census figures and will differ from household estimates for 1990 based on the Current Population Survey shown elsewhere in this book.
Source: TGE Demographics, Inc., Ithaca, New York

Projections of Black Households by Age of Householder, 1990 to 2000

The number of black households is projected to grow five times faster than the number of white households during the 1990s.

(number of black households by age of householder, 1990-2000, and percent change, 1990-2000; numbers in thousands)

	1990	1995	2000	percent change 1990–2000
Total	**10,307**	**11,369**	**12,441**	**20.7%**
Under age 25	686	697	704	2.7
Aged 25 to 34	2,484	2,480	2,478	-0.2
Aged 35 to 44	2,529	3,008	3,252	28.6
Aged 45 to 54	1,614	2,006	2,544	57.6
Aged 55 to 64	1,346	1,394	1,571	16.7
Aged 65 to 74	993	1,037	1,032	3.9
Aged 75 or older	655	747	860	31.3

Note: Household counts for 1990 in this projection series are based on 1990 census figures and will differ from household estimates for 1990 based on the Current Population Survey shown elsewhere in this book.
Source: TGE Demographics, Inc., Ithaca, New York

Projections of Black Households by Type of Household, 1990 to 2000

Most types of black households will increase by at least 20 percent during the 1990s.

(number of black households by type of household, 1990-2000, and percent change, 1990-2000; numbers in thousands)

	1990	1995	2000	percent change 1990–2000
Total	**10,307**	**11,369**	**12,441**	**20.7%**
Family households	**7,355**	**8,128**	**8,883**	**20.8**
Married couples, total	3,696	4,104	4,524	22.4
With children under age 18	2,078	2,325	2,530	21.8
Without children under age 18	1,618	1,779	1,994	23.2
Male householder	441	490	538	22.0
Female householder	3,220	3,537	3,824	18.8
Nonfamily households	**2,953**	**3,241**	**3,558**	**20.5**
Male householder	1,286	1,415	1,543	20.0
Living alone	1,065	1,176	1,286	20.8
Female householder	1,666	1,826	2,015	20.9
Living alone	1,494	1,639	1,813	21.4

Note: Household counts for 1990 in this projection series are based on 1990 census figures and will differ from household estimates for 1990 based on the Current Population Survey shown elsewhere in this book.
Source: TGE Demographics, Inc., Ithaca, New York

Projections of Hispanic Households by Age of Householder, 1990 to 2000

The number of Hispanic households is projected to grow by an enormous 48 percent between 1990 and 2000.

(number of Hispanic households by age of householder, 1990-2000, and percent change, 1990-2000; numbers in thousands)

	1990	1995	2000	percent change 1990–2000
Total	**6,365**	**7,859**	**9,422**	**48.0%**
Under age 25	629	639	703	11.7
Aged 25 to 34	1,865	2,251	2,411	29.3
Aged 35 to 44	1,499	1,977	2,507	67.2
Aged 45 to 54	975	1,302	1,743	78.7
Aged 55 to 64	692	804	990	43.0
Aged 65 to 74	491	623	724	47.5
Aged 75 or older	213	264	344	61.4

Note: Household counts for 1990 in this projection series are based on 1990 census figures and will differ from household estimates for 1990 based on the Current Population Survey shown elsewhere in this book.
Hispanics may be of any race.
Source: TGE Demographics, Inc., Ithaca, New York

Projections of Hispanic Households by Type of Household, 1990 to 2000

Every type of Hispanic household is projected to grow by nearly 50 percent during the 1990s. By 2000 there should be nearly 10 million Hispanic households.

(number of Hispanic households by type of household, 1990-2000, and percent change, 1990-2000; numbers in thousands)

	1990	1995	2000	percent change 1990–2000
Total	6,365	7,859	9,422	48.0%
Family households	5,193	6,432	7,717	48.6
Married couples, total	3,636	4,522	5,431	49.4
With children under age 18	2,448	3,060	3,655	49.3
Without children under age 18	1,188	1,461	1,776	49.5
Male householder	360	430	504	40.0
Female householder	1,199	1,485	1,787	49.0
Nonfamily households	1,172	1,426	1,705	45.5
Male householder	633	766	904	42.8
Living alone	444	544	651	46.6
Female householder	539	661	800	48.4
Living alone	468	578	705	50.6

Note: Household counts for 1990 in this projection series are based on 1990 census figures and will differ from household estimates for 1990 based on the Current Population Survey shown elsewhere in this book.
Hispanics may be of any race.
Source: TGE Demographics, Inc., Ithaca, New York

Married Couples by Age of Householder and Number of Children

Most married couples under age 50 have at least one child at home. The majority of those in their 30s have two or more at home.

(number and percent distribution of married couples by age of householder and number of children under age 18 living at home in 1991, numbers in thousands)

	none		one		two		three or more	
	number	percent	number	percent	number	percent	number	percent
All couples	**27,754**	**53.2%**	**9,316**	**17.9%**	**9,720**	**18.6%**	**5,357**	**10.3%**
Under age 25	737	47.3	521	33.5	234	15.0	65	4.2
Aged 25 to 29	1,593	35.0	1,284	28.2	1,162	25.5	513	11.3
Aged 30 to 34	1,296	20.1	1,573	24.4	2,176	33.7	1,406	21.8
Aged 35 to 39	1,048	15.5	1,380	20.5	2,688	39.9	1,624	24.1
Aged 40 to 44	1,419	21.8	1,869	28.7	2,071	31.8	1,147	17.6
Aged 45 to 49	2,455	47.5	1,412	27.3	884	17.1	414	8.0
Aged 50 to 54	3,109	73.3	699	16.5	315	7.4	117	2.8
Aged 55 to 59	3,454	87.4	331	8.4	122	3.1	43	1.1
Aged 60 to 64	3,705	93.8	172	4.4	54	1.4	18	0.5
Aged 65 to 69	3,591	98.0	53	1.4	11	0.3	8	0.2
Aged 70 to 74	2,616	99.3	17	0.6	0	0.0	2	0.1
Aged 75 or older	2,730	99.7	5	0.2	2	0.1	0	0.0

Source: 1991 Current Population Survey tabulation by TGE Demographics, Inc., Ithaca, New York

A growing share of households contain just one or two people, while a shrinking share contain four or more. The share with three people has remained steady since 1970.

(number and percent distribution of households by size, 1970 to 1990; numbers in thousands)

	1990		1980		1970	
	number	percent	number	percent	number	percent
All households	**93,347**	**100.0%**	**80,776**	**100.0%**	**63,401**	**100.0%**
One person	22,999	24.6	18,296	22.7	10,851	17.1
Two persons	30,114	32.3	25,327	31.4	18,333	28.9
Three persons	16,128	17.3	14,130	17.5	10,949	17.3
Four persons	14,456	15.5	12,666	15.7	9,991	15.8
Five persons	6,213	6.7	6,059	7.5	6,548	10.3
Six persons	2,143	2.3	2,519	3.1	3,534	5.6
Seven or more persons	1,295	1.4	1,778	2.2	3,195	5.0

Source: Bureau of the Census

Living Arrangements of Children Under Age 18

Most white or Hispanic children live with two parents, while most black children live with their mother only. The number of children who live with their fathers has increased rapidly, although these children remain a small minority.

(living arrangements of children under age 18 by race and Hispanic origin, 1980 and 1990; numbers in thousands)

	1990		1980		
All races	number	percent distribution	number	percent distribution	percent change 1980-90
Children under age 18	64,137	100.0%	63,427	100.0%	1.1%
Living with:					
Two parents	46,503	72.5	48,624	76.7	-4.4
One parent	15,867	24.7	12,466	19.7	27.3
Mother only	13,874	21.6	11,406	18.0	21.6
Father only	1,993	3.1	1,060	1.7	88.0
Other relatives	1,422	2.2	1,949	3.1	-27.0
Nonrelatives only	346	0.5	388	0.6	-10.8
White					
Children under age 18	51,390	100.0	52,242	100.0	-1.6
Living with:					
Two parents	40,593	79.0	43,200	82.7	-6.0
One parent	9,870	19.2	7,901	15.1	24.90
Mother only	8,321	16.2	7,059	13.5	17.9
Father only	1,549	3.0	842	1.6	84.0
Other relatives	708	1.4	887	1.7	-20.2
Nonrelatives only	220	0.4	254	0.5	-13.4
Black					
Children under age 18	10,018	100.0	9,375	100.0	6.9
Living with:					
Two parents	3,781	37.7	3,956	42.2	-4.4
One parent	5,485	54.8	4,297	45.8	27.6
Mother only	5,132	51.2	4,117	43.9	24.7
Father only	353	3.5	180	1.9	96.1
Other relatives	654	6.5	999	10.7	-34.5
Nonrelatives only	98	1.0	123	1.3	-20.3
Hispanic					
Children under age 18	7,174	100.0	5,459	100.0	31.4
Living with:					
Two parents	4,789	66.8	4,116	75.4	16.4
One parent	2,154	30.0	1,152	21.1	87.0
Mother only	1,943	27.1	1,069	19.6	81.8
Father only	211	2.9	83	1.5	154.2
Other relatives	177	2.5	183	3.4	-3.3
Nonrelatives only	54	0.8	8	0.1	575.0

Source: Bureau of the Census

Living Arrangements of Young Adults

Most men aged 18 to 24 still live with their parents, while most women in this age group live independently. Fifteen percent of men aged 25 to 34 continue to live with a parent, as do 8 percent of women.

(living arrangements of young adults by age and sex, 1980 and 1990; numbers in thousands)

	1990		1980	
Adults aged 18 to 24	number	percent distribution	number	percent distribution
Total	**25,310**	**100.0%**	**29,122**	**100.0%**
Child of householder	13,367	52.8	14,091	48.4
Family householder or spouse	5,631	22.2	8,408	28.9
Nonfamily householder	2,252	8.9	2,776	9.5
Other	4,060	16.0	3,848	13.2
Male	**12,450**	**100.0**	**14,278**	**100.0**
Child of householder	7,232	58.1	7,755	54.3
Family householder or spouse	1,838	14.8	3,041	21.3
Nonfamily householder	1,228	9.9	1,581	11.1
Other	2,152	17.3	1,902	13.3
Female	**12,860**	**100.0**	**14,844**	**100.0**
Child of householder	6,135	47.7	6,336	42.7
Family householder or spouse	3,793	29.5	5,367	36.2
Nonfamily householder	1,024	8.0	1,195	8.1
Other	1,908	14.8	1,946	13.1
Adults aged 25 to 34				
Total	**43,240**	**100.0**	**36,796**	**100.0**
Child of householder	4,986	11.5	3,194	8.7
Family householder or spouse	27,964	64.7	26,615	72.3
Nonfamily householder	5,618	13.0	4,411	12.0
Other	4,672	10.8	2,577	7.0
Male	**21,462**	**100.0**	**18,107**	**100.0**
Child of householder	3,213	15.0	1,894	10.5
Family householder or spouse	11,998	55.9	12,024	66.4
Nonfamily householder	3,467	16.2	2,765	15.3
Other	2,784	13.0	1,424	7.9
Female	**21,779**	**100.0**	**18,689**	**100.0**
Child of householder	1,774	8.1	1,300	7.0
Family householder or spouse	15,966	73.3	14,591	78.1
Nonfamily householder	2,151	9.9	1,646	8.8
Other	1,888	8.7	1,153	6.2

Source: Census Bureau

Living Arrangements of the Elderly

A majority of women aged 75 or older live alone. Among men, only 28 percent live alone at ages 85 and older.

(living arrangements of the elderly by age and sex, 1990; numbers in thousands)

	total	men	women	percent distribution		
				total	men	women
Aged 65 or older	**29,566**	**12,334**	**17,232**	**100.0%**	**100.0%**	**100.0%**
Living:						
Alone	9,176	1,942	7,233	31.0	15.7	42.0
With spouse	16,003	9,158	6,845	54.1	74.3	39.7
With other relatives	3,734	953	2,782	12.6	7.7	16.1
With nonrelatives only	653	281	372	2.2	2.3	2.2
Aged 65 to 74	**17,979**	**8,013**	**9,966**	**100.0**	**100.0**	**100.0**
Living:						
Alone	4,350	1,042	3,309	24.2	13.0	33.2
With spouse	11,353	6,265	5,089	63.1	78.2	51.1
With other relatives	1,931	528	1,401	10.7	6.6	14.1
With nonrelatives only	345	178	167	1.9	2.2	1.7
Aged 75 to 84	**9,354**	**3,562**	**5,792**	**100.0**	**100.0**	**100.0**
Living:						
Alone	3,774	688	3,086	40.3	19.3	53.3
With spouse	4,145	2,537	1,607	44.3	71.2	27.7
With other relatives	1,237	264	974	13.2	7.4	16.8
With nonrelatives only	198	73	125	2.1	2.0	2.2
Aged 85 or older	**2,233**	**758**	**1,475**	**100.0**	**100.0%**	**100.0**
Living:						
Alone	1,051	213	838	47.1	28.1	56.8
With spouse	505	356	150	22.6	47.0	10.2
With other relatives	567	160	406	25.4	21.1	27.5
With nonrelatives only	110	29	81	4.9	3.8	5.5

Source: Bureau of the Census

Characteristics of American Grandparents

Fully 77 percent of Americans aged 60 or older have grandchildren. But only 38 percent have grandchildren under age 6.

(number and age of grandchildren by age of grandparents, 1989; in percent of population of given ages)

	age of grandparent		
	30 to 44	*45 to 59*	*60 or older*
Number of grandchildren			
Any	8%	50%	77%
1 to 2	5	24	16
3 to 4	2	10	22
5 to 7	1	10	17
8 or more	-	4	17
Median number for those with grandchildren	2.0	3.0	4.0
Age of grandchildren			
Under age 6	81	81	38
Aged 6 to 12	35	57	57
Aged 13 to 17	5	21	49
Aged 18 to 24	5	9	51
Aged 25 or older	2	2	29
Median age of grandchildren	5 years	6 years	15 years

Source: Roper Reports 89-5

Characteristics of
In-Household Caregivers

Nearly 6 million Americans help someone in their household with daily activities. Most helpers are women, and nearly half are spouses.

(number of persons who provided assistance to one or more household members by selected characteristics and type of assistance, 1986; numbers in thousands)

			activities assisted with			
	one or more activities	personal care	getting around outside	preparing meals	doing housework	keeping track of bills and/or money
Total providers	**5,791**	**2,469**	**2,894**	**3,734**	**3,927**	**1,815**
Age						
Under age 18	557	149	124	299	452	6
Aged 18 to 29	728	226	230	453	560	126
Aged 30 to 44	1,045	437	538	668	660	248
Aged 45 to 64	1,944	890	1,207	1,249	1,233	751
Aged 65 or older	1,518	767	795	1,065	1,022	684
Sex						
Male	2,558	795	1,333	1,603	1,872	534
Female	3,233	1,673	1,561	2,130	2,055	1,282
Relationship to recipient						
Son	692	182	311	394	457	132
Daughter	1,063	452	441	753	864	392
Spouse	2,549	1,112	1,419	1,666	1,662	694
Other relative	1,150	566	556	686	702	469
Nonrelative	337	156	167	235	243	128

Source: Bureau of the Census

Characteristics of
Out-of-Household Caregivers

Fifteen million Americans help someone in another household with daily activities. One-third of helpers are not related to the person they help.

(number of persons aged 15 and older who provided assistance to a person outside their household by selected characteristics and type of assistance, 1986; numbers in thousands)

	one or more activities	personal care	getting around outside	preparing meals	doing housework	keeping track of bills and/or money
			activities assisted with			
Total providers	**15,099**	**3,790**	**11,656**	**6,794**	**7,475**	**3,456**
Age						
Under age 18	368	107	137	163	292	44
Aged 18 to 29	2,853	685	2,101	1,312	1,632	404
Aged 30 to 44	4,820	1,279	3,834	2,285	2,563	1,070
Aged 45 to 64	4,861	1,288	3,886	2,146	2,276	1,522
Aged 65 or older	2,197	432	1,698	889	712	415
Sex						
Male	4,970	986	3,967	1,400	1,877	1,218
Female	10,130	2,805	7,689	5,395	5,598	2,238
Relationship to recipient						
Son	1,808	447	1,503	545	754	681
Daughter	3,359	1,020	2,822	1,883	2,187	1,216
Other relative	4,922	1,349	3,709	2,343	2,628	1,088
Nonrelative	5,011	974	3,622	2,024	1,906	470

Source: Bureau of the Census

Characteristics of People Needing Assistance in Daily Life

More than 8 million Americans need help with at least one daily activity. Among those aged 85 or older, nearly half need help.

(number and percent of persons 15 years and older by need for assistance status and selected characteristics, 1986; numbers in thousands)

	total	**needed assistance with:**						did not need assistance
		one or more activities	personal care	getting around outside	preparing meals	doing housework	keeping track of bills and/ or money	
Total, number	**186,022**	**8,206**	**3,211**	**5,213**	**4,830**	**5,927**	**3,039**	**177,816**
Age								
Under age 65	158,359	3,794	1,383	2,077	2,315	2,821	1,050	154,564
Aged 65 or older	27,663	4,412	1,827	3,136	2,515	3,106	1,990	23,252
Aged 65 to 69	9,615	890	285	546	484	635	274	8,724
Aged 70 to 74	7,391	806	336	525	472	566	299	6,586
Aged 75 to 79	5,434	1,026	408	678	554	710	408	4,408
Aged 80 to 84	3,126	738	311	595	365	473	334	2,388
Aged 85 or older	2,097	952	487	791	639	722	674	1,145
Living arrangement								
Family member	154,866	5,601	2,426	3,553	3,610	4,034	2,026	149,264
Not a family member	31,156	2,605	785	1,660	1,220	1,893	1,013	28,552
Lives alone	21,907	2,269	631	1,426	1,000	1,632	834	19,638
Monthly household income								
Under $600	16,227	1,916	669	1,219	1,030	1,379	712	14,310
$600 to $1,199	25,066	2,056	772	1,323	1,091	1,465	882	23,010
$1,200 to $1,999	37,483	1,731	713	1,102	1,073	1,196	574	35,752
$2,000 to $2,999	39,737	1,205	492	729	777	896	458	38,532
$3,000 or more	67,509	1,297	565	841	859	991	412	66,212
Total, percent	**100.0%**	**4.4%**	**1.7%**	**2.8%**	**2.6%**	**3.2%**	**1.6%**	**95.6%**
Age								
Under age 65	100.0	2.4	0.9	1.3	1.5	1.8	0.7	97.6
Aged 65 or older	100.0	16.0	6.6	11.3	9.1	11.2	7.2	84.1
Aged 65 to 69	100.0	9.3	3.0	5.7	5.0	6.6	2.8	90.7
Aged 70 to 74	100.0	10.9	4.5	7.1	6.4	7.7	4.0	89.1
Aged 75 to 79	100.0	18.9	7.5	12.5	10.2	13.1	7.5	81.1
Aged 80 to 84	100.0	23.6	10.0	19.0	11.7	15.1	10.7	76.4
Aged 85 or older	100.0	45.4	23.2	37.7	30.5	34.4	32.1	54.6
Living arrangement								
Family member	100.0	3.6	1.6	2.3	2.3	2.6	1.3	96.4
Not a family member	100.0	8.4	2.5	5.3	3.9	6.1	3.3	91.6
Lives alone	100.0	10.4	2.9	6.5	4.6	7.4	3.8	89.6

(continued on next page)

(continued from previous page)

(number and percent of persons 15 years and older by need for assistance status and selected characteristics, 1986; numbers in thousands)

	total	one or more activities	personal care	getting around outside	preparing meals	doing housework	keeping track of bills and/ or money	did not need assistance
Monthly household income								
Under $600	100.0%	11.8%	4.1%	7.5%	6.3%	8.5%	4.4%	88.2%
$600 to $1,199	100.0	8.2	3.1	5.3	4.4	5.8	3.5	91.8
$1,200 to $1,999	100.0	4.6	1.9	2.9	2.9	3.2	1.5	95.4
$2,000 to $2,999	100.0	3.0	1.2	1.8	2.0	2.3	1.2	97.0
$3,000 or more	100.0	1.9	0.8	1.2	1.3	1.5	0.6	98.1

Source: Bureau of the Census

Characteristics of
Single-Person Households

Two-thirds of women who live alone are aged 55 or older. Sixty percent of men who live alone are aged 25 to 54.

(number and percent distribution of persons living alone by age and sex, 1990; numbers in thousands)

	number	percent distribution
Both sexes	**22,999**	**100.0%**
Aged 15 to 24	1,210	5.3
Aged 25 to 34	3,972	17.3
Aged 35 to 44	3,138	13.6
Aged 45 to 54	2,422	10.5
Aged 55 to 64	3,080	13.4
Aged 65 to 74	4,350	18.9
Aged 75 or older	4,825	21.0
Median age	58	-
Men	**9,049**	**100.0**
Aged 15 to 24	674	7.4
Aged 25 to 34	2,395	26.5
Aged 35 to 44	1,836	20.3
Aged 45 to 54	1,167	12.9
Aged 55 to 64	1,036	11.4
Aged 65 to 74	1,042	11.5
Aged 75 or older	901	10.0
Median age	43	-
Women	**13,950**	**100.0**
Aged 15 to 24	536	3.8
Aged 25 to 34	1,578	11.3
Aged 35 to 44	1,303	9.3
Aged 45 to 54	1,256	9.0
Aged 55 to 64	2,044	14.7
Aged 65 to 74	3,309	23.7
Aged 75 or older	3,924	28.1
Median age	66	-

Source: Bureau of the Census

Characteristics of Single-Parent Households

More than eight out of ten single-parent families are headed by women. Seventy percent of those women are aged 25 to 44.

(number and percent distribution of single-parent families with children under age 18 by sex, age, race, and Hispanic origin of householder, 1990; numbers in thousands)

	number	percent
Total	**7,752**	**100.0%**
Female householders	**6,599**	**100.0**
Under age 25	786	11.9
Aged 25 to 29	1,139	17.3
Aged 30 to 34	1,486	22.5
Aged 35 to 39	1,380	20.9
Aged 40 to 44	961	14.6
Aged 45 to 54	707	10.7
Aged 55 or older	138	2.1
Male householders	**1,153**	**100.0**
Under age 25	96	8.3
Aged 25 to 29	164	14.2
Aged 30 to 34	185	16.0
Aged 35 to 39	240	20.8
Aged 40 to 44	218	18.9
Aged 45 to 54	193	16.7
Aged 55 or older	58	5.0
White	**5,138**	**100.0**
Female	4,199	81.7
Male	939	18.3
Black	**2,405**	**100.0**
Female	2,232	92.8
Male	173	7.2
Hispanic	**863**	**100.0**
Female	745	86.3
Male	118	13.7

Source: Bureau of the Census

Marital Status by Age

Most people aged 25 or older are married. The never-married are a majority of those under age 25, while widows are a majority of women aged 75 or older.

(number and percent distribution of men and women aged 15 or older by age and marital status, 1990; numbers in thousands)

	total		never married		married		widowed		divorced	
	number	*percent*	*number*	*percent*	*number*	*percent*	*number*	*percent*	*number*	*percent*
Men	**91,955**	**100.0%**	**27,505**	**29.9%**	**55,833**	**60.7%**	**2,333**	**2.5%**	**6,283**	**6.8%**
Under age 20	8,722	100.0	8,595	98.5	123	1.4	-	0.0	3	0.0
Aged 20 to 24	8,811	100.0	6,985	79.3	1,732	19.7	-	0.0	95	1.1
Aged 25 to 29	10,515	100.0	4,749	45.2	5,268	50.1	6	0.1	493	4.7
Aged 30 to 34	10,947	100.0	2,955	27.0	7,108	65.0	18	0.2	867	7.9
Aged 35 to 39	9,844	100.0	1,450	14.7	7,284	74.0	35	0.4	1,075	10.9
Aged 40 to 44	8,487	100.0	895	10.5	6,588	77.6	42	0.5	962	11.3
Aged 45 to 54	12,292	100.0	778	6.3	10,007	81.4	144	1.2	1,364	11.1
Aged 55 to 64	10,002	100.0	576	5.8	8,279	82.8	334	3.3	813	8.1
Aged 65 to 74	8,013	100.0	376	4.7	6,426	80.2	733	9.2	478	6.0
Aged 75 to 84	3,562	100.0	119	3.3	2,631	73.8	693	19.5	118	3.3
Aged 85 or older	758	100.0	27	3.5	388	51.1	329	43.4	15	2.0
Women	**99,838**	**100.0**	**22,718**	**22.8**	**56,797**	**56.8**	**11,477**	**11.5**	**8,845**	**8.9**
Under age 20	8,544	100.0	8,117	95.0	413	4.8	-	-	16	0.2
Aged 20 to 24	9,177	100.0	5,762	62.8	3,143	34.3	10	0.1	261	2.8
Aged 25 to 29	10,685	100.0	3,318	31.1	6,559	61.4	47	0.4	760	7.1
Aged 30 to 34	11,094	100.0	1,824	16.4	8,017	72.3	86	0.8	1,167	10.5
Aged 35 to 39	10,047	100.0	1,045	10.4	7,468	74.3	145	1.4	1,389	13.8
Aged 40 to 44	8,817	100.0	704	8.0	6,517	73.9	202	2.3	1,395	15.8
Aged 45 to 54	13,012	100.0	655	5.0	9,790	75.3	688	5.3	1,879	14.4
Aged 55 to 64	11,230	100.0	443	3.9	7,747	69.0	1,931	17.2	1,107	9.9
Aged 65 to 74	9,966	100.0	460	4.6	5,297	53.2	3,597	36.1	613	6.2
Aged 75 to 84	5,792	100.0	299	5.2	1,690	29.1	3,593	62.0	209	3.6
Aged 85 or older	1,475	100.0	92	6.2	157	10.6	1,177	79.8	50	3.4

Source: Bureau of the Census
Note: (-) means that the number is too small to be reliable and is not reported.

Marriages and Remarriages, 1980 to 1988

Just 55 percent of all marriages today are between single men and women. In nearly 20 percent of marriages, both the bride and groom are previously divorced.

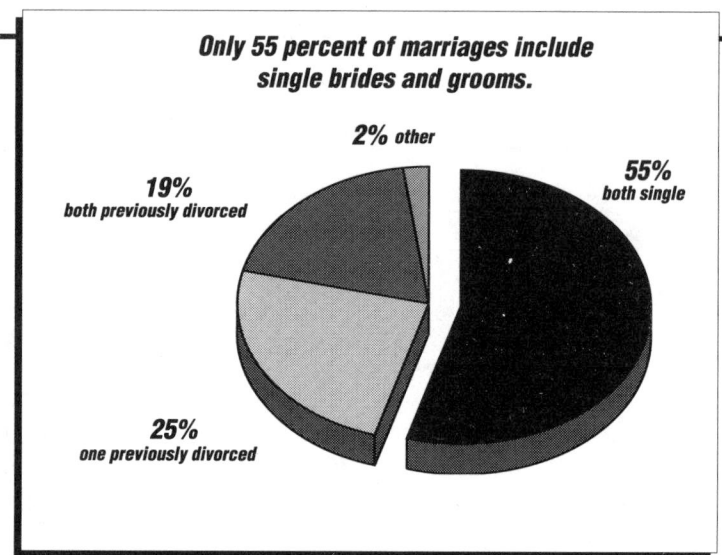

Only 55 percent of marriages include single brides and grooms.

2% other
19% both previously divorced
55% both single
25% one previously divorced

(percent distribution of marriages by previous marital status of both bride and groom, 1980 to 1988)

	total	wife previously single and husband previously:			wife previously divorced and husband previously:			wife previously widowed and husband previously:		
		single	divorced	widowed	single	divorced	widowed	single	divorced	widowed
1988	100.0%	54.5%	10.7%	0.4%	10.9%	19.0%	1.3%	0.5%	1.4%	1.3%
1987	100.0	54.3	11.0	0.4	10.7	19.1	1.3	0.5	1.4	1.4
1986	100.0	54.4	11.0	0.3	10.7	18.9	1.3	0.5	1.4	1.4
1985	100.0	54.7	11.1	0.3	10.4	18.8	1.3	0.5	1.4	1.5
1984	100.0	55.0	11.1	0.4	10.2	18.8	1.3	0.5	1.4	1.5
1983	100.0	54.8	11.2	0.4	10.0	18.9	1.3	0.5	1.5	1.5
1982	100.0	55.1	11.3	0.4	9.8	18.8	1.3	0.5	1.4	1.5
1981	100.0	54.9	11.4	0.4	9.6	18.8	1.3	0.5	1.5	1.5
1980	100.0	56.5	10.8	0.4	9.3	17.8	1.4	0.5	1.5	1.6

Source: National Center for Health Statistics

Median Age at First Marriage, 1890 to 1990

The median age at first marriage for men now matches the record level it set back in 1890. Women are marrying at a later age than ever before.

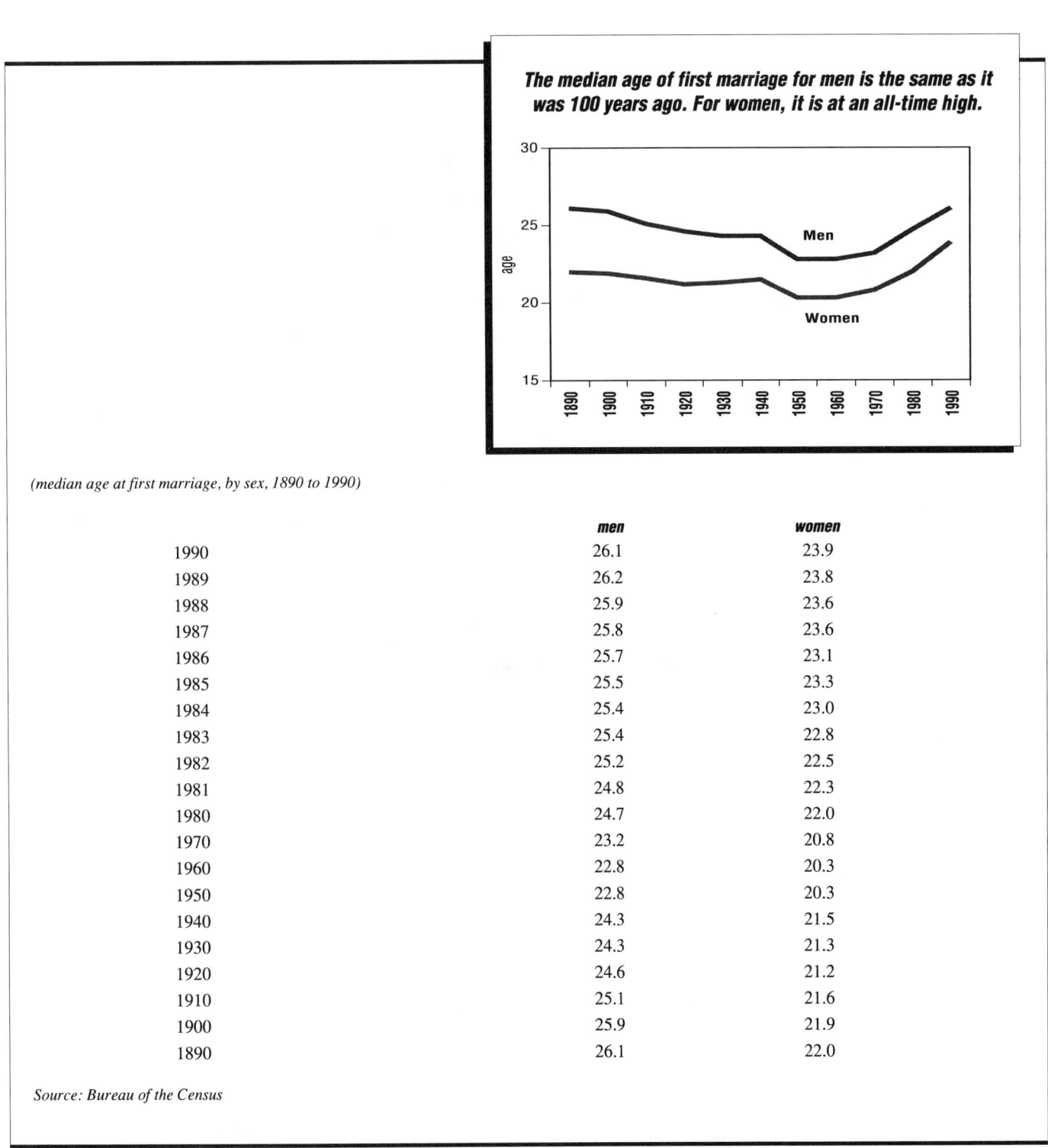

The median age of first marriage for men is the same as it was 100 years ago. For women, it is at an all-time high.

(median age at first marriage, by sex, 1890 to 1990)

	men	women
1990	26.1	23.9
1989	26.2	23.8
1988	25.9	23.6
1987	25.8	23.6
1986	25.7	23.1
1985	25.5	23.3
1984	25.4	23.0
1983	25.4	22.8
1982	25.2	22.5
1981	24.8	22.3
1980	24.7	22.0
1970	23.2	20.8
1960	22.8	20.3
1950	22.8	20.3
1940	24.3	21.5
1930	24.3	21.3
1920	24.6	21.2
1910	25.1	21.6
1900	25.9	21.9
1890	26.1	22.0

Source: Bureau of the Census

Marriage and Divorce Rates, 1940 to 1991

Both marriage and divorce rates peaked in the early 1980s and have fallen since then. But the divorce rate remains higher than it was prior to 1970.

(marriages and divorces per 1,000 population, 1940 to 1991)

	marriage rate	divorce rate
1991	9.7	4.7
1990	9.7	4.7
1989	9.7	4.6
1988	9.7	4.7
1987	9.9	4.8
1986	10.0	4.9
1985	10.1	5.0
1984	10.5	5.0
1983	10.5	4.9
1982	10.6	5.0
1981	10.6	5.3
1980	10.6	5.2
1975	10.0	4.8
1970	10.6	3.5
1960	8.5	2.2
1950	11.1	2.6
1940	12.1	2.0

Characteristics of Cohabiting Couples

Most unmarried couples are under the age of 35, but a significant share are older. In 18 percent of cohabiting couples, the man is aged 45 or older.

(number and percent distribution of adults in unmarried-couple households, by age and sex, 1990; numbers in thousands)

		female partner				
Male partner	*total*	*under age 25*	*aged 25 to 34*	*aged 35 to 44*	*aged 45 to 64*	*65+*
Male partner	2,856	788	1,170	494	320	83
Under age 25	530	381	141	8	3	-
Aged 25 to 34	1,189	333	726	113	15	3
Aged 35 to 44	618	55	236	270	55	2
Aged 45 to 64	390	19	54	100	195	24
Aged 65 or older	129	4	13	4	55	54
Percent distribution	100.0%	27.6%	41.0%	17.3%	11.2%	2.9%
Under age 25	18.6	13.3	4.9	0.3	0.1	-
Aged 25 to 34	41.6	11.7	25.4	4.0	0.5	0.1
Aged 35 to 44	21.6	1.9	8.3	9.5	1.9	0.1
Aged 45 to 64	13.7	0.7	1.9	3.5	6.8	0.8
Aged 65 or older	4.5	0.1	0.5	0.1	1.9	1.9

Source: Bureau of the Census

Sexual Behavior of Americans

The average American adult has had seven sexual partners since age 18. Those in their 30s average eight partners and have the greatest frequency of sexual intercourse.

(various measures of sexual behavior for persons aged 18 or older, by sex, marital status, and age, 1989)

	average number of partners in past year	average number of partners since age 18	number of times had intercourse in past year
All	1.2	7.2	57.4
Sex			
Men	1.5	12.3	66.4
Women	0.9	3.3	50.6
Marital status			
Married	1.0	5.7	67.3
Widowed	0.2	3.0	5.7
Divorced	1.3	13.3	55.2
Separated	2.4	11.8	66.1
Never married	1.8	8.7	54.9
Age			
Aged 18 to 29	1.8	6.1	77.8
Aged 30 to 39	1.3	8.4	78.3
Aged 40 to 49	1.3	9.7	66.9
Aged 50 to 59	1.0	9.3	46.1
Aged 60 to 69	0.7	4.7	22.6
Aged 70 or older	0.4	3.5	8.2

Source: General Social Survey, National Opinion Research Center

Number of Births, 1960 to 1995

The number of births in the U.S. bottomed out in 1973 before climbing to over 4 million in 1989. Births are expected to decline gradually through the mid-1990s.

(number of births in 1960 to 1990 and projections for 1991 to 1995; numbers in thousands)

	number of births
1995	3,924
1994	4,009
1993	4,095
1992	4,180
1991	4,159
1990	4,179
1989	4,021
1988	3,910
1987	3,809
1986	3,757
1985	3,761
1984	3,669
1983	3,639
1982	3,681
1981	3,629
1980	3,612
1979	3,494
1978	3,333
1977	3,327
1976	3,168
1975	3,144
1974	3,160
1973	3,137
1972	3,258
1971	3,556
1970	3,731
1969	3,600
1968	3,502
1967	3,521
1966	3,606
1965	3,760
1964	4,027
1963	4,098
1962	4,167
1961	4,268
1960	4,258

Source: National Center for Health Statistics and American Demographics magazine, July 1991

Births by Age of Mother

Despite an increase in the number of older mothers in recent years, nearly 60 percent of babies are born to mothers in their twenties.

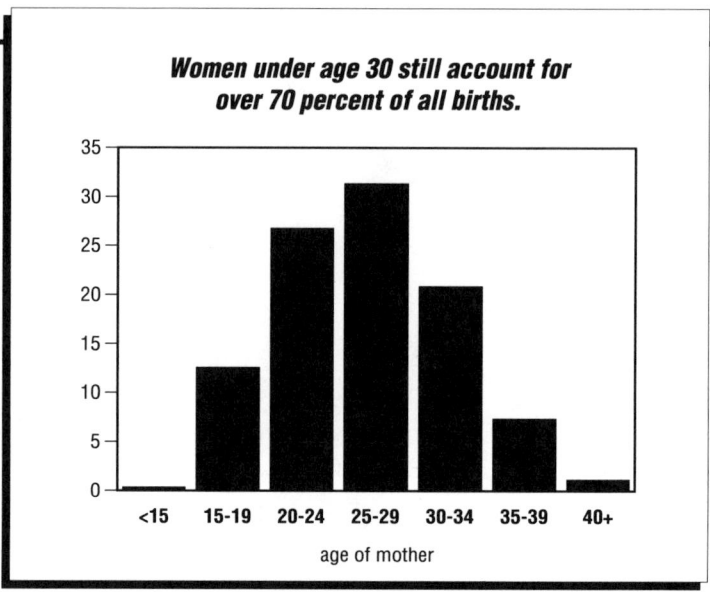

Women under age 30 still account for over 70 percent of all births.

age of mother

(number and percent distribution of live births by age of mother, 1989)

Age of mother	number	percent
Total births	**4,040,958**	**100.0%**
Under age 15	11,486	0.3
Aged 15 to 19	506,503	12.5
Aged 20 to 24	1,077,598	26.7
Aged 25 to 29	1,263,098	31.3
Aged 30 to 34	842,395	20.8
Aged 35 to 39	293,878	7.3
Aged 40 or older	46,000	1.1

Source: National Center for Health Statistics

Birth Order, 1950 to 1989

The share of all births accounted for by first births peaked in 1980 at 43 percent. Now that baby boomers are having their second and third children, the first-birth share is declining.

(percent of all births that are first, second, or higher-order births, 1950-89)

	first	*second*	*third or more*
1989	41%	32%	27%
1985	42	33	25
1980	43	32	25
1975	42	32	26
1970	39	27	34
1965	31	24	45
1960	26	25	49
1955	28	27	45
1950	32	30	38

Source: National Center for Health Statistics

Births by Race and Ethnicity

White babies are the majority of all births in the U.S. But black or Hispanic newborns account for a significant share of births.

(number and percent distribution of live births by race and Hispanic origin of child, 1989)

	number	percent
Total births	**4,040,958**	**100.0%**
White	3,192,355	79.0
Black	673,124	16.7
American Indian	39,478	1.0
Chinese	20,982	0.5
Japanese	8,689	0.2
Hawaiian	5,609	0.1
Filipino	24,585	0.6
Other	73,210	1.8
Births of Hispanics (47 reporting states)		
Total births in reporting states (all races)	3,903,012	100.0%
Total non-Hispanic	3,370,763	86.4
Total Hispanic	532,249	13.6
Mexican	327,233	8.4
Puerto Rican	56,229	1.4
Cuban	10,842	0.3
Central and South American	72,443	1.9
Other	65,502	1.7

Source: National Center for Health Statistics
Note: Hispanics may be of any race.

Fertility Status of American Women

After the age of 35, most women are no longer fertile. Over half have been surgically sterilized, while 11 percent have impaired fecundity.

(number of women aged 15 to 44 and percent distribution by fecundity status, by age and number of children, 1988; numbers in thousands)

	number	percent	fecund	surgically sterile	impaired fecundity
All women					
Aged 15 to 44	57,900	100.0%	63.6%	28.0%	8.4%
Aged 15 to 24	18,592	100.0	93.0	2.2	4.8
Aged 25 to 34	21,726	100.0	64.7	25.6	9.6
Aged 35 to 44	17,582	100.0	31.0	58.3	10.6
Women with no children					
Aged 15 to 44	25,129	100.0	86.9	4.3	8.8
Aged 15 to 24	14,978	100.0	95.7	0.2	4.1
Aged 25 to 34	7,252	100.0	82.0	4.7	13.4
Aged 35 to 44	2,899	100.0	53.6	25.0	21.4
Women with one or more child(ren)					
Aged 15 to 44	32,771	100.0	45.8	46.1	8.1
Aged 15 to 24	3,614	100.0	81.8	10.5	7.7
Aged 25 to 34	14,474	100.0	56.1	36.1	7.8
Aged 35 to 44	14,683	100.0	26.7	64.8	8.5

Source: National Center for Health Statistics

Out-of-Wedlock Births

Over one-fourth of all newborns in the U.S. are born out of wedlock. Among blacks, two-thirds are born out of wedlock.

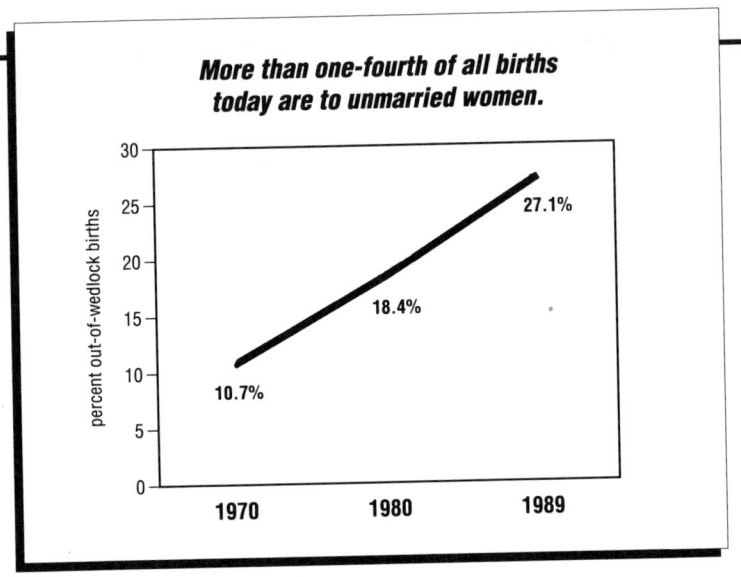

More than one-fourth of all births today are to unmarried women.

(number and percent distribution of out-of-wedlock births by age and race of mother, 1989)

	total	percent	white	percent	black	percent
Total number of births	4,040,958	100.0%	3,192,355	100.0%	673,124	100.0%
Out of wedlock	1,094,169	27.1	613,543	19.2	442,395	65.7
Out of wedlock by age, total		100.0		100.0		100.0
Under age 20	347,880	31.8	192,173	31.3	145,176	32.8
Aged 20 to 24	378,122	34.6	211,815	34.5	153,551	34.7
Aged 25 to 29	215,477	19.7	120,640	19.7	86,846	19.6
Aged 30 to 34	106,344	9.7	60,344	9.8	41,468	9.4
aged 35 to 39	39,030	3.6	23,730	3.9	13,333	3.0
Aged 40 or older	7,316	0.7	4,841	0.8	2,021	0.5

Source: National Center for Health Statistics

Women With Adopted Children

Fewer than 2 percent of women aged 20 to 44 have ever adopted a child. Women with more education and higher incomes are more likely than others to have adopted a child.

(percent of ever-married women aged 20 to 44 who have ever adopted a child, by selected characteristics of women and relationship to child, 1987)

	number of ever-married women (in thousands)	percent who have adopted		
		any child	unrelated child	related child
Total	38,077	1.7%	1.3%	0.4%
Current age				
Aged 20 to 24	4,598	0.1	0.1	0.0
Aged 25 to 29	8,218	0.6	0.3	0.2
Aged 30 to 34	9,186	1.5	1.1	0.3
Aged 35 to 39	8,799	2.4	1.9	0.3
Aged 40 to 44	7,277	3.4	2.8	0.4
Marital status				
Currently married	31,695	1.8	1.4	0.2
Previously married	6,382	1.3	1.0	0.4
Race				
White	32,894	1.8	1.4	0.2
Black	3,770	1.5	0.8	0.6
Hispanic origin				
Hispanic	3,111	0.8	0.4	0.4
Non-Hispanic	34,788	1.8	1.4	0.3
Education, years of school completed				
Less than 12 years	5,367	1.0	0.5	0.5
12 years	16,705	1.5	1.1	0.2
13 years or more	15,842	2.2	1.9	0.2
Family income				
Under $15,000	6,399	0.9	0.4	0.4
$15,000 to $24,999	7,482	1.6	1.2	0.3
$25,000 to $34,999	7,398	1.8	1.4	0.2
$35,000 or more	12,713	2.3	1.9	0.2

Source: National Center for Health Statistics
Note: The sum of the percents who adopted unrelated and related children may not equal the percent who adopted any child because of missing information and women who adopted children in both categories. "Total" includes women of other races and women for whom information on specific characteristics is not ascertained. Hispanics may be of any race.

3

Income Trends

American incomes rose steadily during most of the 1980s, reaching a record high in 1989. Both household and personal incomes rose, after adjusting for inflation. By the end of the decade, a record proportion of households had incomes of $50,000 or more. Those making the greatest income gains were the college-educated, dual-earners, married couples, and women. The recession of 1990-91 cut the incomes of most Americans, but the 1990s promise renewed growth in affluence.

Major Income Trends

☞   The 1990s will be the most affluent decade in American history, once the country recovers from the effects of the recession.

☞   The middle-aging of the well-educated baby-boom generation will boost household incomes to record highs. The most affluent households are college-educated, middle-aged, married couples aged 45 to 64. As the baby boom inflates this household segment, a rising proportion of households will have incomes of $75,000 or more.

☞   Women's incomes will continue to gain on men's as well-educated younger women replace older women in the labor force. This should help to reduce poverty rates among children.

Distribution of Aggregate Household Income, 1980 to 1990

The amount of income accruing to the poorest households fell during the 1980s, while the amount accruing to the richest households rose. Nearly 19 percent of all household income in 1990 went to the top 5 percent of households.

(aggregate income received by each quintile and top 5 percent of households, in percent of income, 1980-90; numbers in thousands)

	all households	lowest quintile	second quintile	third quintile	fourth quintile	fifth quintile	top 5 percent
				percent distribution of aggregate income			
1990	94,312	3.9%	9.6%	15.9%	24.0%	46.6%	18.6%
1989	93,347	3.8	9.5	15.8	24.0	46.8	18.9
1988	92,830	3.8	9.6	16.0	24.3	46.3	18.3
1987	91,124	3.8	9.6	16.1	24.3	46.2	18.2
1986	89,479	3.8	9.7	16.2	24.3	46.1	18.0
1985	88,458	3.8	9.8	16.2	24.4	45.6	17.6
1984	86,789	3.9	9.9	16.3	24.6	45.2	17.1
1983	85,290	4.0	9.9	16.4	24.6	45.1	17.1
1982	83,918	4.0	10.0	16.5	24.5	45.0	17.0
1981	83,527	4.0	10.1	16.7	24.8	44.4	16.5
1980	82,368	4.1	10.2	16.8	24.8	44.1	16.5

Source: Bureau of the Census

Household Income Distribution, 1980 to 1990

Households are migrating up the income scale. The proportion of households with incomes of $100,000 or more nearly doubled between 1980 and 1990, after adjusting for inflation.

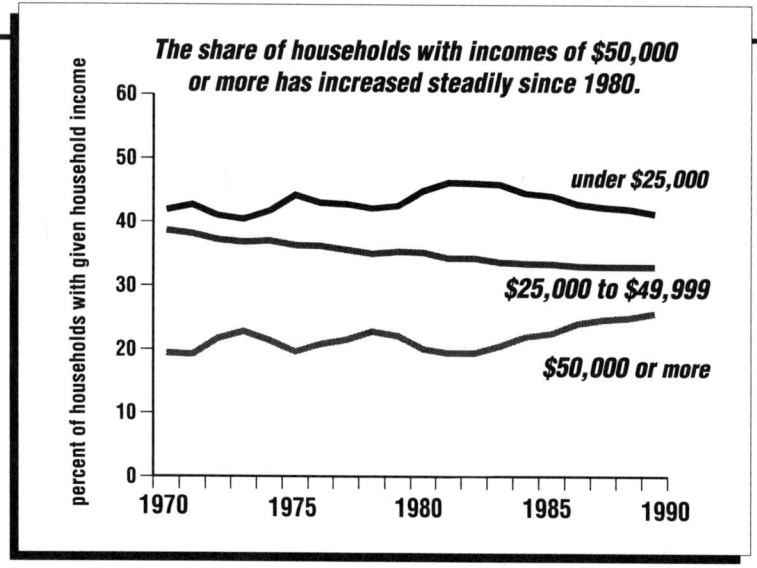

The share of households with incomes of $50,000 or more has increased steadily since 1980.

(percent of households with given household income — under $25,000; $25,000 to $49,999; $50,000 or more — 1970, 1975, 1980, 1985, 1990)

(percent distribution of households by income, 1980-90, in 1990 dollars; numbers in thousands)

	all households	total	under $15,000	$15,000 to $24,999	$25,000 to $34,999	$35,000 to $49,999	$50,000 to $74,999	$75,000 to $99,999	$100,000 or more
1990	94,312	100.0%	24.4%	17.7%	15.8%	17.5%	14.9%	5.4%	4.3%
1989	93,347	100.0	24.1	17.2	15.6	17.4	15.5	5.7	4.5
1988	92,830	100.0	24.6	17.4	15.3	17.7	15.3	5.4	4.3
1987	91,124	100.0	24.9	17.4	15.3	17.7	15.3	5.4	4.0
1986	89,479	100.0	25.1	17.7	15.2	17.9	15.1	5.2	3.8
1985	88,458	100.0	25.8	18.3	15.7	17.7	14.5	4.7	3.3
1984	86,789	100.0	26.0	18.5	16.2	17.3	14.3	4.6	3.1
1983	85,290	100.0	26.8	19.1	16.3	17.4	13.5	4.2	2.8
1982	83,918	100.0	27.3	18.8	16.8	17.5	13.0	3.8	2.6
1981	83,527	100.0	27.1	19.1	16.2	18.1	13.4	3.8	2.2
1980	82,368	100.0	26.0	18.9	16.6	18.6	13.6	4.1	2.3

Source: Bureau of the Census

Median Household Income by Race and Hispanic Origin, 1980 to 1990

Household income rose during the 1980s, after adjusting for inflation, regardless of race or ethnicity. Between 1980 and 1990, median household income for all households increased 7 percent.

(median household income by race and Hispanic origin of householder, 1980-90, in 1990 dollars)

	all households	white	black	Hispanic
1990	$29,943	$31,231	$18,676	$22,330
1989	30,468	32,049	19,060	23,105
1988	30,079	31,798	18,127	22,493
1987	29,984	31,591	18,031	22,247
1986	29,690	31,214	17,983	21,885
1985	28,688	30,255	18,000	21,214
1984	28,197	29,747	16,946	21,375
1983	27,581	28,915	16,368	20,726
1982	27,320	28,601	16,210	20,557
1981	27,425	28,977	16,261	21,999
1980	28,091	29,636	17,073	21,653

Source: Bureau of the Census
Note: Hispanics may be of any race.

Median Household Income by Race, Hispanic Origin, and Type of Household

Married couples are the most affluent household type among whites, blacks, and Hispanics. Women who live alone are the poorest.

(median household income by type of household, race and Hispanic origin of householder, 1990)

	all households	white	black	Hispanic
All households	**$29,943**	**$31,231**	**$18,676**	**$22,330**
Family households	**35,707**	**37,219**	**21,899**	**24,552**
Married couple	39,996	40,433	33,893	28,584
Male householder	31,552	32,869	24,048	25,456
Female householder	18,069	20,867	12,537	12,603
Nonfamily households	**17,690**	**18,449**	**11,789**	**14,274**
Male householder	22,489	23,778	15,451	17,689
Living alone	19,964	20,900	13,126	13,716
Female householder	14,099	14,629	8,661	10,750
Living alone	12,548	13,094	7,674	8,993

Source: Bureau of the Census
Note: Hispanics may be of any race.

Median Family Income by Race and Hispanic Origin, 1980 to 1990

White and black median family income grew in the 1980s, while Hispanic income stagnated. The median income of black and white families was up by just over 6 percent, after adjusting for inflation.

(median family income by race and Hispanic origin of householder, 1980-90, in 1990 dollars)

	all households	white	black	Hispanic
1990	$35,353	$36,915	$21,423	$23,431
1989	36,062	37,919	21,301	24,713
1988	35,565	37,470	21,355	24,051
1987	35,632	37,260	21,177	23,356
1986	35,129	36,740	20,993	23,844
1985	33,689	35,410	20,390	23,112
1984	33,251	34,827	19,411	23,690
1983	32,378	33,905	19,108	22,216
1982	31,738	33,322	18,417	21,978
1981	32,190	33,814	19,074	23,582
1980	33,346	34,743	20,103	23,342

Source: Bureau of the Census
Note: Hispanics may be of any race.

Median Family Income by Number of Earners, 1980 to 1990

Median incomes rose during the 1980s for all families except those with one earner. Since 1988, most families have had a drop in income, even those with two or three earners.

(median family income by number of earners, 1980-90, in 1990 dollars)

	no earners	one earner	two earners	three earners	four earners or more
1990	$15,047	$25,878	$42,146	$53,721	$67,700
1989	15,057	26,589	42,855	54,555	69,273
1988	15,168	26,374	42,759	54,111	71,725
1987	15,009	26,590	42,338	54,755	69,664
1986	14,914	26,605	41,867	52,836	66,370
1985	14,665	25,739	40,583	50,780	62,227
1984	14,312	25,525	39,885	50,101	63,246
1983	13,812	25,531	39,146	48,980	62,713
1982	13,424	25,616	38,022	48,485	60,147
1981	13,530	25,343	38,620	49,315	60,374
1980	13,580	26,511	39,111	50,492	62,810

Source: Bureau of the Census

Aggregate Household Income by Age of Householder

Nearly half of aggregate household income went to householders aged 25 to 44 in 1990, or more than $1.6 billion.

(distribution of aggregate household income by income category and age of householder, 1990; in millions of dollars)

Income category	all ages	under 25	25 to 34	35 to 44	45 to 54	55 to 64	65 to 74	75+
				age of householder				
Under $10,000	$70,420	$6,714	$12,074	$8,347	$6,184	$8,396	$12,869	$15,836
$10,000-$19,999	258,314	19,555	53,568	39,674	23,464	30,962	50,134	40,957
$20,000-$29,999	398,200	26,021	100,473	80,970	52,078	51,161	57,737	29,761
$30,000-$39,999	481,545	22,720	128,780	123,555	72,979	62,638	49,616	21,256
$40,000-$49,999	453,337	11,925	115,959	132,464	82,512	61,025	37,130	12,324
$50,000-$59,999	402,294	7,926	89,971	130,770	83,383	55,989	23,934	10,321
$60,000-$69,999	320,890	4,257	61,956	103,333	77,354	46,384	20,721	6,885
$70,000-$79,999	252,363	1,583	40,018	85,200	67,523	39,488	13,863	4,687
$80,000-$89,999	185,767	1,413	30,300	53,040	56,535	26,541	13,198	4,740
$90,000-$99,999	133,539	1,392	18,896	36,346	43,255	19,958	11,590	2,102
$100,000 or more	570,871	1,390	48,832	166,622	172,319	116,672	44,548	20,471
Total household income	$3,527,540	$104,894	$700,827	$960,320	$737,585	$519,217	$335,340	$169,340
Percent distribution of household income	100.0%	3.0%	19.9%	27.2%	20.9%	14.7%	9.5%	4.8%
Percent distribution of households	100.0%	5.2%	21.5%	22.6%	15.6%	13.3%	12.7%	9.0%

Percent distribution of aggregate household income within age groups

Income category	all ages	under 25	25 to 34	35 to 44	45 to 54	55 to 64	65 to 74	75+
				age of householder				
Under $10,000	2.0%	6.4%	1.7%	0.9%	0.8%	1.6%	3.8%	9.4%
$10,000-$19,999	7.3	18.6	7.6	4.1	3.2	6.0	15.0	17.6
$20,000-$29,999	11.3	24.8	14.3	8.4	7.1	9.9	17.2	12.6
$30,000-$39,999	13.7	21.7	18.4	12.9	9.9	12.1	14.8	7.3
$40,000-$49,999	12.9	11.4	16.5	13.8	11.2	11.8	11.1	6.1
$50,000-$59,999	11.4	7.6	12.8	13.6	11.3	10.8	7.1	4.1
$60,000-$69,999	9.1	4.1	8.8	10.8	10.5	8.9	6.2	2.8
$70,000-$79,999	7.2	1.5	5.7	8.9	9.2	7.6	4.1	2.8
$80,000-$89,999	5.3	1.3	4.3	5.5	7.7	5.1	3.9	1.2
$90,000-$99,999	3.8	1.3	2.7	3.8	5.9	3.8	3.5	12.1
$100,000 or more	16.2	1.3	7.0	17.4	23.4	22.5	13.3	100.0%
Total	100.0%	100.0%	100.0%	100.0%	100.0%	100.0%	100.0%	100.0%

Source: 1991 Current Population Survey tabulation by TGE Demographics, Inc., Ithaca, New York

Household Income Distribution by Age, 1990

Householders aged 45 to 54 had the highest incomes in 1990, nearly $42,000. Those aged 35 to 44 had the second-highest incomes.

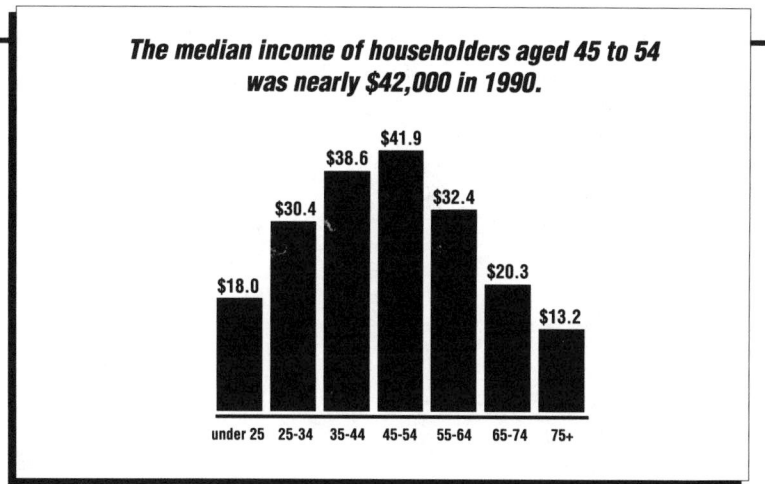

The median income of householders aged 45 to 54 was nearly $42,000 in 1990.

(distribution of households by household income in 1990 and age of householder in 1991; numbers in thousands)

	all households	under 25	25 to 34	35 to 44	45 to 54	55 to 64	65 to 74	75+
Total	**94,312**	**4,882**	**20,323**	**21,304**	**14,751**	**12,524**	**12,001**	**8,526**
Under $5,000	4,901	648	1,017	701	493	687	613	740
$5,000 to $9,999	9,184	694	1,397	968	743	992	1,961	2,427
$10,000 to $14,999	8,925	715	1,659	1,235	782	1,054	1,870	1,610
$15,000 to $19,999	8,296	589	1,912	1,410	783	1,010	1,472	1,120
$20,000 to $24,999	8,427	595	2,105	1,569	1,041	1,079	1,334	703
$25,000 to $29,999	7,501	445	1,914	1,670	1,042	967	975	487
$30,000 to $34,999	7,363	365	2,010	1,848	1,042	922	812	364
$35,000 to $39,999	6,395	284	1,669	1,682	1,043	867	606	244
$40,000 to $44,999	5,372	147	1,417	1,510	952	755	442	148
$45,000 to $49,999	4,702	118	1,160	1,434	882	601	383	125
$50,000 to $54,999	4,088	72	956	1,372	778	562	247	100
$55,000 to $59,999	3,227	72	680	1,005	738	456	188	88
$60,000 to $64,999	2,767	35	586	902	644	390	147	63
$65,000 to $69,999	2,170	30	367	688	546	324	172	43
$70,000 to $74,999	1,809	15	304	592	483	286	95	35
$75,000 to $79,999	1,555	6	230	544	417	241	90	28
$80,000 to $84,999	1,204	15	191	331	359	177	90	41
$85,000 to $89,999	982	2	166	293	306	135	66	15
$90,000 to $94,999	769	10	95	221	260	100	69	15
$95,000 to $99,999	590	4	88	157	176	105	53	7
$100,000 or more	4,085	19	400	1,172	1,240	813	317	123
Median income	**$29,943**	**$18,002**	**$30,359**	**$38,561**	**$41,922**	**$32,365**	**$20,292**	**$13,150**

Source: Bureau of the Census

Household Income Distribution
by Age, 2000

By 2000, nearly one in four households headed by a 45-to-54-year-old will have an income of $75,000 or more, up from 19 percent in 1990.

(number and percent distribution of households by household income and age of householder in 2000; income in 1989 dollars; numbers in thousands)

Number	total	under 25	25 to 34	35 to 44	45 to 54	55 to 64	65+
All households	**102,440**	**4,298**	**17,457**	**24,050**	**20,651**	**13,804**	**22,180**
Under $10,000	14,275	996	1,752	1,821	1,593	1,753	6,360
$10,000 to $15,000	8,769	539	1,261	1,236	1,057	1,128	3,548
$15,000 to $20,000	8,277	540	1,422	1,377	1,059	1,075	2,804
$20,000 to $25,000	7,843	502	1,600	1,515	1,132	1,000	2,094
$25,000 to $30,000	7,524	430	1,646	1,635	1,236	989	1,588
$30,000 to $35,000	7,167	354	1,562	1,753	1,290	975	1,233
$35,000 to $40,000	6,581	268	1,452	1,828	1,288	847	898
$40,000 to $50,000	11,133	313	2,318	3,331	2,551	1,455	1,165
$50,000 to $60,000	8,621	166	1,645	2,685	2,150	1,201	774
$60,000 to $75,000	8,594	104	1,363	2,794	2,477	1,203	653
$75,000 to $100,000	7,180	61	896	2,266	2,396	1,044	517
$100,000 or more	6,480	24	541	1,810	2,424	1,135	546
Percent distribution							
All households	**100.0%**	**100.0%**	**100.0%**	**100.0%**	**100.0%**	**100.0%**	**100.0%**
Under $10,000	13.9	23.2	10.0	7.6	7.7	12.7	28.7
$10,000 to $15,000	8.6	12.5	7.2	5.1	5.1	8.2	16.0
$15,000 to $20,000	8.1	12.6	8.1	5.7	5.1	7.8	12.6
$20,000 to $25,000	7.7	11.7	9.2	6.3	5.5	7.2	9.4
$25,000 to $30,000	7.3	10.0	9.4	6.8	6.0	7.2	7.2
$30,000 to $35,000	7.0	8.2	8.9	7.3	6.2	7.1	5.6
$35,000 to $40,000	6.4	6.2	8.3	7.6	6.2	6.1	4.0
$40,000 to $50,000	10.9	7.3	13.3	13.9	12.4	10.5	5.3
$50,000 to $60,000	8.4	3.9	9.4	11.2	10.4	8.7	3.5
$60,000 to $75,000	8.4	2.4	7.8	11.6	12.0	8.7	2.9
$75,000 to $100,000	7.0	1.4	5.1	9.4	11.6	7.6	2.3
$100,000 or more	6.3	0.6	3.1	7.5	11.7	8.2	2.5

Source: The Conference Board

Household Income Distribution by Household Type

Married couples, with a median income of nearly $40,000, are the most affluent type of household. Women who live alone have the smallest incomes.

(distribution of households by household income in 1990 and type of household in 1991; numbers in thousands)

	all households	family households total	type of family married-couple	type of family male householder, no wife present	type of family female householder, no husband present	nonfamily households total	sex of householder male total	sex of householder male living alone	sex of householder female total	sex of householder female living alone
Total	**94,312**	**66,322**	**52,147**	**2,907**	**11,268**	**27,990**	**12,150**	**9,450**	**15,840**	**14,141**
Under $5,000	4,901	2,241	674	101	1,466	2,660	853	806	1,807	1,771
$5,000 to $9,999	9,184	3,712	1,700	189	1,823	5,471	1,468	1,378	4,003	3,918
$10,000 to $14,999	8,925	4,841	3,102	233	1,506	4,084	1,589	1,349	2,494	2,365
$15,000 to $19,999	8,296	5,176	3,626	293	1,257	3,120	1,412	1,200	1,708	1,578
$20,000 to $24,999	8,427	5,601	4,175	298	1,128	2,826	1,314	1,066	1,512	1,318
$25,000 to $29,999	7,501	5,325	4,127	246	952	2,176	1,046	827	1,130	974
$30,000 to $34,999	7,363	5,483	4,437	285	761	1,881	1,002	772	878	717
$35,000 to $39,999	6,395	5,049	4,235	220	594	1,346	712	491	634	490
$40,000 to $44,999	5,372	4,415	3,782	213	420	957	500	335	457	318
$45,000 to $49,999	4,702	3,930	3,425	183	323	772	508	317	264	165
$50,000 to $54,999	4,088	3,469	3,107	123	239	619	374	220	245	178
$55,000 to $59,999	3,227	2,784	2,491	117	176	442	271	139	172	91
$60,000 to $64,999	2,767	2,443	2,235	95	114	324	225	122	99	51
$65,000 to $69,999	2,170	1,975	1,788	55	131	195	108	52	87	41
$70,000 to $74,999	1,809	1,612	1,463	56	93	198	134	68	63	32
$75,000 to $79,999	1,555	1,405	1,306	34	66	150	98	54	52	23
$80,000 to $84,999	1,204	1,089	1,025	24	40	115	73	26	41	27
$85,000 to $89,999	982	875	827	19	29	106	82	46	24	7
$90,000 to $94,999	769	690	633	25	31	79	43	11	36	15
$95,000 to $99,999	590	538	504	17	18	52	30	14	22	8
$100,000 or more	4,085	3,666	3,485	82	100	419	305	157	113	56
Median income	**$29,943**	**$35,707**	**$39,996**	**$31,552**	**$18,069**	**$17,690**	**$22,489**	**$19,964**	**$14,099**	**$12,548**

Source: Bureau of the Census

Income Distribution of Married Couples With Children

The most affluent couples are those with one school-aged child in the home. Most of these couples are in their peak earning years and will soon become empty-nesters.

(income distribution of married couples by presence, number, and age of children under age 18; income in 1990; households in 1991; numbers in thousands)

	all households	no related children	one child			two children or more			
			total	under 6	6 to 17	total	all under 6	some under 6 some 6 to 17	all 6 to 17
All married couples	**52,147**	**26,737**	**9,765**	**4,093**	**5,672**	**15,646**	**2,714**	**6,018**	**6,914**
Under $5,000	678	410	110	62	48	157	41	59	58
$5,000 to $9,999	1,717	976	282	130	153	459	115	213	131
$10,000 to $14,999	3,122	1,929	433	247	186	759	148	332	280
$15,000 to $19,999	3,645	2,113	531	294	237	1,001	211	454	335
$20,000 to $24,999	4,203	2,316	677	322	355	1,210	214	554	442
$25,000 to $29,999	4,115	2,141	715	355	360	1,260	279	487	494
$30,000 to $34,999	4,432	2,142	867	395	473	1,422	228	582	612
$35,000 to $39,999	4,244	2,000	814	339	475	1,430	254	556	620
$40,000 to $44,999	3,790	1,707	711	291	420	1,372	234	536	602
$45,000 to $49,999	3,426	1,600	683	319	364	1,143	176	406	561
$50,000 to $54,999	3,090	1,406	678	248	430	1,006	173	353	481
$55,000 to $59,999	2,490	1,212	496	179	318	782	80	292	409
$60,000 to $64,999	2,225	1,031	491	200	292	703	99	268	336
$65,000 to $69,999	1,780	856	393	113	280	532	86	164	281
$70,000 to $74,999	1,456	691	313	108	204	452	73	138	242
$75,000 to $79,999	1,297	678	286	91	195	333	45	110	178
$80,000 to $84,999	1,022	518	243	82	161	261	34	75	152
$85,000 to $89,999	830	405	182	61	121	242	29	70	142
$90,000 to $94,999	628	333	132	38	94	164	26	53	85
$95,000 to $99,999	491	271	104	38	66	115	14	37	64
$100,000 or more	3,466	2,002	622	182	440	842	156	278	408
Median income	**$39,895**	**$38,254**	**$43,057**	**$38,446**	**$46,632**	**$40,404**	**$37,018**	**$37,545**	**$43,888**

Source: Bureau of the Census

Distribution of Income by Household Type, Householders Under Age 25

Most households headed by people under age 25 had incomes of less than $20,000 in 1990, regardless of household type.

(number of households headed by householders under age 25 by household income and household type; income in 1990, households in 1991; numbers in thousands)

	all households	all family households			all nonfamilies			
		married couples	male-headed	female-headed	male-headed	men living alone	female-headed	women living alone
Total	**4,879**	**1,559**	**249**	**919**	**1,200**	**622**	**955**	**518**
Under $10,000	1,758	176	44	616	255	206	251	210
$10,000-$19,999	1,707	446	51	162	379	230	266	173
$20,000-$29,999	1,264	435	53	58	271	136	224	87
$30,000-$39,999	721	316	45	47	129	32	112	40
$40,000-$49,999	280	95	19	14	80	8	57	7
$50,000-$59,999	156	47	12	13	49	10	23	2
$60,000-$69,999	64	26	8	2	17	0	11	0
$70,000-$79,999	21	6	2	3	6	0	4	0
$80,000-$89,999	17	5	3	1	7	0	1	0
$90,000-$99,999	14	4	3	1	2	0	4	0
$100,000 or more	19	4	8	0	5	0	2	0

Note: Household totals may not match those elsewhere in this book because of rounding.
Source: 1991 Current Population Survey tabulations by TGE Demographics, Inc., Ithaca, New York

Distribution of Income by Household Type, Householders Aged 25 to 34

A majority of married couples headed by someone aged 25 to 34 had incomes between $20,000 and $50,000 in 1990.

(number of households headed by householders aged 25 to 34 by household income and household type; income in 1990, households in 1991; numbers in thousands)

	all households	all family households			all nonfamilies			
		married couples	male-headed	female headed	male-headed	men living alone	female-headed	women living alone
Total	**20,325**	**11,003**	**720**	**2,866**	**3,578**	**2,491**	**2,155**	**1,626**
Under $10,000	2,416	455	72	1,194	426	386	269	252
$10,000-$19,999	3,571	1,348	159	808	788	659	468	412
$20,000-$29,999	4,018	2,032	162	423	823	651	578	496
$30,000-$39,999	3,680	2,289	120	211	641	443	419	311
$40,000-$49,999	2,577	1,834	106	105	343	185	189	84
$50,000-$59,999	1,636	1,221	46	52	224	75	93	36
$60,000-$69,999	953	729	26	21	123	39	54	15
$70,000-$79,999	534	409	13	27	60	12	25	4
$80,000-$89,999	356	281	2	11	44	8	18	6
$90,000-$99,999	200	135	5	6	36	15	18	5
$100,000 or more	384	272	10	8	70	18	24	7

Note: Household totals may not match those elsewhere in this book because of rounding.
Source: 1991 Current Population Survey tabulations by TGE Demographics, Inc., Ithaca, New York

Distribution of Income by Household Type, Householders Aged 35 to 44

Households headed by people aged 35 to 44 are the second most affluent. Most married couples in this age group had incomes above $40,000 in 1990.

(number of households headed by householders aged 35 to 44 by household income and household type; income in 1990, households in 1991; numbers in thousands)

	all households	all family households			all nonfamilies			
		married couples	male-headed	female-headed	male-headed	men living alone	female-headed	women living alone
Total	**21,308**	**13,246**	**758**	**3,075**	**2,536**	**2,008**	**1,690**	**1,394**
Under $10,000	1,670	342	74	731	295	280	228	214
$10,000-$19,999	2,645	924	109	786	491	428	335	316
$20,000-$29,999	3,240	1,544	130	692	488	409	386	340
$30,000-$39,999	3,531	2,222	149	414	441	359	305	246
$40,000-$49,999	2,943	2,192	112	195	277	207	167	133
$50,000-$59,999	2,379	1,866	74	107	187	120	145	95
$60,000-$69,999	1,589	1,359	48	59	86	56	37	15
$70,000-$79,999	1,137	970	24	30	83	54	30	14
$80,000-$89,999	624	532	12	14	52	32	14	7
$90,000-$99,999	382	312	13	15	27	8	15	2
$100,000 or more	1,168	984	14	33	109	56	28	12

Note: Household totals may not match those elsewhere in this book because of rounding.
Source: 1991 Current Population Survey tabulations by TGE Demographics, Inc., Ithaca, New York

Distribution of Income by Household Type, Householders Aged 45 to 54

Households headed by people aged 45 to 54 are the most affluent of all. Thirty percent of married couples in this age group had incomes of $70,000 or more in 1990.

(number of households headed by householders aged 45 to 54 by household income and household type; income in 1990, households in 1991; numbers in thousands)

	all households	all family households			all nonfamilies			
		married couples	male-headed	female headed	male-headed	men living alone	female-headed	women living alone
Total	**14,749**	**9,407**	**492**	**1,803**	**1,493**	**1,240**	**1,556**	**1,367**
Under $10,000	1,237	262	34	329	252	233	360	346
$10,000-$19,999	1,564	582	56	316	282	253	328	304
$20,000-$29,999	2,084	988	80	369	292	259	355	314
$30,000-$39,999	2,084	1,248	69	315	219	179	233	206
$40,000-$49,999	1,833	1,266	83	209	150	115	125	100
$50,000-$59,999	1,517	1,211	57	99	96	77	54	43
$60,000-$69,999	1,190	981	40	73	60	39	36	24
$70,000-$79,999	900	778	24	36	40	30	22	13
$80,000-$89,999	664	593	10	15	35	18	11	2
$90,000-$99,999	455	411	17	10	10	7	7	6
$100,000 or more	1,221	1,086	23	32	56	32	24	9

Note: Household totals may not match those elsewhere in this book because of rounding.
Source: 1991 Current Population Survey tabulations by TGE Demographics, Inc., Ithaca, New York

Distribution of Income by Household Type, Householders Aged 55 to 64

Incomes begin to fall for households headed by 55-to-64-year-olds because many are retired. Still, most married couples in this age group had incomes of $40,000 or more in 1990.

(number of households headed by householders aged 55 to 64 by household income and household type; income in 1990, households in 1991; numbers in thousands)

	all households	all family households			all nonfamilies			
		married couples	male-headed	female-headed	male-headed	men living alone	female-headed	women living alone
Total	**12,522**	**7,898**	**310**	**1,117**	**1,225**	**1,079**	**1,973**	**1,864**
Under $10,000	1,679	384	21	182	335	326	757	740
$10,000-$19,999	2,063	935	47	261	305	274	515	491
$20,000-$29,999	2,046	1,202	56	253	185	159	350	330
$30,000-$39,999	1,789	1,240	57	148	163	138	181	164
$40,000-$49,999	1,356	1,050	38	113	87	72	68	57
$50,000-$59,999	1,017	820	36	69	45	37	47	44
$60,000-$69,999	714	618	10	37	26	23	23	17
$70,000-$79,999	526	439	16	24	31	18	16	11
$80,000-$89,999	313	275	14	10	10	7	4	3
$90,000-$99,999	210	183	6	10	8	8	3	3
$100,000 or more	809	752	9	9	29	18	10	4

Note: Household totals may not match those elsewhere in this book because of rounding.
Source: 1991 Current Population Survey tabulations by TGE Demographics, Inc., Ithaca, New York

Distribution of Income by Household Type, Householders Aged 65 to 74

Incomes are much lower for householders aged 65 to 74 than for middle-aged households, regardless of household type, because most are retired.

(number of households headed by householders aged 65 to 74 by household income and household type; income in 1990, households in 1991; numbers in thousands)

	all households	all family households			all nonfamilies			
		married couples	male-headed	female-headed	male-headed	men living alone	female-headed	women living alone
Total	**12,003**	**6,299**	**233**	**841**	**1,169**	**1,096**	**3,460**	**3,397**
Under $10,000	2,574	428	26	118	371	370	1,631	1,623
$10,000-$19,999	3,342	1,492	62	217	411	376	1,160	1,144
$20,000-$29,999	2,309	1,512	44	168	199	182	386	373
$30,000-$39,999	1,419	1,025	36	145	74	72	139	128
$40,000-$49,999	825	627	19	72	45	40	62	51
$50,000-$59,999	435	324	8	49	25	25	29	29
$60,000-$69,999	319	244	16	34	11	8	14	14
$70,000-$79,999	184	139	9	16	12	8	8	7
$80,000-$89,999	155	130	2	10	0	0	13	12
$90,000-$99,999	123	99	3	5	6	5	10	7
$100,000 or more	318	278	10	7	14	10	9	9

Note: Household totals may not match those elsewhere in this book because of rounding.
Source: 1991 Current Population Survey tabulations by TGE Demographics, Inc., Ithaca, New York

Distribution of Income by Household Type, Householders Aged 75 or Older

Householders aged 75 or older have the lowest incomes. Most women in this age group live alone, and most had incomes below $10,000 in 1990.

(number of households headed by householders aged 75 or older by household income and household type; income in 1990, households in 1991; numbers in thousands)

	all households	all family households			all nonfamilies			
		married couples	male-headed	female-headed	male-headed	men living alone	female-headed	women living alone
Total	**8,526**	**2,737**	**143**	**647**	**950**	**914**	**4,049**	**3,973**
Under $10,000	3,167	327	20	120	386	383	2,314	2,304
$10,000-$19,999	2,731	1,001	42	212	345	330	1,131	1,102
$20,000-$29,999	1,190	590	19	117	102	96	362	353
$30,000-$39,999	608	333	29	75	48	41	123	111
$40,000-$49,999	274	143	18	35	26	26	52	51
$50,000-$59,999	188	110	8	26	19	15	25	20
$60,000-$69,999	105	67	1	19	9	9	9	8
$70,000-$79,999	62	27	3	21	0	0	11	7
$80,000-$89,999	56	37	0	8	7	7	4	4
$90,000-$99,999	22	14	0	2	3	2	3	1
$100,000 or more	123	88	4	11	5	5	15	13

Note: Household totals may not match those elsewhere in this book because of rounding.
Source: 1991 Current Population Survey tabulations by TGE Demographics, Inc., Ithaca, New York

Income Distribution of White Householders by Age

White householders in their peak earning years had a median income of over $44,000. Nearly one in ten had an income of $100,000 or more.

(distribution of white households in 1991 by household income in 1990, by age of householder; numbers in thousands)

	all white households	under 25	25 to 34	35 to 44	45 to 54	55 to 64	65 to 74	75+
Total	**80,968**	**4,046**	**17,069**	**18,013**	**12,534**	**10,876**	**10,663**	**7,768**
Under $5,000	3,256	433	582	419	338	487	432	564
$5,000 to $9,999	7,161	522	958	681	529	728	1,586	2,156
$10,000 to $14,999	7,460	587	1,294	917	584	893	1,687	1,498
$15,000 to $19,999	7,034	511	1,562	1,094	636	856	1,343	1,033
$20,000 to $24,999	7,262	522	1,743	1,295	883	933	1,220	667
$25,000 to $29,999	6,558	394	1,691	1,421	848	846	885	472
$30,000 to $34,999	6,494	337	1,760	1,618	876	803	755	346
$35,000 to $39,999	5,576	241	1,466	1,431	864	781	566	226
$40,000 to $44,999	4,809	138	1,255	1,330	846	675	418	147
$45,000 to $49,999	4,187	104	1,030	1,255	784	547	344	123
$50,000 to $54,999	3,679	64	852	1,225	692	513	236	97
$55,000 to $59,999	2,953	68	630	910	664	428	169	83
$60,000 to $64,999	2,540	30	532	823	594	358	143	59
$65,000 to $69,999	1,962	27	348	619	489	284	152	43
$70,000 to $74,999	1,626	13	288	523	418	265	91	28
$75,000 to $79,999	1,404	6	206	484	379	216	87	26
$80,000 to $84,999	1,079	15	168	286	327	161	82	41
$85,000 to $89,999	899	2	162	259	265	134	63	15
$90,000 to $94,999	689	9	85	199	223	92	66	15
$95,000 to $99,999	549	3	87	147	162	96	48	7
$100,000 or more	3,791	18	368	1,077	1,133	782	290	123
Median income	**$31,231**	**$19,662**	**$31,859**	**$40,423**	**$44,098**	**$34,249**	**$21,089**	**$13,714**

Source: Bureau of the Census

Income Distribution of
Black Householders by Age

Even in their peak earning years, the median income of black householders falls below $30,000. Only one in five householders aged 45 to 54 has an income of $50,000 or more.

(distribution of black households in 1991 by household income in 1990, by age of householder; numbers in thousands)

	all black households	under 25	25 to 34	35 to 44	45 to 54	55 to 64	65 to 74	75+
Total	**10,671**	**683**	**2,591**	**2,578**	**1,693**	**1,337**	**1,118**	**671**
Under $5,000	1,500	197	396	247	143	178	166	173
$5,000 to $9,999	1,786	150	393	242	200	238	327	236
$10,000 to $14,999	1,240	99	306	271	174	141	150	99
$15,000 to $19,999	1,050	68	284	253	131	128	111	76
$20,000 to $24,999	988	54	313	230	135	126	96	34
$25,000 to $29,999	741	36	163	208	155	100	68	11
$30,000 to $34,999	695	19	208	187	115	105	50	11
$35,000 to $39,999	613	28	159	202	115	64	29	15
$40,000 to $44,999	412	5	105	130	89	68	13	2
$45,000 to $49,999	378	11	78	139	77	39	33	-
$50,000 to $54,999	293	3	71	115	54	38	11	2
$55,000 to $59,999	197	2	25	77	54	19	16	3
$60,000 to $64,999	128	5	25	47	27	20	4	-
$65,000 to $69,999	132	3	16	48	41	11	13	-
$70,000 to $74,999	113	2	7	35	47	11	4	7
$75,000 to $79,999	96	-	15	36	25	16	3	2
$80,000 to $84,999	69	-	10	25	19	11	4	-
$85,000 to $89,999	51	-	-	27	22	-	2	-
$90,000 to $94,999	44	-	4	17	18	6	-	-
$95,000 to $99,999	23	-	1	6	10	5	-	-
$100,000 or more	122	1	11	36	43	13	18	-
Median income	**$18,676**	**$9,816**	**$18,339**	**$26,011**	**$26,910**	**$19,226**	**$11,974**	**$7,831**

Source: Bureau of the Census

Income Distribution of Hispanic Householders by Age

The median income of Hispanic households is higher than that of black households in every age group. Still, it never rises above $30,000.

(distribution of Hispanic households in 1991 by household income in 1990, by age of householder; numbers in thousands)

	all Hispanic households	under 25	25 to 34	35 to 44	45 to 54	55 to 64	65 to 74	75+
Total	**6,220**	**594**	**1,808**	**1,524**	**957**	**682**	**434**	**220**
Under $5,000	466	83	122	91	45	48	45	33
$5,000 to $9,999	849	109	195	163	106	81	114	79
$10,000 to $14,999	804	110	260	152	97	84	69	32
$15,000 to $19,999	679	60	256	136	81	60	51	34
$20,000 to $24,999	633	68	189	162	84	71	43	16
$25,000 to $29,999	531	50	166	144	92	48	26	6
$30,000 to $34,999	498	37	145	144	86	49	30	9
$35,000 to $39,999	404	31	138	120	57	42	16	-
$40,000 to $44,999	286	14	71	93	62	35	12	-
$45,000 to $49,999	233	6	77	69	41	30	6	5
$50,000 to $54,999	182	5	52	58	38	25	4	1
$55,000 to $59,999	121	3	27	34	42	14	1	-
$60,000 to $64,999	99	-	31	32	19	12	4	1
$65,000 to $69,999	95	7	19	20	31	14	3	1
$70,000 to $74,999	71	1	19	24	14	11	2	-
$75,000 to $79,999	53	1	8	21	11	9	1	1
$80,000 to $84,999	40	1	6	11	10	9	3	-
$85,000 to $89,999	24	1	6	7	5	6	-	-
$90,000 to $94,999	30	-	6	12	6	6	-	-
$95,000 to $99,999	9	-	3	2	2	1	1	1
$100,000 or more	111	9	15	30	28	25	4	1
Median income	**$22,330**	**$14,732**	**$21,695**	**$26,598**	**$28,195**	**$24,757**	**$14,123**	**$9,850**

Source: Bureau of the Census
Note: Hispanics may be of any race.

Income Distribution of Married Couples by Race and Hispanic Origin

Married couples have relatively high incomes regardless of race or ethnicity. But white couples' median income was 19 percent higher than that of black couples in 1990, and 41 percent higher than that of Hispanic couples.

(distribution of married-couples by household income in 1990 and by race and Hispanic origin of householder in 1991; numbers in thousands)

		married couples		
	all households	white	black	Hispanic
Total	**52,147**	**47,014**	**3,569**	**3,454**
Under $5,000	674	552	73	97
$5,000 to $9,999	1,700	1,380	272	251
$10,000 to $14,999	3,102	2,722	280	390
$15,000 to $19,999	3,626	3,202	309	385
$20,000 to $24,999	4,175	3,739	358	359
$25,000 to $29,999	4,127	3,784	236	321
$30,000 to $34,999	4,437	4,015	329	328
$35,000 to $39,999	4,235	3,795	311	279
$40,000 to $44,999	3,782	3,438	242	209
$45,000 to $49,999	3,425	3,100	235	174
$50,000 to $54,999	3,107	2,819	198	135
$55,000 to $59,999	2,491	2,291	140	90
$60,000 to $64,999	2,235	2,067	92	81
$65,000 to $69,999	1,788	1,621	98	73
$70,000 to $74,999	1,463	1,323	83	57
$75,000 to $79,999	1,306	1,190	73	47
$80,000 to $84,999	1,025	927	48	37
$85,000 to $89,999	827	760	39	20
$90,000 to $94,999	633	562	40	24
$95,000 to $99,999	504	469	23	6
$100,000 or more	3,485	3,257	90	89
Median income	**$39,996**	**$40,433**	**$33,893**	**$28,584**

Source: Bureau of the Census
Note: Hispanics may be of any race.

Income Distribution of Female-Headed Families by Race and Hispanic Origin

White female-headed families have household incomes two-thirds larger than families headed by black or Hispanic women.

(distribution of female-headed families by household income in 1990, and by race and Hispanic origin of householders in 1991; numbers in thousands)

		female-headed families		
	all households	white	black	Hispanic
Total	**11,268**	**7,512**	**3,430**	**1,186**
Under $5,000	1,466	726	719	186
$5,000 to $9,999	1,823	1,035	710	287
$10,000 to $14,999	1,506	975	494	186
$15,000 to $19,999	1,257	868	363	121
$20,000 to $24,999	1,128	786	304	104
$25,000 to $29,999	952	683	245	92
$30,000 to $34,999	761	570	159	60
$35,000 to $39,999	594	437	138	43
$40,000 to $44,999	420	336	77	25
$45,000 to $49,999	323	250	67	27
$50,000 to $54,999	239	195	43	17
$55,000 to $59,999	176	147	23	10
$60,000 to $64,999	114	92	13	7
$65,000 to $69,999	131	104	24	5
$70,000 to $74,999	93	77	13	6
$75,000 to $79,999	66	48	15	2
$80,000 to $84,999	40	36	5	-
$85,000 to $89,999	29	22	6	-
$90,000 to $94,999	31	28	1	3
$95,000 to $99,999	18	14	-	1
$100,000 or more	100	83	10	7
Median income	**$18,069**	**$20,867**	**$12,537**	**$12,603**

Source: Bureau of the Census
Note: Hispanics may be of any race.

Income Distribution of Male-Headed Families by Race and Hispanic Origin

Male-headed families had a median income of over $30,000 in 1990. Even those headed by black or Hispanic men had median incomes of more than $20,000.

(distribution of male-headed families by household income in 1990, and by race and Hispanic origin of householder in 1991; numbers in thousands)

	male-headed families			
	all households	white	black	Hispanic
Total	**2,907**	**2,276**	**472**	**342**
Under $5,000	101	61	31	8
$5,000 to $9,999	189	131	43	40
$10,000 to $14,999	233	164	61	31
$15,000 to $19,999	293	226	55	48
$20,000 to $24,999	298	237	53	41
$25,000 to $29,999	246	185	47	25
$30,000 to $34,999	285	220	49	41
$35,000 to $39,999	220	177	34	30
$40,000 to $44,999	213	179	26	18
$45,000 to $49,999	183	136	27	14
$50,000 to $54,999	123	111	7	12
$55,000 to $59,999	117	103	8	8
$60,000 to $64,999	95	80	10	3
$65,000 to $69,999	55	51	3	4
$70,000 to $74,999	56	51	1	6
$75,000 to $79,999	34	26	2	1
$80,000 to $84,999	24	20	2	1
$85,000 to $89,999	19	14	3	1
$90,000 to $94,999	25	23	2	1
$95,000 to $99,999	17	16	-	-
$100,000 or more	82	65	6	9
Median income	**$31,552**	**$32,869**	**$24,048**	**$25,456**

Source: Bureau of the Census
Note: Hispanics may be of any race.

Income Distribution of Nonfamily Households by Race and Hispanic Origin

Nonfamily households have relatively low incomes. Those headed by blacks have the lowest incomes of all.

(distribution of nonfamily households by household income in 1990, and by race and Hispanic origin of householder in 1991; numbers in thousands)

	nonfamily households			
	all households	white	black	Hispanic
Total	**27,990**	**24,166**	**3,200**	**1,238**
Under $5,000	2,660	1,917	676	177
$5,000 to $9,999	5,471	4,614	760	270
$10,000 to $14,999	4,084	3,599	404	197
$15,000 to $19,999	3,120	2,738	323	126
$20,000 to $24,999	2,826	2,501	273	129
$25,000 to $29,999	2,176	1,905	213	93
$30,000 to $34,999	1,881	1,689	158	69
$35,000 to $39,999	1,346	1,167	130	53
$40,000 to $44,999	957	856	67	34
$45,000 to $49,999	772	700	49	18
$50,000 to $54,999	619	553	46	18
$55,000 to $59,999	442	412	25	13
$60,000 to $64,999	324	301	13	9
$65,000 to $69,999	195	187	7	14
$70,000 to $74,999	198	175	16	2
$75,000 to $79,999	150	140	6	2
$80,000 to $84,999	115	96	15	2
$85,000 to $89,999	106	104	3	3
$90,000 to $94,999	79	75	2	2
$95,000 to $99,999	52	51	-	2
$100,000 or more	419	385	15	6
Median income	**$17,690**	**$18,449**	**$11,789**	**$14,274**

Source: Bureau of the Census
Note: Hispanics may be of any race.

Income Distribution of Dual-Earner Couples

Most dual-earner married couples in which husbands and wives work full time have incomes exceeding $50,000 a year.

(income distribution of dual-earner married couples in which both husband and wife work year-round, full-time, by presence, number, and age of children under age 18 at home, income in 1990; households in 1991; numbers in thousands)

	all households	no related children	one child			two children or more			
			total	under 6	6 to 17	total	all under 6	some under 6 some 6 to 17	all 6 to 17
Total	**13,656**	**6,665**	**3,253**	**1,190**	**2,063**	**3,738**	**486**	**1,283**	**1,968**
Under $5,000	30	23	2	-	2	5	1	4	-
$5,000 to $9,999	24	13	6	4	3	4	-	2	-
$10,000 to $14,999	101	41	26	5	21	34	6	16	3
$15,000 to $19,999	220	94	45	15	30	80	12	28	12
$20,000 to $24,999	418	192	91	41	50	135	19	61	41
$25,000 to $29,999	623	269	154	78	76	201	31	78	55
$30,000 to $34,999	962	420	233	110	123	309	39	115	92
$35,000 to $39,999	1,091	498	273	103	169	321	54	106	154
$40,000 to $44,999	1,088	474	229	94	135	385	51	142	160
$45,000 to $49,999	1,106	523	253	104	150	330	44	119	192
$50,000 to $54,999	1,151	541	286	100	186	324	44	94	166
$55,000 to $59,999	984	500	236	93	143	248	13	99	186
$60,000 to $64,999	994	461	239	99	140	294	37	119	136
$65,000 to $69,999	774	363	198	55	143	212	24	70	137
$70,000 to $74,999	676	314	170	64	106	191	23	49	118
$75,000 to $79,999	588	316	152	42	111	120	14	30	119
$80,000 to $84,999	491	252	130	37	93	109	11	25	76
$85,000 to $89,999	391	201	93	28	65	97	7	29	73
$90,000 to $94,999	316	163	88	17	71	65	8	19	62
$95,000 to $99,999	226	140	52	20	32	34	3	14	39
$100,000 or more	1,401	867	295	82	213	240	44	64	18
Median income	**$55,068**	**$57,348**	**$55,551**	**$51,819**	**$57,693**	**$50,898**	**$48,151**	**$48,870**	132
									$52,757

Source: Bureau of the Census

Income by Age and Education of Householder, All Households

Households headed by college-educated 25-to-64-year-olds have median annual incomes far above the all-household median of $29,949.

(number, percent distribution, and median income of households by age and educational attainment of householder; income in 1990; all households in 1991; numbers in thousands)

	number	percent	median income
All households	**94,312**	**100.0%**	**$29,949**
Under age 25			
Total	4,882	100.0	18,259
Less than 4 years high school	944	19.3	9,965
High school graduate only	2,130	43.6	18,228
1 to 3 years college	1,180	24.2	15,656
4 or more years college	628	12.9	25,835
Aged 25 to 44			
Total	41,628	100.0	34,220
Less than 4 years high school	5,112	12.3	18,570
High school graduate only	15,441	37.1	30,312
1 to 3 years college	9,446	22.7	36,205
4 or more years college	11,628	27.9	48,655
Aged 45 to 64			
Total	27,274	100.0	37,614
Less than 4 years high school	6,303	23.1	21,490
High school graduate only	9,918	36.4	35,327
1 to 3 years college	4,642	17.0	42,148
4 or more years college	6,412	23.5	63,159
Aged 65 or older			
Total	20,527	100.0	17,010
Less than 4 years high school	8,808	42.9	12,302
High school graduate only	6,684	32.6	18,030
1 to 3 years college	2,363	11.5	23,615
4 or more years college	2,672	13.0	35,321

Source: 1991 Current Population Survey tabulation by TGE Demographics, Inc., Ithaca, New York

Income by Age and Education of Householder, Married Couples

Half of college-educated married couples headed by a 45-to-64-year-old have annual incomes above $73,562. These are the most affluent households in the country.

(number, percent distribution, and median income of households by age and educational attainment of householder; income in 1990; married-couple households in 1991; numbers in thousands)

	number	percent	median income
Married couples	**52,147**	**100.0%**	**$39,996**
Under age 25			
Total	1,558	100.0	23,200
Less than 4 years high school	312	20.0	16,639
High school graduate only	803	51.6	22,693
1 to 3 years college	289	18.5	27,255
4 or more years college	154	9.9	30,842
Aged 25 to 44			
Total	24,249	100.0	42,286
Less than 4 years high school	2,758	11.4	24,788
High school graduate only	9,144	37.7	36,785
1 to 3 years college	5,284	21.8	45,160
4 or more years college	7,062	29.1	59,121
Aged 45 to 64			
Total	17,305	100.0	47,717
Less than 4 years high school	3,639	21.0	29,003
High school graduate only	6,252	36.1	48,578
1 to 3 years college	2,862	16.5	53,435
4 or more years college	4,552	26.3	73,562
Aged 65 or older			
Total	9,036	100.0	25,551
Less than 4 years high school	3,502	38.8	18,566
High school graduate only	2,888	32.0	26,688
1 to 3 years college	1,090	12.1	32,594
4 or more years college	1,555	17.2	44,891

Source: 1991 Current Population Survey tabulation by TGE Demographics, Inc., Ithaca, New York

Income by Age and Education of Householder, Female-Headed Families

Though families headed by women typically have low incomes, those with a college-educated householder aged 25 or older have median incomes above the all-household median.

(number, percent distribution, and median income of households by age and educational attainment of householder; income in 1990; female-headed families in 1991; numbers in thousands)

	number	percent	median income
Female-headed families	**14,008**	**100.0%**	**$18,332**
Under age 25			
Total	919	100.0	6,953
Less than 4 years high school	372	40.5	4,373
High school graduate only	419	45.6	7,955
1 to 3 years college	113	12.3	11,768
4 or more years college	15	1.6	21,914
Aged 25 to 44			
Total	5,941	100.0	16,114
Less than 4 years high school	1,300	21.9	8,931
High school graduate only	2,644	44.5	15,399
1 to 3 years college	1,282	21.6	20,634
4 or more years college	715	12.0	31,933
Aged 45 to 64			
Total	2,920	100.0	25,523
Less than 4 years high school	915	31.3	15,850
High school graduate only	1,123	38.5	25,737
1 to 3 years college	479	16.4	31,863
4 or more years college	402	13.8	41,962
Aged 65 or older			
Total	4,228	100.0	22,485
Less than 4 years high school	3,502	82.8	17,980
High school graduate only	492	11.6	27,876
1 to 3 years college	124	2.9	26,153
4 or more years college	110	2.6	37,442

Source: 1991 Current Population Survey tabulation by TGE Demographics, Inc., Ithaca, New York

Income by Age and Education of Householder, Male-Headed Nonfamilies

Nonfamily households headed by college-educated men aged 25 to 64 have median annual incomes well above the all-household median.

(number, percent distribution, and median income of households by age and educational attainment of householder; income in 1990; male-headed nonfamilies in 1991; numbers in thousands)

	number	percent	median income
Nonfamilies, male householder	**12,150**	**100.0%**	**$22,864**
Under age 25			
Total	1,200	100.0	18,906
Less than 4 years high school	125	10.4	13,889
High school graduate only	461	38.4	18,155
1 to 3 years college	396	33.0	17,623
4 or more years college	218	18.2	25,373
Aged 25 to 44			
Total	6,114	100.0	27,793
Less than 4 years high school	531	8.7	16,134
High school graduate only	2,037	33.3	23,180
1 to 3 years college	1,564	25.6	28,479
4 or more years college	1,982	32.4	36,645
Aged 45 to 64			
Total	2,718	100.0	23,821
Less than 4 years high school	739	27.2	12,354
High school graduate only	864	31.8	22,989
1 to 3 years college	494	18.2	28,164
4 or more years college	621	22.8	41,065
Aged 65 or older			
Total	2,118	100.0	13,296
Less than 4 years high school	1,087	51.3	10,128
High school graduate only	560	26.4	14,900
1 to 3 years college	217	10.2	19,644
4 or more years college	254	12.0	27,209

Source: 1991 Current Population Survey tabulation by TGE Demographics, Inc., Ithaca, New York

Income by Age and Education of Householder, Female-Headed Nonfamilies

Even for female-headed nonfamily households, which typically have the lowest incomes, a college degree makes a big difference in living standards.

(number, percent distribution, and median income of households by age and educational attainment of householder; income in 1990; female-headed nonfamilies in 1991; numbers in thousands)

	number	percent	median income
Nonfamilies, female householder	**15,840**	**100.0%**	**$14,230**
Under age 25			
Total	956	100.0	18,391
Less than 4 years high school	66	6.9	6,103
High school graduate only	326	34.1	16,756
1 to 3 years college	337	35.2	18,894
4 or more years college	228	23.8	22,575
Aged 25 to 44			
Total	3,845	100.0	26,317
Less than 4 years high school	225	5.9	9,500
High school graduate only	990	25.7	19,639
1 to 3 years college	965	25.1	24,501
4 or more years college	1,665	43.3	32,731
Aged 45 to 64			
Total	3,530	100.0	17,478
Less than 4 years high school	798	22.6	7,511
High school graduate only	1,381	39.1	16,449
1 to 3 years college	691	19.6	22,086
4 or more years college	660	18.7	34,035
Aged 65 or older			
Total	7,509	100.0	9,681
Less than 4 years high school	3,244	43.2	7,868
High school graduate only	2,661	35.4	11,107
1 to 3 years college	897	11.9	14,395
4 or more years college	708	9.4	19,855

Source: 1991 Current Population Survey tabulation by TGE Demographics, Inc., Ithaca, New York

People Living in Poverty

Children are most likely to be poor, with more than 20 percent in poverty in 1990. The middle-aged are least likely to be poor.

(number of persons living in poverty and poverty rates by age and sex, 1990; number of persons in 1991; numbers in thousands)

Both sexes	all persons	persons living in poverty	
		number	percent of age group
Total	**248,644**	**33,585**	**13.5%**
Under age 18	65,049	13,431	20.6
Aged 18 to 24	24,901	3,964	15.9
Aged 25 to 34	42,905	5,201	12.1
Aged 35 to 44	38,665	3,268	8.5
Aged 45 to 54	25,686	2,002	7.8
Aged 55 to 59	10,692	963	9.0
Aged 60 to 64	10,654	1,098	10.3
Aged 65 or older	30,093	3,658	12.2
Aged 65 to 74	18,238	1,765	9.7
Aged 75 or older	11,855	1,893	16.0
Males			
Total	**121,073**	**14,211**	**11.7**
Under age 18	33,311	6,841	20.5
Aged 18 to 24	12,275	1,499	12.2
Aged 25 to 34	21,319	1,923	9.0
Aged 35 to 44	19,032	1,342	7.1
Aged 45 to 54	12,428	821	6.6
Aged 55 to 59	5,179	384	7.4
Aged 60 to 64	4,982	443	8.9
Aged 65 or older	12,547	959	7.6
Aged 65 to 74	8,156	524	6.4
Aged 75 or older	4,391	434	9.9
Females			
Total	**127,571**	**19,373**	**15.2**
Under age 18	31,738	6,591	20.8
Aged 18 to 24	12,627	2,465	19.5
Aged 25 to 34	21,586	3,278	15.2
Aged 35 to 44	19,633	1,926	9.8
Aged 45 to 54	13,258	1,181	8.9
Aged 55 to 59	5,512	579	10.5
Aged 60 to 64	5,671	656	11.6
Aged 65 or older	17,546	2,699	15.4
Aged 65 to 74	10,081	1,240	12.3
Aged 75 or older	7,464	1,459	19.5

Source: Bureau of the Census

Whites Living in Poverty

Among whites, poverty rates were highest for the young and the old in 1990. Thirty-nine percent of poor whites are children or young adults.

(number of whites living in poverty and poverty rate by age and sex, 1990; number of persons in 1991; numbers in thousands)

		whites living in poverty	
Both sexes	*all whites*	*number*	*percent of age group*
Total	**208,611**	**22,326**	**10.7%**
Under age 18	51,929	8,232	15.9
Aged 18 to 24	20,383	2,753	13.5
Aged 25 to 34	35,902	3,578	10.0
Aged 35 to 44	32,905	2,250	6.8
Aged 45 to 54	22,030	1,358	6.2
Aged 55 to 59	9,248	681	7.4
Aged 60 to 64	9,316	768	8.2
Aged 65 or older	26,898	2,707	10.1
Aged 65 to 74	16,209	1,234	7.6
Aged 75 or older	10,689	1,472	13.8
Males			
Total	**102,159**	**9,543**	**9.3**
Under age 18	26,643	4,240	15.9
Aged 18 to 24	10,121	1,067	10.5
Aged 25 to 34	18,054	1,404	7.8
Aged 35 to 44	16,434	1,020	6.2
Aged 45 to 54	10,748	585	5.4
Aged 55 to 59	4,525	274	6.0
Aged 60 to 64	4,398	320	7.3
Aged 65 or older	11,235	634	5.6
Aged 65 to 74	7,267	325	4.5
Aged 75 or older	3,968	309	7.8
Females			
Total	**106,453**	**12,783**	**12.0**
Under age 18	25,286	3,992	15.8
Aged 18 to 24	10,262	1,686	16.4
Aged 25 to 34	17,848	2,174	12.2
Aged 35 to 44	16,471	1,230	7.5
Aged 45 to 54	11,282	773	6.9
Aged 55 to 59	4,723	407	8.6
Aged 60 to 64	4,918	448	9.1
Aged 65 or older	15,663	2,073	13.2
Aged 65 to 74	8,942	909	10.2
Aged 75 or older	6,721	1,164	17.3

Source: Bureau of the Census

Blacks Living in Poverty

The poverty rate for black children was more than double the national average in 1990. Nearly half of poor blacks are children.

(number of blacks living in poverty and poverty rates by age and sex, 1990; number of persons in 1991; numbers in thousands)

Both sexes	all blacks	blacks living in poverty	
		number	percent of age group
Total	**30,806**	**9,837**	**31.9%**
Under age 18	10,162	4,550	44.8
Aged 18 to 24	3,549	1,051	29.6
Aged 25 to 34	5,435	1,434	26.4
Aged 35 to 44	4,272	839	19.7
Aged 45 to 54	2,694	569	21.1
Aged 55 to 59	1,115	246	22.0
Aged 60 to 64	1,033	288	27.9
Aged 65 or older	2,547	860	33.8
Aged 65 to 74	1,581	468	29.6
Aged 75 or older	966	392	40.6
Males			
Total	**14,439**	**4,030**	**27.9**
Under age 18	5,145	2,263	44.0
Aged 18 to 24	1,669	370	22.2
Aged 25 to 34	2,496	442	17.7
Aged 35 to 44	1,931	259	13.4
Aged 45 to 54	1,198	203	17.0
Aged 55 to 59	505	97	19.3
Aged 60 to 64	465	109	23.5
Aged 65 or older	1,031	286	27.8
Aged 65 to 74	694	170	24.6
Aged 75 or older	337	116	34.4
Females			
Total	**16,367**	**5,807**	**35.5**
Under age 18	5,016	2,287	45.6
Aged 18 to 24	1,881	681	36.2
Aged 25 to 34	2,938	992	33.8
Aged 35 to 44	2,341	580	24.8
Aged 45 to 54	1,496	365	24.4
Aged 55 to 59	610	148	24.4
Aged 60 to 64	569	179	31.4
Aged 65 or older	1,516	574	37.9
Aged 65 to 74	887	298	33.6
Aged 75 or older	629	276	43.9

Source: Bureau of the Census

Hispanics Living in Poverty

Among Hispanics, poverty rates were highest for those under age 18 in 1990. Nearly 40 percent of poor Hispanics are children.

(number of Hispanics living in poverty and poverty rates by age and sex, 1990; number of persons in 1991; numbers in thousands)

	all Hispanics	Hispanics living in poverty	
		number	percent of age group
Both sexes			
Total	**21,405**	**6,006**	**28.1%**
Under age 18	7,457	2,865	38.4
Aged 18 to 24	2,741	752	27.5
Aged 25 to 34	4,219	1,004	23.8
Aged 35 to 44	2,920	603	20.6
Aged 45 to 54	1,737	311	17.9
Aged 55 to 59	658	122	18.5
Aged 60 to 64	582	105	18.1
Aged 65 or older	1,091	245	22.5
Aged 65 to 74	737	152	20.6
Aged 75 or older	354	93	26.2
Males			
Total	**10,745**	**2,814**	**26.2**
Under age 18	3,812	1,508	39.5
Aged 18 to 24	1,424	323	22.7
Aged 25 to 34	2,190	416	19.0
Aged 35 to 44	1,475	260	17.6
Aged 45 to 54	811	134	16.5
Aged 55 to 59	318	50	15.6
Aged 60 to 64	255	38	14.7
Aged 65 or older	461	86	18.6
Aged 65 to 74	323	58	18.0
Aged 75 or older	137	28	20.1
Females			
Total	**10,660**	**3,193**	**29.9**
Under age 18	3,645	1,357	37.2
Aged 18 to 24	1,317	430	32.6
Aged 25 to 34	2,029	587	28.9
Aged 35 to 44	1,445	343	23.7
Aged 45 to 54	926	177	19.1
Aged 55 to 59	340	72	21.1
Aged 60 to 64	327	68	20.7
Aged 65 or older	631	159	25.3
Aged 65 to 74	414	94	22.7
Aged 75 or older	217	65	30.1

Source: Bureau of the Census
Note: Hispanics may be of any race.

Poverty Status of Families

Only 11 percent of families are poor, but among blacks, the proportion is nearly 30 percent. One in four Hispanic families is poor.

(poverty status of families and percent of families in poverty by age, race, and Hispanic origin of householder, 1990; number of families in 1991; numbers in thousands)

| | families in poverty | | | | | | | |
| | all races | | white | | black | | Hispanic | |
	number	*percent*	*number*	*percent*	*number*	*percent*	*number*	*percent*
All family householders	**7,098**	**10.7%**	**4,622**	**8.1%**	**2,193**	**29.3%**	**1,244**	**25.0%**
Under age 25	955	35.0	617	28.5	311	65.3	182	43.0
Aged 25 to 34	2,377	16.3	1,568	12.9	734	37.8	441	29.5
Aged 35 to 44	1,648	9.6	1,063	7.4	482	23.8	322	24.4
Aged 45 to 64	1,433	6.8	930	5.1	443	21.0	229	17.2
Aged 65 or older	686	6.3	443	4.5	224	24.2	69	17.0

Source: Bureau of the Census
Note: Hispanics may be of any race.

Poverty Status of Married Couples

Only 6 percent of married couples are poor, but among Hispanics, the proportion is nearly 18 percent. Among blacks, the figure is 13 percent.

(poverty status of married couples and percent of married couples in poverty by age, race, and Hispanic origin of householder, 1990; number of married couples in 1991; numbers in thousands)

	all races		white		black		Hispanic	
	number	*percent*	*number*	*percent*	*number*	*percent*	*number*	*percent*
All married-couple householders	**2,981**	**5.7%**	**2,386**	**5.1%**	**448**	**12.6%**	**605**	**17.5%**
Under age 25	226	14.5	197	13.9	23	22.2	71	30.0
Aged 25 to 34	844	7.7	726	7.3	80	10.0	226	21.5
Aged 35 to 44	667	5.0	532	4.5	87	9.1	144	15.7
Aged 45 to 64	794	4.6	610	3.9	143	12.2	117	12.3
Aged 65 or older	450	5.0	321	3.8	115	21.5	46	15.7

(column header for grouped section: married-couple families in poverty)

Source: Bureau of the Census
Note: Hispanics may be of any race.

Poverty Status of Female-Headed Families

Poverty rates are highest for families headed by women under age 25. Black and Hispanic female-headed families are nearly twice as likely to be poor as their white counterparts.

(poverty status of female-headed families and percent of female-headed families in poverty by age, race, and Hispanic origin of householder, 1990; number of female-headed families in 1991; numbers in thousands)

	all races		**white**		**black**		**Hispanic**	
	number	**percent**	**number**	**percent**	**number**	**percent**	**number**	**percent**
All female family householders	**3,768**	**33.4%**	**2,010**	**26.8%**	**1,648**	**48.1%**	**573**	**48.3%**
Under age 25	679	73.9	386	70.1	278	80.9	92	79.9
Aged 25 to 34	1,428	49.8	778	43.8	619	61.0	200	61.2
Aged 35 to 44	889	28.9	465	22.9	377	40.3	160	48.4
Aged 45 to 64	574	19.7	283	14.1	276	33.6	103	31.9
Aged 65 or older	198	13.3	97	8.5	98	31.2	18	19.5

female-headed families in poverty

Source: Bureau of the Census
Note: Hispanics may be of any race.

Sources of Income

People under age 65 are most likely to receive money from wages and salaries, while people aged 65 or older are most likely to receive Social Security.

(selected sources of income in 1990 for persons aged 15 or older by age; number of persons with income from source and average income from source; numbers in thousands)

	all persons aged 15 or older		persons under age 65		persons aged 65 or older	
	number with income	average income	number with income	average income	number with income	average income
Total	**180,465**	**$19,842**	**150,730**	**$20,791**	**29,734**	**$15,029**
Wages and salary	124,604	20,979	120,638	21,203	3,966	14,152
Nonfarm self-employment	12,744	16,558	11,786	16,875	958	12,656
Social Security	35,418	5,923	8,039	5,107	27,380	6,163
Public assistance	5,131	3,219	4,987	3,258	145	1,856
Veterans' benefits	2,622	4,082	1,434	4,679	1,188	3,361
Disability benefits	1,875	7,720	1,567	7,599	309	8,329
Pensions	14,518	8,769	4,868	10,640	9,650	7,825
Interest	108,508	1,592	87,900	1,073	20,608	3,805
Dividends	23,281	1,695	17,989	1,231	5,292	3,272
Rents, royalties, estates or trusts	13,543	3,257	10,582	3,029	2,961	4,072
Education	7,915	2,394	7,871	2,401	44	-
Child support	4,136	2,850	4,126	2,852	10	-

Source: Bureau of the Census

Child-Support Payments by Characteristics of Mother

Among the 58 percent of women who are supposed to receive child-support payments, three out of four do receive payments.

(child-support payments awarded and received from absent fathers by award status, 1989, by selected characteristics of women with children present; numbers in thousands)

	total	percent awarded child-support payments	supposed to receive child support in 1989				
				actually received child support in 1989			
			total	percent	average child support	average total income	child support as percent of total income
All women							
Total	**9,955**	**57.7%**	**4,953**	**75.2%**	**$2,995**	**$16,171**	**18.5%**
Current marital status							
Married	2,531	79.0	1,685	72.1	2,931	14,469	20.3
Divorced	3,056	76.8	2,123	77.0	3,322	19,456	17.1
Separated	1,352	47.9	527	79.7	3,060	14,891	20.5
Widowed	65	-	34	-	-	-	-
Never married	2,950	23.9	583	73.2	1,888	9,495	19.9
Race and Hispanic origin							
White	6,905	67.5	4,048	76.5	3,132	16,632	18.8
Black	2,770	34.5	791	69.7	2,263	13,898	16.3
Hispanic	1,112	40.6	364	69.8	2,965	14,758	20.1
Age							
Aged 15 to 17	128	18.0	23	-	-	-	-
Aged 18 to 29	3,086	45.6	1,208	75.6	1,981	9,938	19.9
Aged 30 to 39	4,175	64.3	2,413	74.4	3,032	17,006	17.8
Aged 40 or older	2,566	63.6	1,309	76.2	3,903	20,668	18.9
Years of school completed							
Less than 12 years	2,372	36.9	741	66.7	1,754	8,201	21.4
4 years high school	4,704	62.0	2,470	76.4	2,698	13,535	19.9
1 to 3 years college	1,988	65.0	1,139	76.6	3,338	18,462	18.1
4 or more years college	891	74.5	603	77.9	4,850	30,872	15.7
Number of own children present from an absent father							
One child	5,721	57.2	2,742	75.8	2,425	15,799	15.3
Two children	2,873	63.1	1,608	75.6	3,527	17,465	20.2
Three children	1,030	52.1	488	70.1	4,509	14,863	30.3
Four children or more	331	37.8	115	77.4	3,226	12,217	26.4

Source: Bureau of the Census
(-) means sample too small to be reliable.
Note: Hispanics may be of any race.

Child-Support Payments by Characteristics of Absent Father

Women are more likely to receive child support payments from fathers who have joint custody or visitation rights.

(percent of women who receive child support payments by visitation provisions and residence of absent father, 1989; numbers in thousands)

All women	total	percent awarded child-support payments	supposed to receive child support in 1989				
				actually received child support in 1989			
			total	percent	average child support	average total income	child support as percent of total income
Total	**9,955**	**57.7%**	**4,953**	**75.2%**	**$2,995**	**$16,171**	**18.5%**
Visitation and custodial provisions of absent fathers:							
Father has visitation privileges	5,461	77.7	3,876	79.1	2,917	16,006	18.2
Father has joint custody	726	65.3	396	90.2	4,031	19,158	21.0
Father has neither	3,768	27.3	681	44.5	2,563	14,327	17.9
Resident of absent father:							
Same state as mother	6,345	61.0	3,385	81.1	3,021	16,441	18.4
Different state from mother	2,549	58.9	1,319	65.6	3,012	15,768	19.1
Father's residence other	1,061	35.7	249	46.6	2,253	12,818	17.6

Source: Bureau of the Census

Average Taxes Paid, 1990

INCOME

The tax bite amounts to more than $10,000 for households paying the average in federal, Social Security, and state taxes. For those in the highest income quintile, it amounts to over $24,000 a year.

(average taxes paid by household income quintiles in 1990; households in 1991; numbers in thousands)

	Federal Income Tax	Social Security Tax	State Income Tax
All households paying tax	**71,311**	**71,002**	**63,660**
Average tax paid	**$5,912**	**$2,689**	**$1,942**
Lowest quintile			
Upper limit ($)	$7,126	$7,223	$7,219
Number paying tax	1,157	5,100	3,374
Average amount paid	$208	$305	$76
Second quintile			
Upper limit ($)	$18,894	$20,324	$18,532
Number paying tax	13,891	14,229	13,535
Average amount paid	$986	$1,091	$348
Third quintile			
Upper limit ($)	$30,752	$34,028	$29,763
Number paying tax	18,548	16,532	15,225
Average amount paid	$2,359	$2,051	$951
Fourth quintile			
Upper limit ($)	$47,143	$53,563	$45,137
Number paying tax	18,895	17,301	15,675
Average amount paid	$4,593	$3,116	$1,817
Highest quintile			
Number paying tax	18,820	17,840	15,853
Average amount paid	$14,725	$4,822	$4,775

Source: Bureau of the Census

Discretionary Income by Age of Householder

More than 30 percent of households headed by people aged 30 to 59 have discretionary income.
The amount of discretionary income ranges from nearly $8,000 to over $14,000 per year.

(discretionary income of households in 1986 by age of householder; households in 1987; numbers in thousands)

| | households | | households with discretionary income | | | | |
| | | | average income | | spendable discretionary income | | |
	number	percent of households	before taxes	after taxes	aggregate (billions)	average	per capita
Total	**25,869**	**28.9%**	**$56,605**	**$41,940**	**$319.0**	**$12,332**	**$4,633**
Aged 15 to 24	972	18.7	38,241	30,124	7.6	7,790	3,022
Aged 25 to 29	2,646	27.4	48,547	36,618	24.2	9,130	3,306
Aged 30 to 34	3,419	31.5	54,243	40,067	37.3	10,919	3,713
Aged 35 to 39	3,349	33.0	60,049	43,585	41.5	12,405	4,195
Aged 40 to 44	2,605	30.5	66,133	47,891	36.5	13,999	4,679
Aged 45 to 49	2,299	33.4	69,412	49,968	33.2	14,448	4,572
Aged 50 to 54	2,008	31.8	68,181	49,079	27.2	13,550	4,899
Aged 55 to 59	2,252	35.0	61,480	44,906	32.8	14,584	5,759
Aged 60 to 64	1,848	28.8	61,001	44,262	26.5	14,356	6,188
Aged 65 to 69	1,523	25.0	50,447	38,968	19.7	12,921	6,280
Aged 70 or older	2,946	22.8	39,117	32,344	32.5	11,015	6,073

Source: A Marketer's Guide to Discretionary Income, a joint study by the Consumer Research Center, The Conference Board, and the U.S. Bureau of the Census
Note: Households with discretionary income are those with a spendable income at least 30 percent higher than the average household of a similar size and age.

Distribution of Men's Income, 1980 to 1990

A growing proportion of men make $50,000 or more a year, but most men have annual incomes of less than $25,000.

(percent distribution of men aged 15 or older by income, 1980-90, in 1990 dollars; numbers in thousands)

| | number of men | number with income | total | percent distribution of men with income | | | | | | |
				under $5,000	$5,000 to $9,999	$10,000 to $14,999	$15,000 to $24,999	$25,000 to $49,999	$50,000 to $74,999	$75,000 or more
1990	92,840	88,220	100.0%	12.3%	12.8%	12.8%	21.7%	29.2%	7.3%	3.9%
1989	91,955	87,454	100.0	12.2	12.6	12.6	20.8	29.9	7.5	4.3
1988	91,034	86,584	100.0	12.8	12.6	12.1	21.0	30.3	7.2	4.0
1987	90,256	85,713	100.0	13.3	12.4	12.9	20.4	29.7	7.5	3.7
1986	89,368	84,471	100.0	13.5	12.9	12.2	20.4	29.9	7.2	3.7
1985	88,478	83,631	100.0	14.3	13.0	12.6	21.0	29.1	6.9	3.2
1984	87,304	82,183	100.0	14.5	13.3	12.1	20.4	29.5	6.9	3.2
1983	86,014	80,795	100.0	15.3	13.3	12.3	21.4	28.6	6.3	2.9
1982	84,955	79,722	100.0	15.2	13.5	12.9	21.0	28.7	6.0	2.8
1981	83,958	79,688	100.0	14.7	13.1	12.8	20.8	29.9	6.2	2.4
1980	82,949	78,661	100.0	13.9	13.0	11.6	21.8	31.3	5.7	2.8

Source: Bureau of the Census

Distribution of Women's Income, 1980 to 1990

A growing proportion of women are making their way into the higher income categories. Still, most women have an annual income below $10,000.

(percent distribution of women aged 15 or older by income, 1980-90, in 1990 dollars; numbers in thousands)

	number of women	number with income	percent distribution of women with income							
			total	under $5,000	$5,000 to $9,999	$10,000 to $14,999	$15,000 to $24,999	$25,000 to $49,999	$50,000 to $74,999	$75,000 or more
1990	100,680	92,245	100.0%	28.5%	21.2%	14.7%	19.0%	14.3%	1.7%	0.6%
1989	99,838	91,399	100.0	28.7	21.3	14.7	18.9	14.1	1.6	0.6
1988	99,019	90,593	100.0	29.8	21.5	14.3	18.8	13.6	1.4	0.5
1987	98,225	89,661	100.0	30.6	21.6	14.6	18.4	13.1	1.3	0.5
1986	97,320	87,822	100.0	31.6	22.0	14.3	18.0	12.5	1.1	0.5
1985	96,354	86,531	100.0	32.9	22.0	14.3	17.7	11.6	1.1	0.3
1984	95,282	85,555	100.0	32.7	22.5	14.3	18.0	11.2	1.0	0.4
1983	94,269	83,781	100.0	34.0	22.2	14.5	18.0	10.1	0.8	0.3
1982	93,145	82,505	100.0	35.6	22.5	15.0	16.9	9.1	0.6	0.3
1981	92,228	82,139	100.0	35.8	22.5	15.6	17.0	8.4	0.5	0.2
1980	91,133	80,826	100.0	36.5	22.5	14.3	17.6	8.3	0.6	0.2

Source: Bureau of the Census

Men's Median Income by Race and Hispanic Origin, 1980 to 1990

Men's incomes barely grew during the 1980s, up by just 2 percent after adjusting for inflation. Hispanic men saw their incomes decline sharply.

(median income of males aged 15 or older with income, by race and Hispanic origin, 1980-90, in 1990 dollars)

	all males	white	black	Hispanic
1990	$20,293	$21,170	$12,868	$13,470
1989	20,968	21,990	13,290	14,124
1988	20,890	22,051	13,306	14,396
1987	20,463	21,751	12,903	14,071
1986	20,409	21,537	12,905	13,752
1985	19,813	20,784	13,080	13,889
1984	19,624	20,715	11,885	13,964
1983	19,239	20,240	11,836	14,244
1982	18,894	19,975	11,970	14,182
1981	19,372	20,555	12,223	14,670
1980	19,875	21,140	12,704	15,321

Source: Bureau of the Census
Note: Hispanics may be of any race.

Women's Median Income by Race and Hispanic Origin, 1980 to 1990

Women's incomes have grown substantially during the 1980s, regardless of race or ethnicity. Women saw their median income increase by nearly 30 percent between 1980 and 1990.

(median income of females aged 15 or older with income, by race and Hispanic origin, 1980-90, in 1990 dollars)

	all females	white	black	Hispanic
1990	$10,070	$10,317	$8,328	$7,532
1989	10,144	10,342	8,301	8,060
1988	9,815	10,057	8,119	7,723
1987	9,544	9,788	7,995	7,628
1986	9,075	9,254	7,830	7,558
1985	8,766	8,936	7,625	7,312
1984	8,640	8,741	7,754	7,334
1983	8,405	8,552	7,308	7,076
1982	7,973	8,082	7,128	6,962
1981	7,848	7,935	7,050	7,275
1980	7,804	7,847	7,265	6,987

Source: Bureau of the Census
Note: Hispanics may be of any race.

Change in Personal Income, 1980 to 1990

The incomes of older men rose during the 1980s, while those of younger men fell. Women of all ages saw their incomes grow.

(median income of persons with income by selected characteristics, 1980 and 1990; in 1990 dollars)

	1990	1980	percent change 1980 to 1990
Males, aged 15 or older	$20,293	$19,875	2.1%
White	21,170	21,141	0.1
Black	12,868	12,703	1.3
Hispanic	13,470	15,320	-13.7
Males, aged 25 or older	23,341	25,714	-10.2
Aged 25 to 34	21,393	24,713	-15.5
Aged 35 to 44	29,773	31,782	-6.7
Aged 45 to 54	31,007	31,682	-2.2
Aged 55 to 64	24,804	25,242	-1.8
Aged 65 or older	14,183	11,646	17.9
Years of school completed			
High school, 1-3 years	15,131	19,334	-27.8
High school, 4 years	21,713	27,316	-25.8
College, 4 years or more	37,860	37,875	0.0
Females, aged 15 or older	10,070	7,804	22.5
White	10,317	7,847	23.9
Black	8,328	7,264	12.8
Hispanic	7,532	6,987	7.2
Females, aged 25 or older	11,272	8,571	24.0
Aged 25 to 34	12,589	11,060	12.1
Aged 35 to 44	14,504	10,255	29.3
Aged 45 to 54	14,230	10,157	28.6
Aged 55 to 64	9,400	7,814	16.9
Aged 65 or older	8,044	6,703	16.7
Years of school completed			
High school, 1-3 years	7,042	6,955	1.2
High school, 4 years	10,653	9,395	11.8
College, 4 years or more	22,509	17,499	22.3

Source: Bureau of the Census

Median Incomes of Full-Time Workers

Among full-time workers, the incomes of younger women are 90 percent as great as the incomes of younger men.

(median income of male and female year-round, full-time workers and female-to-male income ratio, by age, 1990)

	male	female	female-to-male income ratio
All	$28,979	$20,591	71.1%
Under age 25	15,462	13,944	90.2
Aged 25 to 34	25,355	20,184	79.6
Aged 35 to 44	32,607	22,505	69.0
Aged 45 to 54	35,732	21,938	61.4
Aged 55 to 64	33,169	20,755	62.6
Aged 65 to 74	35,872	22,978	64.1
Aged 75 or older	31,665	22,895	72.3

Source: Bureau of the Census

Income of Households by Education of Householder

Households headed by high school graduates had a median income of $28,744 in 1990. Those headed by college graduates had a median income of $47,083.

(number, percent distribution, and median income of householders aged 25 or older by education of householder, income in 1990; number of householders in 1991; numbers in thousands)	number of households	percent of households	median income
All levels	**89,429**	**100.0%**	**$30,757**
8 years or less	10,146	11.3	13,523
High school, 1 to 3 years	10,077	11.3	18,191
High school, 4 years	32,043	35.8	28,744
College, total	37,163	41.6	43,112
College, 1 to 3 years	16,451	18.4	35,724
College, 4 years	11,443	12.8	47,083
College, 5+ years	9,269	10.4	54,636

Source: Bureau of the Census

Earnings Distribution of Men by Education

The most educated men have the highest earnings. Over one-third of men with graduate-level training earned at least $50,000 in 1990.

(earnings distribution of men aged 25 or older in 1991 by education; income in 1990; numbers in thousands)

| | all men | 8 years or less | high school | | college | | | |
			1 to 3 years	4 years	total	1 to 3 years	4 years	5 years or more
Total	75,487	8,317	7,887	27,189	32,094	13,720	10,230	8,143
Without earnings	15,735	4,438	2,522	5,076	3,698	1,774	1,074	850
With earnings	59,753	3,879	5,365	22,113	28,396	11,946	9,156	7,294
Under $2,500	2,464	418	362	878	806	367	233	206
$2,500 to $4,999	1,890	307	343	662	579	328	134	117
$5,000 to $7,499	2,539	422	435	954	728	387	188	153
$7,500 to $9,999	2,265	364	349	926	627	293	217	117
$10,000 to $12,499	3,597	485	590	1,404	1,118	598	299	220
$12,500 to $14,999	2,629	255	373	1,169	831	459	215	157
$15,000 to $17,499	3,671	337	487	1,746	1,102	633	302	167
$17,500 to $19,999	2,943	205	368	1,336	1,033	587	302	144
$20,000 to $22,499	4,445	252	450	2,085	1,658	957	463	239
$22,500 to $24,999	2,439	128	225	1,071	1,015	506	340	169
$25,000 to $29,999	6,195	271	410	2,681	2,832	1,422	888	523
$30,000 to $34,999	5,852	176	401	2,296	2,979	1,406	978	595
$35,000 to $39,999	4,472	108	217	1,625	2,521	1,105	869	547
$40,000 to $44,999	3,533	60	127	1,219	2,128	827	749	552
$45,000 to $49,999	2,397	44	73	676	1,605	576	543	486
$50,000 to $54,999	2,331	18	78	527	1,708	491	598	619
$55,000 to $64,999	2,133	19	46	440	1,629	461	530	637
$65,000 to $74,999	1,159	2	11	142	1,003	177	443	383
$75,000 to $84,999	904	1	6	107	791	129	301	361
$85,000 to $99,999	494	2	3	42	447	61	149	237
$100,000 or more	1,400	5	11	129	1,255	175	416	664
Median earnings	**$25,613**	**$12,212**	**$16,181**	**$22,378**	**$32,241**	**$27,308**	**$35,079**	**$41,825**

Source: Bureau of the Census

Earnings Distribution of Women by Education

The most educated women have the highest earnings. Nearly 10 percent of women with graduate-level training earned at least $50,000 in 1990.

(earnings distribution of women aged 25 or older in 1991 by education; income in 1990; numbers in thousands)

	all women	8 years or less	high school 1 to 3 years	high school 4 years	college total	college 1 to 3 years	college 4 years	college 5 years or more
Total	83,207	8,532	9,492	34,083	31,101	15,449	9,871	5,781
Without earnings	33,114	6,472	5,596	13,202	7,843	4,462	2,335	1,046
With earnings	50,093	2,059	3,895	20,881	23,257	10,987	7,535	4,735
Under $2,500	5,491	405	680	2,486	1,920	1,115	571	234
$2,500 to $4,999	3,640	335	505	1,680	1,120	666	314	139
$5,000 to $7,499	4,203	334	502	2,027	1,341	807	353	181
$7,500 to $9,999	3,787	287	453	1,862	1,185	700	343	142
$10,000 to $12,499	4,846	245	477	2,474	1,651	979	450	222
$12,500 to $14,999	3,218	124	329	1,660	1,105	693	269	143
$15,000 to $17,499	4,322	116	324	2,145	1,736	1,039	513	185
$17,500 to $19,999	2,994	54	165	1,341	1,434	752	463	219
$20,000 to $22,499	3,746	47	173	1,528	1,998	988	695	314
$22,500 to $24,999	2,140	22	69	784	1,265	559	482	224
$25,000 to $29,999	4,210	38	107	1,375	2,691	1,122	945	624
$30,000 to $34,999	2,795	27	48	712	2,008	706	724	579
$35,000 to $39,999	1,676	14	17	335	1,310	368	545	397
$40,000 to $44,999	1,130	6	15	187	922	221	325	376
$45,000 to $49,999	621	5	11	108	498	106	179	213
$50,000 to $54,999	453	1	5	46	401	72	139	190
$55,000 to $64,999	374	-	5	67	302	51	91	161
$65,000 to $74,999	144	-	4	23	116	14	44	58
$75,000 to $84,999	123	1	3	16	103	7	42	54
$85,000 to $99,999	62	-	-	10	52	11	20	21
$100,000 or more	118	-	3	17	98	11	26	61
Median earnings	$14,893	$7,173	$8,936	$12,412	$20,171	$16,284	$21,763	$27,332

Source: Bureau of the Census

Income of Men and Women by Education

Among full-time workers, women who were high school graduates earned just 67 percent as much as their male counterparts. Women with four years of college earned 72 percent as much as men with the same education.

(median income of male and female year-round, full-time workers by education, and female-to-male income ratio, 1990)

	males	females	female-to-male income ratio
All persons	**$29,987**	**$20,556**	**68.5%**
8 years or less	16,840	11,831	70.3
High school, 1 to 3 years	20,452	13,858	67.8
High school, 4 years	25,872	17,412	67.3
College, total	36,115	25,274	70.0
College, 1 to 3 years	30,865	21,324	69.1
College, 4 years	37,283	26,828	72.0
College, 5+ years	47,131	31,969	67.8

Source: Bureau of the Census

Income of Full-Time Workers by Age and Education

Income peaks at more than $52,000 for men aged 55 to 64 with graduate-level training. For women, peak earnings are nearly $36,000 for those aged 45 to 54 with graduate-level training.

(median income of male and female year-round, full-time workers by education and age, 1990)

	25 to 34		35 to 44		45 to 54		55 to 64		65 or older	
	male	*female*	*male*	*female*	*male*	*female*	*male*	*female*	*male*	*female*
All levels	**$25,168**	**$19,623**	**$32,119**	**$21,688**	**$34,669**	**$20,991**	**$30,933**	**$18,890**	**$26,804**	**$18,194**
8 years or less	13,098	10,804	16,223	12,150	18,337	12,069	20,735	12,531	12,180	-
High school, 1 to 3 years	17,394	12,618	21,149	14,280	22,186	14,335	22,662	13,722	14,607	-
High school, 4 years	22,098	16,232	26,880	18,534	30,856	18,537	27,780	17,203	24,098	17,926
College, total	29,558	23,302	38,251	26,390	42,059	26,834	42,594	25,387	39,975	21,206
College, 1 to 3 years	26,179	19,913	32,369	22,078	36,137	23,227	31,856	21,785	29,902	-
College, 4 years	31,058	25,695	40,617	29,273	44,352	26,859	47,789	26,017	40,027	-
College, 5+ years	35,229	29,819	48,847	32,066	51,625	35,751	52,224	32,755	50,173	-

Source: Bureau of the Census
Note: (-) means sample too small to be reliable.

Median Weekly Earnings by Sex and Occupation

Overall, women who work full time make just 74 percent as much as their male counterparts. But women in some professions, such as engineering and computer science make at least 85 percent as much as men.

(median weekly earnings of full-time wage and salary workers aged 16 or older by selected occupations and sex, and female-male earnings ratio, 1991)

	males	females	female-to-male earnings ratio
All full-time wage and salary workers	**$497**	**$368**	**74%**
Managerial and professional specialty	**753**	**527**	**70**
Executive, administrative, and managerial	758	504	66
Financial managers	953	559	59
Accountants and auditors	699	501	72
Professional specialty	748	559	75
Engineers	863	740	86
Computer systems analysts and scientists	822	732	89
Natural scientists	726	571	79
Physicians	1,155	623	54
Teachers, college and university	824	659	80
Social scientists and urban planners	704	533	76
Lawyers	1,091	821	75
Technical, sales, and administrative support	**509**	**350**	**69**
Technicians	576	445	77
Sales occupations	518	308	59
Insurance sales	596	440	74
Real estate sales	642	488	76
Securities and financial services sales	823	541	66
Administrative support, including clerical	459	348	76
Service occupations	**330**	**244**	**74**
Police and detectives	685	483	71
Waiters and waitresses	281	205	73
Precision production, craft, and repair	**494**	**341**	**69**
Mechanics and repairers	489	506	103
Construction trades	484	-	-
Precision production occupations	508	317	62
Operators, fabricators, and laborers	**387**	**273**	**71**
Transportation and material moving occupations	**423**	**339**	**80**
Handlers, equipment cleaners, helpers, and laborers	**315**	**261**	**83**
Farming, forestry, and fishing	**269**	**224**	**83**

(-) means less than 50,000 in occupation.
Source: Bureau of Labor Statistics

Median Income by Metropolitan Status and Region of Residence

Households in the suburbs have the highest median income—$38,831 in 1990. Those in the Northeast and West have incomes that are higher than the national median.

(number of households and median household income by metropolitan residence status and region of residence; income in 1990; households in 1991; numbers in thousands)

	number of households	median income
All households	**94,312**	**$29,943**
Residence status		
Inside metropolitan areas	73,135	31,823
One million or more	46,601	33,826
Inside central cities	18,388	26,732
Outside central cities	28,213	38,831
Under 1 million	26,534	28,579
Inside central cities	11,509	24,900
Outside central cities	15,025	31,395
Outside metropolitan areas	21,177	23,709
Region		
Northeast	19,271	32,676
Midwest	23,223	29,897
South	32,312	26,942
West	19,506	31,761

Source: Bureau of the Census

Median Income of Households by State

Median household income was highest in New Hampshire in 1990 and lowest in Mississippi. The gap in income between those two states was more than $20,000.

(median household income by state, 1990)

	median income		median income
Alabama	$23,357	Montana	$23,375
Alaska	39,298	Nebraska	27,482
Arizona	29,224	Nevada	32,023
Arkansas	22,786	New Hampshire	40,805
California	33,290	New Jersey	38,734
Colorado	30,733	New Mexico	25,039
Connecticut	38,870	New York	31,591
Delaware	30,804	North Carolina	26,329
District of Columbia	27,392	North Dakota	25,264
Florida	26,685	Ohio	30,013
Georgia	27,561	Oklahoma	24,384
Hawaii	38,921	Oregon	29,281
Idaho	25,305	Pennsylvania	29,005
Illinois	32,542	Rhode Island	31,968
Indiana	26,928	South Carolina	28,735
Iowa	27,288	South Dakota	24,571
Kansas	29,917	Tennessee	22,592
Kentucky	24,780	Texas	28,228
Louisiana	22,405	Utah	30,142
Maine	27,464	Vermont	31,098
Maryland	38,857	Virginia	35,073
Massachusetts	36,247	Washington	32,112
Michigan	29,937	West Virginia	22,137
Minnesota	31,465	Wisconsin	30,711
Mississippi	20,178	Wyoming	29,460
Missouri	27,332		

Source: Bureau of the Census

CHAPTER

4

Spending & Wealth Trends

Americans sharply reduced their spending in 1990 as the recession set in. They spent less on a wide variety of products and services, causing a dramatic restructuring of the nation's businesses. But behind the clouds of gloom and doom is a silver lining: the rapid middle-aging of the population assures spending growth in the 1990s. Householders aged 35 to 54 (typically, the biggest spenders) will control the majority of spending on nearly every product and service category by 1995.

Major Spending & Wealth Trends

☞ Spending will grow again, but consumers will continue to be cautious, planning their spending carefully. Now that baby boomers have families to support, impulse spending is a thing of the past.

☞ Look for the saving rate to grow as increasingly cautious, middle-aged consumers begin to save for their children's college educations and their own retirement. This should boost net worth in the 1990s.

☞ Expect homeownership rates to reach record highs by the end of the decade as lower interest rates and rising incomes allow many more middle-aged baby boomers to buy homes.

Household Spending Trends, 1986 to 1990

Household spending fell by 0.3 percent between 1986 and 1990, after adjusting for inflation. The biggest drop was in spending on new cars and trucks and other vehicles such as motorcycles.

(average annual expenditures for all households, 1986 to 1990; number of households in thousands; expenditures in 1990 dollars)

	1990	1989	1988	1987	1986	percent change 1986-90
Number of households*	**96,968**	**95,818**	**94,862**	**94,150**	**94,044**	3.1%
Income before taxes	**$31,889**	**$33,000**	**$31,532**	**$31,439**	**$30,362**	5.0
Average number of persons per household	**2.6**	**2.6**	**2.6**	**2.6**	**2.6**	0.0
Average annual expenditures	**$28,369**	**$29,313**	**$28,606**	**$28,089**	**$28,461**	-0.3
Food	**$4,296**	**$4,376**	**$4,141**	**$4,216**	**$4,112**	4.5%
Food at home	2,485	2,519	2,360	2,415	2,377	4.6
Cereals and bakery products	368	378	345	344	328	12.2
Cereals and cereal products	129	138	120	120	111	16.3
Bakery products	240	240	224	223	218	10.0
Meats, poultry, fish, and eggs	668	644	609	658	670	-0.3
Beef	218	213	201	220	225	-3.3
Pork	132	122	122	133	138	-4.6
Other meats	99	94	91	95	94	5.1
Poultry	108	105	93	100	101	6.5
Fish and seafood	82	75	72	76	76	7.4
Eggs	30	35	31	32	36	-16.1
Dairy products	295	320	303	315	299	-1.4
Fresh milk and cream	140	156	148	152	145	-3.8
Other dairy products	155	165	156	163	153	1.5
Fruits and vegetables	408	430	412	410	382	6.9
Fresh fruits	127	133	134	130	122	4.4
Fresh vegetables	118	134	122	127	110	7.6
Processed fruits	93	94	94	90	86	8.3
Processed vegetables	70	70	63	63	64	8.7
Other food at home	746	746	691	652	661	12.9
Sugar and other sweets	94	91	86	85	88	6.5
Fats and oils	68	62	61	59	61	11.8
Miscellaneous foods	336	331	292	285	281	19.4
Nonalcoholic beverages	213	228	220	223	230	-7.5
Food prep. by hh, out-of-town trips	35	35	33	36	37	-5.3
Food away from home	1,811	1,857	1,781	1,801	1,735	4.4
Alcoholic beverages	**293**	**299**	**297**	**333**	**323**	**-9.3**
Housing	**8,886**	**9,074**	**8,926**	**8,708**	**8,696**	2.2
Shelter	5,032	5,096	4,964	4,779	4,745	6.0
Owned dwellings	2,953	3,004	2,838	2,733	2,749	7.4
Mortgage interest	1,817	1,835	1,733	1,681	1,706	6.5

(continued on next page)

(continued from previous page)

(average annual expenditures for all households, 1986 to 1990; number of households in thousands; expenditures in 1990 dollars)

	1990	1989	1988	1987	1986	percent change 1986-90
Property taxes	$597	$606	$557	$534	$498	19.8%
Maintenance, repairs, insurance, other	540	562	548	517	544	-0.7
Rented dwellings	1,533	1,581	1,622	1,547	1,505	1.9
Other lodging	545	511	504	499	491	10.9
Utilities, fuels, and public services	1,890	1,934	1,930	1,923	1,962	-3.7
Natural gas	246	260	259	267	296	-16.8
Electricity	758	778	783	796	804	-5.7
Fuel oil and other fuels	100	106	108	108	128	-21.6
Telephone	592	598	593	574	562	5.4
Water and other public services	193	192	188	176	173	11.6
Household operations	446	485	435	427	422	5.6
Personal services	219	231	189	196	200	9.3
Other household expenses	227	254	246	231	222	2.3
Housekeeping supplies	406	415	399	392	377	7.7
Laundry and cleaning supplies	113	113	112	112	110	3.0
Other household products	171	174	162	160	150	13.8
Postage and stationery	122	129	125	121	117	4.4
Household furnishings and equipment	1,111	1,145	1,197	1,187	1,190	-6.6
Household textiles	99	111	104	105	125	-20.9
Furniture	310	329	360	362	363	-14.5
Floor coverings	92	74	72	79	66	40.3
Major appliances	147	156	187	184	186	-21.0
Small appliances, misc. housewares	61	69	66	66	67	-8.7
Miscellaneous household equipment	402	407	408	391	384	4.7
Apparel and services	**1,617**	**1,667**	**1,645**	**1,664**	**1,605**	**0.7**
Men and boys	393	418	429	415	409	-3.9
Men, aged 16 or older	324	342	344	339	332	-2.3
Boys, aged 2 to 15	70	78	85	76	79	-11.1
Women and girls	672	692	649	680	649	3.6
Women, aged 16 or older	585	594	544	587	563	3.9
Girls, aged 2 to 15	87	98	105	93	86	1.3
Babies under age 2	70	76	68	67	67	4.8
Footwear	225	199	217	212	199	13.0
Other apparel products and services	258	280	284	289	281	-8.3
Transportation	**5,122**	**5,467**	**5,627**	**5,292**	**5,774**	**-11.3**
Vehicle purchases (net outlay)	2,129	2,415	2,608	2,326	2,788	-23.6
Cars and trucks, new	1,159	1,284	1,497	1,315	1,687	-31.3
Cars and trucks, used	948	1,108	1,085	989	1,065	-11.0
Other vehicles	22	23	25	21	35	-36.4
Gasoline and motor oil	1,047	1,038	1,030	1,022	1,091	-4.0
Other vehicle expenses	1,644	1,715	1,680	1,630	1,600	2.7
Vehicle finance charges	300	319	314	322	321	-6.5
Maintenance and repairs	591	591	611	591	587	0.7

(continued on next page)

(continued from previous page)

(average annual expenditures for all households, 1986 to 1990; number of households in thousands; expenditures in 1990 dollars)

	1990	1989	1988	1987	1986	percent change 1986-90
Vehicle insurance	$563	$606	$561	$532	$501	12.4%
Vehicle rental, licenses, other charges	190	198	196	184	192	-1.0
Public transportation	302	299	308	314	296	2.1
Health care	**1,480**	**1,483**	**1,434**	**1,306**	**1,354**	**9.3**
Health insurance	581	566	524	451	442	31.3
Medical services	562	571	584	537	599	-6.1
Drugs	252	253	246	234	229	10.1
Medical supplies	85	92	78	84	82	3.3
Entertainment	**1,422**	**1,501**	**1,468**	**1,373**	**1,370**	**3.8**
Fees and admissions	371	397	390	372	367	1.0
Television, radios, sound equipment	454	452	460	436	442	2.6
Pets, toys, and playground equipment	276	262	254	251	241	14.6
Other supplies, equipment, and services	321	389	365	314	320	0.4
Personal-care products and services	**364**	**386**	**369**	**380**	**361**	**0.7**
Reading	**153**	**165**	**166**	**163**	**167**	**-8.4**
Education	**406**	**387**	**378**	**388**	**374**	**8.4**
Tobacco products and smoking supplies	**274**	**275**	**267**	**267**	**274**	**-0.1**
Cash contributions	**816**	**949**	**766**	**853**	**890**	**-8.3**
Personal insurance and pensions	**2,592**	**2,606**	**2,485**	**2,502**	**2,536**	**2.2**
Life and other personal insurance	345	365	347	338	348	-0.9
Pensions and Social Security	2,248	2,240	2,138	2,164	2,187	2.8
Miscellaneous	**645**	**678**	**639**	**647**	**622**	**3.6**

*The Consumer Expenditure Survey uses consumer units as its sampling unit. See Glossary for definition of consumer unit.
Source: Bureau of Labor Statistics
Note: Numbers may not add to total due to rounding.

Market Shares of the Youth, Middle-Aged, and Mature Market in 1990

SPENDING & WEALTH

In 1990, households headed by 35-to-54-year-olds accounted for slightly less than half of spending in most product or service categories.

(youth are householders under age 35, middle-aged are householders aged 35 to 54, mature are householders aged 55 or older)

	all households	youth	middle-aged	mature
Average annual expenditures	**100.0%**	**24.5%**	**48.0%**	**27.5%**
Food	**100.0**	**24.1**	**47.7**	**28.2**
Food at home	100.0	23.1	46.8	30.1
Cereals and bakery products	100.0	22.1	47.1	30.8
Cereals and cereal products	100.0	24.1	46.7	29.2
Bakery products	100.0	21.0	47.4	31.6
Meats, poultry, fish, and eggs	100.0	22.6	46.2	31.1
Beef	100.0	23.8	45.7	30.5
Pork	100.0	21.0	47.2	31.8
Other meats	100.0	22.9	46.5	30.6
Poultry	100.0	22.5	45.4	32.2
Fish and seafood	100.0	21.4	48.1	30.4
Eggs	100.0	24.1	43.6	32.3
Dairy products	100.0	24.2	46.5	29.3
Fresh milk and cream	100.0	25.1	45.8	29.2
Other dairy products	100.0	23.4	47.1	29.5
Fruits and vegetables	100.0	21.8	44.4	33.7
Fresh fruits	100.0	21.1	42.2	36.7
Fresh vegetables	100.0	21.4	45.6	33.0
Processed fruits	100.0	22.6	44.7	32.7
Processed vegetables	100.0	23.0	46.1	30.9
Other food at home	100.0	24.3	48.4	27.3
Sugar and other sweets	100.0	21.3	48.7	30.0
Fats and oils	100.0	20.6	47.6	31.8
Miscellaneous foods	100.0	26.0	49.0	25.0
Nonalcoholic beverages	100.0	24.3	48.2	27.6
Food prep. by hh, out-of-town trips	100.0	23.7	45.0	31.3
Food away from home	100.0	25.5	49.0	25.4
Alcoholic beverages	**100.0**	**33.2**	**45.8**	**21.0**
Housing	**100.0**	**25.6**	**47.0**	**27.4**
Shelter	100.0	27.6	47.7	24.7
Owned dwellings	100.0	21.4	52.5	26.0
Mortgage interest	100.0	27.2	59.3	13.5
Property taxes	100.0	11.0	44.2	44.8
Maintenance, repairs, insurance, other	100.0	13.9	38.9	47.3
Rented dwellings	100.0	44.8	35.7	19.5
Other lodging	100.0	14.6	53.9	31.5

(continued on next page)

(youth are householders under age 35, middle-aged are householders aged 35 to 54, mature are householders aged 55 or older)

	all households	youth	middle-aged	mature
Utilities, fuels, and public services	100.0%	21.7%	44.4%	33.9%
Natural gas	100.0	19.3	43.5	37.2
Electricity	100.0	21.1	44.2	34.7
Fuel oil and other fuels	100.0	14.3	40.8	44.9
Telephone	100.0	26.0	45.3	28.7
Water and other public services	100.0	17.9	45.4	36.8
Household operations	100.0	29.2	41.2	29.7
Personal services	100.0	47.4	40.2	12.4
Other household expenses	100.0	12.2	42.1	45.7
Housekeeping supplies	100.0	21.9	45.4	32.8
Laundry and cleaning supplies	100.0	23.8	46.7	29.5
Other household products	100.0	20.7	46.0	33.3
Postage and stationery	100.0	21.8	43.1	35.1
Household furnishings and equipment	100.0	23.4	51.2	25.4
Household textiles	100.0	19.2	50.2	30.6
Furniture	100.0	27.7	47.9	24.4
Floor coverings	100.0	13.0	61.6	25.4
Major appliances	100.0	24.2	44.2	31.7
Small appliances, misc. housewares	100.0	22.5	46.2	31.3
Miscellaneous household equipment	100.0	23.5	54.8	21.7
Apparel and services	**100.0**	**24.5**	**52.5**	**23.0**
Men and boys	100.0	26.0	54.5	19.5
Men, aged 16 or older	100.0	25.3	53.3	21.4
Boys, aged 2 to 15	100.0	29.3	59.7	11.0
Women and girls	100.0	20.7	53.0	26.3
Women, aged 16 or older	100.0	20.0	51.2	28.8
Girls, aged 2 to 15	100.0	25.2	65.1	9.7
Babies under age 2	100.0	49.2	35.7	15.2
Footwear	100.0	22.3	54.1	23.6
Other apparel products and services	100.0	27.3	51.4	21.3
Transportation	**100.0**	**26.5**	**47.7**	**25.8**
Vehicle purchases (net outlay)	100.0	28.7	48.1	23.2
Cars and trucks, new	100.0	26.8	48.3	24.8
Cars and trucks, used	100.0	30.6	48.0	21.5
Other vehicles	100.0	45.6	44.0	10.3
Gasoline and motor oil	100.0	26.0	46.9	27.1
Other vehicle expenses	100.0	25.4	47.8	26.7
Vehicle finance charges	100.0	30.2	51.4	18.4
Maintenance and repairs	100.0	24.8	46.4	28.8
Vehicle insurance	100.0	22.9	47.0	30.0
Vehicle rental, licenses, other charges	100.0	27.3	49.2	23.5
Public transportation	100.0	19.0	46.7	34.3
Health care	**100.0**	**15.6**	**37.6**	**46.7**
Health insurance	100.0	15.3	33.7	51.0
Medical services	100.0	16.7	43.5	39.8
Drugs	100.0	12.9	30.5	56.6
Medical supplies	100.0	18.9	46.7	34.4

(continued on next page)

(continued from previous page)
(youth are householders under age 35, middle-aged are householders aged 35 to 54, mature are householders aged 55 or older)

	all households	youth	middle-aged	mature
Entertainment	**100.0%**	**25.4%**	**49.9%**	**24.7%**
Fees and admissions	100.0	22.9	49.5	27.5
Television, radios, sound equipment	100.0	28.1	48.9	23.0
Pets, toys, and playground equipment	100.0	26.2	51.7	22.1
Other supplies, equipment, and services	100.0	23.9	50.3	25.8
Personal-care products and services	**100.0**	**21.8**	**47.6**	**30.6**
Reading	**100.0**	**21.4**	**45.7**	**32.9**
Education	**100.0**	**29.2**	**55.1**	**15.7**
Tobacco products and smoking supplies	**100.0**	**25.9**	**45.9**	**28.2**
Cash contributions	**100.0**	**11.7**	**48.1**	**40.3**
Personal insurance and pensions	**100.0**	**24.7**	**54.1**	**21.1**
Life and other personal insurance	100.0	14.5	52.5	33.0
Pensions and Social Security	100.0	26.3	54.4	19.3
Miscellaneous	**100.0**	**24.4**	**47.5**	**28.2**

Source: Bureau of Labor Statistics and tabulations by New Strategist Publications

Market Shares of the Youth, Middle-Aged, and Mature Market in 1995

By 1995, households headed by 35-to-54-year-olds will account for over half of spending in most product and service categories. For some items, such as children's clothing, they will account for nearly two-thirds of household spending.

(youth are householders under age 35, middle-aged are householders aged 35 to 54, mature are householders aged 55 or older)

	all households	youth	middle-aged	mature
Average annual expenditures	**100.0%**	**21.9%**	**51.9%**	**26.2%**
Food	**100.0**	**21.6**	**51.6**	**26.8**
Food at home	100.0	20.7	50.5	28.8
Cereals and bakery products	100.0	19.8	50.8	29.4
Cereals and cereal products	100.0	21.6	50.4	28.0
Bakery products	100.0	18.8	51.1	30.2
Meats, poultry, fish, and eggs	100.0	20.2	50.1	29.7
Beef	100.0	21.4	49.6	29.1
Pork	100.0	18.7	51.1	30.3
Other meats	100.0	20.5	50.4	29.1
Poultry	100.0	20.1	49.2	30.7
Fish and seafood	100.0	19.1	51.8	29.0
Eggs	100.0	21.6	47.3	31.0
Dairy products	100.0	21.7	50.2	28.1
Fresh milk and cream	100.0	22.5	49.5	28.0
Other dairy products	100.0	20.9	50.8	28.2
Fruits and vegetables	100.0	19.6	48.0	32.4
Fresh fruits	100.0	18.9	45.7	35.3
Fresh vegetables	100.0	19.2	49.3	31.5
Processed fruits	100.0	20.2	48.2	31.6
Processed vegetables	100.0	20.6	49.8	29.7
Other food at home	100.0	21.7	52.2	26.0
Sugar and other sweets	100.0	19.0	52.4	28.6
Fats and oils	100.0	18.3	51.3	30.3
Miscellaneous foods	100.0	23.3	52.8	23.9
Nonalcoholic beverages	100.0	21.7	52.0	26.3
Food prep. by hh, out-of-town trips	100.0	21.3	49.0	29.7
Food away from home	100.0	22.8	53.1	24.1
Alcoholic beverages	**100.0**	**30.1**	**49.9**	**20.1**
Housing	**100.0**	**22.9**	**50.8**	**26.2**
Shelter	100.0	24.7	51.6	23.7
Owned dwellings	100.0	19.1	56.3	24.7
Mortgage interest	100.0	24.1	63.4	12.5
Property taxes	100.0	9.8	47.5	42.7
Maintenance, repairs, insurance, other	100.0	12.4	42.1	45.6
Rented dwellings	100.0	41.2	39.4	19.4
Other lodging	100.0	12.9	57.8	29.4

(continued on next page)

(continued from previous page)

(youth are householders under age 35, middle-aged are householders aged 35 to 54, mature are householders aged 55 or older)

	all households	youth	middle-aged	mature
Utilities, fuels, and public services	100.0%	19.4%	48.1%	32.5%
Natural gas	100.0	17.2	47.2	35.6
Electricity	100.0	18.9	47.9	33.2
Fuel oil and other fuels	100.0	12.7	44.0	43.3
Telephone	100.0	23.3	49.2	27.5
Water and other public services	100.0	15.9	48.9	35.1
Household operations	100.0	26.4	44.4	29.1
Personal services	100.0	43.7	43.4	12.9
Other household expenses	100.0	10.9	45.4	43.7
Housekeeping supplies	100.0	19.6	49.1	31.3
Laundry and cleaning supplies	100.0	21.3	50.5	28.2
Other household products	100.0	18.5	49.7	31.7
Postage and stationery	100.0	19.5	46.8	33.7
Household furnishings and equipment	100.0	20.9	55.1	24.0
Household textiles	100.0	17.1	54.2	28.7
Furniture	100.0	24.9	52.0	23.1
Floor coverings	100.0	11.4	65.0	23.7
Major appliances	100.0	21.7	48.0	30.3
Small appliances, misc. housewares	100.0	20.2	50.1	29.8
Miscellaneous household equipment	100.0	20.9	58.7	20.4
Apparel and services	**100.0**	**21.8**	**56.5**	**21.7**
Men and boys	100.0	23.1	58.7	18.2
Men, aged 16 or older	100.0	22.5	57.6	19.9
Boys, aged 2 to 15	100.0	26.2	63.5	10.3
Women and girls	100.0	18.4	56.9	24.7
Women, aged 16 or older	100.0	17.8	55.2	27.1
Girls, aged 2 to 15	100.0	22.4	68.5	9.1
Babies under age 2	100.0	45.5	39.8	14.7
Footwear	100.0	19.8	57.9	22.3
Other apparel products and services	100.0	24.4	55.5	20.1
Transportation	**100.0**	**23.7**	**51.8**	**24.5**
Vehicle purchases (net outlay)	100.0	25.7	52.3	22.1
Cars and trucks, new	100.0	24.0	52.4	23.6
Cars and trucks, used	100.0	27.4	52.2	20.4
Other vehicles	100.0	41.6	48.7	9.7
Gasoline and motor oil	100.0	23.3	51.0	25.7
Other vehicle expenses	100.0	22.8	51.9	25.3
Vehicle finance charges	100.0	27.0	55.7	17.3
Maintenance and repairs	100.0	22.2	50.4	27.4
Vehicle insurance	100.0	20.5	51.0	28.5
Vehicle rental, licenses, other charges	100.0	24.5	53.3	22.2
Public transportation	100.0	16.9	50.7	32.4

(continued on next page)

(continued from previous page)
(youth are householders under age 35, middle-aged are householders aged 35 to 54, mature are householders aged 55 or older)

	all households	youth	middle-aged	mature
Health care	100.0%	14.0%	40.8%	45.2%
Health insurance	100.0	13.7	36.7	49.5
Medical services	100.0	14.9	46.9	38.2
Drugs	100.0	11.5	33.2	55.2
Medical supplies	100.0	16.7	50.3	32.9
Entertainment	100.0	22.7	54.0	23.2
Fees and admissions	100.0	20.5	53.3	26.2
Television, radios, sound equipment	100.0	25.2	53.0	21.9
Pets, toys, and playground equipment	100.0	23.3	55.9	20.8
Other supplies, equipment, and services	100.0	21.3	54.8	23.9
Personal-care products and services	100.0	19.5	51.4	29.1
Reading	100.0	19.2	49.3	31.5
Education	100.0	25.9	59.7	14.5
Tobacco products and smoking supplies	100.0	23.2	50.0	26.7
Cash contributions	100.0	10.3	51.4	38.3
Personal insurance and pensions	100.0	22.0	58.3	19.6
Life and other personal insurance	100.0	12.8	56.4	30.8
Pensions and Social Security	100.0	23.5	58.7	17.9
Miscellaneous	100.0	21.9	51.4	26.8

Source: Bureau of Labor Statistics and tabulations by New Strategist Publications

Market Shares of the Youth, Middle-Aged, and Mature Market in 2000

By 2000, households headed by 35-to-54-year-olds will dominate spending in all but a handful of product and service categories. The share controlled by householders under age 35 will slip below 20 percent.

(youth are householders under age 35, middle-aged are householders aged 35 to 54, mature are householders aged 55 or older)

	all households	youth	middle-aged	mature
Average annual expenditures	**100.0%**	**19.6%**	**54.2%**	**26.3%**
Food	**100.0**	**19.3**	**53.8**	**26.9**
Food at home	100.0	18.5	52.7	28.9
Cereals and bakery products	100.0	17.6	52.9	29.5
Cereals and cereal products	100.0	19.3	52.6	28.1
Bakery products	100.0	16.7	53.1	30.2
Meats, poultry, fish, and eggs	100.0	18.1	52.2	29.7
Beef	100.0	19.1	51.7	29.2
Pork	100.0	16.6	53.1	30.3
Other meats	100.0	18.3	52.5	29.2
Poultry	100.0	18.0	51.3	30.8
Fish and seafood	100.0	17.0	53.9	29.0
Eggs	100.0	19.4	49.5	31.2
Dairy products	100.0	19.4	52.4	28.2
Fresh milk and cream	100.0	20.1	51.7	28.2
Other dairy products	100.0	18.7	53.0	28.3
Fruits and vegetables	100.0	17.5	50.1	32.5
Fresh fruits	100.0	16.9	47.7	35.4
Fresh vegetables	100.0	17.1	51.3	31.6
Processed fruits	100.0	18.0	50.3	31.7
Processed vegetables	100.0	18.4	51.9	29.8
Other food at home	100.0	19.4	54.5	26.1
Sugar and other sweets	100.0	16.9	54.5	28.6
Fats and oils	100.0	16.3	53.3	30.3
Miscellaneous foods	100.0	20.8	55.2	24.0
Nonalcoholic beverages	100.0	19.4	54.2	26.4
Food prep. by hh, out-of-town trips	100.0	19.1	51.2	29.8
Food away from home	100.0	20.4	55.4	24.2
Alcoholic beverages	**100.0**	**27.1**	**52.6**	**20.3**
Housing	**100.0**	**20.5**	**53.1**	**26.4**
Shelter	100.0	22.1	54.0	23.8
Owned dwellings	100.0	16.9	58.4	24.6
Mortgage interest	100.0	21.5	66.0	12.5
Property taxes	100.0	8.6	49.0	42.4
Maintenance, repairs, insurance, other	100.0	11.0	43.6	45.4
Rented dwellings	100.0	37.7	42.3	20.0
Other lodging	100.0	11.3	59.6	29.1

(continued on next page)

(continued from previous page)

(youth are householders under age 35, middle-aged are householders aged 35 to 54, mature are householders aged 55 or older)

	all households	youth	middle-aged	mature
Utilities, fuels, and public services	100.0%	17.3%	50.1%	32.6%
Natural gas	100.0	15.4	49.0	35.6
Electricity	100.0	16.8	49.9	33.2
Fuel oil and other fuels	100.0	11.3	45.5	43.2
Telephone	100.0	20.9	51.5	27.7
Water and other public services	100.0	14.1	50.8	35.1
Household operations	100.0	23.8	46.7	29.5
Personal services	100.0	40.2	46.5	13.3
Other household expenses	100.0	9.6	46.9	43.5
Housekeeping supplies	100.0	17.5	51.2	31.4
Laundry and cleaning supplies	100.0	19.0	52.7	28.3
Other household products	100.0	16.5	51.7	31.8
Postage and stationery	100.0	17.4	48.8	33.8
Household furnishings and equipment	100.0	18.6	57.4	24.0
Household textiles	100.0	15.2	56.2	28.6
Furniture	100.0	22.3	54.4	23.2
Floor coverings	100.0	10.0	66.7	23.3
Major appliances	100.0	19.4	50.2	30.4
Small appliances, misc. housewares	100.0	18.0	52.2	29.8
Miscellaneous household equipment	100.0	18.6	61.0	20.4
Apparel and services	**100.0**	**19.4**	**58.9**	**21.7**
Men and boys	100.0	20.6	61.1	18.2
Men, aged 16 or older	100.0	20.1	60.0	20.0
Boys, aged 2 to 15	100.0	23.4	66.3	10.3
Women and girls	100.0	16.3	59.0	24.7
Women, aged 16 or older	100.0	15.8	57.2	27.0
Girls, aged 2 to 15	100.0	19.9	71.0	9.1
Babies under age 2	100.0	41.9	42.8	15.3
Footwear	100.0	17.6	60.1	22.2
Other apparel products and services	100.0	21.9	58.0	20.2
Transportation	**100.0**	**21.2**	**54.2**	**24.6**
Vehicle purchases (net outlay)	100.0	23.0	54.8	22.2
Cars and trucks, new	100.0	21.5	54.8	23.7
Cars and trucks, used	100.0	24.6	54.7	20.6
Other vehicles	100.0	38.1	52.0	10.0
Gasoline and motor oil	100.0	20.8	53.3	25.8
Other vehicle expenses	100.0	20.3	54.2	25.4
Vehicle finance charges	100.0	24.2	58.4	17.4
Maintenance and repairs	100.0	19.8	52.7	27.5
Vehicle insurance	100.0	18.3	53.2	28.6
Vehicle rental, licenses, other charges	100.0	21.9	55.7	22.4
Public transportation	100.0	15.0	52.6	32.4
Health care	**100.0**	**12.4**	**42.4**	**45.2**
Health insurance	100.0	12.2	38.2	49.6
Medical services	100.0	13.2	48.6	38.1
Drugs	100.0	10.3	34.6	55.2
Medical supplies	100.0	14.9	52.2	32.9

(continued on next page)

(continued from previous page)

(youth are householders under age 35, middle-aged are householders aged 35 to 54, mature are householders aged 55 or older)

	all households	youth	middle-aged	mature
Entertainment	**100.0%**	**20.3%**	**56.4%**	**23.3%**
Fees and admissions	100.0	18.3	55.5	26.2
Television, radios, sound equipment	100.0	22.6	55.4	22.0
Pets, toys, and playground equipment	100.0	20.8	58.3	20.9
Other supplies, equipment, and services	100.0	19.0	57.1	23.9
Personal-care products and services	**100.0**	**17.4**	**53.5**	**29.1**
Reading	**100.0**	**17.1**	**51.4**	**31.5**
Education	**100.0**	**23.1**	**62.3**	**14.5**
Tobacco products and smoking supplies	**100.0**	**20.8**	**52.3**	**26.9**
Cash contributions	**100.0**	**9.0**	**53.0**	**37.9**
Personal insurance and pensions	**100.0**	**19.6**	**60.7**	**19.6**
Life and other personal insurance	100.0	11.3	58.1	30.5
Pensions and Social Security	100.0	20.9	61.1	17.9
Miscellaneous	**100.0**	**19.5**	**53.6**	**26.9**

Source: Bureau of Labor Statistics and tabulations by New Strategist Publications

Spending by Age

Households headed by 45-to-54-year-olds have the highest incomes and spend the most—30 percent more than the average household in 1990.

(average annual expenditures for households by age of householder, 1990; number of households in thousands)

	all households	under 25	25 to 34	35 to 44	45 to 54	55 to 64	65 to 74	75 +
Number of households*	**96,968**	**7,581**	**21,287**	**21,003**	**14,855**	**12,162**	**11,318**	**8,761**
Income before taxes	**$31,889**	**$14,089**	**$32,325**	**$41,208**	**$43,451**	**$35,309**	**$21,501**	**$15,435**
Average number of persons								
per household	**2.6**	**1.8**	**2.8**	**3.3**	**2.9**	**2.3**	**1.9**	**1.6**
Average annual expenditures	**$28,369**	**$16,518**	**$28,107**	**$35,579**	**$36,996**	**$29,244**	**$20,895**	**$15,448**
Food	**$4,296**	**$2,761**	**$4,100**	**$5,380**	**$5,490**	**$4,430**	**$3,305**	**$2,406**
Food at home	2,485	1,285	2,340	3,134	3,008	2,601	2,106	1,654
Cereals and bakery products	368	183	332	475	440	378	324	268
Cereals and cereal products	129	72	125	170	143	129	103	88
Bakery products	240	111	206	305	297	249	221	179
Meats, poultry, fish, and eggs	668	296	628	801	850	747	598	405
Beef	218	97	217	262	268	231	207	116
Pork	132	59	114	156	180	153	117	85
Other meats	99	48	93	116	130	115	82	55
Poultry	108	39	103	126	136	125	98	70
Fish and seafood	82	35	73	107	102	90	66	57
Eggs	30	17	29	34	35	33	27	22
Dairy products	295	156	292	377	345	291	247	201
Fresh milk and cream	140	81	142	175	162	128	122	101
Other dairy products	155	75	150	202	184	163	126	101
Fruits and vegetables	408	188	366	490	468	447	392	347
Fresh fruits	127	46	113	141	144	155	128	120
Fresh vegetables	118	57	103	145	140	131	115	85
Processed fruits	93	48	85	114	104	88	89	90
Processed vegetables	70	37	65	89	80	72	61	52
Other food at home	746	462	722	991	904	737	545	433
Sugar and other sweets	94	48	81	124	119	95	79	69
Fats and oils	68	31	57	88	83	72	64	48
Miscellaneous foods	336	241	342	462	394	303	221	182
Nonalcoholic beverages	213	127	207	274	267	216	154	124
Food prep. by hh, out-of-town trips	35	15	35	43	41	51	27	10
Food away from home	1,811	1,476	1,760	2,246	2,482	1,830	1,199	752
Alcoholic beverages	**293**	**318**	**365**	**370**	**324**	**254**	**166**	**71**
Housing	**8,886**	**4,845**	**9,349**	**11,354**	**10,719**	**8,610**	**6,591**	**5,527**
Shelter	5,032	3,025	5,667	6,528	6,130	4,390	3,339	2,857
Owned dwellings	2,953	311	2,904	4,324	3,954	2,872	2,081	1,619
Mortgage interest	1,817	233	2,261	3,081	2,625	1,249	568	107

(continued on next page)

(continued from previous page)

(average annual expenditures for households by age of householder, 1990; number of households in thousands)

	all households	under 25	25 to 34	35 to 44	45 to 54	55 to 64	65 to 74	75 +
Property taxes	$597	$27	$304	$718	$711	$850	$824	$677
Maintenance, repairs, insurance, other	540	51	339	525	618	772	689	835
Rented dwellings	1,533	2,504	2,441	1,531	1,221	873	734	974
Other lodging	545	210	322	673	956	646	524	264
Utilities, fuels, public services	1,890	906	1,684	2,153	2,357	2,160	1,838	1,515
Natural gas	246	94	199	274	306	291	286	215
Electricity	758	317	668	860	947	918	733	606
Fuel oil and other fuels	100	17	63	109	111	129	129	148
Telephone	592	430	604	682	750	590	476	376
Water and other public services	193	48	150	229	244	232	215	169
Household operations	446	146	568	610	315	386	342	460
Personal services	219	100	449	354	54	57	29	189
Other household expenses	227	46	119	256	261	328	313	271
Housekeeping supplies	406	178	368	494	483	488	362	273
Laundry and cleaning supplies	113	47	113	142	137	125	86	70
Other household products	171	59	150	218	198	225	147	105
Postage and stationery	122	72	105	133	148	138	130	98
Household furnishings, equip.	1,111	590	1,063	1,570	1,433	1,186	709	422
Household textiles	99	39	79	124	145	122	90	34
Furniture	310	254	334	408	374	370	146	91
Floor coverings	92	9	54	153	150	91	56	53
Major appliances	147	65	150	173	175	188	115	89
Small appliances, misc. housewares	61	29	57	72	80	71	53	37
Misc. household equipment	402	194	390	640	508	345	250	117
Apparel and services	**1,617**	**1,034**	**1,571**	**2,310**	**2,165**	**1,557**	**972**	**489**
Men and boys	393	315	392	562	571	358	174	75
Men, aged 16 or older	324	303	300	420	503	325	152	71
Boys, aged 2 to 15	70	13	92	141	68	34	22	4
Women and girls	672	315	567	979	903	687	518	241
Women, aged 16 or older	585	289	471	775	827	657	490	230
Girls, aged 2 to 15	87	26	96	204	77	30	29	10
Babies under age 2	70	84	134	69	58	51	19	13
Footwear	225	94	209	347	288	217	134	87
Other apparel products and services	258	226	268	353	345	243	127	73
Transportation	**5,122**	**3,498**	**5,415**	**6,082**	**7,051**	**5,298**	**3,466**	**2,132**
Vehicle purchases (net outlay)	2,129	1,591	2,421	2,523	2,967	2,014	1,163	921
Cars and trucks, new	1,159	734	1,257	1,351	1,673	1,144	702	562
Cars and trucks, used	948	835	1,123	1,148	1,267	853	461	359
Other vehicles	22	23	41	25	27	16	1	0
Gasoline and motor oil	1,047	722	1,080	1,245	1,391	1,134	792	396
Other vehicle expenses	1,644	1,006	1,691	1,987	2,242	1,737	1,240	633
Vehicle finance charges	300	194	371	395	429	262	142	28

(continued on next page)

(continued from previous page)

(average annual expenditures for households by age of householder, 1990; number of households in thousands)

	all households	under 25	25 to 34	35 to 44	45 to 54	55 to 64	65 to 74	75 +
Maintenance and repairs	$591	$393	$581	$695	$778	$658	$493	$249
Vehicle insurance	563	323	521	651	784	646	470	296
Vehicle rental, licenses, other charges	190	97	217	247	251	170	135	60
Public transportation	302	179	223	326	450	414	271	182
Health care	**1,480**	**403**	**981**	**1,415**	**1,597**	**1,791**	**2,197**	**2,223**
Health insurance	581	106	391	485	583	700	1,014	960
Medical services	562	190	391	646	664	654	656	674
Drugs	252	65	135	183	236	340	455	501
Medical supplies	85	41	64	100	113	96	73	88
Entertainment	**1,422**	**833**	**1,472**	**1,837**	**1,966**	**1,507**	**914**	**423**
Fees and admissions	371	218	342	527	438	365	329	153
Television, radios, sound equip.	454	344	503	583	592	390	307	161
Pets, toys, and playground equip.	276	117	307	359	410	255	161	83
Other supplies, equip., services	321	155	321	367	527	497	116	26
Personal-care products, services	**364**	**212**	**315**	**447**	**478**	**412**	**305**	**218**
Reading	**153**	**75**	**134**	**188**	**184**	**163**	**156**	**112**
Education	**406**	**817**	**325**	**465**	**732**	**376**	**48**	**61**
Tobacco pdts., smoking supplies	**274**	**216**	**275**	**316**	**361**	**326**	**209**	**91**
Cash contributions	**816**	**146**	**411**	**876**	**1,299**	**903**	**937**	**1,141**
Personal insurance and pensions	**2,592**	**972**	**2,761**	**3,700**	**3,847**	**2,958**	**1,071**	**261**
Life and other personal insurance	345	49	225	444	555	467	341	131
Pensions and Social Security	2,248	922	2,536	3,256	3,292	2,491	730	130
Miscellaneous	**645**	**388**	**634**	**837**	**784**	**658**	**558**	**292**

*The Consumer Expenditure Survey uses consumer units as its sampling unit. See Glossary for definition of consumer unit.
Source: Bureau of Labor Statistics
Note: Numbers may not add to total due to rounding.

Indexed Spending by Age

Households headed by 35-to-54-year-olds spend far more than the average American household on almost every product and service category.

(indexed average annual expenditures for households by age of householder, 1990; number of households in thousands)

	all households	under 25	25 to 34	35 to 44	45 to 54	55 to 64	65 to 74	75 +
Number of households*	96,968	7,581	21,287	21,003	14,855	12,162	11,318	8,761
Income before taxes	$31,889	$14,089	$32,325	$41,208	$43,451	$35,309	$21,501	$15,435
Average number of persons per household	2.6	1.8	2.8	3.3	2.9	2.3	1.9	1.6
Average annual expenditures	100	58	99	125	130	103	74	54
Food	100	64	95	125	128	103	77	56
Food at home	100	52	94	126	121	105	85	67
Cereals and bakery products	100	50	90	129	120	103	88	73
Cereals and cereal products	100	56	97	132	111	100	80	68
Bakery products	100	46	86	127	124	104	92	75
Meats, poultry, fish, and eggs	100	44	94	120	127	112	90	61
Beef	100	44	100	120	123	106	95	53
Pork	100	45	86	118	136	116	89	64
Other meats	100	48	94	117	131	116	83	56
Poultry	100	36	95	117	126	116	91	65
Fish and seafood	100	43	89	130	124	110	80	70
Eggs	100	57	97	113	117	110	90	73
Dairy products	100	53	99	128	117	99	84	68
Fresh milk and cream	100	58	101	125	116	91	87	72
Other dairy products	100	48	97	130	119	105	81	65
Fruits and vegetables	100	46	90	120	115	110	96	85
Fresh fruits	100	36	89	111	113	122	101	94
Fresh vegetables	100	48	87	123	119	111	97	72
Processed fruits	100	52	91	123	112	95	96	97
Processed vegetables	100	53	93	127	114	103	87	74
Other food at home	100	62	97	133	121	99	73	58
Sugar and other sweets	100	51	86	132	127	101	84	73
Fats and oils	100	46	84	129	122	106	94	71
Miscellaneous foods	100	72	102	138	117	90	66	54
Nonalcoholic beverages	100	60	97	129	125	101	72	58
Food prep. by hh, out-of-town trips	100	43	100	123	117	146	77	29
Food away from home	100	82	97	124	137	101	66	42
Alcoholic beverages	100	109	125	126	111	87	57	24
Housing	100	55	105	128	121	97	74	62
Shelter	100	60	113	130	122	87	66	57
Owned dwellings	100	11	98	146	134	97	70	55
Mortgage interest	100	13	124	170	144	69	31	6

(continued on next page)

(indexed average annual expenditures for households by age of householder, 1990; number of households in thousands)

	all households	under 25	25 to 34	35 to 44	45 to 54	55 to 64	65 to 74	75 +
Property taxes	100	5	51	120	119	142	138	113
Maintenance, repairs, insurance, other	100	9	63	97	114	143	128	155
Rented dwellings	100	163	159	100	80	57	48	64
Other lodging	100	39	59	123	175	119	96	48
Utilities, fuels, public services	100	48	89	114	125	114	97	80
Natural gas	100	38	81	111	124	118	116	87
Electricity	100	42	88	113	125	121	97	80
Fuel oil and other fuels	100	17	63	109	111	129	129	148
Telephone	100	73	102	115	127	100	80	64
Water and other public services	100	25	78	119	126	120	111	88
Household operations	100	33	127	137	71	87	77	103
Personal services	100	46	205	162	25	26	13	86
Other household expenses	100	20	52	113	115	144	138	119
Housekeeping supplies	100	44	91	122	119	120	89	67
Laundry and cleaning supplies	100	42	100	126	121	111	76	62
Other household products	100	35	88	127	116	132	86	61
Postage and stationery	100	59	86	109	121	113	107	80
Household furnishings, equip.	100	53	96	141	129	107	64	38
Household textiles	100	39	80	125	146	123	91	34
Furniture	100	82	108	132	121	119	47	29
Floor coverings	100	10	59	166	163	99	61	58
Major appliances	100	44	102	118	119	128	78	61
Small appliances, misc. housewares	100	48	93	118	131	116	87	61
Misc. household equipment	100	48	97	159	126	86	62	29
Apparel and services	**100**	**64**	**97**	**143**	**134**	**96**	**60**	**30**
Men and boys	100	80	100	143	145	91	44	19
Men, aged 16 or older	100	94	93	130	155	100	47	22
Boys, aged 2 to 15	100	19	131	201	97	49	31	6
Women and girls	100	47	84	146	134	102	77	36
Women, aged 16 or older	100	49	81	132	141	112	84	39
Girls, aged 2 to 15	100	30	110	234	89	34	33	11
Babies under age 2	100	120	191	99	83	73	27	19
Footwear	100	42	93	154	128	96	60	39
Other apparel products, services	100	88	104	137	134	94	49	28
Transportation	**100**	**68**	**106**	**119**	**138**	**103**	**68**	**42**
Vehicle purchases (net outlay)	100	75	114	119	139	95	55	43
Cars and trucks, new	100	63	108	117	144	99	61	48
Cars and trucks, used	100	88	118	121	134	90	49	38
Other vehicles	100	105	186	114	123	73	5	0
Gasoline and motor oil	100	69	103	119	133	108	76	38
Other vehicle expenses	100	61	103	121	136	106	75	39
Vehicle finance charges	100	65	124	132	143	87	47	9
Maintenance and repairs	100	66	98	118	132	111	83	42
Vehicle insurance	100	57	93	116	139	115	83	53
Vehicle rental, licenses, other charges	100	51	114	130	132	89	71	32

(continued on next page)

(continued from previous page)
(indexed average annual expenditures for households by age of householder, 1990; number of households in thousands)

	all households	under 25	25 to 34	35 to 44	45 to 54	55 to 64	65 to 74	75 +
Public transportation	100	59	74	108	149	137	90	60
Health care	**100**	**27**	**66**	**96**	**108**	**121**	**148**	**150**
Health insurance	100	18	67	83	100	120	175	165
Medical services	100	34	70	115	118	116	117	120
Drugs	100	26	54	73	94	135	181	199
Medical supplies	100	48	75	118	133	113	86	104
Entertainment	**100**	**59**	**104**	**129**	**138**	**106**	**64**	**30**
Fees and admissions	100	59	92	142	118	98	89	41
Television, radios, sound equip.	100	76	111	128	130	86	68	35
Pets, toys, playground equip.	100	42	111	130	149	92	58	30
Other supplies, equip., services	100	48	100	114	164	155	36	8
Personal-care products, services	**100**	**58**	**87**	**123**	**131**	**113**	**84**	**60**
Reading	**100**	**49**	**88**	**123**	**120**	**107**	**102**	**73**
Education	**100**	**201**	**80**	**115**	**180**	**93**	**12**	**15**
Tobacco products, smoking supplies	**100**	**79**	**100**	**115**	**132**	**119**	**76**	**33**
Cash contributions	**100**	**18**	**50**	**107**	**159**	**111**	**115**	**140**
Personal insurance and pensions	**100**	**38**	**107**	**143**	**148**	**114**	**41**	**10**
Life and other personal insurance	100	14	65	129	161	135	99	38
Pensions and Social Security	100	41	113	145	146	111	32	6
Miscellaneous	**100**	**60**	**98**	**130**	**122**	**102**	**87**	**45**

*The Consumer Expenditure Survey uses consumer units as its sampling unit. See Glossary for definition of consumer unit.
Source: Bureau of Labor Statistics
Note: An index of 100 is the average for all households. An index of 132 means that spending for that group is 32 percent greater than the average for all households. An index of 68 means that spending is 32 percent below average.

Spending by Income

Not surprisingly, households with the highest incomes spend the most. Those with the lowest incomes spend more than they make, which may be an artifact of income underreporting.

(average annual expenditures for households by total household income, 1990; number of households in thousands; complete income reporters only)

	all households	under $10,000	$10,000 to $19,999	$20,000 to $29,999	$30,000 to $39,999	$40,000 to $49,999	$50,000 or more
Number of households*	83,424	17,151	17,467	14,690	10,726	7,819	15,572
Income before taxes	$31,889	$5,751	$14,614	$24,676	$34,422	$44,648	$78,711
Average number of persons per household	2.5	2	2	2.6	2.8	3	3.2
Avg. annual expenditures	$29,050	$12,880	$18,392	$24,535	$31,298	$38,397	$56,295
Food	**$4,352**	**$2,396**	**$3,119**	**$3,838**	**$4,681**	**$5,842**	**$7,143**
Food at home	2,509	1,593	2,071	2,341	2,744	3,278	3,492
Cereals and bakery products	370	229	306	339	394	479	536
Cereals and cereal products	130	85	111	126	131	166	177
Bakery products	241	144	195	213	263	313	359
Meats, poultry, fish, and eggs	667	462	554	643	717	865	877
Beef	220	157	168	221	245	298	281
Pork	130	95	118	130	137	166	154
Other meats	99	66	86	95	106	122	131
Poultry	107	75	90	95	120	139	146
Fish and seafood	81	47	62	71	78	105	132
Eggs	30	23	30	30	32	36	33
Dairy products	301	192	258	289	340	384	400
Fresh milk and cream	143	102	135	142	162	174	161
Other dairy products	159	90	123	147	178	209	239
Fruits and vegetables	412	273	341	380	434	526	581
Fresh fruits	128	82	106	117	135	150	193
Fresh vegetables	119	79	104	109	120	149	166
Processed fruits	94	60	77	86	98	129	129
Processed vegetables	71	52	54	69	81	97	91
Other food at home	759	438	612	690	859	1,024	1,097
Sugar and other sweets	95	58	79	82	106	133	134
Fats and oils	68	48	59	65	71	92	85
Miscellaneous foods	341	190	255	311	393	469	512
Nonalcoholic beverages	218	131	199	203	246	275	292
Food prep. by hh, out-of-town trips	36	11	21	28	42	55	73
Food away from home	1,843	804	1,048	1,497	1,937	2,564	3,651
Alcoholic beverages	**309**	**127**	**195**	**275**	**326**	**442**	**563**
Housing	**8,895**	**4,450**	**5,984**	**7,573**	**9,111**	**11,171**	**16,930**
Shelter	5,036	2,413	3,329	4,232	5,192	6,355	9,827
Owned dwellings	2,949	858	1,310	1,987	2,909	4,218	7,390

(continued on next page)

(continued from previous page)

(average annual expenditures for households by total household income, 1990; number of households in thousands; complete income reporters only)

	all households	under $10,000	$10,000 to $19,999	$20,000 to $29,999	$30,000 to $39,999	$40,000 to $49,999	$50,000 or more
Mortgage interest	$1,825	$303	$514	$1,090	$1,841	$2,828	$5,151
Property taxes	588	278	375	400	586	773	1,252
Maintenance, repairs, insurance, other	536	276	420	497	482	617	987
Rented dwellings	1,539	1,366	1,775	1,917	1,779	1,503	962
Other lodging	547	189	244	328	504	633	1,475
Utilities, fuels, and public services	1,870	1,216	1,586	1,847	1,969	2,241	2,679
Natural gas	241	164	204	219	254	294	351
Electricity	748	476	641	746	796	895	1,064
Fuel oil and other fuels	99	67	85	109	94	125	131
Telephone	590	401	503	589	616	701	823
Water and other public services	192	107	153	185	208	226	309
Household operations	436	179	243	305	391	490	1,061
Personal services	228	78	113	162	236	312	537
Other household expenses	208	101	130	144	155	178	525
Housekeeping supplies	430	239	277	377	464	566	742
Laundry and cleaning supplies	119	73	90	111	134	158	172
Other household products	181	89	109	152	197	249	330
Postage and stationery	131	78	78	114	134	159	240
Household furnishings, equip.	1,123	403	549	810	1,095	1,519	2,620
Household textiles	100	57	53	76	106	107	212
Furniture	294	85	169	229	334	429	629
Floor coverings	99	20	31	49	38	207	283
Major appliances	148	69	98	141	171	179	265
Small appliances, misc. housewares	66	28	40	49	72	82	141
Misc. household equipment	416	145	159	267	376	515	1,090
Apparel and services	**1,663**	**679**	**965**	**1,327**	**1,857**	**1,971**	**3,452**
Men and boys	401	150	201	301	387	503	924
Men, aged 16 or older	333	102	147	245	327	403	818
Boys, aged 2 to 15	68	48	53	56	60	99	106
Women and girls	690	289	394	570	861	813	1,346
Women, aged 16 or older	603	260	346	494	751	690	1,179
Girls, aged 2 to 15	87	28	47	76	110	123	166
Babies under age 2	71	30	51	70	77	110	116
Footwear	238	101	166	182	260	256	474
Other apparel products, services	263	110	154	203	271	288	593
Transportation	**5,199**	**2,003**	**3,420**	**4,556**	**6,034**	**7,185**	**9,731**
Vehicle purchases (net outlay)	2,171	758	1,484	1,760	2,637	2,957	4,168
Cars and trucks, new	1,149	229	659	826	1,262	1,531	2,747
Cars and trucks, used	996	512	819	923	1,355	1,322	1,388
Other vehicles	26	18	8	10	20	104	33

(continued on next page)

(continued from previous page)

(average annual expenditures for households by total household income, 1990; number of households in thousands; complete income reporters only)

	all households	under $10,000	$10,000 to $19,999	$20,000 to $29,999	$30,000 to $39,999	$40,000 to $49,999	$50,000 or more
Gasoline and motor oil	$1,054	$522	$764	$1,084	$1,236	$1,418	$1,630
Other vehicle expenses	1,671	609	1,022	1,496	1,875	2,517	3,153
Vehicle finance charges	301	69	159	277	377	484	595
Maintenance and repairs	606	267	385	541	679	937	1,060
Vehicle insurance	569	216	375	530	626	811	1,050
Vehicle rental, licenses, other charges	195	57	103	148	193	285	448
Public transportation	303	115	150	216	286	293	780
Health care	**1,497**	**1,016**	**1,429**	**1,427**	**1,510**	**1,606**	**2,098**
Health insurance	585	413	596	606	590	644	707
Medical services	565	330	451	511	555	619	982
Drugs	257	218	286	240	266	241	283
Medical supplies	90	54	96	70	98	102	127
Entertainment	**1,451**	**550**	**707**	**1,127**	**1,502**	**2,241**	**3,137**
Fees and admissions	375	98	154	301	400	536	902
Television, radios, sound equipment	461	208	297	404	527	639	843
Pets, toys, playground equip.	279	136	160	264	309	391	504
Other supplies, equip., svcs.	334	107	97	158	267	675	887
Personal-care products, svcs.	**375**	**182**	**241**	**323**	**422**	**522**	**659**
Reading	**156**	**62**	**98**	**142**	**182**	**202**	**298**
Education	**400**	**352**	**172**	**246**	**298**	**380**	**932**
Tobacco products and smoking supplies	**278**	**200**	**267**	**302**	**322**	**342**	**291**
Cash contributions	**875**	**231**	**449**	**739**	**912**	**982**	**2,113**
Personal insurance, pensions	**2,920**	**323**	**931**	**2,058**	**3,349**	**4,504**	**7,732**
Life, other personal insurance	349	118	173	266	352	449	830
Pensions and Social Security	2,570	206	759	1,792	2,997	4,055	6,902
Miscellaneous	**680**	**305**	**414**	**602**	**794**	**1,009**	**1,215**

*The Consumer Expenditure Survey uses consumer units as its sampling unit. See Glossary for definition of consumer unit.
Source: Bureau of Labor Statistics
Note: Numbers may not add to total due to rounding.

Indexed Spending by Income

Households with the highest incomes spend more than twice as much as the average household on many products and services, such as new cars and trucks, and personal insurances and pensions.

(indexed average annual expenditures for households by total household income, 1990; number of households in thousands; complete income reporters only)

	all households	under $10,000	$10,000 to $19,999	$20,000 to $29,999	$30,000 to $39,999	$40,000 to $49,999	$50,000 or more
Number of households*	83,424	17,151	17,467	14,690	10,726	7,819	15,572
Income before taxes	$31,889	$5,751	$14,614	$24,676	$34,422	$44,648	$78,711
Average number of persons per household	2.5	1.8	2.3	2.6	2.8	3.0	3.2
Average annual expenditures	100	44	63	84	108	132	194
Food	**100**	**55**	**72**	**88**	**108**	**134**	**164**
Food at home	100	64	83	93	109	131	139
Cereals and bakery products	100	62	83	92	106	129	145
Cereals and cereal products	100	65	86	97	101	128	136
Bakery products	100	60	81	88	109	130	149
Meats, poultry, fish, and eggs	100	69	83	96	107	130	131
Beef	100	71	76	100	111	135	128
Pork	100	73	91	100	105	128	118
Other meats	100	66	87	96	107	123	132
Poultry	100	70	84	89	112	130	136
Fish and seafood	100	58	77	88	96	130	163
Eggs	100	77	100	100	107	120	110
Dairy products	100	64	86	96	113	128	133
Fresh milk and cream	100	71	94	99	113	122	113
Other dairy products	100	56	77	92	112	131	150
Fruits and vegetables	100	66	83	92	105	128	141
Fresh fruits	100	64	83	91	105	117	151
Fresh vegetables	100	66	87	92	101	125	139
Processed fruits	100	64	82	91	104	137	137
Processed vegetables	100	73	76	97	114	137	128
Other food at home	100	58	81	91	113	135	145
Sugar and other sweets	100	61	83	86	112	140	141
Fats and oils	100	70	86	96	104	135	125
Miscellaneous foods	100	56	75	91	115	138	150
Nonalcoholic beverages	100	60	91	93	113	126	134
Food prep. by hh, out-of-town trips	100	31	58	78	117	153	203
Food away from home	100	44	57	81	105	139	198
Alcoholic beverages	**100**	**41**	**63**	**89**	**106**	**143**	**182**
Housing	**100**	**50**	**67**	**85**	**102**	**126**	**190**
Shelter	100	48	66	84	103	126	195
Owned dwellings	100	29	44	67	99	143	251

(continued on next page)

(indexed average annual expenditures for households by total household income, 1990; number of households in thousands; complete income reporters only)

	all households	under $10,000	$10,000 to $19,999	$20,000 to $29,999	$30,000 to $39,999	$40,000 to $49,999	$50,000 or more
Mortgage interest	100	17	28	60	101	155	282
Property taxes	100	47	64	68	100	131	213
Maintenance, repairs, insurance, other	100	52	78	93	90	115	184
Rented dwellings	100	89	115	125	116	98	63
Other lodging	100	35	45	60	92	116	270
Utilities, fuels, public services	100	65	85	99	105	120	143
Natural gas	100	68	85	91	105	122	146
Electricity	100	64	86	100	106	120	142
Fuel oil and other fuels	100	68	85	110	95	126	132
Telephone	100	68	85	100	104	119	139
Water and other public services	100	56	80	96	108	118	161
Household operations	100	41	56	70	90	112	243
Personal services	100	34	49	71	104	137	236
Other household expenses	100	49	62	69	75	86	252
Housekeeping supplies	100	56	64	88	108	132	173
Laundry and cleaning supplies	100	61	76	93	113	133	145
Other household products	100	49	60	84	109	138	182
Postage and stationery	100	59	60	87	102	121	183
Household furnishings, equip.	100	36	49	72	98	135	233
Household textiles	100	57	53	76	106	107	212
Furniture	100	29	58	78	114	146	214
Floor coverings	100	20	31	49	38	209	286
Major appliances	100	47	66	95	116	121	179
Small appliances, misc. housewares	100	42	61	74	109	124	214
Misc. household equipment	100	35	38	64	90	124	262
Apparel and services	**100**	**41**	**58**	**80**	**112**	**119**	**208**
Men and boys	100	37	50	75	97	125	230
Men, aged 16 or older	100	31	44	74	98	121	246
Boys, aged 2 to 15	100	70	78	82	88	146	156
Women and girls	100	42	57	83	125	118	195
Women, aged 16 or older	100	43	57	82	125	114	196
Girls, aged 2 to 15	100	32	54	87	126	141	191
Babies under age 2	100	42	72	99	108	155	163
Footwear	100	42	70	76	109	108	199
Other apparel products, services	100	42	59	77	103	110	225
Transportation	**100**	**39**	**66**	**88**	**116**	**138**	**187**
Vehicle purchases (net outlay)	100	35	68	81	121	136	192
Cars and trucks, new	100	20	57	72	110	133	239
Cars and trucks, used	100	51	82	93	136	133	139
Other vehicles	100	69	32	38	77	400	127
Gasoline and motor oil	100	50	72	103	117	135	155
Other vehicle expenses	100	36	61	90	112	151	189
Vehicle finance charges	100	23	53	92	125	161	198
Maintenance and repairs	100	44	63	89	112	155	175

(continued on next page)

(continued from previous page)

(indexed average annual expenditures for households by total household income, 1990; number of households in thousands; complete income reporters only)

	all households	under $10,000	$10,000 to $19,999	$20,000 to $29,999	$30,000 to $39,999	$40,000 to $49,999	$50,000 or more
Vehicle insurance	100	38	66	93	110	143	185
Vehicle rental, licenses, other charges	100	29	53	76	99	146	230
Public transportation	100	38	49	71	94	97	257
Health care	**100**	**68**	**95**	**95**	**101**	**107**	**140**
Health insurance	100	71	102	104	101	110	121
Medical services	100	58	80	90	98	110	174
Drugs	100	85	111	93	104	94	110
Medical supplies	100	60	107	78	109	113	141
Entertainment	**100**	**38**	**49**	**78**	**104**	**154**	**216**
Fees and admissions	100	26	41	80	107	143	241
Television, radios, sound equip.	100	45	64	88	114	139	183
Pets, toys, playground equip.	100	49	57	95	111	140	181
Other supplies, equip., services	100	32	29	47	80	202	266
Personal-care products, services	**100**	**48**	**64**	**86**	**113**	**139**	**176**
Reading	**100**	**40**	**63**	**91**	**117**	**129**	**191**
Education	**100**	**88**	**43**	**62**	**75**	**95**	**233**
Tobacco products and smoking supplies	**100**	**72**	**96**	**109**	**116**	**123**	**105**
Cash contributions	**100**	**26**	**51**	**84**	**104**	**112**	**241**
Personal insurance, pensions	**100**	**11**	**32**	**70**	**115**	**154**	**265**
Life, other personal insurance	100	34	50	76	101	129	238
Pensions and Social Security	100	8	30	70	117	158	269
Miscellaneous	**100**	**45**	**61**	**89**	**117**	**148**	**179**

*The Consumer Expenditure Survey uses consumer units as its sampling unit. See Glossary for definition of consumer unit.
Source: Bureau of Labor Statistics
Note: An index of 100 is the average for all households. An index of 132 means that spending for that group is 32 percent greater than the average for all households. An index of 68 means that spending is 32 percent below average.

Spending by Household Type

Married couples with children spend more than other types of households, partly because their households are larger than others.

(average annual expenditures for households by household type, 1990; number of households in thousands)

	all households	all married couples	married couple only	married couples with children	single parents	single persons	all others
Number of households*	96,968	52,649	20,653	27,991	6,074	27,263	10,982
Income before taxes	$31,889	$41,599	$36,196	$45,181	$17,415	$18,678	$26,140
Average number of persons per household	2.6	3.2	2.0	3.9	2.9	1.0	2.7
Avg. annual expenditures	$28,369	$35,992	$31,509	$38,999	$19,230	$17,126	$24,789
Food	**$4,296**	**$5,422**	**$4,567**	**$6,006**	**$3,539**	**$2,302**	**$4,267**
Food at home	2,485	3,167	2,507	3,589	2,397	1,130	2,628
Cereals and bakery products	368	471	356	548	359	169	373
Cereals and cereal products	129	164	117	196	141	55	138
Bakery products	240	307	239	352	219	114	243
Meats, poultry, fish, and eggs	668	851	697	941	693	272	760
Beef	218	283	240	309	246	79	236
Pork	132	166	132	185	138	51	167
Other meats	99	127	100	142	100	43	103
Poultry	108	135	113	150	106	49	126
Fish and seafood	82	104	85	114	70	37	95
Eggs	30	37	28	41	32	14	35
Dairy products	295	377	276	444	289	134	305
Fresh milk and cream	140	177	119	215	149	64	146
Other dairy products	155	200	157	229	140	71	156
Fruits and vegetables	408	511	445	544	362	206	441
Fresh fruits	127	160	149	164	99	66	136
Fresh vegetables	118	148	129	156	101	60	128
Processed fruits	93	115	95	128	92	48	100
Processed vegetables	70	88	72	95	70	32	78
Other food at home	746	957	732	1,113	693	348	752
Sugar and other sweets	94	122	97	140	90	43	89
Fats and oils	68	87	71	97	64	31	71
Miscellaneous foods	336	431	311	517	330	152	341
Nonalcoholic beverages	213	268	206	311	193	107	224
Food prep. by hh, out-of-town trips	35	49	47	47	16	15	28
Food away from home	1,811	2,255	2,061	2,417	1,142	1,172	1,639
Alcoholic beverages	**293**	**309**	**337**	**297**	**164**	**261**	**367**
Housing	**8,886**	**10,842**	**9,593**	**11,769**	**7,007**	**6,012**	**7,683**
Shelter	5,032	5,896	5,186	6,408	3,980	3,865	4,369
Owned dwellings	2,953	4,029	3,356	4,508	1,555	1,599	1,929

(continued on next page)

(continued from previous page)

(average annual expenditures for households by household type, 1990; number of households in thousands)

	all households	all married couples	married couple only	married couples with children	single parents	single persons	all others
Mortgage interest	$1,817	$2,565	$1,744	$3,135	$997	$838	$1,115
Property taxes	597	793	806	790	256	370	409
Maintenance, repairs, insurance, other	540	671	807	583	301	391	414
Rented dwellings	1,533	1,132	1,027	1,207	2,223	1,922	2,108
Other lodging	545	736	803	693	203	345	315
Utilities, fuels, public services	1,890	2,280	2,040	2,406	1,598	1,198	1,900
Natural gas	246	293	249	318	219	156	259
Electricity	758	941	850	988	632	446	725
Fuel oil and other fuels	100	131	129	137	48	57	87
Telephone	592	664	588	695	550	440	647
Water and other public services	193	251	224	267	150	100	170
Household operations	446	586	383	766	579	222	257
Personal services	219	307	47	521	432	44	114
Other household expenses	227	279	336	244	147	178	144
Housekeeping supplies	406	538	489	571	271	200	359
Laundry and cleaning supplies	113	149	121	169	98	46	115
Other household products	171	233	207	251	104	77	144
Postage and stationery	122	155	161	151	70	77	104
Household furnishings, equip.	1,111	1,542	1,494	1,619	577	526	792
Household textiles	99	144	129	158	34	40	66
Furniture	310	410	406	422	208	175	222
Floor coverings	92	139	87	185	29	36	41
Major appliances	147	199	196	196	112	68	113
Small appliances, misc. housewares	61	81	85	76	25	36	47
Misc. household equipment	402	569	591	583	170	172	301
Apparel and services	**1,617**	**2,032**	**1,657**	**2,274**	**1,502**	**886**	**1,506**
Men and boys	393	517	397	600	291	215	297
Men, aged 16 or older	324	422	376	449	83	207	278
Boys, aged 2 to 15	70	95	21	151	208	8	28
Women and girls	672	845	748	907	654	352	647
Women, aged 16 or older	585	720	724	708	482	340	603
Girls, aged 2 to 15	87	124	23	199	172	12	49
Babies under age 2	70	102	32	144	67	11	65
Footwear	225	270	235	293	265	123	240
Other apparel products, services	258	299	246	331	224	185	261
Transportation	**5,122**	**6,812**	**5,748**	**7,464**	**2,708**	**2,661**	**4,465**
Vehicle purchases (net outlay)	2,129	2,993	2,381	3,404	1,028	888	1,677
Cars and trucks, new	1,159	1,710	1,569	1,839	174	439	850
Cars and trucks, used	948	1,257	795	1,534	823	440	797
Other vehicles	22	26	17	31	31	9	30
Gasoline and motor oil	1,047	1,362	1,137	1,490	615	556	995

(continued on next page)

(continued from previous page)

(average annual expenditures for households by household type, 1990; number of households in thousands)

	all households	all married couples	married couple only	married couples with children	single parents	single persons	all others
Other vehicle expenses	$1,644	$2,109	$1,836	$2,267	$924	$948	$1,541
Vehicle finance charges	300	404	297	480	137	138	294
Maintenance and repairs	591	729	655	765	348	391	560
Vehicle insurance	563	728	648	762	307	315	529
Vehicle rental, licenses, other charges	190	248	237	259	131	105	156
Public transportation	302	347	393	304	142	268	259
Health care	**1,480**	**1,898**	**2,091**	**1,691**	**629**	**977**	**1,195**
Health insurance	581	744	859	640	229	389	471
Medical services	562	728	714	711	272	356	438
Drugs	252	321	402	246	84	173	210
Medical supplies	85	105	116	94	44	58	79
Entertainment	**1,422**	**1,863**	**1,668**	**2,016**	**880**	**841**	**1,050**
Fees and admissions	371	487	442	527	219	235	237
Television, radios, sound equip.	454	552	443	623	397	290	423
Pets, toys, playground equip.	276	358	282	408	166	168	212
Other supplies, equip., services	321	466	501	458	97	148	179
Personal-care products, services	**364**	**467**	**418**	**500**	**270**	**209**	**307**
Reading	**153**	**190**	**186**	**193**	**79**	**109**	**126**
Education	**406**	**500**	**253**	**682**	**261**	**312**	**269**
Tobacco products and smoking supplies	**274**	**321**	**269**	**340**	**208**	**156**	**378**
Cash contributions	**816**	**1,035**	**1,197**	**935**	**351**	**609**	**537**
Personal insurance, pensions	**2,592**	**3,546**	**2,875**	**4,022**	**1,157**	**1,293**	**2,037**
Life, other personal insurance	345	518	448	545	137	112	209
Pensions and Social Security	2,248	3,028	2,427	3,477	1,020	1,180	1,839
Miscellaneous	**645**	**754**	**650**	**811**	**475**	**499**	**579**

*The Consumer Expenditure Survey uses consumer units as its sampling unit. See Glossary for definition of consumer unit.

Source: Bureau of Labor Statistics

Note: Numbers may not add to total due to rounding.

Indexed Spending by Household Type

Above-average spending is the norm for married couples. Other types of households spend more than average on only a handful of products and services, such as rent.

(indexed average annual expenditures for households by household type, 1990; number of households in thousands)

	all households	all married couples	married couple only	married couples with children	single parents	single persons	all others
Number of households*	96,968	52,649	20,653	27,991	6,074	27,263	10,982
Income before taxes	$31,889	$41,599	$36,196	$45,181	$17,415	$18,678	$26,140
Average number of persons per household	2.6	3.2	2.0	3.9	2.9	1.0	2.7
Average annual expenditures	**100**	**127**	**111**	**137**	**68**	**60**	**87**
Food	**100**	**126**	**106**	**140**	**82**	**54**	**99**
Food at home	100	127	101	144	96	45	106
Cereals and bakery products	100	128	97	149	98	46	101
Cereals and cereal products	100	127	91	152	109	43	107
Bakery products	100	128	100	147	91	48	101
Meats, poultry, fish, and eggs	100	127	104	141	104	41	114
Beef	100	130	110	142	113	36	108
Pork	100	126	100	140	105	39	126
Other meats	100	128	101	143	101	43	104
Poultry	100	125	105	139	98	45	117
Fish and seafood	100	127	104	139	85	45	116
Eggs	100	123	93	137	107	47	117
Dairy products	100	128	94	151	98	45	103
Fresh milk and cream	100	126	85	154	106	46	105
Other dairy products	100	129	101	148	90	46	101
Fruits and vegetables	100	125	109	133	89	50	108
Fresh fruits	100	126	117	129	78	52	107
Fresh vegetables	100	125	109	132	86	51	108
Processed fruits	100	124	102	138	99	52	107
Processed vegetables	100	126	103	136	100	46	111
Other food at home	100	128	98	149	93	47	101
Sugar and other sweets	100	130	103	149	96	46	94
Fats and oils	100	128	104	143	94	46	104
Miscellaneous foods	100	128	93	154	98	45	101
Nonalcoholic beverages	100	126	97	146	91	50	105
Food prep. by hh, out-of-town trips	100	140	134	134	46	43	80
Food away from home	100	125	114	133	63	65	90
Alcoholic beverages	**100**	**105**	**115**	**101**	**56**	**89**	**125**
Housing	**100**	**122**	**108**	**132**	**79**	**68**	**86**
Shelter	100	117	103	127	79	77	87

(continued on next page)

(indexed average annual expenditures for households by household type, 1990; number of households in thousands)

	all households	all married couples	married couple only	married couples with children	single parents	single persons	all others
Owned dwellings	100	136	114	153	53	54	65
Mortgage interest	100	141	96	173	55	46	61
Property taxes	100	133	135	132	43	62	69
Maintenance, repairs, insurance, other	100	124	149	108	56	72	77
Rented dwellings	100	74	67	79	145	125	138
Other lodging	100	135	147	127	37	63	58
Utilities, fuels, public services	100	121	108	127	85	63	101
Natural gas	100	119	101	129	89	63	105
Electricity	100	124	112	130	83	59	96
Fuel oil and other fuels	100	131	129	137	48	57	87
Telephone	100	112	99	117	93	74	109
Water and other public services	100	130	116	138	78	52	88
Household operations	100	131	86	172	130	50	58
Personal services	100	140	21	238	197	20	52
Other household expenses	100	123	148	107	65	78	63
Housekeeping supplies	100	133	120	141	67	49	88
Laundry and cleaning supplies	100	132	107	150	87	41	102
Other household products	100	136	121	147	61	45	84
Postage and stationery	100	127	132	124	57	63	85
Household furnishings, equip.	100	139	134	146	52	47	71
Household textiles	100	145	130	160	34	40	66
Furniture	100	132	131	136	67	56	72
Floor coverings	100	151	95	201	32	39	44
Major appliances	100	135	133	133	76	46	77
Small appliances, misc. housewares	100	133	139	125	41	59	77
Misc. household equipment	100	142	147	145	42	43	75
Apparel and services	**100**	**126**	**102**	**141**	**93**	**55**	**93**
Men and boys	100	132	101	153	74	55	76
Men, aged 16 or older	100	130	116	139	26	64	86
Boys, aged 2 to 15	100	136	30	216	297	11	40
Women and girls	100	126	111	135	97	52	96
Women, aged 16 or older	100	123	124	121	82	58	103
Girls, aged 2 to 15	100	143	26	229	198	14	56
Babies under age 2	100	146	46	206	96	16	92
Footwear	100	120	104	130	118	55	107
Other apparel products, services	100	116	95	128	87	72	101
Transportation	**100**	**133**	**112**	**146**	**53**	**52**	**87**
Vehicle purchases (net outlay)	100	141	112	160	48	42	79
Cars and trucks, new	100	148	135	159	15	38	73
Cars and trucks, used	100	133	84	162	87	46	84
Other vehicles	100	118	77	141	141	41	137
Gasoline and motor oil	100	130	109	142	59	53	95
Other vehicle expenses	100	128	112	138	56	58	94
Vehicle finance charges	100	135	99	160	46	46	98
Maintenance and repairs	100	123	111	129	59	66	95

(continued on next page)

(continued from previous page)

(indexed average annual expenditures for households by household type, 1990; number of households in thousands)

	all households	all married couples	married couple only	married couples with children	single parents	single persons	all others
Vehicle insurance	100	129	115	135	55	56	94
Vehicle rental, licenses, other charges	100	131	125	136	69	55	82
Public transportation	100	115	130	101	47	89	86
Health care	**100**	**128**	**141**	**114**	**43**	**66**	**81**
Health insurance	100	128	148	110	39	67	81
Medical services	100	130	127	127	48	63	78
Drugs	100	127	160	98	33	69	83
Medical supplies	100	124	136	111	52	68	93
Entertainment	**100**	**131**	**117**	**142**	**62**	**59**	**74**
Fees and admissions	100	131	119	142	59	63	64
Television, radios, sound equip.	100	122	98	137	87	64	93
Pets, toys, playground equip.	100	130	102	148	60	61	77
Other supplies, equip., services	100	145	156	143	30	46	56
Personal-care products, services	**100**	**128**	**115**	**137**	**74**	**57**	**84**
Reading	**100**	**124**	**122**	**126**	**52**	**71**	**82**
Education	**100**	**123**	**62**	**168**	**64**	**77**	**66**
Tobacco products and smoking supplies	**100**	**117**	**98**	**124**	**76**	**57**	**138**
Cash contributions	**100**	**127**	**147**	**115**	**43**	**75**	**66**
Personal insurance and pensions	**100**	**137**	**111**	**155**	**45**	**50**	**79**
Life and other personal insurance	100	150	130	158	40	32	61
Pensions and Social Security	100	135	108	155	45	52	82
Miscellaneous	**100**	**117**	**101**	**126**	**74**	**77**	**90**

*The Consumer Expenditure Survey uses consumer units as its sampling unit. See Glossary for definition of consumer unit.

Source: Bureau of Labor Statistics

Note: An index of 100 is the average for all households. An index of 132 means that spending for that group is 32 percent greater than the average for all households. An index of 68 means that spending is 32 percent below average.

Spending by Married Couples

Married couples with children aged 18 or older at home earn and spend more than other married couples. Many of these households have three or more earners.

(average annual expenditures for married-couple households with and without children, 1990; number of households in thousands)

	all households	all married couples	married couple only	married couples with children	oldest child under 6	oldest child 6 to 17	oldest child 18 or older	other married couples
				married couples with children				
Number of households*	96,968	52,649	20,653	27,991	6,403	13,701	7,886	4,005
Income before taxes	$31,889	$41,599	$36,196	$45,181	$40,687	$44,628	$50,200	$44,902
Average number of persons per household	2.6	3.2	2.0	3.9	3.4	4.2	3.9	4.9
Average annual expenditures	$28,369	$35,992	$31,509	$38,999	$35,009	$38,779	$42,785	$38,327
Food	**$4,296**	**$5,422**	**$4,567**	**$6,006**	**$4,660**	**$6,187**	**$6,887**	**$5,933**
Food at home	2,485	3,167	2,507	3,589	2,972	3,660	4,034	3,788
Cereals and bakery products	368	471	356	548	424	575	610	550
Cereals and cereal products	129	164	117	196	162	209	202	196
Bakery products	240	307	239	352	262	366	408	354
Meats, poultry, fish, and eggs	668	851	697	941	751	925	1,157	1,063
Beef	218	283	240	309	241	302	387	338
Pork	132	166	132	185	150	181	228	223
Other meats	99	127	100	142	105	139	185	162
Poultry	108	135	113	150	115	152	178	155
Fish and seafood	82	104	85	114	105	110	131	132
Eggs	30	37	28	41	34	41	47	54
Dairy products	295	377	276	444	389	454	474	451
Fresh milk and cream	140	177	119	215	194	216	231	230
Other dairy products	155	200	157	229	195	238	243	221
Fruits and vegetables	408	511	445	544	459	550	611	646
Fresh fruits	127	160	149	164	129	171	183	186
Fresh vegetables	118	148	129	156	129	156	182	193
Processed fruits	93	115	95	128	125	121	145	135
Processed vegetables	70	88	72	95	77	101	101	132
Other food at home	746	957	732	1,113	950	1,156	1,182	1,078
Sugar and other sweets	94	122	97	140	95	156	152	130
Fats and oils	68	87	71	97	76	100	112	102
Miscellaneous foods	336	431	311	517	488	531	517	472
Nonalcoholic beverages	213	268	206	311	247	318	357	296
Food prep. by hh, out-of-town trips	35	49	47	47	44	50	44	79
Food away from home	1,811	2,255	2,061	2,417	1,687	2,527	2,853	2,145
Alcoholic beverages	**293**	**309**	**337**	**297**	**266**	**289**	**341**	**238**
Housing	**8,886**	**10,842**	**9,593**	**11,769**	**12,723**	**11,672**	**11,171**	**10,807**
Shelter	5,032	5,896	5,186	6,408	7,060	6,375	5,934	5,986

(continued on next page)

(continued from previous page)

(average annual expenditures for married-couple households with and without children, 1990; number of households in thousands)

	all households	all married couples	married couple only	married couples with children	married couples with children	married couples with children	married couples with children	other married couples
				married couples with children	oldest child under 6	oldest child 6 to 17	oldest child 18 or older	
Owned dwellings	$2,953	$4,029	$3,356	$4,508	$4,526	$4,618	$4,301	$4,147
Mortgage interest	1,817	2,565	1,744	3,135	3,425	3,343	2,539	2,810
Property taxes	597	793	806	790	628	718	1,044	746
Maintenance, repairs, insurance, other	540	671	807	583	473	557	717	591
Rented dwellings	1,533	1,132	1,027	1,207	2,006	1,077	785	1,148
Other lodging	545	736	803	693	527	681	848	691
Utilities, fuels, public services	1,890	2,280	2,040	2,406	2,033	2,367	2,775	2,634
Natural gas	246	293	249	318	256	309	385	338
Electricity	758	941	850	988	822	987	1,125	1,083
Fuel oil and other fuels	100	131	129	137	96	143	162	100
Telephone	592	664	588	695	651	650	810	833
Water and other public services	193	251	224	267	207	279	293	280
Household operations	446	586	383	766	1,576	669	276	379
Personal services	219	307	47	521	1,325	423	39	156
Other household expenses	227	279	336	244	250	246	238	223
Housekeeping supplies	406	538	489	571	470	594	621	574
Laundry and cleaning supplies	113	149	121	169	135	175	190	164
Other household products	171	233	207	251	189	271	269	255
Postage and stationery	122	155	161	151	146	147	163	155
Household furnishings, equip.	1,111	1,542	1,494	1,619	1,584	1,667	1,565	1,234
Household textiles	99	144	129	158	135	142	212	123
Furniture	310	410	406	422	442	459	341	351
Floor coverings	92	139	87	185	240	198	100	87
Major appliances	147	199	196	196	182	200	202	237
Small appliances, misc. housewares	61	81	85	76	65	69	100	89
Misc. household equipment	402	569	591	583	520	600	610	347
Apparel and services	**1,617**	**2,032**	**1,657**	**2,274**	**1,881**	**2,373**	**2,450**	**2,323**
Men and boys	393	517	397	600	405	664	651	573
Men, aged 16 or older	324	422	376	449	317	429	608	479
Boys, aged 2 to 15	70	95	21	151	88	235	44	94
Women and girls	672	845	748	907	605	967	1,080	918
Women, aged 16 or older	585	720	724	708	487	669	993	786
Girls, aged 2 to 15	87	124	23	199	118	298	87	132
Babies under age 2	70	102	32	144	370	75	70	184
Footwear	225	270	235	293	209	332	293	300
Other apparel products, services	258	299	246	331	291	335	356	348
Transportation	**5,122**	**6,812**	**5,748**	**7,464**	**6,229**	**7,163**	**8,993**	**7,744**
Vehicle purchases (net outlay)	2,129	2,993	2,381	3,404	2,767	3,411	3,907	3,285
Cars and trucks, new	1,159	1,710	1,569	1,839	1,552	1,832	2,084	1,534
Cars and trucks, used	948	1,257	795	1,534	1,190	1,549	1,786	1,707
Other vehicles	22	26	17	31	25	30	37	45

(continued on next page)

(continued from previous page)

(average annual expenditures for married-couple households with and without children, 1990; number of households in thousands)

	all households	all married couples	married couple only	married couples with children				other married couples
				married couples with children	oldest child under 6	oldest child 6 to 17	oldest child 18 or older	
Gasoline and motor oil	$1,047	$1,362	$1,137	$1,490	$1,190	$1,454	$1,797	$1,627
Other vehicle expenses	1,644	2,109	1,836	2,267	2,007	2,035	2,882	2,416
Vehicle finance charges	300	404	297	480	477	436	560	430
Maintenance and repairs	591	729	655	765	636	709	971	861
Vehicle insurance	563	728	648	762	632	654	1,054	904
Vehicle rental, licenses, other charges	190	248	237	259	263	236	297	221
Public transportation	302	347	393	304	265	263	407	415
Health care	**1,480**	**1,898**	**2,091**	**1,691**	**1,551**	**1,597**	**1,969**	**2,356**
Health insurance	581	744	859	640	578	574	806	879
Medical services	562	728	714	711	718	705	715	916
Drugs	252	321	402	246	197	221	330	435
Medical supplies	85	105	116	94	58	97	119	125
Entertainment	**1,422**	**1,863**	**1,668**	**2,016**	**1,613**	**2,216**	**1,992**	**1,803**
Fees and admissions	371	487	442	527	350	610	527	439
Television, radios, sound equip.	454	552	443	623	499	684	620	613
Pets, toys, playground equip.	276	358	282	408	407	449	335	402
Other supplies, equip., services	321	466	501	458	357	473	511	349
Personal-care products, services	**364**	**467**	**418**	**500**	**370**	**499**	**620**	**497**
Reading	**153**	**190**	**186**	**193**	**184**	**193**	**200**	**188**
Education	**406**	**500**	**253**	**682**	**255**	**555**	**1,247**	**506**
Tobacco products and smoking supplies	**274**	**321**	**269**	**340**	**249**	**324**	**441**	**460**
Cash contributions	**816**	**1,035**	**1,197**	**935**	**535**	**868**	**1,374**	**897**
Personal insurance, pensions	**2,592**	**3,546**	**2,875**	**4,022**	**3,795**	**4,011**	**4,226**	**3,685**
Life, other personal insurance	345	518	448	545	377	570	636	694
Pensions and Social Security	2,248	3,028	2,427	3,477	3,417	3,440	3,590	2,991
Miscellaneous	**645**	**754**	**650**	**811**	**699**	**832**	**873**	**891**

*The Consumer Expenditure Survey uses consumer units as its sampling unit. See Glossary for definition of consumer unit.
Source: Bureau of Labor Statistics
Note: Other married couples are those who are living with extended family members or unrelated individuals. Numbers may not add to total due to rounding.

Indexed Spending by Married Couples

Married couples with children under age 6 spend six times as much as the average household on personal services—largely day-care costs.

(indexed average annual expenditures for married-couple households with and without children, 1990; number of households in thousands)

	all households	all married couples	married couple only	married couples with children	oldest child under 6	oldest child 6 to 17	oldest child 18 or older	other married couples
				married couples with children				
Number of households*	96,968	52,649	20,653	27,991	6,403	13,701	7,886	4,005
Income before taxes	$31,889	$41,599	$36,196	$45,181	$40,687	$44,628	$50,200	$44,902
Average number of persons per household	2.6	3.2	2.0	3.9	3.4	4.2	3.9	4.9
Average annual expenditures	100	127	111	137	123	137	151	135
Food	**100**	**126**	**106**	**140**	**108**	**144**	**160**	**138**
Food at home	100	127	101	144	120	147	162	152
Cereals and bakery products	100	128	97	149	115	156	166	149
Cereals and cereal products	100	127	91	152	126	162	157	152
Bakery products	100	128	100	147	109	153	170	148
Meats, poultry, fish, and eggs	100	127	104	141	112	138	173	159
Beef	100	130	110	142	111	139	178	155
Pork	100	126	100	140	114	137	173	169
Other meats	100	128	101	143	106	140	187	164
Poultry	100	125	105	139	106	141	165	144
Fish and seafood	100	127	104	139	128	134	160	161
Eggs	100	123	93	137	113	137	157	180
Dairy products	100	128	94	151	132	154	161	153
Fresh milk and cream	100	126	85	154	139	154	165	164
Other dairy products	100	129	101	148	126	154	157	143
Fruits and vegetables	100	125	109	133	113	135	150	158
Fresh fruits	100	126	117	129	102	135	144	146
Fresh vegetables	100	125	109	132	109	132	154	164
Processed fruits	100	124	102	138	134	130	156	145
Processed vegetables	100	126	103	136	110	144	144	189
Other food at home	100	128	98	149	127	155	158	145
Sugar and other sweets	100	130	103	149	101	166	162	138
Fats and oils	100	128	104	143	112	147	165	150
Miscellaneous foods	100	128	93	154	145	158	154	140
Nonalcoholic beverages	100	126	97	146	116	149	168	139
Food prep. by hh, out-of-town trips	100	140	134	134	126	143	126	226
Food away from home	100	125	114	133	93	140	158	118
Alcoholic beverages	**100**	**105**	**115**	**101**	**91**	**99**	**116**	**81**
Housing	**100**	**122**	**108**	**132**	**143**	**131**	**126**	**122**
Shelter	100	117	103	127	140	127	118	119
Owned dwellings	100	136	114	153	153	156	146	140

(continued on next page)

(indexed average annual expenditures for married-couple households with and without children, 1990; number of households in thousands)

	all households	all married couples	married couple only	married couples with children	oldest child under 6	oldest child 6 to 17	oldest child 18 or older	other married couples
				married couples with children				
Mortgage interest	100	141	96	173	188	184	140	155
Property taxes	100	133	135	132	105	120	175	125
Maintenance, repairs, insurance, other	100	124	149	108	88	103	133	109
Rented dwellings	100	74	67	79	131	70	51	75
Other lodging	100	135	147	127	97	125	156	127
Utilities, fuels, public services	100	121	108	127	108	125	147	139
Natural gas	100	119	101	129	104	126	157	137
Electricity	100	124	112	130	108	130	148	143
Fuel oil and other fuels	100	131	129	137	96	143	162	100
Telephone	100	112	99	117	110	110	137	141
Water and other public services	100	130	116	138	107	145	152	145
Household operations	100	131	86	172	353	150	62	85
Personal services	100	140	21	238	605	193	18	71
Other household expenses	100	123	148	107	110	108	105	98
Housekeeping supplies	100	133	120	141	116	146	153	141
Laundry and cleaning supplies	100	132	107	150	119	155	168	145
Other household products	100	136	121	147	111	158	157	149
Postage and stationery	100	127	132	124	120	120	134	127
Household furnishings, equip.	100	139	134	146	143	150	141	111
Household textiles	100	145	130	160	136	143	214	124
Furniture	100	132	131	136	143	148	110	113
Floor coverings	100	151	95	201	261	215	109	95
Major appliances	100	135	133	133	124	136	137	161
Small appliances, misc. housewares	100	133	139	125	107	113	164	146
Misc. household equipment	100	142	147	145	129	149	152	86
Apparel and services	**100**	**126**	**102**	**141**	**116**	**147**	**152**	**144**
Men and boys	100	132	101	153	103	169	166	146
Men, aged 16 or older	100	130	116	139	98	132	188	148
Boys, aged 2 to 15	100	136	30	216	126	336	63	134
Women and girls	100	126	111	135	90	144	161	137
Women, aged 16 or older	100	123	124	121	83	114	170	134
Girls, aged 2 to 15	100	143	26	229	136	343	100	152
Babies under age 2	100	146	46	206	529	107	100	263
Footwear	100	120	104	130	93	148	130	133
Other apparel products, services	100	116	95	128	113	130	138	135
Transportation	**100**	**133**	**112**	**146**	**122**	**140**	**176**	**151**
Vehicle purchases (net outlay)	100	141	112	160	130	160	184	154
Cars and trucks, new	100	148	135	159	134	158	180	132
Cars and trucks, used	100	133	84	162	126	163	188	180
Other vehicles	100	118	77	141	114	136	168	205
Gasoline and motor oil	100	130	109	142	114	139	172	155
Other vehicle expenses	100	128	112	138	122	124	175	147
Vehicle finance charges	100	135	99	160	159	145	187	143
Maintenance and repairs	100	123	111	129	108	120	164	146

(continued on next page)

(continued from previous page)
(indexed average annual expenditures for married-couple households with and without children, 1990; number of households in thousands)

	all households	all married couples	married couple only	married couples with children				other married couples
				married couples with children	oldest child under 6	oldest child 6 to 17	oldest child 18 or older	
Vehicle insurance	100	129	115	135	112	116	187	161
Vehicle rental, licenses, other charges	100	131	125	136	138	124	156	116
Public transportation	100	115	130	101	88	87	135	137
Health care	**100**	**128**	**141**	**114**	**105**	**108**	**133**	**159**
Health insurance	100	128	148	110	99	99	139	151
Medical services	100	130	127	127	128	125	127	163
Drugs	100	127	160	98	78	88	131	173
Medical supplies	100	124	136	111	68	114	140	147
Entertainment	**100**	**131**	**117**	**142**	**113**	**156**	**140**	**127**
Fees and admissions	100	131	119	142	94	164	142	118
Television, radios, sound equip.	100	122	98	137	110	151	137	135
Pets, toys, playground equip.	100	130	102	148	147	163	121	146
Other supplies, equip., services	100	145	156	143	111	147	159	109
Personal care products, services	**100**	**128**	**115**	**137**	**102**	**137**	**170**	**137**
Reading	**100**	**124**	**122**	**126**	**120**	**126**	**131**	**123**
Education	**100**	**123**	**62**	**168**	**63**	**137**	**307**	**125**
Tobacco products and smoking supplies	**100**	**117**	**98**	**124**	**91**	**118**	**161**	**168**
Cash contributions	**100**	**127**	**147**	**115**	**66**	**106**	**168**	**110**
Personal insurance and pensions	**100**	**137**	**111**	**155**	**146**	**155**	**163**	**142**
Life and other personal insurance	100	150	130	158	109	165	184	201
Pensions and Social Security	100	135	108	155	152	153	160	133
Miscellaneous	**100**	**117**	**101**	**126**	**108**	**129**	**135**	**138**

*The Consumer Expenditure Survey uses consumer units as its sampling unit. See Glossary for definition of consumer unit.
Source: Bureau of Labor Statistics
Note: An index of 100 is the average for all households. An index of 132 means that spending for that group is 32 percent greater than the average for all households. An index of 68 means that spending is 32 percent below average. Other married couples are those who are living with extended family members or unrelated individuals.

Spending by Household Size

Household income and spending rise with household size through four people. Both incomes and spending are less for households with five or more people.

(average annual expenditures for households by household size, 1990; number of households in thousands)

	all households	one person	two or more persons	two persons	three persons	four persons	five or more persons
Number of households*	96,968	27,263	69,705	29,508	15,999	14,107	10,091
Income before taxes	$31,889	$18,678	$37,187	$32,790	$37,719	$43,545	$40,602
Average number of persons per household	2.6	1.0	3.2	2.0	3.0	4.0	5.6
Avg. annual expenditures	$28,369	$17,126	$32,768	$28,836	$33,672	$37,477	$36,260
Food	**$4,296**	**$2,302**	**$5,077**	**$4,295**	**$5,119**	**$5,879**	**$6,183**
Food at home	2,485	1,130	3,016	2,393	2,977	3,565	4,135
Cereals and bakery products	368	169	446	339	440	552	622
Cereals and cereal products	129	55	157	112	147	196	252
Bakery products	240	114	289	227	292	356	370
Meats, poultry, fish, and eggs	668	272	823	666	834	910	1,144
Beef	218	79	272	225	268	301	373
Pork	132	51	164	129	175	177	229
Other meats	99	43	121	95	116	139	177
Poultry	108	49	131	106	132	146	178
Fish and seafood	82	37	100	82	107	107	130
Eggs	30	14	36	28	35	40	56
Dairy products	295	134	359	267	346	450	520
Fresh milk and cream	140	64	170	118	165	208	277
Other dairy products	155	71	189	149	181	242	243
Fruits and vegetables	408	206	486	423	469	541	625
Fresh fruits	127	66	151	140	137	160	192
Fresh vegetables	118	60	141	123	138	149	187
Processed fruits	93	48	110	91	111	133	133
Processed vegetables	70	32	85	69	83	99	113
Other food at home	746	348	901	699	889	1,111	1,224
Sugar and other sweets	94	43	114	91	102	140	167
Fats and oils	68	31	83	67	83	90	118
Miscellaneous foods	336	152	407	300	412	511	568
Nonalcoholic beverages	213	107	254	201	251	325	319
Food prep. by hh, out-of-town trips	35	15	43	40	41	45	52
Food away from home	1,811	1,172	2,061	1,902	2,142	2,314	2,048
Alcoholic beverages	**293**	**261**	**306**	**340**	**308**	**309**	**199**
Housing	**8,886**	**6,012**	**10,010**	**8,941**	**10,025**	**11,448**	**11,104**
Shelter	5,032	3,865	5,488	4,930	5,447	6,275	6,089

(continued on next page)

(continued from previous page)
(average annual expenditures for households by household size, 1990; number of households in thousands)

	all households	one person	two or more persons	two persons	three persons	four persons	five or more persons
Owned dwellings	$2,953	$1,599	$3,483	$2,906	$3,414	$4,363	$4,050
Mortgage interest	1,817	838	2,199	1,545	2,275	3,019	2,846
Property taxes	597	370	686	679	629	772	680
Maintenance, repairs, insurance, other	540	391	598	683	510	572	524
Rented dwellings	1,533	1,922	1,381	1,355	1,515	1,314	1,341
Other lodging	545	345	624	669	517	598	698
Utilities, fuels, public services	1,890	1,198	2,161	1,925	2,175	2,366	2,544
Natural gas	246	156	282	242	269	310	380
Electricity	758	446	880	785	885	993	994
Fuel oil and other fuels	100	57	117	115	113	119	129
Telephone	592	440	652	582	681	681	769
Water and other public services	193	100	230	200	227	264	272
Household operations	446	222	534	368	630	767	543
Personal services	219	44	288	87	410	534	335
Other household expenses	227	178	247	281	220	233	207
Housekeeping supplies	406	200	486	446	480	559	512
Laundry and cleaning supplies	113	46	139	112	142	171	169
Other household products	171	77	208	187	201	251	220
Postage and stationery	122	77	139	147	137	138	124
Household furnishings, equip.	1,111	526	1,340	1,273	1,294	1,480	1,416
Household textiles	99	40	122	110	114	155	122
Furniture	310	175	364	346	328	449	352
Floor coverings	92	36	114	68	139	104	220
Major appliances	147	68	178	173	168	189	198
Small appliances, misc. housewares	61	36	71	74	72	71	62
Misc. household equipment	402	172	492	503	473	512	462
Apparel and services	**1,617**	**886**	**1,903**	**1,564**	**2,016**	**2,233**	**2,257**
Men and boys	393	215	463	348	496	600	557
Men, aged 16 or older	324	207	370	317	404	430	383
Boys, aged 2 to 15	70	8	94	31	91	170	174
Women and girls	672	352	797	705	844	857	908
Women, aged 16 or older	585	340	680	675	739	642	654
Girls, aged 2 to 15	87	12	117	30	105	214	254
Babies under age 2	70	11	93	31	138	124	157
Footwear	225	123	264	231	233	324	331
Other apparel products, services	258	185	286	249	306	328	305
Transportation	**5,122**	**2,661**	**6,085**	**5,134**	**6,636**	**7,122**	**6,545**
Vehicle purchases (net outlay)	2,129	888	2,614	2,026	3,085	3,157	2,824
Cars and trucks, new	1,159	439	1,440	1,266	1,627	1,616	1,404
Cars and trucks, used	948	440	1,146	746	1,390	1,518	1,408

(continued on next page)

(continued from previous page)

(average annual expenditures for households by household size, 1990; number of households in thousands)

	all households	one person	two or more persons	two persons	three persons	four persons	five or more persons
Other vehicles	$22	$9	$28	$14	$69	$22	$12
Gasoline and motor oil	1,047	556	1,239	1,065	1,247	1,443	1,447
Other vehicle expenses	1,644	948	1,917	1,707	2,014	2,213	1,962
Vehicle finance charges	300	138	363	274	423	474	377
Maintenance and repairs	591	391	670	622	674	749	693
Vehicle insurance	563	315	660	598	700	721	696
Vehicle rental, licenses, other charges	190	105	223	214	216	269	196
Public transportation	302	268	316	335	290	308	312
Health care	**1,480**	**977**	**1,677**	**1,796**	**1,618**	**1,581**	**1,555**
Health insurance	581	389	657	729	627	618	548
Medical services	562	356	642	629	638	648	682
Drugs	252	173	282	336	266	231	226
Medical supplies	85	58	95	103	88	85	99
Entertainment	**1,422**	**841**	**1,649**	**1,461**	**1,572**	**1,975**	**1,866**
Fees and admissions	371	235	424	382	376	510	507
Television, radios, sound equip.	454	290	518	428	527	642	591
Pets, toys, playground equip.	276	168	319	256	304	399	413
Other supplies, equip., services	321	148	389	395	366	425	354
Personal care products, services	**364**	**209**	**425**	**376**	**442**	**493**	**447**
Reading	**153**	**109**	**170**	**168**	**165**	**185**	**166**
Education	**406**	**312**	**443**	**263**	**456**	**654**	**658**
Tobacco products and smoking supplies	**274**	**156**	**321**	**281**	**350**	**325**	**383**
Cash contributions	**816**	**609**	**897**	**1,014**	**868**	**696**	**884**
Personal insurance, pensions	**2,592**	**1,293**	**3,101**	**2,575**	**3,375**	**3,744**	**3,305**
Life, other personal insurance	345	112	436	365	462	497	517
Pensions and Social Security	2,248	1,180	2,665	2,210	2,914	3,247	2,788
Miscellaneous	**645**	**499**	**703**	**627**	**721**	**835**	**709**

*The Consumer Expenditure Survey uses consumer units as its sampling unit. See Glossary for definition of consumer unit.
Source: Bureau of Labor Statistics
Note: Numbers may not add to total due to rounding.

Spending by Region

Households in the Northeast and West have above-average incomes and spending, while those in the South and Midwest are below average on both counts.

(average annual expenditures for households by region of residence, 1990; number of households in thousands)

	all households	Northeast	Midwest	South	West
Number of households*	96,968	20,259	24,205	32,651	19,853
Income before taxes	$31,889	$35,521	$29,012	$29,599	$35,385
Average number of persons per household	2.6	2.5	2.5	2.5	2.6
Average annual expenditures	$28,369	$29,489	$25,919	$27,011	$32,445
Food	$4,296	$4,623	$4,022	$4,077	$4,658
Food at home	2,485	2,599	2,313	2,381	2,749
Cereals and bakery products	368	407	347	345	392
Cereals and cereal products	129	132	119	127	139
Bakery products	240	275	228	218	252
Meats, poultry, fish, and eggs	668	751	591	655	700
Beef	218	226	197	213	241
Pork	132	130	130	142	122
Other meats	99	111	98	94	96
Poultry	108	139	82	105	111
Fish and seafood	82	112	61	72	94
Eggs	30	33	24	29	35
Dairy products	295	313	280	271	337
Fresh milk and cream	140	152	132	130	155
Other dairy products	155	161	148	141	182
Fruits and vegetables	408	444	372	380	459
Fresh fruits	127	136	121	114	145
Fresh vegetables	118	128	101	110	144
Processed fruits	93	109	88	81	101
Processed vegetables	70	72	62	75	69
Other food at home	746	684	723	730	861
Sugar and other sweets	94	89	91	93	105
Fats and oils	68	61	65	72	73
Miscellaneous foods	336	290	337	328	392
Nonalcoholic beverages	213	213	203	207	234
Food prep. by hh, out-of-town trips	35	32	28	29	57
Food away from home	1,811	2,024	1,709	1,696	1,909
Alcoholic beverages	293	332	293	249	328
Housing	8,886	9,789	7,837	8,000	10,699
Shelter	5,032	5,855	4,217	4,177	6,592
Owned dwellings	2,953	3,305	2,566	2,428	3,932
Mortgage interest	1,817	1,852	1,443	1,506	2,747

(continued on next page)

(average annual expenditures for households by region of residence, 1990; number of households in thousands)

	all households	Northeast	Midwest	South	West
Property taxes	$597	$884	$639	$391	$594
Maintenance, repairs, insurance, other	540	569	484	531	591
Rented dwellings	1,533	1,832	1,200	1,264	2,077
Other lodging	545	718	451	485	583
Utilities, fuels, and public services	1,890	1,981	1,838	2,000	1,681
Natural gas	246	285	373	150	212
Electricity	758	695	668	950	616
Fuel oil and other fuels	100	257	83	56	33
Telephone	592	589	547	616	611
Water and other public services	193	154	167	227	209
Household operations	446	378	365	468	580
Personal services	219	184	203	212	286
Other household expenses	227	194	162	256	294
Housekeeping supplies	406	426	390	380	447
Laundry and cleaning supplies	113	122	110	109	114
Other household products	171	170	164	166	189
Postage and stationery	122	134	115	105	145
Household furnishings and equipment	1,111	1,149	1,027	975	1,399
Household textiles	99	88	101	95	113
Furniture	310	341	291	280	352
Floor coverings	92	158	105	48	79
Major appliances	147	145	131	153	160
Small appliances, misc. housewares	61	53	58	57	81
Miscellaneous household equipment	402	363	341	342	614
Apparel and services	**1,617**	**1,808**	**1,357**	**1,549**	**1,852**
Men and boys	393	416	332	380	467
Men, aged 16 or older	324	338	268	313	395
Boys, aged 2 to 15	70	78	64	67	72
Women and girls	672	743	576	660	736
Women, aged 16 or older	585	652	492	579	638
Girls, aged 2 to 15	87	91	84	81	98
Babies under age 2	70	71	63	66	83
Footwear	225	305	164	193	270
Other apparel products and services	258	273	222	251	296
Transportation	**5,122**	**4,813**	**4,794**	**5,310**	**5,529**
Vehicle purchases (net outlay)	2,129	1,920	2,068	2,275	2,174
Cars and trucks, new	1,159	1,170	891	1,306	1,231
Cars and trucks, used	948	739	1,155	942	915
Other vehicles	22	11	22	27	28
Gasoline and motor oil	1,047	867	1,000	1,152	1,115
Other vehicle expenses	1,644	1,596	1,517	1,635	1,865
Vehicle finance charges	300	238	300	346	287
Maintenance and repairs	591	535	535	604	697
Vehicle insurance	563	630	485	544	624
Vehicle rental, licenses, other charges	190	193	197	141	257
Public transportation	302	430	209	249	375

(continued on next page)

(continued from previous page)

(average annual expenditures for households by region of residence, 1990; number of households in thousands)

	all households	Northeast	Midwest	South	West
Health care	**$1,480**	**$1,396**	**$1,336**	**$1,600**	**$1,544**
Health insurance	581	553	550	637	558
Medical services	562	559	457	573	676
Drugs	252	205	248	297	230
Medical supplies	85	80	82	93	80
Entertainment	**1,422**	**1,331**	**1,356**	**1,266**	**1,853**
Fees and admissions	371	398	347	306	482
Television, radios, sound equipment	454	429	433	439	528
Pets, toys, and playground equipment	276	270	270	271	299
Other supplies, equipment, and services	321	235	306	250	543
Personal-care products and services	**364**	**352**	**328**	**359**	**428**
Reading	**153**	**171**	**160**	**131**	**164**
Education	**406**	**593**	**394**	**319**	**375**
Tobacco products and smoking supplies	**274**	**279**	**298**	**286**	**221**
Cash contributions	**816**	**708**	**745**	**839**	**975**
Personal insurance and pensions	**2,592**	**2,690**	**2,408**	**2,395**	**3,042**
Life and other personal insurance	345	341	355	368	298
Pensions and Social Security	2,248	2,349	2,053	2,027	2,744
Miscellaneous	**645**	**604**	**593**	**631**	**776**

*The Consumer Expenditure Survey uses consumer units as its sampling unit. See Glossary for definition of consumer unit.
Source: Bureau of Labor Statistics
Note: Numbers may not add to total due to rounding.

Spending by Income, Householders Under Age 25

Although young householders with incomes of $40,000 or more spend the most, few in this age group fall into that income category.

(annual average expenditures for householders under age 25 by income, 1989-90; number of households in thousands; complete income reporters only)

	all households	under $10,000	$10,000 to $19,999	$20,000 to $29,999	$30,000 to $39,999	$40,000 or more
Number of households*	**6,798**	**1,802**	**1,376**	**916**	**512**	**269**
Income before taxes	**$14,478**	**$4,683**	**$14,377**	**$24,635**	**$34,009**	**$59,102**
Average number of persons per household	**1.8**	**1.5**	**2.0**	**2.1**	**2.4**	**2.5**
Average annual expenditures	**$16,918**	**$10,191**	**$16,944**	**$25,013**	**$30,967**	**$36,792**
Food	**$2,592**	**$1,836**	**$2,510**	**$3,191**	**$4,210**	**$4,922**
Food at home	1,240	773	1,311	1,541	2,201	2,359
Cereals and bakery products	184	129	188	206	325	333
Cereals and cereal products	70	52	76	78	99	118
Bakery products	113	77	112	129	227	215
Meats, poultry, fish, and eggs	279	161	302	337	548	551
Beef	95	52	110	114	200	165
Pork	51	31	55	48	83	135
Other meats	43	26	53	50	80	61
Poultry	40	23	36	48	102	94
Fish and seafood	32	17	30	59	50	58
Eggs	17	11	17	18	34	39
Dairy products	163	110	163	212	307	234
Fresh milk and cream	83	53	96	103	146	115
Other dairy products	80	57	67	109	161	120
Fruits and vegetables	178	107	186	221	355	325
Fresh fruits	49	33	45	57	106	96
Fresh vegetables	52	26	62	63	106	105
Processed fruits	44	31	45	54	78	64
Processed vegetables	32	16	34	48	64	60
Other food at home	436	266	473	564	666	916
Sugar and other sweets	45	30	43	53	84	88
Fats and oils	27	16	30	35	46	56
Miscellaneous foods	231	130	257	312	335	528
Nonalcoholic beverages	118	80	128	138	186	208
Food prep. by hh, out-of-town trips	14	8	15	26	15	35
Food away from home	1,353	1,062	1,199	1,650	2,009	2,563
Alcoholic beverages	**319**	**210**	**260**	**512**	**359**	**705**
Housing	**4,888**	**2,817**	**5,062**	**7,218**	**9,616**	**10,679**
Shelter	3,071	1,844	3,191	4,372	5,797	7,079
Owned dwellings	323	33	163	638	1,245	2,061
Mortgage interest	239	19	113	464	994	1,531

(continued on next page)

(continued from previous page)

(annual average expenditures for householders under age 25 by income, 1989-90; number of households in thousands; complete income reporters only)

	all households	under $10,000	$10,000 to $19,999	$20,000 to $29,999	$30,000 to $39,999	$40,000 or more
Property taxes	$33	$1	$13	$67	$117	$269
Maintenance, repairs, insurance, other	51	12	38	106	134	262
Rented dwellings	2,572	1,600	2,950	3,573	4,209	4,831
Other lodging	176	211	79	161	343	187
Utilities, fuels, and public services	907	598	972	1,310	1,531	1,528
Natural gas	89	53	80	148	205	166
Electricity	329	189	395	489	544	542
Fuel oil and other fuels	18	8	21	33	24	39
Telephone	424	326	426	556	646	682
Water and other public services	47	22	49	84	111	99
Household operations	137	50	150	217	394	302
Personal services	93	21	109	173	329	97
Other household expenses	44	29	41	45	65	206
Housekeeping supplies	178	98	166	313	285	294
Laundry and cleaning supplies	51	25	57	67	118	87
Other household products	51	22	61	66	73	141
Postage and stationery	76	51	47	180	94	66
Household furnishings and equipment	597	228	584	1,007	1,610	1,474
Household textiles	26	7	24	71	31	36
Furniture	264	82	259	456	900	578
Floor coverings	11	2	12	23	10	82
Major appliances	79	25	92	84	245	300
Small appliances, misc. housewares	32	17	39	42	62	64
Miscellaneous household equipment	185	94	159	331	362	414
Apparel and services	**1,144**	**694**	**1,095**	**1,614**	**1,907**	**2,406**
Men and boys	286	159	262	313	510	927
Men, aged 16 or older	276	154	248	299	489	922
Boys, aged 2 to 15	10	5	14	14	21	5
Women and girls	426	295	391	681	372	681
Women, aged 16 or older	410	282	376	660	338	673
Girls, aged 2 to 15	16	13	14	21	34	8
Babies under age 2	86	45	85	122	193	180
Footwear	115	48	148	135	326	187
Other apparel products and services	232	147	209	363	506	431
Transportation	**3,803**	**1,922**	**4,173**	**6,488**	**7,157**	**7,784**
Vehicle purchases (net outlay)	1,915	838	2,143	3,676	3,878	3,268
Cars and trucks, new	822	286	844	2,242	1,612	663
Cars and trucks, used	1,077	544	1,285	1,379	2,260	2,605
Other vehicles	16	8	14	56	5	0
Gasoline and motor oil	725	478	814	996	1,097	1,385
Other vehicle expenses	998	445	1,083	1,666	1,940	2,770
Vehicle finance charges	212	47	237	436	474	716
Maintenance and repairs	335	206	351	492	578	674

(continued on next page)

(continued from previous page)

(annual average expenditures for householders under age 25 by income, 1989-90; number of households in thousands; complete income reporters only)

	all households	under $10,000	$10,000 to $19,999	$20,000 to $29,999	$30,000 to $39,999	$40,000 or more
Vehicle insurance	$356	$136	$400	$605	$700	$1,132
Vehicle rental, licenses, other charges	95	56	95	133	187	247
Public transportation	165	161	132	149	242	361
Health care	**393**	**198**	**394**	**752**	**770**	**706**
Health insurance	113	32	117	236	257	334
Medical services	184	101	182	367	367	216
Drugs	58	37	56	100	97	72
Medical supplies	38	27	38	48	50	84
Entertainment	**913**	**587**	**807**	**1,316**	**1,630**	**2,592**
Fees and admissions	226	174	178	307	397	583
Television, radios, sound equipment	364	228	375	554	624	733
Pets, toys, and playground equipment	132	60	106	261	299	279
Other supplies, equipment, and services	191	125	148	193	311	998
Personal-care products and services	**235**	**137**	**275**	**314**	**301**	**465**
Reading	**79**	**51**	**87**	**107**	**145**	**148**
Education	**765**	**1,056**	**434**	**593**	**630**	**516**
Tobacco products and smoking supplies	**211**	**125**	**292**	**270**	**357**	**172**
Cash contributions	**143**	**86**	**123**	**198**	**187**	**706**
Personal insurance and pensions	**1,090**	**267**	**1,086**	**1,982**	**3,032**	**4,113**
Life and other personal insurance	68	17	76	77	308	135
Pensions and Social Security	1,022	250	1,010	1,905	2,724	3,979
Miscellaneous	**341**	**205**	**347**	**457**	**667**	**877**

*The Consumer Expenditure Survey uses consumer units as its sampling unit. See Glossary for definition of consumer unit.

Source: Bureau of Labor Statistics

Note: The data here for all households in the age group will differ from those for the age groups given on pages 176 through 178 because combined data from 1989-1990 were used for this crosstabulation. Numbers may not add to total due to rounding.

Indexed Spending by Income, Householders Under Age 25

Spending rises directly with income for householders under age 25, except for a few categories such as education and other lodging.

(indexed annual average expenditures for householders under age 25 by income, 1989-90; number of households in thousands; complete income reporters only)

	all households	under $10,000	$10,000 to $19,999	$20,000 to $29,999	$30,000 to $39,999	$40,000 or more
Number of households*	6,798	1,802	1,376	916	512	269
Income before taxes	$14,478	$4,683	$14,377	$24,635	$34,009	$59,102
Average number of persons per household	1.8	1.5	2.0	2.1	2.4	2.5
Average annual expenditures	100	60	100	148	183	217
Food	100	71	97	123	162	190
Food at home	100	62	106	124	178	190
Cereals and bakery products	100	70	102	112	177	181
Cereals and cereal products	100	75	109	111	141	169
Bakery products	100	68	99	114	201	190
Meats, poultry, fish, and eggs	100	58	108	121	196	197
Beef	100	55	116	120	211	174
Pork	100	62	108	94	163	265
Other meats	100	60	124	116	186	142
Poultry	100	57	91	120	255	235
Fish and seafood	100	52	94	184	156	181
Eggs	100	66	101	106	200	229
Dairy products	100	68	100	130	188	144
Fresh milk and cream	100	64	116	124	176	139
Other dairy products	100	72	84	136	201	150
Fruits and vegetables	100	60	104	124	199	183
Fresh fruits	100	68	92	116	216	196
Fresh vegetables	100	51	120	121	204	202
Processed fruits	100	71	103	123	177	145
Processed vegetables	100	52	105	150	200	188
Other food at home	100	61	108	129	153	210
Sugar and other sweets	100	67	95	118	187	196
Fats and oils	100	59	110	130	170	207
Miscellaneous foods	100	56	111	135	145	229
Nonalcoholic beverages	100	68	109	117	158	176
Food prep. by hh, out-of-town trips	100	59	105	186	107	250
Food away from home	100	79	89	122	148	189
Alcoholic beverages	100	66	81	161	113	221
Housing	100	58	104	148	197	218
Shelter	100	60	104	142	189	231
Owned dwellings	100	10	50	198	385	638
Mortgage interest	100	8	47	194	416	641

(continued on next page)

(indexed annual average expenditures for householders under age 25 by income, 1989-90; number of households in thousands; complete income reporters only)

	all households	under $10,000	$10,000 to $19,999	$20,000 to $29,999	$30,000 to $39,999	$40,000 or more
Property taxes	100	4	38	203	355	815
Maintenance, repairs, insurance, other	100	24	74	208	263	514
Rented dwellings	100	62	115	139	164	188
Other lodging	100	120	45	91	195	106
Utilities, fuels, and public services	100	66	107	144	169	168
Natural gas	100	60	90	166	230	187
Electricity	100	57	120	149	165	165
Fuel oil and other fuels	100	46	118	183	133	217
Telephone	100	77	100	131	152	161
Water and other public services	100	46	104	179	236	211
Household operations	100	36	110	158	288	220
Personal services	100	23	117	186	354	104
Other household expenses	100	66	92	102	148	468
Housekeeping supplies	100	55	93	176	160	165
Laundry and cleaning supplies	100	49	112	131	231	171
Other household products	100	44	120	129	143	276
Postage and stationery	100	67	61	237	124	87
Household furnishings and equipment	100	38	98	169	270	247
Household textiles	100	28	94	273	119	138
Furniture	100	31	98	173	341	219
Floor coverings	100	18	107	209	91	745
Major appliances	100	32	116	106	310	380
Small appliances, misc. housewares	100	54	121	131	194	200
Miscellaneous household equipment	100	51	86	179	196	224
Apparel and services	**100**	**61**	**96**	**141**	**167**	**210**
Men and boys	100	56	92	109	178	324
Men, aged 16 or older	100	56	90	108	177	334
Boys, aged 2 to 15	100	48	139	140	210	50
Women and girls	100	69	92	160	87	160
Women, aged 16 or older	100	69	92	161	82	164
Girls, aged 2 to 15	100	83	89	131	213	50
Babies under age 2	100	52	99	142	224	209
Footwear	100	41	129	117	283	163
Other apparel products and services	100	63	90	156	218	186
Transportation	**100**	**51**	**110**	**171**	**188**	**205**
Vehicle purchases (net outlay)	100	44	112	192	203	171
Cars and trucks, new	100	35	103	273	196	81
Cars and trucks, used	100	50	119	128	210	242
Other vehicles	100	53	87	350	31	0
Gasoline and motor oil	100	66	112	137	151	191
Other vehicle expenses	100	45	109	167	194	278
Vehicle finance charges	100	22	112	206	224	338
Maintenance and repairs	100	61	105	147	173	201
Vehicle insurance	100	38	112	170	197	318
Vehicle rental, licenses, other charges	100	59	100	140	197	260
Public transportation	100	97	80	90	147	219

(continued on next page)

(continued from previous page)

(indexed annual average expenditures for householders under age 25 by income, 1989-90; number of households in thousands; complete income reporters only)

	all households	under $10,000	$10,000 to $19,999	$20,000 to $29,999	$30,000 to $39,999	$40,000 or more
Health care	**100**	**50**	**100**	**191**	**196**	**180**
Health insurance	100	29	104	209	227	296
Medical services	100	55	99	199	199	117
Drugs	100	64	97	172	167	124
Medical supplies	100	72	101	126	132	221
Entertainment	**100**	**64**	**88**	**144**	**179**	**284**
Fees and admissions	100	77	79	136	176	258
Television, radios, sound equipment	100	63	103	152	171	201
Pets, toys, and playground equipment	100	45	80	198	227	211
Other supplies, equipment, and services	100	65	78	101	163	523
Personal-care products and services	**100**	**58**	**117**	**134**	**128**	**198**
Reading	**100**	**65**	**110**	**135**	**184**	**187**
Education	**100**	**138**	**57**	**78**	**82**	**67**
Tobacco products and smoking supplies	**100**	**59**	**138**	**128**	**169**	**82**
Cash contributions	**100**	**60**	**86**	**138**	**131**	**494**
Personal insurance and pensions	**100**	**25**	**100**	**182**	**278**	**377**
Life and other personal insurance	100	25	111	113	453	199
Pensions and Social Security	100	24	99	186	267	389
Miscellaneous	**100**	**60**	**102**	**134**	**196**	**257**

*The Consumer Expenditure Survey uses consumer units as its sampling unit. See Glossary for definition of consumer unit.
Source: Bureau of Labor Statistics
Note: The data here for all households in the age group will differ from those for the age groups given on pages 176 through 178 because combined data from 1989-1990 were used for this crosstabulation. An index of 100 is the average for all households. An index of 132 means that spending for that group is 32 percent greater than the average for all households. An index of 68 means that spending is 32 percent below average.

Spending by Income, Householders Aged 25 to 34

Over one-fourth of households headed by 25-to-34-year-olds fall into the top income and spending category, with average expenditures of nearly $44,000 in 1990.

(annual average expenditures for householders aged 25 to 34 by income, 1989-90; number of households in thousands; complete income reporters only)

	all households	under $10,000	$10,000 to $19,999	$20,000 to $29,999	$30,000 to $39,999	$40,000 or more
Number of households*	18,492	690	1,656	4,026	3,522	4,940
Income before taxes	$31,498	$6,209	$14,851	$24,713	$34,161	$59,462
Average number of persons per household	2.8	2.7	2.6	2.7	2.7	3.0
Average annual expenditures	$28,331	$13,236	$18,328	$24,356	$31,094	$43,917
Food	$4,108	$2,751	$3,044	$3,780	$4,398	$5,477
Food at home	2,303	1,838	1,854	2,194	2,555	2,724
Cereals and bakery products	334	269	261	300	385	403
Cereals and cereal products	128	109	110	116	141	149
Bakery products	206	160	151	184	244	254
Meats, poultry, fish, and eggs	586	492	498	576	636	658
Beef	202	166	165	221	222	219
Pork	106	109	97	101	118	106
Other meats	88	67	75	92	101	95
Poultry	97	71	80	80	103	127
Fish and seafood	63	50	55	55	62	81
Eggs	29	29	28	26	30	30
Dairy products	297	246	240	274	341	347
Fresh milk and cream	146	132	134	139	158	158
Other dairy products	151	113	106	135	183	190
Fruits and vegetables	361	312	271	330	374	457
Fresh fruits	105	100	80	96	95	137
Fresh vegetables	106	89	81	98	107	135
Processed fruits	83	66	59	71	93	110
Processed vegetables	67	57	50	65	79	75
Other food at home	725	520	583	714	818	858
Sugar and other sweets	82	58	65	81	93	97
Fats and oils	55	42	43	55	68	61
Miscellaneous foods	347	255	263	340	406	412
Nonalcoholic beverages	209	153	191	215	215	234
Food prep. by hh, out-of-town trips	32	11	21	23	35	55
Food away from home	1,804	913	1,190	1,586	1,843	2,753
Alcoholic beverages	384	243	280	356	405	525
Housing	9,329	4,551	6,160	7,850	9,532	14,954
Shelter	5,538	2,683	3,630	4,626	5,613	8,996
Owned dwellings	2,826	420	716	1,782	2,780	6,413
Mortgage interest	2,193	281	498	1,356	2,224	5,015

(continued on next page)

(continued from previous page)

(annual average expenditures for householders aged 25 to 34 by income, 1989-90; number of households in thousands; complete income reporters only)

	all households	under $10,000	$10,000 to $19,999	$20,000 to $29,999	$30,000 to $39,999	$40,000 or more
Property taxes	$316	$74	$89	$193	$268	$734
Maintenance, repairs, insurance, other	317	66	128	233	289	665
Rented dwellings	2,399	2,138	2,768	2,690	2,501	1,939
Other lodging	314	125	146	154	332	644
Utilities, fuels, and public services	1,660	1,145	1,352	1,568	1,739	2,150
Natural gas	205	171	162	172	200	286
Electricity	649	475	520	647	655	826
Fuel oil and other fuels	64	31	48	62	82	81
Telephone	592	377	525	561	650	729
Water and other public services	148	91	97	126	152	229
Household operations	611	129	334	518	605	1,126
Personal services	484	85	267	434	495	866
Other household expenses	128	44	67	84	110	261
Housekeeping supplies	377	225	258	322	424	531
Laundry and cleaning supplies	117	87	99	104	127	144
Other household products	153	80	85	129	168	237
Postage and stationery	107	57	74	89	129	150
Household furnishings and equipment	1,143	370	586	816	1,151	2,150
Household textiles	92	23	48	73	118	150
Furniture	364	120	209	209	367	719
Floor coverings	59	2	11	24	22	168
Major appliances	149	57	121	136	169	209
Small appliances, misc. housewares	66	21	37	41	74	121
Miscellaneous household equipment	414	147	161	332	402	783
Apparel and services	**1,634**	**1,068**	**1,037**	**1,334**	**1,767**	**2,450**
Men and boys	427	340	241	332	416	673
Men, aged 16 or older	328	145	173	257	330	564
Boys, aged 2 to 15	100	195	69	74	86	109
Women and girls	573	314	374	471	692	828
Women, aged 16 or older	473	237	310	378	582	692
Girls, aged 2 to 15	100	76	64	93	110	136
Babies under age 2	143	78	99	124	140	216
Footwear	207	190	131	187	222	274
Other apparel products and services	284	147	191	220	297	459
Transportation	**5,351**	**2,088**	**3,550**	**4,588**	**6,662**	**7,919**
Vehicle purchases (net outlay)	2,350	807	1,457	1,892	3,230	3,488
Cars and trucks, new	1,211	165	423	907	1,396	2,409
Cars and trucks, used	1,092	544	1,018	960	1,791	1,017
Other vehicles	46	98	16	26	44	62
Gasoline and motor oil	1,036	498	814	1,040	1,146	1,374
Other vehicle expenses	1,733	665	1,140	1,512	2,032	2,642
Vehicle finance charges	386	79	209	351	494	615
Maintenance and repairs	591	335	486	501	639	828

(continued on next page)

(continued from previous page)

(annual average expenditures for householders aged 25 to 34 by income, 1989-90; number of households in thousands; complete income reporters only)

	all households	under $10,000	$10,000 to $19,999	$20,000 to $29,999	$30,000 to $39,999	$40,000 or more
Vehicle insurance	$534	$198	$346	$509	$601	$804
Vehicle rental, licenses, other charges	222	53	99	151	298	396
Public transportation	233	118	139	143	254	414
Health care	**955**	**422**	**695**	**938**	**1,050**	**1,343**
Health insurance	367	148	280	366	452	475
Medical services	389	160	250	370	406	603
Drugs	138	94	119	145	127	173
Medical supplies	61	20	46	58	65	91
Entertainment	**1,470**	**702**	**818**	**1,202**	**1,610**	**2,424**
Fees and admissions	339	98	160	263	364	631
Television, radios, sound equipment	500	309	353	459	532	708
Pets, toys, and playground equipment	302	234	186	281	315	426
Other supplies, equipment, and services	328	62	118	199	399	660
Personal-care products and services	**347**	**180**	**229**	**292**	**390**	**515**
Reading	**140**	**52**	**79**	**115**	**151**	**237**
Education	**270**	**271**	**217**	**195**	**240**	**390**
Tobacco products and smoking supplies	**266**	**228**	**306**	**283**	**261**	**242**
Cash contributions	**475**	**135**	**254**	**426**	**553**	**783**
Personal insurance and pensions	**2,961**	**359**	**1,226**	**2,315**	**3,383**	**5,709**
Life and other personal insurance	241	70	112	190	274	438
Pensions and Social Security	2,720	289	1,114	2,125	3,109	5,271
Miscellaneous	**643**	**186**	**433**	**681**	**690**	**950**

*The Consumer Expenditure Survey uses consumer units as its sampling unit. See Glossary for definition of consumer unit.

Source: Bureau of Labor Statistics

Note: The data here for all households in the age group will differ from those for the age groups given on pages 176 through 178 because combined data from 1989-90 were used for this crosstabulation. Numbers may not add to total due to rounding.

Indexed Spending by Income, Householders Aged 25 to 34

Except for those in the top income category, households headed by 25-to-34-year-olds spend less than average or just an average amount on most products and services.

(indexed annual average expenditures for householders aged 25 to 34 by income, 1989-90; number of households in thousands; complete income reporters only)

	all households	under $10,000	$10,000 to $19,999	$20,000 to $29,999	$30,000 to $39,999	$40,000 or more
Number of households*	18,492	690	1,656	4,026	3,522	4,940
Income before taxes	$31,498	$6,209	$14,851	$24,713	$34,161	$59,462
Average number of persons per household	2.8	2.7	2.6	2.7	2.7	3.0
Average annual expenditures	100	47	65	86	110	155
Food	100	67	74	92	107	133
Food at home	100	80	80	95	111	118
Cereals and bakery products	100	81	78	90	115	121
Cereals and cereal products	100	85	86	91	110	116
Bakery products	100	78	73	89	118	123
Meats, poultry, fish, and eggs	100	84	85	98	109	112
Beef	100	82	82	109	110	108
Pork	100	103	92	95	111	100
Other meats	100	76	85	105	115	108
Poultry	100	73	82	82	106	131
Fish and seafood	100	79	87	87	98	129
Eggs	100	99	95	90	103	103
Dairy products	100	83	81	92	115	117
Fresh milk and cream	100	90	92	95	108	108
Other dairy products	100	75	70	89	121	126
Fruits and vegetables	100	86	75	91	104	127
Fresh fruits	100	95	76	91	90	130
Fresh vegetables	100	84	76	92	101	127
Processed fruits	100	79	72	86	112	133
Processed vegetables	100	85	75	97	118	112
Other food at home	100	72	80	98	113	118
Sugar and other sweets	100	71	79	99	113	118
Fats and oils	100	76	77	100	124	111
Miscellaneous foods	100	73	76	98	117	119
Nonalcoholic beverages	100	73	91	103	103	112
Food prep. by hh, out-of-town trips	100	35	67	72	109	172
Food away from home	100	51	66	88	102	153
Alcoholic beverages	100	63	73	93	105	137
Housing	100	49	66	84	102	160
Shelter	100	48	66	84	101	162
Owned dwellings	100	15	25	63	98	227
Mortgage interest	100	13	23	62	101	229

(continued on next page)

(continued from previous page)

(indexed annual average expenditures for householders aged 25 to 34 by income, 1989-90; number of households in thousands; complete income reporters only)

	all households	under $10,000	$10,000 to $19,999	$20,000 to $29,999	$30,000 to $39,999	$40,000 or more
Property taxes	100	24	28	61	85	232
Maintenance, repairs, insurance, other	100	21	40	74	91	210
Rented dwellings	100	89	115	112	104	81
Other lodging	100	40	47	49	106	205
Utilities, fuels, and public services	100	69	81	94	105	130
Natural gas	100	83	79	84	98	140
Electricity	100	73	80	100	101	127
Fuel oil and other fuels	100	48	76	97	128	127
Telephone	100	64	89	95	110	123
Water and other public services	100	61	65	85	103	155
Household operations	100	21	55	85	99	184
Personal services	100	17	55	90	102	179
Other household expenses	100	35	52	66	86	204
Housekeeping supplies	100	60	68	85	112	141
Laundry and cleaning supplies	100	75	85	89	109	123
Other household products	100	53	56	84	110	155
Postage and stationery	100	53	69	83	121	140
Household furnishings and equipment	100	32	51	71	101	188
Household textiles	100	25	52	79	128	163
Furniture	100	33	57	57	101	198
Floor coverings	100	4	19	41	37	285
Major appliances	100	38	81	91	113	140
Small appliances, misc. housewares	100	31	56	62	112	183
Miscellaneous household equipment	100	35	39	80	97	189
Apparel and services	**100**	**65**	**63**	**82**	**108**	**150**
Men and boys	100	80	56	78	97	158
Men, aged 16 or older	100	44	53	78	101	172
Boys, aged 2 to 15	100	195	69	74	86	109
Women and girls	100	55	65	82	121	145
Women, aged 16 or older	100	50	66	80	123	146
Girls, aged 2 to 15	100	76	64	93	110	136
Babies under age 2	100	54	69	87	98	151
Footwear	100	92	64	90	107	132
Other apparel products and services	100	52	67	77	105	162
Transportation	**100**	**39**	**66**	**86**	**125**	**148**
Vehicle purchases (net outlay)	100	34	62	81	137	148
Cars and trucks, new	100	14	35	75	115	199
Cars and trucks, used	100	50	93	88	164	93
Other vehicles	100	212	35	57	96	135
Gasoline and motor oil	100	48	79	100	111	133
Other vehicle expenses	100	38	66	87	117	152
Vehicle finance charges	100	20	54	91	128	159
Maintenance and repairs	100	57	82	85	108	140
Vehicle insurance	100	37	65	95	113	151
Vehicle rental, licenses, other charges	100	24	45	68	134	178
Public transportation	100	51	60	61	109	178

(continued on next page)

(continued from previous page)

(indexed annual average expenditures for householders aged 25 to 34 by income, 1989-90; number of households in thousands; complete income reporters only)

	all households	under $10,000	$10,000 to $19,999	$20,000 to $29,999	$30,000 to $39,999	$40,000 or more
Health care	**100**	**44**	**73**	**98**	**110**	**141**
Health insurance	100	40	76	100	123	129
Medical services	100	41	64	95	104	155
Drugs	100	68	86	105	92	125
Medical supplies	100	33	75	95	107	149
Entertainment	**100**	**48**	**56**	**82**	**110**	**165**
Fees and admissions	100	29	47	78	107	186
Television, radios, sound equipment	100	62	71	92	106	142
Pets, toys, and playground equipment	100	78	62	93	104	141
Other supplies, equipment, and services	100	19	36	61	122	201
Personal-care products and services	**100**	**52**	**66**	**84**	**112**	**148**
Reading	**100**	**37**	**56**	**82**	**108**	**169**
Education	**100**	**100**	**80**	**72**	**89**	**144**
Tobacco products and smoking supplies	**100**	**86**	**115**	**106**	**98**	**91**
Cash contributions	**100**	**29**	**53**	**90**	**116**	**165**
Personal insurance and pensions	**100**	**12**	**41**	**78**	**114**	**193**
Life and other personal insurance	100	29	46	79	114	182
Pensions and Social Security	100	11	41	78	114	194
Miscellaneous	**100**	**29**	**67**	**106**	**107**	**148**

The Consumer Expenditure Survey uses consumer units as its sampling unit. See Glossary for definition of consumer unit.
Source: Bureau of Labor Statistics
Note: The data here for all households in the age group will differ from those for the age groups given on pages 176 through 178 because combined data from 1989-90 were used for this crosstabulation. An index of 100 is the average for all households. An index of 132 means that spending for that group is 32 percent greater than the average for all households. An index of 68 means that spending is 32 percent below average.

Spending by Income, Householders Aged 35 to 44

Nearly half of households headed by 35-to-44-year-olds are in the top income category, spending more than $50,000 in 1990.

(annual average expenditures for householders aged 35 to 44 by income, 1989-90; number of households in thousands; complete income reporters only)

	all households	under $10,000	$10,000 to $19,999	$20,000 to $29,999	$30,000 to $39,999	$40,000 or more
Number of households*	**17,748**	**706**	**1,090**	**2,839**	**2,997**	**7,469**
Income before taxes	**$41,063**	**$5,308**	**$15,175**	**$24,615**	**$34,563**	**$67,697**
Average number of persons per household	**3.3**	**2.8**	**3.0**	**3.1**	**3.2**	**3.5**
Average annual expenditures	**$36,688**	**$16,555**	**$20,869**	**$26,012**	**$33,712**	**$52,243**
Food	**$5,408**	**$3,309**	**$3,686**	**$4,325**	**$5,000**	**$7,031**
Food at home	3,088	2,249	2,524	2,755	2,853	3,682
Cereals and bakery products	469	312	383	413	437	565
Cereals and cereal products	172	122	157	172	149	197
Bakery products	296	190	227	241	288	367
Meats, poultry, fish, and eggs	773	663	666	697	675	903
Beef	257	202	215	230	234	303
Pork	141	146	115	140	133	152
Other meats	116	99	103	104	90	139
Poultry	123	96	115	112	108	142
Fish and seafood	100	80	82	73	78	131
Eggs	36	40	35	38	31	37
Dairy products	386	291	316	354	365	449
Fresh milk and cream	181	166	167	174	178	194
Other dairy products	205	126	149	180	188	256
Fruits and vegetables	491	361	388	442	450	588
Fresh fruits	141	93	109	128	131	172
Fresh vegetables	147	110	122	138	138	170
Processed fruits	116	89	89	97	100	144
Processed vegetables	87	68	68	79	80	103
Other food at home	970	622	770	850	927	1,177
Sugar and other sweets	118	72	85	105	110	147
Fats and oils	81	64	70	79	73	93
Miscellaneous foods	446	264	355	389	450	537
Nonalcoholic beverages	277	200	243	248	257	325
Food prep. by hh, out-of-town trips	47	21	18	28	37	74
Food away from home	2,320	1,061	1,162	1,570	2,146	3,349
Alcoholic beverages	**372**	**225**	**273**	**314**	**305**	**489**
Housing	**11,244**	**5,643**	**6,966**	**7,618**	**9,476**	**16,173**
Shelter	6,518	3,250	4,063	4,332	5,423	9,445
Owned dwellings	4,389	1,299	1,704	2,001	3,265	7,442
Mortgage interest	3,193	899	1,062	1,369	2,317	5,545

(continued on next page)

(continued from previous page)

(annual average expenditures for householders aged 35 to 44 by income, 1989-90; number of households in thousands; complete income reporters only)

	all households	under $10,000	$10,000 to $19,999	$20,000 to $29,999	$30,000 to $39,999	$40,000 or more
Property taxes	$677	$226	$305	$302	$528	$1,119
Maintenance, repairs, insurance, other	519	175	337	330	420	777
Rented dwellings	1,507	1,790	2,134	2,048	1,593	978
Other lodging	622	161	225	284	564	1,026
Utilities, fuels, and public services	2,116	1,435	1,717	1,873	2,042	2,544
Natural gas	264	192	207	208	282	316
Electricity	865	586	704	767	838	1,038
Fuel oil and other fuels	101	55	53	92	90	138
Telephone	653	467	591	622	605	751
Water and other public services	232	136	161	184	227	301
Household operations	597	170	241	266	393	1,033
Personal services	343	103	146	162	272	568
Other household expenses	254	68	95	104	121	464
Housekeeping supplies	530	313	333	370	437	742
Laundry and cleaning supplies	148	129	103	129	129	181
Other household products	236	95	128	152	187	355
Postage and stationery	146	89	102	90	121	206
Household furnishings and equipment	1,483	474	611	777	1,180	2,409
Household textiles	120	35	51	77	95	187
Furniture	398	77	220	262	349	610
Floor coverings	131	16	33	37	65	254
Major appliances	183	71	110	115	158	270
Small appliances, misc. housewares	84	24	36	41	64	138
Miscellaneous household equipment	568	251	159	245	450	949
Apparel and services	**2,317**	**959**	**1,215**	**1,743**	**2,207**	**3,254**
Men and boys	569	170	238	352	454	898
Men, aged 16 or older	418	116	129	234	322	692
Boys, aged 2 to 15	151	53	108	119	131	206
Women and girls	985	454	518	913	1,030	1,264
Women, aged 16 or older	778	369	379	774	829	978
Girls, aged 2 to 15	207	86	138	139	201	286
Babies under age 2	76	38	45	40	76	110
Footwear	317	137	208	179	366	427
Other apparel products and services	370	161	208	258	282	555
Transportation	**6,459**	**3,036**	**3,804**	**4,856**	**6,823**	**8,682**
Vehicle purchases (net outlay)	2,817	1,300	1,772	2,111	3,346	3,609
Cars and trucks, new	1,502	359	593	947	1,880	2,158
Cars and trucks, used	1,292	922	1,176	1,158	1,437	1,416
Other vehicles	23	19	2	7	30	36
Gasoline and motor oil	1,239	714	839	1,106	1,259	1,549
Other vehicle expenses	2,082	895	1,057	1,457	1,952	3,017
Vehicle finance charges	402	135	224	261	408	580
Maintenance and repairs	751	419	363	520	700	1,073

(continued on next page)

(continued from previous page)

(annual average expenditures for householders aged 35 to 44 by income, 1989-90; number of households in thousands; complete income reporters only)

	all households	under $10,000	$10,000 to $19,999	$20,000 to $29,999	$30,000 to $39,999	$40,000 or more
Vehicle insurance	$661	$240	$350	$523	$648	$930
Vehicle rental, licenses, other charges	269	101	121	154	196	434
Public transportation	320	127	137	182	267	507
Health care	**1,394**	**739**	**1,133**	**1,053**	**1,323**	**1,807**
Health insurance	465	214	331	400	501	584
Medical services	633	357	465	452	558	857
Drugs	196	135	165	145	182	246
Medical supplies	99	33	170	56	82	119
Entertainment	**2,010**	**694**	**818**	**1,189**	**1,715**	**3,173**
Fees and admissions	534	182	146	285	427	894
Television, radios, sound equipment	586	285	390	445	551	796
Pets, toys, and playground equipment	367	152	181	257	376	519
Other supplies, equipment, and services	522	75	100	202	361	964
Personal-care products and services	**458**	**250**	**252**	**359**	**428**	**624**
Reading	**194**	**75**	**97**	**136**	**185**	**282**
Education	**449**	**200**	**146**	**233**	**295**	**759**
Tobacco products and smoking supplies	**329**	**330**	**337**	**377**	**343**	**301**
Cash contributions	**952**	**218**	**379**	**681**	**980**	**1,423**
Personal insurance and pensions	**4,191**	**502**	**1,344**	**2,463**	**3,673**	**6,952**
Life and other personal insurance	483	175	200	280	473	739
Pensions and Social Security	3,708	326	1,145	2,183	3,200	6,213
Miscellaneous	**913**	**376**	**420**	**663**	**960**	**1,293**

*The Consumer Expenditure Survey uses consumer units as its sampling unit. See Glossary for definition of consumer unit.

Source: Bureau of Labor Statistics

Note: The data here for all households in the age group will differ from those for the age groups given on pages 176 through 178 because combined data from 1989-1990 were used for this crosstabulation. Numbers may not add to total due to rounding.

Indexed Spending by Income, Householders Aged 35 to 44

Among households headed by 35-to-44-year-olds, only those in the top income category spend less than the average household in their age group on rent.

(indexed annual average expenditures for householders aged 35 to 44 by income, 1989-90; number of households in thousands; complete income reporters only)

	all households	under $10,000	$10,000 to $19,999	$20,000 to $29,999	$30,000 to $39,999	$40,000 or more
Number of households*	17,748	706	1,090	2,839	2,997	7,469
Income before taxes	$41,063	$5,308	$15,175	$24,615	$34,563	$67,697
Average number of persons per household	3.3	2.8	3.0	3.1	3.2	3.5
Average annual expenditures	100	45	57	71	92	142
Food	**100**	**61**	**68**	**80**	**92**	**130**
Food at home	100	73	82	89	92	119
Cereals and bakery products	100	66	82	88	93	120
Cereals and cereal products	100	71	91	100	87	115
Bakery products	100	64	77	81	97	124
Meats, poultry, fish, and eggs	100	86	86	90	87	117
Beef	100	79	84	89	91	118
Pork	100	104	82	99	94	108
Other meats	100	86	89	90	78	120
Poultry	100	78	94	91	88	115
Fish and seafood	100	80	82	73	78	131
Eggs	100	110	97	106	86	103
Dairy products	100	75	82	92	95	116
Fresh milk and cream	100	92	92	96	98	107
Other dairy products	100	62	73	88	92	125
Fruits and vegetables	100	73	79	90	92	120
Fresh fruits	100	66	77	91	93	122
Fresh vegetables	100	75	83	94	94	116
Processed fruits	100	77	77	84	86	124
Processed vegetables	100	78	79	91	92	118
Other food at home	100	64	79	88	96	121
Sugar and other sweets	100	61	72	89	93	125
Fats and oils	100	79	86	98	90	115
Miscellaneous foods	100	59	80	87	101	120
Nonalcoholic beverages	100	72	88	90	93	117
Food prep. by hh, out-of-town trips	100	44	37	60	79	157
Food away from home	100	46	50	68	93	144
Alcoholic beverages	**100**	**61**	**73**	**84**	**82**	**131**
Housing	**100**	**50**	**62**	**68**	**84**	**144**
Shelter	100	50	62	66	83	145
Owned dwellings	100	30	39	46	74	170
Mortgage interest	100	28	33	43	73	174

(continued on next page)

(indexed annual average expenditures for householders aged 35 to 44 by income, 1989-90; number of households in thousands; complete income reporters only)

	all households	under $10,000	$10,000 to $19,999	$20,000 to $29,999	$30,000 to $39,999	$40,000 or more
Property taxes	100	33	45	45	78	165
Maintenance, repairs, insurance, other	100	34	65	64	81	150
Rented dwellings	100	119	142	136	106	65
Other lodging	100	26	36	46	91	165
Utilities, fuels, and public services	100	68	81	89	97	120
Natural gas	100	73	78	79	107	120
Electricity	100	68	81	89	97	120
Fuel oil and other fuels	100	54	53	91	89	137
Telephone	100	71	91	95	93	115
Water and other public services	100	58	70	79	98	130
Household operations	100	28	40	45	66	173
Personal services	100	30	43	47	79	166
Other household expenses	100	27	37	41	48	183
Housekeeping supplies	100	59	63	70	82	140
Laundry and cleaning supplies	100	87	70	87	87	122
Other household products	100	40	54	64	79	150
Postage and stationery	100	61	70	62	83	141
Household furnishings and equipment	100	32	41	52	80	162
Household textiles	100	29	43	64	79	156
Furniture	100	19	55	66	88	153
Floor coverings	100	13	26	28	50	194
Major appliances	100	39	60	63	86	148
Small appliances, misc. housewares	100	28	43	49	76	164
Miscellaneous household equipment	100	44	28	43	79	167
Apparel and services	**100**	**41**	**52**	**75**	**95**	**140**
Men and boys	100	30	42	62	80	158
Men, aged 16 or older	100	28	31	56	77	166
Boys, aged 2 to 15	100	35	72	79	87	136
Women and girls	100	46	53	93	105	128
Women, aged 16 or older	100	47	49	99	107	126
Girls, aged 2 to 15	100	41	67	67	97	138
Babies under age 2	100	50	60	53	100	145
Footwear	100	43	66	56	115	135
Other apparel products and services	100	43	56	70	76	150
Transportation	**100**	**47**	**59**	**75**	**106**	**134**
Vehicle purchases (net outlay)	100	46	63	75	119	128
Cars and trucks, new	100	24	39	63	125	144
Cars and trucks, used	100	71	91	90	111	110
Other vehicles	100	84	7	30	130	157
Gasoline and motor oil	100	58	68	89	102	125
Other vehicle expenses	100	43	51	70	94	145
Vehicle finance charges	100	34	56	65	101	144
Maintenance and repairs	100	56	48	69	93	143
Vehicle insurance	100	36	53	79	98	141
Vehicle rental, licenses, other charges	100	38	45	57	73	161
Public transportation	100	40	43	57	83	158

(continued on next page)

(continued from previous page)

(indexed annual average expenditures for householders aged 35 to 44 by income, 1989-90; number of households in thousands; complete income reporters only)

	all households	under $10,000	$10,000 to $19,999	$20,000 to $29,999	$30,000 to $39,999	$40,000 or more
Health care	100	53	81	76	95	130
Health insurance	100	46	71	86	108	126
Medical services	100	56	74	71	88	135
Drugs	100	69	84	74	93	126
Medical supplies	100	34	172	57	83	120
Entertainment	100	35	41	59	85	158
Fees and admissions	100	34	27	53	80	167
Television, radios, sound equipment	100	49	67	76	94	136
Pets, toys, and playground equipment	100	42	49	70	102	141
Other supplies, equipment, and services	100	14	19	39	69	185
Personal-care products and services	100	55	55	78	93	136
Reading	100	39	50	70	95	145
Education	100	45	33	52	66	169
Tobacco products and smoking supplies	100	100	102	115	104	91
Cash contributions	100	23	40	72	103	149
Personal insurance and pensions	100	12	32	59	88	166
Life and other personal insurance	100	36	41	58	98	153
Pensions and Social Security	100	9	31	59	86	168
Miscellaneous	100	41	46	73	105	142

The Consumer Expenditure Survey uses consumer units as its sampling unit. See Glossary for definition of consumer unit.
Source: Bureau of Labor Statistics
Note: The data here for all households in the age group will differ from those for the age groups given on pages 176 through 178 because combined data from 1989-90 were used for this crosstabulation. An index of 100 is the average for all households. An index of 132 means that spending for that group is 32 percent greater than the average for all households. An index of 68 means that spending is 32 percent below average.

Spending by Income, Householders Aged 45 to 54

Households headed by 45-to-54-year-olds in the top income category spend more than any other households, just over $54,000 in 1990.

(annual average expenditures for householders aged 45 to 54 by income, 1989-90; number of households in thousands; complete income reporters only)

	all households	under $10,000	$10,000 to $19,999	$20,000 to $29,999	$30,000 to $39,999	$40,000 or more
Number of households*	12,376	521	861	1,980	1,657	5,404
Income before taxes	$42,716	$4,832	$14,743	$24,676	$34,693	$71,583
Average number of persons per household	2.9	2.2	2.6	2.8	3.0	3.2
Average annual expenditures	$37,358	$16,592	$19,618	$25,850	$33,008	$54,090
Food	**$5,528**	**$3,056**	**$3,732**	**$3,863**	**$5,148**	**$7,251**
Food at home	3,025	2,155	2,450	2,337	3,098	3,562
Cereals and bakery products	433	284	348	318	429	526
Cereals and cereal products	143	112	123	114	130	167
Bakery products	290	172	226	204	299	358
Meats, poultry, fish, and eggs	838	652	703	697	886	944
Beef	277	213	214	217	298	318
Pork	171	155	159	143	190	181
Other meats	130	89	142	122	131	137
Poultry	130	103	87	104	139	154
Fish and seafood	93	59	62	73	87	116
Eggs	38	34	39	38	40	38
Dairy products	359	254	311	300	367	409
Fresh milk and cream	165	126	178	156	179	166
Other dairy products	195	128	132	144	188	243
Fruits and vegetables	478	352	381	348	517	560
Fresh fruits	146	108	114	105	156	173
Fresh vegetables	147	107	136	106	150	169
Processed fruits	104	72	67	73	122	126
Processed vegetables	81	64	64	64	89	92
Other food at home	916	612	706	674	899	1,124
Sugar and other sweets	112	72	106	78	102	134
Fats and oils	77	58	76	62	75	85
Miscellaneous foods	396	276	264	242	409	504
Nonalcoholic beverages	286	192	239	261	278	328
Food prep. by hh, out-of-town trips	47	14	21	31	35	73
Food away from home	2,503	902	1,282	1,526	2,050	3,689
Alcoholic beverages	**338**	**142**	**173**	**230**	**325**	**468**
Housing	**10,610**	**5,885**	**6,061**	**8,266**	**8,874**	**14,791**
Shelter	6,025	3,329	3,355	4,624	5,002	8,506
Owned dwellings	3,912	1,529	1,249	2,626	2,968	6,245
Mortgage interest	2,536	1,000	740	1,479	1,798	4,191

(continued on next page)

(continued from previous page)

(annual average expenditures for householders aged 45 to 54 by income, 1989-90; number of households in thousands; complete income reporters only)

	all households	under $10,000	$10,000 to $19,999	$20,000 to $29,999	$30,000 to $39,999	$40,000 or more
Property taxes	$723	$253	$257	$539	$566	$1,127
Maintenance, repairs, insurance, other	653	276	251	607	605	928
Rented dwellings	1,264	1,432	1,854	1,618	1,407	834
Other lodging	849	368	252	381	627	1,428
Utilities, fuels, and public services	2,279	1,569	1,701	2,068	2,178	2,778
Natural gas	296	208	216	262	289	363
Electricity	912	614	671	817	835	1,134
Fuel oil and other fuels	104	49	62	97	108	135
Telephone	728	554	589	682	701	847
Water and other public services	238	144	162	211	246	298
Household operations	337	98	93	142	233	590
Personal services	83	11	23	43	47	150
Other household expenses	254	87	70	99	186	441
Housekeeping supplies	511	257	313	409	445	678
Laundry and cleaning supplies	139	88	98	106	144	172
Other household products	209	98	121	158	174	287
Postage and stationery	163	71	95	145	127	219
Household furnishings and equipment	1,458	632	600	1,022	1,016	2,239
Household textiles	147	185	50	81	110	211
Furniture	373	133	226	206	302	571
Floor coverings	142	0	48	66	67	251
Major appliances	174	60	69	164	147	254
Small appliances, misc. housewares	89	48	36	52	78	134
Miscellaneous household equipment	532	206	171	452	312	818
Apparel and services	**2,143**	**901**	**1,092**	**1,389**	**2,108**	**3,019**
Men and boys	563	185	237	304	453	872
Men, aged 16 or older	494	157	193	260	400	773
Boys, aged 2 to 15	69	28	45	44	53	100
Women and girls	893	354	487	619	893	1,223
Women, aged 16 or older	794	307	415	537	790	1,097
Girls, aged 2 to 15	99	47	71	82	103	126
Babies under age 2	59	26	29	45	117	66
Footwear	280	144	204	205	344	332
Other apparel products and services	347	191	134	217	301	526
Transportation	**7,057**	**2,574**	**3,676**	**4,424**	**6,341**	**10,593**
Vehicle purchases (net outlay)	3,001	798	1,652	1,391	2,433	4,817
Cars and trucks, new	1,592	131	406	639	1,056	2,907
Cars and trucks, used	1,376	668	1,215	752	1,350	1,853
Other vehicles	33	0	31	0	28	56
Gasoline and motor oil	1,354	771	810	1,177	1,391	1,754
Other vehicle expenses	2,270	834	1,012	1,640	2,230	3,319
Vehicle finance charges	431	141	171	268	460	650
Maintenance and repairs	786	272	409	575	811	1,109

(continued on next page)

(continued from previous page)

(annual average expenditures for householders aged 45 to 54 by income, 1989-90; number of households in thousands; complete income reporters only)

	all households	under $10,000	$10,000 to $19,999	$20,000 to $29,999	$30,000 to $39,999	$40,000 or more
Vehicle insurance	$806	$345	$352	$632	$748	$1,170
Vehicle rental, licenses, other charges	247	76	81	165	210	390
Public transportation	431	171	202	216	288	704
Health care	**1,509**	**908**	**1,055**	**1,231**	**1,519**	**1,922**
Health insurance	536	361	386	470	570	649
Medical services	626	276	376	502	547	877
Drugs	236	213	219	177	296	251
Medical supplies	110	57	75	81	107	146
Entertainment	**1,901**	**1,040**	**678**	**1,305**	**1,383**	**2,932**
Fees and admissions	457	108	143	243	342	772
Television, radios, sound equipment	557	277	289	388	514	798
Pets, toys, and playground equipment	362	223	199	434	315	447
Other supplies, equipment, and services	525	432	46	240	213	915
Personal-care products and services	**486**	**207**	**290**	**324**	**476**	**666**
Reading	**191**	**82**	**92**	**136**	**190**	**275**
Education	**667**	**239**	**201**	**302**	**512**	**1,125**
Tobacco products and smoking supplies	**355**	**351**	**340**	**332**	**375**	**363**
Cash contributions	**1,384**	**191**	**401**	**667**	**990**	**2,427**
Personal insurance and pensions	**4,298**	**598**	**1,360**	**2,524**	**3,854**	**7,093**
Life and other personal insurance	501	228	236	301	512	738
Pensions and Social Security	3,797	370	1,124	2,223	3,342	6,355
Miscellaneous	**890**	**416**	**467**	**856**	**913**	**1,166**

*The Consumer Expenditure Survey uses consumer units as its sampling unit. See Glossary for definition of consumer unit.

Source: Bureau of Labor Statistics

Note: The data for all households in the age group will differ from those for the age groups given on pages 176 through 178 because combined data from 1989-90 were used for this crosstabulation. Numbers may not add to total due to rounding.

Indexed Spending by Income, Householders Aged 45 to 54

The most affluent households headed by 45-to-54-year-olds spend less than the average household in this age group only on rent. They spend nearly twice as much on new cars and trucks.

(indexed annual average expenditures for householders aged 45 to 54 by income, 1989-90; number of households in thousands; complete income reporters only)

	all households	under $10,000	$10,000 to $19,999	$20,000 to $29,999	$30,000 to $39,999	$40,000 or more
Number of households*	12,376	521	861	1,980	1,657	5,404
Income before taxes	$42,716	$4,832	$14,743	$24,676	$34,693	$71,583
Average number of persons per household	2.9	2.2	2.6	2.8	3.0	3.2
Average annual expenditures	100	44	53	69	88	145
Food	100	55	68	70	93	131
Food at home	100	71	81	77	102	118
Cereals and bakery products	100	66	80	73	99	121
Cereals and cereal products	100	79	86	80	91	117
Bakery products	100	59	78	70	103	123
Meats, poultry, fish, and eggs	100	78	84	83	106	113
Beef	100	77	77	78	108	115
Pork	100	90	93	84	111	106
Other meats	100	68	109	94	101	105
Poultry	100	79	67	80	107	118
Fish and seafood	100	63	67	78	94	125
Eggs	100	90	104	100	105	100
Dairy products	100	71	87	84	102	114
Fresh milk and cream	100	77	108	95	108	101
Other dairy products	100	65	68	74	96	125
Fruits and vegetables	100	74	80	73	108	117
Fresh fruits	100	74	78	72	107	118
Fresh vegetables	100	73	93	72	102	115
Processed fruits	100	69	64	70	117	121
Processed vegetables	100	79	79	79	110	114
Other food at home	100	67	77	74	98	123
Sugar and other sweets	100	64	95	70	91	120
Fats and oils	100	75	98	81	97	110
Miscellaneous foods	100	70	67	61	103	127
Nonalcoholic beverages	100	67	84	91	97	115
Food prep. by hh, out-of-town trips	100	30	44	66	74	155
Food away from home	100	36	51	61	82	147
Alcoholic beverages	100	42	51	68	96	138
Housing	100	55	57	78	84	139
Shelter	100	55	56	77	83	141
Owned dwellings	100	39	32	67	76	160
Mortgage interest	100	39	29	58	71	165

(continued on next page)

(indexed annual average expenditures for householders aged 45 to 54 by income, 1989-90; number of households in thousands; complete income reporters only)

	all households	under $10,000	$10,000 to $19,999	$20,000 to $29,999	$30,000 to $39,999	$40,000 or more
Property taxes	100	35	36	75	78	156
Maintenance, repairs, insurance, other	100	42	38	93	93	142
Rented dwellings	100	113	147	128	111	66
Other lodging	100	43	30	45	74	168
Utilities, fuels, and public services	100	69	75	91	96	122
Natural gas	100	70	73	89	98	123
Electricity	100	67	74	90	92	124
Fuel oil and other fuels	100	47	60	93	104	130
Telephone	100	76	81	94	96	116
Water and other public services	100	60	68	89	103	125
Household operations	100	29	28	42	69	175
Personal services	100	13	27	52	57	181
Other household expenses	100	34	28	39	73	174
Housekeeping supplies	100	50	61	80	87	133
Laundry and cleaning supplies	100	63	71	76	104	124
Other household products	100	47	58	76	83	137
Postage and stationery	100	44	58	89	78	134
Household furnishings and equipment	100	43	41	70	70	154
Household textiles	100	126	34	55	75	144
Furniture	100	36	61	55	81	153
Floor coverings	100	0	34	46	47	177
Major appliances	100	34	40	94	84	146
Small appliances, misc. housewares	100	54	40	58	88	151
Miscellaneous household equipment	100	39	32	85	59	154
Apparel and services	**100**	**42**	**51**	**65**	**98**	**141**
Men and boys	100	33	42	54	80	155
Men, aged 16 or older	100	32	39	53	81	156
Boys, aged 2 to 15	100	41	65	64	77	145
Women and girls	100	40	55	69	100	137
Women, aged 16 or older	100	39	52	68	99	138
Girls, aged 2 to 15	100	48	72	83	104	127
Babies under age 2	100	45	48	76	198	112
Footwear	100	51	73	73	123	119
Other apparel products and services	100	55	39	63	87	152
Transportation	**100**	**36**	**52**	**63**	**90**	**150**
Vehicle purchases (net outlay)	100	27	55	46	81	161
Cars and trucks, new	100	8	25	40	66	183
Cars and trucks, used	100	49	88	55	98	135
Other vehicles	100	0	95	0	85	170
Gasoline and motor oil	100	57	60	87	103	130
Other vehicle expenses	100	37	45	72	98	146
Vehicle finance charges	100	33	40	62	107	151
Maintenance and repairs	100	35	52	73	103	141
Vehicle insurance	100	43	44	78	93	145
Vehicle rental, licenses, other charges	100	31	33	67	85	158
Public transportation	100	40	47	50	67	163

(continued on next page)

(continued from previous page)
(indexed annual average expenditures for householders aged 45 to 54 by income, 1989-90; number of households in thousands; complete income reporters only)

	all households	under $10,000	$10,000 to $19,999	$20,000 to $29,999	$30,000 to $39,999	$40,000 or more
Health care	**100**	**60**	**70**	**82**	**101**	**127**
Health insurance	100	67	72	88	106	121
Medical services	100	44	60	80	87	140
Drugs	100	90	93	75	125	106
Medical supplies	100	52	68	74	97	133
Entertainment	**100**	**55**	**36**	**69**	**73**	**154**
Fees and admissions	100	24	31	53	75	169
Television, radios, sound equipment	100	50	52	70	92	143
Pets, toys, and playground equipment	100	62	55	120	87	123
Other supplies, equipment, and services	100	82	9	46	41	174
Personal-care products and services	**100**	**43**	**60**	**67**	**98**	**137**
Reading	**100**	**43**	**48**	**71**	**99**	**144**
Education	**100**	**36**	**30**	**45**	**77**	**169**
Tobacco products and smoking supplies	**100**	**99**	**96**	**94**	**106**	**102**
Cash contributions	**100**	**14**	**29**	**48**	**72**	**175**
Personal insurance and pensions	**100**	**14**	**32**	**59**	**90**	**165**
Life and other personal insurance	100	46	47	60	102	147
Pensions and Social Security	100	10	30	59	88	167
Miscellaneous	**100**	**47**	**52**	**96**	**103**	**131**

*The Consumer Expenditure Survey uses consumer units as its sampling unit. See Glossary for definition of consumer unit.
Source: Bureau of Labor Statistics
Note: The data here for all households in the age group will differ from those for the age groups given on pages 176 through 178 because combined data from 1989-90 were used for this crosstabulation. An index of 100 is the average for all households. An index of 132 means that spending for that group is 32 percent greater than the average for all households. An index of 68 means that spending is 32 percent below average.

Spending by Income, Householders Aged 55 to 64

Income and spending levels begin to drop among householders aged 55 to 64 because many are retired.

(annual average expenditures for householders aged 55 to 64 by income, 1989-90; number of households in thousands; complete income reporters only)

	all households	under $10,000	$10,000 to $19,999	$20,000 to $29,999	$30,000 to $39,999	$40,000 or more
Number of households*	9,844	564	1,195	1,789	1,148	3,060
Income before taxes	$35,041	$5,428	$14,736	$24,738	$34,883	$72,002
Average number of persons per household	2.3	1.7	2.0	2.1	2.6	2.7
Average annual expenditures	$29,681	$14,528	$18,791	$24,462	$31,215	$48,410
Food	$4,476	$2,673	$3,320	$4,234	$4,795	$6,391
Food at home	2,635	1,922	2,320	2,593	2,863	3,231
Cereals and bakery products	388	281	348	398	402	475
Cereals and cereal products	127	107	121	127	131	144
Bakery products	261	174	227	271	271	331
Meats, poultry, fish, and eggs	739	592	671	696	785	883
Beef	232	183	194	222	273	275
Pork	153	143	143	154	159	165
Other meats	110	74	99	99	127	137
Poultry	119	102	108	118	117	137
Fish and seafood	90	60	87	66	73	133
Eggs	36	30	39	37	37	37
Dairy products	306	220	276	323	352	352
Fresh milk and cream	138	115	139	147	160	137
Other dairy products	168	106	137	176	192	215
Fruits and vegetables	453	320	377	450	491	575
Fresh fruits	149	91	118	144	181	197
Fresh vegetables	142	115	124	142	136	176
Processed fruits	89	64	73	95	87	114
Processed vegetables	72	49	62	69	87	89
Other food at home	748	509	648	727	831	945
Sugar and other sweets	94	64	72	78	125	123
Fats and oils	72	66	64	65	77	84
Miscellaneous foods	304	190	272	322	299	389
Nonalcoholic beverages	233	161	213	228	256	283
Food prep. by hh, out-of-town trips	46	29	28	33	75	66
Food away from home	1,841	750	1,001	1,640	1,933	3,160
Alcoholic beverages	265	82	148	215	277	479
Housing	8,205	4,974	5,650	6,957	8,054	12,592
Shelter	4,302	2,593	2,866	3,451	4,019	6,867
Owned dwellings	2,840	1,177	1,571	2,186	2,959	4,999
Mortgage interest	1,186	372	514	858	1,146	2,320

(continued on next page)

(continued from previous page)

(annual average expenditures for householders aged 55 to 64 by income, 1989-90; number of households in thousands; complete income reporters only)

	all households	under $10,000	$10,000 to $19,999	$20,000 to $29,999	$30,000 to $39,999	$40,000 or more
Property taxes	$857	$386	$517	$645	$938	$1,454
Maintenance, repairs, insurance, other	796	420	541	683	875	1,224
Rented dwellings	783	1,250	953	880	463	462
Other lodging	679	166	342	385	597	1,406
Utilities, fuels, and public services	2,059	1,530	1,714	1,961	2,118	2,635
Natural gas	301	212	255	278	351	379
Electricity	836	644	723	783	873	1,041
Fuel oil and other fuels	130	86	86	172	105	171
Telephone	575	436	470	535	565	753
Water and other public services	217	153	179	193	224	290
Household operations	319	135	153	221	179	647
Personal services	48	40	13	51	7	90
Other household expenses	271	95	141	170	171	557
Housekeeping supplies	462	268	312	477	487	666
Laundry and cleaning supplies	120	84	92	144	137	141
Other household products	199	106	121	205	193	312
Postage and stationery	142	77	99	128	157	214
Household furnishings and equipment	1,063	449	604	847	1,251	1,778
Household textiles	122	71	85	83	168	178
Furniture	263	83	115	244	256	480
Floor coverings	106	47	46	58	132	197
Major appliances	166	54	119	188	237	224
Small appliances, misc. housewares	69	26	39	58	62	126
Miscellaneous household equipment	337	168	201	215	395	574
Apparel and services	**1,586**	**619**	**939**	**1,137**	**1,787**	**2,780**
Men and boys	347	95	196	261	333	659
Men, aged 16 or older	312	81	165	215	293	618
Boys, aged 2 to 15	35	14	31	46	40	41
Women and girls	726	296	420	503	1,022	1,186
Women, aged 16 or older	690	277	402	468	978	1,133
Girls, aged 2 to 15	36	19	18	34	44	53
Babies under age 2	49	22	45	43	48	74
Footwear	221	94	158	184	175	388
Other apparel products and services	244	113	119	148	209	473
Transportation	**5,503**	**2,570**	**3,445**	**4,553**	**6,528**	**8,775**
Vehicle purchases (net outlay)	2,304	1,102	1,275	1,735	2,795	3,847
Cars and trucks, new	1,289	549	514	818	1,496	2,442
Cars and trucks, used	992	553	761	916	1,287	1,335
Other vehicles	23	0	0	1	12	69
Gasoline and motor oil	1,127	650	893	1,055	1,355	1,516
Other vehicle expenses	1,725	666	1,118	1,549	1,980	2,766
Vehicle finance charges	252	90	125	222	325	423
Maintenance and repairs	619	246	435	548	708	975

(continued on next page)

(annual average expenditures for householders aged 55 to 64 by income, 1989-90; number of households in thousands; complete income reporters only)

	all households	under $10,000	$10,000 to $19,999	$20,000 to $29,999	$30,000 to $39,999	$40,000 or more
Vehicle insurance	$672	$268	$452	$613	$809	$1,036
Vehicle rental, licenses, other charges	183	62	106	166	138	331
Public transportation	347	152	158	214	397	647
Health care	**1,829**	**1,027**	**1,696**	**1,680**	**1,737**	**2,505**
Health insurance	686	393	747	649	680	835
Medical services	694	320	544	633	531	1,108
Drugs	346	258	331	307	415	407
Medical supplies	103	56	73	91	111	154
Entertainment	**1,478**	**586**	**690**	**913**	**1,533**	**2,843**
Fees and admissions	393	116	162	223	384	811
Television, radios, sound equipment	398	184	268	328	458	630
Pets, toys, and playground equipment	254	124	171	171	267	431
Other supplies, equipment, and services	433	161	88	191	423	971
Personal-care products and services	**425**	**222**	**360**	**339**	**448**	**635**
Reading	**174**	**72**	**109**	**149**	**184**	**288**
Education	**328**	**216**	**94**	**226**	**192**	**663**
Tobacco products and smoking supplies	**333**	**292**	**314**	**371**	**415**	**316**
Cash contributions	**1,115**	**286**	**489**	**951**	**1,236**	**2,068**
Personal insurance and pensions	**3,294**	**607**	**1,047**	**2,180**	**3,431**	**6,972**
Life and other personal insurance	450	177	223	388	423	809
Pensions and Social Security	2,844	430	824	1,793	3,008	6,163
Miscellaneous	**670**	**304**	**488**	**556**	**599**	**1,103**

*The Consumer Expenditure Survey uses consumer units as its sampling unit. See Glossary for definition of consumer unit.
Source: Bureau of Labor Statistics
Note: The data here for all households in the age group will differ from those for the age groups given on pages 176 through 178 because combined data from 1989-90 were used for this crosstabulation. Numbers may not add to total due to rounding.

Indexed Spending by Income, Householders Aged 55 to 64

The most affluent households headed by 55-to-64-year-olds spend more than twice as much as the average household in their age group on items such as pensions, insurance, education (for their grandchildren), and fees and admissions.

(indexed annual average expenditures for householders aged 55 to 64 by income, 1989-90; number of households in thousands; complete income reporters only)

	all households	under $10,000	$10,000 to $19,999	$20,000 to $29,999	$30,000 to $39,999	$40,000 or more
Number of households*	9,844	564	1,195	1,789	1,148	3,060
Income before taxes	$35,041	$5,428	$14,736	$24,738	$34,883	$72,002
Average number of persons per household	2.3	1.7	2.0	2.1	2.6	2.7
Average annual expenditures	100	49	63	82	105	163
Food	**100**	**60**	**74**	**95**	**107**	**143**
Food at home	100	73	88	98	109	123
Cereals and bakery products	100	72	90	103	104	122
Cereals and cereal products	100	84	95	100	103	113
Bakery products	100	67	87	104	104	127
Meats, poultry, fish, and eggs	100	80	91	94	106	119
Beef	100	79	83	96	118	119
Pork	100	93	93	101	104	108
Other meats	100	67	90	90	115	125
Poultry	100	86	91	99	98	115
Fish and seafood	100	67	97	73	81	148
Eggs	100	85	109	103	103	103
Dairy products	100	72	90	106	115	115
Fresh milk and cream	100	83	101	107	116	99
Other dairy products	100	63	81	105	114	128
Fruits and vegetables	100	71	83	99	108	127
Fresh fruits	100	61	79	97	121	132
Fresh vegetables	100	81	88	100	96	124
Processed fruits	100	72	82	107	98	128
Processed vegetables	100	69	85	96	121	124
Other food at home	100	68	87	97	111	126
Sugar and other sweets	100	68	76	83	133	131
Fats and oils	100	92	89	90	107	117
Miscellaneous foods	100	62	89	106	98	128
Nonalcoholic beverages	100	69	91	98	110	121
Food prep. by hh, out-of-town trips	100	63	60	72	163	143
Food away from home	100	41	54	89	105	172
Alcoholic beverages	**100**	**31**	**56**	**81**	**105**	**181**
Housing	**100**	**61**	**69**	**85**	**98**	**153**
Shelter	100	60	67	80	93	160
Owned dwellings	100	41	55	77	104	176
Mortgage interest	100	31	43	72	97	196

(continued on next page)

(indexed annual average expenditures for householders aged 55 to 64 by income, 1989-90; number of households in thousands; complete income reporters only)

	all households	under $10,000	$10,000 to $19,999	$20,000 to $29,999	$30,000 to $39,999	$40,000 or more
Property taxes	100	45	60	75	109	170
Maintenance, repairs, insurance, other	100	53	68	86	110	154
Rented dwellings	100	160	122	112	59	59
Other lodging	100	24	50	57	88	207
Utilities, fuels, and public services	100	74	83	95	103	128
Natural gas	100	70	85	92	117	126
Electricity	100	77	87	94	104	125
Fuel oil and other fuels	100	66	66	132	81	132
Telephone	100	76	82	93	98	131
Water and other public services	100	70	83	89	103	134
Household operations	100	42	48	69	56	203
Personal services	100	84	26	106	15	188
Other household expenses	100	35	52	63	63	206
Housekeeping supplies	100	58	67	103	105	144
Laundry and cleaning supplies	100	70	77	120	114	118
Other household products	100	53	61	103	97	157
Postage and stationery	100	54	70	90	111	151
Household furnishings and equipment	100	42	57	80	118	167
Household textiles	100	58	70	68	138	146
Furniture	100	32	44	93	97	183
Floor coverings	100	45	43	55	125	186
Major appliances	100	33	72	113	143	135
Small appliances, misc. housewares	100	37	57	84	90	183
Miscellaneous household equipment	100	50	60	64	117	170
Apparel and services	**100**	**39**	**59**	**72**	**113**	**175**
Men and boys	100	27	56	75	96	190
Men, aged 16 or older	100	26	53	69	94	198
Boys, aged 2 to 15	100	41	89	131	114	117
Women and girls	100	41	58	69	141	163
Women, aged 16 or older	100	40	58	68	142	164
Girls, aged 2 to 15	100	52	50	94	122	147
Babies under age 2	100	45	92	88	98	151
Footwear	100	42	72	83	79	176
Other apparel products and services	100	46	49	61	86	194
Transportation	**100**	**47**	**63**	**83**	**119**	**159**
Vehicle purchases (net outlay)	100	48	55	75	121	167
Cars and trucks, new	100	43	40	63	116	189
Cars and trucks, used	100	56	77	92	130	135
Other vehicles	100	0	0	4	52	300
Gasoline and motor oil	100	58	79	94	120	135
Other vehicle expenses	100	39	65	90	115	160
Vehicle finance charges	100	36	50	88	129	168
Maintenance and repairs	100	40	70	89	114	158
Vehicle insurance	100	40	67	91	120	154
Vehicle rental, licenses, other charges	100	34	58	91	75	181
Public transportation	100	44	46	62	114	186

(continued on next page)

(continued from previous page)

(indexed annual average expenditures for householders aged 55 to 64 by income, 1989-90; number of households in thousands; complete income reporters only)

	all households	under $10,000	$10,000 to $19,999	$20,000 to $29,999	$30,000 to $39,999	$40,000 or more
Health care	**100**	**56**	**93**	**92**	**95**	**137**
Health insurance	100	57	109	95	99	122
Medical services	100	46	78	91	77	160
Drugs	100	75	96	89	120	118
Medical supplies	100	55	71	88	108	150
Entertainment	**100**	**40**	**47**	**62**	**104**	**192**
Fees and admissions	100	29	41	57	98	206
Television, radios, sound equipment	100	46	67	82	115	158
Pets, toys, and playground equipment	100	49	67	67	105	170
Other supplies, equipment, and services	100	37	20	44	98	224
Personal-care products and services	**100**	**52**	**85**	**80**	**105**	**149**
Reading	**100**	**41**	**63**	**86**	**106**	**166**
Education	**100**	**66**	**29**	**69**	**59**	**202**
Tobacco products and smoking supplies	**100**	**88**	**94**	**111**	**125**	**95**
Cash contributions	**100**	**26**	**44**	**85**	**111**	**185**
Personal insurance and pensions	**100**	**18**	**32**	**66**	**104**	**212**
Life and other personal insurance	100	39	50	86	94	180
Pensions and Social Security	100	15	29	63	106	217
Miscellaneous	**100**	**45**	**73**	**83**	**89**	**165**

*The Consumer Expenditure Survey uses consumer units as its sampling unit. See Glossary for definition of consumer unit.
Source: Bureau of Labor Statistics
Note: The data here for all households in the age group will differ from those for the age groups given on pages 176 through 178 because combined data from 1989-90 were used for this crosstabulation. An index of 100 is the average for all households. An index of 132 means that spending for that group is 32 percent greater than the average for all households. An index of 68 means that spending is 32 percent below average.

Spending by Income, Householders Aged 65 or Older

The majority of householders aged 65 or older had incomes below $30,000 in 1990 and spent less than $25,000.

(annual average expenditures for householders aged 65 or older by income, 1989-90; number of households in thousands; complete income reporters only)

	all households	under $10,000	$10,000 to $19,999	$20,000 to $29,999	$30,000 to $39,999	$40,000 or more
Number of households*	**17,934**	**1,437**	**5,111**	**2,666**	**1,218**	**1,647**
Income before taxes	**$19,269**	**$6,543**	**$14,268**	**$24,344**	**$34,443**	**$68,218**
Average number of persons per household	**1.8**	**1.4**	**1.8**	**2.1**	**2.2**	**2.3**
Average annual expenditures	**$19,047**	**$10,877**	**$16,868**	**$23,455**	**$28,638**	**$46,265**
Food	**$2,957**	**$1,873**	**$2,883**	**$3,644**	**$4,651**	**$5,672**
Food at home	1,959	1,430	2,008	2,352	2,894	2,815
Cereals and bakery products	310	231	315	359	445	458
Cereals and cereal products	105	84	107	117	137	146
Bakery products	205	147	209	242	309	312
Meats, poultry, fish, and eggs	516	382	517	644	821	685
Beef	166	135	160	209	270	181
Pork	103	78	104	137	126	143
Other meats	70	52	74	81	108	80
Poultry	89	63	91	98	143	146
Fish and seafood	61	31	59	93	132	101
Eggs	27	21	30	25	42	33
Dairy products	236	181	249	267	316	330
Fresh milk and cream	118	97	122	133	153	146
Other dairy products	119	84	127	135	163	183
Fruits and vegetables	388	277	399	470	606	562
Fresh fruits	132	86	126	166	251	224
Fresh vegetables	112	83	121	128	167	146
Processed fruits	87	62	96	104	117	114
Processed vegetables	57	45	56	72	71	77
Other food at home	508	359	526	612	706	781
Sugar and other sweets	72	58	67	81	118	109
Fats and oils	56	41	64	62	74	72
Miscellaneous foods	208	144	217	259	254	340
Nonalcoholic beverages	149	111	162	173	213	185
Food prep. by hh, out-of-town trips	23	5	16	37	47	75
Food away from home	998	443	875	1,292	1,757	2,856
Alcoholic beverages	**138**	**45**	**113**	**187**	**354**	**433**
Housing	**6,148**	**4,210**	**5,667**	**7,042**	**8,403**	**12,648**
Shelter	3,032	2,067	2,738	3,362	4,179	6,532
Owned dwellings	1,782	1,013	1,535	2,165	2,735	4,396
Mortgage interest	369	175	278	350	816	1,165

(continued on next page)

(continued from previous page)

(annual average expenditures for householders aged 65 or older by income, 1989-90; number of households in thousands; complete income reporters only)

	all households	under $10,000	$10,000 to $19,999	$20,000 to $29,999	$30,000 to $39,999	$40,000 or more
Property taxes	$690	$385	$609	$836	$1,110	$1,646
Maintenance, repairs, insurance, other	722	452	648	979	809	1,585
Rented dwellings	860	950	950	640	796	591
Other lodging	389	105	252	557	648	1,545
Utilities, fuels, and public services	1,685	1,285	1,694	2,015	2,077	2,422
Natural gas	253	192	265	304	279	348
Electricity	680	503	688	802	885	1,000
Fuel oil and other fuels	138	118	145	160	130	170
Telephone	429	345	416	506	542	606
Water and other public services	185	128	180	242	242	298
Household operations	385	249	299	415	455	1,135
Personal services	95	99	77	36	134	213
Other household expenses	290	150	222	379	320	921
Housekeeping supplies	364	213	398	451	573	637
Laundry and cleaning supplies	85	62	88	112	118	108
Other household products	156	79	199	178	234	253
Postage and stationery	124	73	112	161	220	276
Household furnishings and equipment	682	396	538	799	1,119	1,922
Household textiles	85	29	76	114	206	232
Furniture	151	87	131	163	201	421
Floor coverings	49	28	41	57	64	151
Major appliances	110	80	93	122	151	242
Small appliances, misc. housewares	49	28	48	53	116	87
Miscellaneous household equipment	237	146	150	290	381	788
Apparel and services	**820**	**354**	**707**	**1,128**	**1,453**	**2,359**
Men and boys	174	51	166	257	296	512
Men, aged 16 or older	154	37	147	220	279	488
Boys, aged 2 to 15	20	14	19	36	17	24
Women and girls	403	175	335	549	809	1,192
Women, aged 16 or older	381	165	321	522	756	1,118
Girls, aged 2 to 15	22	11	15	27	53	74
Babies under age 2	18	5	18	19	31	61
Footwear	110	63	106	158	117	257
Other apparel products and services	114	60	81	146	201	336
Transportation	**3,054**	**1,382**	**2,678**	**4,203**	**5,043**	**7,720**
Vehicle purchases (net outlay)	1,207	492	1,039	1,577	2,027	3,436
Cars and trucks, new	683	191	666	869	1,094	2,097
Cars and trucks, used	522	300	372	708	926	1,339
Other vehicles	1	0	1	0	7	0
Gasoline and motor oil	614	334	597	870	932	1,139
Other vehicle expenses	994	474	898	1,391	1,692	2,261
Vehicle finance charges	102	39	94	168	189	206
Maintenance and repairs	389	202	336	551	716	831

(continued on next page)

(continued from previous page)

(annual average expenditures for householders aged 65 or older by income, 1989-90; number of households in thousands; complete income reporters only)

	all households	under $10,000	$10,000 to $19,999	$20,000 to $29,999	$30,000 to $39,999	$40,000 or more
Vehicle insurance	$401	$197	$380	$528	$630	$908
Vehicle rental, licenses, other charges	103	35	88	144	157	315
Public transportation	239	82	144	364	391	884
Health care	**2,188**	**1,534**	**2,254**	**2,638**	**2,704**	**3,508**
Health insurance	981	713	1,078	1,239	1,101	1,197
Medical services	639	407	618	767	926	1,214
Drugs	451	349	462	541	541	621
Medical supplies	117	66	96	90	136	476
Entertainment	**713**	**257**	**546**	**1,052**	**1,214**	**2,227**
Fees and admissions	245	48	148	359	450	1,033
Television, radios, sound equipment	244	129	223	304	327	624
Pets, toys, and playground equipment	140	54	108	293	224	304
Other supplies, equipment, and services	84	27	66	96	213	266
Personal-care products and services	**280**	**146**	**280**	**369**	**449**	**600**
Reading	**140**	**65**	**130**	**201**	**218**	**314**
Education	**65**	**34**	**40**	**99**	**103**	**198**
Tobacco products and smoking supplies	**154**	**116**	**133**	**215**	**219**	**239**
Cash contributions	**1,136**	**368**	**684**	**1,370**	**1,685**	**5,010**
Personal insurance and pensions	**786**	**150**	**394**	**808**	**1,429**	**4,195**
Life and other personal insurance	274	124	239	313	316	902
Pensions and Social Security	512	27	155	494	1,113	3,292
Miscellaneous	**467**	**343**	**358**	**499**	**714**	**1,142**

*The Consumer Expenditure Survey uses consumer units as its sampling unit. See Glossary for definition of consumer unit.
Source: Bureau of Labor Statistics
Note: The data here for all households in the age group will differ from those for the age groups given on pages 176 through 178 because combined data from 1989-90 were used for this crosstabulation. Numbers may not add to total due to rounding.

Indexed Spending by Income, Householders Aged 65 or Older

The spending of affluent householders aged 65 or older contrasts sharply with the spending of the average household in this age group. Those in the highest income category spend three and four times as much as the average on a variety of products and services.

(indexed annual average expenditures for householders aged 65 or older by income, 1989-90; number of households in thousands; complete income reporters only)

	all households	under $10,000	$10,000 to $19,999	$20,000 to $29,999	$30,000 to $39,999	$40,000 or more
Number of households*	17,934	1,437	5,111	2,666	1,218	1,647
Income before taxes	$19,269	$6,543	$14,268	$24,344	$34,443	$68,218
Average number of persons per household	1.8	1.4	1.8	2.1	2.2	2.3
Average annual expenditures	100	57	89	123	150	243
Food	**100**	**63**	**97**	**123**	**157**	**192**
Food at home	100	73	103	120	148	144
Cereals and bakery products	100	75	102	116	144	148
Cereals and cereal products	100	80	102	111	130	139
Bakery products	100	72	102	118	151	152
Meats, poultry, fish, and eggs	100	74	100	125	159	133
Beef	100	81	96	126	163	109
Pork	100	76	101	133	122	139
Other meats	100	75	106	116	154	114
Poultry	100	71	102	110	161	164
Fish and seafood	100	51	97	152	216	166
Eggs	100	79	110	93	156	122
Dairy products	100	77	106	113	134	140
Fresh milk and cream	100	82	104	113	130	124
Other dairy products	100	70	107	113	137	154
Fruits and vegetables	100	71	103	121	156	145
Fresh fruits	100	65	95	126	190	170
Fresh vegetables	100	74	108	114	149	130
Processed fruits	100	71	110	120	134	131
Processed vegetables	100	79	99	126	125	135
Other food at home	100	71	104	120	139	154
Sugar and other sweets	100	81	93	113	164	151
Fats and oils	100	74	115	111	132	129
Miscellaneous foods	100	69	104	125	122	163
Nonalcoholic beverages	100	74	109	116	143	124
Food prep. by hh, out-of-town trips	100	23	68	161	204	326
Food away from home	100	44	88	129	176	286
Alcoholic beverages	**100**	**32**	**82**	**136**	**257**	**314**
Housing	**100**	**68**	**92**	**115**	**137**	**206**
Shelter	100	68	90	111	138	215
Owned dwellings	100	57	86	121	153	247
Mortgage interest	100	47	75	95	221	316

(continued on next page)

(indexed annual average expenditures for householders aged 65 or older by income, 1989-90; number of households in thousands; complete income reporters only)

	all households	under $10,000	$10,000 to $19,999	$20,000 to $29,999	$30,000 to $39,999	$40,000 or more
Property taxes	100	56	88	121	161	239
Maintenance, repairs, insurance, other	100	63	90	136	112	220
Rented dwellings	100	110	110	74	93	69
Other lodging	100	27	65	143	167	397
Utilities, fuels, and public services	100	76	101	120	123	144
Natural gas	100	76	105	120	110	138
Electricity	100	74	101	118	130	147
Fuel oil and other fuels	100	85	105	116	94	123
Telephone	100	80	97	118	126	141
Water and other public services	100	69	97	131	131	161
Household operations	100	65	78	108	118	295
Personal services	100	105	81	38	141	224
Other household expenses	100	52	77	131	110	318
Housekeeping supplies	100	58	109	124	157	175
Laundry and cleaning supplies	100	73	104	132	139	127
Other household products	100	51	127	114	150	162
Postage and stationery	100	59	90	130	177	223
Household furnishings and equipment	100	58	79	117	164	282
Household textiles	100	34	90	134	242	273
Furniture	100	58	87	108	133	279
Floor coverings	100	57	83	116	131	308
Major appliances	100	72	85	111	137	220
Small appliances, misc. housewares	100	57	97	108	237	178
Miscellaneous household equipment	100	61	63	122	161	332
Apparel and services	**100**	**43**	**86**	**138**	**177**	**288**
Men and boys	100	29	95	148	170	294
Men, aged 16 or older	100	24	96	143	181	317
Boys, aged 2 to 15	100	70	94	180	85	120
Women and girls	100	43	83	136	201	296
Women, aged 16 or older	100	43	84	137	198	293
Girls, aged 2 to 15	100	48	67	123	241	336
Babies under age 2	100	28	100	106	172	339
Footwear	100	57	97	144	106	234
Other apparel products and services	100	53	71	128	176	295
Transportation	**100**	**45**	**88**	**138**	**165**	**253**
Vehicle purchases (net outlay)	100	41	86	131	168	285
Cars and trucks, new	100	28	97	127	160	307
Cars and trucks, used	100	58	71	136	177	257
Other vehicles	100	0	78	0	700	0
Gasoline and motor oil	100	54	97	142	152	186
Other vehicle expenses	100	48	90	140	170	227
Vehicle finance charges	100	38	93	165	185	202
Maintenance and repairs	100	52	86	142	184	214
Vehicle insurance	100	49	95	132	157	226
Vehicle rental, licenses, other charges	100	34	85	140	152	306
Public transportation	100	34	60	152	164	370

(continued on next page)

(continued from previous page)

(indexed annual average expenditures for householders aged 65 or older by income, 1989-90; number of households in thousands; complete income reporters only)

	all households	under $10,000	$10,000 to $19,999	$20,000 to $29,999	$30,000 to $39,999	$40,000 or more
Health care	**100**	**70**	**103**	**121**	**124**	**160**
Health insurance	100	73	110	126	112	122
Medical services	100	64	97	120	145	190
Drugs	100	77	102	120	120	138
Medical supplies	100	56	82	77	116	407
Entertainment	**100**	**36**	**77**	**148**	**170**	**312**
Fees and admissions	100	20	60	147	184	422
Television, radios, sound equipment	100	53	92	125	134	256
Pets, toys, and playground equipment	100	39	77	209	160	217
Other supplies, equipment, and services	100	32	79	114	254	317
Personal-care products and services	**100**	**52**	**100**	**132**	**160**	**214**
Reading	**100**	**46**	**93**	**144**	**156**	**224**
Education	**100**	**52**	**62**	**152**	**158**	**305**
Tobacco products and smoking supplies	**100**	**75**	**86**	**140**	**142**	**155**
Cash contributions	**100**	**32**	**60**	**121**	**148**	**441**
Personal insurance and pensions	**100**	**19**	**50**	**103**	**182**	**534**
Life and other personal insurance	100	45	87	114	115	329
Pensions and Social Security	100	5	30	96	217	643
Miscellaneous	**100**	**73**	**77**	**107**	**153**	**245**

The Consumer Expenditure Survey uses consumer units as its sampling unit. See Glossary for definition of consumer unit.
Source: Bureau of Labor Statistics
Note: The data here for all households in the age group will differ from those for the age groups given on pages 176 through 178 because combined data from 1989-90 were used for this crosstabulation. An index of 100 is the average for all households. An index of 132 means that spending for that group is 32 percent greater than the average for all households. An index of 68 means that spending is 32 percent below average.

Saving Trends, 1965 to 1991

The personal saving rate was recovering from its low of 2.9 percent in 1987, but the recession reduced savings in 1991.

(savings as a percent of disposable personal income, 1965 to June 1991)

	personal saving rate
1991*	4.2%
1990	4.6
1989	4.6
1988	4.2
1987	2.9
1986	4.1
1985	4.4
1984	6.1
1983	5.4
1982	6.8
1981	7.5
1980	7.1
1979	6.8
1978	7.1
1977	6.6
1976	7.6
1975	9.2
1970	8.1
1965	7.0

*For the first half of 1991.
Source: Department of Commerce

Household Debt Relative to Disposable Income, 1980 to 1990

Household debt reached nearly 84 percent of disposable household income in 1990, up from 65 percent in 1980. The largest component is mortgage debt.

(household debt as a percent of disposable household income, 1980 to 1990)

	total debt (mortgage + consumer)	home mortgage debt	consumer debt	
			total	installment
1990	83.5%	63.1%	20.4%	18.5%
1989	81.3	60.8	20.5	18.7
1988	78.9	58.3	20.6	18.6
1987	77.2	56.3	20.8	18.6
1986	73.1	52.2	20.9	18.4
1985	68.5	48.6	19.9	17.3
1984	64.6	46.5	18.1	15.6
1983	62.5	45.7	16.8	14.3
1982	63.0	46.3	16.7	14.2
1981	63.6	46.6	17.0	14.5
1980	65.4	47.3	18.2	15.6

Source: Board of Governors of the Federal Reserve System

Composition of Household Assets and Debts, 1983 and 1989

Financial assets are a growing share of Americans' total assets. Mortgage debt is a declining share of total debt, while home equity and credit-card debt are growing.

(percent distribution of household assets and debts, 1983 and 1989, and percentage point change in distribution, 1983 to 1989)

Assets	1989	1983	percentage point change 1983-89
Total	**100.0%**	**100.0%**	**0.0**
Financial	27.7	25.6	2.1
Nonfinancial	72.3	74.4	-2.1
Vehicles	3.9	3.6	0.3
Principal residence	32.2	33.4	-1.2
Real estate and land investment	15.1	16.0	-0.9
Business investment (excluding real estate)	17.8	20.4	-2.6
Other	3.3	1.0	2.3
Debts			
Total	**100.0%**	**100.0%**	**0.0**
Home mortgages	53.1	58.1	-5.0
Investment real estate mortgages	25.0	20.5	4.5
Home equity lines of credit	2.6	0.5	2.1
Other lines of credit	1.0	2.8	-1.8
Credit cards	2.2	1.8	0.4
Car loans	8.0	6.1	1.9
Other debts	8.1	10.2	-2.1

Source: Board of Governors of the Federal Reserve System

Ownership of Financial Assets by Age

A majority of American households had a savings account in 1983, but this proportion fell to just 44 percent by 1989.

(percent of households owning selected financial assets, by age of householder, 1983 and 1989, and percentage point change in ownership, 1983-89)

1989	all households	under 35	35 to 44	45 to 54	55 to 64	65 to 74	75+
Percent owning:							
Total	87.5%	82.2%	88.4%	90.4%	87.5%	91.5%	90.6%
Checking accounts	75.4	68.4	76.1	78.9	76.7	79.9	79.3
Savings accounts	43.5	45.0	50.0	44.6	38.9	37.7	36.2
Money market accounts	22.2	14.9	20.4	27.0	23.0	28.3	30.5
CDs	19.6	8.5	15.5	21.1	20.9	31.6	39.4
Retirement accounts	33.3	23.0	44.0	45.5	42.6	30.0	6.6
Stocks	19.0	11.4	21.2	23.1	22.0	20.8	21.3
Bonds	4.4	0.8	3.4	3.5	5.9	9.1	9.6
Nontaxable bonds	4.4	0.9	3.5	4.3	7.5	9.4	4.9
Trusts	3.4	2.5	2.8	3.1	3.0	6.4	4.8
Other	47.7	39.5	56.8	52.9	49.6	48.4	35.5
1983							
Percent owning:							
Total	87.8%	85.0%	90.1%	88.7%	90.1%	88.2%	85.9%
Checking accounts	78.6	71.9	82.9	81.8	81.2	82.5	76.2
Savings accounts	61.7	62.6	68.4	64.9	59.0	55.4	48.9
Money market accounts	15.0	8.5	16.5	14.9	20.0	22.4	15.3
CDs	20.1	8.6	15.5	18.1	20.3	36.9	38.3
Retirement accounts	24.2	17.2	31.0	35.5	36.3	14.8	1.7
Stocks	20.4	12.9	22.8	23.2	25.7	26.1	19.9
Bonds	3.0	1.0	2.5	3.2	4.9	6.7	2.2
Nontaxable bonds	2.1	0.2	1.7	2.1	3.0	6.1	2.2
Trusts	4.0	4.0	3.6	6.0	3.8	3.1	2.9
Other	44.0	36.0	50.2	48.6	47.5	49.2	35.4
Percentage point change, 1983-89:							
Total	-0.3	-2.8	-1.7	1.7	-2.6	3.3	4.7
Checking accounts	-3.2	-3.5	-6.8	-2.9	-4.5	-2.6	3.1
Savings accounts	-18.2	-17.6	-18.4	-20.3	-20.1	-17.7	-12.7
Money market accounts	7.2	6.4	3.9	12.1	3.0	5.9	15.2
CDs	-0.5	-0.1	0.0	3.0	0.6	-5.3	1.1
Retirement accounts	9.1	5.8	13.0	10.0	6.3	15.2	4.9
Stocks	-1.4	-1.5	-1.6	-0.1	-3.7	-5.3	1.4
Bonds	1.4	-0.2	0.9	0.3	1.0	2.4	7.4
Nontaxable bonds	2.3	0.7	1.8	2.2	4.5	3.3	2.7
Trusts	-0.6	-1.5	-0.8	-2.9	-0.8	3.3	1.9
Other	3.7	3.5	6.6	4.3	2.1	-0.8	0.1

Source: Board of Governors of the Federal Reserve System

Value of Financial Assets by Age

The median net worth of Americans grew by 10.5 percent, after adjusting for inflation, between 1983 and 1989.

(median net worth and median value of selected financial assets of households holding such assets, by age of householder, 1983 and 1989, and percent change in net worth and asset value, 1983-89; in thousands of 1989 dollars)

1989	*all households*	*under 35*	*35 to 44*	*45 to 54*	*55 to 64*	*65 to 74*	*75+*
Median net worth	**$47.2**	**$6.8**	**$52.8**	**$86.7**	**$91.3**	**$77.6**	**$66.1**
Median value of:							
Total	10.4	2.5	11.2	14.5	20.0	18.2	21.0
Checking accounts	0.9	0.6	0.9	1.0	1.0	1.0	1.0
Savings accounts	1.5	0.7	1.5	1.5	4.5	2.0	5.0
Money market accounts	5.0	2.6	5.0	2.7	11.0	10.0	8.0
CDs	11.0	5.0	10.0	9.0	12.0	17.0	25.0
Retirement accounts	10.0	4.0	8.0	14.0	22.0	15.0	25.0
Stocks	7.5	2.7	3.0	6.0	18.3	25.0	18.0
Bonds	17.3	0.1	6.2	12.0	20.0	20.0	26.0
Non-taxable bonds	25.0	15.0	11.7	10.0	25.0	32.0	50.0
Trusts	23.0	26.0	10.0	10.0	32.0	48.0	32.0
Other	2.5	1.0	2.5	3.5	5.0	3.0	3.7
1983							
Median net worth	**$42.7**	**$8.5**	**$49.8**	**$69.4**	**$84.4**	**$76.3**	**$49.8**
Median value of:							
Total	4.5	1.5	4.4	5.7	11.7	17.2	15.6
Checking accounts	0.6	0.4	0.6	0.7	1.2	1.2	1.1
Savings accounts	1.4	0.6	1.4	1.7	2.0	2.5	3.7
Money market accounts	11.0	5.6	7.5	17.4	12.5	16.3	16.8
CDs	12.5	5.0	10.0	10.6	15.4	23.0	23.0
Retirement accounts	5.0	2.0	5.0	5.6	7.5	12.5	5.0
Stocks	6.2	1.9	5.0	5.0	11.2	16.8	14.9
Bonds	12.5	12.5	8.7	12.5	18.7	31.1	6.2
Nontaxable bonds	52.9	149.4	52.9	54.0	56.3	62.3	18.7
Trusts	12.5	3.7	10.0	12.5	32.4	95.9	12.5
Other	3.0	1.9	2.9	3.9	6.2	2.6	1.9
Percent change, 1983-89							
Median net worth	**10.5%**	**-20.0%**	**6.0%**	**24.9%**	**8.2%**	**1.7%**	**32.7%**
Median value of:							
Total	131.1	66.7	154.5	154.4	70.9	5.8	34.6
Checking accounts	50.0	50.0	50.0	42.9	-16.7	-16.7	-9.1
Savings accounts	7.1	16.7	7.1	-11.8	125.0	-20.0	35.1
Money market accounts	-54.5	-53.6	-33.3	-84.5	-12.0	-38.7	-52.4

(continued on next page)

(continued from previous page)

(median net worth and median value of selected financial assets of households holding such assets, by age of householder, 1983 and 1989, and percent change in net worth and asset value, 1983-89; in thousands of 1989 dollars)

	all households	under 35	35 to 44	45 to 54	55 to 64	65 to 74	75+
CDs	-12.0%	0.0%	0.0%	-15.1%	-22.1%	-26.1%	8.7%
Retirement accounts	100.0	100.0	60.0	150.0	193.3	20.0	400.0
Stocks	21.0	42.1	-40.0	20.0	63.4	48.8	20.8
Bonds	38.4	-99.2	-28.7	-4.0	7.0	-35.7	319.4
Nontaxable bonds	-52.7	-89.9	-77.9	-81.5	-55.6	-48.6	167.4
Trusts	84.0	602.7	0.0	-20.0	-1.2	-49.9	156.0
Other	-16.7	-47.4	-13.8	-10.3	-19.4	15.4	94.7

Source: Board of Governors of the Federal Reserve System

Ownership of Financial Assets by Income and Housing Status

The most affluent households and homeowners are more likely to own all types of assets than is the average household.

(percent of households owning selected financial assets, by household income and housing status, 1983 and 1989, and percentage point change in ownership, 1983-89)

	all households	under $10,000	$10,000 to $19,999	$20,000 to $29,999	$30,000 to $49,999	$50,000 or more	own	rent or other
				income			**housing status**	
1989								
Percent owning:								
Total	87.5%	59.1%	85.6%	95.2%	98.2%	99.7%	95.6%	72.7%
Checking accounts	75.4	46.2	69.7	80.3	88.8	91.5	84.9	57.8
Savings accounts	43.5	21.9	40.7	47.6	52.9	53.9	49.2	32.9
Money market accounts	22.2	7.8	14.6	21.0	23.2	44.7	27.2	13.1
CDs	19.6	8.6	21.2	20.6	21.0	26.5	24.6	10.4
Retirement accounts	33.3	3.1	14.9	34.4	44.9	69.2	43.6	14.5
Stocks	19.0	2.0	10.9	16.9	20.8	44.6	25.2	7.6
Bonds	4.4	0.8	2.4	3.0	5.0	12.7	6.1	1.2
Non-taxable bonds	4.4	-	-	4.2	4.2	12.6	5.8	2.0
Trusts	3.4	-	3.1	3.0	3.6	7.1	4.6	1.4
Other	47.7	16.6	35.6	49.4	63.5	72.3	58.0	28.7
1983								
Percent owning:								
Total	87.8%	64.0%	84.5%	93.7%	97.5%	98.8%	93.7%	77.6%
Checking accounts	78.6	49.2	71.7	83.7	92.4	96.0	87.8	62.6
Savings accounts	61.7	36.9	53.4	67.2	76.6	73.8	67.6	51.4
Money market accounts	15.0	2.7	9.0	12.0	17.4	37.1	18.5	8.9
CDs	20.1	8.1	18.4	19.4	22.7	33.1	26.5	9.0
Retirement accounts	24.2	1.9	8.4	19.8	34.5	61.7	30.6	13.0
Stocks	20.4	4.4	10.6	18.0	25.2	48.3	25.7	11.4
Bonds	3.0	-	1.6	1.9	2.4	10.0	3.7	1.9
Non-taxable bonds	2.1	-	-	1.0	1.0	9.3	2.9	0.6
Trusts	4.0	2.6	1.9	2.7	4.4	9.6	4.5	3.2
Other	44.0	22.7	34.5	45.8	54.5	64.6	52.4	29.5
Percentage point change, 1983-89:								
Total	-0.3	-4.9	1.1	1.5	0.7	0.9	1.9	-4.9
Checking accounts	-3.2	-3.0	-2.0	-3.4	-3.6	-4.5	-2.9	-4.8
Savings accounts	-18.2	-15.0	-12.7	-19.6	-23.7	-19.9	-18.4	-18.5
Money market accounts	7.2	5.1	5.6	9.0	5.8	7.6	8.7	4.2
CDs	-0.5	0.5	2.8	1.2	-1.7	-6.6	-1.9	1.4
Retirement accounts	9.1	1.2	6.5	14.6	10.4	7.5	13.0	1.5
Stocks	-1.4	-2.4	0.3	-1.1	-4.4	-3.7	-0.5	-3.8
Bonds	1.4	-	0.8	1.1	2.6	2.7	2.4	-0.7
Non-taxable bonds	2.3	-	-	3.2	3.2	3.3	2.9	1.4
Trusts	-0.6	-	1.2	0.3	-0.8	-2.5	0.1	-1.8
Other	3.7	-6.1	1.1	3.6	9.0	7.7	5.6	-0.8

Source: Board of Governors of the Federal Reserve System
Note: (-) means the sample is too small to be reliable.

Value of Financial Assets by Income and Housing Status

SPENDING & WEALTH

The median net worth of the most affluent households rose by just 5 percent between 1983 and 1989, less than the increase for all households.

(median net worth and median value of selected financial assets of households holding such assets, by household income and housing status, 1983 and 1989, and percent change in net worth and asset value, 1983-89; in thousands of 1989 dollars)

1989	all households	income					housing status	
		under $10,000	$10,000 to $19,999	$20,000 to $29,999	$30,000 to $49,999	$50,000 or more	own	rent or other
Median net worth	**$47.2**	**$2.3**	**$27.1**	**$37.0**	**$69.2**	**$185.6**	**$97.3**	**$2.2**
Median value of:								
Total	10.4	1.3	4.5	6.8	12.2	41.5	16.2	2.3
Checking accounts	0.9	0.4	0.7	0.8	1.0	1.5	1.0	0.6
Savings accounts	1.5	1.0	1.0	1.2	2.0	3.0	2.0	0.9
Money market accounts	5.0	4.0	5.0	3.5	4.0	10.0	6.4	3.0
CDs	11.0	10.0	10.0	10.0	12.0	15.0	13.0	8.0
Retirement accounts	10.0	3.3	4.0	6.0	8.5	21.2	12.4	4.0
Stocks	7.5	30.0	7.0	4.0	5.5	12.0	8.0	5.0
Bonds	17.3	13.0	15.0	6.2	26.0	20.0	16.0	30.0
Non-taxable bonds	25.0	-	-	5.0	25.0	35.0	30.0	6.3
Trusts	23.0	-	20.0	14.0	30.0	32.0	20.0	26.0
Other	2.5	1.0	2.1	2.0	2.8	4.7	3.0	1.5
1983								
Median net worth	**$42.7**	**$3.8**	**$19.3**	**$36.9**	**$67.7**	**$176.1**	**$80.4**	**$3.0**
Median value of:								
Total	4.5	0.9	2.1	2.8	6.0	31.9	7.8	1.5
Checking accounts	0.6	0.4	0.5	0.5	0.6	1.4	0.7	0.5
Savings accounts	1.4	0.6	0.9	1.3	1.7	3.4	1.9	0.7
Money market accounts	11.0	3.2	8.1	6.2	9.7	14.9	12.5	6.2
CDs	12.5	9.1	12.5	14.7	12.5	15.5	13.1	10.0
Retirement accounts	5.0	2.8	2.5	2.5	3.8	8.1	5.6	2.5
Stocks	6.2	2.4	5.1	3.9	3.1	18.7	6.3	3.1
Bonds	12.5	-	12.5	12.5	8.5	24.9	18.7	11.3
Non-taxable bonds	52.9	-	37.4	15.6	12.6	62.3	52.9	49.8
Trusts	12.5	3.9	3.6	3.7	8.3	24.9	13.7	3.8
Other	3.0	1.6	1.9	1.9	3.9	6.2	3.7	1.6
Percent change, 1983-89								
Median net worth	**10.5%**	**-39.5%**	**40.4%**	**0.3%**	**2.2%**	**5.4%**	**21.0%**	**-26.7%**
Median value of:								
Total	131.1	44.4	114.3	142.9	103.3	30.1	107.7	53.3
Checking accounts	50.0	0.0	40.0	60.0	66.7	7.1	42.9	20.0
Savings accounts	7.1	66.7	11.1	-7.7	17.6	-11.8	5.3	28.6
Money market accounts	-54.5	25.0	-38.3	-43.5	-58.8	-32.9	-48.8	-51.6

(continued on next page)

(continued from previous page)

(median net worth and median value of selected financial assets of households holding such assets, by household income and housing status, 1983 and 1989, and percent change in net worth and asset value, 1983-89; in thousands of 1989 dollars)

	all households	income					housing status	
		under $10,000	$10,000 to $19,999	$20,000 to $29,999	$30,000 to $49,999	$50,000 or more	own	rent or other
CDs	-12.0%	9.9%	-20.0%	-32.0%	-4.0%	-3.2%	-0.8%	-20.0%
Retirement accounts	100.0	17.9	60.0	140.0	123.7	161.7	121.4	60.0
Stocks	21.0	1150.0	37.3	2.6	77.4	-35.8	27.0	61.3
Bonds	38.4	-	20.0	-50.4	205.9	-19.7	-14.4	165.5
Non-taxable bonds	-52.7	-	-	-67.9	98.4	-43.8	-43.3	-87.3
Trusts	84.0	-	455.6	278.4	261.4	28.5	46.0	584.2
Other	-16.7	-37.5	10.5	5.3	-28.2	-24.2	-18.9	-6.3

Source: Board of Governors of the Federal Reserve System
Note: (-) means the sample is too small to be reliable.

Ownership of Financial Assets by Life-Cycle Stage

Retired householders are more likely to own a variety of financial assets, such as CDs and stocks, than the average household.

(percent of households owning selected financial assets, by life-cycle stage of householder, 1983 and 1989, and percentage point change in ownership, 1983-89)

1989	all households	unmarried, no children	married, no children	under age 55		aged 55 or older	
				unmarried, children	married, children	in labor force	retired
Percent owning:							
Total	87.5%	84.7%	92.8%	68.4%	92.7%	95.6%	93.0%
Checking accounts	75.4	71.9	78.9	54.5	80.8	83.9	81.8
Savings accounts	43.5	40.2	52.6	35.7	52.5	44.4	37.6
Money market accounts	22.2	17.2	31.2	9.5	22.7	25.1	31.3
CDs	19.6	10.7	16.3	9.0	16.4	23.2	35.9
Retirement accounts	33.3	26.7	40.2	21.9	43.1	49.1	25.2
Stocks	19.0	16.8	26.9	8.7	19.9	26.1	23.7
Bonds	4.4	1.8	4.8	1.4	2.5	7.2	10.9
Non-taxable bonds	4.4	3.0	5.8	1.9	2.4	9.8	8.4
Trusts	3.4	2.4	2.2	0.7	3.7	4.6	6.0
Other	47.7	30.3	50.2	30.8	61.5	57.3	45.6
1983							
Percent owning:							
Total	87.8%	88.9%	90.6%	73.3%	91.7%	93.1%	85.8%
Checking accounts	78.6	74.7	86.1	58.9	84.1	85.1	77.5
Savings accounts	61.7	61.4	67.7	55.2	69.2	64.9	49.9
Money market accounts	15.0	14.6	20.2	7.4	12.4	24.6	17.1
CDs	20.1	8.6	15.0	9.0	15.4	31.2	34.8
Retirement accounts	24.2	19.5	29.1	12.8	31.9	42.0	7.9
Stocks	20.4	18.2	19.3	12.4	20.4	28.9	22.6
Bonds	3.0	2.7	-	2.3	1.8	5.0	4.9
Non-taxable bonds	2.1	1.1	1.3	0.8	1.2	4.7	3.6
Trusts	4.0	4.6	5.8	4.4	1.2	4.3	2.6
Other	44.0	31.6	46.0	32.9	50.3	54.2	41.5
Percentage point change, 1983-89:							
Total	-0.3	-4.2	2.2	-4.9	1.0	2.5	7.2
Checking accounts	-3.2	-2.8	-7.2	-4.4	-3.3	-1.2	4.3
Savings accounts	-18.2	-21.2	-15.1	-19.5	-16.7	-20.5	-12.3
Money market accounts	7.2	2.6	11.0	2.1	10.3	0.5	14.2
CDs	-0.5	2.1	1.3	0.0	1.0	-8.0	1.1
Retirement accounts	9.1	7.2	11.1	9.1	11.2	7.1	17.3
Stocks	-1.4	-1.4	7.6	-3.7	-0.5	-2.8	1.1
Bonds	1.4	-0.9	-	-0.9	0.7	2.2	6.0
Non-taxable bonds	2.3	1.9	4.5	1.1	1.2	5.1	4.8
Trusts	-0.6	-2.2	-3.6	-3.7	-0.3	0.3	3.4
Other	3.7	-1.3	4.2	-2.1	11.2	3.1	4.1

Source: Board of Governors of the Federal Reserve System. Note: (-) means the sample is too small to be reliable.

Value of Financial Assets by Life-Cycle Stage

The net worth of retired householders is twice as high as that of the average household. It climbed 47 percent between 1983 and 1989, over four times as fast as the average.

(median net worth and median value of selected financial assets of households holding such assets, by life-cycle stage of householder, 1983 and 1989, and percent change in net worth and asset value, 1983-89; in thousands of 1989 dollars)

1989	all households	unmarried, no children	married, no children	under age 55 unmarried, children	under age 55 married, children	aged 55 or older in labor force	aged 55 or older retired
Median net worth	**$47.2**	**$8.4**	**$27.3**	**$5.7**	**$62.0**	**$104.5**	**$94.1**
Median value of:							
Total	10.4	4.9	7.1	3.0	11.0	22.2	22.4
Checking accounts	0.9	0.7	1.0	0.5	0.9	1.0	1.0
Savings accounts	1.5	1.0	1.6	1.0	1.2	3.0	5.0
Money market accounts	5.0	4.5	2.7	1.5	4.0	15.0	10.5
CDs	11.0	10.0	6.2	5.1	7.0	13.0	20.0
Retirement accounts	10.0	5.0	4.9	4.0	10.0	20.0	16.0
Stocks	7.5	3.7	3.6	2.5	3.6	20.0	20.3
Bonds	17.3	30.0	3.0	12.0	6.0	20.0	26.0
Non-taxable bonds	25.0	11.7	7.0	2.0	30.5	50.0	25.0
Trusts	23.0	40.0	8.0	6.0	14.0	32.0	45.0
Other	2.5	1.5	1.0	2.0	2.5	5.0	4.0
1983							
Median net worth	**$42.7**	**$6.0**	**$20.1**	**$10.8**	**$51.3**	**$108.0**	**$63.9**
Median value of:							
Total	4.5	2.0	3.5	1.7	3.5	15.7	12.8
Checking accounts	0.6	0.5	0.6	0.5	0.6	1.2	1.2
Savings accounts	1.4	0.6	1.0	0.8	1.4	2.0	3.0
Money market accounts	11.0	6.8	7.5	6.2	9.3	14.1	14.9
CDs	12.5	5.0	6.2	10.6	7.5	16.2	19.0
Retirement accounts	5.0	3.1	3.6	2.5	5.0	10.0	5.6
Stocks	6.2	2.5	3.7	3.7	4.4	11.8	14.7
Bonds	12.5	12.5	-	5.0	12.5	12.5	24.9
Non-taxable bonds	52.9	54.0	124.5	15.6	47.3	56.3	18.7
Trusts	12.5	0.7	5.0	6.2	10.0	62.3	32.4
Other	3.0	1.8	2.8	1.5	3.4	5.1	2.1
Percent change, 1983-89							
Median net worth	**10.5%**	**40.0%**	**35.8%**	**-47.2%**	**20.9%**	**-3.2%**	**47.3%**
Median value of:							
Total	131.1	145.0	102.9	76.5	214.3	41.4	75.0
Checking accounts	50.0	40.0	66.7	0.0	50.0	-16.7	-16.7
Savings accounts	7.1	66.7	60.0	25.0	-14.3	50.0	66.7
Money market accounts	-54.5	-33.8	-64.0	-75.8	-57.0	6.4	-29.5

(continued on next page)

(continued from previous page)
(median net worth and median value of selected financial assets of households holding such assets, by life-cycle stage of householder, 1983 and 1989, and percent change in net worth and asset value, 1983-89; in thousands of 1989 dollars)

| | all households | unmarried, no children | married, no children | under age 55 | | aged 55 or older | |
				unmarried, children	married, children	in labor force	retired
CDs	-12.0%	100.0%	0.0%	-51.9%	-6.7%	-19.8%	5.3%
Retirement accounts	100.0	61.3	36.1	60.0	100.0	100.0	185.7
Stocks	21.0	48.0	-2.7	-32.4	-18.2	69.5	38.1
Bonds	38.4	140.0	-	140.0	-52.0	60.0	4.4
Non-taxable bonds	-52.7	-78.3	-94.4	-87.2	-35.5	-11.2	33.7
Trusts	84.0	5614.3	60.0	-3.2	40.0	-48.6	38.9
Other	-16.7	-16.7	-64.3	33.3	-26.5	-2.0	90.5

Source: Board of Governors of the Federal Reserve System
Note: (-) means the sample is too small to be reliable.

Ownership of Nonfinancial Assets by Age

A majority of households own a vehicle and a home. Homeownership peaks among householders aged 55 to 64.

(percent of households owning selected nonfinancial assets, by of age householder, 1983 and 1989, and percentage point change in ownership, 1983-89)

1989	all households	under 35	35 to 44	45 to 54	55 to 64	65 to 74	75+
Percent owning:							
Total	90.2%	84.4%	92.8%	93.3%	92.1%	93.8%	87.3%
Vehicles	84.0	80.7	89.5	90.9	86.9	81.9	66.9
Business	11.5	8.4	17.0	16.2	11.3	7.9	4.7
Investment real estate	20.4	8.1	20.9	28.5	31.3	25.6	16.9
Other assets	22.1	20.5	24.9	25.6	23.9	20.4	13.3
Principal residence	64.7	36.8	65.9	76.6	82.2	80.2	72.8
1983							
Percent owning:							
Total	90.3%	87.2%	94.0%	92.7%	93.1%	91.8%	79.6%
Vehicles	84.4	83.3	91.2	90.3	87.7	80.2	57.8
Business	14.2	10.3	18.3	18.2	18.1	12.3	6.4
Investment real estate	20.9	10.4	22.9	24.9	32.6	27.2	16.9
Other assets	7.4	9.1	10.3	6.4	5.9	5.6	1.4
Principal residence	64.4	38.7	68.4	78.0	76.8	78.9	69.5
Percentage point change, 1983-89:							
Total	-0.1	-2.8	-1.2	0.6	-1.0	2.0	7.7
Vehicles	-0.4	-2.6	-1.7	0.6	-0.8	1.7	9.1
Business	-2.7	-1.9	-1.3	-2.0	-6.8	-4.4	-1.7
Investment real estate	-0.5	-2.3	-2.0	3.6	-1.3	-1.6	0.0
Other assets	14.7	11.4	14.6	19.2	18.0	14.8	11.9
Principal residence	0.3	-1.9	-2.5	-1.4	5.4	1.3	3.3

Source: Board of Governors of the Federal Reserve System

Note: Homeownership rates here differ from those in other tables in this chapter because the data are based on different samples.

Value of Nonfinancial Assets by Age

The most valuable asset owned by most Americans is their home. Home values rose by 8 percent for all households between 1983 and 1989.

(median net worth and median value of selected nonfinancial assets of households holding such assets, by age of householder, 1983 and 1989, and percent change in net worth and asset value, 1983-89; in thousands of 1989 dollars)

1989	all households	under 35	35 to 44	45 to 54	55 to 64	65 to 74	75+
Median net worth	**$47.2**	**$6.8**	**$52.8**	**$86.7**	**$91.3**	**$77.6**	**$66.1**
Median value of:							
Total	66.7	15.5	81.3	105.3	93.9	63.1	52.0
Vehicles	6.9	5.7	8.0	9.6	7.1	5.4	3.7
Business	50.0	11.0	50.0	61.6	80.0	53.0	28.5
Investment real estate	39.0	31.5	46.0	50.0	39.0	34.0	35.0
Other assets	5.0	1.6	5.0	8.3	8.0	10.0	10.0
Principal residence	70.0	65.0	80.0	85.0	75.0	58.1	55.0
1983							
Median net worth	**$42.7**	**$8.5**	**$49.8**	**$69.4**	**$84.4**	**$76.3**	**$49.8**
Median value of:							
Total	59.7	13.2	77.4	88.1	81.4	65.5	49.2
Vehicles	5.1	4.4	5.6	6.6	6.3	3.8	2.3
Business	57.0	24.9	55.2	67.5	93.4	94.7	124.5
Investment real estate	43.6	31.1	47.3	36.1	49.8	49.8	39.8
Other assets	6.2	2.5	6.2	10.7	12.5	12.5	5.8
Principal residence	64.7	56.0	80.9	74.7	74.7	57.3	44.8
Percent change, 1983-89							
Median net worth	**10.5%**	**-20.0%**	**6.0%**	**24.9%**	**8.2%**	**1.7%**	**32.7%**
Median value of:							
Total	11.7	17.4	5.0	19.5	15.4	-3.7	5.7
Vehicles	35.3	29.5	42.9	45.5	12.7	42.1	60.9
Business	-12.3	-55.8	-9.4	-8.7	-14.3	-44.0	-77.1
Investment real estate	-10.6	1.3	-2.7	38.5	-21.7	-31.7	-12.1
Other assets	-19.4	-36.0	-19.4	-22.4	-36.0	-20.0	72.4
Principal residence	8.2	16.1	-1.1	13.8	0.4	1.4	22.8

Source: Board of Governors of the Federal Reserve System

Ownership of Nonfinancial Assets by Income and Housing Status

Ownership of all types of nonfinancial assets rises steadily with income. Fully 90 percent of households with incomes of $50,000 or more own a home.

(percent of households owning selected nonfinancial assets, by household income and housing status, 1983 and 1989, and percentage point change in ownership, 1983-89)

1989	all households	income under $10,000	income $10,000 to $19,999	income $20,000 to $29,999	income $30,000 to $49,999	income $50,000 or more	housing status own	housing status rent or other
Percent owning:								
Total	90.2%	66.9%	90.5%	96.7%	98.0%	99.4%	100.0%	72.3%
Vehicles	84.0	51.6	82.1	94.4	95.5	96.8	92.7	67.9
Business	11.5	2.3	8.0	10.1	12.0	25.4	14.4	6.3
Investment real estate	20.4	5.9	14.4	15.0	27.1	38.7	26.0	10.1
Other assets	22.1	12.1	18.5	23.8	25.4	30.7	23.0	20.3
Principal residence	64.7	36.2	57.0	63.5	76.2	90.0	100.0	na
1983								
Percent owning:								
Total	90.3%	67.4%	89.1%	96.1%	98.6%	99.4%	100.0%	73.4%
Vehicles	84.4	50.5	83.2	93.3	97.0	96.4	92.4	70.5
Business	14.2	4.5	6.9	12.0	18.7	31.5	18.8	6.3
Investment real estate	20.9	6.9	14.1	17.9	25.8	42.7	27.1	10.2
Other assets	7.4	3.3	5.5	7.2	8.0	14.3	7.5	7.4
Principal residence	64.4	40.1	52.6	60.3	77.2	88.9	100.0	na
Percentage point change, 1983-89:								
Total	-0.1	-0.5	1.4	0.6	-0.6	0.0	0.0	-1.1
Vehicles	-0.4	1.1	-1.1	1.1	-1.5	0.4	0.3	-2.6
Business	-2.7	-2.2	1.1	-1.9	-6.7	-6.1	-4.4	0.0
Investment real estate	-0.5	-1.0	0.3	-2.9	1.3	-4.0	-1.1	-0.1
Other assets	14.7	8.8	13.0	16.6	17.4	16.4	15.5	12.9
Principal residence	0.3	-3.9	4.4	3.2	-1.0	1.1	0.0	na

Source: Board of Governors of the Federal Reserve System
Note: Homeownership rates here differ from those in other tables in this chapter because the data are based on different samples.
(na) means not applicable.

Value of Nonfinancial Assets by Income and Housing Status

Median net worth rises sharply with income, but even among the most affluent households, their home is their most valuable asset.

(median net worth and median value of selected financial assets of households holding such assets, by household income and housing status, 1983 and 1989, and percent change in net worth and asset value, 1983-89; in thousands of 1989 dollars)

1989	all households	income under $10,000	$10,000 to $19,999	$20,000 to $29,999	$30,000 to $49,999	$50,000 or more	housing status own	rent or other
Median net worth	**$47.2**	**$2.3**	**$27.1**	**$37.0**	**$69.2**	**$185.6**	**$97.3**	**$2.2**
Median value of:								
Total	66.7	11.4	39.2	48.3	84.9	190.0	95.9	5.5
Vehicles	6.9	2.0	4.1	5.8	8.7	13.4	8.3	8.0
Business	50.0	14.3	5.9	40.0	45.0	93.0	60.0	7.2
Investment real estate	39.0	16.7	18.0	30.0	35.0	80.0	40.0	31.0
Other assets	5.0	1.2	3.0	3.0	5.0	15.0	8.0	2.0
Principal residence	70.0	33.0	50.0	57.0	75.0	130.0	70.0	na
1983								
Median net worth	**$42.7**	**$3.8**	**$19.3**	**$36.9**	**$67.7**	**$176.1**	**$80.4**	**$3.0**
Median value of:								
Total	59.7	15.5	31.1	45.9	81.5	163.9	85.0	4.2
Vehicles	5.1	1.8	3.2	4.5	6.4	9.8	6.1	3.4
Business	57.0	41.1	31.4	24.9	44.0	121.0	62.3	26.6
Investment real estate	43.6	13.9	27.9	31.1	39.0	89.0	43.6	36.1
Other assets	6.2	2.5	2.9	3.7	6.2	12.5	8.5	3.1
Principal residence	64.7	32.1	49.8	54.2	74.7	112.1	64.7	na
Percent change, 1983-89								
Median net worth	**10.5%**	**-39.5%**	**40.4%**	**0.3%**	**2.2%**	**5.4%**	**21.0%**	**-26.7%**
Median value of:								
Total	11.7	-26.5	26.0	5.2	4.2	15.9	12.8	31.0
Vehicles	35.3	11.1	28.1	28.9	35.9	36.7	36.1	135.3
Business	-12.3	-65.2	-81.2	60.6	2.3	-23.1	-3.7	-72.9
Investment real estate	-10.6	20.1	-35.5	-3.5	-10.3	-10.1	-8.3	-14.1
Other assets	-19.4	-52.0	3.4	-18.9	-19.4	20.0	-5.9	-35.5
Principal residence	8.2	2.8	0.4	5.2	0.4	16.0	8.2	na

Source: Board of Governors of the Federal Reserve System
Note: (na) means not applicable.

Ownership of Nonfinancial Assets by Life-Cycle Stage

People aged 55 or older are most likely to own a home, as are married couples with children. Homeownership increased for these groups between 1983 and 1989.

(percent of households owning selected nonfinancial assets, by life-cycle stage of householder, 1983 and 1989, and percentage point change in ownership, 1983-89)

				under age 55		aged 55 or older	
1989	all households	unmarried, no children	married, no children	unmarried, children	married, children	in labor force	retired
Percent owning:							
Total	90.2%	82.1%	97.2%	71.6%	97.7%	94.8%	93.5%
Vehicles	84.0	75.5	95.4	64.7	96.6	91.1	82.6
Business	11.5	10.5	13.0	5.0	17.5	17.6	4.7
Investment real estate	20.4	10.9	19.8	9.2	22.3	34.3	25.0
Other assets	22.1	28.6	26.9	22.2	21.6	28.7	17.4
Principal residence	64.7	23.7	56.9	35.2	74.9	82.0	82.2
1983							
Percent owning:							
Total	90.3%	79.1%	97.0%	78.3%	97.8%	95.1%	86.2%
Vehicles	84.4	71.9	96.4	73.1	96.2	89.5	74.4
Business	14.2	9.1	14.3	6.4	19.3	24.1	6.1
Investment real estate	20.9	10.0	14.6	12.0	22.5	36.3	22.1
Other assets	7.4	13.9	13.0	6.2	7.6	7.3	3.4
Principal residence	64.4	23.4	51.8	42.7	73.5	78.1	74.8
Percentage point change, 1983-89:							
Total	-0.1	3.0	0.2	-6.7	-0.1	-0.3	7.3
Vehicles	-0.4	3.6	-1.0	-8.4	0.4	1.6	8.2
Business	-2.7	1.4	-1.3	-1.4	-1.8	-6.5	-1.4
Investment real estate	-0.5	0.9	5.2	-2.8	-0.2	-2.0	2.9
Other assets	14.7	14.7	13.9	16.0	14.0	21.4	14.0
Principal residence	0.3	0.3	5.1	-7.5	1.4	3.9	7.4

Source: Board of Governors of the Federal Reserve System
Note: Homeownership rates here differ from those in other tables in this chapter because the data are based on different samples.

Value of Nonfinancial Assets by Life-Cycle Stage

Older Americans and married couples with children have the highest net worth. Net worth rose from 1983 to 1989 for all household types except single parents and workers aged 55 or older.

(median net worth and median value of selected nonfinancial assets of households holding such assets, by life-cycle stage of householder, 1983 and 1989, and percent change in net worth and asset value, 1983-89; in thousands of 1989 dollars)

	all households	unmarried, no children	married, no children	under age 55 unmarried, children	under age 55 married, children	aged 55 or older in labor force	aged 55 or older retired
1989							
Median net worth	**$47.2**	**$8.4**	**$27.3**	**$5.7**	**$62.0**	**$104.5**	**$94.1**
Median value of:							
Total	66.7	8.8	66.3	22.7	86.4	98.3	67.6
Vehicles	6.9	4.3	9.0	4.8	9.3	7.6	5.5
Business	50.0	8.4	45.0	13.4	52.0	80.0	49.2
Investment real estate	39.0	45.0	94.0	46.0	45.0	43.0	35.7
Other assets	5.0	2.0	4.0	3.0	6.0	8.0	11.4
Principal residence	70.0	84.0	84.0	60.0	80.0	80.0	60.0
1983							
Median net worth	**$42.7**	**$6.0**	**$20.1**	**$10.8**	**$51.3**	**$108.0**	**$63.9**
Median value of:							
Total	59.7	6.2	39.9	39.0	74.3	91.7	55.6
Vehicles	5.1	3.6	6.0	3.6	6.3	6.4	3.4
Business	57.0	15.4	49.8	49.0	50.3	93.4	99.6
Investment real estate	43.6	28.0	53.4	37.0	39.0	56.0	43.6
Other assets	6.2	2.8	3.7	11.2	5.1	18.7	8.7
Principal residence	64.7	56.0	62.3	62.3	74.7	74.7	49.8
Percent change, 1983-89							
Median net worth	**10.5%**	**40.0%**	**35.8%**	**-47.2%**	**20.9%**	**-3.2%**	**47.3%**
Median value of:							
Total	11.7	41.9	66.2	-41.8	16.3	7.2	21.6
Vehicles	35.3	19.4	50.0	33.3	47.6	18.8	61.8
Business	-12.3	-45.5	-9.6	-72.7	3.4	-14.3	-50.6
Investment real estate	-10.6	60.7	76.0	24.3	15.4	-23.2	-18.1
Other assets	-19.4	-28.6	8.1	-73.2	17.6	-57.2	31.0
Principal residence	8.2	50.0	34.8	-3.7	7.1	7.1	20.5

Source: Board of Governors of the Federal Reserve System

Households With Debt by Age

The proportion of American households in debt rose slightly between 1983 and 1989. The greatest increases were for householders aged 45 or older.

(percent of households with selected financial debts, by age of householder, 1983 and 1989, and percentage point change in households with debt, 1983-89)

1989 Percent with:	all households	under 35	35 to 44	45 to 54	55 to 64	65 to 74	75+
Total	72.7%	79.5%	89.6%	85.9%	74.0%	47.9%	23.8%
Home mortgage	38.7	32.8	57.7	56.3	37.5	19.9	8.6
Investment real estate	7.0	2.6	10.2	12.3	10.7	3.9	1.4
Home equity lines	3.3	1.0	4.3	6.3	6.1	1.0	-
Other lines of credit	3.3	4.5	4.7	4.0	1.9	0.6	-
Credit cards	39.9	44.0	52.4	50.0	34.1	25.4	10.6
Car loans	35.1	37.4	51.5	48.7	29.3	14.0	5.3
Other debt	32.3	45.0	43.0	32.9	24.2	13.4	8.1
1983 Percent with:							
Total	69.6%	79.1%	87.1%	81.0%	67.2%	37.1%	16.8%
Home mortgage	36.9	32.6	58.1	53.5	34.4	15.7	3.7
Investment real estate	7.6	5.3	11.7	10.4	10.6	3.5	1.2
Home equity lines	0.5	0.4	0.8	0.8	-	-	-
Other lines of credit	11.2	12.6	17.3	13.6	9.6	3.1	-
Credit cards	37.0	38.4	51.5	45.0	37.5	18.2	6.1
Car loans	28.7	36.9	38.4	35.3	21.9	8.4	-
Other debt	29.6	42.3	38.4	31.1	19.0	9.0	6.2
Percentage point change, 1983-89:							
Total	3.1	0.4	2.5	4.9	6.8	10.8	7.0
Home mortgage	1.8	0.2	-0.4	2.8	3.1	4.2	4.9
Investment real estate	-0.6	-2.7	-1.5	1.9	0.1	0.4	0.2
Home equity lines	2.8	0.6	3.5	5.5	-	-	-
Other lines of credit	-7.9	-8.1	-12.6	-9.6	-7.7	-2.5	-
Credit cards	2.9	5.6	0.9	5.0	-3.4	7.2	4.5
Car loans	6.4	0.5	13.1	13.4	7.4	5.6	-
Other debt	2.7	2.7	4.6	1.8	5.2	4.4	1.9

Source: Board of Governors of the Federal Reserve System
Note: (-) means the sample is too small to be reliable.

Amount of Household Debt by Age

Median household debt rose by 13 percent between 1983 and 1989. The biggest increase was for householders aged 75 or older, although their debt levels are small.

(median debt of households having such debts, by age of householder, 1983 and 1989, and percent change in debt level, 1983-89; in thousands of 1989 dollars)

1989	**all households**	**under 35**	**35 to 44**	**45 to 54**	**55 to 64**	**65 to 74**	**75+**
Median amount of:							
Total	$15.2	$11.0	$31.1	$23.7	$10.8	$5.0	$3.0
Home mortgage	32.0	44.0	40.0	26.0	21.0	11.0	4.5
Investment real estate	30.0	20.0	39.0	21.0	16.3	15.0	18.0
Home equity lines	17.5	18.9	15.0	16.0	30.0	30.0	-
Other lines of credit	2.0	1.7	3.3	1.3	2.0	2.0	-
Credit cards	0.9	1.0	1.2	1.0	0.9	0.5	0.2
Car loans	5.8	5.1	6.6	6.4	5.8	4.0	3.3
Other debt	2.0	2.0	2.0	2.5	1.8	1.1	2.5
1983							
Median amount of:							
Total	$13.4	$8.3	$25.4	$16.1	$10.2	$4.9	$1.2
Home mortgage	27.0	34.0	31.9	20.3	15.9	14.1	4.6
Investment real estate	23.3	23.0	24.2	15.7	29.6	35.6	43.7
Home equity lines	7.5	2.5	30.5	10.0	-	-	-
Other lines of credit	1.2	0.9	1.2	1.4	1.9	0.9	-
Credit cards	0.6	0.6	0.7	0.6	0.6	0.2	0.4
Car loans	3.8	3.2	4.5	4.0	3.7	2.9	
Other debt	1.6	1.4	2.0	2.3	2.9	0.7	0.4
Percent change, 1983-89							
Median amount of:							
Total	13.4%	32.5%	22.4%	47.2%	5.9%	2.0%	150.0%
Home mortgage	18.5	29.4	25.4	28.1	32.1	-22.0	-2.2
Investment real estate	28.8	-13.0	61.2	33.8	-44.9	-57.9	-58.8
Home equity lines	133.3	656.0	-50.8	60.0	-	-	-
Other lines of credit	66.7	88.9	175.0	-7.1	5.3	122.2	-
Credit cards	50.0	66.7	71.4	66.7	50.0	150.0	-50.0
Car loans	52.6	59.4	46.7	60.0	56.8	37.9	-
Other debt	25.0	42.9	0.0	8.7	-37.9	57.1	525.0

Source: Board of Governors of the Federal Reserve System
Note: (-) means the sample is too small to be reliable.

Households With Debt by Income and Housing Status

Affluent households are more likely to have debts than those with smaller incomes, and the proportion of affluent households with debts rose between 1983 and 1989.

(percent of households with selected financial debts, by household income and housing status, 1983 and 1989, and percentage point change in households with debts, 1983-89)

	all households	income					housing status	
		under $10,000	$10,000 to $19,999	$20,000 to $29,999	$30,000 to $49,999	$50,000 or more	own	rent or other
1989								
Percent with:								
Total	72.7%	47.2%	58.7%	79.5%	86.5%	91.8%	78.0%	63.1%
Home mortgage	38.7	8.8	21.3	36.8	53.1	72.4	59.8	na
Investment real estate	7.0	1.0	1.5	4.7	8.8	18.7	9.0	3.4
Home equity lines	3.3	-	1.3	2.4	4.5	7.7	5.0	na
Other lines of credit	3.3	1.5	2.2	1.6	4.1	6.7	2.9	4.0
Credit cards	39.9	15.0	27.3	48.9	55.0	53.1	43.8	32.7
Car loans	35.1	11.1	21.8	39.4	50.9	51.7	39.0	27.9
Other debt	32.3	29.6	31.0	30.0	36.1	34.2	30.7	35.4
1983								
Percent with:								
Total	69.6%	41.3%	58.2%	76.6%	85.3%	87.2%	75.1%	60.0%
Home mortgage	36.9	9.9	20.1	34.0	56.4	66.8	58.3	na
Investment real estate	7.6	1.0	2.6	5.4	9.9	21.3	9.6	4.2
Home equity lines	0.5	-	-	-	0.8	0.7	0.8	na
Other lines of credit	11.2	3.0	7.2	10.7	16.9	18.2	12.0	9.8
Credit cards	37.0	11.9	26.3	45.5	53.0	48.4	41.6	29.1
Car loans	28.7	8.8	21.7	32.9	40.0	40.1	31.0	24.5
Other debt	29.6	24.4	25.1	31.9	34.8	32.1	28.5	31.6
Percentage point change, 1983-89:								
Total	3.1	5.9	0.5	2.9	1.2	4.6	2.9	3.1
Home mortgage	1.8	-1.1	1.2	2.8	-3.3	5.6	1.5	na
Investment real estate	-0.6	0.0	-1.1	-0.7	-1.1	-2.6	-0.6	-0.8
Home equity lines	2.8	-	-	-	3.7	7.0	4.2	na
Other lines of credit	-7.9	-1.5	-5	-9.1	-12.8	-11.5	-9.1	-5.8
Credit cards	2.9	3.1	1.0	3.4	2.0	4.7	2.2	3.6
Car loans	6.4	2.3	0.1	6.5	10.9	11.6	8.0	3.4
Other debt	2.7	5.2	5.9	-1.9	1.3	2.1	2.2	3.8

Source: Board of Governors of the Federal Reserve System
Note: (na) means not applicable. (-) means the sample is too small to be reliable.

Amount of Household Debt by Income and Housing Status

The median amount of debt held by Americans increased from 1983 to 1989 in all income categories.

(median debt of households having such debts, by household income and housing status, 1983 and 1989, and percent change in debt level, 1983-89; in thousands of 1989 dollars)

1989	all households	income under $10,000	$10,000 to $19,999	$20,000 to $29,999	$30,000 to $49,999	$50,000 or more	housing status own	rent or other
Median amount of:								
Total	$15.2	$1.9	$5.0	$12.5	$26.2	$55.5	$32.0	$3.2
Home mortgage	32.0	7.5	13.0	21.0	33.0	48.0	32.0	na
Investment real estate	30.0	3.6	24.0	13.5	17.5	47.0	27.0	39.0
Home equity lines	17.5	-	25.0	8.3	16.0	20.0	17.5	na
Other lines of credit	2.0	2.0	0.9	0.5	2.5	3.3	3.0	1.4
Credit cards	0.9	0.3	0.6	0.8	1.0	1.7	1.0	0.8
Car loans	5.8	1.8	3.0	5.5	6.5	7.2	6.6	4.2
Other debt	2.0	1.2	1.3	2.0	2.3	4.0	2.3	1.7
1983								
Median amount of:								
Total	$13.4	$1.8	$4.0	$8.5	$21.8	$45.1	$25.5	$2.2
Home mortgage	27.0	13.5	17.6	17.7	28.4	39.1	27.0	na
Investment real estate	23.3	2.8	10.2	21.4	15.8	40.0	23.3	24.2
Home equity lines	7.5	-	-	-	2.5	24.9	7.5	na
Other lines of credit	1.2	0.5	1.0	0.9	1.2	1.9	1.2	1.0
Credit cards	0.6	0.4	0.5	0.5	0.7	1.0	0.6	0.6
Car loans	3.8	1.6	2.6	3.0	4.0	5.5	4.2	2.8
Other debt	1.6	0.7	0.9	1.4	2.1	5.0	2.2	1.0
Percent change, 1983-89								
Median amount of:								
Total	13.4%	5.6%	25.0%	47.1%	20.2%	23.1%	25.5%	45.5%
Home mortgage	18.5	-44.4	-26.1	18.6	16.2	22.8	18.5	na
Investment real estate	28.8	28.6	135.3	-36.9	10.8	17.5	15.9	61.2
Home equity lines	133.3	-	-	-	540.0	-19.7	133.3	na
Other lines of credit	66.7	300.0	-10.0	-44.4	108.3	73.7	150.0	40.0
Credit cards	50.0	-25.0	20.0	60.0	42.9	70.0	66.7	33.3
Car loans	52.6	12.5	15.4	83.3	62.5	30.9	57.1	50.0
Other debt	25.0	71.4	44.4	42.9	9.5	-20.0	4.5	70.0

Source: Board of Governors of the Federal Reserve System
Note: (na) means not applicable. (-) means the sample is too small to be reliable.

Households With Debt by Life-Cycle Stage

Nearly all household segments are likely to have debts, but those most likely to be in debt are married couples with children.

(percent of households with selected financial debts, by life-cycle stage of householder, 1983 and 1989, and percentage point change in households with debt, 1983-89)

1989	all households	unmarried, no children	married, no children	under age 55		aged 55 or older	
				unmarried, children	married, children	in labor force	retired
Percent with:							
Total	72.7%	72.8%	89.2%	70.0%	93.6%	79.1%	37.9%
Home mortgage	38.7	18.1	52.0	26.8	63.6	41.2	15.5
Investment real estate	7.0	5.0	9.8	4.2	9.3	12.0	3.7
Home equity lines	3.3	-	-	1.6	5.4	6.6	1.1
Other lines of credit	3.3	5.6	11.0	2.6	4.0	2.7	0.5
Credit cards	39.9	37.5	57.9	33.4	56.7	43.3	15.2
Car loans	35.1	29.8	50.5	29.9	55.0	32.1	12.5
Other debt	32.3	37.6	49.5	38.4	43.1	21.2	11.5
1983							
Percent with:							
Total	69.6%	68.8%	91.1%	70.5%	89.0%	66.7%	33.2%
Home mortgage	36.9	14.8	45.8	31.0	60.0	34.3	13.7
Investment real estate	7.6	4.3	7.4	5.1	11.2	12.3	2.0
Home equity lines	0.5	-	-	-	0.7	-	-
Other lines of credit	11.2	7.7	17.1	12.8	16.4	10.7	1.8
Credit cards	37.0	33.3	52.8	34.3	49.4	37.3	15.5
Car loans	28.7	21.6	45.0	24.6	45.3	21.7	7.2
Other debt	29.6	35.2	46.0	33.4	40.3	18.6	8.8
Percentage point change, 1983-89:							
Total	3.1	4.0	-1.9	-0.5	4.6	12.4	4.7
Home mortgage	1.8	3.3	6.2	-4.2	3.6	6.9	1.8
Investment real estate	-0.6	0.7	2.4	-0.9	-1.9	-0.3	1.7
Home equity lines	2.8	-	-	-	4.7	-	-
Other lines of credit	-7.9	-2.1	-6.1	-10.2	-12.4	-8.0	-1.3
Credit cards	2.9	4.2	5.1	-0.9	7.3	6.0	-0.3
Car loans	6.4	8.2	5.5	5.3	9.7	10.4	5.3
Other debt	2.7	2.4	3.5	5.0	2.8	2.6	2.7

Source: Board of Governors of the Federal Reserve System
Note: (-) means the sample is too small to be reliable.

Amount of Household Debt by Life-Cycle Stage

Married couples without children carry the most debt, a median of $34,200 in 1989, up from just $24,000 in 1983.

(median debt of households holding such debts, by life-cycle stage of householder, 1983 and 1989, and percent change in debt level, 1983-89; in thousands of 1989 dollars)

1989	all households	unmarried, no children	married, no children	under age 55 unmarried, children	under age 55 married, children	aged 55 or older in labor force	aged 55 or older retired
Median amount of:							
Total	$15.2	$5.9	$34.2	$7.3	$31.2	$14.0	$5.8
Home mortgage	32.0	50.0	52.5	26.5	38.0	21.0	7.9
Investment real estate	30.0	53.0	35.0	20.0	31.7	17.0	12.5
Home equity lines	17.5	-	-	16.0	15.0	30.0	4.0
Other lines of credit	2.0	1.4	1.7	3.0	3.0	2.0	1.1
Credit cards	0.9	0.8	0.8	1.0	1.2	0.8	0.5
Car loans	5.8	5.1	7.1	4.3	6.4	4.5	5.8
Other debt	2.0	2.6	4.4	1.5	2.1	2.4	1.8
1983							
Median amount of:							
Total	$13.4	$3.6	$15.3	$7.0	$24.0	$12.4	$3.1
Home mortgage	27.0	28.9	38.4	22.5	29.8	17.8	11.8
Investment real estate	23.3	25.1	43.3	16.4	20.3	32.2	35.6
Home equity lines	7.5	-	-	-	5.0	-	-
Other lines of credit	1.2	1.0	0.9	1.2	1.2	2.4	0.8
Credit cards	0.6	0.5	0.6	0.5	0.7	0.6	0.4
Car loans	3.8	3.3	4.4	2.8	4.0	3.8	3.4
Other debt	1.6	1.6	1.2	1.1	2.0	3.1	0.6
Percent change, 1983-89							
Median amount of:							
Total	13.4%	63.9%	123.5%	4.3%	30.0%	12.9%	87.1%
Home mortgage	18.5	73.0	36.7	17.8	27.5	18.0	-33.1
Investment real estate	28.8	111.2	-19.2	22.0	56.2	-47.2	-64.9
Home equity lines	133.3	-	-	-	200.0	-	-
Other lines of credit	66.7	40.0	88.9	150.0	150.0	-16.7	37.5
Credit cards	50.0	60.0	33.3	100.0	71.4	33.3	25.0
Car loans	52.6	54.5	61.4	53.6	60.0	18.4	70.6
Other debt	25.0	62.5	266.7	36.4	5.0	-22.6	200.0

Source: Board of Governors of the Federal Reserve System
Note: (-) means the sample is too small to be reliable.

Homeownership Rates, 1982 to 1990

During the 1980s, homeownership rates fell for all but the oldest householders. The biggest declines were for those in their 30s.

(homeownership rates by age of householder and percentage point change in ownership, 1982-90)

	1990	1989	1988	1987	1986	1985	1984	1983	1982	percentage point change 1982-90
All households	**63.9%**	**63.9%**	**63.8%**	**64.0%**	**63.8%**	**63.9%**	**64.5%**	**64.6%**	**64.8%**	**-0.9%**
Age of householder										
Under age 25	15.7	16.6	15.8	16.0	17.2	17.2	17.9	18.8	19.3	-3.6
Under age 35	38.5	39.1	39.3	39.5	39.6	39.9	40.5	40.7	41.2	-2.7
Aged 25 to 29	35.2	35.3	35.9	36.4	36.7	37.7	38.6	38.3	38.6	-3.4
Aged 30 to 34	51.8	53.2	53.2	53.5	53.6	54.0	54.8	55.4	57.1	-5.3
Aged 35 to 39	63.0	63.4	63.6	64.1	64.8	65.4	66.1	66.5	67.6	-4.6
Aged 40 to 44	69.8	70.2	70.7	70.8	70.5	71.4	72.3	72.8	73.0	-3.2
Aged 45 to 49	73.9	74.1	74.4	74.6	74.1	74.3	74.6	75.3	76.0	-2.1
Aged 50 or older	77.4	77.2	77.1	77.4	77.2	76.9	77.3	77.4	77.2	0.2
Aged 50 to 54	76.8	77.2	77.1	77.8	78.1	77.5	78.4	78.8	78.8	-2.0
Aged 55 to 59	78.8	79.1	79.3	80.0	80.0	79.2	80.1	80.1	80.0	-1.2
Aged 60 to 64	79.8	80.1	79.8	80.4	79.8	79.9	79.9	79.8	80.1	-0.3
Aged 65 or older	76.3	75.8	75.6	75.5	75.0	74.8	75.1	75.0	74.4	1.9
Aged 65 to 69	80.0	80.0	80.0	79.5	79.4	79.5	79.3	78.7	77.9	2.1
Aged 70 to 74	78.4	77.8	77.7	77.7	77.2	76.8	75.5	75.4	75.2	3.2
Aged 75 or older	72.3	71.2	70.8	70.8	70.0	69.8	71.5	71.9	71.0	1.3

Source: Bureau of the Census
Note: Homeownership rates here differ from those in other tables in this chapter because the data are based on different samples.

Homeownership by Household Type and Age, 1982 to 1990

Homeownership rates fell during the 1980s for married couples and male- and female-headed families. Rates rose for people who live alone, particularly women under age 50.

(homeownership rates by household type and age of householder and percentage point change in ownership, 1982-90)

	1990	1989	1988	1987	1986	1985	1984	1983	1982	percentage point change 1982-90
All households	**63.9%**	**63.9%**	**63.8%**	**64.0%**	**63.8%**	**63.9%**	**64.5%**	**64.6%**	**64.8%**	**-0.9%**
Married couple families	**78.1**	**78.3**	**78.9**	**78.7**	**78.4**	**78.2**	**78.2**	**78.3**	**78.5**	**-0.4**
Under age 35	56.0	56.6	58.0	57.9	57.4	57.6	57.7	57.7	58.2	-2.2
Under age 50	70.8	71.0	71.8	71.4	70.9	70.9	70.9	70.9	71.3	-0.5
Aged 50 or older	89.0	89.1	88.9	88.9	88.8	88.3	88.3	88.3	88.1	0.9
Aged 65 or older	89.2	89.1	88.8	88.5	88.1	87.8	87.2	87.3	86.6	2.6
Male-headed families	**55.2**	**55.7**	**56.1**	**56.5**	**56.8**	**57.8**	**59.2**	**59.2**	**59.3**	**-4.1**
Under age 35	31.8	31.8	31.8	32.3	33.3	34.4	36.3	36.1	35.8	-4.0
Under age 50	45.9	46.2	46.1	46.1	47.0	48.6	49.3	49.4	49.4	-3.5
Aged 50 or older	75.8	75.9	76.4	76.8	75.2	75.0	76.5	75.5	76.1	-0.3
Aged 65 or older	80.7	79.5	80.0	80.7	80.0	78.3	78.4	79.1	75.3	5.4
Female-headed families	**44.0**	**44.1**	**45.3**	**45.8**	**45.3**	**45.8**	**46.9**	**47.0**	**47.1**	**-3.1**
Under age 35	17.2	17.1	18.5	18.0	18.4	19.2	20.4	19.8	20.9	-3.7
Under age 50	32.5	32.1	33.2	33.5	32.8	33.5	34.4	34.7	35.2	-2.7
Aged 50 or older	70.2	71.0	71.4	72.1	72.3	71.7	71.9	71.3	70.9	-0.7
Aged 65 or older	76.9	77.6	78.3	78.1	77.0	76.7	76.7	75.2	75.1	1.8
Persons living alone	**49.0**	**48.2**	**46.3**	**46.3**	**45.9**	**45.8**	**46.5**	**46.2**	**45.6**	**3.4**
Males living alone	42.4	41.8	39.9	39.9	40.0	38.8	38.9	38.3	38.0	4.4
Under age 35	25.0	26.4	24.0	23.3	24.8	23.1	23.4	23.9	23.7	1.3
Under age 50	33.0	33.2	30.8	29.8	30.2	29.6	29.2	28.8	28.5	4.5
Aged 50 or older	57.4	55.9	54.9	56.4	56.0	53.9	54.1	53.3	52.9	4.5
Aged 65 or older	62.4	61.1	60.1	61.0	61.3	59.6	60.3	59.6	58.6	3.8
Females living alone	53.6	52.6	51.8	51.6	50.9	51.3	52.2	52.0	51.2	2.4
Under age 35	19.1	19.3	17.8	17.1	16.4	15.7	15.6	15.0	15.1	4.0
Under age 50	30.2	29.1	27.8	26.7	26.0	25.8	24.6	23.3	23.3	6.9
Aged 50 or older	63.3	62.4	61.8	61.7	60.7	61.2	62.6	62.6	61.6	1.7
Aged 65 or older	64.0	62.6	62.0	62.0	61.2	61.7	63.0	62.7	62.2	1.8
2+-person nonfamily households	**32.0**	**31.2**	**31.5**	**31.6**	**31.2**	**31.1**	**30.4**	**30.6**	**30.1**	**1.9**
Male householder	31.7	31.5	31.3	31.1	29.8	30.1	28.8	29.5	28.3	3.4
Female householder	32.5	30.8	30.5	30.7	31.4	30.6	30.0	29.7	30.1	2.4

Source: Bureau of the Census

Note: Homeownership rates here differ from those in other tables in this chapter because the data are based on different samples.

Housing Characteristics

Half of American homes have more than one bathroom. Most also have a porch or deck and a garage.

(selected characteristics of occupied housing units, 1989; numbers in thousands)	number	percent of total units
Total units	93,683	100.0%
Number of rooms		
3 or fewer rooms	10,187	10.9
4 rooms	17,614	18.8
5 rooms	21,174	22.6
6 rooms	19,435	20.7
7 rooms	12,726	13.6
8 rooms	7,203	7.7
9 rooms	3,176	3.4
10 rooms or more	2,167	2.3
Median number of rooms	5.4	-
Bathrooms		
No bathroom	701	0.7
1 bathroom	46,122	49.2
1 and one-half bathrooms	15,435	16.5
2 or more bathrooms	31,425	33.5
Square footage*		
Less than 500	727	0.8
500 to 749	2,654	2.8
750-999	5,989	6.4
1,000 to 1,499	15,472	16.5
1,500 to 1,999	13,145	14.0
2,000 to 2,499	9,466	10.1
2,500 to 2,999	5,138	5.5
3,000 to 3,999	4,554	4.9
4,000 or more	2,434	2.6
Median for all units	1,688	-
Lot size*		
Less than one-eighth acre	6,266	6.7
One-eighth to one-quarter acre	12,052	12.9
One-quarter to one-half acre	9,160	9.8
One-half to one acre	6,261	6.7
1 to 4 acres	9,521	10.2
5 to 9 acres	1,515	1.6
10 acres or more	3,822	4.1
Median acreage	0.4	-
Amenities:		
Porch, deck, balcony or patio	70,799	75.6
Usable fireplace	29,037	31.0
Separate dining room	40,789	43.5
Two or more living/recreation rooms	29,961	32.0
Garage or carport	53,633	57.2

* Number of single detached and mobile homes only. Source: Bureau of the Census

Pension Coverage

The share of wage and salary workers covered by a pension plan slipped between 1984 and 1987 as coverage fell for workers under age 60.

(pension plan coverage, by selected characteristics of wage and salary workers aged 25 or older, 1984 and 1987; numbers in thousands)

	all workers		percent covered by a pension plan		percent vested in a pension plan	
	1987	**1984**	**1987**	**1984**	**1987**	**1984**
Total	**83,962**	**78,619**	**66.4%**	**67.1%**	**44.8%**	**45.1%**
Sex						
Men	45,047	43,467	68.8	69.8	48.9	50.3
Women	38,916	35,152	63.5	63.7	40.0	38.7
Age						
Aged 25 to 29	16,557	16,039	59.9	60.4	29.1	28.6
Aged 30 to 34	15,230	14,162	63.9	65.9	37.4	40.5
Aged 35 to 39	13,908	12,188	69.2	70.8	48.4	47.5
Aged 40 to 49	19,158	17,190	71.0	72.0	53.2	54.1
Aged 50 to 59	12,812	12,846	70.4	71.1	57.5	58.2
Aged 60 to 64	4,038	4,054	67.8	63.4	53.2	50.4
Aged 65 or older	2,261	2,141	49.5	46.0	29.1	25.7
Industry						
Agriculture, forestry, and fisheries	1,491	1,173	31.8	20.4	19.9	13.0
Mining	675	679	70.4	72.2	53.2	48.9
Construction	4,544	4,078	46.2	50.1	32.5	36.1
Manufacturing, total	18,219	19,428	75.8	76.5	54.0	52.6
Durable goods	11,179	11,391	78.8	78.7	56.3	55.2
Nondurable goods	7,040	8,037	71.1	73.3	50.3	48.9
Transportation, communication, and other public utilities	6,579	6,029	77.3	78.5	57.1	59.3
Wholesale trade	3,706	3,465	55.1	58.2	37.0	40.3
Retail trade	10,823	9,755	46.8	45.9	26.1	25.0
Finance, insurance, and real estate	5,453	4,915	70.5	69.7	45.0	43.9
Business and repair services	3,975	3,130	44.5	38.3	27.4	21.9
Personal services	2,482	2,223	27.3	22.4	13.2	13.0
Entertainment and recreation services	717	585	43.7	40.7	27.2	26.8
Professional and related services	19,950	17,885	75.0	75.0	49.8	50.2
Public administration, total	4,715	4,630	95.3	96.1	74.9	74.4
Federal government	1,404	1,600	97.7	98.6	78.6	79.7
State government	1,516	1,254	94.7	97.6	71.3	78.0
Local government	1,795	1,777	93.9	92.8	75.0	67.0
Armed forces	634	644	99.5	100.0	24.4	29.8
Size of firm						
Under 25 employees	18,389	17,348	22.5	24.7	14.8	15.1
25 to 99 employees	11,239	10,075	51.2	49.7	34.2	33.5
100 to 499 employees	11,847	10,368	70.6	70.5	46.4	46.9
500 to 999 employees	5,080	5,045	80.5	81.8	53.9	55.8
1,000 employees or more	37,407	35,782	89.3	89.5	61.0	60.9

Source: Bureau of the Census

CHAPTER

5

Labor Force Trends

In the 1990s, the American labor force will become increasingly middle-aged and diverse. The middle-aging of the labor force should boost worker productivity, since an experienced work force is more productive than one dominated by entry-level workers. The growing segmentation of the work force will challenge businesses to adapt to the needs of women and minorities. But this diversity should make the U.S. more competitive in a rapidly changing world economy.

Major Labor Force Trends

☛ During the 1990s, a larger proportion of Americans will be working than ever before in our history. With so many people juggling work and family needs, employers will have to become more flexible.

☛ Between 1990 and 2005, the number of workers aged 45 to 54 will grow by 75 percent. The median age of the work force will rise from 37 to 41 years. Productivity and incomes should rise because of the middle-aging of the work force.

☛ The share of the labor force comprised of white men will fall from 43 percent in 1990 to 38 percent by 2005. To find enough skilled workers in the years ahead, employers will have to hire more women and minorities.

Employment Status, 1960 to 1990

The percentage of Americans in the labor force is at a record high of 66 percent because so many women have gone to work. Men's labor force participation rates have fallen over the past three decades.

(employment status of the civilian noninstitutional population aged 16 or older by sex, race, and Hispanic origin, 1960-90; numbers in thousands)

	civilian labor force						not in labor force	
	civilian labor force	percent of population	number employed	percent of labor force	number unemployed	percent of labor force	number	percent of population
All persons								
1990	124,787	66.4%	117,914	94.5%	6,874	5.5%	63,262	33.6%
1985	115,461	64.8	107,150	92.8	8,312	7.2	62,744	35.2
1980	106,940	63.8	99,303	92.9	7,637	7.1	60,806	36.2
1970	82,771	60.4	78,678	95.1	4,093	4.9	54,315	39.6
1960	69,628	59.4	65,778	94.5	3,852	5.5	47,617	40.6
Males								
1990	68,234	76.1	64,435	94.4	3,799	5.6	21,417	23.9
1985	64,411	76.3	59,891	93.0	4,521	7.0	20,058	23.7
1980	61,453	77.4	57,186	93.1	4,267	6.9	17,945	22.7
1970	51,228	79.7	48,990	95.6	2,238	4.4	13,076	20.3
1960	46,388	83.3	43,904	94.6	2,486	5.0	9,274	16.7
Females								
1990	56,554	57.5	53,479	94.6	3,075	5.4	41,845	42.5
1985	51,050	54.5	47,259	92.6	3,791	7.4	42,686	45.5
1980	45,487	51.5	42,117	92.6	3,370	7.4	42,861	48.5
1970	31,543	43.3	29,688	94.1	1,855	5.9	41,239	56.7
1960	23,240	37.7	21,874	94.1	1,366	5.9	38,343	62.3
White								
1990	107,177	66.8	102,087	95.3	5,091	4.7	53,237	33.2
1985	99,926	65.0	93,736	93.8	6,191	6.2	53,753	35.0
1980	93,600	64.1	87,715	93.7	5,884	6.3	52,522	35.9
1970	73,556	60.2	70,217	95.5	3,339	4.5	48,618	39.8
1960	61,915	58.8	58,850	95.0	3,065	5.0	43,367	41.1
Black								
1990	13,493	63.3	11,966	88.7	1,527	11.3	7,808	36.7
1985	12,364	62.9	10,501	84.9	1,864	15.1	7,299	37.1
1980	10,865	61.0	9,313	85.7	1,553	14.3	6,959	39.0
Hispanic								
1990	9,576	67.0	8,808	92.0	769	8.0	4,721	33.0
1985	7,698	64.6	6,888	89.5	811	10.5	4,217	35.4
1980	6,146	64.0	5,527	89.9	620	10.1	3,452	36.0

Source: Bureau of Labor Statistics
Note: The civilian labor force equals the number employed plus the number unemployed. The civilian population equals the number in the labor force plus the number not in the labor force.

Labor Force Participation, 1960 to 1990

Labor force participation rates for women have increased in every age group except the oldest since 1960. Rates for men have fallen in nearly every age group.

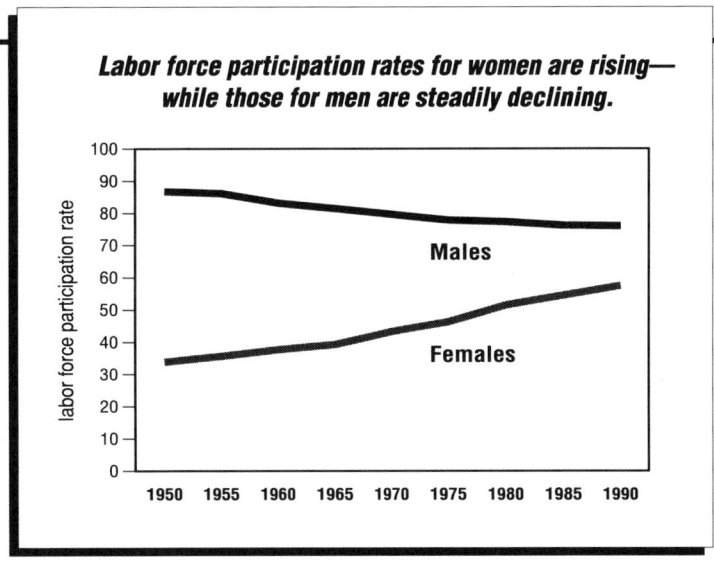

Labor force participation rates for women are rising—while those for men are steadily declining.

(labor force participation rates for persons aged 16 or older by sex and age, 1960-90)

	all	16 to 19	20 to 24	25 to 34	35 to 44	45 to 54	55 to 64	65+
Males								
1990	76.1%	55.7%	84.3%	94.2%	94.4%	90.7%	67.7%	16.4%
1985	76.3	56.8	85.0	94.7	95.0	91.0	67.9	15.8
1980	77.4	60.5	85.9	95.2	95.5	91.2	72.1	19.0
1975	77.9	59.1	84.5	95.2	95.6	92.1	75.6	21.6
1970	79.7	56.1	83.3	96.4	96.9	94.3	83.0	26.8
1960	83.2	55.0	88.1	97.5	97.7	95.7	86.8	33.1
Females								
1990	57.5	51.8	71.6	73.6	76.5	71.2	45.3	8.7
1985	54.5	52.1	71.8	70.9	71.8	64.4	42.0	7.3
1980	51.5	52.9	68.9	65.5	65.5	59.9	41.3	8.1
1975	46.3	49.1	64.1	54.9	55.8	54.6	40.9	8.2
1970	43.3	44.0	57.7	45.0	51.1	54.4	43.0	9.7
1960	37.7	39.3	46.1	36.0	43.4	49.8	37.2	10.8

Source: Bureau of Labor Statistics

Employment Status
by Age and Sex

Among women aged 25 to 54, three out of four are in the labor force. Over 93 percent of men aged 25 to 54 are in the labor force.

(employment status of civilian noninstitutional population by age and sex, 1990; numbers in thousands)

	civilian labor force						not in labor force	
All persons	civilian labor force	percent of population	number employed	percent of labor force	number unemployed	percent of labor force	number	percent of population
aged 16 years or older	**124,787**	**66.4%**	**117,914**	**94.5%**	**6,874**	**5.5%**	**63,262**	**33.6%**
Aged 16 to 19	7,410	53.7	6,261	84.5	1,149	15.5	6,385	46.3
Aged 20 to 24	13,843	77.8	12,622	91.2	1,221	8.8	3,956	22.2
Aged 25 to 54	88,140	83.5	84,139	95.5	4,001	4.5	17,358	16.5
Aged 25 to 34	35,803	83.7	33,831	94.5	1,972	5.5	6,949	16.3
Aged 35 to 44	31,844	85.3	30,543	95.9	1,301	4.1	5,498	14.7
Aged 45 to 54	20,493	80.7	19,765	96.4	728	3.6	4,910	19.3
Aged 55 to 64	11,860	55.9	11,464	96.7	396	3.3	9,369	44.1
Aged 65 or older	3,535	11.9	3,428	97.0	107	3.0	26,195	88.1
Males								
Aged 16 years or older	68,234	76.1	64,435	94.4	3,799	5.6	21,417	23.9
Aged 16 to 19	3,866	55.7	3,237	83.7	629	16.3	3,081	44.4
Aged 20 to 24	7,291	84.3	6,625	90.9	666	9.1	1,356	15.7
Aged 25 to 54	48,259	93.4	46,071	95.5	2,188	4.5	3,383	5.5
Aged 25 to 34	19,813	94.2	18,732	94.5	1,081	5.5	1,224	5.8
Aged 35 to 44	17,268	94.4	16,575	96.0	693	4.0	1,017	5.6
Aged 45 to 54	11,177	90.7	10,764	96.3	413	3.7	1,142	9.3
Aged 55 to 64	6,785	67.7	6,530	96.2	255	3.8	3,238	32.3
Aged 65 or older	2,033	16.4	1,972	97.0	61	3.0	10,359	83.6
Females								
Aged 16 years or older	56,554	57.5	53,479	94.6	3,075	5.4	41,845	42.5
Aged 16 to 19	3,544	51.8	3,024	85.3	519	14.7	3,304	48.3
Aged 20 to 24	6,552	71.6	5,997	91.5	555	8.5	2,600	28.4
Aged 25 to 54	39,881	74.1	38,068	95.5	1,813	4.5	13,975	25.9
Aged 25 to 34	15,990	73.6	15,099	94.4	890	5.6	5,725	26.4
Aged 35 to 44	14,576	76.5	13,967	95.8	608	4.2	4,482	23.5
Aged 45 to 54	9,316	71.2	9,001	96.6	315	3.4	3,768	28.8
Aged 55 to 64	5,075	45.3	4,935	97.2	141	2.8	6,131	54.7
Aged 65 or older	1,502	8.7	1,455	96.9	46	3.1	15,836	91.3

Source: Bureau of Labor Statistics
Note: The civilian labor force equals the number employed plus the number unemployed. The civilian population equals the number in the labor force plus the number not in the labor force.

Employment Status
by Age and Race

In every age group, blacks are slightly less likely to be in the labor force than whites. Unemployment rates for blacks are nearly double what they are for whites.

(employment status of civilian noninstitutional population by age and race, 1990; numbers in thousands)

	civilian labor force						not in labor force	
All persons	civilian labor force	percent of population	number employed	percent of labor force	number unemployed	percent of labor force	number	percent of population
aged 16 years or older	**124,787**	**66.4%**	**117,914**	**94.5%**	**6,874**	**5.5%**	**63,262**	**33.6%**
Aged 16 to 19	7,410	53.7	6,261	84.5	1,149	15.5	6,385	46.3
Aged 20 to 24	13,843	77.8	12,622	91.2	1,221	8.8	3,956	22.2
Aged 25 to 54	88,140	83.5	84,139	95.5	4,001	4.5	17,358	16.5
Aged 25 to 34	35,803	83.7	33,831	94.5	1,972	5.5	6,949	16.3
Aged 35 to 44	31,844	85.3	30,543	95.9	1,301	4.1	5,498	14.7
Aged 45 to 54	20,493	80.7	19,765	96.4	728	3.6	4,910	19.3
Aged 55 to 64	11,860	55.9	11,464	96.7	396	3.3	9,369	44.1
Aged 65 or older	3,535	11.9	3,428	97.0	107	3.0	26,195	88.1
White								
Aged 16 years or older	107,177	66.8	102,087	95.3	5,091	4.7	53,237	33.2
Aged 16 to 19	6,374	57.5	5,518	86.6	856	13.4	4,720	42.5
Aged 20 to 24	11,709	79.7	10,865	92.8	844	7.2	2,974	20.3
Aged 25 to 54	75,418	84.3	72,453	96.1	2,965	3.9	14,035	15.7
Aged 25 to 34	30,318	84.7	28,922	95.4	1,397	4.6	5,476	15.3
Aged 35 to 44	27,371	85.9	26,389	96.4	983	3.6	4,485	14.1
Aged 45 to 54	17,729	81.3	17,143	96.7	586	3.3	4,074	18.7
Aged 55 to 64	10,486	56.6	10,151	96.8	335	3.2	8,054	43.4
Aged 65 or older	3,189	12.0	3,100	97.2	90	2.8	23,454	88.0
Black								
Aged 16 years or older	13,493	63.3	11,966	88.7	1,527	11.3	7,808	36.7
Aged 16 to 19	831	38.6	573	68.9	258	31.1	1,319	61.3
Aged 20 to 24	1,679	68.9	1,344	80.1	335	19.9	758	31.1
Aged 25 to 54	9,643	79.8	8,773	91.0	870	9.0	2,435	20.2
Aged 25 to 34	4,263	79.8	3,763	88.3	500	11.7	1,081	20.2
Aged 35 to 44	3,358	82.3	3,095	92.2	263	7.8	723	17.7
Aged 45 to 54	2,022	76.2	1,915	94.7	107	5.3	631	23.8
Aged 55 to 64	1,060	49.8	1,012	95.4	49	4.6	1,069	50.2
Aged 65 or older	279	11.1	264	94.7	15	5.3	2,227	88.9

Source: Bureau of Labor Statistics
Note: The civilian labor force equals the number employed plus the number unemployed persons. The civilian population equals the number in the labor force plus the number not in the labor force. White and black do not sum to total because other races are not shown.

Employment Status of Hispanics

Hispanic women are less likely to be in the labor force than white or black women. Over half of Puerto Rican women do not work.

(employment status of civilians aged 16 or older of Hispanic and Mexican, Puerto Rican, or Cuban origin by sex, 1990; numbers in thousands)

| | civilian labor force | | | | | | not in labor force | |
Total	civilian labor force	percent of population	number employed	percent of labor force	number unemployed	percent of labor force	number	percent of population
*All Hispanics**	9,576	67.0%	8,808	92.0%	769	8.0%	4,721	33.0%
Mexican	5,970	68.3	5,478	91.8	492	8.2	2,773	31.7
Puerto Rican	859	55.6	780	90.9	79	9.1	687	44.4
Cuban	552	65.1	512	92.8	40	7.2	295	34.8
Males								
*All Hispanics**	5,755	81.2	5,304	92.2	451	7.8	1,332	18.8
Mexican	3,726	82.9	3,431	92.1	295	7.9	768	17.1
Puerto Rican	489	71.9	443	90.7	46	9.3	191	28.1
Cuban	310	74.8	288	93.1	21	6.9	104	25.1
Females								
*All Hispanics**	3,821	53.0	3,504	91.7	317	8.3	3,389	47.0
Mexican	2,244	52.8	2,047	91.2	197	8.8	2,005	47.2
Puerto Rican	370	42.8	337	91.1	33	8.9	495	57.2
Cuban	242	55.9	224	92.5	18	7.5	191	44.1

*Includes persons of Central or South American origin and of other Hispanic origin, not shown separately.
Source: Bureau of Labor Statistics
Note: The civilian labor force equals the number employed plus the number unemployed. The civilian population equals the number in the labor force plus the number not in the labor force.

Full-time and Part-time Workers

The majority of both men and women work full time. Among those who work part time, women are more likely than men to be doing so voluntarily.

(employed civilian labor force by full- and part-time status, 1970-90; numbers in thousands)

	civilian labor force	usually work full time				usually work part time			
		total	percent of labor force	currently on full-time schedule	currently on part-time schedule	total	percent of labor force	voluntary	part time for economic reasons
All persons aged 16 years or older									
1990	117,914	97,994	83.1%	96,113	1,880	19,920	16.9%	16,697	3,223
1985	107,149	88,534	82.6	86,795	1,739	18,615	17.4	14,764	3,851
1980	99,302	82,562	83.1	80,706	1,856	16,740	16.9	14,275	2,465
1975	85,846	71,586	83.4	69,790	1,796	14,260	16.6	12,251	2,008
1970	78,678	66,753	84.8	65,418	1,335	11,925	15.2	10,814	1,110
Males									
1990	64,434	57,982	90.0	56,866	1,116	6,452	10.0	5,118	1,335
1985	59,890	53,862	89.9	52,832	1,030	6,028	10.1	4,486	1,542
1980	57,188	51,717	90.4	50,583	1,134	5,471	9.6	4,498	973
1975	51,858	46,988	90.6	45,858	1,130	4,870	9.4	4,027	843
1970	48,991	44,825	91.5	44,012	813	4,166	8.5	3,681	485
Females									
1990	53,479	40,011	74.8	39,247	764	13,468	25.2	11,580	1,888
1985	47,259	34,672	73.4	33,963	709	12,587	26.6	10,278	2,309
1980	42,115	30,845	73.2	30,123	723	11,270	26.8	9,779	1,492
1975	33,989	24,598	72.4	23,932	666	9,391	27.6	8,225	1,166
1970	29,687	21,929	73.9	21,406	522	7,758	26.1	7,133	626

The shares of full- and part-time workers do not total to 100 percent of the labor force because they do not include the unemployed.
Source: Bureau of Labor Statistics
Note: Part-time employment is less than 35 hours per week.

Employment by School Enrollment Status

Most 20-to-24-year-olds who are in school are also employed. Even among those going to college full time, half also have a job.

(employment status of the civilian noninstitutional population aged 16 to 24 by school enrollment status, age, sex, and years of school completed, 1990; numbers in thousands)

	civilian population	total	percent of population	employed total	full time	part time	unemployed total	percent of labor force
Enrolled in school								
Aged 16 to 24	12,824	6,203	48.4%	5,528	1,189	4,339	675	10.9%
Aged 16 to 19	8,556	3,695	43.2	3,188	361	2,827	507	13.7
Aged 20 to 24	4,268	2,508	58.8	2,339	827	1,512	169	6.7
High school	6,381	2,572	40.3	2,154	165	1,989	419	16.3
College	6,443	3,631	56.4	3,374	1,024	2,350	256	7.1
Full-time students	5,419	2,732	50.4	2,523	479	2,044	209	7.7
Part-time students	1,024	899	87.8	852	545	307	47	5.2
Males								
Aged 16 to 24	6,458	3,079	47.7	2,715	612	2,103	365	11.8
Aged 16 to 19	4,342	1,860	42.9	1,587	195	1,392	273	14.7
Aged 20 to 24	2,117	1,219	57.6	1,127	417	711	91	7.5
High school	3,359	1,370	40.8	1,140	101	1,039	230	16.8
College	3,099	1,709	55.1	1,575	511	1,064	134	7.9
Full-time students	2,645	1,297	49.0	1,189	255	933	109	8.4
Part-time students	454	412	90.7	386	256	130	25	6.2
Females								
Aged 16 to 24	6,366	3,124	49.1	2,813	577	2,236	311	9.9
Aged 16 to 19	4,214	1,835	43.5	1,601	166	1,435	233	12.7
Aged 20 to 24	2,152	1,289	59.9	1,212	411	801	77	6.0
High school	3,023	1,202	39.8	1,014	64	950	188	15.7
College	3,343	1,922	57.5	1,799	513	1,287	122	6.4
Full-time students	2,773	1,434	51.7	1,334	224	1,110	101	7.0
Part-time students	570	487	85.5	466	289	176	22	4.4
Not enrolled in school								
All aged 16 to 24	18,769	15,049	80.2	13,355	10,966	2,389	1,694	11.3
Aged 16 to 19	5,238	3,715	70.9	3,073	1,956	1,116	642	17.3
Aged 20 to 24	13,531	11,335	83.8	10,282	9,010	1,272	1,052	9.3
Less than 4 years high school	5,278	3,340	63.3	2,673	1,883	790	667	20.0
4 years high school	8,664	7,309	84.4	6,550	5,513	1,037	758	10.4
1 to 3 years college	3,304	2,950	89.3	2,756	2,311	445	193	6.6
4 or more years college	1,524	1,451	95.2	1,375	1,259	117	76	5.2

(continued on next page)

(continued from previous page)
(employment status of the civilian noninstitutional population aged 16 to 24 by school status, age, sex, and years of school completed, 1990; numbers in thousands)

| | civilian population | civilian labor force | | employed | | | unemployed | |
		total	percent of population	total	full time	part time	total	percent of labor force
Males								
Aged 16 to 24	9,136	8,078	88.4%	7,147	6,182	965	931	11.5%
Aged 16 to 19	2,605	2,005	77.0	1,649	1,147	502	356	17.8
Aged 20 to 24	6,531	6,073	93.0	5,498	5,035	463	575	9.5
Less than 4 years high school	2,750	2,130	77.5	1,730	1,346	384	400	18.8
4 years high school	4,247	3,933	92.6	3,529	3,141	387	404	10.3
1 to 3 years college	1,484	1,385	93.3	1,293	1,134	159	92	6.6
4 or more years college	655	630	96.1	596	561	34	34	5.5
Females								
Aged 16 to 24	9,633	6,971	72.4	6,208	4,784	1,424	764	11.0
Aged 16 to 19	2,633	1,709	64.9	1,423	809	614	286	16.7
Aged 20 to 24	7,000	5,262	75.2	4,784	3,975	810	478	9.1
Less than 4 years high school	2,528	1,209	47.8	943	537	406	266	22.0
4 years high school	4,417	3,376	76.4	3,022	2,372	650	354	10.5
1 to 3 years college	1,820	1,565	86.0	1,463	1,178	286	102	6.5
4 or more years college	868	821	94.6	780	697	82	42	5.1

Source: Bureau of Labor Statistics
Note: The civilian labor force equals the number employed plus the number unemployed. The civilian population equals the number in the labor force plus the number not in the labor force.

Reasons For Not Being in the Labor Force, by Sex and Age

Most women who are not in the labor force are keeping house. Most men who are not in the labor force are retired.

(persons not in the labor force by reason, sex, and age, 1990; numbers in thousands)

	all persons	age			
		16 to 19	20 to 24	25 to 59	60 or older
Total					
Total not in labor force	63,262	6,385	3,956	20,846	32,075
Do not want a job now	57,789	5,235	3,181	17,892	31,482
Current activity:					
Going to school	6,658	4,178	1,579	880	21
Ill or disabled	4,973	42	123	2,663	2,145
Keeping house	23,626	348	1,112	11,336	10,831
Retired	18,429	-	1	442	17,987
Other activity	4,102	667	367	2,571	497
Want a job now	5,473	1,150	775	2,955	593
Reason for not looking:					
School attendance	1,411	855	277	276	3
Ill or disabled	911	22	50	646	193
Home responsibilities	1,207	62	215	887	42
Think cannot get a job	855	95	119	495	147
Job-market factors	540	45	82	348	66
Personal factors	315	50	37	148	81
Other reasons	1,090	116	115	650	209
Males					
Total not in labor force	21,417	3,081	1,356	4,399	12,581
Do not want a job now	19,449	2,509	1,091	3,537	12,312
Current activity:					
Going to school	3,269	2,107	812	343	7
Ill or disabled	2,569	26	65	1,479	999
Keeping house	459	16	29	186	227
Retired	11,059	-	1	315	10,743
Other activity	2,094	360	184	1,214	336
Want a job now	1,968	572	265	861	269
Reason for not looking:					
School attendance	691	454	139	96	1
Ill or disabled	455	12	22	342	79
Think cannot get a job	367	50	59	191	67
Other reasons	455	56	45	232	122
Females					
Total not in labor force	41,845	3,304	2,600	16,448	19,494

(continued on next page)

(continued from previous page)

(persons not in the labor force by reason, sex, and age, 1990; numbers in thousands)

	all persons	age			
		16 to 19	20 to 24	25 to 59	60 or older
Do not want a job now	38,340	2,726	2,090	14,354	19,170
Current activity:					
Going to school	3,390	2,071	767	538	14
Ill or disabled	2,404	16	58	1,184	1,146
Keeping house	23,167	331	1,082	11,149	10,604
Retired	7,371	-	-	126	7,244
Other activity	2,008	308	183	1,357	161
Want a job now	3,505	578	510	2,093	324
Reason for not looking:					
School attendance	720	400	138	180	2
Ill or disabled	456	10	28	304	113
Home responsibilities	1,207	62	215	887	42
Think cannot get a job	488	45	59	304	80
Other reasons	635	60	70	418	87

Source: Bureau of Labor Statistics
Note: Numbers may not add to total due to rounding and weighting patterns applied to the data.

Reasons For Not Being in the Labor Force by Age, Race, and Hispanic Origin

Most whites and Hispanics who are not in the labor force are either keeping house or retired. Among blacks, the major reasons are more diverse, including being ill or disabled.

(persons not in the labor force by race and Hispanic origin, reason, and age, 1990; numbers in thousands)

	all persons	age 16 to 24	age 25 to 59	age 60 or older	men	women
White						
Total not in labor force	53,237	7,694	16,969	28,574	17,785	35,453
Do not want a job now	49,282	6,384	14,814	28,084	16,359	32,923
Current activity:						
Going to school	5,046	4,365	664	18	2,461	2,585
Ill or disabled	3,827	118	2,008	1,700	1,997	1,829
Keeping house	20,632	1,136	9,690	9,806	340	20,292
Retired	16,498	1	394	16,104	9,933	6,565
Other activity	3,278	764	2,058	456	1,627	1,651
Want a job now	3,932	1,292	2,153	487	1,406	2,526
Reason for not looking:						
School attendance	948	759	188	1	470	479
Ill or disabled	679	55	477	146	342	337
Home responsibilities	879	171	672	36	-	879
Think cannot get a job	589	144	321	124	246	343
Other reasons	836	163	495	179	348	489
Black						
Total not in labor force	7,808	2,077	2,891	2,839	2,859	4,948
Do not want a job now	6,491	1,527	2,221	2,744	2,398	4,093
Current activity:						
Going to school	1,101	1,001	97	3	535	566
Ill or disabled	1,018	42	571	405	497	520
Keeping house	2,185	258	1,125	801	105	2,079
Retired	1,545	-	39	1,505	892	653
Other activity	643	226	389	29	368	275
Want a job now	1,316	551	670	96	461	855
Reason for not looking:						
School attendance	384	316	67	1	172	212
Ill or disabled	204	15	146	43	100	105
Home responsibilities	295	99	191	6	-	295
Think cannot get a job	219	61	140	19	97	122
Other reasons	214	60	127	27	92	121
Hispanic						
Total not in labor force	4,721	1,245	2,219	1,257	1,332	3,389

(continued on next page)

(continued from previous page)

(persons not in the labor force by race and Hispanic origin, reason, and age, 1990; numbers in thousands)

	all persons	age			men	women
		16 to 24	25 to 59	60 or older		
Do not want a job now	4,116	1,022	1,851	1,243	1,138	2,978
Current activity:						
Going to school	637	563	71	3	284	353
Ill or disabled	408	27	257	125	224	184
Keeping house	2,112	335	1,325	452	52	2,060
Retired	666	-	17	649	427	239
Other activity	292	96	182	14	151	142
Want a job now	611	223	354	33	188	422
Reason for not looking:						
School attendance	137	110	27	-	61	75
Ill or disabled	88	10	62	16	47	40
Home responsibilities	169	36	130	3	-	169
Think cannot get a job	120	41	69	10	40	79
Other reasons	98	26	67	4	39	58

Source: Bureau of Labor Statistics
Note: Numbers may not add to total due to rounding and weighting patterns applied to the data.

Volunteering in the U.S.

Those most likely to volunteer are aged 35 to 44, women, white, college educated, and married. Religious organizations get the largest share of volunteers.

(number and percent distribution of persons who performed unpaid volunteer work, by type of organization for which work was performed, and selected characteristics of volunteer workers, 1989; numbers in thousands)

| | volunteer workers | | | percent distribution of workers | | | | | | |
	number	percent of population	total	churches, other religious organizations	schools, other educational organizations	civic or political organizations	hospitals, other health organizations	social or welfare organizations	sport or recreational organizations	other organ.
All persons	38,042	20.4%	100.0%	37.4%	15.1%	13.2%	10.4%	9.9%	7.8%	6.3%
Age										
16 to 19	1,902	13.4	100.0	34.4	26.8	8.9	9.2	7.0	8.2	5.5
20 to 24	2,064	11.4	100.0	30.5	18.5	12.7	11.9	11.6	8.0	6.8
25 to 34	8,680	20.2	100.0	34.9	18.3	13.3	9.1	9.3	8.9	6.1
35 to 44	10,337	28.9	100.0	33.1	20.3	12.6	7.4	8.5	12.1	6.1
45 to 54	5,670	23.0	100.0	40.8	11.8	15.1	10.1	8.8	7.1	6.3
55 to 64	4,455	20.8	100.0	45.7	6.7	16.1	12.4	10.9	2.5	5.7
65 or older	4,934	16.9	100.0	43.3	4.3	11.1	17.8	14.5	1.8	7.2
Sex										
Male	16,681	18.8	100.0	35.9	10.5	17.2	7.0	10.1	11.8	7.5
Female	21,361	21.9	100.0	38.5	18.8	10.1	13.1	9.7	4.6	5.3
Race/Hispanic origin										
White	34,823	21.9	100.0	36.6	15.1	13.5	10.7	9.8	8.0	6.3
Black	2,505	11.9	100.0	50.4	12.4	9.6	7.0	10.4	4.6	5.6
Hispanic	1,289	9.4	100.0	42.2	18.3	9.6	8.5	8.9	6.9	5.6
Educational attainment*										
Less than 4 years high school	2,939	8.3	100.0	48.4	6.6	10.0	10.0	13.1	4.8	7.0
4 years high school	11,105	18.8	100.0	41.5	12.5	11.2	11.1	8.8	8.2	6.7
1 to 3 years college	7,572	28.1	100.0	36.8	14.7	13.3	10.8	10.1	8.0	6.3
4 years college or more	12,459	38.4	100.0	32.9	17.4	16.4	9.7	10.1	7.8	5.7
Marital status										
Never married	6,327	13.7	100.0	29.3	18.6	14.0	10.9	12.4	7.6	7.3
Married, spouse present	26,344	24.8	100.0	40.4	15.2	13.2	9.0	8.4	8.4	5.4
Married, spouse absent	765	13.2	100.0	29.4	17.8	11.6	13.2	12.5	5.0	10.5
Divorced	2,510	17.3	100.0	25.1	12.6	15.1	15.0	15.0	8.2	9.0
Widowed	2,096	15.3	100.0	41.2	5.9	8.1	20.8	13.9	1.3	8.9

*Educational attainment is for persons aged 25 or older.
Source: Bureau of Labor Statistics
Note: Hispanics may be of any race. Numbers may not add to total due to rounding.

Labor Force Projections, 1990 to 2005

The number of workers aged 25 to 34 will decline sharply between 1990 and 2005. The number of workers aged 45 to 54 will grow by 66 percent for men and 85 percent for women.

(civilian labor force and participation rates by sex, age, race, and Hispanic origin, 1990, and moderate growth projections to 2005; numbers in thousands)

	participation rate		number		percent change 1990–2005	annual growth rate 1990–2005
	1990	2005	1990	2005		
Total, aged 16 or older	**66.4%**	**69.0%**	**124,787**	**150,732**	**20.8%**	**1.3%**
Males						
Aged 16 or older	76.1	75.4	68,234	79,338	16.3	1.0
Aged 16 to 19	55.6	57.7	3,866	4,575	18.3	1.1
Aged 20 to 24	84.3	86.1	7,291	7,989	9.6	0.6
Aged 25 to 34	94.2	93.6	19,813	16,955	-14.4	-1.0
Aged 35 to 44	94.4	93.4	17,268	19,237	11.4	0.7
Aged 45 to 54	90.7	90.3	11,177	18,588	66.3	3.4
Aged 55 to 64	67.7	67.9	6,785	9,692	42.8	2.4
Aged 65 or older	16.4	16.0	2,033	2,302	13.2	0.8
Aged 65 to 74	21.4	22.5	1,727	1,860	7.7	0.5
Aged 75 or older	7.1	7.2	307	442	44.0	2.5
Females						
Aged 16 or older	57.5	63.0	56,554	71,394	26.2	1.6
Aged 16 to 19	51.8	54.3	3,544	4,218	19.0	1.2
Aged 20 to 24	71.6	75.3	6,552	7,266	10.9	0.7
Aged 25 to 34	73.6	79.7	15,990	14,724	-7.9	-0.5
Aged 35 to 44	76.5	85.3	14,576	17,829	22.3	1.4
Aged 45 to 54	71.2	81.5	9,316	17,229	84.9	4.2
Aged 55 to 64	45.3	54.3	5,075	8,372	65.0	3.4
Aged 65 or older	8.7	8.8	1,502	1,756	16.9	1.0
Aged 65 to 74	13.1	15.1	1,306	1,492	14.2	0.9
Aged 75 or older	2.7	2.6	196	264	34.7	2.0
White, aged 16 or older	**66.8**	**69.7**	**107,177**	**125,785**	**17.4**	**1.1**
Males	76.9	76.2	59,298	66,851	12.7	0.8
Females	57.5	63.5	47,879	58,934	23.1	1.4
Black, aged 16 or older	**63.3**	**65.6**	**13,493**	**17,766**	**31.7**	**1.9**
Males	70.1	70.2	6,708	8,704	29.8	1.8
Females	57.8	61.7	6,785	9,062	33.6	1.9
Asian and other, aged 16 or older	**64.9**	**66.4**	**4,116**	**7,181**	**74.5**	**3.8**
Males	74.2	75.0	2,226	3,783	69.9	3.6
Females	56.7	58.9	1,890	3,398	79.8	4.0
Hispanic, aged 16 or older	**67.0**	**69.9**	**9,576**	**16,790**	**75.3**	**3.8**
Males	81.2	81.6	5,755	9,902	72.1	3.7
Females	53.0	58.0	3,821	6,888	80.3	4.0

Source: Bureau of Labor Statistics. Note: Hispanics may be of any race.

Median Age of the Labor Force, 1962 to 2005

By 2005, the median age of the labor force will equal what it was in the early 1960s. Hispanics will continue to be the youngest workers, while whites will continue to be the oldest.

(median age of the labor force by sex, race, and Hispanic origin, for selected years, 1962-90, and projections for 1995-2005)

	1962	1970	1975	1980	1985	1990	1995	2000	2005
Total	**40.5**	**39.0**	**35.8**	**34.3**	**35.2**	**36.6**	**38.0**	**39.4**	**40.6**
Males	40.5	39.4	36.5	35.1	35.6	36.7	38.0	39.4	40.5
Females	40.4	38.3	34.8	33.9	34.7	36.4	38.0	39.5	40.6
White	40.9	39.3	35.6	34.8	35.4	36.8	38.3	39.8	41.0
Black	38.3	36.6	34.1	33.3	33.8	34.9	36.2	37.4	38.3
Asian and other	-	-	-	33.8	34.9	36.5	37.2	38.0	38.6
Hispanic	-	-	-	30.7	32.4	33.2	34.2	35.0	35.6

Source: Bureau of Labor Statistics
Note: (−) means data not available.

Workers Entering and Leaving the Labor Force, 1990 to 2005

Only one-third of people entering the labor force between 1990 and 2005 will be white men. Consequently, white men will represent a shrinking share of the labor force, falling from 43 percent in 1990 to 38 percent by 2005.

(civilian labor force aged 16 or older by sex, race, and Hispanic origin, 1990, and projected to 2005, and projected entrants and leavers, 1990–2005; numbers in thousands)

Number	total labor force, 1990	entrants 1990–2005	leavers 1990–2005	total labor force, 2005
Total	**124,786**	**55,798**	**29,851**	**150,732**
Males	68,232	28,197	17,090	79,339
Females	56,554	27,601	12,761	71,394
White, non-Hispanic	**98,013**	**36,425**	**24,423**	**110,015**
Males	53,784	17,965	14,204	57,545
Females	44,229	18,460	10,219	52,470
Black	**13,340**	**7,250**	**3,144**	**17,447**
Males	6,628	3,461	1,553	8,537
Females	6,712	3,789	1,591	8,910
Hispanic	**9,577**	**8,768**	**1,556**	**16,789**
Males	5,756	5,085	939	9,902
Females	3,822	3,683	617	6,888
Asian and other	**3,855**	**3,354**	**728**	**6,482**
Males	2,064	1,686	395	3,356
Females	1,791	1,668	333	3,126
Percent distribution				
Total	**100.0%**	**100.0%**	**100.0%**	**100.0%**
Males	54.7	50.5	57.3	52.6
Females	45.3	49.5	42.7	47.4
White, non-Hispanic	**78.5**	**65.3**	**81.8**	**73.0**
Males	43.1	32.2	47.6	38.2
Females	35.4	33.1	34.2	34.8
Black	**10.7**	**13.0**	**10.5**	**11.6**
Males	5.3	6.2	5.2	5.7
Females	5.4	6.8	5.3	5.9
Hispanic	**7.7**	**15.7**	**5.2**	**11.1**
Males	4.6	9.1	3.1	6.6
Females	3.1	6.6	2.1	4.6
Asian and other	**3.1**	**6.0**	**2.4**	**4.3**
Males	1.7	3.0	1.3	2.2
Females	1.4	3.0	1.1	2.1

Source: Bureau of Labor Statistics

Job Tenure

Americans are not changing jobs more today than in the past. In fact, the number of years people have been employed at their current job has increased for nearly every age group.

(median number of years workers have been employed at their current job by age and sex, 1963 and 1987)

	1987	1963	change 1963–1987
All			
Aged 25 to 34	3.4	3.0	0.4%
Aged 35 to 44	6.1	6.0	0.1
Aged 45 to 54	9.6	9.0	0.6
Aged 55 to 64	12.7	11.8	0.9
Aged 65 or older	12.4	13.8	-1.4
Males			
Aged 25 to 34	3.7	3.5	0.2
Aged 35 to 44	7.6	7.6	0.0
Aged 45 to 54	12.3	11.4	0.9
Aged 55 to 64	15.7	14.7	1.0
Aged 65 or older	15.0	16.6	-1.6
Females			
Aged 25 to 34	3.1	2.0	1.1
Aged 35 to 44	4.9	3.6	1.3
Aged 45 to 54	7.3	6.1	1.2
Aged 55 to 64	10.3	7.8	2.5
Aged 65 or older	10.8	8.8	2.0

Source: Bureau of Labor Statistics

Female-to-Male Earnings Ratio

Women who work full time now earn 74 percent as much as men, up from 63 percent in 1979. This is a record high.

(median weekly earnings and earnings ratio of female to male full-time wage and salary workers aged 16 or older, 1979-91; median weekly earnings in current dollars)

	male	female	female-to-male earnings ratio
1991	$497	$368	74.0%
1990	485	348	71.8
1989	468	328	70.1
1988	449	315	70.2
1987	433	303	70.0
1986	419	290	69.2
1985	406	277	68.2
1984	391	265	67.8
1983	378	252	66.7
1982	364	238	65.4
1981	339	219	64.6
1980	312	201	64.4
1979	291	182	62.5

Source: Bureau of Labor Statistics

Median Weekly Earnings of Families by Earner Status

Families in which both husband and wife work take home the most money each week. Dual-earner families account for nearly half of all families with earners.

(median weekly earnings of families by type of family, number of earners, race, and Hispanic origin, 1990; numbers in thousands)

	number of families	median weekly earnings
Total		
All families with earners	43,759	$653
Married couple families	34,219	732
One earner	12,166	455
Husband	8,994	520
Wife	2,407	267
Two or more earners	22,053	880
Husband and wife	19,599	897
Families maintained by women	7,323	363
One earner	4,983	288
Two or more earners	2,340	607
Families maintained by men	2,218	514
One earner	1,352	396
Two or more earners	866	778
White		
All families with earners	37,239	$681
Married couple families	30,361	745
One earner	10,856	473
Husband	8,162	535
Wife	2,044	270
Two or more earners	19,505	892
Husband and wife	17,354	908
Families maintained by women	5,127	382
Families maintained by men	1,751	539
Black		
All families with earners	5,082	$459
Married couple families	2,724	601
One earner	893	304
Husband	527	345
Wife	290	243
Two or more earners	1,831	748
Husband and wife	1,634	768
Families maintained by women	1,986	314
Families maintained by men	372	397

(continued on next page)

(continued from previous page)
(median weekly earnings of families by type of family, number of earners, race, and Hispanic origin, 1990; numbers in thousands)

	number of families	median weekly earnings
Hispanic		
All families with earners	3,624	$496
Married couple families	2,599	555
One earner	1,050	322
Husband	814	356
Wife	164	236
Two or more earners	1,549	716
Husband and wife	1,204	727
Families maintained by women	691	326
Families maintained by men	334	468

Source: Bureau of Labor Statistics
Note: Hispanics may be of any race. White and black do not sum to total because other races are not shown.

Employment Status of Women by Age and Marital Status

Three out of four working women work full time. Married women are slightly more likely to work 40-hour weeks than divorced or single women.

(females aged 16 or older employed in nonagricultural industries by age, marital status, and full- or part-time employment status, 1990; numbers in thousands)

Number	total employed	on full-time schedules			on part-time schedules		average hours worked/week total	average hours worked/week full-time workers
		total	40 hours or less	41 hours or more	voluntary	involuntary		
All females, aged 16 or older	**49,551**	**36,598**	**27,247**	**9,351**	**10,355**	**2,599**	**35.8**	**41.3**
Aged 16 to 19	2,864	883	730	154	1,684	296	24.4	39.3
Aged 20 or older	46,688	35,714	26,517	9,197	8,671	2,303	36.5	41.4
Aged 20 to 24	5,689	4,072	3,155	917	1,208	410	35.1	40.8
Aged 25 or older	40,999	31,643	23,362	8,280	7,463	1,893	36.8	41.4
Aged 25 to 44	26,941	21,290	15,599	5,691	4,413	1,238	37.2	41.4
Aged 45 to 64	12,753	9,815	7,341	2,474	2,354	584	36.7	41.4
Aged 65 or older	1,304	536	420	115	696	73	27.0	40.9
Marital status								
Married, spouse present	27,228	19,972	15,145	4,827	6,080	1,176	35.6	41.0
Divorced, separated, widowed	10,009	8,163	5,811	2,353	1,246	600	38.2	42.1
Single (never married)	12,314	8,462	6,290	2,171	3,029	824	34.5	41.4

Percent distribution	total employed	on full-time schedules			on part-time schedules			
		total	40 hours or less	41 hours or more	voluntary	involuntary		
All females, aged 16 or older	**100.0%**	**73.9%**	**55.0%**	**18.9%**	**20.9%**	**5.2%**	-	-
Aged 16 to 19	100.0	30.8	25.5	5.4	58.8	10.3	-	-
Aged 20 or older	100.0	76.5	56.8	19.7	18.6	4.9	-	-
Aged 20 to 24	100.0	71.6	55.5	16.1	21.2	7.2	-	-
Aged 25 or older	100.0	77.2	57.0	20.2	18.2	4.6	-	-
Aged 25 to 44	100.0	79.0	57.9	21.1	16.4	4.6	-	-
Aged 45 to 64	100.0	77.0	57.6	19.4	18.5	4.6	-	-
Aged 65 or older	100.0	41.1	32.2	8.8	53.4	5.6	-	-
Marital status								
Married, spouse present	100.0	73.4	55.6	17.7	22.3	4.3	-	-
Divorced, separated, widowed	100.0	81.6	58.1	23.5	12.4	6.0	-	-
Single (never married)	100.0	68.7	51.1	17.6	24.6	6.7	-	-

Source: Bureau of Labor Statistics
Note: Part-time workers are those who usually work 1 to 34 hours per week.

Labor Force Participation of Women With and Without Children

Since 1970, labor force participation rates have increased the most for women with children. Among married women with preschoolers, rates have increased from 30 percent in 1970 to 57 percent in 1988.

(labor force participation rates of women aged 16 or older by marital status and presence and age of children, 1970-88)

	1988	1985	1980	1970
All women	**56.6%**	**54.5%**	**51.5%**	**43.3%**
Married, spouse present	56.5	54.2	50.1	40.8
Separated	60.3	61.2	59.4	52.1
Divorced	75.7	75.0	74.5	71.5
Single	65.2	65.2	61.5	53.0
All with no children under age 18	**51.2**	**50.4**	**48.1**	-
Married, spouse present	48.9	48.2	46.0	42.2
Separated	60.1	60.0	58.9	52.3
Divorced	73.0	72.1	71.4	67.7
Single	67.3	66.9	62.1	-
All with children aged 6 to 17 only	**73.3**	**69.9**	**64.3**	-
Married, spouse present	72.5	67.8	61.7	49.2
Separated	69.3	70.9	66.3	60.6
Divorced	83.9	83.4	82.3	82.4
Single	67.1	64.1	67.6	-
All with children under age 6	**56.1**	**53.5**	**46.8**	-
Married, spouse present	57.1	53.4	45.1	30.3
Separated	53.0	53.2	52.2	45.4
Divorced	70.1	67.5	68.3	63.3
Single	44.7	46.5	44.1	-

Source: Bureau of Labor Statistics
Note: (-) means data not available.

Labor Force Participation of Wives With Preschool Children

Labor force participation rates have increased the most for married women with children under age 3. Among those with children under age 1, only 31 percent were in the work force in 1975. By 1988, 52 percent were working.

(labor force participation rates for married women with spouse present by age of youngest child and race, 1975-88)

	total			white			black		
	1988	**1980**	**1975**	**1988**	**1980**	**1975**	**1988**	**1980**	**1975**
All wives	**56.7%**	**50.2%**	**44.5%**	**55.8%**	**49.3%**	**43.7%**	**66.1%**	**59.3%**	**54.3%**
With no children under age 18	**49.1**	**46.0**	**44.0**	**48.5**	**45.5**	**43.5**	**54.4**	**51.2**	**47.7**
With children under age 18	**65.2**	**54.3**	**44.9**	**64.3**	**53.2**	**43.9**	**75.8**	**65.6**	**58.8**
Youngest child under age 6	57.4	45.3	36.8	56.3	43.5	35.0	71.7	63.4	56.4
Youngest child under age 3	54.8	41.5	32.6	53.3	40.0	30.9	73.0	57.7	52.2
Aged 1 or under	51.9	39.0	30.8	50.5	37.7	29.2	71.5	52.9	50.0
Aged 2	61.7	48.1	37.1	60.2	46.1	35.1	76.2	71.0	56.4
Aged 3 to 5	61.4	51.7	42.2	60.9	49.4	40.3	69.8	72.3	61.7
Aged 3	59.3	51.5	41.2	58.1	48.4	39.0	76.1	73.4	62.7
Aged 4	61.4	51.4	41.2	61.0	49.8	38.7	70.3	66.4	64.9
Aged 5	63.6	52.4	44.4	64.0	50.4	43.8	62.5	77.8	56.3

Source: Bureau of Labor Statistics

Labor Force Participation of Women With Newborns

In 1990, 53 percent of new mothers were in the labor force within a year of giving birth. Nearly 70 percent of new mothers with a college education were in the labor force.

(number and labor force participation rates of women aged 18 to 44 who had a child in the last year by selected characteristics, 1980 and 1990, numbers in thousands)

	1990		1980	
	number	**percent in labor force**	**number**	**percent in labor force**
Total	**3,809**	**53.1%**	**3,247**	**38.0%**
Age				
18 to 24	1,272	45.0	1,396	38.1
25 to 29	1,192	55.3	1,081	38.4
30 to 44	1,346	58.9	770	37.3
Education				
Less than high school	718	30.0	792	28.2
High school, 4 years	1,582	52.0	1,475	39.5
College, 1-3 years	777	62.8	542	43.8
College, 4 or more years	732	68.0	437	43.7
Birth order				
First birth	1,453	60.7	1,299	45.7
Second or higher order birth	2,357	48.4	1,948	32.8
Marital status				
Married, husband present	2,803	56.6	2,660	36.4
Widowed, divorced, or separated	316	50.5	238	49.8
Never married	691	40.2	348	42.2
Race/Hispanic origin				
White	3,075	54.9	2,670	36.5
Black	589	46.2	471	46.8
Asian or other	98	49.4	-	-
Hispanic	478	44.4	320	32.9

(-) means data not available.
Source: Bureau of the Census
Note: Hispanics may be of any race.

Employment by Industry, 1990 to 2005

The service industries are projected to gain the most jobs between 1990 and 2005. By 2005, they will employ more than 80 percent of all wage and salary workers.

(employment by major industry division, 1990, and moderate growth projections to 2005; numbers in thousands)

Number	1990	2005	percent change 1990–2005
Total*, all industries	**122,570**	**147,190**	**20.1%**
Nonfarm wage and salary employment	109,319	132,647	21.3
Goods-producing	24,958	25,242	1.1
Mining	711	668	-6.0
Construction	5,136	6,059	18.0
Manufacturing	19,111	18,514	-3.1
Durable manufacturing	11,115	10,517	-5.4
Nondurable manufacturing	7,995	7,998	0.0
Service-producing	84,363	107,405	27.3
Transportation, communications, utilities	5,826	6,689	14.8
Wholesale trade	6,205	7,210	16.2
Retail trade	19,683	24,804	26.0
Finance, insurance, and real estate	6,739	8,129	20.6
Services	27,588	39,058	41.6
Government	18,322	21,515	17.4
Agriculture	3,276	3,080	-6.0
Private households	1,014	700	-31.0
Nonagricultural self-employed and unpaid family workers	8,961	10,763	20.1

Percent distribution of wage and salary employment			percentage point change 1990–2005
Nonfarm wage and salary employment	100.0%	100.0%	0.0
Goods-producing	22.8	19.0	-3.8
Mining	0.7	0.5	-0.2
Construction	4.7	4.6	-0.1
Manufacturing	17.5	14.0	-3.5
Durable manufacturing	10.2	7.9	-2.3
Nondurable manufacturing	7.3	6.0	-1.3
Service-producing	77.2	81.0	3.8
Transportation, communications, utilities	5.3	5.0	-0.3
Wholesale trade	5.7	5.4	-0.3
Retail trade	18.0	18.7	0.7
Finance, insurance, and real estate	6.2	6.1	-0.1
Services	25.2	29.4	4.2
Government	16.8	16.2	-0.6

* Total employment here is lower than in other tables because it does not include workers in some agricultural services or in nonclassified establishments.
Source: Bureau of Labor Statistics

Fastest Growing and Declining Industries, 1990 to 2005

Computer, health, legal, accounting, and research services will be the some of the fastest-growing industries from 1990 to 2005. Those losing ground include the footwear, luggage, ammunition, and apparel industries.

(employment change in selected industries, 1990-2005, ranked by annual percent change; numbers in thousands)

	1990	2005	change 1990–2005	annual percent change 1990–2005
Fastest growing				
Residential care	469	911	442	4.5%
Computer and data processing services	784	1,494	710	4.4
Health services	697	1,262	565	4.0
Management and public relations	622	1,097	475	3.9
Water and sanitation, including combined services	184	299	115	3.3
Libraries, vocational and other schools	207	335	128	3.3
Offices of health practitioners	2,180	3,470	1,290	3.1
Passenger transportation arrangement	192	299	107	3.0
Individual and miscellaneous social services	638	991	353	3.0
Legal services	919	1,427	508	3.0
Nursing and personal-care facilities	1,420	2,182	762	2.9
Miscellaneous equipment rental and leasing	211	324	113	2.9
Accounting, auditing, and services	575	871	296	2.8
Elementary and secondary schools	457	689	232	2.8
Automotive rentals, without drivers	180	271	91	2.8
Research and testing services	407	609	202	2.7
Miscellaneous publishing	82	123	41	2.7
Business services	937	1,397	460	2.7
Photocopying, commercial art, photofinishing	200	293	93	2.6
Nondepository; holding and investment offices	596	871	275	2.6
Most rapidly declining				
Footwear, except rubber and plastic	80	41	-39	-4.3
Ammunition and ordnance, except small arms	52	30	-22	-3.8
Luggage, handbags, and leather products	52	31	-21	-3.5
Tobacco manufactures	49	34	-15	-2.5
Agricultural chemicals	56	38	-18	-2.5
Private households	1,014	700	-314	-2.4
Stampings, except automotive	84	59	-25	-2.3
Metal cans and shipping containers	50	35	-15	-2.3

(continued on next page)

(continued from previous page)

(employment change in selected industries, 1990-2005, ranked by annual percent change; numbers in thousands)

	1990	2005	change 1990–2005	annual percent change 1990–2005
Forgings	40	29	-11	-2.3%
Petroleum refining	118	85	-33	-2.2
Small arms and small arms ammunition	23	17	-6	-2.1
Guided missiles and space vehicles	134	98	-36	-2.0
Household appliances	125	94	-31	-1.9
Motor vehicles and bodies	328	246	-82	-1.9
Office and accounting machines	43	33	-10	-1.9
Soft drinks and flavorings	121	92	-29	-1.8
Photographic equipment and supplies	100	76	-24	-1.8
Tires and inner tubes	86	65	-21	-1.8
Apparel	839	638	-201	-1.8
Communications, except broadcasting	947	724	-223	-1.8

Source: Bureau of Labor Statistics

Industry Employment, 1990 to 2005

Industry employment is projected to grow 1.3 percent annually between 1990 and 2005, but the annual gain should be greater than 3 percent for health, legal, and social services.

(employment in selected industries in 1990 and moderate growth projections to 2005; numbers in thousands)

	1990	*2005*	*annual growth rate 1990–2005*
Total*, all industries	**122,570**	**147,190**	**1.2%**
Nonfarm wage and salary employment	109,319	132,647	1.3
Mining	711	668	-0.4
Construction	5,136	6,059	1.1
Manufacturing	19,111	18,514	-0.2
Durable manufacturing	11,115	10,517	-0.4
Lumber and wood products	741	722	-0.2
Furniture and fixtures	510	618	1.3
Stone, clay, and glass products	557	516	-0.5
Primary metal industries	756	643	-1.1
Fabricated metal products	1,423	1,238	-0.9
Industrial machinery and equipment	2,095	1,941	-0.5
Electronic and other electric equipment	1,673	1,567	-0.4
Transportation equipment	1,980	1,889	-0.3
Instruments and related products	1,004	1,018	0.1
Miscellaneous manufacturing industries	377	364	-0.2
Nondurable manufacturing	7,995	7,998	0.0
Food and kindred products	1,668	1,560	-0.4
Tobacco manufactures	49	34	-2.5
Textile mill products	691	596	-1.0
Apparel and other textile products	1,043	848	-1.4
Paper and allied products	699	727	0.3
Printing and publishing	1,574	1,900	1.3
Chemicals and allied products	1,093	1,098	0.0
Petroleum and coal products	158	122	-1.7
Leather and leather products	132	72	-4.0
Transportation, communications, utilities	5,826	6,689	0.9
Transportation	3,554	4,427	1.5
Transportation services	350	530	2.8
Communications	1,311	1,143	-0.9
Communications, except broadcasting	947	724	-1.8
Radio and television broadcasting, cable TV	364	419	0.9
Electric, gas, and sanitary services	961	1,119	1.0
Wholesale trade	6,205	7,210	1.0
Retail trade	19,683	24,804	1.6
Retail trade, except eating and drinking places	13,118	16,092	1.4

(continued on next page)

(continued from previous page)

(employment in selected industries in 1990 and moderate growth projections to 2005; numbers in thousands)

	1990	2005	annual growth rate 1990–2005
Eating and drinking places	6,565	8,712	1.9%
Finance, insurance, and real estate	6,739	8,129	1.3
Services	27,588	39,058	2.3
Hotels and other lodging places	1,649	2,174	1.9
Personal services	1,113	1,338	1.2
Laundry, cleaning, and shoe repair	440	499	0.8
Personal services	199	275	2.2
Beauty and barber shops	391	468	1.2
Funeral service and crematories	83	97	1.0
Business services	5,241	7,623	2.5
Auto repair, services, and garages	928	1,245	2.0
Miscellaneous repair shops	390	480	1.4
Motion pictures	408	476	1.0
Videotape rental	132	150	0.8
Amusement and recreation services	1,089	1,428	1.8
Health services	7,844	11,519	2.6
Offices of health practitioners	2,180	3,470	3.1
Nursing and personal-care facilities	1,420	2,182	2.9
Hospitals, private	3,547	4,605	1.8
Health services	697	1,262	4.0
Legal services	919	1,427	3.0
Social services	1,811	2,874	3.1
Individual and miscellaneous social services	638	991	3.0
Job training and related services	247	320	1.7
Child day care services	457	652	2.4
Residential care	469	911	4.5
Museums, zoos, and membership organizations	2,149	2,488	1.0
Engineering, management, and services	2,396	3,660	2.9
Government	18,322	21,515	1.1
Federal government	3,085	3,184	0.2
State and local government	15,237	18,331	1.2
Agriculture	3,276	3,080	-0.4
Private households	1,014	700	-2.4
Nonagricultural self-employed and unpaid family	8,961	10,763	1.2

* Total employment here is lower than in other tables because it does not include workers in some agricultural services or in nonclassified establishments.
Source: Bureau of Labor Statistics
Note: Numbers will not add to total because all categories of industries are not reported.

Employment by Industry and Occupation

The single largest group of employed men are salesmen in wholesale or retail trades. The single largest group of employed women are specialists in service industries such as nurses and teachers.

(employed civilians by sex, industry, and occupation in 1990; numbers in thousands)

| | total employed | managerial & professional specialty | | technical, sales, & administrative support | | |
		executive, administrative, & managerial	professional specialty	technicians & related support	sales	admin. support, inc. clerical
Males						
Agriculture	2,507	69	55	13	13	9
Mining	617	84	53	25	8	15
Construction	7,032	904	121	56	62	51
Manufacturing	14,315	1,874	1,409	582	518	712
Durable goods	9,227	1,160	1,043	435	249	451
Nondurable goods	5,089	714	366	147	269	260
Transportation and public utilities	5,819	627	354	239	137	894
Wholesale/retail trade	12,773	1,175	235	72	4,920	532
Wholesale trade	3,329	341	65	34	1,517	191
Retail trade	9,444	834	170	38	3,403	341
Finance, insurance, and real estate	3,323	1,046	119	75	1,153	465
Services	14,830	2,415	4,893	741	388	764
Private households	150	2	3	1	1	1
Other service industries	14,680	2,414	4,890	740	387	763
Professional services	7,937	1,116	4,109	478	40	417
Public administration	3,218	702	482	151	10	328
Females						
Agriculture	679	26	30	17	11	99
Mining	113	28	10	7	1	58
Construction	664	138	11	8	14	376
Manufacturing	6,868	671	382	177	263	1,643
Durable goods	3,331	370	178	94	78	908
Nondurable goods	3,538	300	204	83	185	735
Transportation and public utilities	2,317	294	104	66	203	1,258
Wholesale/retail trade	11,496	903	232	65	5,147	1,871
Wholesale trade	1,322	187	22	15	352	591
Retail trade	10,174	716	210	50	4,795	1,279
Finance, insurance, and real estate	4,697	1,043	105	79	758	2,600
Services	24,254	2,342	6,919	1,370	570	5,754
Private households	873	2	10	3	1	8
Other service industries	23,381	2,340	6,909	1,367	569	5,746
Professional services	17,398	1,535	6,350	1,231	120	4,321
Public administration	2,390	499	302	99	16	1,211

(continued on next page)

(continued from previous page)

(employed civilians by industry, sex, and occupation in 1990)

	service		precision production, craft & repair	operators, fabricators, & laborers			farming, forestry, & fishing
	private household	other service		machine operators, assemblers, & inspectors	transportation & material moving	handlers, equip. cleaners, helpers, & laborers	
Males							
Agriculture	-	8	39	9	46	15	2,231
Mining	-	8	240	24	122	35	2
Construction	-	25	4,330	109	519	832	22
Manufacturing	-	290	3,311	3,938	753	831	99
Durable goods	-	156	2,290	2,538	393	423	89
Nondurable goods	-	134	1,020	1,400	360	408	9
Transportation and public utilities	-	154	1,192	106	1,665	437	13
Wholesale/retail trade	-	2,011	1,292	178	902	1,433	23
Wholesale trade	-	29	304	83	446	310	7
Retail trade	-	1,982	988	94	456	1,122	16
Finance, insurance, and real estate	-	201	146	14	15	24	65
Services	29	2,410	1,709	435	339	347	361
Private households	29	11	14	1	6	18	65
Other service industries	-	2,399	1,695	434	333	329	296
Professional services	-	1,070	341	99	119	72	77
Public administration	-	1,152	223	29	54	40	48
Females							
Agriculture	-	8	1	4	3	5	476
Mining	-	1	4	1	2	1	-
Construction	-	9	70	4	5	29	1
Manufacturing	-	82	626	2,655	45	321	3
Durable goods	-	40	416	1,101	21	121	1
Nondurable goods	-	42	210	1,554	24	200	1
Transportation and public utilities	-	135	67	16	139	33	1
Wholesale/retail trade	-	2,465	200	149	58	392	14
Wholesale trade	-	9	18	50	13	61	3
Retail trade	-	2,456	182	99	45	331	11
Finance, insurance, and real estate	-	91	8	5	2	1	4
Services	753	5,702	171	381	177	74	41
Private households	753	85	3	1	1	-	5
Other service industries	-	5,617	168	380	176	73	36
Professional services	-	3,455	58	129	158	28	14
Public administration	-	224	11	13	6	4	4

Source: Bureau of Labor Statistics

Characteristics of Workers, 1983 and 1990

Women are the majority of workers in a wide variety of occupations, including health-care managers, therapists, social scientists, and bus drivers.

(percent of employed civilians in selected occupations who are female, black, or Hispanic, 1983 and 1990)

	1990			1983		
	women	**black**	**Hispanic**	**women**	**black**	**Hispanic**
All, aged 16 or older	**45.4%**	**10.1%**	**7.5%**	**43.7%**	**9.3%**	**5.3%**
Managerial and professional specialty	**45.8**	**6.2**	**3.6**	**40.9**	**5.6**	**2.6**
Executive, administrative, and managerial	40.0	5.7	3.9	32.4	4.7	2.8
Officials and administrators, public admin.	42.4	9.2	3.2	38.5	8.3	3.8
Financial managers	44.3	4.1	2.9	38.6	3.5	3.1
Personnel and labor relations managers	55.1	6.7	3.2	43.9	4.9	2.6
Purchasing managers	31.9	4.8	3.5	23.6	5.1	1.4
Managers marketing, advertising, and public relations	31.1	2.9	3.1	21.8	2.7	1.7
Administrators, education and related fields	54.4	9.5	3.8	41.4	11.3	2.4
Managers, medicine and health	66.5	7.5	2.9	57.0	5.0	2.0
Managers, property and real estate	45.2	6.5	5.1	42.8	5.5	5.2
Professional specialty	51.2	6.7	3.4	48.1	6.4	2.5
Architects	18.4	0.9	3.5	12.7	1.6	1.5
Engineers	8.0	3.6	2.8	5.8	2.7	2.2
Mathematical and computer scientists	36.5	6.5	3.4	29.6	5.4	2.6
Natural scientists	26.0	2.7	3.8	20.5	2.6	2.1
Health diagnosing occupations	17.8	3.0	3.7	13.3	2.7	3.3
Physicians	19.3	3.0	4.5	15.8	3.2	4.5
Dentists	9.5	4.9	3.5	6.7	2.4	1.0
Health assessment and treating occupations	86.2	7.4	2.8	85.8	7.1	2.2
Registered nurses	94.5	7.4	2.5	95.8	6.7	1.8
Pharmacists	37.2	4.1	4.1	26.7	3.8	2.6
Dietitians	95.0	20.1	3.5	90.8	21.0	3.7
Therapists	76.6	6.0	2.9	76.3	7.6	2.7
Teachers, college and university	37.7	4.5	2.5	36.3	4.4	1.8
Teachers, except college and university	73.7	8.7	3.5	70.9	9.1	2.7
Librarians, archivists, and curators	81.1	5.3	3.3	84.4	7.8	1.6
Social scientists and urban planners	51.5	5.4	3.3	46.8	7.1	2.1
Economists	43.8	4.0	3.3	37.9	6.3	2.7
Psychologists	58.4	6.6	3.6	57.1	8.6	1.1
Social, recreation, and religious workers	50.4	15.2	4.6	43.1	12.1	3.8
Lawyers and judges	20.8	3.4	2.7	15.8	2.7	1.0
Writers, artists, entertainers, and athletes	47.4	4.5	4.0	42.7	4.8	2.9
Technical, sales, and administrative support	**64.7**	**9.2**	**5.8**	**64.6**	**7.6**	**4.3**
Health technologists and technicians	83.5	14.1	4.5	84.3	12.7	3.1

(continued on next page)

(continued from previous page)

(percent of employed civilians in selected occupations that are female, black, or Hispanic, 1983 and 1990)

	1990			1983		
	women	black	Hispanic	women	black	Hispanic
Engineering and related technologists and technicians	19.8%	7.2%	4.8%	18.4%	6.1%	3.5%
Science technicians	31.9	7.5	7.2	29.1	6.6	2.8
Technicians, except health, engineering, and science	40.2	5.7	3.1	35.3	5.0	2.7
Airplane pilots and navigators	5.1	0.6	3.3	2.1	-	1.6
Computer programmers	36.0	5.8	2.5	32.5	4.4	2.1
Legal assistants	78.8	6.1	3.7	74.0	4.3	3.6
Sales occupations	49.2	6.4	5.3	47.5	4.7	3.7
Supervisors and proprietors	34.8	4.5	4.4	28.4	3.6	3.4
Sales representatives, finance and business services	42.9	4.4	3.6	37.2	2.7	2.2
Sales representatives, commodities, except retail	22.0	2.6	3.3	15.1	2.1	2.2
Sales workers, retail and personal services	67.4	9.5	7.0	69.7	6.7	4.8
Administrative support, including clerical	79.8	11.4	6.5	79.9	9.6	5.0
Supervisors	58.3	11.8	6.5	53.4	9.3	5.0
Computer equipment operators	65.7	13.1	6.9	63.9	12.5	6.0
Secretaries, stenographers, and typists	98.3	8.6	5.4	98.2	7.3	4.5
Information clerks	88.3	9.5	7.3	88.9	8.5	5.5
Records processing occupations, except financial	81.3	14.1	7.2	82.4	13.9	4.8
Financial records processing	91.6	6.2	5.1	89.4	4.6	3.7
Service occupations	**60.1**	**17.3**	**11.2**	**60.1**	**16.6**	**6.8**
Private household	96.3	24.7	19.7	96.1	27.8	8.5
Protective service	14.6	16.6	5.9	12.8	13.6	4.6
Firefighting and fire prevention	2.4	11.0	4.4	1.0	6.7	4.1
Police and detectives	13.8	16.0	5.3	9.4	13.1	4.0
Service occupations, except private household and protective services	64.9	17.0	11.5	64.0	16.0	6.9
Food preparation and service occupations	59.5	12.4	12.5	63.3	10.5	6.8
Health service occupations	90.2	26.3	6.4	89.2	23.5	4.8
Cleaning and building service occupations	44.0	22.4	16.7	38.8	24.4	9.2
Personal service occupations	81.6	12.0	7.3	79.2	11.1	6.0
Hairdressers and cosmetologists	89.8	9.2	7.1	88.7	7.0	5.7
Child-care workers	97.0	12.1	6.4	96.8	12.6	5.2
Precision production, craft, and repair	**8.5**	**7.8**	**8.5**	**8.1**	**6.8**	**6.2**
Mechanics and repairers	3.6	8.1	7.0	3.0	6.8	5.3
Supervisors	7.5	5.8	3.8	7.0	3.7	3.3
Construction trades	1.9	6.9	8.9	1.8	6.6	6.0
Precision production occupations	23.1	8.6	9.8	21.5	7.3	7.4
Supervisors	16.2	8.5	8.0	14.1	6.6	5.7
Precision textile, apparel, and furnishings machine workers	60.8	8.7	13.8	58.9	7.9	12.7
Dressmakers	96.4	9.9	11.8	96.1	8.9	7.9
Upholsterers	25.1	8.3	12.6	26.2	6.9	17.7
Precision workers, assorted materials	54.3	8.9	12.8	56.9	7.5	10.4

(continued on next page)

(continued from previous page)

(percent of employed civilians in selected occupations that are female, black, or Hispanic, 1983 and 1990)

	1990			1983		
	women	black	Hispanic	women	black	Hispanic
Operators, fabricators, and laborers	**25.5%**	**15.0%**	**12.2%**	**26.6%**	**14.0%**	**8.3%**
Machine operators, assemblers, and inspectors	40.0	14.4	13.9	42.1	14.0	9.4
Transportation and material moving occupations	**9.0**	**15.4**	**8.5**	**7.8**	**13.0**	**5.9**
Motor vehicle operators	10.8	15.4	8.6	9.2	13.5	6.0
Bus drivers	51.6	23.4	6.9	45.5	22.2	7.0
Taxi-cab drivers and chauffeurs	9.5	25.3	15.0	10.4	19.6	8.6
Handlers, equipment cleaners, helpers, and laborers	**17.7**	**15.7**	**12.9**	**16.8**	**15.1**	**8.6**
Farming, forestry, and fishing	**16.0**	**6.1**	**14.2**	**16.0**	**7.5**	**8.2**

Source: Bureau of Labor Statistics

Occupations With the Highest Earnings

The most highly paid occupations include lawyers, airline pilots, and physicians. Those in the top 10 percent of the pay scale made close to $100,000 a year in 1989.

(25 occupations with the highest median weekly earnings in 1989; occupations with employment of 50,000 or more)

	1989 median	lower boundary of top 10 percent of earners
1. Lawyers	$990	$1,830
2. Airline pilots and navigators	807	1,855
3. Chemical engineers	807	1,366
4. Electrical and electronics engineers	803	1,201
5. Aerospace engineers	801	1,305
6. Physicians	792	1,849
7. Engineers	775	1,201
8. Mechanical engineers	766	1,142
9. Engineers, not classified elsewhere	761	1,180
10. Managers; marketing, advertising, and public relations	753	1,443
11. Pharmacists	748	935
12. Civil engineers	735	1,079
13. Administrators, education and related fields	712	1,162
14. Computer systems analysts and scientists	711	1,080
15. Teachers, college and university	711	1,177
16. Industrial engineers	710	1,198
17. Economists	704	1,309
18. Locomotive operating occupations	696	-
19. Management analysts	693	1,426
20. Postsecondary teachers, subject not specified	676	1,099
21. Supervisors, police and detectives	674	1,003
22. Personnel and labor relations managers	668	1,192
23. Financial managers	667	1,220
24. Architects	667	1,018
25. Operations and systems researchers and analysts	662	1,030

Source: Bureau of Labor Statistics
Note: (-) means data not available.

Earnings by Occupation and Education

Executives, administrators, and managers with a college degree earn the most, followed by college-educated marketing and sales workers. Those without a high school diploma earn the least, no matter what the occupation.

(median annual earnings by occupation and level of education, 1987)

	total, all levels	less than high school	high school	1–3 years college	4 years or more college
All occupations	$21,543	$15,249	$18,902	$21,975	$31,029
Executive, administrative, and managerial	30,264	22,306	23,286	27,255	37,252
Professional specialty	30,116	19,177	23,233	27,458	31,311
Technicians and related support	24,489	16,207	21,358	23,830	28,004
Marketing and sales	22,220	13,746	17,654	22,546	32,747
Administrative support occupations, including clerical	17,120	15,535	16,554	17,491	20,823
Service occupations	13,443	10,764	13,093	16,937	21,381
Precision, production, craft, and repair	24,856	20,465	25,140	27,042	30,938
Operators, fabricators, and laborers	18,132	15,365	19,303	21,627	22,114
Agriculture, forestry, fishing, and related workers	11,781	10,571	12,730	16,331	17,130

Source: Bureau of Labor Statistics

Employment by Occupation, 1990 and 2005

Some occupations are projected to grow much faster than the 20 percent average between 1990 and 2005, including marketing and computer jobs, psychologists, physical therapists, and travel agents.

(civilian employment by occupation, 1990, and moderate growth projections to 2005; numbers in thousands)

	total employed		change 1990–2005	
	1990	**2005**	**number**	**percent**
Total, all occupations*	**122,573**	**147,191**	**24,618**	**20%**
Executive, administrative, and managerial occupations	**12,451**	**15,866**	**3,414**	**27**
Managerial and administrative occupations	8,838	11,174	2,336	26
General managers and top executives	3,086	3,684	598	19
Industrial production managers	210	251	41	20
Marketing, advertising, and public relations managers	427	630	203	47
Personnel, training, and labor relations managers	178	235	57	32
Property and real estate managers	225	302	76	34
Purchasing managers	248	298	49	20
Management support occupations	3,613	4,691	1,079	30
Professional specialty occupations	**15,800**	**20,907**	**5,107**	**32**
Engineers	1,519	1,919	400	26
Aeronautical and astronautical engineers	73	88	15	20
Chemical engineers	48	54	6	12
Electrical and electronics engineers	426	571	145	34
Mechanical engineers	233	289	56	24
Architects and surveyors	236	284	48	20
Life scientists	174	230	56	32
Computer, mathematical, and operations research analysts	571	987	416	73
Actuaries	13	18	4	34
Systems analysts and computer scientists	463	829	366	79
Operations research analysts	57	100	42	73
Physical scientists	200	241	41	21
Chemists	83	96	13	16
Geologists, geophysicists, and oceanographers	48	58	11	22
Meteorologists	5	7	2	30
Physicists and astronomers	20	21	1	5
All other physical scientists	44	59	15	34
Social scientists	224	320	96	43
Economists	37	45	8	21
Psychologists	125	204	79	64
Social, recreational, and religious workers	1,049	1,376	327	31
Lawyers and judicial workers	633	850	217	34
Teachers, librarians, and counselors	5,687	7,280	1,593	28

(continued on next page)

(continued from previous page)

(civilian employment by occupation, 1990, and moderate growth projections to 2005; numbers in thousands)

	total employed		change 1990–2005	
	1990	**2005**	**number**	**percent**
Teachers, elementary	1,362	1,675	313	23%
Teachers, preschool and kindergarten	425	598	173	41
Teachers, secondary school	1,280	1,717	437	34
College and university faculty	712	846	134	19
Health diagnosing occupations	855	1,101	247	29
Dentists	174	196	21	12
Optometrists	37	45	8	20
Physicians	580	776	196	34
Podiatrists	16	23	7	46
Veterinarians and veterinary inspectors	47	62	14	31
Health assessment and treating occupations	2,305	3,304	999	43
Dieticians and nutritionists	45	56	11	24
Pharmacists	169	204	35	21
Physician assistants	53	72	18	34
Registered nurses	1,727	2,494	767	44
Therapists	311	479	168	54
Physical therapists	88	155	67	76
Respiratory therapists	60	91	31	52
Writers, artists, and entertainers	1,542	1,915	373	24
Technicians and related support occupations	**4,204**	**5,754**	**1,550**	**37**
Health technicians and technologists	1,833	2,595	763	42
Engineering and science technicians and technologists	1,327	1,640	312	24
Technicians, except health and engineering and science	1,044	1,519	475	46
Marketing and sales occupations	**14,088**	**17,489**	**3,401**	**24**
Real estate agents, brokers, and appraisers	413	492	79	19
Salespersons, retail	3,619	4,506	887	24
Securities and financial services sales workers	191	267	76	40
Travel agents	132	214	82	62
Administrative support occupations, including clerical	**21,951**	**24,835**	**2,884**	**13**
Communications equipment operators	345	236	-108	-31
Financial records processing occupations	2,860	2,750	-110	-4
Information clerks	1,418	2,003	584	41
Mail clerks and messengers	280	306	26	9
Postal clerks and mail carriers	439	519	80	18
Records processing occupations, except financial	949	1,045	96	10
Secretaries, stenographers, and typists	4,680	5,110	429	9
Secretaries	3,576	4,116	540	15
Legal secretaries	281	413	133	47
Medical secretaries	232	390	158	68
Stenographers	132	125	-7	-5
Typists and word processors	972	869	-103	-11

(continued on next page)

(continued from previous page)

(civilian employment by occupation, 1990, and moderate growth projections to 2005; numbers in thousands)

	total employed		change 1990–2005	
	1990	**2005**	**number**	**percent**
Service occupations	**19,204**	**24,806**	**5,602**	**29%**
Cleaning and building service occupations, except private household	3,435	4,068	633	18
Food preparation and service occupations	7,705	10,031	2,325	30
Food and beverage service occupations	4,400	5,623	1,223	28
Health service occupations	1,972	2,832	860	44
Ambulance drivers and attendants, except EMTs	12	15	2	20
Dental assistants	176	236	60	34
Medical assistants	165	287	122	74
Pharmacy assistants	83	101	18	22
Physical and corrective therapy assistants and aides	45	74	29	64
Personal service occupations	2,192	3,164	972	44
Child care workers	725	1,078	353	49
Cosmetologists and related workers	636	793	157	25
Flight attendants	101	159	59	59
Homemaker–home health aides	391	733	343	88
Home health aides	287	550	263	92
Personal and home care aides	103	183	79	77
Private household workers	782	555	-227	-29
Protective service occupations	2,266	2,995	729	32
Agriculture, forestry, fishing, and related occupations	**3,506**	**3,665**	**158**	**5**
Farm operators and managers	1,223	1,023	-200	-16
Gardeners and groundskeepers, except farm	874	1,222	348	40
Precision production, craft, and repair occupations	**14,124**	**15,909**	**1,785**	**13**
Construction trades	3,763	4,557	794	21
Mechanics, installers, and repairers	4,900	5,669	769	16
Electrical and electronic equipment mechanics, installers, and repairers	530	540	10	2
Data processing equipment repairers	84	134	50	60
Vehicle and mobile equipment mechanics and repairers	1,568	1,892	324	21
Production occupations, precision	3,134	3,208	74	2
Textile, apparel, and furnishings workers, precision	272	302	29	11
Printing, binding, and related workers	393	466	72	18
Textile and related setters, operators, and related workers	1,090	912	-178	-16
Hand workers, including assemblers and fabricators	2,675	2,307	-368	-14
Transportation and material moving machine and vehicle operators	4,730	5,743	1,013	21
Motor vehicle operators	3,417	4,301	883	26
Operators, fabricators, and laborers	**17,245**	**17,961**	**716**	**4**

* Total employment here is lower than in other tables because it does not include workers in some agricultural services or in nonclassified establishments.
Source: Bureau of Labor Statistics

Fastest-Growing Occupations, 1990 to 2005

The number of jobs in five occupations is projected to grow by more than 75 percent between 1990 and 2005. These occupations are home health aides, paralegals, systems analysts, personal and home care aides, and physical therapists.

(occupations with the largest percentage increase in employment, 1990-2005; numbers in thousands)

	number employed		change	percent change
	1990	**2005**	**1990–2005**	**1990–2005**
Home health aides	287	550	263	91.7%
Paralegals	90	167	77	85.2
Systems analysts and computer scientists	463	829	366	78.9
Personal and home care aides	103	183	79	76.7
Physical therapists	88	155	67	76.0
Medical assistants	165	287	122	73.9
Operations research analysts	57	100	42	73.2
Human services workers	145	249	103	71.2
Radiologic technologists and technicians	149	252	103	69.5
Medical secretaries	232	390	158	68.3
Physical and corrective therapy assistants and aides	45	74	29	64.0
Psychologists	125	204	79	63.6
Travel agents	132	214	82	62.3
Correction officers	230	372	142	61.4
Data processing equipment repairers	84	134	50	60.0
Flight attendants	101	159	59	58.5
Computer programmers	565	882	317	56.1
Occupational therapists	36	56	20	55.2
Surgical technologists	38	59	21	55.2
Medical records technicians	52	80	28	54.3
Management analysts	151	230	79	52.3
Respiratory therapists	60	91	31	52.1
Child-care workers	725	1,078	353	48.8
Marketing, advertising, and public relations managers	427	630	203	47.4
Legal secretaries	281	413	133	47.4
Receptionists and information clerks	900	1,322	422	46.9
Registered nurses	1,727	2,494	767	44.4
Nursing aides, orderlies, and attendants	1,274	1,826	552	43.4
Licensed practical nurses	644	913	269	41.9
Cooks, restaurant	615	872	257	41.8

Source: Bureau of Labor Statistics

Occupations With Largest Job Growth, 1990 to 2005

The occupations projected to gain the most jobs between 1990 and 2005 include retail sales, cashiers, truck drivers, waiters, and secretaries.

(occupations with the largest job gain, 1990-2005; numbers in thousands)

	number employed		change	percent change
	1990	**2005**	**1990–2005**	**1990–2005**
Salespersons, retail	3,619	4,506	887	24.5%
Registered nurses	1,727	2,494	767	44.4
Cashiers	2,633	3,318	685	26.0
General office clerks	2,737	3,407	670	24.5
Truck drivers, light and heavy	2,362	2,979	617	26.1
General managers and top executives	3,086	3,684	598	19.4
Janitors and cleaners, including maids and housekeeping cleaners	3,007	3,562	555	18.5
Nursing aides, orderlies, and attendants	1,274	1,826	552	43.4
Food counter, fountain, and related workers	1,607	2,158	550	34.2
Waiters and waitresses	1,747	2,196	449	25.7
Teachers, secondary school	1,280	1,717	437	34.2
Receptionists and information clerks	900	1,322	422	46.9
Systems analysts and computer scientists	463	829	366	78.9
Food preparation workers	1,156	1,521	365	31.6
Child-care workers	725	1,078	353	48.8
Gardeners and groundskeepers, except farm	874	1,222	348	39.8
Accountants and auditors	985	1,325	340	34.5
Computer programmers	565	882	317	56.1
Teachers, elementary	1,362	1,675	313	23.0
Guards	883	1,181	298	33.7
Teacher aides and educational assistants	808	1,086	278	34.4
Licensed practical nurses	644	913	269	41.9
Clerical supervisors and managers	1,218	1,481	263	21.6
Home health aides	287	550	263	91.7
Cooks, restaurant	615	872	257	41.8
Maintenance repairers, general utility	1,128	1,379	251	22.2
Secretaries, except legal and medical	3,064	3,312	248	8.1
Cooks, short order and fast food	743	989	246	33.0
Stock clerks, sales floor	1,242	1,451	209	16.8
Lawyers	587	793	206	35.1

Source: Bureau of Labor Statistics

Occupations With the Largest Job Losses, 1990 to 2005

While the number of farmers is projected to decline the most between 1990 and 2005, also on the list of losers are bookkeepers, typists, bank tellers, and gas-station attendants.

(occupations with the largest numerical decline in jobs, 1990-2005; numbers in thousands)

	number employed		change 1990–2005	percent change 1990–2005
	1990	2005		
Farmers	1,074	850	-224	-20.9%
Bookkeeping, accounting, and auditing clerks	2,276	2,143	-133	-5.8
Child-care workers, private household	314	190	-124	-39.5
Sewing machine operators, garment	585	469	-116	-19.8
Electrical and electronic assemblers	232	128	-105	-45.1
Typists and word processors	972	869	-103	-10.6
Cleaners and servants, private household	411	310	-101	-24.5
Farm workers	837	745	-92	-11.0
Electrical and electronic equipment assemblers, precision	171	90	-81	-47.5
Textile draw-out and winding machine operators and tenders	199	138	-61	-30.6
Switchboard operators	246	189	-57	-23.2
Machine forming operators and tenders, metal and plastic	174	131	-43	-24.5
Machine tool cutting operators and tenders, metal and plastic	145	104	-42	-28.6
Telephone and cable TV line installers and repairers	133	92	-40	-30.4
Central office and PBX installers and repairers	80	46	-34	-42.5
Central office operators	53	22	-31	-59.2
Statistical clerks	85	54	-31	-36.1
Packaging and filling machine operators and tenders	324	297	-27	-8.3
Station installers and repairers, telephone	47	21	-26	-55.0
Bank tellers	517	492	-25	-4.8
Lathe and turning machine tool setters and set-up operators, metal and plastic	80	61	-20	-24.4
Grinders and polishers, hand	84	65	-19	-22.5
Electromechanical equipment assemblers, precision	49	31	-18	-36.5
Grinding machine setters and set-up operators, metal and plastic	72	54	-18	-25.1
Service-station attendants	246	229	-17	-7.1
Directory-assistance operators	26	11	-16	-59.4
Butchers and meatcutters	234	220	-14	-5.9
Chemical equipment controllers, operators, and tenders	75	61	-14	-19.1
Drilling and boring machine tool setters and set-up operators, metal and plastic	52	39	-13	-25.6
Meter readers, utilities	50	37	-12	-24.8

Source: Bureau of Labor Statistics

Self-employed Workers
1990 and 2005

The number of self-employed is projected to grow by 15 percent between 1990 and 2005, but self employment in some occupations is projected to grow much faster. These include social scientists, psychologists, and cleaners.

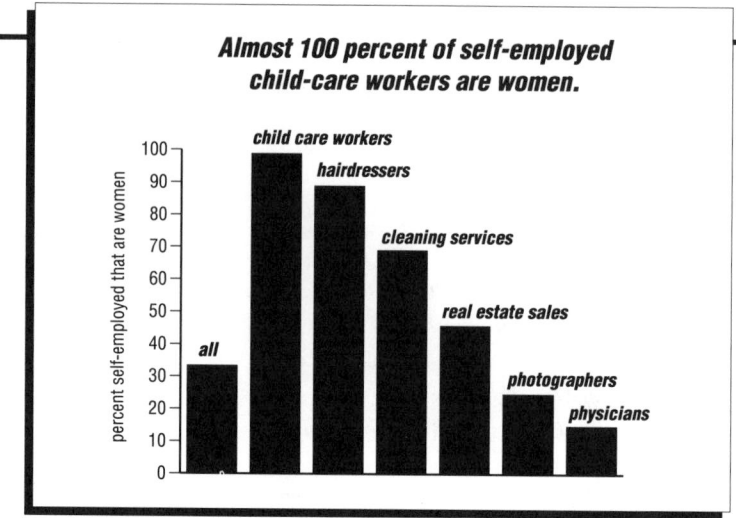

Almost 100 percent of self-employed child-care workers are women.

(number of self-employed workers and self-employed as a percent of total employed in occupation, 1990 and projections for 2005; numbers in thousands)

	1990			2005			change in self-employed 1990–2005	
	total employment	self-employed workers	percent of total employment	total employment	self-employed workers	percent of total employment	number	percent
All occupations	**122,573**	**10,161**	**8.3%**	**147,191**	**11,663**	**7.9%**	**1,502**	**14.8%**
Executive, administrative,								
managerial	**12,451**	**1,598**	**12.8**	**15,866**	**2,106**	**13.3**	**508**	**31.8**
Managerial and administrative	8,838	1,328	15.0	11,174	1,778	15.9	450	33.9
Food service/lodging managers	595	247	41.5	793	280	35.3	33	13.4
Property and real estate managers	225	89	39.5	302	110	36.5	21	23.6
Management support	3,613	270	7.5	4,691	328	7.0	58	21.5
Accountants and auditors	985	102	10.4	1,325	110	8.3	8	7.8
Management analysts	151	68	44.9	230	100	43.4	32	47.1
Professional specialty	**15,800**	**1,446**	**9.2**	**20,907**	**1,727**	**8.3**	**281**	**19.4**
Social scientists	224	65	29.0	320	106	33.1	41	63.1
Psychologists	125	51	40.9	204	90	44.1	39	76.5
Lawyers	587	198	33.8	793	205	25.9	7	3.5
Teachers, librarians, counselors	5,687	134	2.4	7,280	165	2.3	31	23.1
Health diagnosing	855	271	31.7	1,101	310	28.1	39	14.4
Dentists	174	92	52.7	196	103	52.6	11	12.0
Physicians	580	139	24.0	776	160	20.6	21	15.1
Writers, artists, and entertainers	1,542	517	33.5	1,915	603	31.5	86	16.6
Artists and commercial artists	230	143	62.2	303	190	62.8	47	32.9
Designers	339	114	33.6	428	123	28.7	9	7.9
Musicians	252	75	29.7	276	85	30.8	10	13.3
Writers/editors, inc. technical writers	232	78	33.6	292	89	30.5	11	14.1

(continued on next page)

(continued from previous page)
(number of self-employed workers and self-employed as a percent of total employed in occupation, 1990 and projections for 2005; numbers in thousands)

	1990			2005			change in self-employed 1990–2005	
	total employment	self-employed workers	percent of total employment	total employment	self-employed workers	percent of total employment	number	percent
Technicians and related support	**4,204**	**107**	**2.5%**	**5,754**	**132**	**2.3%**	**25**	**22.9%**
Marketing and sales	**14,088**	**1,831**	**13.0**	**17,489**	**1,903**	**10.9**	**72**	**4.0**
Insurance sales workers	439	139	31.7	527	150	28.5	11	7.9
Real estate agents, brokers, appraisers	413	255	61.8	492	281	57.2	26	10.4
Salespersons, retail	3,619	187	5.2	4,506	200	4.4	13	7.0
Administrative support, inc. clerical	**21,951**	**338**	**1.5**	**24,835**	**382**	**1.5**	**44**	**13.0**
Financial records processing	2,860	147	5.1	2,750	164	6.0	17	11.6
Secretaries, stenographers, typists	4,680	88	1.9	5,110	110	2.2	22	25.0
Service occupations	**19,204**	**1,220**	**6.4**	**24,805**	**1,662**	**6.7**	**442**	**36.2**
Cleaning and building service, except private household	3,435	238	6.9	4,068	352	8.7	114	47.9
Food preparation service	7,706	79	1.0	10,031	80	0.8	1	1.3
Personal service	2,192	824	37.6	3,164	1,112	35.1	288	34.9
Barbers	77	59	76.8	76	59	77.8	0	0.0
Child-care workers	725	466	64.3	1,078	676	62.7	210	45.0
Cosmetologists, etc.	636	296	46.5	793	374	47.1	78	26.4
Agriculture, forestry, fishing, etc.	**3,506**	**1,380**	**39.4**	**3,665**	**1,250**	**34.1**	**-131**	**-9.5**
Precision production, craft, repair	**14,124**	**1,686**	**11.9**	**15,909**	**1,932**	**12.1**	**246**	**14.6**
Blue-collar worker supervisors	1,792	130	7.3	1,912	143	7.5	13	10.0
Construction trades	3,763	936	24.9	4,557	1,158	25.4	222	23.7
Carpenters	1,057	373	35.3	1,209	450	37.2	77	20.6
Electricians	548	58	10.6	706	75	10.6	17	29.3
Painters and paperhangers, construction and maintenance	453	214	47.2	564	289	51.2	75	35.0
Plumbers, pipefitters, steamfitters	379	65	17.2	459	75	16.4	10	15.4
Mechanics, installers, repairers	4,900	407	8.3	5,669	411	7.3	4	1.0
Machinery and related mechanics, installers, and repairers	1,675	56	3.3	1,980	65	3.3	9	16.1
Vehicle and mobile equipment mechanics and repairers	1,568	240	15.3	1,892	225	11.9	-15	-6.3
Precision production	3,134	205	6.5	3,208	212	6.6	7	3.4
Textile, apparel, furnishings	272	90	33.0	302	96	31.8	6	6.7
Custom tailors and sewers	116	61	52.7	137	70	51.0	9	14.8
Operators, fabricators, laborers	**17,245**	**555**	**3.2**	**17,961**	**570**	**3.2**	**15**	**2.7**
Motor vehicle operators	3,417	248	7.3	4,301	242	5.6	-6	-2.4
Truckdrivers	2,701	196	7.3	3,360	174	5.2	-22	-11.2

Source: Bureau of Labor Statistics

Employee Benefits in Small Firms

In small firms, professional and technical workers are more likely to receive employee benefits than clerical, sales, or production workers.

(percent of full-time employees participating in selected employee benefit programs, private nonfarm industries employing fewer than 100 workers, 1990)

	all employees	professional, technical, and related employees	clerical and sales employees	production and service employees
Paid				
Holidays	84%	95%	91%	75%
Vacations	88	94	93	83
Personal leave	11	17	13	7
Lunch period	8	7	7	8
Rest time	48	42	46	51
Funeral leave	47	57	54	38
Jury duty leave	54	72	62	43
Military leave	21	29	26	15
Sick leave	47	70	61	29
Maternity leave	2	3	3	1
Paternity leave	(n)	(n)	(n)	(n)
Unpaid				
Maternity leave	17	26	20	12
Paternity leave	8	13	8	5
Sickness and accident insurance	**26**	**25**	**24**	**27**
Wholly employer financed	17	14	15	19
Partly employer financed	9	10	10	9
Long-term disability insurance	**19**	**36**	**25**	**9**
Wholly employer financed	16	30	21	8
Partly employer financed	3	5	4	2
Medical care	**69**	**82**	**75**	**60**
Employee coverage				
Wholly employer financed	40	46	40	37
Partly employer financed	29	36	35	23
Family coverage				
Wholly employer financed	22	23	22	22
Partly employer financed	46	59	53	38
Dental care	**30**	**38**	**35**	**24**
Employee coverage				
Wholly employer financed	17	19	19	15
Partly employer financed	12	18	16	8
Family coverage				
Wholly employer financed	11	11	12	11
Partly employer financed	19	27	23	13

(continued on next page)

(continued from previous page)

(percent of full-time employees participating in selected employee benefit programs, private nonfarm industries employing fewer than 100 workers, 1990)

	all employees	professional, technical, and related employees	clerical and sales employees	production and service employees
Life insurance	64%	79%	70%	55%
Wholly employer financed	53	69	60	43
Partly employer financed	11	11	10	11
All retirement	42	49	47	37
Defined benefit pension	20	20	23	18
Wholly employer financed	19	18	21	18
Partly employer financed	1	2	1	1
Defined contribution*	31	40	36	24
Uses of funds				
Retirement	28	36	32	21
Wholly employer financed	16	19	17	15
Partly employer financed	11	17	16	6
Capital accumulation	4	5	4	2
Wholly employer financed	1	2	2	1
Partly employer financed	2	3	3	2
Types of plans				
Savings and thrift	10	16	15	5
Deferred profit sharing	15	17	17	13
Employee stock ownership	1	1	1	(n)
Money purchase pension	6	9	6	6
Simplified employee pension	1	1	1	(n)
Stock purchase	(n)	(n)	(n)	(n)
Cash only profit-sharing	(n)	-	(n)	-
Flexible benefits plans	1	3	2	1
Reimbursement accounts	8	13	9	4
Other benefits				
Free or subsidized parking	86	84	85	88
Nonproduction bonuses	45	42	47	44
Employer assistance for child care	1	2	2	1
Eldercare	2	5	1	1
Wellness programs	6	10	8	4
Employer-subsidized recreation facilities	6	12	6	4
Employee discounts	38	32	46	36
Educational assistance				
Job-related	35	50	41	27
Not job-related	4	8	5	3

*The total is less than the sum of the individual items because some employees participated in more than one program.

Source: Bureau of Labor Statistics

Note: (n) means less than 0.5 percent. (-) means no employees in this category.

Employee Benefits in Medium and Large Firms

Among employees in medium and large firms, there is little difference in the proportion who receive benefits by occupation. Over 90 percent have employer-provided medical insurance, two-thirds have dental insurance, and over 80 percent have some kind of retirement plan.

(percent of full-time employees participating in selected employee benefit programs, private nonfarm industries employing more than 100 workers, 1989)

	all employees	professional, technical, and related employees	clerical and sales employees	production and service employees
Paid				
Holidays	97%	97%	96%	97%
Vacations	97	98	99	95
Personal leave	22	28	30	14
Lunch period	10	4	4	16
Rest time	71	57	69	80
Funeral leave	84	87	86	80
Jury duty leave	90	95	92	87
Military leave	53	61	57	45
Sick leave	68	93	87	44
Maternity leave	3	4	2	3
Paternity leave	1	2	1	1
Unpaid				
Maternity leave	37	39	37	35
Paternity leave	18	20	17	17
Sickness and accident insurance	**43**	**29**	**29**	**58**
Wholly employer financed	36	22	22	51
Partly employer financed	7	7	7	7
Long-term disability insurance	**45**	**65**	**57**	**27**
Wholly employer financed	35	50	43	23
Partly employer financed	9	15	14	4
Medical care	**92**	**93**	**91**	**93**
Employee coverage				
Wholly employer financed	48	45	41	54
Partly employer financed	44	48	50	39
Family coverage				
Wholly employer financed	31	28	25	37
Partly employer financed	60	64	66	54
Dental care	**66**	**69**	**66**	**65**
Employee coverage				
Wholly employer financed	34	32	31	38
Partly employer financed	32	37	36	27
Family coverage				
Wholly employer financed	25	23	21	28
Partly employer financed	42	46	46	37

(continued on next page)

(continued from previous page)

(percent of full-time employees participating in selected employee benefit programs, private nonfarm industries employing more than 100 workers, 1989)

	all employees	professional, technical, and related employees	clerical and sales employees	production and service employees
Life insurance	94%	95%	94%	93%
Wholly employer financed	82	82	81	83
Partly employer financed	12	13	14	11
All retirement	81	85	81	80
Defined benefit pension	63	64	63	63
Wholly employer financed	60	61	61	60
Partly employer financed	3	3	2	3
Defined contribution*	48	59	52	40
Uses of funds				
Retirement	36	43	39	31
Wholly employer financed	14	15	14	12
Partly employer financed	22	28	24	18
Capital accumulation	14	18	14	11
Wholly employer financed	2	1	1	3
Partly employer financed	12	17	13	8
Types of plans				
Savings and thrift	30	41	35	21
Deferred profit sharing	15	13	13	16
Employee stock ownership	3	4	3	3
Money purchase pension	5	8	6	3
Stock purchase	2	3	2	1
Cash only profit-sharing	1	1	1	1
Flexible benefits plans	9	14	15	3
Reimbursement accounts	23	36	31	11
Other benefits				
Free or subsidized parking	90	85	86	94
Nonproduction bonuses	27	26	28	28
Employer assistance for child care	5	6	6	3
Eldercare	3	4	3	2
Wellness programs	23	30	25	19
Employer-subsidized recreation facilities	28	36	26	24
Employee discounts	54	53	58	52
Educational assistance				
Job-related	69	81	75	59
Not job-related	19	21	17	19

*The total is less than the sum of the individual items because some employees participated in more than one program.
Source: Bureau of Labor Statistics

Child-Care Benefits

Small firms are most likely to offer their employees varied work schedules, but large firms are most likely to provide direct child-care benefits.

(establishments providing child care benefits and/or varied work-schedule policies, by establishment size and sector, 1987, for establishments with ten or more employees; numbers in thousands)

	total	size			sector			
		10–49 employees	50–249 employees	250 or more employees	total	private goods	services	government
All establishments	**1,202**	**919**	**236**	**47**	**1,128**	**272**	**856**	**74**
Percent providing child-care benefits or services	**11.1%**	**9.0%**	**15.3%**	**31.8%**	**10.1%**	**6.3%**	**11.3%**	**26.4%**
Employer-sponsored day care	2.1	1.9	2.2	5.2	1.6	0.3	2.0	9.4
Assisted with child-care expenses	3.1	2.4	4.7	8.9	3.1	1.9	3.5	2.9
Child-care information and referral services	5.1	4.3	6.3	14.0	4.3	2.3	5.0	15.8
Counseling services	5.1	3.8	7.6	17.1	4.2	3.0	4.6	18.2
Percent with varied work-schedule policies aiding child care	**61.2%**	**62.0%**	**58.1%**	**59.4%**	**61.4%**	**51.3%**	**64.6%**	**57.2%**
Flextime	43.2	45.1	37.7	34.9	43.6	31.3	47.5	37.5
Voluntary part-time	34.8	36.0	32.0	25.1	35.3	22.4	39.4	26.7
Job sharing	15.5	16.0	13.7	15.7	15.0	9.0	16.9	23.5
Work at home	8.3	9.2	5.6	3.8	8.5	8.2	8.6	4.0
Flexible leave	42.9	43.8	39.9	40.2	42.9	37.3	44.6	43.7

Source: Bureau of Labor Statistics

Social Security, 1950 to 1988

The average age at which Americans begin to receive Social Security retirement benefits has fallen for both men and women over the past 40 years, with the biggest declines occurring before 1970.

(average age at which retiring workers begin to receive Social Security benefits, by sex, 1950-88)

	age	
	men	*women*
1988	63.7	63.3
1985	63.7	63.4
1980	63.9	63.5
1975	64.0	63.7
1970	64.4	63.9
1965	65.8	66.2
1960	66.8	65.2
1955	68.4	67.8
1950	68.7	68.0

Source: U.S. Department of Health and Human Services

CHAPTER

6

Education Trends

Americans have never been as well-educated as they are today. While many fear that the quality of our educational system is eroding, in fact, high school drop-out rates are declining and SAT scores by race and ethnicity are rising. Today, nearly 60 percent of high school graduates continue on to college. This bodes well for the economic future of millions of Americans, since incomes rise with educational level.

Major Education Trends

☞ As the educational level of Americans rises, the work force will become more sophisticated and flexible—two qualities needed to keep up in a fast-changing world economy.

☞ Women will account for over half of the 1 million Americans graduating from college through the 1990s. But the black and Hispanic share of college graduates may be reduced by rapidly rising college tuitions. Businesses in need of well-trained workers should lobby for increasing the minority share of college students.

☞ An investment in a college education will pay off handsomely for the nation's burgeoning middle-aged work force in the 1990s. The household incomes of the middle-aged should rise sharply, even after adjusting for inflation, because of the growing return to a college education.

Educational Attainment by Sex and Age

More than three-quarters of all adults are high school graduates. Twenty-four percent of men and 17 percent of women have a college degree.

(percentage of men and women aged 25 or older with a high school diploma or a college degree, by age and sex, 1980 and 1990)

	high school graduates		4+ years of college	
	1990	**1980**	**1990**	**1980**
Men				
All men	77.7%	67.7%	23.9%	20.3%
25-34	86.5	84.8	24.5	26.5
35-44	87.1	77.3	30.8	24.5
45-54	79.1	65.8	25.5	19.8
55-64	68.1	56.3	20.7	14.3
65 or older	54.6	37.5	13.6	10.1
Women				
All women	76.9	66.2	17.0	12.9
25-34	87.8	84.1	23.6	20.4
35-44	86.6	76.4	22.5	14.9
45-54	79.2	66.7	15.4	10.5
55-64	70.2	57.6	11.1	8.0
65 or older	55.2	40.1	8.0	7.2

Source: American Demographics magazine, January 1990

Educational Attainment by Age, Sex and Race

Younger blacks and whites are almost equally likely to be high school graduates, but a large gap remains between the percentage of whites and blacks who have at least four years of college.

The median year of school completed by people aged 25 or older is rising.

	all races	white	black and other
1989	12.7	12.7	12.5
1980	12.5	12.5	12.2
1970	12.2	12.2	10.1
1960	10.5	10.8	8.2
1950	9.3	9.7	6.9
1940	8.6	8.7	5.7

Source: National Center for Education Statistics

(percent of all persons aged 25 or older with a high school diploma or at least 4 years of college by sex, age, and race, 1990)

	high school graduate		4+ years of college	
	white	black	white	black
Men				
All men	78.6%	64.2%	25.4%	11.7%
Aged 25 to 34	86.2	81.3	25.8	11.8
Aged 35 to 44	87.9	78.1	32.9	13.4
Aged 45 to 54	80.9	55.4	27.0	11.9
Aged 55 to 64	71.3	48.2	22.7	7.1
Aged 65 or older	56.7	22.1	14.7	2.1
Women				
All women	78.2	65.0	18.5	11.9
Aged 25 to 34	88.2	84.1	24.4	14.6
Aged 35 to 44	87.9	78.5	24.7	16.2
Aged 45 to 54	80.4	63.8	18.3	11.7
Aged 55 to 64	72.4	42.8	12.1	5.5
Aged 65 or older	58.7	26.3	9.6	5.3

Source: Bureau of the Census

Future High School Graduates

As the baby-bust generation moves though its teen years, the number of high school graduates is expected to slump until the mid-1990s.

(number of high school graduates, 1980-89, and projections for 1990 to 2001; numbers in thousands)

year ending	number	percent change from previous year
1980	3,043	-2.3%
1981	3,020	-0.8
1982	2,995	-0.8
1983	2,888	-3.6
1984	2,767	-4.2
1985	2,677	-3.3
1986	2,643	-1.3
1987	2,699	2.1
1988	2,801	3.8
1989	2,820	0.7
1990	2,628	-6.8
1991	2,522	-4.0
1992	2,517	-0.2
1993	2,518	0.0
1994	2,512	-0.2
1995	2,631	4.7
1996	2,670	1.5
1997	2,770	3.7
1998	2,879	3.9
1999	2,923	1.5
2000	2,966	1.5
2001	3,237	9.1

Source: National Center for Education Statistics

High School Drop Outs

High school drop outs are a shrinking share of 16-to-24-year-olds. Blacks, in particular, were much less likely to drop out of high school by 1990 than in 1980.

(percent of persons aged 16 to 24 who are not enrolled in school or who are not high school graduates by sex, race, and Hispanic origin, 1980 and 1990)

	1990	1980
Total	**12.1%**	**14.1%**
White	12.0	13.3
Black	13.2	19.3
Hispanic	32.4	35.2
Men	**12.2**	**15.1**
White	12.7	14.2
Black	11.8	21.1
Hispanic	34.3	37.2
Women	**11.6**	**13.1**
White	11.4	12.3
Black	14.4	17.9
Hispanic	30.3	33.2

Source: National Center for Education Statistics

High School Graduates by State

Residents of Utah and Washington are most likely to be high school graduates. Residents of southern states are least likely to have graduated from high school.

(percent of state populations aged 25 or older with a high school diploma in 1989, ranked by percent)

	percent of population		*percent of population*
Utah	88.2%	Florida	77.9%
Washington	88.2	Ohio	77.6
Alaska	86.9	Idaho	77.3
Wyoming	85.6	Illinois	77.2
Minnesota	85.5	Michigan	77.0
Nevada	84.0	United States	76.9
Oregon	83.9	Maine	76.9
Montana	83.6	Pennsylvania	76.8
Iowa	83.4	New York	76.7
Colorado	83.2	Missouri	75.9
Hawaii	82.3	Oklahoma	75.4
New Hampshire	82.2	New Mexico	74.6
Kansas	82.2	Texas	74.3
Nebraska	82.2	Virginia	74.3
Vermont	81.8	District of Columbia	72.9
North Dakota	81.1	Rhode Island	72.7
Wisconsin	81.1	North Carolina	71.3
Maryland	80.7	Georgia	71.1
Delaware	80.7	Louisiana	70.9
Massachusetts	80.7	South Carolina	69.8
Connecticut	80.6	West Virginia	68.0
Arizona	80.6	Mississippi	67.7
New Jersey	79.4	Arkansas	67.6
California	78.6	Tennessee	65.4
South Dakota	78.3	Kentucky	64.7
Indiana	78.0	Alabama	63.2

Source: Bureau of the Census

College Educated by State

Thirty-five percent of adults living in the District of Columbia have been to college for at least four years. This is three times greater than the share of college graduates in Alabama or West Virginia.

(percent of state populations aged 25 or older with four or more years of college in 1989, ranked by percent)

	percent of population		*percent of population*
District of Columbia	35.2%	Oregon	20.2%
Massachusetts	28.1	Rhode Island	20.2
Connecticut	27.5	Florida	19.8
Maryland	27.4	Nebraska	19.7
Virginia	27.3	Delaware	19.4
Colorado	27.0	Wisconsin	18.9
Vermont	26.7	Pennsylvania	18.6
California	26.4	Maine	18.5
New Jersey	25.7	South Dakota	18.4
Utah	24.2	North Carolina	18.3
Washington	24.1	Georgia	18.2
Hawaii	23.9	Ohio	17.6
New Hampshire	23.5	Michigan	17.3
Alaska	23.4	Nevada	17.2
New York	22.8	Idaho	17.1
Kansas	22.3	Iowa	17.1
North Dakota	22.2	Oklahoma	17.1
Arizona	22.2	South Carolina	16.6
Wyoming	21.9	Louisiana	16.6
Texas	21.7	Tennessee	15.7
Missouri	21.6	Mississippi	15.6
Minnesota	21.5	Kentucky	14.9
United States	21.1	Arkansas	14.8
Montana	21.1	Indiana	13.8
Illinois	21.1	Alabama	11.6
New Mexico	20.6	West Virginia	11.1

Source: Bureau of the Census

Future High School Graduates, by State

The number of high school graduates will rise rapidly in some states during the 1990s, but decline in others. Western states will gain more high school graduates than other areas of the U.S.

(projected number of public high school graduates by state and region of residence in 1989-90 and 1999-2000)

	1989-90	*1999-2000*	*percent change* *1989-90 to 1999-2000*
United States	**2,326,050**	**2,624,810**	**12.8%**
Northeast	**446,700**	**461,820**	**3.4**
Connecticut	27,380	31,290	14.3
Maine	13,180	14,150	7.4
Massachusetts	51,290	52,740	2.8
New Hampshire	10,610	13,630	28.5
New Jersey	68,860	68,200	-1.0
New York	150,720	150,000	-0.5
Pennsylvania	111,380	116,770	4.8
Rhode Island	7,750	8,820	13.8
Vermont	5,530	6,220	12.5
Midwest	**620,640**	**662,060**	**6.7**
Illinois	107,770	108,640	0.8
Indiana	59,650	62,380	4.6
Iowa	31,880	32,010	0.4
Kansas	25,950	30,820	18.8
Michigan	95,530	95,880	0.4
Minnesota	48,880	61,560	25.9
Missouri	49,030	53,450	9.0
Nebraska	17,680	19,070	7.9
North Dakota	7,690	8,080	5.1
Ohio	117,030	119,600	2.2
South Dakota	7,950	9,140	15.0
Wisconsin	51,600	61,430	19.1
South	**802,760**	**888,660**	**10.7**
Alabama	41,160	40,040	-2.7
Arkansas	27,120	26,950	-0.6
Delaware	5,560	7,010	26.1
District of Columbia	3,480	3,160	-9.2
Florida	89,140	125,030	40.3
Georgia	56,450	68,600	21.5
Kentucky	38,120	35,840	-6.0
Louisiana	37,520	37,640	0.3
Maryland	41,930	51,560	23.0
Mississippi	25,570	26,200	2.5
North Carolina	65,210	64,630	-0.9

(continued on next page)

(continued from previous page)

(projected number of public high school graduates by state and region of residence in 1989-1990 and 1999-2000)

	1989-90	1999-2000	percent change 1989-90 to 1999-2000
Oklahoma	34,270	34,420	0.4%
South Carolina	35,720	39,210	9.8
Tennessee	45,760	47,460	3.7
Texas	173,290	198,080	14.3
Virginia	60,520	66,000	9.1
West Virginia	21,940	16,830	-23.3
West	**455,950**	**612,270**	**34.3**
Alaska	5,310	6,140	15.6
Arizona	28,630	39,490	37.9
California	233,080	333,640	43.1
Colorado	32,320	36,630	13.3
Hawaii	9,690	11,370	17.3
Idaho	12,180	13,940	14.4
Montana	9,400	9,870	5.0
Nevada	9,460	16,030	69.5
New Mexico	15,210	19,060	25.3
Oregon	25,670	29,970	16.8
Utah	22,130	28,640	29.4
Washington	47,120	62,070	31.7
Wyoming	5,750	5,420	-5.7

Source: National Center for Education Statistics

Enrollment in Kindergarten Through 12th Grade

The number of students in kindergarten through eighth grade is expected to peak in the mid-1990s, while the number of high school students will begin to rise in the early 1990s.

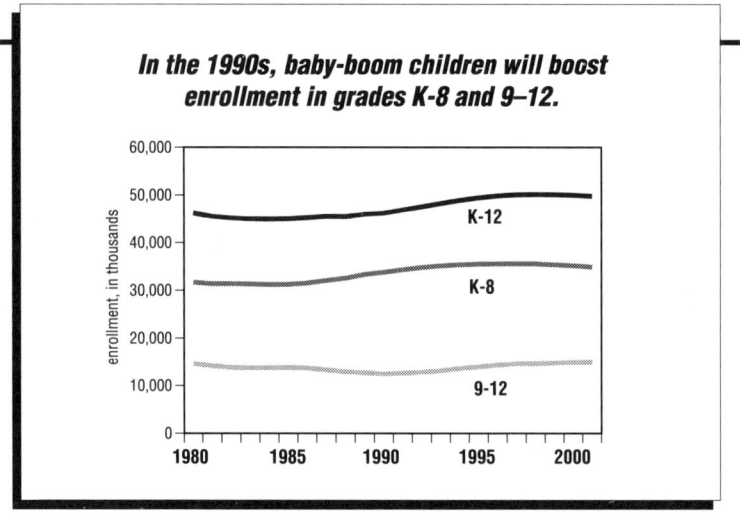

In the 1990s, baby-boom children will boost enrollment in grades K-8 and 9–12.

(students enrolled in public and private schools, 1980-89, and projections for 1990 to 2001; numbers in thousands)

	total K–12	K–8	9–12
1980	46,249	31,669	14,581
1981	45,522	31,370	14,152
1982	45,166	31,358	13,807
1983	44,967	31,294	13,674
1984	44,908	31,201	13,708
1985	44,979	31,225	13,754
1986	45,205	31,535	13,670
1987	45,487	32,048	13,307
1988	45,434	32,537	12,898
1989	45,963	33,309	12,654
1990	46,192	33,765	12,427
1991	46,856	34,291	12,566
1992	47,546	34,767	12,779
1993	48,226	35,120	13,106
1994	48,909	35,347	13,563
1995	49,431	35,496	13,935
1996	49,843	35,545	14,298
1997	50,080	35,534	14,546
1998	50,136	35,539	14,597
1999	50,108	35,357	14,751
2000	49,976	35,145	14,830
2001	49,786	34,887	14,899

Source: National Center for Education Statistics

Private Schools and Private School Enrollment

By the late 1980s, more than 5 million students attended private elementary and secondary schools. Most private school students attend religious schools.

(enrollment in private schools and number of private schools by selected characteristics, 1987-88)

	kindergarten through 12th grade enrollment				number of schools			
	total	Catholic	other religious	non-sectarian	total	Catholic	other religious	non-sectarian
All private schools	**5,479,368**	**2,901,809**	**1,714,852**	**862,707**	**26,807**	**9,527**	**12,132**	**5,148**
School enrollment								
Less than 150	841,262	177,719	449,991	213,552	13,122	1,820	8,058	3,245
150 to 299	1,744,413	938,072	559,389	246,952	8,125	4,225	2,697	1,203
300 to 499	1,291,757	837,426	318,467	135,864	3,454	2,211	868	374
500 to 749	784,027	467,333	189,650	127,044	1,319	801	315	203
750 or more	817,908	481,259	197,354	-	758	470	193	-
Community type*								
Rural/farming	523,494	186,451	216,070	120,973	5,181	1,108	3,359	715
Small city/town	989,361	525,604	317,135	146,621	6,210	2,340	2,916	954
Suburban	1,446,736	786,635	429,390	230,711	5,257	1,925	2,137	1,194
Urban	2,504,081	1,401,756	751,986	350,339	10,150	4,141	3,717	2,292

* Other types of communities are included in the total but are not shown separately.
Source: National Center for Education Statistics
Note: (-) means too few sample cases (fewer than 30) for reliable estimates.

SAT Scores

Average SAT scores increased during the 1980s for almost all racial and ethnic groups. Increases for blacks were particularly sharp.

(average SAT scores by race and Hispanic origin of student, 1979-80 and 1989-90)

	1989–90	1979–80	point change
Verbal SAT			
All students	424	424	0
White	442	442	0
Black	352	330	22
Mexican-American	380	372	8
Puerto Rican	359	350	9
Asian-American	410	396	14
Native American	388	390	-2
Other	410	394	16
Mathematical SAT			
All students	476	466	10
White	491	482	9
Black	385	360	25
Mexican-American	429	413	16
Puerto Rican	405	394	11
Asian-American	528	509	19
Native American	437	426	11
Other	467	449	18

Source: National Center for Education Statistics

College Enrollment by Sex, Race, and Ethnicity

Today, more women than men are enrolled in college. About 85 percent of college students are white, 10 percent are black and just 6 percent are Hispanic.

Among Hispanics aged 25 or older, Cubans have the highest levels of educational attainment.

	high school graduate	college graduate
Total, 25 or older	**77.6%**	**21.3%**
All Hispanics	50.8	9.2
Mexican	44.1	5.4
Puerto Rican	55.5	9.7
Cuban	63.5	20.2
Central & South American	58.5	15.6
Other Hispanic	68.7	15.2

Source: Bureau of the Census

(number and percent distribution of persons aged 15 or older enrolled in college by sex, race, and Hispanic origin, 1989; numbers in thousands)

	number	percent of total
Total	**13,180**	**100.0%**
Male	5,950	45.1
Female	7,231	54.9
White	**11,243**	**85.3**
Male	5,136	39.0
Female	6,107	46.3
Black	**1,287**	**9.8**
Male	480	3.6
Female	807	6.1
Hispanic	**754**	**5.7**
Male	353	2.7
Female	401	3.0

Source: Bureau of the Census
Note: Hispanics may be of any race. White and black do not sum to total because other races are not shown.

College Enrollment Rates

Between 1960 and 1989, the share of female high school graduates who enrolled in college increased nearly 24 percentage points. The figure for males rose by less than 4 percentage points.

(percent of high school graduates going on to college within 12 months of graduating from high school by sex, race, and Hispanic origin, 1960-89)

	total	male	female	white	black	Hispanic
1989	59.6%	57.6%	61.6%	60.4%	52.8%	55.4%
1980	49.3	46.7	51.8	49.9	41.8	52.7
1970	51.8	55.2	48.5	52.0	-	-
1960	45.1	54.0	37.9	45.8	-	-

Source: National Center for Education Statistics
Note: Enrollment in college as of October of each year for persons aged 16 to 24 who graduated from high school during the preceding 12 months.
(-) means data not available.

College Enrollment by Sex, Attendance Status, and Control of Institution

The typical college student through the year 2001 will be a woman who attends a public institution and goes to school full time.

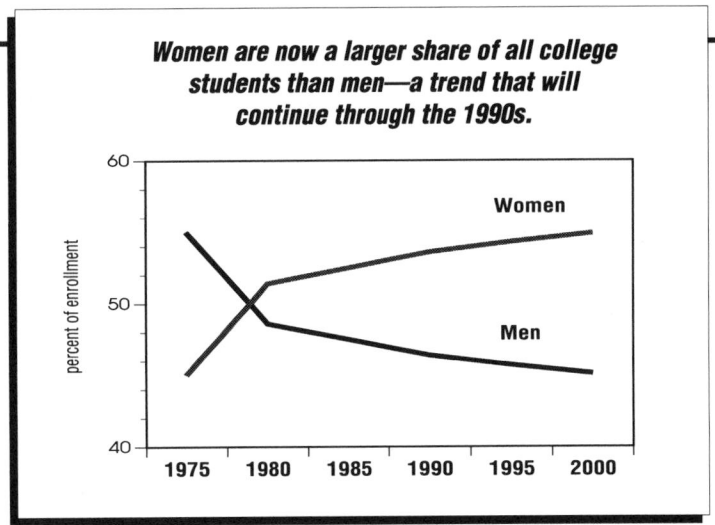

Women are now a larger share of all college students than men—a trend that will continue through the 1990s.

(projected number of persons enrolled in college by sex, attendance status, and control of institution, 1990 to 2001; numbers in thousands)

	total	sex		attendance status		control	
		men	women	full-time	part-time	public	private
1990	13,558	6,292	7,266	7,640	5,918	10,539	3,019
1991	13,643	6,309	7,334	7,627	6,016	10,608	3,035
1992	13,613	6,276	7,337	7,569	6,044	10,587	3,026
1993	13,597	6,254	7,343	7,508	6,089	10,579	3,018
1994	13,579	6,228	7,351	7,456	6,123	10,571	3,008
1995	13,657	6,247	7,410	7,490	6,167	10,637	3,020
1996	13,747	6,271	7,476	7,542	6,205	10,710	3,037
1997	13,906	6,331	7,575	7,654	6,252	10,834	3,072
1998	14,089	6,412	7,677	7,801	6,288	10,977	3,112
1999	14,165	6,395	7,770	7,841	6,324	11,047	3,118
2000	14,326	6,468	7,858	7,970	6,356	11,171	3,155
2001	14,447	6,522	7,925	8,067	6,380	11,264	3,183

Source: National Center for Education Statistics

Enrollment in Two- and Four-Year Colleges

Women will account for more than half of students at both two- and four-year institutions during the 1990s. They are more likely than men to be part-time students.

(share of enrollment in institutions of higher education by type of institution, sex, and enrollment status in 1975-85, and projections for 1990-2000)

	1975	1980	1985	1990	1995	2000
All institutions						
Men	55.0%	48.6%	47.5%	45.5%	45.6%	45.8%
Full time	63.8	62.8	62.0	59.8	58.6	60.4
Part time	36.2	37.2	38.0	40.2	41.4	39.6
Women	45.0	51.4	52.5	54.5	54.4	54.2
Full time	57.9	59.6	53.9	53.2	51.8	53.6
Part time	42.1	45.2	46.1	46.8	48.2	46.4
2-year institutions						
Men	54.6	45.2	44.2	42.5	42.5	42.8
Full time	47.8	43.0	41.2	39.2	38.3	40.2
Part time	6.0	57.0	58.8	60.8	61.7	59.8
Women	45.5	54.8	55.8	57.5	57.5	57.2
Full time	40.2	35.3	34.2	33.4	32.3	33.7
Part time	59.8	64.7	65.8	66.6	67.7	66.3
4-year institutions						
Men	55.2	50.5	49.4	47.3	47.4	47.5
Full time	72.5	73.4	72.9	70.8	69.6	71.3
Part time	27.5	26.6	27.1	29.2	30.4	28.7
Women	44.8	49.4	50.5	52.7	52.6	52.5
Full time	67.8	67.7	66.8	66.1	64.7	66.5
Part time	32.2	32.3	33.2	33.9	35.3	33.5

Source: National Center for Education Statistics

College Students by Age, Sex, and Attendance Status

The number of older college students will grow faster than those of traditional age through 2001. Most students aged 35 or older attend college part time.

(projections of the number of persons aged 14 or older enrolled in college full time and part time by sex and age, 1989 to 2001; numbers in thousands)

	1989			1996			2001		
	total	*full-time*	*part-time*	*total*	*full-time*	*part-time*	*total*	*full-time*	*part-time*
Total	**13,419**	**7,596**	**5,823**	**13,747**	**7,542**	**6,205**	**14,447**	**8,067**	**6,380**
Aged 14 to 17	193	150	43	210	153	57	231	161	71
Aged 18 to 19	2,965	2,611	355	2,911	2,553	358	3,248	2,842	406
Aged 20 to 21	2,521	2,070	451	2,497	2,012	485	2,861	2,296	565
Aged 22 to 24	1,991	1,238	753	1,904	1,182	723	2,018	1,245	773
Aged 25 to 29	1,935	747	1,188	1,699	665	1,034	1,545	610	936
Aged 30 to 34	1,371	356	1,015	1,344	367	978	1,142	252	889
35 or older	2,443	423	2,019	3,180	611	2,569	3,400	662	2,738
Men	**6,260**	**3,781**	**2,479**	**6,271**	**3,735**	**2,535**	**6,522**	**3,980**	**2,542**
Aged 14 to 17	78	61	17	83	62	21	89	65	25
Aged 18 to 19	1,382	1,230	152	1,370	1,217	153	1,549	1,369	180
Aged 20 to 21	1,248	1,030	218	1,254	1,016	239	1,446	1,176	270
Aged 22 to 24	1,058	700	357	1,008	666	342	1,067	706	361
Aged 25 to 29	993	439	554	863	382	481	781	346	436
Aged 30 to 34	624	167	457	602	161	440	449	49	400
35 or older	878	154	724	1,091	232	859	1,140	270	870
Women	**7,159**	**3,815**	**3,344**	**7,476**	**3,806**	**3,670**	**7,925**	**4,087**	**3,838**
Aged 14 to 17	115	90	26	128	91	36	142	96	46
Aged 18 to 19	1,583	1,381	203	1,541	1,335	206	1,699	1,473	227
Aged 20 to 21	1,273	1,041	232	1,243	997	247	1,415	1,120	295
Aged 22 to 24	934	538	396	896	516	381	952	539	413
Aged 25 to 29	943	308	635	836	283	553	764	264	500
Aged 30 to 34	747	189	558	743	205	537	692	203	489
35 or older	1,565	269	1,296	2,090	380	1,710	2,260	392	1,868

Source: National Center for Education Statistics

College Graduates by Level of Degree

The number of people receiving college degrees is not expected to change much from 1991 through 2001. About 1 million people a year will be receiving bachelor's degrees.

(number of degrees conferred by level of degree, 1980-89, and projections for 1990-2001)

	Bachelor's	Master's	Doctor's
1980	929,417	298,081	32,615
1981	935,140	295,739	32,958
1982	952,998	295,546	32,707
1983	969,510	289,921	32,775
1984	974,309	284,263	33,209
1985	979,477	286,251	32,943
1986	987,823	288,567	33,653
1987	991,339	289,557	34,120
1988	993,362	298,733	34,839
1989	1,016,728	307,682	35,379
1990	1,017,000	319,000	35,600
1991	1,024,000	321,000	35,900
1992	1,060,000	322,000	35,900
1993	1,063,000	323,000	36,100
1994	1,058,000	323,000	36,200
1995	1,047,000	324,000	36,300
1996	1,031,000	324,000	36,400
1997	1,015,000	324,000	36,400
1998	1,012,000	324,000	36,400
1999	1,010,000	325,000	36,400
2000	1,019,000	326,000	36,300
2001	1,037,000	327,000	36,200

Source: National Center for Education Statistics

Degrees Conferred by Sex of Student and Level of Degree

In 1980 women received fewer than half of all degrees except associate degrees. By 2001, women will receive the majority of associate, master's, and doctor's degrees.

(number and percent distribution of degrees conferred by level of degree and sex of degree-holder, 1980, and projections for 1990 and 2001)

	1980		1990		2001	
	number	percent	number	percent	number	percent
Associate degree	**400,910**	**100.0%**	**458,000**	**100.0%**	**489,000**	**100.0%**
Men	183,737	45.8	201,000	43.9	211,000	43.1
Women	217,173	54.2	257,000	56.1	278,000	56.9
Bachelor's degree	**929,417**	**100.0**	**1,017,000**	**100.0**	**1,037,000**	**100.0**
Men	473,611	51.0	481,000	47.3	522,000	50.3
Women	455,806	49.0	536,000	52.7	515,000	49.7
Master's degree	**298,081**	**100.0**	**319,000**	**100.0**	**327,000**	**100.0**
Men	150,749	50.6	156,000	48.9	149,000	45.6
Women	147,332	49.4	163,000	51.1	178,000	54.4
Doctor's degree	**32,615**	**100.0**	**35,600**	**100.0**	**36,200**	**100.0**
Men	22,943	70.3	22,600	63.5	17,300	47.8
Women	9,672	29.7	13,000	36.5	18,900	52.2
First-professional degree	**70,131**	**100.0**	**74,100**	**100.0**	**71,300**	**100.0**
Men	52,716	75.2	47,600	64.2	41,400	58.1
Women	17,415	24.8	26,500	35.8	29,900	41.9

Source: National Center for Education Statistics

Bachelor's Degrees Conferred by Sex of Student and Field of Study

Women receive the majority of college degrees in many fields, including communications, life sciences, public affairs, foreign languages, and visual arts.

(number of Bachelor's degrees conferred by all institutions of higher education by sex of student and field of study, 1988-89)

	total	men	women	percent women
All fields	**1,015,239**	**481,687**	**533,552**	**52.6%**
Agriculture and natural resources	13,488	9,295	4,193	31.1
Architecture and environmental design	9,191	5,580	3,611	39.3
Business and management	246,659	131,419	115,240	46.7
Communications	48,625	19,263	29,362	60.4
Computer and information sciences	30,637	21,221	9,416	30.7
Education	96,988	21,662	75,326	77.7
Engineering and engineering technologies	85,273	73,651	11,622	13.6
Foreign languages	10,774	2,879	7,895	73.3
Health sciences	59,111	8,926	50,185	84.9
Home economics	14,717	1,380	13,337	90.6
Law	1,976	785	1,191	60.3
Letters	43,323	14,237	29,086	67.1
Liberal/general studies	23,459	10,051	13,408	57.2
Library and archival sciences	122	16	106	86.9
Life sciences	36,079	17,970	18,109	50.2
Mathematics	15,237	8,221	7,016	46.0
Parks and recreation	4,171	1,709	2,462	59.0
Philosophy and religion	6,411	4,122	2,289	35.7
Physical sciences and science technologies	17,204	12,097	5,107	29.7
Protective services	14,626	9,074	5,552	38.0
Psychology	48,516	14,181	34,335	70.8
Public affairs	15,254	4,948	10,306	67.6
Social sciences	107,714	59,924	47,790	44.4
Visual and performing arts	37,781	14,558	23,223	61.5

Source: National Center for Education Statistics
Note: Numbers do not add to total because all fields are not shown.

Master's and Doctor's Degrees Conferred by Sex of Student and Field of Study

Women receive about one-third of all Doctor's degrees, but a majority of those in such fields as education, psychology, and foreign languages.

(number of Master's and Doctor's degrees conferred by all institutions of higher education by sex of student and field of study, 1988-89)

	Master's degrees				Doctor's degrees			
	total	men	women	percent women	total	men	women	percent women
All fields	**308,872**	**148,486**	**160,386**	**51.9%**	**35,692**	**22,651**	**13,041**	**36.5%**
Agriculture and natural resources	3,245	2,231	1,014	31.2	1,184	952	232	19.6
Architecture and environmental design	3,378	2,191	1,187	35.1	86	63	23	26.7
Business and management	73,154	48,557	24,597	33.6	1,150	844	306	26.6
Communications	4,233	1,710	2,523	59.6	248	137	111	44.8
Computer and information sciences	9,392	6,769	2,623	27.9	538	457	81	15.1
Education	82,238	20,286	61,952	75.3	6,783	2,894	3,889	57.3
Engineering and engineering technologies	24,541	21,355	3,186	13.0	4,533	4,133	400	8.8
Foreign languages	1,911	602	1,309	68.5	422	169	253	60.0
Health sciences	19,255	4,210	15,045	78.1	1,439	612	827	57.5
Home economics	2,174	311	1,863	85.7	263	59	204	77.6
Law	2,098	1,491	607	28.9	76	46	30	39.5
Letters	6,608	2,272	4,336	65.6	1,238	559	679	54.8
Liberal/general studies	1,408	495	913	64.8	32	16	16	50.0
Library and archival sciences	3,940	816	3,124	79.3	61	27	34	55.7
Life sciences	4,933	2,484	2,449	49.6	3,533	2,235	1,298	36.7
Mathematics	3,424	2,058	1,366	39.9	882	711	171	19.4
Parks and recreation	460	213	247	53.7	36	28	8	22.2
Philosophy and religion	1,274	755	519	40.7	464	341	123	26.5
Physical sciences	5,737	4,204	1,533	26.7	3,852	3,093	759	19.7
Protective services	1,046	722	324	31.0	27	19	8	29.6
Psychology	8,579	2,799	5,780	67.4	3,263	1,429	1,834	56.2
Public affairs	17,928	6,398	11,530	64.3	417	208	209	50.1
Social sciences	10,854	6,493	4,361	40.2	2,878	1,939	939	32.6
Visual and performing arts	8,234	3,598	4,636	53.0	755	443	312	41.3

Source: National Center for Education Statistics
Note: Numbers do not add to total because all fields are not shown.

First-Professional Degrees Conferred by Sex of Student and Field of Study

Women receive over half of first-professional degrees in pharmacy and in veterinary medicine. They receive fewer than one-fourth of degrees in theology and podiatry.

(number of first-professional degrees conferred by all institutions of higher education by sex of student and field of study, 1988-89)

	total	men	women	percent women
Total, all institutions	**70,758**	**45,067**	**25,691**	**36.3%**
Dentistry (D.D.S. or D.M.D.)	4,247	3,139	1,108	26.1
Medicine (M.D.)	15,454	10,326	5,128	33.2
Optometry (O.D.)	1,093	683	410	37.5
Osteopathic medicine (D.O.)	1,635	1,183	452	27.6
Pharmacy (D.Phar.)	1,074	422	652	60.7
Podiatry (Pod.D. or D.P.) or podiatric medicine (D.P.M.)	636	487	149	23.4
Veterinary medicine (D.V.M.)	2,157	981	1,176	54.5
Chiropractic (D.C. or D.C.M.)	2,890	2,159	731	25.3
Law, general (LL.B. or J.D.)	35,567	21,048	14,519	40.8
Theological professions, general (B.D., M.Div., Rabbi)	6,005	4,639	1,366	22.7

Source: National Center for Education Statistics

Educational Attainment by Age of Householder

More than 16 percent of householders aged 35 to 44 are college graduates. This compares with fewer than 8 percent of householders aged 60 or older.

(number and percent distribution of householders by age of householder and highest level of school completed, 1990; numbers in thousands)

		educational attainment of householder					
Number	all households	grade school or less	some high school	high school graduate	some college	college graduate	graduate school
Total	**93,347**	**10,904**	**10,813**	**33,422**	**17,122**	**11,805**	**9,281**
Under age 25	5,122	208	724	2,196	1,279	617	98
Aged 25 to 29	9,423	339	961	3,670	2,021	1,704	728
Aged 30 to 34	11,048	420	960	4,252	2,474	1,791	1,151
Aged 35 to 39	10,892	419	781	3,851	2,568	1,827	1,446
Aged 40 to 44	9,661	457	658	3,369	2,166	1,464	1,547
Aged 45 to 49	7,936	566	771	2,887	1,485	1,057	1,170
Aged 50 to 54	6,579	700	770	2,499	1,130	699	781
Aged 55 to 59	6,101	809	851	2,261	898	619	663
Aged 60 to 64	6,429	1,150	991	2,145	927	619	597
Aged 65 to 69	6,312	1,333	993	2,212	786	533	455
Aged 70 to 74	5,421	1,354	955	1,886	556	389	281
Aged 75 or older	8,423	3,149	1,398	2,194	832	486	364
Percent distribution							
Total	**100.0%**	**11.7%**	**11.6%**	**35.8%**	**18.3%**	**12.6%**	**9.9%**
Under age 25	100.0	4.1	14.1	42.9	25.0	12.0	1.9
Aged 25 to 29	100.0	3.6	10.2	38.9	21.4	18.1	7.7
Aged 30 to 34	100.0	3.8	8.7	38.5	22.4	16.2	10.4
Aged 35 to 39	100.0	3.8	7.2	35.4	23.6	16.8	13.3
Aged 40 to 44	100.0	4.7	6.8	34.9	22.4	15.2	16.0
Aged 45 to 49	100.0	7.1	9.7	36.4	18.7	13.3	14.7
Aged 50 to 54	100.0	10.6	11.7	38.0	17.2	10.6	11.9
Aged 55 to 59	100.0	13.3	13.9	37.1	14.7	10.1	10.9
Aged 60 to 64	100.0	17.9	15.4	33.4	14.4	9.6	9.3
Aged 65 to 69	100.0	21.1	15.7	35.0	12.5	8.4	7.2
Aged 70 to 74	100.0	25.0	17.6	34.8	10.3	7.2	5.2
Aged 75 or older	100.0	37.4	16.6	26.0	9.9	5.8	4.3

Source: The Conference Board

Education of Husband by Education of Wife

Husbands and wives tend to have similar levels of education, but husbands generally are better educated than their wives.

(number of years of school completed by husbands aged 18 or older, by number of years of school completed by wives, for married couples only, 1989; numbers in thousands)

			education of wife						
			elementary			high school		college		
Education of husband										
Husbands, aged 18	total	0–4 years	5–7 years	8 years	1–3 years	4 years	1–3 years	4 years	5+ years
or older	52,920	743	1,573	2,017	5,696	23,675	9,510	6,205	3,500
Elementary									
0 to 4 years	1,111	357	226	148	193	151	28	5	3
5 to 7 years	2,098	180	588	264	486	488	66	23	4
8 years	2,575	51	205	618	564	970	123	28	16
High school									
1 to 3 years	5,710	72	267	398	1,831	2,557	432	95	59
4 years	19,153	50	208	477	2,018	12,470	2,666	887	376
College									
1 to 3 years	9,200	23	54	77	448	4,107	2,989	1,073	429
4 years	7,044	8	23	28	125	1,891	1,929	2,323	717
5 or more years	6,029	3	3	8	29	1,040	1,277	1,771	1,898

Source: Bureau of the Census

Household Income by Educational Attainment of Householder, 1990

In 1990, just 18 percent of householders with a high school diploma had incomes of $50,000 or more. In contrast, 43 percent of those with a college degree had an income that high.

(number and percent distribution of householders by household income in 1989, and by education of householder in 1990; numbers in thousands)

		educational attainment of householder					
Number of householders	**all households**	**grade school or less**	**some high school**	**high school graduate**	**some college**	**college graduate**	**graduate school**
Total	**93,347**	**10,904**	**10,813**	**33,422**	**17,122**	**11,805**	**9,281**
Under $10,000	14,592	4,391	3,138	4,643	1,611	538	271
$10,000 to $15,000	9,057	1,777	1,640	3,596	1,266	511	267
$15,000 to $20,000	8,619	1,332	1,338	3,473	1,491	653	332
$20,000 to $25,000	8,135	934	1,001	3,368	1,489	837	506
$25,000 to $30,000	7,778	676	909	3,276	1,513	892	512
$30,000 to $35,000	7,062	464	641	2,960	1,541	879	577
$35,000 to $40,000	6,153	327	557	2,437	1,443	799	590
$40,000 to $50,000	10,029	464	673	3,762	2,269	1,666	1,195
$50,000 to $60,000	7,061	249	402	2,461	1,682	1,311	956
$60,000 to $75,000	6,462	147	299	1,856	1,382	1,465	1,313
$75,000 to $100,000	4,802	91	152	1,034	893	1,246	1,386
$100,000 or more	3,597	51	66	556	541	1,009	1,374
Percent distribution							
Total	**100.0%**	**100.0%**	**100.0%**	**100.0%**	**100.0%**	**100.0%**	**100.0%**
Under $10,000	15.6	40.3	29.0	13.9	9.4	4.6	2.9
$10,000 to $15,000	9.7	16.3	15.2	10.8	7.4	4.3	2.9
$15,000 to $20,000	9.2	12.2	12.4	10.4	8.7	5.5	3.6
$20,000 to $25,000	8.7	8.6	9.3	10.1	8.7	7.1	5.5
$25,000 to $30,000	8.3	6.2	8.4	9.8	8.8	7.6	5.5
$30,000 to $35,000	7.6	4.3	5.9	8.9	9.0	7.4	6.2
$35,000 to $40,000	6.6	3.0	5.2	7.3	8.4	6.8	6.4
$40,000 to $50,000	10.7	4.3	6.2	11.3	13.3	14.1	12.9
$50,000 to $60,000	7.6	2.3	3.7	7.4	9.8	11.1	10.3
$60,000 to $75,000	6.9	1.3	2.8	5.6	8.1	12.4	14.1
$75,000 to $100,000	5.1	0.8	1.4	3.1	5.2	10.6	14.9
$100,000 or more	3.9	0.5	0.6	1.7	3.2	8.5	14.8

Source: The Conference Board

Household Income by Educational Attainment of Householder, 2000

The importance of education to a high income is projected to increase during the 1990s. By 2000, 16 percent of householders with a college diploma will have an income of $100,000-plus, up from 11 percent in 1990.

(number and percent distribution of householders by household income in 1999, and by education of householder in 2000; numbers in thousands)

| | | educational attainment of householder | | | | | |
Number of householders	all households	grade school or less	some high school	high school graduate	some college	college graduate	graduate school
Total	**102,442**	**8,341**	**10,154**	**37,437**	**20,903**	**14,440**	**11,167**
Under $10,000	13,410	3,236	2,790	4,746	1,755	585	298
$10,000 to $15,000	8,536	1,357	1,489	3,573	1,323	516	278
$15,000 to $20,000	8,331	1,012	1,225	3,562	1,534	652	346
$20,000 to $25,000	8,046	727	948	3,463	1,611	809	488
$25,000 to $30,000	7,839	531	828	3,375	1,621	926	558
$30,000 to $35,000	7,404	375	644	3,189	1,645	958	593
$35,000 to $40,000	6,837	266	522	2,827	1,649	936	637
$40,000 to $50,000	11,433	366	691	4,357	2,859	1,823	1,337
$50,000 to $60,000	8,722	211	419	3,101	2,185	1,643	1,163
$60,000 to $75,000	8,570	133	325	2,610	2,109	1,882	1,511
$75,000 to $100,000	7,057	79	184	1,643	1,520	1,848	1,783
$100,000 or more	6,257	48	89	991	1,092	1,862	2,175
Percent distribution							
Total	**100.0%**	**100.0%**	**100.0%**	**100.0%**	**100.0%**	**100.0%**	**100.0%**
Under $10,000	13.1	38.8	27.5	12.7	8.4	4.1	2.7
$10,000 to $15,000	8.3	16.3	14.7	9.5	6.3	3.6	2.5
$15,000 to $20,000	8.1	12.1	12.1	9.5	7.3	4.5	3.1
$20,000 to $25,000	7.9	8.7	9.3	9.3	7.7	5.6	4.4
$25,000 to $30,000	7.7	6.4	8.2	9.0	7.8	6.4	5.0
$30,000 to $35,000	7.2	4.5	6.3	8.5	7.9	6.6	5.3
$35,000 to $40,000	6.7	3.2	5.1	7.6	7.9	6.5	5.7
$40,000 to $50,000	11.2	4.4	6.8	11.6	13.7	12.6	12.0
$50,000 to $60,000	8.5	2.5	4.1	8.3	10.5	11.4	10.4
$60,000 to $75,000	8.4	1.6	3.2	7.0	10.1	13.0	13.5
$75,000 to $100,000	6.9	0.9	1.8	4.4	7.3	12.8	16.0
$100,000 or more	6.1	0.6	0.9	2.6	5.2	12.9	19.5

Source: The Conference Board

Discretionary Income by Education of Householder

Over half of households headed by someone with a college degree have discretionary income to spend, amounting to more than $5,000 per capita.

(years of school completed by householder in 1987 by discretionary income in 1986; numbers in thousands)

| | households | | households with discretionary income | | | | |
| | | | average income | | spendable discretionary income | | |
Education	*number*	*proportion of households*	*before taxes*	*after taxes*	*aggregate (billions)*	*average*	*per capita*
Total	**25,869**	**28.9%**	**$56,605**	**$41,940**	**$319.0**	**$12,332**	**$4,633**
Less than 12 years	2,604	11.3	43,783	34,508	21.9	8,416	3,076
12 years	7,850	24.5	48,448	37,296	70.6	8,999	3,381
College: total	15,414	44.8	62,925	45,561	226.5	14,692	5,546
1 to 3 years	5,051	32.7	54,253	40,904	56.7	11,226	4,174
4 years	5,249	50.4	63,043	45,427	76.4	14,559	5,643
5 years or more	5,115	59.6	71,369	50,298	93.3	18,250	6,810

Source: A Marketer's Guide to Discretionary Income, a joint study by the Consumer Research Center, The Conference Board, and the U.S. Bureau of the Census

Occupation by Sex and Educational Attainment

Nearly 30 percent of employed people have four or more years of college. But a majority of professional and managerial workers have a college degree.

(occupation of employed civilians aged 25 or older by sex and years of school completed, 1988; numbers in thousands)

Number	total		managerial/professional		technical, sales, administrative	
	male	female	male	female	male	female
Total	**49,918**	**40,476**	**14,688**	**11,570**	**9,738**	**17,472**
Less than 4 years of high school	7,807	4,812	460	287	617	1,048
4 years of high school only	18,402	17,437	2,212	2,273	3,287	9,225
1 to 3 years of college	9,342	8,640	2,427	2,508	2,694	4,663
4 years of college or more	14,367	9,586	9,588	6,502	3,140	2,537
Percent distribution						
Total	**100.0%**	**100.0%**	**100.0%**	**100.0%**	**100.0%**	**100.0%**
Less than 4 years of high school	15.6	11.9	3.1	2.5	6.3	6.0
4 years of high school only	36.9	43.1	15.1	19.6	33.8	52.8
1 to 3 years of college	18.7	21.3	16.5	21.7	27.7	26.7
4 years of college or more	28.8	23.7	65.3	56.2	32.2	14.5

Number	service		precision production		operators/fabricators	
	male	female	male	female	male	female
Total	**3,907**	**6,435**	**10,151**	**965**	**9,678**	**3,685**
Less than 4 years of high school	908	1,830	2,257	227	2,967	1,330
4 years of high school only	1,776	3,275	5,418	513	4,936	1,982
1 to 3 years of college	812	997	1,885	155	1,296	269
4 years of college or more	410	333	591	69	479	103
Percent distribution						
Total	**100.0%**	**100.0%**	**100.0%**	**100.0%**	**100.0%**	**100.0%**
Less than 4 years of high school	23.2	28.4	22.2	23.5	30.7	36.1
4 years of high school only	45.5	50.9	53.4	53.2	51.0	53.8
1 to 3 years of college	20.8	15.5	18.6	16.1	13.4	7.3
4 years of college or more	10.5	5.2	5.8	7.2	4.9	2.8

Source: Bureau of the Census

7

Health Trends

Most Americans under the age of 65 report being in good or excellent health. Even after age 65, fewer than one-third report that their health is only fair or poor. Americans feel healthy because they're taking better care of themselves. Fewer Americans smoke cigarettes than 20 years ago, and drug use has declined as well. But as the population middle-ages in the 1990s, many more people will develop serious health problems. This assures that health care will remain at the top of the nation's political agenda.

Major Health Trends

☛ Health problems become much more prevalent after the age of 45. With the baby-boom generation inflating the 45-to-54 age group in the 1990s, the number of people with serious health conditions will grow rapidly.

☛ As millions of Americans reach the ages at which health problems increase, demands for a better health-care system will grow. Expect health-care financing to change dramatically before the end of the decade.

☛ The importance of AIDS as a leading cause of death is growing. Already, it ranks among the top ten causes of death for children ages 1-4, and for adults ages 15-64. As the 1990s progress, AIDS will dominate health-care issues.

Health Status of Americans

A majority of Americans rate their health as very good to excellent until ages 65 or older. Even at ages 75 and older, only one-third of Americans rate their health as fair or poor.

(percent distribution of self-assessed or parent-assessed health status by selected characteristics, 1989)

	all persons	excellent	very good	good	fair or poor
Age					
Under 5 years	100.0%	54.8%	26.9%	15.7%	2.6%
Aged 5 to 14	100.0	52.9	27.0	17.7	2.3
Aged 15 to 44	100.0	43.4	30.3	20.6	5.6
Aged 45 to 64	100.0	28.9	26.9	28.0	16.1
Aged 65 to 74	100.0	17.8	24.0	31.9	26.3
Aged 75 or older	100.0	14.3	21.7	32.0	32.0
Sex					
Male	100.0	43.0	27.5	20.8	8.6
Female	100.0	38.5	28.4	23.5	9.5
Race					
White	100.0	42.6	28.4	20.8	8.2
Black	100.0	30.4	24.9	28.9	15.9
Household income					
Less than $14,000	100.0	27.6	23.8	29.3	19.4
$14,000 to $24,999	100.0	35.7	28.9	25.2	10.1
$25,000 to $34,999	100.0	41.9	30.2	21.1	6.9
$35,000 to $49,999	100.0	46.0	29.7	19.2	5.1
$50,000 or more	100.0	54.2	26.9	15.2	3.7

Source: National Center for Health Statistics

Average Weight of Americans

About one-fourth of all Americans are overweight, a share that rises with age for women and peaks at ages 45 to 54 for men.

(average weight, in pounds, and percent overweight by sex, race, and Hispanic origin, and age)

| | all adults | age | | | | | |
		18-24	25-34	35-44	45-54	55-64	65-74
Men							
Average weight, in pounds							
All races	172.2	162.7	173.4	178.4	178.4	173.7	164.9
White	173.0	163.5	174.3	179.4	178.6	174.0	166.2
Black	171.6	159.3	172.5	181.9	181.7	173.3	161.7
Hispanic							
Mexican	166.0	155.3	170.1	170.6	172.5	167.5	158.6
Cuban	167.9	164.1	175.2	167.4	167.4	166.6	161.3
Puerto Rican	163.2	156.9	163.9	169.3	168.0	158.2	158.3
Percent overweight							
All races	24.4%	12.1%	20.4%	28.9%	31.0%	28.1%	25.2%
White	24.4	12.7	20.9	28.2	30.5	28.6	25.8
Black	26.3	5.5	17.5	40.9	41.4	26.0	26.4
Hispanic							
Mexican	31.2	15.5	29.2	37.2	36.9	37.5	30.3
Cuban	28.5	21.2	27.9	25.8	34.6	31.7	31.1
Puerto Rican	25.7	15.8	18.9	33.4	32.9	26.4	31.6
Women							
Average weight, in pounds							
All races	144.2	133.6	141.6	147.8	149.9	149.6	146.8
White	143.0	133.2	140.2	145.6	148.4	148.1	145.9
Black	157.0	139.2	152.7	165.9	171.2	167.2	159.6
Hispanic							
Mexican	144.4	134.6	142.3	149.5	153.2	153.4	144.3
Cuban	140.4	126.6	131.8	142.8	148.1	147.8	139.4
Puerto Rican	141.7	132.2	137.2	148.5	150.1	146.2	147.2
Percent overweight							
All races	26.7%	11.4%	20.0%	27.0%	32.5%	37.0%	38.5%
White	24.6	9.6	17.9	24.8	29.9	34.8	36.5
Black	45.1	23.7	33.5	40.8	61.2	59.4	60.8
Hispanic							
Mexican	41.5	21.9	31.8	43.8	52.0	57.3	49.7
Cuban	31.9	13.6	23.8	32.7	37.2	51.4	39.6
Puerto Rican	39.8	23.6	26.5	42.7	50.2	49.0	61.0

Source: National Center for Health Statistics; white and black data are from 1976-80; Hispanic data are from 1982-84.
Note: Data for overweight include adults aged 20 to 74. For overweight, the age group 18 to 24 includes only those aged 20 to 24. Overweight excludes pregnant women. Weight includes clothing weight, estimated as ranging from 0.20 to 0.62 pounds. Overweight is defined in terms of a body mass index which is determined by dividing weight in kilograms by height in meters squared. Overweight people have a body mass index equal to or greater than that at the 85th percentile of men and women aged 20 to 29.

Average Height of Americans

The average American man stands five feet nine inches tall. The average American woman is about five feet four inches tall. Men and women both lose about two inches in height during their adulthood.

(average height, in inches, by sex, race, and Hispanic origin, and age)

	all adults	18-24	25-34	35-44	45-54	55-64	65-74
Men							
Average height, in inches							
All races	69.1	69.7	69.6	69.4	69.0	68.4	67.4
White	69.2	69.8	69.7	69.6	69.1	68.4	67.6
Black	69.1	69.6	69.6	69.5	68.6	68.6	67.4
Hispanic							
Mexican	67.1	67.4	67.3	67.1	66.9	66.1	65.6
Cuban	67.4	68.5	68.4	67.3	66.6	66.8	66.0
Puerto Rican	67.0	67.9	68.0	66.4	66.3	65.3	65.1
Women							
Average height, in inches							
All races	63.7	64.3	64.2	64.1	63.5	63.0	62.2
White	63.8	64.4	64.3	64.1	63.6	63.0	62.3
Black	63.8	64.3	63.9	64.3	63.7	63.4	62.5
Hispanic							
Mexican	61.8	62.3	62.1	61.8	61.4	61.1	60.3
Cuban	61.8	62.9	62.0	61.9	62.1	61.3	60.6
Puerto Rican	61.8	62.6	62.4	61.4	61.3	60.8	60.2

Source: National Center for Health Statistics; white and black data are from 1976-80; Hispanic data are from 1982-84.
Note: Height is without shoes.

Cigarette Smoking

The percentage of Americans who smoke has declined sharply, particularly among men. Those most likely to smoke are black men aged 25 to 64.

(current cigarette smoking status of persons aged 18 or older by sex, age, and race, 1965, 1974, and 1987; percent of the population)

	1987	1974	1965
All persons aged 18 or older	28.7%	37.2%	42.3%
Men, all races			
All aged 18 or older	31.0	42.9	51.6
Aged 18 to 24	28.2	42.1	54.1
Aged 25 to 34	34.8	50.5	60.7
Aged 35 to 44	36.6	51.0	58.2
Aged 45 to 64	33.5	42.6	51.9
Aged 65 or older	17.2	24.8	28.5
Men, white			
All aged 18 or older	30.4	41.7	50.8
Aged 18 to 24	29.2	40.8	53.0
Aged 25 to 34	33.8	49.5	60.1
Aged 35 to 44	36.2	50.1	57.3
Aged 45 to 64	32.4	41.2	51.3
Aged 65 or older	16.0	24.3	27.7
Men, black			
All aged 18 or older	39.0	54.0	59.2
Aged 18 to 24	24.9	54.9	62.8
Aged 25 to 34	44.9	58.5	68.4
Aged 35 to 44	44.0	61.5	67.3
Aged 45 to 64	44.3	57.8	57.9
Aged 65 or older	30.3	29.7	36.4
Women, all races			
All aged 18 or older	26.7	32.5	34.0
Aged 18 to 24	26.1	34.1	38.1
Aged 25 to 34	31.8	38.8	43.7
Aged 35 to 44	29.6	39.8	43.7
Aged 45 to 64	28.6	33.4	32.0
Aged 65 or older	13.7	12.0	9.6
Women, white			
All aged 18 or older	27.2	32.3	34.3
Aged 18 to 24	27.8	34.0	38.4
Aged 25 to 34	31.9	38.6	43.4
Aged 35 to 44	29.2	39.3	43.9
Aged 45 to 64	29.0	33.0	32.7
Aged 65 or older	13.9	12.3	9.8
Women, black			
All aged 18 or older	27.2	35.9	32.1
Aged 18 to 24	20.4	35.6	37.1
Aged 25 to 34	35.8	42.2	47.8
Aged 35 to 44	35.3	46.4	42.8
Aged 45 to 64	28.4	38.9	25.7
Aged 65 or older	11.7	8.9	7.1

Source: National Center for Health Statistics
Note: A current smoker is a person who has smoked at least 100 cigarettes and who now smokes. Includes occasional smokers.

Drug-Use Trends Among Young People

Drug and alcohol use among young people peaked in 1979 and declined during the 1980s. In 1990, 41 percent of those aged 12 to 17 said they drank alcohol in the last year.

(percent of persons aged 12 to 17 and aged 18 to 25 reporting drug use in the past year, 1974 to 1990)

	1990	1988	1985	1982	1979	1976	1974
Persons aged 12 to 17							
Any illicit drug use	15.9%	16.8%	23.7%	22.0%	26.0%	-	-
Marijuana/hashish	11.3	12.6	19.7	20.6	24.1	22.3%	18.5%
Cocaine	2.2	2.9	4.0	4.1	4.2	2.6	2.7
Inhalants	4.0	3.9	5.1	-	4.6	2.2	2.4
Hallucinogens	2.4	2.8	2.7	3.6	4.7	3.1	4.3
Heroin	0.6	0.4	-	-	-	0.6	-
Nonmedical use of psychotherapeutics	7.0	5.4	8.5	8.3	5.6	-	-
Stimulants	3.0	2.8	4.3	5.6	2.9	3.7	3.0
Sedatives	2.2	1.7	2.9	3.7	2.2	2.0	2.0
Tranquilizers	1.5	1.5	3.4	3.3	2.7	2.9	2.0
Analgesics	4.8	3.0	3.8	3.7	2.2	-	-
Alcohol	41.0	44.6	51.7	52.4	53.6	47.5	51.0
Persons aged 18 to 25							
Any illicit drug use	28.7	32.0	42.6	43.4	49.4	-	-
Marijuana/hashish	24.6	27.9	36.9	40.4	46.9	35.0	34.2
Cocaine	7.5	12.1	16.3	18.8	19.6	7.0	8.1
Inhalants	3.0	4.1	2.1	-	3.8	1.4	1.2
Hallucinogens	3.9	5.6	4.0	6.9	9.9	6.0	6.1
Heroin	0.5	0.3	0.6	-	0.8	0.6	0.8
Nonmedical use of psychotherapeutics	7.0	11.3	15.6	16.1	16.3	-	-
Stimulants	3.4	6.4	9.9	10.8	10.1	8.8	8.0
Sedatives	2.0	3.3	5.0	8.7	7.3	5.7	4.2
Tranquilizers	2.4	4.6	6.4	5.9	7.1	6.2	4.6
Analgesics	4.1	5.5	6.6	4.4	5.2	-	-
Alcohol	80.2	81.7	87.2	87.1	86.6	77.9	77.1

Source: National Institute on Drug Abuse, US Department of Health and Human Services
Note: Use of an illicit drug means using that drug at least once. Nonmedical use of psychotherapeutics does not include over-the-counter medications. The exclusion of inhalants from the survey in 1982 is believed to have resulted in underestimates in any illicit use for that year, especially among persons aged 12 to 17. (-) means no estimate available or unreliable estimate.

Drug-Use Trends Among Adults

The use of illicit drugs peaked among adults in the middle of the 1980s. By 1990, only 10 percent admitted using illicit drugs in the past year.

(percent of persons aged 26 or older reporting drug use in the past year and in the lifetime, 1974 to 1990)

	1990	1988	1985	1982	1979	1976	1974
Reported drug use in past year							
Any illicit drug use	10.1%	10.2%	13.3%	11.8%	10.0%	-	-
Marijuana/hashish	7.3	6.9	9.5	10.6	9.0	5.4%	3.8%
Cocaine	2.4	2.7	4.2	3.8	2.0	0.6	-
Inhalants	0.5	0.4	0.8	-	1.0	-	-
Hallucinogens	0.4	0.6	1.0	0.8	0.5	-	-
Heroin	0.1	0.2	-	-	-	-	-
Nonmedical use of psychotherapeutics	3.4	4.7	6.2	3.1	2.3	-	-
Stimulants	1.0	1.7	2.6	1.7	1.3	0.8	-
Sedatives	0.8	1.2	2.0	1.4	0.8	0.6	-
Tranquilizers	1.0	1.8	2.8	1.1	0.9	1.2	-
Analgesics	1.9	2.1	2.9	1.0	0.5	-	-
Alcohol	66.6	68.6	73.6	72.0	72.4	64.2	62.7
Reported drug use in lifetime							
Illicit drug use	35.3	33.7	31.5	24.7	23.0	-	-
Marijuana/hashish	31.8	30.7	27.2	23.0	19.6	12.9	9.9
Cocaine	10.9	9.9	9.5	8.5	4.3	1.6	0.9
Inhalants	3.8	3.9	5.0	-	3.9	1.9	1.2
Hallucinogens	7.4	6.6	6.2	6.4	4.5	1.6	1.3
Heroin	0.9	1.1	1.1	1.1	1.0	0.5	0.5
Nonmedical use of psychotherapeutics	11.5	11.3	13.8	8.8	9.2	-	-
Stimulants	6.9	6.6	7.9	6.2	5.8	5.6	3.0
Sedatives	3.7	3.3	5.2	4.8	3.5	2.4	2.0
Tranquilizers	4.2	4.5	7.2	3.6	3.1	2.7	2.0
Analgesics	5.1	4.5	5.6	3.2	2.7	-	-
Alcohol	86.8	88.6	89.4	88.2	91.5	74.7	73.2

Source: National Institute on Drug Abuse, US Department of Health and Human Services
Note: Use of an illicit drug means using that drug at least once. Nonmedical use of psychotherapeutics does not include over-the-counter medications. The exclusion of inhalants from the survey in 1982 is believed to have resulted in underestimates in any illicit use for that year, especially among persons aged 12 to 17. (-) means no estimate available or unreliable estimate.

Strenuous Exercisers

About one-third of all Americans say they exercise strenuously several times a week. Although the share of strenuous exercisers declines with age, the share of those who walk for exercise increases.

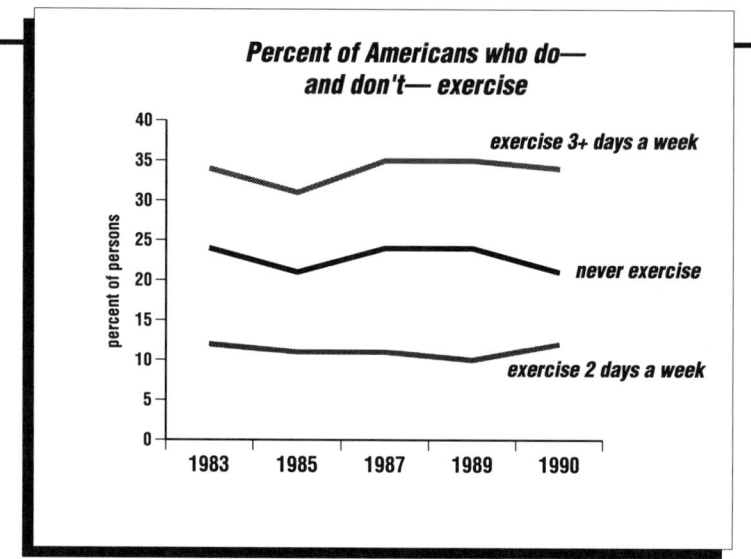

Percent of Americans who do— and don't— exercise

(percent of adults who exercise strenuously three or more days a week or walk several times a week for exercise by selected characteristics, 1990)

	exercise strenuously three or more times a week	walk several times a week or more		exercise strenuously three or more times a week	walk several times a week or more
All persons	**34%**	**45%**	$35,001 to $50,000	38%	44%
Sex			$50,001 or more	39	43
Male	41	44	**Education**		
Female	28	46	Not high school graduate	31	44
Age			High school graduate	32	48
Aged 18 to 29	46	43	Some college	34	42
Aged 30 to 39	36	42	Four or more years college	38	44
Aged 40 to 49	34	42	**Region**		
Aged 50 to 64	30	46	East	34	42
Aged 65 or older	17	54	South	37	45
Household income			Midwest	32	46
$7,500 or less	23	51	West	32	48
$7,501 to $15,000	32	46	**Self-described health status**		
$15,001 to $25,000	35	46	Excellent	43	44
$25,001 to $35,000	34	43	Very good or good	32	44
			Fair or poor	26	49

Source: The 1991 Prevention Index, Rodale Press, Inc.

Eating and Dieting

More than one-third of Americans are trying to lose weight, a proportion that peaks among the middle-aged. Eighty-two percent of those who are trying to lose weight say they are eating less; 60 percent are exercising more.

(percent distribution of persons with selected health habits and knowledge by age and sex, 1985)

	all ages	age 18-29	age 30-44	age 45-64	age 65+	sex male	sex female
Total	100%	100%	100%	100%	100%	100%	100%
1. How often do you eat breakfast?							
Almost every day	55	41	46	62	87	54	56
Sometimes	20	27	23	17	6	20	19
Rarely or never	25	32	31	21	8	26	24
2. Including evening snacks, how often do you eat between meals?							
Almost every day	39	42	41	37	30	40	37
Sometimes	32	37	33	29	26	29	34
Rarely or never	29	21	26	34	44	30	29
3. In your opinion, which of these are the two best ways to lose weight?							
Don't eat at bedtime	29	29	26	30	31	31	27
Eat fewer calories	74	70	76	77	72	69	79
Take diet pills	2	2	2	1	1	2	2
Increase physical activity	73	83	81	67	53	74	73
Eat no fat	11	7	7	12	20	12	10
Eat grapefruit with every meal	4	4	3	5	6	5	4
Don't know	7	4	5	8	17	9	5
4. Are you now trying to lose weight?							
Yes	37	35	42	41	26	27	46
5. If yes to question 4, are you eating fewer calories to lose weight?							
Yes	82	77	83	86	81	77	85
6. If yes to question 4, have you increased your physical activity to lose weight?							
Yes	60	74	63	51	40	62	59
7. Do you consider yourself overweight, underweight, or just about right? If overweight, would you say you are very overweight, somewhat overweight, or only a little overweight?							
Very overweight	8	5	9	11	6	3	12
Somewhat overweight	17	13	19	21	14	13	21
Only a little overweight	21	18	22	22	20	20	22
Just about right	48	56	45	41	52	55	42
Underweight	6	8	4	4	7	8	4

Source: National Center for Health Statistics

Current Knowledge About AIDS

Fifteen percent of Americans know or have known someone with the AIDS virus. Eighty percent say there is no chance that they have the AIDS virus, but only 10 percent have been tested for the virus recently.

(percent of persons aged 18 or older with selected AIDS knowledge and attitudes, 1990)

AIDS knowledge or attitude	total	age			education		
		18 to 29	30 to 49	50+	<12 years	12 years	12+ years
	100%	100%	100%	100%	100%	100%	100%
1. How much would you say you know about AIDS?							
A lot	19	22	22	12	9	15	27
Some	47	53	54	35	29	50	54
A little	24	21	20	30	31	27	17
Nothing	11	4	4	23	30	8	3
Don't know	0	-	0	0	0	0	0
2. AIDS is an infectious disease caused by a virus.							
Definitely true	69	76	77	56	55	68	78
Probably true	16	15	13	19	19	17	12
Probably false	2	2	2	3	3	2	2
Definitely false	3	2	3	3	2	3	3
Don't know	10	5	5	19	20	10	4
3. ANY person with the AIDS virus can pass it on to someone else through sexual intercourse.							
Definitely true	87	92	90	81	81	89	90
Probably true	9	6	7	12	11	8	8
Probably false	1	1	1	0	0	1	0
Definitely false	0	0	0	0	0	0	0
Don't know	3	1	1	6	7	2	1
4. There is a vaccine available to the public that protects a person from getting the AIDS virus.							
Definitely true	2	3	2	3	5	2	2
Probably true	4	4	3	4	6	4	2
Probably false	9	10	9	10	11	10	8
Definitely false	69	71	76	60	48	69	80
Don't know	15	12	10	24	29	15	8
5. There is no cure for AIDS at present.							
Definitely true	85	86	89	81	74	86	91
Probably true	7	6	6	8	8	8	5
Probably false	1	2	1	1	2	1	1
Definitely false	2	2	1	2	3	1	1
Don't know	5	3	3	8	12	4	2
How likely do you think it is that a person will get AIDS or the AIDS virus infection from:							
6. Working near someone with the AIDS virus?							
Very likely	2	2	2	3	4	2	2

(continued on next page)

(continued from previous page)

(percent of persons aged 18 or older with selected AIDS knowledge and attitudes, 1990)

AIDS knowledge or attitude	total	age			education		
		18 to 29	30 to 49	50+	<12 years	12 years	12+ years
Somewhat likely	6%	7%	6%	6%	9%	6%	5%
Somewhat unlikely	9	10	9	9	10	10	8
Very unlikely	40	40	40	40	32	41	43
Definitely not possible	36	40	39	31	31	36	40
Don't know	6	2	4	11	14	5	2

7. Eating in a restaurant where the cook has the AIDS virus?

Very likely	5	4	5	7	8	6	4
Somewhat likely	17	17	17	17	18	18	15
Somewhat unlikely	13	15	13	11	12	12	14
Very unlikely	34	33	37	32	25	34	39
Definitely not possible	21	25	22	18	18	21	24
Don't know	10	6	6	16	19	10	5

8. Sharing plates, forks, or glasses with someone who has the AIDS virus?

Very likely	10	8	9	11	12	10	8
Somewhat likely	22	20	22	22	24	21	20
Somewhat unlikely	13	15	13	12	11	14	14
Very unlikely	29	30	31	26	21	28	34
Definitely not possible	18	22	19	13	15	18	19
Don't know	9	5	6	15	17	9	5

9. Using public toilets?

Very likely	5	6	4	6	9	6	3
Somewhat likely	14	13	13	16	20	14	10
Somewhat unlikely	11	12	11	11	10	13	11
Very unlikely	36	35	39	35	26	36	43
Definitely not possible	25	29	28	18	18	25	29
Don't know	8	5	5	14	16	7	4

10. Sharing needles for drug use with someone who has the AIDS virus?

Very likely	95	97	97	92	90	96	97
Somewhat likely	2	1	1	3	4	2	1
Somewhat unlikely	0	0	0	0	0	0	0
Very unlikely	0	0	0	0	1	0	1
Definitely not possible	0	0	0	0	0	0	0
Don't know	2	1	1	4	5	1	1

11. Being coughed or sneezed on by someone who has the AIDS virus?

Very likely	8	7	7	10	10	8	6
Somewhat likely	20	16	20	23	23	20	18
Somewhat unlikely	15	16	15	13	12	15	16
Very unlikely	30	34	32	26	23	30	35
Definitely not possible	17	22	18	12	14	17	18
Don't know	10	5	7	17	19	10	6

12. Have you ever discussed AIDS with any of your children aged 10 to 17?

Yes	68	56	69	62	51	67	75

(continued on next page)

(percent of persons aged 18 or older with selected AIDS knowledge and attitudes, 1990)

AIDS knowledge or attitude	total	age			education		
		18 to 29	30 to 49	50+	<12 years	12 years	12+ years
No	32%	44%	31%	38%	49%	33%	24%
Don't know	0	-	0	-	-	-	0

13. Have any or all of your children aged 10 to 17 had instruction at school about AIDS

Yes	75	67	77	69	68	77	76
No	9	13	9	9	14	8	9
Don't know	15	20	14	22	18	15	15

14. To the best of your knowledge, are blood donations routinely tested for the AIDS virus infection?

Yes	68	72	77	54	47	66	81
No	4	4	4	4	4	4	4
Don't know	6	6	6	8	9	7	5
Never heard of test	21	18	13	34	40	22	11

15. Do you think the present supply of blood is safe for transfusions?

Yes	46	51	49	39	33	43	56
No	31	31	31	32	35	34	26
Don't know	23	18	20	29	32	23	18

16. Except for blood donations since 1985, have you had your blood tested for the AIDS virus infection?

Yes	10	16	12	3	8	9	12
No	66	64	73	60	50	67	74
Don't know	2	2	2	3	2	2	3
Never heard of test	21	18	13	34	40	22	11

17. Were the blood tests, including those you had before the past 12 months, required or did you go for them voluntarily, or were there some of each? *

All required	52	57	50	47	57	48	54
All volunteered	43	39	46	45	40	47	41
Some of each	3	2	3	3	2	2	3
Don't know	2	1	1	5	1	2	2

18. Was your last test required or did you go for it voluntarily? *

Required	53	58	51	47	58	49	55
Voluntary	44	40	47	48	41	49	42
Don't know	2	1	2	5	1	2	2

19. Was the test required for:*

Hospitalization or a surgical procedure?	9	7	8	19	11	8	9
Health insurance?	3	3	3	3	2	4	4
Life insurance?	6	3	9	3	2	3	9
Employment?	7	7	7	2	3	8	7
Military induction or military service?	9	15	5	4	2	11	10
Immigration?	7	6	8	5	25	3	3
Other	12	16	10	10	12	13	13
Don't know	-	-	-	-	-	-	-

20. Before your last blood test for the AIDS virus infection, were you counseled about the AIDS virus and the meaning of the test? *

Yes	39	40	40	28	38	39	39

(continued on next page)

(continued from previous page)

(percent of persons aged 18 or older with selected AIDS knowledge and attitudes, 1990)

AIDS knowledge or attitude	total	age			education		
		18 to 29	30 to 49	50+	<12 years	12 years	12+ years
No	60%	59%	58%	71%	61%	60%	59%
Don't know	1	0	1	0	-	1	1
21. Did you get the results of your last test? *							
Yes	74	76	72	76	79	74	72
No	25	23	27	23	19	25	26
Don't know	0	0	0	1	-	1	0
22. Did you want the results of your last test? **							
Yes	29	32	27	23	55	23	26
No	67	60	71	74	45	72	69
Don't know	4	8	2	4	-	5	5
23. How effective do you think the use of a condom is to prevent getting the AIDS virus through sexual activity?							
Very effective	27	33	30	20	19	26	32
Somewhat effective	52	54	55	47	42	54	55
Not at all effective	4	5	4	5	7	5	3
Don't know how effective	14	7	10	23	25	13	8
Don't know method	3	2	1	5	7	2	1
24. What are your chances of having the AIDS virus?							
High	0	1	0	0	1	0	0
Medium	2	3	2	2	2	2	2
Low	15	21	18	9	9	14	20
None	80	74	78	87	84	82	77
Don't know	2	2	1	2	4	1	1
25. What are your chances of getting the AIDS virus?							
High	0	0	0	0	0	0	0
Medium	3	3	3	2	2	3	3
Low	21	27	25	12	12	19	27
None	73	66	70	82	80	75	68
Don't know	2	2	2	3	5	2	1
N/A—High chance of already having the AIDS virus	0	1	0	0	1	0	0
26. Have you ever personally known anyone with AIDS or the AIDS virus?							
Yes	15	13	19	11	8	11	21
No	84	86	80	88	91	88	78
Don't know	1	1	1	1	2	1	1

* Based on persons answering yes to question 16. ** Based on persons answering no or don't know to question 21. (-) means that the percentage of responses is too small to be reported.
Source: National Center for Health Statistics

Acute Health Conditions, All Americans

On average, each American comes down with 1.7 acute conditions per year, such as a cold, the flu, or another short-term illness.

(number of acute conditions reported for all persons in thousands, and number of acute conditions per 100 persons in 1988)

	number of acute conditions	
	all persons	per 100 persons, all ages
All acute conditions	**422,277**	**172**
Infective and parasitic diseases	**53,783**	**22**
Common childhood diseases	5,452	2
Intestinal virus, unspecified	11,455	5
Viral infections, unspecified	16,969	7
Other	19,908	8
Respiratory conditions	**209,342**	**85**
Common cold	68,692	28
Other acute upper-respiratory infections	21,993	9
Influenza	103,167	42
Acute bronchitis	8,137	3
Pneumonia	3,007	1
Other respiratory conditions	4,347	2
Digestive system conditions	**15,080**	**6**
Dental conditions	2,910	1
Indigestion, nausea, and vomiting	8,177	3
Other digestive conditions	3,995	2
Injuries	59,161	24
Fractures and dislocations	7,750	3
Sprains and strains	14,517	6
Open wounds and lacerations	13,231	5
Contusions and superficial injuries	11,314	5
Other current injuries	12,349	5
Selected other acute conditions	**58,579**	**24**
Eye conditions	2,864	1
Acute ear infections	19,070	8
Other ear conditions	2,803	1
Acute urinary conditions	6,851	3
Menstruation disorders	1,133	1
Other disorders of female genital tract	1,788	1
Delivery and other conditions of pregnancy	4,494	2
Skin conditions	5,866	2
Acute musculoskeletal conditions	7,889	3
Headache, excluding migraine	2,265	1
Fever, unspecified	3,557	1
All other acute conditions	**26,330**	**11**

Source: National Center for Health Statistics
Note: An acute condition is defined by the National Health Interview Survey as an illness or injury that usually lasts less than three months and was first noticed less than three months before the respondent's interview. The acute condition must also have caused the person to restrict activities for at least half a day or to contact a physician.

Acute Health Conditions, Americans Under Age 5

Preschoolers are most susceptible to acute health conditions, coming down with an average of 3.7 per year. Colds account for a large share of those illnesses.

(number of acute conditions reported for children under age 5 in thousands, share of all acute conditions accounted for by children under age 5, and number of acute conditions per 100 children under age 5 in 1988)

	children under age 5		
	number of acute conditions	**share of acute conditions**	**number of acute conditions per 100 children**
All acute conditions	**66,694**	**16%**	**365**
Infective and parasitic diseases	**9,405**	**17**	**51**
Common childhood diseases	2,135	39	12
Intestinal virus, unspecified	1,630	14	9
Viral infections, unspecified	2,551	15	14
Other	3,090	16	17
Respiratory conditions	**30,393**	**15**	**166**
Common cold	13,010	19	71
Other acute upper-respiratory infections	3,701	17	20
Influenza	10,033	10	55
Acute bronchitis	2,066	25	11
Pneumonia	647	22	4
Other respiratory conditions	937	22	5
Digestive system conditions	**2,035**	**13**	**11**
Dental conditions	612	21	3
Indigestion, nausea, and vomiting	831	10	5
Other digestive conditions	592	15	3
Injuries	**4,934**	**8**	**27**
Fractures and dislocations	280	4	2
Sprains and strains	241	2	1
Open wounds and lacerations	1,846	14	10
Contusions and superficial injuries	868	8	5
Other current injuries	1,698	14	9
Selected other acute conditions	**15,697**	**27**	**86**
Eye conditions	441	15	2
Acute ear infections	10,694	56	59
Other ear conditions	663	24	4
Acute urinary conditions	247	4	1
Menstruation disorders	-	0	0
Other disorders of female genital tract	49	3	0
Delivery and other conditions of pregnancy	-	0	0
Skin conditions	1,648	28	9
Acute musculoskeletal conditions	99	1	1
Headache, excluding migraine	-	0	0
Fever, unspecified	1854	52	10
All other acute conditions	**4230**	**16**	**23**

Source: National Center for Health Statistics. Note: An acute condition is defined by the National Health Interview Survey as an illness or injury that usually lasts less than three months and was first noticed less than three months before the respondent's interview. The acute condition must also have caused the person to restrict activities for at least half a day or to contact a physician.

Acute Health Conditions, Children Aged 5 to 17

School-aged children get between two and three acute conditions per year, with colds and flu being the most common.

(number of acute conditions reported for children aged 5 to 17 in thousands, share of all acute conditions accounted for by children aged 5 to 17, and number of acute conditions per 100 children aged 5 to 17 in 1988)

	children aged 5 to 17		
	number of acute conditions	share of acute conditions	number of acute conditions per 100 children
All acute conditions	**112,018**	**27%**	**247**
Infective and parasitic diseases	**21,083**	**39**	**46**
Common childhood diseases	2,995	55	7
Intestinal virus, unspecified	3,602	31	8
Viral infections, unspecified	5,649	33	12
Other	8,836	44	19
Respiratory conditions	**59,413**	**28**	**131**
Common cold	18,843	27	42
Other acute upper-respiratory infections	8,248	38	18
Influenza	29,053	28	64
Acute bronchitis	1,799	22	4
Pneumonia	520	17	1
Other respiratory conditions	951	22	2
Digestive system conditions	**3,664**	**24**	**8**
Dental conditions	582	20	1
Indigestion, nausea, and vomiting	2,636	32	6
Other digestive conditions	446	11	1
Injuries	**13,498**	**23**	**30**
Fractures and dislocations	2,044	26	5
Sprains and strains	3,620	25	8
Open wounds and lacerations	2,602	20	6
Contusions and superficial injuries	2,825	25	6
Other current injuries	2,407	19	5
Selected other acute conditions	**11,583**	**20**	**26**
Eye conditions	489	17	1
Acute ear infections	5,491	29	12
Other ear conditions	923	33	2
Acute urinary conditions	320	5	1
Menstruation disorders	254	22	1
Other disorders of female genital tract	0	0	0
Delivery and other conditions of pregnancy	271	6	1
Skin conditions	1,028	18	2
Acute musculoskeletal conditions	696	9	2
Headache, excluding migraine	804	35	2
Fever, unspecified	1,307	37	3
All other acute conditions	**2,776**	**11**	**6**

Source: National Center for Health Statistics. Note: An acute condition is defined by the National Health Interview Survey as an illness or injury that usually lasts less than three months and was first noticed less than three months before the respondent's interview. The acute condition must also have caused the person to restrict activities for at least half a day or to contact a physician.

Acute Health Conditions, People Aged 18 to 24

Only about one in four 18-to-24-year-olds gets a cold each year. More than one-third get the flu. Sprains and strains affect one in ten.

(number of acute conditions reported for persons aged 18 to 24 in thousands, share of all acute conditions accounted for by persons aged 18 to 24, and number of acute conditions per 100 persons aged 18 to 24 in 1988)

	persons aged 18 to 24		
	number of acute conditions	share of acute conditions	number of acute conditions per 100 persons
All acute conditions	**42,663**	**10%**	**159**
Infective and parasitic diseases	**12,909**	**24**	**48**
Common childhood diseases	182	3	1
Intestinal virus, unspecified	1,451	13	5
Viral infections, unspecified	1,176	7	4
Other	2,065	10	8
Respiratory conditions	**20,025**	**10**	**74**
Common cold	6,752	10	25
Other acute upper-respiratory infections	1,980	9	7
Influenza	10,033	10	37
Acute bronchitis	490	6	2
Pneumonia	113	4	0
Other respiratory conditions	656	15	2
Digestive system conditions	**1,675**	**11**	**6**
Dental conditions	432	15	2
Indigestion, nausea, and vomiting	880	11	3
Other digestive conditions	363	9	1
Injuries	**8,406**	**14**	**31**
Fractures and dislocations	1,045	13	4
Sprains and strains	2,812	19	10
Open wounds and lacerations	1,992	15	7
Contusions and superficial injuries	1,269	11	5
Other current injuries	1,287	10	5
Selected other acute conditions	**5,703**	**10**	**21**
Eye conditions	130	5	0
Acute ear infections	545	3	2
Other ear conditions	192	7	1
Acute urinary conditions	868	13	3
Menstruation disorders	428	38	2
Other disorders of female genital tract	386	22	1
Delivery and other conditions of pregnancy	1,447	32	5
Skin conditions	285	5	1
Acute musculoskeletal conditions	849	11	3
Headache, excluding migraine	522	23	2
Fever, unspecified	52	1	0
All other acute conditions	**1,980**	**8**	**7**

Source: National Center for Health Statistics. Note: An acute condition is defined by the National Health Interview Survey as an illness or injury that usually lasts less than three months and was first noticed less than three months before the respondent's interview. The acute condition must also have caused the person to restrict activities for at least half a day or to contact a physician.

Acute Health Conditions, People Aged 25 to 34

Colds and flu are the most common acute conditions suffered by 25-to-34-year-olds. They account for more than 40 percent of all acute illnesses in this age group.

(number of acute conditions reported for persons aged 25 to 34 in thousands, share of all acute conditions accounted for by persons aged 25 to 34, and number of acute conditions per 100 persons aged 25 to 34 in 1988)

	persons aged 25 to 34		
	number of acute conditions	share of acute conditions	number of acute conditions per 100 persons
All acute conditions	**70,909**	**17%**	**162**
Infective and parasitic diseases	**8,638**	**16**	**20**
Common childhood diseases	139	3	0
Intestinal virus, unspecified	2,275	20	5
Viral infections, unspecified	3,054	18	7
Other	3,171	16	7
Respiratory conditions	**35,799**	**17**	**82**
Common cold	11,349	17	26
Other acute upper-respiratory infections	3,364	15	8
Influenza	19,291	19	44
Acute bronchitis	1,032	13	2
Pneumonia	212	7	0
Other respiratory conditions	550	13	1
Digestive system conditions	**2,162**	**14**	**5**
Dental conditions	532	18	1
Indigestion, nausea, and vomiting	1,357	17	3
Other digestive conditions	273	7	1
Injuries	**11,605**	**20**	**26**
Fractures and dislocations	1,353	17	3
Sprains and strains	3,130	22	7
Open wounds and lacerations	2,874	22	7
Contusions and superficial injuries	1,886	17	4
Other current injuries	2,362	19	5
Selected other acute conditions	**9,121**	**16**	**21**
Eye conditions	513	18	1
Acute ear infections	660	3	2
Other ear conditions	345	12	1
Acute urinary conditions	1,587	23	4
Menstruation disorders	201	18	0
Other disorders of female genital tract	739	41	2
Delivery and other conditions of pregnancy	2,472	55	6
Skin conditions	479	8	1
Acute musculoskeletal conditions	1,592	20	4
Headache, excluding migraine	392	17	1
Fever, unspecified	142	4	0
All other acute conditions	**3,584**	**14**	**8**

Source: National Center for Health Statistics. Note: An acute condition is defined by the National Health Interview Survey as an illness or injury that usually lasts less than three months and was first noticed less than three months before the respondent's interview. The acute condition must also have caused the person to restrict activities for at least half a day or to contact a physician.

Acute Health Conditions, People Aged 35 to 44

Only one-fifth of 35-to-44-year-olds get a cold each year, but over 40 percent get the flu. About one-fifth of people in this age group are injured each year.

(number of acute conditions reported for persons aged 35 to 44 in thousands, share of all acute conditions accounted for by persons aged 35 to 44, and number of acute conditions per 100 persons aged 35 to 44 in 1988)

	persons aged 35 to 44		
	number of acute conditions	**share of acute conditions**	**number of acute conditions per 100 persons**
All acute conditions	**49,580**	**12%**	**140**
Infective and parasitic diseases	**4,566**	**8**	**13**
Common childhood diseases	0	0	0
Intestinal virus, unspecified	1,237	11	4
Viral infections, unspecified	1,611	9	5
Other	1,718	9	5
Respiratory conditions	**25,868**	**12**	**73**
Common cold	7,046	10	20
Other acute upper-respiratory infections	2,477	11	7
Influenza	14,603	14	41
Acute bronchitis	1,052	13	3
Pneumonia	336	11	1
Other respiratory conditions	353	8	1
Digestive system conditions	**1,814**	**12**	**5**
Dental conditions	174	6	0
Indigestion, nausea, and vomiting	723	9	2
Other digestive conditions	367	9	1
Injuries	**7,897**	**13**	**22**
Fractures and dislocations	1,150	15	3
Sprains and strains	1,956	13	6
Open wounds and lacerations	1,472	11	4
Contusions and superficial injuries	1,851	16	5
Other current injuries	1,469	12	4
Selected other acute conditions	**5,875**	**10**	**17**
Eye conditions	249	9	1
Acute ear infections	828	4	2
Other ear conditions	105	4	0
Acute urinary conditions	1,134	17	3
Menstruation disorders	196	17	1
Other disorders of female genital tract	366	20	1
Delivery and other conditions of pregnancy	304	7	1
Skin conditions	730	12	2
Acute musculoskeletal conditions	1,508	19	4
Headache, excluding migraine	355	16	1
Fever, unspecified	100	3	0
All other acute conditions	**3,560**	**14**	**10**

Source: National Center for Health Statistics. Note: An acute condition is defined by the National Health Interview Survey as an illness or injury that usually lasts less than three months and was first noticed less than three months before the respondent's interview. The acute condition must also have caused the person to restrict activities for at least half a day or to contact a physician.

Acute Health Conditions, People Aged 45 to 54

People aged 45 to 54 suffer from an average of only one acute condition per year as colds and the flu become less troublesome.

(number of acute conditions reported for persons aged 45 to 54 in thousands, share of all acute conditions accounted for by persons aged 45 to 54, and number of acute conditions per 100 persons aged 45 to 54 in 1988)

	persons aged 45 to 54		
	number of acute conditions	*share of acute conditions*	*number of acute conditions per 100 persons*
All acute conditions	**26,182**	**6%**	**108**
Infective and parasitic diseases	**2,187**	**4**	**9**
Common childhood diseases	0	0	0
Intestinal virus, unspecified	633	6	3
Viral infections, unspecified	1,200	7	5
Other	354	2	1
Respiratory conditions	**14,319**	**7**	**59**
Common cold	4,079	6	17
Other acute upper-respiratory infections	998	5	4
Influenza	7,947	8	33
Acute bronchitis	640	8	3
Pneumonia	519	17	2
Other respiratory conditions	137	3	1
Digestive system conditions	**775**	**5**	**3**
Dental conditions	116	4	0
Indigestion, nausea, and vomiting	276	3	1
Other digestive conditions	382	10	2
Injuries	**3,569**	**6**	**15**
Fractures and dislocations	543	7	2
Sprains and strains	1,140	8	5
Open wounds and lacerations	581	4	2
Contusions and superficial injuries	675	6	3
Other current injuries	631	5	3
Selected other acute conditions	**3,154**	**5**	**13**
Eye conditions	340	12	1
Acute ear infections	351	2	1
Other ear conditions	160	6	1
Acute urinary conditions	630	9	3
Menstruation disorders	54	5	0
Other disorders of female genital tract	145	8	1
Delivery and other conditions of pregnancy	-	0	0
Skin conditions	419	7	2
Acute musculoskeletal conditions	1,828	23	8
Headache, excluding migraine	96	4	0
Fever, unspecified	50	1	0
All other acute conditions	**2,178**	**8**	**9**

Source: National Center for Health Statistics. Note: An acute condition is defined by the National Health Interview Survey as an illness or injury that usually lasts less than three months and was first noticed less than three months before the respondent's interview. The acute condition must also have caused the person to restrict activities for a least a half day or to have contacted a physician.

Acute Health Conditions, People Aged 55 to 64

Colds are uncommon among people aged 55 to 64, but the flu continues to strike nearly one-third of them each year.

(number of acute conditions reported for persons aged 55 to 64 in thousands, share of all acute conditions accounted for by persons aged 55 to 64, and number of acute conditions per 100 persons aged 55 to 64 in 1988)

	persons aged 55 to 64		
	number of acute conditions	share of acute conditions	number of acute conditions per 100 persons
All acute conditions	**22,996**	**5%**	**105**
Infective and parasitic diseases	**1,414**	**3**	**6**
Common childhood diseases	0	0	0
Intestinal virus, unspecified	264	2	1
Viral infections, unspecified	734	4	3
Other	416	2	2
Respiratory conditions	**10,938**	**5**	**50**
Common cold	3,085	4	14
Other acute upper-respiratory infections	615	3	3
Influenza	6,485	6	30
Acute bronchitis	116	1	1
Pneumonia	256	9	1
Other respiratory conditions	381	9	2
Digestive system conditions	**1,133**	**8**	**5**
Dental conditions	169	6	1
Indigestion, nausea, and vomiting	521	6	2
Other digestive conditions	442	11	2
Injuries	**3,339**	**6**	**15**
Fractures and dislocations	534	7	2
Sprains and strains	770	5	4
Open wounds and lacerations	577	4	3
Contusions and superficial injuries	489	4	2
Other current injuries	970	8	4
Selected other acute conditions	**2,985**	**5**	**14**
Eye conditions	260	9	1
Acute ear infections	286	1	1
Other ear conditions	85	3	0
Acute urinary conditions	788	12	4
Menstruation disorders	-	0	0
Other disorders of female genital tract	53	3	0
Delivery and other conditions of pregnancy	-	0	0
Skin conditions	586	10	3
Acute musculoskeletal conditions	896	11	4
Headache, excluding migraine	0	0	0
Fever, unspecified	51	1	0
All other acute conditions	**3,188**	**12**	**15**

Source: National Center for Health Statistics. Note: An acute condition is defined by the National Health Interview Survey as an illness or injury that usually lasts less than three months and was first noticed less than three months before the respondent's interview. The acute condition must also have caused the person to restrict activities for a least a half day or to have contacted a physician.

Acute Health Conditions, People Aged 65 to 74

People aged 65 to 74 come down with an average of only one acute health condition per year, much less than among younger people.

(number of acute conditions reported for persons aged 65 to 74 in thousands, share of all acute conditions accounted for by persons aged 65 to 74, and number of acute conditions per 100 persons aged 65 to 74 in 1988)

	persons aged 65 to 74		
	number of acute conditions	share of acute conditions	number of acute conditions per 100 persons
All acute conditions	**18,938**	**4%**	**106**
Infective and parasitic diseases	**1,235**	**2**	**7**
Common childhood diseases	0	0	0
Intestinal virus, unspecified	268	2	1
Viral infections, unspecified	752	4	4
Other	214	1	1
Respiratory conditions	**8,557**	**4**	**48**
Common cold	2,689	4	15
Other acute upper-respiratory infections	406	2	2
Influenza	4,271	4	24
Acute bronchitis	652	8	4
Pneumonia	252	8	1
Other respiratory conditions	288	7	2
Digestive system conditions	**684**	**5**	**4**
Dental conditions	106	4	1
Indigestion, nausea, and vomiting	379	5	2
Other digestive conditions	199	5	1
Injuries	**3,140**	**5**	**18**
Fractures and dislocations	484	6	3
Sprains and strains	423	3	2
Open wounds and lacerations	840	6	5
Contusions and superficial injuries	655	6	4
Other current injuries	738	6	4
Selected other acute conditions	**2,432**	**4**	**14**
Eye conditions	96	3	1
Acute ear infections	165	1	1
Other ear conditions	211	8	1
Acute urinary conditions	505	7	3
Menstruation disorders	-	0	0
Other disorders of female genital tract	-	0	0
Delivery and other conditions of pregnancy	-	0	0
Skin conditions	530	9	3
Acute musculoskeletal conditions	877	11	5
Headache, excluding migraine	47	2	0
Fever, unspecified	0	0	0
All other acute conditions	**2,889**	**11**	**16**

Source: National Center for Health Statistics. Note: An acute condition is defined by the National Health Interview Survey as an illness or injury that usually lasts less than three months and was first noticed less than three months before the respondent's interview. The acute condition must also have caused the person to restrict activities for a least a half day or to have contacted a physician.

Acute Health Conditions, People Aged 75 or older

People aged 75 or older are more likely to be injured than they are to catch a cold or the flu. This age group accounts for just 3 percent of all acute conditions suffered each year.

(number of acute conditions reported for persons aged 75 or older in thousands, share of all acute conditions accounted for by persons aged 75 or older, and number of acute conditions per 100 persons aged 75 or older in 1988)

	persons aged 75 or older		
	number of acute conditions	share of acute conditions	number of acute conditions per 100 persons
All acute conditions	**12,297**	**3%**	**98**
Infective and parasitic diseases	**379**	**1**	**3**
Common childhood diseases	0	0	0
Intestinal virus, unspecified	93	1	1
Viral infections, unspecified	242	1	2
Other	45	0	0
Respiratory conditions	**4,031**	**2**	**32**
Common cold	1,839	3	15
Other acute upper-respiratory infections	203	1	2
Influenza	1,452	1	12
Acute bronchitis	291	4	2
Pneumonia	152	5	1
Other respiratory conditions	94	2	1
Digestive system conditions	**1,137**	**8**	**9**
Dental conditions	0	0	0
Indigestion, nausea, and vomiting	483	6	4
Other digestive conditions	654	16	5
Injuries	**2,773**	**5**	**22**
Fractures and dislocations	317	4	3
Sprains and strains	425	3	3
Open wounds and lacerations	445	3	4
Contusions and superficial injuries	798	7	6
Other current injuries	789	6	6
Selected other acute conditions	**2,030**	**3**	**16**
Eye conditions	349	12	3
Acute ear infections	50	0	0
Other ear conditions	118	4	1
Acute urinary conditions	771	11	6
Menstruation disorders	-	0	0
Other disorders of female genital tract	50	3	0
Delivery and other conditions of pregnancy	-	0	0
Skin conditions	160	3	1
Acute musculoskeletal conditions	483	6	4
Headache, excluding migraine	49	2	0
Fever, unspecified	0	0	0
All other acute conditions	**1,945**	**7**	**16**

Source: National Center for Health Statistics. Note: An acute condition is defined by the National Health Interview Survey as an illness or injury that usually lasts less than three months and was first noticed less than three months before the respondent's interview. The acute condition must also have caused the person to restrict activities for a least a half day or to have contacted a physician.

Chronic Health Conditions, All Americans

The most common chronic condition among Americans is sinusitis, followed by arthritis and high blood pressure.

(number of chronic conditions reported for all persons in thousands, and number of chronic conditions per 100 persons in 1988)

	number of chronic conditions	
	all persons	per 100 persons, all ages
Selected skin and musculoskeletal conditions		
Arthritis	31,291	12.7
Gout, including gouty arthritis	2,050	0.8
Trouble with bunions	2,616	1.1
Bursitis, unclassified	4,428	1.8
Sebaceous skin cyst	1,480	0.6
Trouble with acne	4,533	1.8
Psoriasis	2,267	0.9
Dermatitis	9,025	3.7
Trouble with dry, itching skin, unclassified	4,788	1.9
Trouble with ingrown nails	6,177	2.5
Trouble with corns and calluses	4,534	1.8
Selected respiratory conditions		
Chronic bronchitis	11,893	4.8
Asthma	9,934	4.0
Hay fever or allergic rhinitis without asthma	22,413	9.1
Chronic sinusitis	33,657	13.7
Chronic disease of tonsils or adenoids	3,659	1.5
Emphysema	1,905	0.8
Selected digestive conditions		
Ulcer	3,847	1.6
Hernia of abdominal cavity	4,744	1.9
Gastritis or duodenitis	2,716	1.1
Frequent indigestion	5,817	2.4
Enteritis or colitis	2,510	1.0
Spastic colon	1,421	0.6
Diverticula of intestines	1,850	0.8
Frequent constipation	4,580	1.9
Selected circulatory conditions		
Ischemic heart disease	7,482	3.0
Tachycardia or rapid heart	1,727	0.7
Heart murmurs	4,634	1.9
Other heart rhythm disorders	1,702	0.7
Other heart diseases	4,072	1.7
High blood pressure (hypertension)	29,256	11.9
Cerebrovascular disease	2,516	1.0

(continued on next page)

(continued from previous page)

(number of chronic conditions reported for all persons in thousands, and number of chronic conditions per 100 persons in 1988)

	number of chronic conditions	
	all persons	per 100 persons, all ages
Hardening of the arteries	2,710	1.1
Varicose veins	7,632	3.1
Hemorrhoids	11,041	4.5
Selected other chronic conditions		
Goiter or other disorders of the thyroid	4,012	1.6
Diabetes	6,221	2.5
Anemia	3,987	1.6
Epilepsy	911	0.4
Migraine headache	9,222	3.7
Kidney trouble	3,310	1.3
Bladder disorders	3,076	1.3
Diseases of prostate	1,502	0.6
Prostate malignancy	221	0.1
Inflammatory female genital diseases	297	0.1
Noninflammatory female genital diseases	929	0.4
Menstrual disorders	2,029	0.8
Breast malignancy	698	0.3
Benign neoplasm of breast/female genital	907	0.4
Selected impairments		
Visual impairment	8,364	3.4
Cataracts	6,104	2.5
Glaucoma	1,866	0.8
Hearing impairment	21,863	8.9
Tinnitus	6,360	2.6

Source: National Center for Health Statistics
Note: Chronic conditions are defined by the National Health Interview Survey as conditions that either a) were noticed three months or more before the date of the interview or, b) belong to a group of conditions (such as heart disease or diabetes) that are considered chronic regardless of when they began. Totals for all chronic conditions are not shown because the National Health Interview Survey does not measure the total number of chronic conditions for each person.

Chronic Health Conditions, Children Under Age 5

Preschoolers are most likely to suffer from acute conditions but are least likely to have any chronic conditions.

(number of chronic conditions reported for children under age 5 in thousands, share of all chronic conditions accounted for by children under age 5, and number of chronic conditions per 100 children under age 5 in 1988)

	children under age 5		
	number of chronic conditions	share of chronic conditions	number of chronic conditions per 100 persons
Selected skin and musculoskeletal conditions			
Arthritis	11	0.0%	0.1
Gout, including gouty arthritis	0	0.0	0.0
Trouble with bunions	0	0.0	0.0
Bursitis, unclassified	15	0.3	0.1
Sebaceous skin cyst	0	0.0	0.0
Trouble with acne	12	0.3	0.1
Psoriasis	51	2.2	0.3
Dermatitis	754	8.4	4.1
Trouble with dry, itching skin, unclassified	127	2.7	0.7
Trouble with ingrown nails	39	0.6	0.2
Trouble with corns and calluses	0	0.0	0.0
Selected respiratory conditions			
Chronic bronchitis	1,121	9.4	6.1
Asthma	617	6.2	3.4
Hay fever or allergic rhinitis without asthma	493	2.2	2.7
Chronic sinusitis	460	1.4	2.5
Chronic disease of tonsils or adenoids	429	11.7	2.3
Emphysema	0	0.0	0.0
Selected digestive conditions			
Ulcer	0	0.0	0.0
Hernia of abdominal cavity	230	4.8	1.3
Gastritis or duodenitis	21	0.8	0.1
Frequent indigestion	33	0.6	0.2
Enteritis or colitis	183	7.3	1.0
Spastic colon	0	0.0	0.0
Diverticula of intestines	0	0.0	0.0
Frequent constipation	251	5.5	1.4
Selected circulatory conditions			
Ischemic heart disease	0	0.0	0.0
Tachycardia or rapid heart	19	1.1	0.1
Heart murmurs	324	7.0	1.8
Other heart rhythm disorders	5	0.3	0.0
Other heart diseases	33	0.8	0.2
High blood pressure (hypertension)	11	0.0	0.1
Cerebrovascular disease	17	0.7	0.1

(continued on next page)

(continued from previous page)

(number of chronic conditions reported for children under age 5 in thousands, share of all chronic conditions accounted for by children under age 5, and number of chronic conditions per 100 children under age 5 in 1988)

	children under age 5		
	number of chronic conditions	share of chronic conditions	number of chronic conditions per 100 persons
Hardening of the arteries	0	0.0%	0.0
Varicose veins	0	0.0	0.0
Hemorrhoids	13	0.1	0.1
Selected other chronic conditions			
Goiter or other disorders of the thyroid	4	0.1	0.0
Diabetes	20	0.3	0.1
Anemia	362	9.1	2.0
Epilepsy	62	6.8	0.3
Migraine headache	12	0.1	0.1
Kidney trouble	22	0.7	0.1
Bladder disorders	21	0.7	0.1
Diseases of prostate	0	0.0	0.0
Prostate malignancy	0	0.0	0.0
Inflammatory female genital diseases	0	0.0	0.0
Noninflammatory female genital diseases	0	0.0	0.0
Menstrual disorders	0	0.0	0.0
Breast malignancy	0	0.0	0.0
Benign neoplasm of breast/female genital	0	0.0	0.0
Selected impairments			
Visual impairment	0	0.0	0.0
Cataracts	11	0.2	0.1
Glaucoma	0	0.0	0.0
Hearing impairment	151	0.7	0.8
Tinnitus	0	0.0	0.0

Source: National Center for Health Statistics
Note: Chronic conditions are defined by the National Health Interview Survey as conditions that either a) were noticed three months or more before the date of the interview or, b) belong to a group of conditions (such as heart disease or diabetes) that are considered chronic regardless of when they began. Totals for all chronic conditions are not shown because the National Health Interview Survey does not measure the total number of conditions for each person.

Chronic Health Conditions, Children Aged 5 to 17

School-aged children account for over one-third of all Americans who suffer from acne and for over half of those who have problems with tonsils or adenoids.

(number of chronic conditions reported for children aged 5 to 17 in thousands, share of all chronic conditions accounted for by children aged 5 to 17, and number of chronic conditions per 100 children aged 5 to 17 in 1988)

	children aged 5 to 17		
	number of chronic conditions	share of chronic conditions	number of chronic conditions per 100 persons
Selected skin and musculoskeletal conditions			
Arthritis	138	0.4%	0.3
Gout, including gouty arthritis	0	0.0	0.0
Trouble with bunions	44	1.7	0.1
Bursitis, unclassified	21	0.5	0.0
Sebaceous skin cyst	119	8.0	0.3
Trouble with acne	1,685	37.2	3.7
Psoriasis	174	7.7	0.4
Dermatitis	1,467	16.3	3.2
Trouble with dry, itching skin, unclassified	483	10.1	1.1
Trouble with ingrown nails	479	7.8	1.1
Trouble with corns and calluses	55	1.2	0.1
Selected respiratory conditions			
Chronic bronchitis	2,332	19.6	5.1
Asthma	2,554	25.7	5.6
Hay fever or allergic rhinitis without asthma	3,534	15.8	7.8
Chronic sinusitis	3,443	10.2	7.6
Chronic disease of tonsils or adenoids	1,877	51.3	4.1
Emphysema	0	0.0	0.0
Selected digestive conditions			
Ulcer	28	0.7	0.1
Hernia of abdominal cavity	135	2.8	0.3
Gastritis or duodenitis	121	4.5	0.3
Frequent indigestion	188	3.2	0.4
Enteritis or colitis	78	3.1	0.2
Spastic colon	0	0.0	0.0
Diverticula of intestines	0	0.0	0.0
Frequent constipation	326	7.1	0.7
Selected circulatory conditions			
Ischemic heart disease	0	0.0	0.0
Tachycardia or rapid heart	45	2.6	0.1
Heart murmurs	802	17.3	1.8
Other heart rhythm disorders	0	0.0	0.0
Other heart diseases	22	0.5	0.0
High blood pressure (hypertension)	135	0.5	0.3
Cerebrovascular disease	10	0.4	0.0

(continued on next page)

(continued from previous page)

(number of chronic conditions reported for children aged 5 to 17 in thousands, share of all chronic conditions accounted for by children aged 5 to 17, and number of chronic conditions per 100 children aged 5 to 17 in 1988)

	children aged 5 to 17		
	number of chronic conditions	*share of chronic conditions*	*number of chronic conditions per 100 persons*
Hardening of the arteries	0	0.0%	0.0
Varicose veins	0	0.0	0.0
Hemorrhoids	66	0.6	0.1
Selected other chronic conditions			
Goiter or other disorders of the thyroid	36	0.9	0.1
Diabetes	118	1.9	0.3
Anemia	297	7.4	0.7
Epilepsy	80	8.8	0.2
Migraine headache	893	9.7	2.0
Kidney trouble	175	5.3	0.4
Bladder disorders	240	7.8	0.5
Diseases of prostate	0	0.0	0.0
Prostate malignancy	0	0.0	0.0
Inflammatory female genital diseases	12	4.0	0.0
Noninflammatory female genital diseases	26	2.8	0.1
Menstrual disorders	196	9.7	0.4
Breast malignancy	0	0.0	0.0
Benign neoplasm of breast/female genital	0	0.0	0.0
Selected impairments			
Visual impairment	578	6.9	1.3
Cataracts	52	0.9	0.1
Glaucoma	0	0.0	0.0
Hearing impairment	925	4.2	2.0
Tinnitus	70	1.1	0.2

Source: National Center for Health Statistics
Note: Chronic conditions are defined by the National Health Interview Survey as conditions that either a) were noticed three months or more before the date of the interview or, b) belong to a group of conditions (such as heart disease or diabetes) that are considered chronic regardless of when they began. Totals for all chronic conditions are not shown because the National Health Interview Survey does not measure the total number conditions for each person.

Chronic Health Conditions, People Aged 18 to 24

Young adults account for more than one-fourth of Americans with acne, and for one in ten migraine sufferers.

(number of chronic conditions reported for persons aged 18 to 24 in thousands, share of all chronic conditions accounted for by persons aged 18 to 24, and number of chronic conditions per 100 persons aged 18 to 24 in 1988)

	persons aged 18 to 24		
	number of chronic conditions	*share of chronic conditions*	*number of chronic conditions per 100 persons*
Selected skin and musculoskeletal conditions			
Arthritis	503	1.6%	1.9
Gout, including gouty arthritis	0	0.0	0.0
Trouble with bunions	157	6.0	0.6
Bursitis, unclassified	129	2.9	0.5
Sebaceous skin cyst	113	7.6	0.4
Trouble with acne	1,145	25.3	4.3
Psoriasis	174	7.7	0.6
Dermatitis	934	10.3	3.5
Trouble with dry, itching skin, unclassified	472	9.9	1.8
Trouble with ingrown nails	669	10.8	2.5
Trouble with corns and calluses	276	6.1	1.0
Selected respiratory conditions			
Chronic bronchitis	886	7.4	3.3
Asthma	1,032	10.4	3.8
Hay fever or allergic rhinitis without asthma	2,671	11.9	9.9
Chronic sinusitis	3,346	9.9	12.4
Chronic disease of tonsils or adenoids	466	12.7	1.7
Emphysema	0	0.0	0.0
Selected digestive conditions			
Ulcer	344	8.9	1.3
Hernia of abdominal cavity	78	1.6	0.3
Gastritis or duodenitis	125	4.6	0.5
Frequent indigestion	391	6.7	1.5
Enteritis or colitis	98	3.9	0.4
Spastic colon	49	3.4	0.2
Diverticula of intestines	0	0.0	0.0
Frequent constipation	205	4.5	0.8
Selected circulatory conditions			
Ischemic heart disease	25	0.3	0.1
Tachycardia or rapid heart	104	6.0	0.4
Heart murmurs	381	8.2	1.4
Other heart rhythm disorders	73	4.3	0.3
Other heart diseases	85	2.1	0.3
High blood pressure (hypertension)	657	2.2	2.4
Cerebrovascular disease	0	0.0	0.0

(continued on next page)

(continued from previous page)

(number of chronic conditions reported for persons aged 18 to 24 in thousands, share of all chronic conditions accounted for by persons aged 18 to 24, and number of chronic conditions per 100 persons aged 18 to 24 in 1988)

	persons aged 18 to 24		
	number of chronic conditions	share of chronic conditions	number of chronic conditions per 100 persons
Hardening of the arteries	0	0.0%	0.0
Varicose veins	297	3.9	1.1
Hemorrhoids	514	4.7	1.9
Selected other chronic conditions			
Goiter or other disorders of the thyroid	125	3.1	0.5
Diabetes	77	1.2	0.3
Anemia	500	12.5	1.9
Epilepsy	83	9.1	0.3
Migraine headache	965	10.5	3.6
Kidney trouble	393	11.9	1.5
Bladder disorders	227	7.4	0.8
Diseases of prostate	0	0.0	0.0
Prostate malignancy	0	0.0	0.0
Inflammatory female genital diseases	96	32.3	0.4
Noninflammatory female genital diseases	104	11.2	0.4
Menstrual disorders	395	19.5	1.5
Breast malignancy	0	0.0	0.0
Benign neoplasm of breast/female genital	57	6.3	0.2
Selected impairments			
Visual impairment	536	6.4	2.0
Cataracts	54	0.9	0.2
Glaucoma	11	0.6	0.0
Hearing impairment	921	4.2	3.4
Tinnitus	233	3.7	0.9

Source: National Center for Health Statistics
Note: Chronic conditions are defined by the National Health Interview Survey as conditions that either a) were noticed three months or more before the date of the interview or, b) belong to a group of conditions (such as heart disease or diabetes) that are considered chronic regardless of when they began. Totals for all chronic conditions are not shown because the National Health Interview Survey does not measure the total number of conditions for each person.

Chronic Health Conditions, People Aged 25 to 34

People aged 25 to 34 account for more than one in five cases of many chronic conditions such as acne, hay fever, and menstrual disorders.

(number of chronic conditions reported for persons aged 25 to 34 in thousands, share of all chronic conditions accounted for by persons aged 25 to 34, and number of chronic conditions per 100 persons aged 25 to 34 in 1988)

	persons aged 25 to 34		
	number of chronic conditions	share of chronic conditions	number of chronic conditions per 100 persons
Selected skin and musculoskeletal conditions			
Arthritis	1,778	5.7%	4.1
Gout, including gouty arthritis	118	5.8	0.3
Trouble with bunions	287	11.0	0.7
Bursitis, unclassified	477	10.8	1.1
Sebaceous skin cyst	459	31.0	1.0
Trouble with acne	1,081	23.8	2.5
Psoriasis	388	17.1	0.9
Dermatitis	1,973	21.9	4.5
Trouble with dry, itching skin, unclassified	997	20.8	2.3
Trouble with ingrown nails	1,166	18.9	2.7
Trouble with corns and calluses	619	13.7	1.4
Selected respiratory conditions			
Chronic bronchitis	1,721	14.5	3.9
Asthma	1,621	16.3	3.7
Hay fever or allergic rhinitis without asthma	4,948	22.1	11.3
Chronic sinusitis	6,655	19.8	15.2
Chronic disease of tonsils or adenoids	491	13.4	1.1
Emphysema	24	1.3	0.1
Selected digestive conditions			
Ulcer	763	19.8	1.7
Hernia of abdominal cavity	259	5.5	0.6
Gastritis or duodenitis	512	18.9	1.2
Frequent indigestion	1,081	18.6	2.5
Enteritis or colitis	491	19.6	1.1
Spastic colon	266	18.7	0.6
Diverticula of intestines	11	0.6	0.0
Frequent constipation	488	10.7	1.1
Selected circulatory conditions			
Ischemic heart disease	55	0.7	0.1
Tachycardia or rapid heart	143	8.3	0.3
Heart murmurs	832	18.0	1.9
Other heart rhythm disorders	96	5.6	0.2
Other heart diseases	195	4.8	0.4
High blood pressure (hypertension)	2,266	7.7	5.2
Cerebrovascular disease	54	2.1	0.1

(continued on next page)

(continued from previous page)

(number of chronic conditions reported for persons aged 25 to 34 in thousands, share of all chronic conditions accounted for by persons aged 25 to 34, and number of chronic conditions per 100 persons aged 25 to 34 in 1988)

	persons aged 25 to 34		
	number of chronic conditions	share of chronic conditions	number of chronic conditions per 100 persons
Hardening of the arteries	0	0.0%	0.0
Varicose veins	1,200	15.7	2.7
Hemorrhoids	2,479	22.5	5.7
Selected other chronic conditions			
Goiter or other disorders of the thyroid	366	9.1	0.8
Diabetes	318	5.1	0.7
Anemia	822	20.6	1.9
Epilepsy	207	22.7	0.5
Migraine headache	2,483	26.9	5.7
Kidney trouble	630	19.0	1.4
Bladder disorders	462	15.0	1.1
Diseases of prostate	54	3.6	0.1
Prostate malignancy	0	0.0	0.0
Inflammatory female genital diseases	102	34.3	0.2
Noninflammatory female genital diseases	354	38.1	0.8
Menstrual disorders	711	35.0	1.6
Breast malignancy	0	0.0	0.0
Benign neoplasm of breast/female genital	174	19.2	0.4
Selected impairments			
Visual impairment	1,144	13.7	2.6
Cataracts	113	1.9	0.3
Glaucoma	44	2.4	0.1
Hearing impairment	1,760	8.1	4.0
Tinnitus	674	10.6	1.5

Source: National Center for Health Statistics
Note: Chronic conditions are defined by the National Health Interview Survey as conditions that either a) were noticed three months or more before the date of the interview or, b) belong to a group of conditions (such as heart disease or diabetes) that are considered chronic regardless of when they began. Totals for all chronic conditions are not shown because the National Health Interview Survey does not measure the total number of conditions for each person.

Chronic Health Conditions, People Aged 35 to 44

People aged 35 to 44 account for a significant share of those who suffer from a variety of chronic conditions such as indigestion, hemorrhoids, and migraines.

(number of chronic conditions reported for persons aged 35 to 44 in thousands, share of all chronic conditions accounted for by persons aged 35 to 44, and number of chronic conditions per 100 persons aged 35 to 44 in 1988)

	persons aged 35 to 44		
	number of chronic conditions	share of chronic conditions	number of chronic conditions per 100 persons
Selected skin and musculoskeletal conditions			
Arthritis	3,216	10.3%	9.1
Gout, including gouty arthritis	202	9.9	0.6
Trouble with bunions	407	15.6	1.2
Bursitis, unclassified	940	21.2	2.7
Sebaceous skin cyst	318	21.5	0.9
Trouble with acne	473	10.4	1.3
Psoriasis	423	18.7	1.2
Dermatitis	1,474	16.3	4.2
Trouble with dry, itching skin, unclassified	619	12.9	1.8
Trouble with ingrown nails	1,067	17.3	3.0
Trouble with corns and calluses	814	18.0	2.3
Selected respiratory conditions			
Chronic bronchitis	1,416	11.9	4.0
Asthma	1,335	13.4	3.8
Hay fever or allergic rhinitis without asthma	4,190	18.7	11.9
Chronic sinusitis	6,225	18.5	17.6
Chronic disease of tonsils or adenoids	183	5.0	0.5
Emphysema	39	2.0	0.1
Selected digestive conditions			
Ulcer	698	18.1	2.0
Hernia of abdominal cavity	616	13.0	1.7
Gastritis or duodenitis	506	18.6	1.4
Frequent indigestion	1,346	23.1	3.8
Enteritis or colitis	502	20.0	1.4
Spastic colon	218	15.3	0.6
Diverticula of intestines	123	6.6	0.3
Frequent constipation	641	14.0	1.8
Selected circulatory conditions			
Ischemic heart disease	382	5.1	1.1
Tachycardia or rapid heart	267	15.5	0.8
Heart murmurs	779	16.8	2.2
Other heart rhythm disorders	181	10.6	0.5
Other heart diseases	343	8.4	1.0
High blood pressure (hypertension)	3,742	12.8	10.6
Cerebrovascular disease	157	6.2	0.4

(continued on next page)

(continued from previous page)

(number of chronic conditions reported for persons aged 35 to 44 in thousands, share of all chronic conditions accounted for by persons aged 35 to 44, and number of chronic conditions per 100 persons aged 35 to 44 in 1988)

	persons aged 35 to 44		
	number of chronic conditions	share of chronic conditions	number of chronic conditions per 100 persons
Hardening of the arteries	98	3.6%	0.3
Varicose veins	1,247	16.3	3.5
Hemorrhoids	2,553	23.1	7.2
Selected other chronic conditions			
Goiter or other disorders of the thyroid	693	17.3	2.0
Diabetes	552	8.9	1.6
Anemia	653	16.4	1.8
Epilepsy	100	11.0	0.3
Migraine headache	2,272	24.6	6.4
Kidney trouble	565	17.1	1.6
Bladder disorders	384	12.5	1.1
Diseases of prostate	214	14.2	0.6
Prostate malignancy	0	0.0	0.0
Inflammatory female genital diseases	41	13.8	0.1
Noninflammatory female genital diseases	319	34.3	0.9
Menstrual disorders	589	29.0	1.7
Breast malignancy	45	6.4	0.1
Benign neoplasm of breast/female genital	351	38.7	1.0
Selected impairments			
Visual impairment	1,327	15.9	3.8
Cataracts	80	1.3	0.2
Glaucoma	95	5.1	0.3
Hearing impairment	2,339	10.7	6.6
Tinnitus	738	11.6	2.1

Source: National Center for Health Statistics
Note: Chronic conditions are defined by the National Health Interview Survey as conditions that either a) were noticed three months or more before the date of the interview or, b) belong to a group of conditions (such as heart disease or diabetes) that are considered chronic regardless of when they began. Totals for all chronic conditions are not shown because the National Health Interview Survey does not measure the total number of conditions for each person.

Chronic Health Conditions, People Aged 45 to 54

Beginning in the 45-to-54 age group, some chronic conditions become common complaints—particularly arthritis, sinusitis, and high blood pressure.

(number of chronic conditions reported for persons aged 45 to 54 in thousands, share of all chronic conditions accounted for by persons aged 45 to 54, and number of chronic conditions per 100 persons aged 45 to 54 in 1988)

	persons aged 45 to 54		
	number of chronic conditions	*share of chronic conditions*	*number of chronic conditions per 100 persons*
Selected skin and musculoskeletal conditions			
Arthritis	4,598	14.7%	19.0
Gout, including gouty arthritis	293	14.3	1.2
Trouble with bunions	393	15.0	1.6
Bursitis, unclassified	1,000	22.6	4.1
Sebaceous skin cyst	151	10.2	0.6
Trouble with acne	74	1.6	0.3
Psoriasis	393	17.3	1.6
Dermatitis	854	9.5	3.5
Trouble with dry, itching skin, unclassified	623	13.0	2.6
Trouble with ingrown nails	717	11.6	3.0
Trouble with corns and calluses	516	11.4	2.1
Selected respiratory conditions			
Chronic bronchitis	1,142	9.6	4.7
Asthma	622	6.3	2.6
Hay fever or allergic rhinitis without asthma	2,474	11.0	10.2
Chronic sinusitis	4,743	14.1	19.6
Chronic disease of tonsils or adenoids	78	2.1	0.3
Emphysema	191	10.0	0.8
Selected digestive conditions			
Ulcer	553	14.4	2.3
Hernia of abdominal cavity	794	16.7	3.3
Gastritis or duodenitis	443	16.3	1.8
Frequent indigestion	880	15.1	3.6
Enteritis or colitis	333	13.3	1.4
Spastic colon	255	17.9	1.1
Diverticula of intestines	136	7.4	0.6
Frequent constipation	448	9.8	1.9
Selected circulatory conditions			
Ischemic heart disease	874	11.7	3.6
Tachycardia or rapid heart	245	14.2	1.0
Heart murmurs	402	8.7	1.7
Other heart rhythm disorders	126	7.4	0.5
Other heart diseases	348	8.5	1.4
High blood pressure (hypertension)	4,806	16.4	19.9
Cerebrovascular disease	311	12.4	1.3

(continued on next page)

(continued from previous page)

(number of chronic conditions reported for persons aged 45 to 54, share of all chronic conditions accounted for by persons aged 45 to 54 in thousands, and number of chronic conditions per 100 persons aged 45 to 54 in 1988)

	persons aged 45 to 54		
	number of chronic conditions	share of chronic conditions	number of chronic conditions per 100 persons
Hardening of the arteries	198	7.3%	0.8
Varicose veins	1,086	14.2	4.5
Hemorrhoids	1,820	16.5	7.5
Selected other chronic conditions			
Goiter or other disorders of the thyroid	723	18.0	3.0
Diabetes	816	13.1	3.4
Anemia	333	8.4	1.4
Epilepsy	138	15.1	0.6
Migraine headache	1,336	14.5	5.5
Kidney trouble	355	10.7	1.5
Bladder disorders	376	12.2	1.6
Diseases of prostate	86	5.7	0.4
Prostate malignancy	23	10.4	0.1
Inflammatory female genital diseases	0	0.0	0.0
Noninflammatory female genital diseases	87	9.4	0.4
Menstrual disorders	120	5.9	0.5
Breast malignancy	80	11.5	0.3
Benign neoplasm of breast/female genital	216	23.8	0.9
Selected impairments			
Visual impairment	1,105	13.2	4.6
Cataracts	266	4.4	1.1
Glaucoma	146	7.8	0.6
Hearing impairment	2,903	13.3	12.0
Tinnitus	853	13.4	3.5

Source: National Center for Health Statistics
Note: Chronic conditions are defined by the National Health Interview Survey as conditions that either a) were noticed three months or more before the date of the interview or, b) belong to a group of conditions (such as heart disease or diabetes) that are considered chronic regardless of when they began. Totals for all chronic conditions are not shown because the National Health Interview Survey does not measure the total number of conditions for each person.

Chronic Health Conditions, People Aged 55 to 64

Over one-fourth of people aged 55 to 64 have arthritis. High blood pressure is a problem for nearly one-third.

(number of chronic conditions reported for persons aged 55 to 64 in thousands, share of all chronic conditions accounted for by persons aged 55 to 64, and number of chronic conditions per 100 persons aged 55 to 64 in 1988)

	persons aged 55 to 64		
	number of chronic conditions	*share of chronic conditions*	*number of chronic conditions per 100 persons*
Selected skin and musculoskeletal conditions			
Arthritis	5,659	18.1%	26.0
Gout, including gouty arthritis	589	28.7	2.7
Trouble with bunions	413	15.8	1.9
Bursitis, unclassified	1,010	22.8	4.6
Sebaceous skin cyst	158	10.7	0.7
Trouble with acne	65	1.4	0.3
Psoriasis	373	16.5	1.7
Dermatitis	985	10.9	4.5
Trouble with dry, itching skin, unclassified	553	11.5	2.5
Trouble with ingrown nails	747	12.1	3.4
Trouble with corns and calluses	1,033	22.8	4.7
Selected respiratory conditions			
Chronic bronchitis	1,416	11.9	6.5
Asthma	965	9.7	4.4
Hay fever or allergic rhinitis without asthma	2,053	9.2	9.4
Chronic sinusitis	3,825	11.4	17.5
Chronic disease of tonsils or adenoids	124	3.4	0.6
Emphysema	573	30.1	2.6
Selected digestive conditions			
Ulcer	776	20.2	3.6
Hernia of abdominal cavity	979	20.6	4.5
Gastritis or duodenitis	366	13.5	1.7
Frequent indigestion	724	12.4	3.3
Enteritis or colitis	317	12.6	1.5
Spastic colon	215	15.1	1.0
Diverticula of intestines	453	24.5	2.1
Frequent constipation	550	12.0	2.5
Selected circulatory conditions			
Ischemic heart disease	2,214	29.6	10.2
Tachycardia or rapid heart	387	22.4	1.8
Heart murmurs	336	7.3	1.5
Other heart rhythm disorders	410	24.1	1.9
Other heart diseases	705	17.3	3.2
High blood pressure (hypertension)	6,941	23.7	31.8
Cerebrovascular disease	528	21.0	2.4

(continued on next page)

(continued from previous page)

(number of chronic conditions reported for persons aged 55 to 64 in thousands, share of all chronic conditions accounted for by persons aged 55 to 64, and number of chronic conditions per 100 persons aged 55 to 64 in 1988)

	persons aged 55 to 64		
	number of chronic conditions	share of chronic conditions	number of chronic conditions per 100 persons
Hardening of the arteries	648	23.9%	3.0
Varicose veins	1,500	19.7	6.9
Hemorrhoids	1,746	15.8	8.0
Selected other chronic conditions			
Goiter or other disorders of the thyroid	902	22.5	4.1
Diabetes	1,671	26.9	7.7
Anemia	264	6.6	1.2
Epilepsy	129	14.2	0.6
Migraine headache	732	7.9	3.4
Kidney trouble	434	13.1	2.0
Bladder disorders	438	14.2	2.0
Diseases of prostate	400	26.6	1.8
Prostate malignancy	62	28.1	0.3
Inflammatory female genital diseases	25	8.4	0.1
Noninflammatory female genital diseases	30	3.2	0.1
Menstrual disorders	19	0.9	0.1
Breast malignancy	156	22.3	0.7
Benign neoplasm of breast/female genital	42	4.6	0.2
Selected impairments			
Visual impairment	1,066	12.7	4.9
Cataracts	719	11.8	3.3
Glaucoma	398	21.3	1.8
Hearing impairment	3,822	17.5	17.5
Tinnitus	1,388	21.8	6.4

Source: National Center for Health Statistics
Note: Chronic conditions are defined by the National Health Interview Survey as conditions that either a) were noticed three months or more before the date of the interview or, b) belong to a group of conditions (such as heart disease or diabetes) that are considered chronic regardless of when they began. Totals for all chronic conditions are not shown because the National Health Interview Survey does not measure the total number of conditions for each person.

Chronic Health Conditions, People Aged 65 to 74

People aged 65 to 74 account for as many as one-third of those suffering from some chronic condition, including emphysema, diverticulitis, hardening of the arteries, prostate disease, and cataracts.

(number of chronic conditions reported for persons aged 65 to 74 in thousands, share of all chronic conditions accounted for by persons aged 65 to 74, and number of chronic conditions per 100 persons aged 65 to 74 in 1988)

	persons aged 65 to 74		
	number of chronic conditions	**share of chronic conditions**	**number of chronic conditions per 100 persons**
Selected skin and musculoskeletal conditions			
Arthritis	7,810	25.0%	43.7
Gout, including gouty arthritis	521	25.4	2.9
Trouble with bunions	621	23.7	3.5
Bursitis, unclassified	621	14.0	3.5
Sebaceous skin cyst	100	6.8	0.6
Trouble with acne	13	0.3	0.1
Psoriasis	162	7.1	0.9
Dermatitis	530	5.9	3.0
Trouble with dry, itching skin, unclassified	549	11.5	3.1
Trouble with ingrown nails	652	10.6	3.6
Trouble with corns and calluses	822	18.1	4.6
Selected respiratory conditions			
Chronic bronchitis	1,153	9.7	6.5
Asthma	764	7.7	4.3
Hay fever or allergic rhinitis without asthma	1,388	6.2	7.8
Chronic sinusitis	3,095	9.2	17.3
Chronic disease of tonsils or adenoids	0	0.0	0.0
Emphysema	623	32.7	3.5
Selected digestive conditions			
Ulcer	471	12.2	2.6
Hernia of abdominal cavity	941	19.8	5.3
Gastritis or duodenitis	369	13.6	2.1
Frequent indigestion	704	12.1	3.9
Enteritis or colitis	367	14.6	2.1
Spastic colon	260	18.3	1.5
Diverticula of intestines	653	35.3	3.7
Frequent constipation	591	12.9	3.3
Selected circulatory conditions			
Ischemic heart disease	2,224	29.7	12.4
Tachycardia or rapid heart	330	19.1	1.8
Heart murmurs	489	10.6	2.7
Other heart rhythm disorders	517	30.4	2.9
Other heart diseases	1,164	28.6	6.5
High blood pressure (hypertension)	6,545	22.4	36.6
Cerebrovascular disease	695	27.6	3.9

(continued on next page)

(continued from previous page)

(number of chronic conditions reported for persons aged 65 to 74 in thousands, share of all chronic conditions accounted for by persons aged 65 to 74, and number of chronic conditions per 100 persons aged 65 to 74 in 1988)

	persons aged 65 to 74		
	number of chronic conditions	*share of chronic conditions*	*number of chronic conditions per 100 persons*
Hardening of the arteries	899	33.2%	5.0
Varicose veins	1,332	17.5	7.5
Hemorrhoids	1,120	10.1	6.3
Selected other chronic conditions			
Goiter or other disorders of the thyroid	640	16.0	3.6
Diabetes	1,673	26.9	9.4
Anemia	277	6.9	1.5
Epilepsy	89	9.8	0.5
Migraine headache	427	4.6	2.4
Kidney trouble	379	11.5	2.1
Bladder disorders	474	15.4	2.7
Diseases of prostate	510	34.0	2.9
Prostate malignancy	106	48.0	0.6
Inflammatory female genital diseases	11	3.7	0.1
Noninflammatory female genital diseases	10	1.1	0.1
Menstrual disorders	0	0.0	0.0
Breast malignancy	178	25.5	1.0
Benign neoplasm of breast/female genital	57	6.3	0.3
Selected impairments			
Visual impairment	1,184	14.2	6.6
Cataracts	2,074	34.0	11.6
Glaucoma	553	29.6	3.1
Hearing impairment	4,807	22.0	26.9
Tinnitus	1,571	24.7	8.8

Source: National Center for Health Statistics
Note: Chronic conditions are defined by the National Health Interview Survey as conditions that either a) were noticed three months or more before the date of the interview or, b) belong to a group of conditions (such as heart disease or diabetes) that are considered chronic regardless of when they began. Totals for all chronic conditions are not shown because the National Health Interview Survey does not measure the total number of conditions for each person.

Chronic Health Conditions, People Aged 75 or older

Among people aged 75 or older, nearly half have arthritis, one-third have high blood pressure, and one-third have hearing problems.

(number of chronic conditions reported for persons aged 75 or older in thousands, share of all chronic conditions accounted for by persons aged 75 or older, and number of chronic conditions per 100 persons aged 75 or older in 1988)

	persons aged 75 or older		
	number of chronic conditions	*share of chronic conditions*	*number of chronic conditions per 100 persons*
Selected skin and musculoskeletal conditions			
Arthritis	6,119	19.6%	48.8
Gout, including gouty arthritis	253	12.3	2.0
Trouble with bunions	278	10.6	2.2
Bursitis, unclassified	401	9.1	3.2
Sebaceous skin cyst	62	4.2	0.5
Trouble with acne	12	0.3	0.1
Psoriasis	139	6.1	1.1
Dermatitis	251	2.8	2.0
Trouble with dry, itching skin, unclassified	477	10.0	3.8
Trouble with ingrown nails	641	10.4	5.1
Trouble with corns and calluses	399	8.8	3.2
Selected respiratory conditions			
Chronic bronchitis	706	5.9	5.6
Asthma	423	4.3	3.4
Hay fever or allergic rhinitis without asthma	659	2.9	5.3
Chronic sinusitis	1,865	5.5	14.9
Chronic disease of tonsils or adenoids	11	0.3	0.1
Emphysema	453	23.8	3.6
Selected digestive conditions			
Ulcer	214	5.6	1.7
Hernia of abdominal cavity	712	15.0	5.7
Gastritis or duodenitis	252	9.3	2.0
Frequent indigestion	469	8.1	3.7
Enteritis or colitis	142	5.7	1.1
Spastic colon	157	11.0	1.3
Diverticula of intestines	474	25.6	3.8
Frequent constipation	1,081	23.6	8.6
Selected circulatory conditions			
Ischemic heart disease	1,709	22.8	13.6
Tachycardia or rapid heart	187	10.8	1.5
Heart murmurs	290	6.3	2.3
Other heart rhythm disorders	295	17.3	2.4
Other heart diseases	1,176	28.9	9.4
High blood pressure (hypertension)	4,153	14.2	33.1
Cerebrovascular disease	743	29.5	5.9

(continued on next page)

(continued from previous page)

(number of chronic conditions reported for persons aged 75 or older in thousands, share of all chronic conditions accounted for by persons aged 75 or older, and number of chronic conditions per 100 persons aged 75 or older in 1988)

	persons aged 75 or older		
	number of chronic conditions	**share of chronic conditions**	**number of chronic conditions per 100 persons**
Hardening of the arteries	868	32.0%	6.9
Varicose veins	969	12.7	7.7
Hemorrhoids	729	6.6	5.8
Selected other chronic conditions			
Goiter or other disorders of the thyroid	523	13.0	4.2
Diabetes	976	15.7	7.8
Anemia	480	12.0	3.8
Epilepsy	23	2.5	0.2
Migraine headache	102	1.1	0.8
Kidney trouble	356	10.8	2.8
Bladder disorders	454	14.8	3.6
Diseases of prostate	238	15.8	1.9
Prostate malignancy	30	13.6	0.2
Inflammatory female genital diseases	10	3.4	0.1
Noninflammatory female genital diseases	0	0.0	0.0
Menstrual disorders	0	0.0	0.0
Breast malignancy	238	34.1	1.9
Benign neoplasm of breast/female genital	9	1.0	0.1
Selected impairments			
Visual impairment	1,419	17.0	11.3
Cataracts	2,735	44.8	21.8
Glaucoma	621	33.3	5.0
Hearing impairment	4,232	19.4	33.8
Tinnitus	835	13.1	6.7

Source: National Center for Health Statistics
Note: Chronic conditions are defined by the National Health Interview Survey as conditions that either a) were noticed three months or more before the date of the interview or, b) belong to a group of conditions (such as heart disease or diabetes) that are considered chronic regardless of when they began. Totals for all chronic conditions are not shown because the National Health Interview Survey does not measure the total number of chronic conditions for each person.

Activity Restrictions

The average American restricts his or her activities because of acute or chronic illnesses 15 days a year. The number of restricted activity days is greatest for women, older people, and those with low incomes.

(number of days of activity restriction and number of days per person per year of activity restriction due to acute or chronic conditions, by type of restriction and sex, age, and family income, 1988)

	number of activity restriction days (in millions)			number of days per person per year		
	all types	bed disability	work/school loss day	all types	bed disability	work/school loss day
All persons*	**3,536**	**1,519**	**831**	**14.7**	**6.3**	**3.5**
Sex						
Male	1,487	607	414	12.7	5.2	3.5
Female	2,049	912	417	16.5	7.3	3.4
Age						
Under age 5	196	98	0	10.7	5.3	0.0
Aged 5 to 17	403	181	222	8.9	4.0	4.9
Aged 18 to 24	240	100	84	9.4	3.9	3.3
Aged 25 to 34	503	193	191	11.8	4.5	4.5
Aged 35 to 44	448	173	146	12.9	5.0	4.2
Aged 45 to 54	359	147	92	15.0	6.2	3.9
Aged 55 to 64	508	215	74	23.5	9.9	3.4
Aged 65 to 74	469	220	18	26.7	12.5	1.0
Aged 75 or older	410	192	3	36.9	17.3	0.3
Household income						
Under $10,000	754	347	87	26.6	12.2	3.0
$10,000 to $19,999	751	334	151	17.8	7.9	3.6
$20,000 to $34,999	734	293	230	12.3	4.9	3.9
$35,000 or more	726	288	251	9.7	3.8	3.4

*Includes persons with unknown income.
Source: National Center for Health Statistics
Note: Numbers may not add to total due to rounding. Restriction days: 1) bed days are those during which a person stayed in bed more than half a day because of illness or injury; includes hospital days of any duration, 2) work-loss days on which an employed person aged 18 or older missed at least half a day of work, 3) school-loss days on which a student aged 5 to 17 missed at least half a day of school, and 4) cut-down days on which a person cuts down on normal activities for a least half a day. The number of cut-down days is not detailed here.

Americans With Work-Related Disabilities

Nearly 9 percent of Americans have a disability that prevents them from working or limits the kind of work they can do. The share of people with work-related disabilities is highest among older Americans and those with less education.

(number and percent of persons aged 16 to 64 with a work disability, by selected characteristics, 1988; numbers in thousands)

		with a work disability						
		both sexes			**males**		**females**	
		total with disability		**severe disability**	**total with disability**	**severe disability**	**total with disability**	**severe disability**
	number of persons	**number**	**percent**					
All persons	**156,542**	**13,420**	**8.6%**	**4.8%**	**8.7%**	**4.9%**	**8.4%**	**4.6%**
Age								
Aged 16 to 24	33,453	1,285	3.8	1.7	4.1	1.9	3.6	1.6
Aged 25 to 34	42,970	2,414	5.6	2.7	5.9	3.1	5.4	2.4
Aged 35 to 44	34,682	2,455	7.1	3.6	7.7	4.3	6.5	3.0
Aged 45 to 54	23,795	2,443	10.3	6.0	10.3	6.0	10.2	6.0
Aged 55 to 64	21,642	4,825	22.3	14.0	22.4	13.7	22.2	14.2
Years of school completed								
All persons aged 25 to 64	123,089	12,135	9.9	5.6	10.0	5.8	9.7	5.4
Less than 8 years	5,756	1,709	29.7	23.4	29.1	23.2	30.3	23.7
8 years	3,843	944	24.6	16.8	23.9	15.8	25.2	17.8
1 to 3 years high school	13,332	2,363	17.7	11.6	17.5	11.7	17.9	11.4
4 years high school	49,528	4,342	8.8	4.5	9.3	5.1	8.4	4.1
1 to 3 years college	22,868	1,726	7.5	3.2	8.4	3.4	6.7	3.0
4 years or more college	27,761	1,051	3.8	1.3	3.8	1.4	3.8	1.2
Ratio of household/personal income to poverty level, 1987								
Less than 1.00	17,287	3,791	21.9	15.5	24.4	17.9	20.3	13.8
1.00 to 1.24	5,627	1,002	17.8	12.4	19.0	14.6	16.8	10.5
1.25 to 1.49	5,815	778	13.4	8.3	13.4	8.6	13.4	8.1
1.50 to 1.99	12,642	1,424	11.3	6.9	12.8	8.4	9.9	5.6
2.00 or higher	115,170	6,426	5.6	2.4	5.8	2.4	5.3	2.3
Veteran status (males only)	20,554	2,597	-	-	12.6	6.8	-	-
Vietnam era	7,360	607	-	-	8.3	3.7	-	-
Korean conflict	4,051	614	-	-	15.2	9.2	-	-
World War II	3,301	871	-	-	26.4	15.3	-	-
Other service	5,842	504	-	-	8.6	4.3	-	-
Nonveteran	56,162	4,109	-	-	7.3	4.3	-	-
Selected sources of income/benefits, 1987								
Social Security income	7,944	3,963	49.9	41.2	60.7	52.1	41.3	32.5
Supplemental Security income	2,069	2,069	100.0	100.0	100.0	100.0	100.0	100.0
Earnings	124,195	4,969	4.0	0.7	4.2	0.7	3.8	0.7
Food stamps	10,102	2,526	25.0	17.6	27.9	20.3	23.3	16.0

(continued on next page)

(continued from previous page)
(number and percent of persons aged 16 to 64 with a work disability, by selected characteristics, 1988; numbers in thousands)

		with a work disability						
		both sexes			males		females	
	number of persons	total with disability		severe disability	total with disability	severe disability	total with disability	severe disability
		number	percent					
Medicaid	7,553	2,904	38.4%	32.2%	54.7%	48.5%	31.7%	25.5%
Public housing	2,887	620	21.5	15.8	21.8	17.9	21.3	14.8
Subsidized housing	1,448	390	27.0	18.9	29.7	22.5	25.8	17.3
Race and Hispanic origin								
White	132,992	10,544	7.9	4.1	8.2	4.3	7.7	3.9
Black	18,299	2,512	13.7	9.9	13.7	10.3	13.8	9.5
Hispanic	12,362	1,011	8.2	5.6	8.4	5.9	7.9	5.2

Source: Bureau of the Census
Note: A work disability is operationally defined as a health problem or disability that prevents someone from working or that limits the kind or amount of work they can do. The income/poverty level ratio compares family or personal income to an official poverty threshold. A ratio of less than 1.00 means that the person is part of the official poverty population. Hispanics may be of any race.

Americans With Activity-Related Disabilities

Fourteen percent of Americans have a chronic illness-related disability that interferes with their daily activities. Women are more likely than men to have activity-related disabilities.

(percent distribution of persons by degree of activity limitation due to chronic conditions, by selected characteristics, 1989; numbers in thousands)

	all persons number	all persons percent	with no activity limitation	with activity limitation	with limitation in major activity	unable to carry on major activity	limited in amount or kind of major activity	limited but not in major activity
All persons*	**243,532**	**100.0%**	**85.9%**	**14.1%**	**9.6%**	**4.1%**	**5.4%**	**4.5%**
Age								
Under age 18	64,003	100.0	94.7	5.3	3.8	0.6	3.2	1.5
Aged 18 to 44	104,196	100.0	91.0	9.0	6.3	2.6	3.7	2.7
Aged 45 to 64	46,114	100.0	77.8	22.2	16.5	8.8	7.7	5.6
Aged 65 to 69	9,903	100.0	63.1	36.9	29.2	15.7	13.4	7.7
Aged 70 or older	19,316	100.0	61.0	39.0	19.5	7.2	12.3	19.4
All males	**118,009**	**100.0**	**86.3**	**13.7**	**9.7**	**4.6**	**5.0**	**4.0**
Under age 18	32,752	100.0	93.7	6.3	4.6	0.6	4.0	1.7
Aged 18 to 44	51,044	100.0	90.9	9.1	6.7	2.9	3.8	2.4
Aged 45 to 64	22,070	100.0	78.6	21.4	16.9	10.4	6.5	4.5
Aged 65 to 69	4,553	100.0	61.7	38.3	33.4	20.8	12.6	4.9
Aged 70 or older	7,590	100.0	61.3	38.7	16.2	7.2	9.0	22.5
All females	**125,523**	**100.0**	**85.6**	**14.4**	**9.5**	**3.6**	**5.8**	**4.9**
Under age 18	31,251	100.0	95.7	4.3	3.0	0.5	2.5	1.3
Aged 18 to 44	53,152	100.0	91.0	9.0	6.0	2.3	3.7	3.0
Aged 45 to 64	24,044	100.0	77.2	22.8	16.1	7.3	8.9	6.7
Aged 65 to 69	5,350	100.0	64.3	35.7	25.5	11.4	14.1	10.1
Aged 70 or older	11,726	100.0	60.9	39.1	21.7	7.2	14.5	17.4
Race								
White	205,312	100.0	85.8	14.2	9.5	3.9	5.5	4.7
Black	29,891	100.0	85.1	14.9	11.3	5.9	5.3	3.6
Household income								
Under $10,000	26,185	100.0	73.2	26.8	19.4	9.7	9.6	7.4
$10,000 to $19,999	41,040	100.0	80.6	19.4	13.4	6.1	7.3	6.0
$20,000 to $34,999	56,718	100.0	88.1	11.9	7.9	3.0	4.9	3.9
$35,000 or more	80,203	100.0	91.8	8.2	5.1	1.7	3.4	3.0

*Includes persons of other races and with unknown family income.

Source: National Center for Health Statistics

Note: Persons are classified as limited in activity if one or more chronic conditions are reported as the cause of activity limitation. Activity limitation refers to the major activity usually associated with the age groups: (a) ordinary play for persons under age 5, (b) attending school for persons aged 5 to 17, (c) working or keeping house for persons aged 18 to 69, and (d) capacity for independent living—ability to dress, eat, shop, bathe, etc. without help—for persons aged 70 or older.

Life Expectancy, 1900–1988

Life expectancy for blacks has doubled since the turn of the century, from only 33 years for black men in 1900 to nearly 65 years by 1988.

(expectation of life at selected ages, by race and sex, 1900-1988, and percent change, 1900-1988)

	all persons	white male	white female	black male	black female
At birth					
1988	74.9	72.3	78.9	64.9	73.4
1987	75.0	72.2	78.9	65.2	73.6
1979-1981	73.9	70.8	78.2	64.1	72.9
1969-1971	70.8	68.0	75.5	60.0	68.3
1959-1961	69.9	67.6	74.2	na	na
1900-1902	49.2	48.2	51.1	32.5	35.0
Percent change, 1900-1902 to 1988	52%	50%	54%	100%	110%
At age 1 year					
1988	74.7	72.0	78.5	65.2	73.6
1987	74.7	71.9	78.5	65.5	73.8
1979-1981	73.8	70.7	78.0	64.6	73.3
1969-1971	71.2	68.3	75.7	61.2	69.4
1959-1961	70.8	68.3	74.7	na	na
1900-1902	55.2	54.6	56.4	42.5	43.5
Percent change, 1900-1902 to 1988	35%	32%	39%	53%	69%
At age 20 years					
1988	56.3	53.6	59.9	47.0	55.1
1987	56.3	53.6	59.9	47.3	55.3
1979-1981	55.5	52.5	59.4	46.5	54.9
1969-1971	53.0	50.2	57.2	43.5	51.2
1959-1961	52.6	50.3	56.3	na	na
1900-1902	42.8	42.2	43.8	35.1	36.9
Percent change, 1900-1902 to 1988	32%	27%	37%	34%	49%
At age 65 years					
1988	16.9	14.9	18.7	13.4	16.9
1987	16.9	14.9	18.8	13.5	17.1
1979-1981	16.5	14.3	18.6	13.3	17.1
1969-1971	15.0	13.0	16.9	12.5	15.7
1959-1961	14.4	13.0	15.9	na	na
1900-1902	11.9	11.5	12.2	10.4	11.4
Percent change, 1900-1902 to 1988	42%	30%	53%	29%	48%

Source: National Center for Health Statistics
Note: na means data not available.

Average Remaining Lifetime

At birth, a newborn can expect to live 75 years. White females have the longest life expectancy; black males the shortest.

(average number of years of life remaining at birth in 1988 and 1990* and for persons who reached a given age in 1988, by race and sex)

	all races			white			black		
	both sexes	**male**	**female**	**both sexes**	**male**	**female**	**both sexes**	**male**	**female**
At birth, 1990	75.4	72.0	78.8	76.0	72.6	79.3	70.3	66.0	74.5
At birth, 1988	74.9	71.5	78.3	75.6	72.3	78.9	69.2	64.9	73.4
Age 5	70.8	67.5	74.2	71.4	68.1	74.6	65.7	61.4	69.8
Age 10	65.9	62.5	69.2	66.5	63.2	69.7	60.8	56.5	64.9
Age 15	61.0	57.6	64.3	61.6	58.3	64.8	55.9	51.6	60.0
Age 20	56.3	53.0	59.4	56.8	53.6	59.9	51.2	47.0	55.1
Age 25	51.6	48.4	54.6	52.1	49.0	55.0	46.6	42.7	50.4
Age 30	46.9	43.8	49.8	47.4	44.4	50.2	42.1	38.4	45.7
Age 35	42.2	39.3	45.0	42.7	39.8	45.4	37.8	34.3	41.1
Age 40	37.6	34.8	40.2	38.0	35.2	40.6	33.6	30.3	36.6
Age 45	33.0	30.3	35.5	33.4	30.7	35.8	29.5	26.5	32.2
Age 50	28.6	26.0	31.0	28.9	26.3	31.2	25.5	22.8	28.0
Age 55	24.4	22.0	26.6	24.6	22.2	26.8	21.8	19.4	24.0
Age 60	20.5	18.2	22.5	20.7	18.4	22.6	18.4	16.2	20.3
Age 65	16.9	14.9	18.6	17.0	14.9	18.7	15.4	13.4	16.9
Age 70	13.6	11.8	15.0	13.6	11.8	15.0	12.6	10.9	13.8
Age 75	10.7	9.1	11.7	10.7	9.1	11.7	10.0	8.6	10.9
Age 80	8.1	6.9	8.7	8.0	6.8	8.7	7.8	6.8	8.4
Age 85	6.0	5.1	6.3	5.9	5.1	6.3	6.3	5.5	6.6

*Provisional data for 1990; final data for 1988.
Source: National Center for Health Statistics

Ten Leading Causes of Death in the U.S.

Heart disease is the leading cause of death in the U.S., accounting for more than one-third of all deaths each year.

(number and percent distribution of deaths for the ten leading causes of death for all persons, 1989)

	number	*percent*
All causes	**2,150,466**	**100.0%**
1. Heart diseases	733,867	34.1
2. Cancer	496,152	23.1
3. Cerebrovascular diseases	145,551	6.8
4. Accidents and adverse effects	95,028	4.4
Motor vehicle accidents	47,575	2.2
All other accidents and adverse effects	47,453	2.2
5. Chronic obstructive pulmonary diseases and allied conditions	84,344	3.9
6. Pneumonia and influenza	76,550	3.6
7. Diabetes mellitus	46,833	2.2
8. Suicide	30,232	1.4
9. Chronic liver disease and cirrhosis	26,694	1.2
10. Homicide and legal intervention	22,909	1.1
All other causes	**392,306**	**18.2**

Source: National Center for Health Statistics

Infant Mortality

Birth defects are the leading cause of death among infants, followed by sudden infant death syndrome.

(number and percent distribution of deaths for the ten leading causes of death for infants under 1 year, 1988)

	number	percent
All causes	**39,655**	**100.0%**
1. Congenital anomalies	8,120	20.5
2. Sudden infant death syndrome	5,634	14.2
3. Disorders relating to short gestation and unspecified low birthweight	3,931	9.9
4. Respiratory distress syndrome	3,631	9.2
5. Newborn affected by maternal complications of pregnancy	1,534	3.9
6. Accidents and adverse effects	996	2.5
7. Newborn affected by complications of placenta, cord, and membranes	984	2.5
8. Infections specific to the perinatal period	892	2.2
9. Intrauterine hypoxia and birth asphyxia	725	1.8
10. Pneumonia and influenza	636	1.6
All other causes	**12,572**	**31.7**

Source: National Center for Health Statistics

Leading Causes of Death, Children Aged 1 to 4

Accidents are the leading cause of death for children aged 1 to 4, accounting for more than one-third of all deaths in this age group. AIDS is the eighth leading cause of death.

(number and percent distribution of deaths for the ten leading causes of death for children aged 1 to 4, 1989)

	number	percent
All causes	**7,292**	**100.0%**
1. Accidents and adverse effects	2,774	38.0
Motor vehicle accidents	1,005	13.8
All other accidents and adverse effects	1,769	24.3
2. Congenital anomalies	928	12.7
3. Cancer	506	6.9
4. Homicide and legal intervention	393	5.4
5. Heart diseases	281	3.9
6. Pneumonia and influenza	228	3.1
7. Certain conditions originating in the perinatal period	134	1.8
8. Human immunodeficiency virus infection	112	1.5
9. Meningitis	99	1.4
10. Septicemia	94	1.3
All other causes	**1,743**	**23.9**

Source: National Center for Health Statistics

Leading Causes of Death, Children Aged 5 to 14

Accidents are the leading cause of death for children aged 5 to 14, accounting for nearly half of deaths. Cancer is second, accounting for 13 percent of deaths in this age group.

(number and percent distribution of deaths for the ten leading causes of death for children aged 5 to 14, 1989)

	number	percent
All causes	**8,914**	**100.0%**
1. Accidents and adverse effects	4,090	45.9
Motor vehicle accidents	2,266	25.4
All other accidents and adverse effects	1,824	20.5
2. Cancer	1,155	13.0
3. Homicide and legal intervention	510	5.7
4. Congenital anomalies	480	5.4
5. Heart diseases	295	3.3
6. Suicide	240	2.7
7. Pneumonia and influenza	122	1.4
8. Chronic obstructive pulmonary diseases and allied conditions	113	1.3
9. Benign neoplasms, carcinoma in situ, and neoplasms of uncertain behavior and of unspecified nature	85	1.0
10. Cerebrovascular diseases	83	0.9
All other causes	**1,741**	**19.5**

Source: National Center for Health Statistics

Leading Causes of Death, People Aged 15 to 24

While accidents are the leading cause of death in this age group, homicide and suicide rank second and third. AIDS ranks sixth.

(number and percent distribution of deaths for the ten leading causes of death for persons aged 15 to 24, 1989)

	number	percent
All causes	**36,488**	**100.0%**
1. Accidents and adverse effects	16,738	45.9
Motor vehicle accidents	12,941	35.5
All other accidents and adverse effects	3,797	10.4
2. Homicide and legal intervention	6,185	17.0
3. Suicide	4,870	13.3
4. Cancer	1,851	5.1
5. Heart diseases	938	2.6
6. Human immunodeficiency virus infection	613	1.7
7. Congenital anomalies	474	1.3
8. Pneumonia and influenza	271	0.7
9. Cerebrovascular diseases	232	0.6
10. Chronic obstructive pulmonary diseases and allied conditions	176	0.5
All other causes	**4,140**	**11.3**

Source: National Center for Health Statistics

Leading Causes of Death, People Aged 25 to 44

Accidents are the leading cause of death for people aged 25 to 44, followed by cancer. AIDS is in third place.

(number and percent distribution of deaths for the ten leading causes of death for persons aged 25 to 44, 1989)

	number	*percent*
All causes	**141,443**	**100.0%**
1. Accidents and adverse effects	28,429	20.1
Motor vehicle accidents	16,571	11.7
All other accidents and adverse effects	11,858	8.4
2. Cancer	21,056	14.9
3. Human immunodeficiency virus infection	16,322	11.5
4. Heart diseases	15,244	10.8
5. Suicide	11,896	8.4
6. Homicide and legal intervention	11,154	7.9
7. Chronic liver disease and cirrhosis	4,584	3.2
8. Cerebrovascular diseases	3,267	2.3
9. Pneumonia and influenza	2,296	1.6
10. Diabetes mellitus	2,119	1.5
All other causes	**25,076**	**17.7**

Source: National Center for Health Statistics

Leading Causes of Death, People Aged 45 to 64

Cancer is the leading cause of death among people aged 45 to 64, followed by heart diseases. AIDS ranks tenth as a cause of death.

(number and percent distribution of deaths for the ten leading causes of death for persons aged 45 to 64, 1989)

	number	percent
All causes	**378,324**	**100.0%**
1. Cancer	135,249	35.7
2. Heart diseases	112,273	29.7
3. Cerebrovascular diseases	15,124	4.0
4. Accidents and adverse effects	15,046	4.0
Motor vehicle accidents	7,287	1.9
All other accidents and adverse effects	7,759	2.1
5. Chronic obstructive pulmonary diseases and allied conditions	13,031	3.4
6. Chronic liver disease and cirrhosis	11,477	3.0
7. Diabetes mellitus	9,726	2.6
8. Suicide	6,984	1.8
9. Pneumonia and influenza	5,587	1.5
10. Human immunodeficiency virus infection	4,429	1.2
All other causes	**49,398**	**13.1**

Source: National Center for Health Statistics

Leading Causes of Death, People Aged 65 or Older

Heart disease is the number one killer of the elderly, followed by cancer and cerebrovascular diseases.

(number and percent distribution of deaths for the ten leading causes of death for persons aged 65 or older, 1989)

	number	percent
All causes	**1,537,788**	**100.0%**
1. Heart diseases	603,968	39.3
2. Cancer	336,206	21.9
3. Cerebrovascular diseases	126,660	8.2
4. Chronic obstructive pulmonary diseases and allied conditions	69,965	4.5
5. Pneumonia and influenza	67,395	4.4
6. Diabetes mellitus	34,798	2.3
7. Accidents and adverse effects	26,832	1.7
Motor vehicle accidents	7,251	0.5
All other accidents and adverse effects	19,581	1.3
8. Atherosclerosis	18,413	1.2
9. Nephritis, nephrotic syndrome, and nephrosis	17,508	1.1
10. Septicemia	15,428	1.0
All other causes	**220,615**	**14.3**

Source: National Center for Health Statistics

Ten Leading Causes of Death, White Males

While heart disease is the leading cause of death for white males, accidents rank third and AIDS ranks tenth.

(number and percent distribution of deaths for the ten leading causes of death for white males, 1989)

	number	percent
All causes	**950,852**	**100.0%**
1. Heart diseases	325,397	34.2
2. Cancer	228,301	24.0
3. Accidents and adverse effects	52,691	5.5
Motor vehicle accidents	27,621	2.9
All other accidents and adverse effects	25,070	2.6
4. Cerebrovascular diseases	48,563	5.1
5. Chronic obstructive pulmonary diseases and allied conditions	44,046	4.6
6. Pneumonia and influenza	30,892	3.2
7. Suicide	21,858	2.3
8. Diabetes mellitus	16,282	1.7
9. Chronic liver disease and cirrhosis	14,414	1.5
10. Human immunodeficiency virus infection	14,114	1.5
All other causes	**154,294**	**16.2**

Source: National Center for Health Statistics

Ten Leading Causes of Death, White Females

Heart disease and cancer are the biggest killers of white females. Accidents rank sixth. AIDS does not make it into the top ten for white females.

(number and percent distribution of deaths for the ten leading causes of death for white females, 1989)

	number	percent
All causes	**902,989**	**100.0%**
1. Heart diseases	323,469	35.8
2. Cancer	205,855	22.8
3. Cerebrovascular diseases	76,953	8.5
4. Pneumonia and influenza	36,961	4.1
5. Chronic obstructive pulmonary diseases and allied conditions	33,835	3.7
6. Accidents and adverse effects	26,448	2.9
Motor vehicle accidents	12,870	1.4
All other accidents and adverse effects	13,578	1.5
7. Diabetes mellitus	21,771	2.4
8. Atherosclerosis	11,139	1.2
9. Septicemia	8,829	1.0
10. Nephritis, nephrotic syndrome, and nephrosis	8,514	0.9
All other causes	**149,215**	**16.5**

Source: National Center for Health Statistics

Ten Leading Causes of Death, Black Males

Chronic diseases—heart diseases and cancer—are the leading killers of black men, but homicide ranks fourth, and AIDS ranks sixth.

(number and percent distribution of deaths for the ten leading causes of death for black males, 1989)

	number	percent
All causes	**146,393**	**100.0%**
1. Heart diseases	38,321	26.2
2. Cancer	31,452	21.5
3. Accidents and adverse effects	9,503	6.5
Motor vehicle accidents	4,120	2.8
All other accidents and adverse effects	5,383	3.7
4. Homicide and legal intervention	8,888	6.1
5. Cerebrovascular diseases	7,739	5.3
6. Human immunodeficiency virus infection	5,475	3.7
7. Pneumonia and influenza	4,168	2.8
8. Certain conditions originating in the perinatal period	3,813	2.6
9. Chronic obstructive pulmonary diseases and allied conditions	3,593	2.5
10. Diabetes mellitus	3,072	2.1
All other causes	**30,369**	**20.7**

Source: National Center for Health Statistics

Ten Leading Causes of Death, Black Females

Among black women, heart disease and cancer are the leading killers, but accidents rank fifth and homicide ranks tenth.

(number and percent distribution of deaths for the ten leading causes of death for black females, 1989)

	number	percent
All causes	**121,249**	**100.0%**
1. Heart diseases	39,110	32.3
2. Cancer	24,112	19.9
3. Cerebrovascular diseases	10,240	8.4
4. Diabetes mellitus	4,883	4.0
5. Accidents and adverse effects	3,901	3.2
Motor vehicle accidents	1,491	1.2
All other accidents and adverse effects	2,410	2.0
6. Pneumonia and influenza	3,417	2.8
7. Certain conditions originating in the perinatal period	3,152	2.6
8. Nephritis, nephrotic syndrome, and nephrosis	2,119	1.7
9. Chronic obstructive pulmonary diseases and allied conditions	2,078	1.7
10. Homicide and legal intervention	2,074	1.7
All other causes	**26,163**	**21.6**

Source: National Center for Health Statistics

Americans Without Health Insurance

Fourteen percent of Americans don't have health insurance, but among the unemployed the proportion climbs to 38 percent.

(percent of persons without health insurance by age and selected characteristics, 1989)

	all ages	all under age 65	under age 18	18-24	25-44	45-64	65+
All persons without health insurance	13.9%	15.7%	14.9%	27.4%	15.5%	10.5%	1.2%
Sex							
Male	15.1	16.7	15.1	31.3	17.6	9.6	1.3
Female	12.7	14.6	14.7	23.7	13.6	11.2	1.2
Race							
White	12.8	14.5	14.0	26.3	14.4	9.4	1.0
Black	20.2	21.9	18.9	34.3	22.5	17.5	2.5
Other	19.7	20.4	18.9	27.8	20.7	17.5	8.4
Household income							
Less than $5,000	27.1	31.3	25.5	27.3	42.4	35.5	1.5
$5,000 to $9,999	27.7	36.9	31.6	43.5	43.5	32.2	1.6
$10,000 to $19,999	24.3	30.1	30.2	37.5	32.0	21.3	1.1
$20,000 to $34,999	10.6	11.6	10.9	22.1	11.8	6.8	1.0
$35,000 to $49,999	5.8	6.0	4.0	18.4	5.8	3.9	0.8
$50,000 or more	3.6	3.7	2.3	12.9	3.7	1.9	1.6
Poverty status							
In poverty	32.5	36.0	32.5	35.9	42.2	35.9	2.3
Not in poverty	10.3	11.5	9.6	23.5	11.7	7.6	1.1
Employment status of persons aged 18 or older							
Currently employed	13.9	14.3	-	26.6	13.6	9.0	1.5
Unemployed	38.3	39.2	-	44.5	40.8	26.5	-
Not in labor force	10.8	18.5	-	26.0	21.2	12.8	1.2
Education of persons aged 18 or older							
Less than 12 years	20.8	30.1	-	42.1	35.5	19.9	1.5
12 years	14.4	16.6	-	29.8	16.8	8.5	0.7
More than 12 years	8.4	9.2	-	16.0	9.0	5.8	1.3
Region of residence							
Northeast	9.6	11.0	9.9	22.0	10.9	6.6	1.7
Midwest	9.6	10.8	8.8	22.3	10.6	7.6	0.8
South	17.5	19.7	20.5	30.9	19.2	13.4	1.1
West	17.1	18.9	16.7	32.7	19.7	13.1	1.6

Source: National Center for Health Statistics

Americans With Private Health Insurance

Three-quarters of Americans are covered by private health insurance, including 95 percent of those with incomes of $50,000 or more.

(percent of persons with private health insurance by age and selected characteristics, 1989)

	all ages	all under age 65	under age 18	18-24	25-44	45-64	65+
All persons with private health insurance	**76.1%**	**75.9%**	**71.8%**	**64.4%**	**79.0%**	**82.6%**	**77.2%**
Sex							
Male	76.3	76.1	71.9	65.1	78.9	83.5	78.1
Female	75.8	75.7	71.7	63.9	79.1	81.8	76.6
Race							
White	79.3	79.1	76.3	67.4	81.4	85.0	80.8
Black	56.6	57.8	51.6	48.8	64.4	64.8	43.7
Other	64.2	65.1	58.2	58.8	70.0	71.4	48.5
Household income							
Less than $5,000	30.5	28.7	15.0	57.1	17.1	20.6	42.1
$5,000 to $9,999	35.8	26.0	19.5	34.9	25.0	33.4	64.3
$10,000 to $19,999	62.1	57.4	51.3	52.1	59.4	67.8	81.5
$20,000 to $34,999	84.4	84.2	82.9	72.6	85.7	89.3	85.9
$35,000 to $49,999	91.7	91.9	92.8	78.7	93.0	94.1	88.2
$50,000 or more	94.9	95.2	96.5	85.6	95.7	96.8	86.7
Poverty status							
In poverty	28.3	26.3	21.4	43.4	23.9	24.0	46.2
Not in poverty	84.3	84.6	85.0	71.6	85.8	88.1	82.3
Employment status of persons aged 18 or older							
Currently employed	83.6	83.5	-	70.0	84.6	89.0	86.0
Unemployed	48.4	47.6	-	42.1	44.7	64.4	81.5
Not in labor force	67.8	61.4	-	54.1	56.4	69.2	75.9
Education of persons aged 18 or older							
Less than 12 years	58.4	54.3	-	42.2	48.8	64.8	67.0
12 years	78.5	77.5	-	61.9	77.6	86.7	84.3
More than 12 years	88.2	88.2	-	80.7	88.7	91.2	88.6
Region of residence							
Northeast	81.3	81.9	78.9	71.7	84.1	87.2	77.5
Midwest	81.7	81.5	79.1	70.0	84.1	86.8	82.7
South	71.7	71.4	65.9	60.6	75.4	78.5	73.9
West	71.7	71.2	67.6	57.2	74.2	79.4	75.8

Source: National Center for Health Statistics

8

Attitude Trends

Americans' changing attitudes toward work, family, and social issues are a consequence of the middle-aging of the huge baby-boom generation. The increasingly pro-family stance of society at large reflects the baby-boom's preoccupation with raising children. The growing importance of leisure is a consequence of the baby boom shifting its focus from career toward family. Changes in American attitudes toward social issues—such as women's roles and race relations—are due to the coming-of-age of the socially liberal generation.

Major Attitude Trends

☛ Time pressures will build during the 1990s as more baby-boom families include two and even three children. Convenience will continue to be an important marketing tool during the next ten years.

☛ Women are more career-oriented than ever before. Though they may long for the simple life, most cannot afford to stop working. By the end of the 1990s, time pressures on working women will ease as young children become teenagers.

☛ Attitudes toward women's roles, race relations, and other social issues will become more liberal as younger generations replace older ones. But in the area of sexuality, expect to see more conservative attitudes because of AIDS.

The Career Ladder

Two out of three baby boomers say they are moving up on the career ladder, but one in four older boomers say they are at the peak of their careers.

(percent of employed Americans, by selected demographic characteristics, 1991)

	"Where are you on the career ladder?"			
	starting out	moving up	at the peak	on way to retirement
National	17%	49%	15%	18%
Baby boomers*	11	65	17	6
Sex				
Male	14	52	16	18
Boomer males	8	68	18	6
Female	22	46	13	17
Boomer females	16	61	15	7
Age				
Aged 18-29	41	54	4	0
Aged 30-49	9	60	21	9
Aged 50 or older	1	12	16	69
Boomer men				
Aged 26-35	11	75	12	2
Aged 36-45	4	58	27	10
Boomer women				
Aged 26-35	20	70	9	-
Aged 36-45	11	49	24	15
Region				
East	16	47	17	20
Midwest	19	48	17	16
South	16	48	15	20
West	19	56	7	15
Race				
White	17	49	15	18
Nonwhite	19	50	7	3
Education				
College graduate	13	56	18	12
Some college	24	47	16	13
High school graduate	17	50	13	19
Some high school	20	31	10	39
Income				
$50,000 or more	12	48	22	18
$30,000-$49,999	15	48	17	19
$20,000-$29,999	23	50	9	18
Under $20,000	28	53	7	12

(-) means less than one percent.
* Aged 26 to 45
Source: The Gallup Monthly Poll, April 1991, p. 40

Americans Think Highly of Their Families

Americans may believe the family is in trouble, but they rank their own families highly on a variety of characteristics.

(scale: 1 = not at all well; 4 = very well)

"On a scale of 1 to 4, how well does each characteristic describe your family?"

	ranking
Caring	3.73%
Loving	3.72
Honest	3.63
Provided me with good ethical values	3.57
Can always be counted on to help when needed	3.57
Taught me responsibility	3.56
Taught me respect for authority	3.55
Fun to be with	3.55
Respectful of each other	3.53
Taught me discipline	3.52
Provides emotional support	3.51
Close	3.50
Understanding	3.47
In touch with each other	3.44
Lets me be myself	3.36
Helps me financially when necessary	3.33
Spends time together	3.30
Tolerant	3.26
Doing things together	3.26
Communicates well	3.25
Is a place to get away from the pressures of the outside world	3.22
Has traditions	3.17
Makes decisions democratically	3.14
Religious	2.95
Financially secure	2.93
Financially well-off	2.74

Source: "Family Time, Family Values," Mark Mellman, Edward Lazarus, Allan Rivlin, in Rebuilding the Nest: A New Commitment to the American Family, *ed. by David Blankenhorn, Steven Bayme, Jean Bethke Elshtain (Family Service America, Milwaukee, WI), p. 76*

Family Activities

Parents and children are more likely to do a variety of activities today than they were in the mid-1970s. The only thing families are not as likely to do is eat main meals together.

(percent of families doing selected activities together frequently or fairly often, 1990 and 1976; based on families with children aged 7 to 17)

	1990	1976
Have the main meal together on weekends	86%	88%
Sit and talk together	86	80
Watch TV together	85	78
Have the main meal together on weekdays	84	87
Visit friends or family together	80	74
Do things together for fun and recreation	78	71
Take a vacation together	71	67
Go out to eat together	72	53
Entertain friends or family at home together	68	68
Go shopping together	64	-
Attend religious services together	62	56
Go sightseeing, attend concerts, art museums, etc.	46	41
Read together	46	-

Source: The Public Pulse Research Supplement, Jan. 1991, p. 1, The Roper Organization, Inc., New York
Note: (-) means not asked in 1976.

Closing the Generation Gap

High school seniors are more likely to agree with their parents about some issues today, like what to do with your life or roles for women, than they were in the mid-1970s.

(percentage of high school seniors indicating that they agree with their parents about selected issues, 1990 and 1975)

	1990	*1975*
What to do with your life	71%	67%
How to dress	62	63
How to spend money	41	48
What is permitted on a date	47	41
Value of an education	86	82
Roles for women	71	61
Environmental issues	55	58
Racial issues	64	56
Religion	69	65
Politics	48	49

Source: University of Michigan, Institute for Social Research, Monitoring the Future, in Youth Indicators 1991, U.S. Dept. of Education, p. 132

A 25-Year Perspective on College Freshmen

The attitudes of the nation's college freshmen have changed considerably over the past two decades. Freshmen are more concerned with making money, but just as interested in raising a family.

(attitudes and behavior of college freshmen, 1990 and 1966 or earliest year asked, in percent)

	1990		1966 (or earliest year)	
Percent of students rating themselves above average in:				
Academic ability	53.7%		57.4%	
Leadership ability	50.9		38.1	
Intellectual self-confidence	48.3		36.0	
Social self-confidence	44.0		29.8	
Activities students report doing frequently or occasionally in past year:				
Participated in organized demonstration	39.4		15.5	
Checked a book out of school library	26.7		51.6	
Smoked cigarettes	10.6		16.6	
Drank beer	58.2		53.5	
Very important reasons for going to college:				
My parents wanted me to go	35.2		22.9	(1971)
To be able to make more money	73.2		49.9	(1971)
To prepare myself for graduate school	53.1		34.5	(1971)
Student estimates chances are very good that he/she:				
Will join fraternity or sorority	17.2		30.8	(1967)
Will need extra time to finish degree	8.2		4.8	(1972)
Will participate in student demonstrations	7.1		4.7	(1967)
Will have to work at an outside job	20.2		34.7	(1972)
Concern about ability to finance college education				
None	35.7	(1989)	35.1	
Some concern	51.2	(1989)	56.3	
Major concern	13.1	(1989)	8.6	
Present political views				
Far left/liberal	24.4		36.6	(1970)
Middle of the road	54.7		45.4	(1970)
Conservative/far right	20.9		18.1	(1970)
Objectives considered essential or very important				
Raising a family	69.5		71.4	(1969)
Being very well-off financially	73.7		43.8	
Developing a meaningful philosophy of life	43.2		82.9	(1967)
Keeping up with political affairs	42.4		57.8	
Percent who strongly or somewhat agree				
Chief benefit of a college education is increased earning power	70.7		56.0	(1967)
Marijuana should be legalized	18.6		19.4	(1968)
Abortion should be legal	64.9		55.7	(1977)
Capital punishment should be abolished	21.5		53.9	(1969)
Laws should prohibit homosexual relations	44.4		47.0	(1976)
Activities of married women are best confined to home and family	25.2		56.6	(1967)

Source: The American Freshman: Twenty-Five Year Trends, by Eric L. Day,
Alexander W. Astin, William S. Korn (Los Angeles: Higher Education Research Institute, UCLA), 1991

American Lifestyles

Americans long for more free time and less chaos, and many are considering doing something to make this happen.

(percent of Americans agreeing to lifestyle questions, 1991)

	percent of Americans agreeing
Have only a little free time or none at all	47%
Would like to slow down and live a more relaxed life	69
Think earning a living today requires so much effort that it's difficult to find time to enjoy life	61
Are the kind of person who always likes to have the very best	53
Say the following activities are becoming more important to them:	
Spending time with family	89
Looking for products that represent the best quality	63
Spending time on personal interests and hobbies	56
Spending time on household chores	54
Doing volunteer work	52
Working hard to get ahead in career	50
Are considering making the following changes in their lifestyles:	
Taking a job that lets them spend more time with family	29
Taking a less stressful job	17
Working part-time instead of full-time*	15
Quitting work entirely	12

Asked only of full-time workers.
Source: Time/CNN Poll, 1991

Time Versus Money

Although Americans were suffering through a recession in 1991, they were even more willing than five years earlier to opt for convenience in a variety of ways.

(percent doing selected activities often or sometimes, 1986 and 1991)

	1991	1986
Postpone household cleaning chores	77%	64%
Eat at fast food restaurants	70	59
Bring home take-out meals	60	47
Shop in convenience store despite the higher prices	55	43
Eat frozen-prepared meals	42	31
Cook the main course of a meal with a microwave oven	31	-
Order by phone/mail/computer instead of shopping in stores	29	22
Pay someone to do the household cleaning	14	11

Source: Roper Reports 91-7, The Roper Organization, New York City
Note: (-) means not asked in 1986.

Time Pressures

More than half of Americans feel like they don't have enough time to do what they want. Those most pressed for time are people aged 30 to 49.

(percent of Americans saying they don't have enough time to do what they want, by age, 1990)

	percent
Total	**51%**
Aged 18 to 29	56
Aged 30 to 49	66
Aged 50 or older	32

Source: The Gallup Poll Monthly, *November 1990, p. 43*

Parents' Weekend Time Use

Mothers and fathers would prefer spending more of their weekends pursuing personal interests and less time cleaning and running errands.

(estimated weekend hours spent in selected activities and preferred number of hours in selected activities, for mothers and fathers, 1991)

	estimated weekend hours		preferred hours	
	mothers	*fathers*	*mothers*	*fathers*
Cleaning	6.0	3.0	1.5	1.0
Pursuing hobbies/personal interests	4.5	6.0	9.0	11.5
Running errands	4.0	3.0	1.5	1.0
Working at job	6.5	6.5	2.5	3.0
Dining out	1.5	2.0	3.5	3.0
Playing with kids	11.0	7.5	11.0	11.0

Source: 1991 Hilton Time Values Survey

Parents' Attitudes Toward Time

Mothers are more likely than fathers to feel under stress because they don't have enough time to do all the things they want to do.

(percent of mothers and fathers agreeing with selected statements, 1991)

	percent in agreement	
	mothers	fathers
I often feel under stress when I don't have enough time.	59%	40%
At the end of the day, I often feel I haven't accomplished what I set out to do.	39	22
I feel that I'm constantly under stress— trying to accomplish more than I can handle.	47	26
I feel trapped in a daily routine.	38	27

Source: 1991 Hilton Time Values Survey

Men, Women, and Lifestyles

Men and women are in agreement about the lifestyle that appeals to them most. About half prefer a marriage of shared responsibilities.

(percent of men and women saying selected lifestyles are the most satisfying, 1990 and 1974)

	1990		1974	
	women	*men*	*women*	*men*
Marriage where husband and wife share responsibilities—work, housekeeping, and child care.	53%	50%	46%	44%
Traditional marriage in which husband works and wife runs house and takes care of children	38	39	50	48
Other	9	12	7	5

Source: The 1990 Virginia Slims Opinion Poll, conducted by The Roper Organization, New York City, 1990, p. 45

Better Off Than Before

Most Americans think they are currently better off than their parents were when they were children. This is particularly true for blacks.

(percent of Americans saying they are better off, worse off, or no different than their parents were when they were children, 1991)

	better off	worse off	no different
National	78%	12%	9%
Baby boomers*	73	16	11
Sex			
Male	79	13	8
Boomer males	70	19	11
Female	77	11	10
Boomer females	75	13	12
Age			
Aged 18 to 29	78	11	10
Aged 30 to 49	73	16	10
Aged 50 or older	84	8	6
Boomer men			
Aged 26 to 35	66	20	14
Aged 36 to 45	75	16	9
Boomer women			
Aged 26 to 35	75	12	13
Aged 36 to 45	76	14	10
Region			
East	79	11	9
Midwest	76	13	9
South	82	11	7
West	74	14	10
Race			
White	78	13	8
Black	81	8	11
Other	67	17	13
Education			
College graduate	76	13	10
Some college	76	13	11
High school graduate	75	15	9
Some high school	90	4	4
Income			
$50,000 or more	87	5	8
$30,000 to $49,999	76	13	11
$20,000 to $29,999	77	13	9
Under $20,000	76	15	7

* Ages 26 to 45.
Source: The Gallup Poll Monthly, April 1991, p. 31
Note: Numbers may not total to 100 percent because of "no opinion."

Americans Not Likely to Strike It Rich

Most Americans don't think they will ever be rich, but among those under age 30, over half think it is at least somewhat likely they will be rich someday.

(in percent, by selected demographic characteristics, 1990)

"How likely is it that you will ever be rich?"

	very	somewhat	not very	not at all
National	9%	23%	32%	35%
Sex				
Male	11	28	30	30
Female	7	19	34	39
Age				
Aged 18 to 29	17	45	27	10
Aged 30 to 49	8	28	38	25
Aged 50 or older	5	5	28	61
Region				
East	8	20	32	38
Midwest	7	22	39	32
South	8	25	27	39
West	12	27	32	27
Race				
White	8	24	33	34
Black	16	21	20	42
Other	17	17	31	33
Education				
College graduate	12	28	36	23
Some college	9	31	30	30
High school graduate	9	20	36	34
Some high school	5	18	22	55
Income				
$50,000 or more	14	33	36	16
$30,000 to $49,999	8	25	40	26
$20,000 to $29,999	9	30	32	28
Under $20,000	7	14	24	54

Source: The Gallup Poll Monthly, July 1990, p. 36
Note: Numbers may not total to 100 percent because of "no opinion."

Importance of Religion

Most Americans says religion is very important in their life. Those least likely to regard it as very important are young people, men, and whites.

(in percent, by selected demographic characteristics, 1991)

"How important is religion in your life?"

	very	fairly	not very
National	55%	31%	14%
Baby boomers*	48	36	15
Sex			
Male	47	35	18
Boomer males	39	42	18
Female	63	27	10
Boomer females	58	31	11
Age			
Aged 18 to 29	38	45	17
Aged 30 to 49	50	34	16
Aged 50 or older	73	18	9
Boomer men			
Aged 26 to 35	38	45	17
Aged 36 to 45	39	40	19
Boomer women			
Aged 26 to 35	58	31	11
Aged 36 to 45	69	21	10
Region			
East	51	31	18
Midwest	54	30	15
South	68	24	8
West	45	41	14
Race			
White	53	32	15
Black	85	14	1
Other	54	37	9
Education			
College graduate	52	30	18
Some college	49	36	15
High school graduate	57	29	14
Some high school	65	30	5
Income			
$50,000 or more	47	31	22
$30,000 to $49,999	55	30	15
$20,000 to $29,999	58	33	9
Under $20,000	59	31	10

* Aged 26 to 45.
Source: The Gallup Poll Monthly, April 1991, p. 41
Note: Numbers may not total to 100 percent because of "no opinion."

Few Americans Lonely

Americans are rarely lonely. Those most likely to feel lonely are women, those aged 50 or older, and those with annual incomes below $20,000.

(in percent, by selected demographic characteristics, 1990)

| | **"How often do you ever feel lonely?"** | | | |
	frequently	sometimes	seldom	never
National	10%	26%	40%	23%
Sex				
Male	8	20	43	28
Female	11	32	37	20
Age				
Aged 18 to 29	10	31	41	18
Aged 30 to 49	8	27	43	22
Aged 50 or older	12	22	36	29
Region				
East	10	32	34	23
Midwest	10	23	43	23
South	10	26	39	24
West	10	25	43	22
Race				
White	10	25	41	23
Nonwhite	12	32	34	22
Education				
College graduate	6	23	47	24
Some college	10	25	45	19
High school graduate	10	29	38	23
Some high school	16	26	31	26
Income				
$50,000 or more	5	22	46	27
$30,000 to $49,999	7	23	45	24
$20,000 to $29,999	11	29	39	21
Under $20,000	16	30	34	19
Number of friends				
1 to 9	17	33	30	19
10 to 20	8	28	42	22
Over 20	8	20	43	29

Source: The Gallup Poll Monthly, March 1990, p. 31
Note: Numbers may not total to 100 percent because of "no opinion."

Losing Weight

Slightly more than half of Americans would like to lose weight, including nearly two out of three women.

(in percent, by selected demographic characteristics, 1990)

"Do you want to lose weight?"

	yes	no, gain	no, stay same
National	**52%**	**7%**	**40%**
Sex			
Male	42	10	47
Female	62	3	34
Age			
Aged 18 to 29	44	11	44
Aged 30 to 49	56	5	39
Aged 50 or older	55	6	39
Region			
East	52	6	42
Midwest	54	6	40
South	53	8	39
West	51	7	40
Race			
White	63	3	33
Black	51	8	39
Other	43	10	47
Education			
College graduate	50	6	44
Some college	55	5	40
High school graduate	55	6	39
Some high school	49	11	39
Income			
$50,000 or more	54	7	39
$30,000 to $49,999	58	4	38
$20,000 to $29,999	47	6	47
Under $20,000	52	9	38

Source: The Gallup Poll Monthly, December 1990, p. 31
Note: Numbers may not total to 100 percent because of "no opinion."

Americans Think They Are Average

Only 5 percent of Americans think they are beautiful or handsome. The majority rate themselves average in looks.

(in percent, by selected demographic characteristics, 1990)

| | "How would you describe your physical appearance?" | | | | |
	beautiful/ handsome	*above average*	*average*	*below average*	*unattractive*
National	5%	31%	59%	3%	1%
Sex					
Male	9	27	60	1	2
Female	2	35	57	3	1
Age					
Aged 18 to 29	5	39	53	1	1
Aged 30 to 49	7	36	53	2	1
Aged 50 or older	4	21	68	3	2
Region					
East	6	31	59	1	1
Midwest	4	32	58	4	1
South	5	27	62	3	1
West	6	35	55	1	2
Race					
White	5	32	59	2	1
Black	11	27	55	2	2
Other	5	18	66	7	2
Education					
College graduate	6	45	47	1	-
Some college	7	36	52	3	1
High school graduate	4	30	61	2	1
Some high school	5	12	74	6	2
Income					
$50,000 or more	6	44	50	-	-
$30,000 to $49,999	5	29	61	3	1
$20,000 to $29,999	5	30	58	5	1
Under $20,000	5	25	64	2	2
Weight situation					
Want to lose	3	30	61	3	1
Satisfied	7	32	57	2	1
Want to gain	11	36	51	1	1

Source: The Gallup Poll Monthly, December 1990, p. 34
Note: Numbers may not add to 100 percent because of "no opinion."
(-) means less than 1 percent.

Women's Attitudes Toward Men

Women have a more negative attitude toward men today than they did in 1970. Most women think men want to keep women down.

(percent of women holding selected attitudes toward men, 1990 and 1970)

	1990	1970
Most men think only their own opinions about the world are important.	58%	50%
Most men find it necessary for their egos to keep women down.	55	49
Most men look at a woman and immediately think how it would be to go to bed with her.	54	41
Most men are interested in their work and life outside the home and don't pay much attention to things going on at home.	53	39
Most men are basically kind, gentle, and thoughtful.	51	67
Most men are more interested in their own, rather than a woman's, sexual satisfaction.	50	40
Most men are basically selfish and self-centered.	42	32

Source: The 1990 Virginia Slims Opinion Poll, conducted by The Roper Organization, New York City, 1990, p. 54

Americans and the Environment

Americans believe more should be done to solve environmental problems, but they place the burden on business and government rather than on themselves.

(American attitudes toward selected environmental issues, in percent, 1990)

	percent
Feel the quality of the environment in the U.S. is:	
Fair or poor	71%
Getting worse	60
Feel the quality of the environment in the area where they live is:	
Fair or poor	47
Getting worse	39
Think the following groups are not doing enough to improve the nation's environment:	
State governments	60
Consumers	69
Federal government	75
Business	76
Think business community's compliance with environmental regulations has been poor	56
Feel they personally should be doing more about the environment	64
Feel guilty about not doing more to protect the environment	48
Think environmental information is sometimes too confusing to know what to do	80
Regularly do the following things:	
Return cans/bottles to a store or recycling center	64
Shop for products that are environmentally safe	53
Save newspapers for recycling	50
Buy products made from recycled materials	47
Avoid products of companies with poor environmental records	29
Contribute money to environmental groups	18
Car pool to work	17

Source: Time/CNN Poll, 1990

Interracial Marriage

Only 42 percent of Americans disapprove of interracial marriage. In 1968, fully 72 percent disapproved.

(in percent, by selected demographic characteristics, 1991)

"Do you approve or disapprove of marriage between blacks and whites?"

	approve	disapprove	no opinion
National	**48%**	**42%**	**10%**
Sex			
Male	52	37	11
Female	44	46	10
Age			
Aged 18 to 29	64	28	8
Aged 30 to 49	56	34	10
Aged 50 or older	27	61	12
Region			
East	54	36	10
Midwest	50	42	8
South	33	54	13
West	60	31	9
Community size			
Large city	65	25	10
Medium city	50	40	10
Suburbs	53	36	11
Small town	41	52	7
Rural area	32	52	16
Race			
White	44	45	11
Black	70	19	11
Education			
College graduate	70	20	10
Some college	58	34	8
High school graduate	40	47	13
Some high school	26	66	8
Income			
$50,000 or more	61	34	5
$30,000 to $49,999	52	33	15
$20,000 to $29,999	49	44	7
Under $20,000	37	51	12

Source: The Gallup Poll Monthly, August 1991, p. 62

How Americans Feel About
Social Change Since the 1960s

Americans are having second thoughts about social changes rooted in the 1960s. They feel positive about changes in women's roles, but negative about more liberal attitudes toward drugs and tolerance of homosexuality.

(percent of Americans who believe social change was good for society, by type of change and age, 1989)

	age in 1989		
	18 to 29	*30 to 49*	*50 or older*
More liberal attitudes toward drugs	24%	16%	6%
More openness about sex and the human body	79	77	49
Greater tolerance of homosexuality as an alternative lifestyle	37	33	20
More liberal acceptance of premarital sex	57	46	19
More willingness to question authority of government	87	88	79
Changes in the role of women in society	91	85	72

Source: The Gallup Report #287, August 1989, pp. 37, 38

Social Attitudes by Age

Older Americans are much more conservative on social issues than younger Americans. The biggest differences of opinion center on sex and women's roles.

(percent of Americans agreeing with the following statements by age, 1986-91)

	age					
	18 to 29	**30 to 44**	**45 to 59**	**60 to 69**	**70 to 79**	**80+**
Most people are fair.	48%	58%	61%	67%	67%	69%
Premarital sex is almost always wrong.	21	26	40	53	62	71
Divorce should be more difficult to obtain.	44	45	50	59	62	68
The man should be the achiever outside the home, while the woman takes care of home and family.	27	28	47	63	75	82
Women should be able to get abortions if they want one for any reason.	41	45	37	30	31	25

Source: Surveys by National Opinion Research Center, 1986–91 data combined, in The Public Perspective, Vol. 3 No. 1, Nov./Dec. 1991, The Roper Center for Public Opinion Research, Storrs, CT, pp. 102, 103

Date Rape

Women are more likely than men, and younger people more likely than older ones, to call it rape under a variety of circumstances.

(percent of Americans considering circumstances rape, and percent saying a women who is raped is partly to blame given conditions, by sex and age, 1991)

	sex		age		
	women	**men**	**18 to 34**	**35 to 49**	**50+**
It's a rape when:					
A man has sex with a woman who has passed out after drinking too much	88%	77%	85%	89%	74%
A married man has sex with his wife, though she does not want to	61	56	69	67	40
A man argues with a woman who does not want to have sex until she agrees to have sex	42	33	39	39	35
A man uses emotional pressure, but no physical force, to get a woman to have sex	39	33	38	46	26
A man and a woman get drunk and have sex	7	5	7	4	6
A woman who is raped is partly to blame if:					
She is under the influence of drugs or alcohol	42	39	31	35	57
She initially says 'yes' to having sex and then changes her mind	37	43	34	43	43
She dresses provocatively	37	38	28	31	53
She agrees to go to the man's room or home	34	34	20	29	53

Source: Survey by Yankelovich Clancy Shulman for Time and CNN, May 8, 1991

American Concerns About Privacy

Americans are increasingly concerned about privacy because of the growing amount of computerized information collected about people.

(American attitudes toward privacy, in percent, 1991)

	percent
Are very or somewhat concerned about threats to personal privacy:	
1991	79%
1978	64
Have been a victim of an improper invasion of privacy:	
1991	25
1978	19
Are very or somewhat concerned about the amount of computerized information about people collected by:	
Credit organizations	78
Insurance companies	77
Federal government	78
Companies marketing products	69
Banks	69
Employers	70
Think companies should be prohibited from selling information about their:	
Arrest record	61
Product purchases	68
Medical history	83
Bill-paying history	86
Household income	90
Think employers should be allowed to:	
Require employees to take drug tests	76
Require job applicants to take psychological tests	46
Scan work areas with video cameras	38
Check credit history of job applicants	31
Listen in on employee phone conversations	4

Source: Harris-Equifax Consumer Privacy Survey 1991, Equifax Inc., 1600 Peachtree St., N.W., Atlanta, GA 30309; Yankelovich Clancy Shulman Time/ CNN Poll on Privacy, November 13, 1991

CHAPTER

For More Information

The federal government is a rich source of information on virtually any topic. Best of all, most of what the various agencies offer is either free or very inexpensive.

Bureau of the Census

Customer Services
Washington, DC 20233
301-763-4100

The Census Bureau collects information about the nation's people and its institutions, producing some 2,000 reports each year. Population and housing, the main subjects of the census, are also covered in surveys between censuses. The Current Population Survey provides current estimates of population characteristics, such as the number of persons with a college education, changes in household income, and characteristics of persons in poverty. The Census Bureau also prepares estimates of the population by age, race, and sex, and projections of future population for the U.S. and individual states. It conducts special local censuses sponsored and paid for by state and local governments.

The American Housing Survey furnishes data comparable to those of the decennial census (but with considerably less geographic detail) as well as many other data items, such as housing inventory change, indicators of housing and neighborhood quality, and rental of new apartments.

Every five years, for years ending in "2" and "7," the Census Bureau conducts censuses of governments and economic activities. The census of governments shows organization, employment, and finances for state and local governments. Annual surveys keep the information current.

Census Bureau focuses on economic activities in the censuses of agriculture, wholesale and retail trade, service industries, construction industries, manufactures, mineral industries, and transportation. To keep pace with new developments, the bureau also publishes results from a variety of monthly, quarterly, and annual surveys on areas of economic activity. In addition, it compiles annual statistics on foreign trade and on other countries.

There are many publications which outline all that you can get from the Census Bureau:

■ *1990 Census of Population and Housing Tabulation and Publication Program*

This report gives complete descriptions of 1990 census products, estimated publication dates, and a comparison of 1990 products with those of 1980. Free from Customer Services.

■ *Census ABCs—Applications in Business and Community*

A report which highlights key information about the 1990 census and illustrates a variety of ways the data can be used. Free from Customer Services.

■ *1990 Census of Population and Housing Guide*

The primary guide to the 1990 census provides detailed information about all aspects of the census and includes a comprehensive glossary of census terms. Free from Customer Services.

■ *Census and You*

The Census Bureau's monthly newsletter for data users. It reports on the latest 1990 census developments, selected new publications and computer tapes, other censuses and surveys, developments in Census Bureau services to users, and upcoming conferences and training courses. $12.00 a year from Superintendent of Documents,

U.S. Government Printing Office, Washington, DC 20402; or call 202-783-3238 and charge to MasterCard, Visa, or your GPO deposit account.

■ 1990 Census Publication Order Forms

For a brief description, prices, and stock numbers on ordering 1990 census reports, contact Customer Services to get on the mailing list to receive order forms as the reports are published.

■ Monthly Product Announcement

A monthly listing of all new Census Bureau publications; microfiche; maps; data files on tape, diskettes, or CD-ROMs; and technical documentation. Free from Customer Services.

■ Census Catalog and Guide

A comprehensive annual description of Census Bureau data products, statistical programs, and services. It provides abstracts of the publications, data files, microfiche, maps, and items online. In addition, it gives information about censuses and surveys, and telephone contact lists for data specialists at the bureau, the state data centers, and other data processing service centers. It's $21.00 from the Superintendent of Documents (see *Census and You* listing above for the address).

Telephone Contacts at the Census Bureau

■ Regional Information Services

Atlanta, GA	404-347-2274
Boston, MA	617-565-7078
Charlotte, NC	704-371-6142
Chicago, IL	312-353-0980
Dallas, TX	214-767-7105
Denver, CO	303-969-7750
Detroit, MI	313-354-4654
Kansas City, KS	816-891-7562
Los Angeles, CA	818-904-6339
New York, NY	212-264-4730
Philadelphia, PA	215-597-8313
Seattle, WA	206-728-5314

■ Frequently Called Numbers

Census Customer Services	301-763-4100
Census Customer Services FAX	763-4794
Census Personnel Locator	763-7662
Congressional Affairs	763-2446
General Information	763-4100
Population Information	763-5002/5020
Press	763-4040

■ Key User Contacts

Age Search (Access to Personal Census Records) - Staff	301-763-7936
Bulletin Board - Staff	763-1580
Business/Industry Data Centers - John Rowe	763-1580
Census Catalog - John McCall	763-1584
CD-ROM - Staff	763-4673
CENDATA - Staff	763-2074

Census and You (Monthly Newsletter) - Jackson Morton, Neil Tillman .301-763-1584
Census Awareness (Regional Offices) - Staff 763-4683
Census History - Frederick Bohme 763-7936
Clearinghouse for Census Data Services - Staff 763-1580
Confidentiality and Privacy Issues - Jerry Gates 763-5062
County and City, State and Metropolitan Area Data Books - Wanda Cevis ..763-1034
Customer Services - Staff 763-4100
Education and Curriculum Support Projects - Staff 763-1510
Exhibits, Conventions - Joanne Dickinson 763-2370
Guides - Gary Young..763-1584
Historical Statistics - Staff 763-7936
International Visitors Program - Nina Pane Pinto, Gene Vandrovec 763-2839
Legislation - Valerie Gregg, Velma Lacy 763-7787/4001
Library - Staff..763-5042
Monthly Product Announcement - Bernice L. Baker 763-1584
National Services Information Centers - Sam Johnson 763-1384
Ordering Information (Computer Software/Tapes,
Microfiche, Publications, etc.) - Customer Services 763-4100
Public-Use Microdata Samples - Carmen Campbell 763-2005
State Data Center Program - Larry Carbaugh 763-1580
Statistical Abstract - Glenn King..763-5299
Statistical Briefs - Robert Bernstein 763-1584
Training Courses - Staff 763-1510
Year 2000 Research and Development - Staff 763-8601

■ Demographic Programs

Decennial Census

Content (General) - Al Paez 301-763-4251
Content and Tabulations (Program Design) - Patricia Berman 763-7094
Count Questions, 1990 Census - Ed Kobilarcik 763-4894
Counts for Current Boundaries - Joel Miller 763-5720
Count Information, Decennial Census - Staff 763-5002/5020
Demographic Analysis - Gregg Robinson..763-5590
Litigation - Valerie Gregg 763-7787
Post-Enumeration Surveys - Howard Hogan 763-1794
Reapportionment/Redistricting - Marshall Turner, Cathy Talbert 763-5820/4070
Sampling Methods, Decennial Census - Henry Woltman 763-5987
Special Tabulations of Housing Data - Bill Downs..763-8553
Special Tabulations of Population Data - Rosemarie Cowan 763-7947
Tabulations and Publications (General) -
Cheryl Landman, Gloria Porter..763-3938/4908
User-Defined Areas Program (Neighborhood Statistics) -
Adrienne Quasney 763-4282

Housing and Income

American Housing Survey - Edward Montfort 301-763-8551
Components of Inventory Change Survey - Jane Maynard 763-8551
Income Statistics - Staff 763-8576
Information, Decennial Census - Bill Downs 763-8553
Market Absorption/Residential Finance - Anne Smoler, Peter Fronczek 763-8552
New York City Housing and Vacancy Survey - Margaret Harper 763-8552
Vacancy Data - Wallace Fraser 763-8165

- State Boundary Certification - Louise Stewart 301-763-3827
Census Geographic Concepts - Staff 763-5720
Census Tracts:
- Address Locations - Ernie Swapshur 763-5720
- Boundaries, Codes, Delineation - Cathy Miller 763-3827
Centers of Population - Don Hirschfeld 763-5720
Congressional Districts:
- Address Locations - Ernie Swapshur 763-5692
- Boundaries, Component Areas - Robert Hamill 763-5720
GBF/DIME System - Staff 763-1580
Maps:
- 1980 Census Map Orders - Leila Baxter 812/288-3192
- 1990 Census Maps - Staff 763-4100
- Cartographic Operations - Staff 763-3973
- Computer Mapping - Fred Broome 763-3973
Metropolitan Areas (MSAs, PMSAs, and CMSAs) -
James Fitzsimmons, Richard Forstall 763-5158
Outlying Areas - Staff 763-2903
Statistical Areas - Staff 763-3827
TIGER System:
- Applications - Larry Carbaugh 763-1580
- Future Plans - Staff 763-4664
- Products - Staff 763-4100
Urban/Rural Residence - Staff 763-7962
Voting Districts - Cathy McCully 763-3827
ZIP Codes:
- Demographic Data - Staff 763-4100
- Economic Data - Anne Russell 763-7038
- Geographic Relationships - Rose Quarato 763-4667

Statistical Standards and Methodology

Statistical Research for Demographic Programs - Lawrence Ernest 301-763-7880
Statistical Research for Economic Programs - Nash J. Monsour 763-5702

State Data Centers

These agencies can provide you with a wealth of census data, population estimates and projections, employment and earnings data, vital statistics, and other valuable information for all states and U.S. territories. Depending on your need, many of them can also produce customized reports.

Alabama Annette Watters, University of Alabama,
Center for Business and Economic Research 205-248-6191

Alaska Kathryn Lizik, Department of Labor,
Alaska State Data Center 907-465-4500

Arizona Betty Jeffries, Arizona Department of Economic Security 602-542-5984

Arkansas Sarah Breshears, University of Arkansas-
Little Rock, State Data Center 501-569-8530

California Linda Gage, State Census Data Center,
Department of Finance 916-322-4651

Colorado Reid Reynolds, Colorado Department of Local Affairs 303-866-2156

International Statistics

Africa, Asia, Latin America, North America,
and Oceania - Frank Hobbs 301-763-4221
China, People's Republic - Judith Banister 763-4012
Europe - Godfrey Baldwin 763-4022
Health - Peter Way 763-4086
International Data Base - Peter Johnson 763-4811
Soviet Union - Barry Kostinsky 763-4022
Women in Development - Ellen Jamison 763-4086

Population

Age and Sex (States, Counties) - Staff..301-763-5072
Age and Sex (U.S.) - Staff 763-7950
Aging Population - Arnold Goldstein 763-7883
Apportionment - Robert Speaker 763-7962
Child Care - Martin O'Connell, Amara Bachu 763-5303
Citizenship - Staff 763-7955
Commuting: Means of Transportation; Place of Work -
Phil Salopek, Celia Boertlein 763-3850
Consumer Expenditure Survey - Gail Hoff 763-2063
Crime - Larry McGinn...763-1735
Current Population Survey - Ronald Tucker 763-2773
Disability - Jack McNeil 763-8300
Education - Staff 763-1154
Employment, Unemployment - Thomas Palumbo, Selwyn Jones 763-8574
Estimates - Staff 763-7722
Families - Staff 763-7987
Farm Population - Don Dahmann 763-5158
Fertility/Births - Martin O'Connell, Amara Bachu 763-5303
Foreign Born - Staff 763-7955
Group Quarters Population - Denise Smith...763-7883
Health Surveys - Robert Mangold 763-5508
Hispanic and Other Ethnic Population Statistics - Staff 763-7955
Homeless Population - Cynthia Taeuber 763-7883
Household Estimates for States and Counties - Staff 763-5221
Household Wealth - Enrique Lamas 763-8578
Households and Families - Staff 763-7987
Immigration (Legal/Undocumented), Emigration - Karen Woodrow 763-5590
Journey to Work - Phil Salopek, Gloria Swieczkowski 763-3850
Language - Staff 763-1154
Longitudinal Surveys - Ronald Dopkowski 763-2767
Marital Status; Living Arrangements - Arlene Saluter 763-7987
Metropolitan Areas (MSAs) - Richard Forstall...763-5158
Migration - Diana DeAre 763-3850
National Estimates and Projections - Staff 763-7950
Occupation and Industry Statistics - John Priebe, Wilfred Masumura 763-8574
Outlying Areas - Michael Levin 763-5134
Place of Birth - Kristin Hansen 763-3850
Population Information - Staff...763-5002/5020
Poverty Statistics - Staff 763-8578
Prisoner Surveys - Larry McGinn...763-1735
Race Statistics - Staff...763-2607/7572

Sampling Methods - Preston J. Waite 301-763-2672
School District Data - Jane Ingold 763-3476
Special Population Censuses - Ronald Dopkowski 763-2767
Special Surveys - Ronald Dopkowski 763-2767
State Projections - Staff 763-1902
State and Outlying Areas Estimates - Staff 763-5072
Survey of Income and Program Participation (SIPP):
  • SIPP: General Information - Staff 763-2764
  • SIPP: Statistical Methods - Raj Singh 763-7944
  • SIPP: Products - Carmen Campbell 763-2005
Travel Surveys - John Cannon 763-5468
Veterans Status - Thomas Palumbo, Selwyn Jones 763-8574
Voting and Registration - Jerry Jennings 763-4547
Women - Denise Smith 763-7883

■ Economic Programs

Agriculture
Crop Statistics - Donald Jahnke...301-763-8567
Data Requirements and Outreach - Douglas Miller 763-8561
Farm Economics - James Liefer..763-8566
General Information - Tom Manning 763-1113
Irrigation and Horticulture Statistics and
Special Surveys - John Blackledge..763-8560
Livestock Statistics - Linda Hutton 763-8569
Puerto Rico, Virgin Islands, Guam, and Northern Marianas - Kent Hoover .763-8564

Business
Business Owners - Donna McCutcheon..301-763-5517
County Business Patterns - Zigmund Decker 763-5430
Minority and Women-Owned Businesses - Donna McCutcheon 763-5517

Foreign Trade
Trade Data Services - Staff, Haydn Mearkle 301-763-5140/7754
Shipper's Export Declaration - Hal Blyweiss...763-5310

Retail Trade
Advance Monthly Sales, Annual Sales, Monthly
Inventories - Ronald Piencykoski 301-763-5294
Census - Anne Russell...763-7038
Monthly Retail Trade Report - Irving True...763-7128

Service Industries
Census - Jack Moody 301-763-7039
Current Selected Services Reports - Thomas Zabelsky 763-1725
Finance, Insurance, and Real Estate - Sidney Marcus 763-1386
Utilities, Communication, and Transportation
Census - Dennis Shoemaker..763-2662

Wholesale Trade
Census - John Trimble 301-763-5281
Current Sales and Inventories - Dale Gordon 763-3916

Construction
Building Permits (C40 Series) - Linda Hoyle..301-763-7244
Census - Bill Visnansky 763-7546
New Residential Construction:
  • Characteristics, Price Index, Sales (C25/27 Series) - Steve Berman 763-7842

  • Housing Stats (C20 Series)/Completions (C22 Series) -
David Fondelier 301-763-5731
  • New Construction in Selected MSAs (C21 Series) - Dale Jacobson 763-7842
Survey of Residential Improvements and
Repairs (C50 Series) - George Roff 763-5705
Value of New Construction Put in Place (C30 Series) - Allan Meyer 763-5717

Governments
Criminal Justice Statistics - Diana Cull 301-763-7789
Employment - Alan Stevens 763-5086
Federal Expenditure Data - David Kellerman 763-5276
Finance - Henry Wulf 763-7664
Governmental Organization - Diana Cull...763-7789
Operations Support and Analysis - William Fanning 763-4403
Survey Operations - Genevieve Speight 763-7783
Taxation - Gerard Keffer 763-5356

Manufacturing
Concentration, Exports from Manufacturing Establishments,
and Production Index - Bruce Goldhirsch 301-763-1503
Durables (Census/Annual Survey) - Kenneth Hansen 763-7304
Durables (Current Industrial Reports) - Malcolm Bernhardt 763-2518
Fuels/Electric Energy Consumed - John McNamee 763-5938
Industries - John P. Govoni 763-7666
Monthly Shipments, Inventories, Orders - Ruth Runyan 763-2502
Nondurables (Census/Annual Survey) - Michael Zampogna 763-2510
Nondurables (Current Industrial Reports) - Thomas Flood ....763-591'
Research and Development, Capacity,
Pollution Abatement - Elinor Champion ....763-5(

Special Topics
County Business Patterns - Zigmund Decker 301-763
Economic Census Products - Paul Zeisset 76
Employment/Unemployment Statistics - Thomas Palumbo 7
Enterprise Statistics - Johnny Monaco ....'
Geographic Areas of the Economic Censuses - Staff ....
Industry and Commodity Classification - Alvin Venning ....
Investment in Plant and Equipment - John Gates.................................
Mineral Industries - John McNamee...
Quarterly Financial Report - Paul Zarrett ....
  • Accounting and Related Issues - Ronald Lee ....
  • Classification - Frank Hartman ....

Puerto Rico, Virgin Islands, Guam
Censuses of Agriculture, Construction, Manufactures, Retail Trad
Services, and Wholesale Trade - Odell Larson, Kent Hoover ....

Transportation
Truck Inventory and Use - William Bostic ....

Geographic Concepts and Products
Area Measurement - Don Hirschfeld ....
Boundaries of Legal Areas:
  • Annexations, Boundary Changes - Nancy Goodman ....

Connecticut Theron Schnure, Connecticut Office
of Policy and Management 203-566-8285

Delaware Judy McKinney-Cherry, Delaware Development Office 302-739-4271

District of Columbia Gan Ahuja, Mayor's Office of Planning 202-727-6533

Florida Steve Kimble, Florida State Data Center 904-487-2814

Georgia Marty Sik, Georgia Office of Planning and Budget 404-656-0911

Guam Peter Barcinas, Guam Department of Commerce 671-646-5841

Hawaii Emogene Estores, Department of Business and
Economic Development 808-548-3082

Idaho Alan Porter, Idaho Department of Commerce 208-334-2470

Illinois Sue Ebetsch, Illinois State Data Center Coop.,
Illinois Bureau of the Budget...217-782-1381

Indiana Roberta Eads, Indiana State Library,
Indiana State Data Center 317-232-3733

Iowa Beth Henning, State Library 515-281-4350

Kansas Marc Galbraith, State Library 913-296-3296

Kentucky Ron Crouch, Kentucky State Data Center,
Urban Research Institute 502-588-7990

Louisiana Karen Paterson, Louisiana Planning and Budget 504-342-7410

Maine Jean Martin, Maine Department of Labor 207-289-2271

Maryland Michel Lettre, Maryland Office of Planning.............................301-225-4450

Massachusetts Steve Coelen, University of Massachusetts,
Massachusetts Institute for Social and Economic Research 413-545-3460

Michigan Eric Swanson, Michigan Information Center,
Department of Management and Budget 517-373-7910

Minnesota David Birkholz, Minnesota State Planning
Agency, State Demographic Unit..612-297-2360

Minnesota David Rademacher, Minnesota State
Demographer's Office..612-297-3255

Mississippi Pattie Byrd, University of Mississippi, Center
for Population Studies 601-232-7288

Missouri Marlys Davis, Missouri State Library 314-751-3615

Montana Patricia Roberts, Montana Department of Commerce 406-444-2896

Nebraska Jerome Deichert, University of Nebraska-Omaha,
Center for Public Affairs Research 402-595-2311

Nevada Betty McNeal, Nevada State Library and Archives 702-687-5160

New Hampshire Thomas J. Duffy, Office of State Planning 603-271-2155

New Jersey Connie O. Hughes, New Jersey Department of Labor 609-984-2593

New Mexico Juliana Boyle, University of New Mexico, Bureau of Business and Economic Research 505-277-2216

New York Robert Scardamalia, Department of Economic Development 518-474-6005

North Carolina Francine Stephenson, State Data Center, North Carolina Office of State Budget and Management 919-733-7061

North Dakota Richard Rathge, North Dakota State University, Department of Agricultural Economics 701-237-8621

Ohio Barry Bennett, Ohio Department of Development 614-466-2115

Oklahoma Karen Selland, Oklahoma Department of Commerce, Oklahoma State Data Center 405-841-5184

Oregon Maria Wilson-Figueroa, Portland State University, Center for Population Research and Census 503-725-3922

Pennsylvania Michael Behney, Pennsylvania State University at Harrisburg, Pennsylvania State Data Center 717-948-6336

Puerto Rico Lillian Torres Aguirre, Puerto Rico Planning Board 809-728-4430

Rhode Island Paul Egan, Rhode Island Department of Administration, Office of Municipal Affairs 401-277-6493

South Carolina Mike MacFarlane, South Carolina Budget and Control Board 803-734-3780

South Dakota DeVee Dykstra, University of South Dakota, Business Research Bureau 605-677-5287

Tennessee Charles Brown, Tennessee State Planning Office 615-741-1676

Texas Susan Tully, Texas Department of Commerce 512-472-5059

Utah Linda Smith, Office of Planning and Budget 801-538-1036

Vermont Office of Policy Research and Coordination 802-828-3326

Virgin Islands Frank Mills, University of the Virgin Islands 809-776-9200

Virginia Dan Jones, Virginia Employment Commission 804-786-8308

Washington Sharon Estee, Office of Financial Management 206-586-2504

West Virginia Mary C. Harless, Governor's Office of Community and Industrial Development 304-348-4010

Wisconsin Robert Naylor, Demographic Services Center, Department of Administration 608-266-1927

Wyoming Mary Byrnes, Department of Administration and Fiscal Control 307-777-7504

Department of Agriculture

Information Division
Economic Research Service and
National Agricultural Statistics Service
Room 228, 1301 New York Ave., N.W.
Washington, DC 20005
800-999-6779
202-219-0494

The Department of Agriculture's Economic Research Service (ERS) analyzes trade, production, rural development, farm inputs, etc. Working with it is the National Agricultural Statistics Service (NASS), which produces estimates of production, stocks, inventories, disposition, utilization, and prices of agricultural commodities and related items such as labor and farm numbers. Call or write for their free catalog of periodicals and listing of information contacts.

Materials cover banking and farm credit, commodities, farm programs, farm workers and farm employment, farm operations and finance, farmland, conservation, and farm policies. Some of the latest research they have available includes:

■ Food Spending in American Households, 1980-88

Presents information on trends in household food expenditures for major food groups by selected demographic variables, as well as information on food price trends. $11.00.

■ Food Consumption, Prices, and Expenditures, 1968-89

Historical data on food consumption, prices, and expenditures, and U.S. income and population. Americans spent $546 billion for food in 1990 and another $80 billion for alcoholic beverages. Away-from-home meals and snacks captured 46 percent of the U.S. food dollar in 1990, up from 34 percent in 1970 and 24 percent in 1950. $14.00.

■ Foreign Ownership of U.S. Agricultural Land Through December 31, 1990

This annual report finds that foreigners owned 14.4 million acres of U.S. agricultural land as of December 31, 1990. This is slightly more than 1 percent of all privately held agricultural land and 0.6 percent of all land in the United States. $8.00.

■ Agricultural Resources: Agricultural Land Values

This annual report finds that U.S. farm real estate values rose 2 percent during 1990, marking the fourth straight increase since their slide in the mid-1980s. $4.00.

■ The Economic Well-Being of Nonmetro Children

Analyzes the economic well-being of children living in families with at least one parent present, by metro-nonmetro residence. Twenty-four percent of children residing in nonmetro areas are in families below the official poverty line, 12 percent are near poor, and 64 percent are in families of at least modest means. $8.00.

■ Employment Trends in Farm and Farm-Related Industries, 1975-87

Shows that agricultural production jobs have declined, some-farm-related industries have declined or remained stable, and other industries that process, market, and sell agricultural products have seen employment growth. $8.00.

Bureau of Economic Analysis

Public Information Office, BE-53
Bureau of Economic Analysis
U.S. Department of Commerce
Washington, DC 20230
202-523-0777

The Bureau of Economic Analysis (BEA) provides basic information on such key issues as economic growth, inflation, regional development, and the nation's role in the world economy. Its products and services are related to the BEA's four program areas: national economics, regional economics, international economics, and tools for measuring, analyzing, and forecasting. You can find out what they have available by calling for a free copy of *A User's Guide to BEA Information*.

Some of their many publications, reports, and other data products include:

■ BEA Reports

Five sets of reports presenting the information contained in the BEA news releases for the following areas: gross national product, personal income and outlays, regional reports, international reports, and composite indexes of leading, coincident, and lagging indicators. The reports contain summary estimates and are mailed the day after estimates are released. All five sets, a total of about 55 printed reports, are available for $110.00 a year.

■ Survey of Current Business

This monthly journal contains estimates and analyses of U.S. economic activity. It includes a review of current economic developments and estimates of the national income and product accounts. It also has economic data from various public and private sources. Recent articles examined regional and state projections of income, employment, and population to the year 2000; U.S. international sales and purchases of services; and an evaluation of the state personal income estimates. An annual subscription is $23.00.

■ Business Statistics, 1961-88

This publication presents monthly or quarterly data on such topics as business sales, inventories, and orders; prices; employment and unemployment; construction; banking and finance; transportation, etc. It includes definitions of terms, sources of data, and methods of compilation. $16.00.

■ Economic Data for All U.S. Counties and Metro Areas

A CD-ROM containing annual data for 3,107 counties and 337 metropolitan areas for 1969-89, including personal income by major source, per capita personal income, regional economic profiles, full- and part-time employment by one-digit SIC industry, farm income and expenses, etc. The package includes a program on a separate floppy disk that allows you to display, print, or copy the tables. $35.00.

■ Recorded Telephone Messages

These 3- to 5-minute recorded telephone messages summarize key estimates immediately after their release and are available 24 hours a day for several days following release. The numbers to dial are:

• Leading indicators: 202-898-2450

- Gross National Product: 202-898-2451

- Personal Income and Outlays: 202-898-2452

- Merchandise Trade, Balance of Payments Basis, or
  U.S. International Transactions: 202-898-2453

■ Economic Bulletin Board

You can access the BEA's bulletin board via personal computer, computer terminal, or word processor equipped with a modem. It gives you regular access to such government reports as personal income statistics, consumer and producer price indexes, daily trade opportunities, economic indicators, exchange rates and money supply reports, etc. Call the Commerce Department's Office of Business Analysis at 202-377-1986 for more information.

National Center for Education Statistics

Information Services
Office of Educational Research and Improvement
U.S. Department of Education
555 New Jersey Ave., N.W.
Washington, DC 20208
800-424-1616
626-9853 in metro Washington, DC

The National Center for Education Statistics (NCES) conducts surveys and publishes reports intended to inform those who make education policy decisions, those in the media who write about education, and the general public. Their free listing of current and forthcoming publications is updated quarterly, but unfortunately gives little information about contents or prices. It does list identification numbers that you need for ordering reports and ordering addresses for publications.

You can get data from the NCES on elementary, secondary, and postsecondary education; for example:

■ Digest of Education Statistics

This publication includes statistics on institutions, resources, and faculty, as well as students, outcomes, public and private support.

Other reports and publications available from NCES include:

- Projections of Education Statistics to 2001

- The Condition of Education: Elementary, Secondary, and Postsecondary Education Indicators of Trends and Status

- Dropout Rates in the United States

- Key Statistics on Public Elementary/Secondary Education by State, Region, Local, and Wealth Clusters.

- School Effects on Educational Achievement in Mathematics and Science

- Who Majors in Science? Science, Engineering and Mathematics College Graduates

- Characteristics of the 100 Largest Public Elementary and Secondary School   Districts in the U.S., 1988-89

- Targeted Forecast: Elementary and Secondary Enrollment

- Status of Minority Participants in Public Schools

- Selected Statistics on Student Financial Aid Awards: 1989-90

- Racial/Ethnic Trends in Degrees Conferred by Higher Education Institutions

- Profile of Undergraduates in American Postsecondary Institutions

- Mathematics Achievement by State

Energy Information Administration

National Energy Information Center (NEIC)
Room 1F-048, Forrestal Bldg.
1000 Independence Ave., S.W.
Washington, DC 20585
202-586-8800
For the hearing impaired: 202-586-1181

The Energy Information Administration (EIA) is the Department of Energy's statistical and analytical arm. It collects and publishes data and prepares analyses on energy production, consumption, prices, and resources. It also does projections of energy supply and demand. You can find out what they have available from their free *EIA Publications Directory*, which is issued annually.

Some of what you can get from the EIA include:

■ Energy Information Administration's Annual Report to Congress

Begun in 1982, the EIA annual report gives a general overview for the calendar year followed by descriptions of significant agency activities. Selected energy statistics and facts for several years are provided in separate sections. Active models and data collection surveys are described in the appendices along with a listing of publications and periodicals published during the year. Free.

■ EIA New Releases

This is a free bimonthly, current awareness newsletter which lists and describes newly released EIA publications. Recent issues discussed the U.S.'s energy efficiency over the next 20 years, the release of a biofuels consumption study, U.S. energy industry financial trends, the decline in operating expenditures for nuclear power plants, the release of preliminary data on uranium industry trends, and how electric utilities are trying to reduce sulfur emissions. Free.

■ Energy Information Sheets

These 20 information sheets examine various aspects of coal, electricity, petroleum, or natural gas. Some sheets explain renewable types of energy, nuclear fuel, and the

meaning of such terms as "degree days" and "British thermal units." Written for the lay person, the sheets are free and updated yearly.

■ Energy Facts

This is an annual pocket-sized handbook that provides a quick reference to a broad range of domestic and international data. $1.50.

■ Monthly Energy Review

This publication provides a complete overview of the nation's energy picture. It provides data on petroleum, natural gas, coal, electricity, nuclear energy, oil and gas resource development, prices, consumption, and the international energy situation. $62.00 for an annual subscription; $7.00 for single copies.

■ Short-Term Energy Outlook, Quarterly Projections

This report discusses world oil prices, macroeconomic activities, energy product prices, petroleum demand and supply, and outlooks for other major energy sources. $14.00 for an annual subscription; $3.75 for single copies.

■ Geothermal Energy in the Western United States and Hawaii: Resources and Projected Electricity Generation Supplies

This report provides information on the status of the geothermal industry, the electric power generation potential from geothermal resources, and a description and quantification of the geothermal resource base. $4.25.

■ The Motor Gasoline Industry: Past, Present, and Future

This publication presents an historical overview of the gasoline industry and discusses motor gasoline supply, storage, distribution and marketing, prices and demand, and alternative fuels. The report also presents a motor gasoline outlook containing forecasts of motor gasoline demand to 2010. $3.50.

National Center for Health Statistics

6525 Belcrest Rd.
Hyattsville, MD 20782
301-436-8500

The National Center for Health Statistics conducts a continuing interview survey of the U.S. civilian noninstitutionalized population called the National Health Interview Survey. It also collects data through direct examination, testing, and measurement of national samples in its National Health Examination Survey and National Health and Nutrition Examination Survey.

Data from these surveys and other studies are presented in hundreds of free or inexpensive reports. Call for a catalog of publications and ordering information.

A sampling of catalog items includes:

• Trends in Hospital Utilization
• Physician Contacts by Sociodemographic and Health Characteristics

- Use of Dental Services and Dental Health
- Health Indicators for Hispanic, Black, and White Americans
- In-Patient Utilization of Short-Stay Hospitals, by Diagnosis
- Health Characteristics by Geographic Region and Large Metropolitan Areas
- Nursing Home Utilization by Current Residents
- Prevalence of Selected Impairments
- Diet and Dental Health, A Study of Relationships
- Height and Weight of Adults by Socioeconomic and Geographic Variables
- Basic Data on Health Care Needs of Adults Ages 25-74 Years
- Eye Conditions and Related Need for Medical Care
- AIDS Knowledge and Attitudes
- Trends and Variations in First Births to Older Women
- Selected Demographic Characteristics of Teenage Wives and Mothers
- Eye Care Visits and Use of Eyeglasses or Contact Lenses
- Americans Assess Their Health
- Serum Cholesterol Levels by Socioeconomic Characteristics
- Decayed, Missing, and Filled Teeth Among Persons 1-74 Years
- Dietary Intake and Cardiovascular Risk Factors
- Blood Pressure Levels for Persons Aged 6 Months-74 Years

■ *Health, United States, 1990*

This annual report to Congress on the nation's health presents easy-to-read and up-to-date facts and statistics on trends in AIDS, smoking, hospital use, life expectancy and mortality, etc. The prevention profile tracks progress toward meeting the nation's health objectives. $19.00

■ *Vital Statistics of the United States*

These annual reports present detailed statistics on births, deaths, marriages, divorces, and infant deaths with brief analyses. Price varies.

Department of Housing and Urban Development

HUD USER
P.O. Box 6091
Rockville, MD 20850
800-245-2691
301-251-5154

HUD USER is sponsored by HUD's Office of Policy Development and Research. It is a research information service and clearinghouse for people who are working toward improving housing and strengthening community development. HUD USER collects, develops, and distributes housing-related information, and its reference specialists are available to help individuals find information. Call for a free copy of *HUD USER: A Guide to Publications and Services.*

HUD's publications span various topics in the fields of housing and urban development: affordable housing and building technology, community planning and urban development, energy and infrastructure, housing programs, and housing statistics.

You can find out what's available through HUD USER ONLINE, a database containing bibliographic references to about 5,500 reports, articles, case studies, and manuals. A Standard Search can be done by the HUD research staff for $5.00 per topic. The standard topics are: federal housing programs, homelessness, housing for the elderly, local economic development, and public housing. If you need information on a subject not included in the Standard Search list, you can get a custom search for $20.00 per topic.

Immigration and Naturalization Service

425 Eye St., N.W.
Washington, DC 20536
202-376-3069

The Statistics Division of the U.S. Immigration and Naturalization Service (INS), which is a branch of the U.S. Department of Justice, collects data on immigrant admissions, refugee arrivals, asylee approvals, and nonimmigrant admissions. A call for a free packet of information will get you details about:

■ Statistical Yearbook of the Immigration and Naturalization Service

This annual yearbook includes summary tables on the demographics of legal immigrants. Characteristics include: port of entry, month and year of admission, age, country of birth, marital status, sex, nationality, labor certification, country of last permanent residence, zip code of intended residence, and occupation.

The Statistical Yearbook is available for 1965 through 1990 in a softbound book for $23.00 per year, and on microfiche for $8.00 per year. You can also get the data on magnetic tape, the cost of which varies by density; call 703-487-4763 for prices and ordering information.

■ Commissioner's Fact Book: Summary of Recent Immigration Data

This annual booklet provides a quick summary of the data in the larger *Statistical Yearbook.* Full of tables, it gives you the latest numbers on such topics as the number of immigrants admitted from 1820 through 1990; the number of drug seizures, amount seized, and estimated dollar value; persons naturalized in 1990 for top 20 states of residence, etc. Free.

■ Immigration Profiles

In June 1991 the INS issued a 13-page *Immigration Profile of Canada*, and will continue to profile other countries periodically. The report examines the demographics of

Canadian immigrants to the U.S.: their age and sex, state of intended residence, marital status, occupation, port of entry, etc. Free.

■ INS Bulletins

Several times a year the Statistics Division publishes bulletins on a variety of topics ranging from new immigrant and nonimmigrant data; parolee data; emigration from the U.S., INS drug seizures, U.S. border patrol apprehensions, and nonimmigrant overstays. Free.

Internal Revenue Service

Statistics of Income Division
P.O. Box 2608
Washington, DC 20013-2608
202-874-0410

The Internal Revenue Service (IRS) has many reports and bulletins on taxes and who is paying them in the U.S. Publications include:

■ Statistics of Income Bulletin

The *SOI Bulletin* provides the earliest published annual financial statistics from the various types of tax and information returns filed with the IRS. Historical data are provided for selected types of taxpayers, as well as state data and gross internal revenue collections. Some of the topics which have been described and analyzed in recent *SOI Bulletins* include: estate tax returns, income by age or sex of taxpayer, high income returns, foreign recipients of U.S. income, historical summary of income and taxes, personal wealth, taxpayers aged 65 or older, unreported income, etc. An annual subscription is $20.00; individual copies are approximately $7.50.

■ Individual Income Tax Returns

This annual report presents in-depth data on sources of income, exemptions, itemized deductions, and tax computations. The data are presented by size of adjusted gross income and marital status. $9.00.

■ Area to Area Migration Data

These data show migration patterns, from where to where, by state and county, based on year-to-year changes in the tax return address for selected time periods between 1978 and 1988. The numbers are based on income tax returns from the Individual Master File, which includes a record for every Form 1040, 1040A, and 1040EZ Individual Income Tax return filed with the IRS. Available on tape for $495 for one time period and $350.00 for each additional time period.

■ County Income Data

For each county, the following data are provided: number of returns and exemptions; aggregate adjusted gross income, wages and salaries, gross dividends, gross interest income, and gross rents and royalties. Available for $5 per page (32 counties per page), or $495 on tape for each tax year.

Department of Justice

National Institute of Justice/NCJRS
User Services
Box 6000
Rockville, MD 20850
800-851-3420
301-251-5500

The U.S. Department of Justice is organized into several agencies, including the Bureau of Justice Statistics, which collects data, and the National Institute of Justice, which does primary research. The findings of these two agencies, and others within the Department of Justice, are available through the National Criminal Justice Reference Service (NCJRS), a clearinghouse that provides the latest criminal justice research findings. Most of their publications are free.

The NCJRS reference specialists can answer questions about a whole range of criminal justice issues, such as law enforcement, drugs and crime, courts, corrections, juvenile justice, criminology, victims, corrections construction, etc.

For more information call or write for free copies of *The NIJ Publications Catalog: Your Guide to NIJ Research Findings* and *User Guide to NCJRS Products and Services*.

Products and services of interest to researchers include:

■ Justice Statistics Clearinghouse

The Bureau of Justice Statistics (BJS) supports this clearinghouse for those seeking crime and criminal justice data. Call 800-732-3277 to get details about its document data base searches, statistics information packages, referrals, and other related products and services.

■ Mailing Lists

The BJS publishes many reports and bulletins on the following topics; call 800-732-3277 to get your name on the mailing lists of interest to you:

- Law enforcement reports—Police Departments in Large Cities, Profile of State and Local Law Enforcement Agencies, etc.
- Drugs and crime data—National Household Survey on Drug Abuse: Population Estimates 1990, Drug Forecasting Annual Report, etc.
- Justice spending and employment
- White-collar crime
- National Crime Survey (annual; details below)
- Corrections (annual; details below)
- Courts—Felony Sentences in State Courts, Felony Case-Processing Time, etc.
- Privacy and security of criminal history information and information policy—Strategies for Improving Data Quality, Survey of Criminal History Information
- Federal justice statistics
- BJS bulletins and special reports (approximately twice a month)
- Sourcebook of Criminal Justice Statistics (annual; details below)

■ National Crime Survey

There are a number of reports and bulletins that come out of this annual survey of crime victims aged 12 or older. They cover such topics as handgun crime victims, violent crime by strangers and non-strangers, preventing domestic violence against women, household burglary, teenage victims of crime, the seasonality of crime victimization, etc.

■ Corrections

The results of this survey are packaged into many bulletins and special reports, which examine such topics as women in prison, capital punishment, population density in state prisons, prisoners at midyear, drunk driving, and the prevalence of imprisonment.

■ Drugs and Crime CD-ROM Library

The library provides abstracts, full-text books, journal articles, images, and data sets from the Departments of Justice, State, Health and Human Services, Education, Transportation, Treasury, and Defense, as well as from foreign governments, the U.N., and private sources. Call NCJRS for details.

■ Sourcebook of Criminal Justice Statistics

This free annual publication has six sections:

1. Characteristics of the criminal justice systems: number and types of criminal justice agencies and employees, criminal justice expenditures, workload of agency personnel, etc.

2. Public attitudes toward crime and criminal-justice-related topics: results of nationwide public opinion polls on such matters as fear of victimization, the death penalty, prison reform, gun control, drug use, etc.

3. Nature and distribution of known offenses: proportions of persons reporting that they have used various drugs or participated in other illegal activities, surveys of individuals and households that may have been victims of crimes, etc.

4. Characteristics and distribution of persons arrested: counts of arrestees by age, sex, race, and area; counts of illegal goods seized, etc.

5. Judicial processing of defendants: number of juveniles and adults processed through the courts, characteristics and sentences of defendants, etc.

6. Persons under correctional supervision: data about persons on probation and parole, population and movement of inmates of state and federal prisons, offenders executed and currently under sentence of death, etc.

The *Sourcebook* also includes a useful list of sources and references for researchers who want to get more information about particular subjects.

■ Bureau of Justice Statistics Slide Presentation

Report to the Nation on Crime and Justice is a comprehensive presentation of statistical information on crime and the administration of justice. The report's charts, maps, and graphs have been made into slides which present a comprehensive picture of the extent of crime, its costs, and the criminal justice system's response. Call NCJRS User Services for details.

■ Federal Criminal Justice Research Data Base

Provides information on current or recently completed government-funded research in criminal justice. It features more than 1,700 studies dealing with such topics as corrections, law enforcement, child abuse, drugs and crime, courts, juvenile justice, forensics, and crime prevention. Contact NCJRS User Services for a search.

■ NCJRS Electronic Bulletin Board

Free and available around the clock, the bulletin board was created to help individuals and organizations involved in criminal justice policy and research obtain and share information, experiences, and views. Call 301-738-8895 for information on how to log on.

■ National Archive of Criminal Justice Data

Public-use tapes of BJS data sets and other criminal justice data are available from the National Archive of Criminal Justice Data, P.O. Box 1248, Ann Arbor, Michigan 48106; 800-999-0960.

Bureau of Labor Statistics

441 G Street, N.W.
Washington, DC 20212
202-523-1221

The Bureau of Labor Statistics (BLS) is the main data-gathering agency of the federal government in the broad field of labor economics. Most of the bureau's data come from voluntary responses to surveys of businesses or households conducted by BLS staff, by the Bureau of the Census (on a contract basis), or in conjunction with cooperating state and federal agencies.

The BLS has a huge array of publications and reports on such topics as employment and unemployment, prices and living conditions, compensation and working conditions, productivity and technology, and employment projections. Some of what you can get include:

■ BLS Update

A quarterly bulletin to help data users keep informed of developments in BLS programs and information. Free

■ Major Programs of the Bureau of Labor Statistics

An annual publication that describes the Bureau's major statistical programs, the data available, the form of publication, some of the uses of the data, and selected publications and data tapes. Free

■ How to Get Information From the Bureau of Labor Statistics

A brochure summarizing the kinds of information the Bureau produces, and how to obtain BLS publications. Free.

■ Where to Find BLS Statistics on Women

A periodically updated report describing where various data series on women are published and the frequency of publication. Free.

■ Monthly Labor Review

Each issue includes analytical articles, 53 pages of current statistics, reports on industrial relations, book reviews, and other features. A recent issue reported on the weakened labor market in the U.S., characteristics of volunteer workers, trends in employer-provided health care benefits, and employer-sponsored prescription drug benefits. $24.00 for an annual subscription; $5.50 per copy.

■ *Occupational Outlook Quarterly*

Each issue keeps guidance counselors, career planners, and others informed of changing career opportunities. $6.50 for an annual subscription; $2.50 per copy.

■ *CPI Detailed Report*

This monthly publication provides a comprehensive report on price movements for the month, plus statistical tables, charts, and technical notes. $21.00 for an annual subscription; $7.00 per copy.

■ *Compensation and Working Conditions*

Reports monthly on employee compensation, including selected wage and benefit changes; work stoppages; major agreements due to expire; industry wages; white-collar pay; occupational safety and health; and statistical summaries. Recent issues discussed the characteristics of union membership, the new BLS census of fatal occupational injuries, and employee benefits in small private establishments. $15.00 for an annual subscription; $3 per copy.

■ *Employment and Earnings*

This monthly report covers employment and unemployment developments in the previous month, plus statistical tables on national, state, and area employment, hours, and earnings. $29.00 for an annual subscription; $9.50 per copy.

■ *24-Hour Current Data Hotline: 202-523-1221*

The BLS also has a phone system for getting recorded messages about the Consumer Price Index, Producer Price Indexes, the Employment Situation, the Employment Cost Index, and scores of other topics. You can dial into it 24 hours a day.

Once you dial 202-523-1221, follow the instructions you'll hear. Staff members are available to answer questions Monday through Friday, from 8:30 a.m. to 4:30 p.m., Eastern time. Some of the many Data Hotline category codes are:

To hear ....*immediately press*
A summary of major BLS Indicators 115
Release dates for major BLS Indicators 1165
Telephone numbers for BLS subject specialists 1166
How to order BLS sales publications 1161
How to order BLS data diskettes and tapes 1162
How to order BLS electronic news releases 1163
How to get on BLS mailing lists..1164

National Technical Information Service

U.S. Department of Commerce
Springfield, VA 22161
703-487-4650

The National Technical Information Service (NTIS) is a unique government agency sustained only by its sales revenue. All costs of NTIS salaries, marketing, postage, and other operating costs are paid for from this revenue, so they are anxious to let customers know what is available and how to order. Call for a free copy of the *NTIS Products and Services Catalog.*

Every week NTIS adds an average of 1,200 titles to its collection—the results of research and studies sponsored by the U.S. and foreign governments. It contains current data not readily available from any other source. Some of the many topics covered include agriculture and food, behavior and society, business and economics, health care, medicine and biology, problem solving information for state and local governments, transportation, and telecommunications.

Some of NTIS's vast number of titles and periodicals include:

■ Abstract Newsletters

Abstract Newsletters are valuable reference sources for researchers and other professionals who need to keep up with the latest developments in their fields. Twenty-six different newsletters cover everything from agriculture and food, to business and economics, to health care. Every week these newsletters summarize the latest research projects and their findings. The source for information is included, usually as a technical report available directly from NTIS. A yearly subject index is available for each newsletter. $35.00.

■ Published Searches

Each *Published Search* contains up to 100 or more citations of reports and studies in a particular subject area. Customers are notified automatically every time their searches are updated. For a catalog listing the 3,000 *Published Searches* available call 703-487-4650 and ask for #PR-186-827.

■ Economic Bulletin Board

This online service allows users to find the latest statistical releases from federal agencies. Data include figures relating to the gross national product, personal income, consumer price index, and the nation's employment situation. $35.00 per year plus connect time charges.

■ The World Factbook 1990

This publication prepared by the CIA gives you accurate, up-to-date facts about all the countries of the world. It provides current geographic, economic, and demographic information, and includes small maps for each country's entry and fold-out color maps of major world regions. $33.50. (Also available on tape and diskette.)

■ National Center for Health Statistics Datafiles

The datafiles provide statistical data on vital events of the American people, including: marriages and divorces, natality and mortality, health interview and examination, nutrition, family growth, utilization of health resources, personal health practices and consequences, medical care utilization expenditures. Call NTIS for more information and a free brochure #PR-716-827.

■ Nutrition and Food Composition Data

These datafiles relate to food composition, the food consumption of individuals, and the food used by households in the U.S. Included are the Department of Agriculture Nutrient Database for Standard Reference, Nationwide Food Consumption Survey, and Nutritive Value of Foods. Call for the free brochure #PR-814-827.

■ NTIS Bibliographic Database

The NTIS Bibliographic Database contains summaries of completed government-sponsored studies from 1964 to the present—representing hundreds of billions of dollars of U.S. and foreign government research. The studies range from adhesives and administration to urban planning and zoology—70,000 new items each year.

To access the database online, contact a commercial service listed below. These vendors will provide a password and instructions. If you do not have a personal computer, check with either your company's library or a public or academic library—most have access to the database.

The NTIS Bibliographic Database is available from:

- BIOSIS Connection, 800-523-4806
- BRS, 800-345-4277
- CISTI, in Canada, 613-993-1210
- DATA-STAR, 800-221-7754
- DIALOG, 800-334-2564
- OCLC's EPIC, 800-848-5878
- ORBIT, 800-456-7248; in Virginia 703-442-0900
- STN International, 800-848-6533; in Ohio and Canada, 800-848-6538
- Batch searching and SDI service is available from NERAC, 203-872-7000.

■ Available on CD-ROM

The database is also available on CD-ROM. It covers the last six years and is updated quarterly. You will need a personal computer and a CD-ROM drive to read the disc. Contact the following companies for more information:

- DIALOG, 800-334-2564
- SilverPlatter, 800-343-0064
- OCLC, 800-848-5878; in Ohio, 800-848-8286

■ Online Help Desk

The Help Desk will answer your questions about the database and its subject content. Call 703-487-4640 between 8:00 a.m. and 5:00 p.m., Eastern time.

■ Free Search Guides

These guides help you search for the material you need and help you take advantage of the subject categories used by NTIS. To get your free copies, call 703-487-4650.

- NTIS Subject Category Descriptions, #PR-832/827

- Search Guide to the NTIS Bibliographic Database:

  on BRS, #PR-831-827

  on DIALOG, #PR-829-827

  on ORBIT, #PR-830-827

  on STN, #PR-837-827

■ NTIS Online Newsletter

The *NTIS Online Alert* gives you search techniques and new information about the NTIS Bibliographic and FEDRIP databases. Call 703-487-4929 to receive this free quarterly newsletter, #PR-862.

■ Federal Research in Progress (FEDRIP) Database

FEDRIP summarizes 120,000 U.S. government-funded research projects currently in progress. These summaries make it possible to determine progress in specific areas before technical reports or journal literature become available. The database content focuses on health, physical sciences, agriculture, engineering, and life sciences.

The database can be searched through DIALOG, 800-334-2564. Batch searching and SDI services are available from NERAC, Inc., 203-872-7000.

National Park Service

Socio-Economic Studies, WASO-TNT
P.O. Box 25287
Denver, CO 80225-0287
303-969-2060

The National Park Service, a division of the U.S. Department of Interior, publishes an annual statistical abstract, which is available for free from Socio-Economic Studies. Replete with tables and charts, the 42-page 1990 edition examined:

- Recreation visits, acreages, areas administered, and areas reporting recreation visits in the national park system by classification. National recreation areas drew the most visitors, while the 22.19-acre international historic site didn't attract anyone.

- Recreation visits by National Park Service Region: California was tops, followed by Washington, DC, Virginia, and North Carolina. Guam came in last with 61,200 visits. A bar chart of the number of visits each year reveals a drop in 1985, followed by steady increases every year thereafter, to almost 260 million visits by 1990. Gettysburg is the favorite Civil War park, while Fort Jefferson comes in last.

- The abstract also details overnight stays in National Park Service Areas by type of accommodation, broken out by individual area. For example, RVs are tops at the Whiskeytown-Shasta-Trinity NRA, while tents are the accommodation of choice in Joshua Tree.

Social Security Administration

Office of Research and Statistics
Room 209 Van Ness Centre
4301 Connecticut Ave., N.W.
Washington, DC 20008
202-282-7138

The Office of Research and Statistics develops and conducts the Social Security Administration's research and statistical program. Its publications include statistics on the Old-Age, Survivors, and Disability Insurance (OASDI) and Supplemental Security Income (SSI) programs and other social insurance and income support programs. Call or write for their free catalog of research and statistics publications.

Some of what you can get from the Social Security Administration include:

■ *Social Security Bulletin*

This monthly publication, which includes an Annual Statistical Supplement, provides data on income-maintenance programs, Social Security trust funds, OASDI cash benefits, SSI payments, Aid to Families with Dependent Children (AFDC) payments, and data from programs related to Social Security, such as workers' compensation, veterans' programs, unemployment insurance, civil service, railroad, retirement, etc. $19.00 a year.

■ *Social Security Programs in the United States*

This is a layperson's guide to the nation's network of publicly funded cash and in-kind income-maintenance programs and the health insurance and medical assistance programs under the Social Security Act. The social insurance systems covered include OASDI, Medicare, unemployment insurance, workers' compensation, and temporary disability insurance or cash sickness insurance. The major income-supported programs discussed include SSI, AFDC, Medicaid, and food stamps. Programs for veterans, public employees, and railroad employees are also discussed. $3.25.

■ *Annual Statistical Supplement to the Social Security Bulletin*

A yearly compilation of current and historical data on Social Security beneficiaries and covered workers and the economy in general. Contains more than 250 detailed tables, as well as sections dealing with program definitions, historical program summaries, and current legislative developments in a variety of areas. The Supplement is included in a subscription to the *Social Security Bulletin* or can be ordered separately for $17.00.

■ *Income and Resources of the Population 65 and Over: Chartbook*

A series of 20 charts detailing the economic status of the aged; the sources of their income; the proportion of their income from Social Security, other pensions, assets, and earnings; and their Social Security benefit levels. Two charts deal with living arrangements of the aged and their health insurance coverage. $2.00.

■ *Income of the Population 55 or Older*

This publication presents a broad income picture of a cross-section of the population aged 55 or older with special emphasis on some aspects of the income of the

■ *Income of the Population 55 or Older*

This publication presents a broad income picture of a cross-section of the population aged 55 or older with special emphasis on some aspects of the income of the population

aged 65 or older. The tabulations focus on the major sources and amounts of income, both separately and combined, for these age groups. $6.00.

■ Social Security Programs Throughout the World

This research report charts the principal features of the social insurance programs of 145 countries and territories. The programs covered include: old age, invalidity, and death; sickness and maternity; work injury; unemployment; and family allowances. The data are based on laws, implementing decrees, and regulations in force at the beginning of 1987. $18.00.

■ Fast Facts and Figures About Social Security

Here are answers to the most frequently asked questions on OASDI beneficiaries and SSI recipients, and the Medicare, Medicaid, and AFDC programs are reflected in this publication. $2.25.

Department of Veterans Affairs

Office of Planning
Management Sciences Service (008B2)
810 Vermont Ave., N.W.
Washington, DC 20420
202-535-8403

There are many reports available from the VA, and they are all listed in *Publications From Management Sciences Services*, which you can order from the above address. The recurring and non-recurring reports cover the veteran population, compensation and pension, female veterans, aging veterans, minority veterans, and employment, education and income,

Some of the currently available reports include:

■ Veteran Population

This annual report contains estimates of the number of living veterans by period of military service, state of residence, sex, and age. Free.

■ Data on Female Veterans

A recurring report, it contains statistical information on female veterans relating to three major areas—population, health care, and compensation and pension. Free.

■ Estimates and Projections of the Veteran Population: 1980 to 2040

This non-recurring report highlights findings from the 1989 series of veteran population estimates and projections which cover the years 1980 to 2040. The main focus of this report is a series of graphs and text which highlight trends in the size and composition of the veteran population over the next 50 years. Data are shown by state and for selected ages and period of service. Free.

■ *Survey of Female Veterans: A Study of the Needs, Attitudes and Experiences of Women Veterans*

This report summarizes the findings of a face-to-face interview survey of 3,003 female veterans. Data collected include demographic and socioeconomic information, health status, medical services utilization and health care coverage, attitudes and experiences concerning VA hospital care, and use of and satisfaction with veterans' benefits and services. Free.

■ *Current Health Status and the Future Demand for Health Care Programs and Social Support Services*

This report presents information on the current health status of veterans aged 55 and over as it relates to their future demand for health care programs and social support services. Free.

■ *Survey of Aging Veterans: A Study of the Means, Resources and Future Expectations of Veterans Aged 55 and Over*

This report summarizes the findings of a personal interview survey of 3,013 veterans aged 55 years old and over. Data collected include demographic and socioeconomic information, health status, health insurance and medical services utilization, use of and satisfaction with veterans' benefits and services, and future expectations of aging veterans. Free.

■ *The VA Market Share of Medical Care Users*

Focusing on the issue of VA versus non-VA medical care usage, this report combines data from several surveys to result in a descriptive analysis of the VA market share of medical care users. Separate sets of market share statistics are presented for the inpatient and out-patient modalities of care. VA market share statistics are also compared over time. In addition, the reasons why otherwise eligible veterans use non-VA medical care are investigated. Free.

Glossary

B

baby boom Americans born between 1946 and 1964. There are 77.8 million baby boomers in 1992.

baby bust The relatively small generation born between 1965 and 1976. There are 43.6 million baby busters in 1992.

C

complete income reporters (on spending tables only) Survey respondents who told government interviewers how much money they received from major sources of income, such as wages and salaries, self-employment income, and Social Security income.

consumer unit For convenience, called household in this book.
—(1) All members of a household who are related by blood, marriage, adoption, or other legal arrangements.
—(2) A person living alone or sharing a household with others or living as a roomer in a private home or lodging house or in permanent living quarters in a hotel or motel, but who is financially independent. Financial independence is determined by the three major expense categories: housing, food, and other living expenses. To be considered financially independent, at least two of the three major expense categories have to be provided by the respondent.
—(3) Two persons or more living together who pool their income to make joint expenditure decisions.

D

dual-earner couple A married couple in which both the householder and the householder's spouse are in the labor force.

E

employed All civilians who did any work as a paid employee or farmer/self-employed worker, or who worked 15 hours or more as an unpaid farm worker or in a family-owned business, during the reference period. All those who have jobs but who are temporarily absent from their jobs due to illness, bad weather, vacation, labor management dispute, or personal reasons are considered employed.

expenditure The transaction cost including excise and sales taxes of goods and services acquired during the survey period. The full cost of each purchase is recorded even though full payment may not have been made at the date of purchase. Expenditure estimates include gifts.

F

family A group of two or more people (one of whom is the householder) related by birth, marriage, or adoption and residing together.

family household A household maintained by a householder who lives with one or more people related by blood, marriage, or adoption.

female/male householder A male or female who maintains a household without a spouse present. May head family or nonfamily households.

G

geographic regions The four major regions and nine census divisions of the United States are state groupings as shown below:
Northeast:
—New England: Connecticut, Maine, Massachusetts, New Hampshire, Rhode Island, and Vermont
—Middle Atlantic: New Jersey, New York, and Pennsylvania
Midwest
—East North Central: Illinois, Indiana, Michigan, Ohio, and Wisconsin
—West North Central: Iowa, Kansas, Minnesota, Missouri, Nebraska, North Dakota, and South Dakota
South:
—South Atlantic: Delaware, District of Columbia, Florida, Georgia, Maryland, North Carolina, South Carolina, Virginia, and West Virginia
—East South Central: Alabama, Kentucky, Mississippi, and Tennessee
—West South Central: Arkansas, Louisiana, Oklahoma, and Texas
West:
—Mountain: Arizona, Colorado, Idaho, Montana, Nevada, New Mexico, Utah, and Wyoming
—Pacific: Alaska, California, Hawaii, Oregon, and Washington

H

Hispanic Persons/householders who say that their origin is Mexican, Puerto Rican, Central or South American or some other Hispanic origin. Persons of Hispanic origin may be of any race.

household All the persons who occupy a housing unit. A household includes the related family members and all the unrelated persons, if any, such as lodgers, foster children, wards, or employees who share the housing unit. A person living alone or a group of unrelated persons sharing a housing unit as partners is also counted as a household. Households do not include group quarters such as college dormitories, prisons, or nursing homes.

household, race/ethnicity of Households are categorized according to the race or ethnicity of the householder only.

householder The householder refers to the person (or one of the persons) in whose name the housing unit is owned or rented or, if there is no such person, any adult member. With married couples, the householder may be either the husband or wife. The householder is the reference person for the household.

householder, age of The age of the householder is used to categorize households into age groups such as those used in this book. Married couples, for example, are classified according to the age of either the husband or wife.

I

income Money received in the preceding calendar year for each person 15 years old and over from each of the following sources: (1) earnings from longest job (or self-employment); (2) earnings from jobs other than longest job; (3) unemployment compensation; (4) workers' compensation; (5) Social Security; (6) Supplemental Security income; (7) public assistance; (8) veterans' payments; (9) survivor benefits; (10) disability benefits; (11) retirement pensions; (12) interest; (13) dividends; (14) rents and royalties or estates and trusts; (15) educational assistance; (16) alimony; (17) child support; (18) financial assistance from outside the household, and other periodic income. Income is reported in several ways in this book. Household income is the combined income of all household members. Income of persons is all income accruing to a person from all sources. Earnings is the amount of money a person received from his or her job.

industry Refers to the industry in which a person worked longest in the preceding calendar year.

L

labor force All the labor force tables in this book are based on the civilian labor force, which is made up of all civilians classified as employed or unemployed.

labor force participation rate The percent of the population in the labor force. Labor force participation rates appearing in this book are all based on the civilian labor force and civilian population. Labor force participation rates may also be calculated for sex–age groups or other special populations such as mothers of children of a given age.

M

married couples with or without children under age 18 Refers to married couples with or without children under age 18 living in the same household. Those without children under age 18 could be parents with grown children living elsewhere or childless couples.

median The median is the measure (of age or years of school completed, for example) which divides the population or households into two equal portions; one below and one above the median.

metropolitan area An area qualifies for recognition as a metropolitan area if (1) it includes a city of at least 50,000 population, or (2) it includes a Census Bureau-defined urbanized area of at least 50,000 with a total metropolitan population of at least 100,000 (75,000 in

New England). In addition to the county containing the main city or urbanized area, a metropolitan area may include other counties having strong commuting ties to the central county.

N

nonfamily household A household maintained by a householder who lives alone or who is not related to other household members.

nonfamily/nonfamily householder A householder maintaining a household while living alone or with nonrelatives only.

O

occupation Refers to the job held longest in the preceding calendar year.

P

part-time or full-time employment Part-time indicates less than 35 hours of work per week in a majority of the weeks worked during the year. Full-time indicates 35 hours or more per week during a majority of the weeks worked.

percent change The change (either positive or negative) in a measure that is expressed as a proportion of the starting measure.

percentage point change The change (either positive or negative) in a value which is already expressed as a percentage. When a labor force participation rate changes from 70 percent to 75 percent, for example, this is a 5 percentage point increase.

proportion or share The value of a part expressed as a percentage of the whole. If there are 44 million people aged 25 to 43 and 33 million of them are white, then the white proportion is 74 percent.

R

race Race is self-reported and usually appears in three categories in this book: white, black, Asian and other. A household is assigned the race of the householder.

T

tenure A housing unit is "owner occupied" if the owner lives in the unit,

even if it is mortgaged or not fully paid for. A cooperative or condominium unit is "owner occupied" only if the owner lives in it. All other occupied units are classified as "renter occupied," or "occupied without payment of cash rent."

total income (on spending tables only) The before-tax combined income of all consumer unit members aged 14 and older during the 12 months preceding the interview. Sources of income may include wages and salaries; self-employment income; Social Security, private, and government retirement benefits; interest, dividends, rental and other property income; unemployment, workers' compensation, and veterans' benefits; public assistance, supplemental security income, and food stamps; alimony, child support, and other regular contributions for support; and other income including such things as scholarships and payment for support of foster children.

Y

year-round, full-time Indicates 50 or more weeks of full-time employment during the previous calendar year.

Index